mural:

A Formal Development Support System

C.B. Jones • K.D. Jones • P.A. Lindsay • R. Moore

mural:
A Formal Development
Support System

With contributions from: J. Bicarregui
M. Elvang-Gøransson
R.E. Fields
R. Kneuper
B. Ritchie
A.C. Wills

Springer-Verlag
London Berlin Heidelberg New York
Paris Tokyo Hong Kong
Barcelona Budapest

C.B. Jones, DPhil,
Department of Computer Science,
University of Manchester,
Manchester M13 9PL

K.D. Jones, PhD,
Digital Equipment Corporation,
System Research Center, 130 Lytton Avenue,
Palo Alto, CA 94555, USA

P.A. Lindsay, PhD,
Computer Science Department,
University of New South Wales,
PO Box 1, Kensington,
NSW 2033, Australia

R.D. Moore, PhD,
Department of Computer Science,
University of Manchester,
Manchester M13 9PL

British Library Cataloguing in Publication Data
mural: a formal development support system.
1. Computers. Design
I. Jones, Clifford Bryn
004.22
ISBN 978-3-540-19651-8
Library of Congress Cataloging-in-Publication Data
A formal development support system/ editors, C.B. Jones ... [et al.].
p. cm.
Includes bibliographical references.
ISBN-13: 978-3-540-19651-8   e-ISBN-13: 978-1-4471-3180-9
DOI: 10.1007/ 978-1-4471-3180-9
1. Computer software–Development. I. Jones, C.B. (Cliff B.), *1944–* .
QA76.76.D47F67 1991   90–29090
005.1–dc20   CIP

The use of registered names, trademarks etc. in this publication does not imply,
even in the absence of a specific statement, that such names are exempt from
the relevant laws and regulations and therefore free for general use.

34/3830543210–Printed on acid-free paper.

Foreword

Programs and software constitute the most formal products known today since they must be processed by actual automata. Yet this software should solve problems in many areas, not all of which are supported by adequate scientific descriptions, let alone formalized ones. This major challenge of software design and engineering is often taken up in two phases which are logically distinct but can be carried out in parallel: in the first one, a clear and truthful formalization, viz. the 'requirements specification', of the problem at hand is built up; in the second one, a correct and efficient software system for the solution is designed on the basis of that formal specification. The first phase may well require the elaboration of adequate scientific models or theories, as close as possible to the semantic universe of the problems considered: bias towards specific solutions is thus usually minimized.

The present book focusses on the second phase, including the issue of correctness. The viewpoint it adopts is that the final programs are derived from the initial specifications through a design process which is decomposed systematically into manageable design steps. Each such step yields (on the basis of the previous version) a new intermediate formal version of the system under construction; the correctness of each new version is ensured by its correct derivation from, or by a verification against, the previous one. The composition of the records of the design steps serves as a record of the entire design process; the latter is correct providing each step and the overall composition are correct.

This viewpoint clearly restricts the scope of software design: the problem of building up an adequate problem description is played down; the design process is assumed to be decomposable into well-defined steps, each of which can be validated completely and on its own. These restrictive assumptions actually characterize 'software design by formal methods' which may use property-based formalisms, such as specific logics or abstract data types, or model-based formalisms such as function algebras, VDM, or Z. Significant industrial applications have been developed using such precise approaches.

Each formal method supplies specific notations, from algebraic ones to graphical ones, and specific correctness criteria, from mathematical proofs to plausibility arguments. Since the final system version is intended for computer processing, at least that version must be recorded on computer. The previous versions, starting with the specifications, can be recorded mentally, on paper, or in a computer. It is of course tempting to edit these intermediate documents with computer aid, as for very much the same reasons, was the present foreword: adaptability and communicability can be enhanced significantly. But then the computer aid should hinder as little as possible the suppleness and expressiveness provided by the use of the dear pencil and paper; it should rather improve on these, e.g. by organized handling of substantial bodies of formal texts or by fast display of beautiful texts. Similarly, the correctness of the design steps can also be ensured by mind-and-paper or by mind-and-computer. Ensuring a new version is correctly designed with respect to a previous one is akin to proving a proposed conclusion can be derived from given assumptions; hence, the correctness of design steps may need the proof of theorems. Hand proofs of machine-generated texts risk becoming inhuman, or being boiled down to proofs by trust; it is thus tempting also to support precise design steps by computer. In fact, once computer aid enters the design process somewhere, it tends to propagate everywhere.

The problem is to ensure this computer 'aid' really aids: computers must serve minds, not conversely. Effective aid depends on the ease of using the notations associated with a given method, on the help provided in elaborating derivations and proofs, and on the speed. As a matter of fact, not many useful computer support systems are currently available. Moreover, most assist designers in editing rather than in reasoning, and each generally supports only one variant of one method; intellectual communication between related methods is thus handicapped.

The work reported in the present book aims at building and using a system which supports not only the strict verification of design steps, but also a reasonable range of formal methods. Indeed, design choices and correctness arguments are often similar across different methods. A generic system could in principle support complementary methods in different parts, for different levels, or at different times of the same design project; remember the mindpower required by industrial projects may exceed tens of mind/years. This aim of genericity is shared by related projects on 'logical frameworks' which essentially focus on theorem proving; little research on generic support systems is carried out for precise and scalable software design. The present book guides us in an unchartered ocean where navigation could become active and attractive. A much needed chart should indicate reasonable boundaries for the domains of human ideas and for the areas of mechanizable arguments.

The results reported herein must be seen as careful observations from a scientific experiment rather than as definitive, indisputable answers. They certainly provide valuable contributions in areas as varied as logical foundations, syntactical context-sensitivity, execution of specifications as prototypes, interactive proof generation, organized composition of formal texts, efficient recording and accessing of such texts, pleasant mind-computer interface, support of specific methods and of specific system designs. Each of these issues deserves a book or a project of its own; many alternatives can be imagined at various levels. The originality and importance of the present work is in presenting an entire system approach which integrates all these aspects consistently and which already proves usable, albeit with some initial sweating.

A number of related systems are under experiment, for instance the generic logical frameworks for theorem proving. All experiments on such systems must benefit from one another, so that a gradual consensus emerges on the basis of the best technical characteristics. It is an essential merit of the present book to be indeed a remarkably substantial step in this crucial direction of scientific cooperation.

Michel Sintzoff

Preface

Formal methods bring mathematical precision to the development of computer systems. This book describes the outcome of a project which designed and built a support tool for formal methods such as VDM. The tool is known as *mural* and is so named because it was developed jointly by (the Computer Science department at) Manchester University and (the Software Engineering Division at SERC's) Rutherford Appleton Laboratories. The major component of *mural* is an interactive proof assistant; another component helps with the creation of formal specifications and designs. Work on the animation of specifications is also reported.

The so-called software crisis has been recognised for many years. Software development is claimed to be unpredictable and often results in products which are 'bug ridden'. In fact there is no reason to confine the criticism to software: the task of developing any major digital system often appears to be beyond the methods employed by its developers. 'Formal methods' are seen as one way of bringing order and precision into the development of systems where errors cannot be accepted lightly. The importance of formal methods is becoming widely recognised. Brian Oakley, who was Director of the UK Alvey Programme, is quoted as saying:

> ...the main achievement of the Alvey Software Engineering Programme is the success with which 'Formal Methods' from the academic world have been pulled through to industrial use. The implications of this achievement are difficult to overestimate, for these Formal Methods are the route to much better software writing, and the economic consequences will be considerable – on a par with those of the revolution in civil engineering in the last century.

The industrial relevance of one particular formal method, VDM, can be gauged from the series of CEC-funded international symposia [BJMN87, BJM88, BHL90].

The term 'formal methods' embraces the use of precise notation in specifications, and verification in design, of computer systems. Such precise specifications employ mathematical notation extended to make it easier to present specifications of computer-related concepts like programs. These extensions are given a precise semantics in terms of more basic mathematical concepts. Examples of such specification languages are 'Meta-IV' (the specification language of VDM) [BJ78, Jon80], 'Z' [Hay87, WL88, Spi89, MN89], 'Larch' [GHW85], COLD-K [Jon88], VVSL [Mid90] and RSL (the specification language of the RAISE project) [HH90]. Having a formally-based specification language makes it possible to convert the claim that an implementation (or even a design) satisfies a specification into the statement of a mathematical theorem. Proof of such a theorem establishes satisfaction for all cases. Examples of formal development methods with documented proof obligations include VDM [BJ82, Jon80, Jon90a] and RAISE [BG90].

There are, however, many real obstacles in the way of an organisation which wishes to apply formal methods. The greatest obstacle is certainly changing the approach of both managers and engineers because – in an industry as young as computing – few have been exposed to a systematic engineering approach to the design of computer systems. A major commitment to education is the only way to overcome this obstacle. The lack of standards is also a brake on the adoption of formal methods although work is now underway within both BSI and ISO towards a standard for VDM.

One of the consequences of the lack of standards has been the limited availability of support for formal methods. Of all of the supposed inhibitors to the wider use of formal methods, this is the most over-estimated! Although this book is about the provision of such support tools, it is worthwhile trying to identify the real needs if only to avoid the trap of assuming that the appearance of tools will, of itself, result in the widespread adoption of the methods which they support. Large specifications, such as [BBH+74, Ped87] have been handled with nothing more powerful than a text processing system. This historical fact is not to be seen as an argument *for* under-provision. In fact, relatively simple parsers and type checkers (e.g. 'SpecBox' [BFM89] for VDM or 'fuzz' for Z) certainly detect many simple errors in specifications. Furthermore, they help minimize the dangers of what is undoubtedly the most difficult task with formal specifications: errors are far more likely to creep in during changes to a specification than during its initial creation. A system to support formal methods must therefore provide tools to enter and type check specifications.

Millennia of mathematics, and even a century of formal logic, show that proofs can be constructed with pencil and paper. Given today's technology, it is not difficult to become more productive at a full-screen editor, if only because of the ability to insert lines in proofs. This is especially true of so-called 'natural deduction' proofs because of the way they grow from the outside boxes to fill in the internal lines. Providing it is done conscientiously, the *process* of constructing even an outline proof should detect most errors in the statement of a supposed theorem because of the way it cross-checks the original claim (an obvious example is the way that, in proving that the body of a loop preserves an invariant, the invariant provides a sideways look at the purpose of the loop; such an alternative point of view is likely to uncover any error in coding the body).

But the formal development of computer systems can involve large specifications and many proofs of considerable size. In business environments, requirements are likely to change part way through development (cf. [Leh89]). Appropriate support tools can greatly improve the productivity of engineers who are employing formal methods. The project which is reported in this book addressed the provision of such tools.

This book has been produced by revising a collection of the papers which were written during the project. They have been edited to make a more coherent text and material has also been specifically written for this book. In some places, this gives rise to repetition; this has been left in the hope that the reader can read separate chapters independently of one another. A good overview of the work can be obtained by reading Chapters 1–3, 6, 7 and 11. Chapters 1 and 2 are introductory. The main component of the *mural* system is a proof assistant – this is described in detail Chapters 3 to 6 of this book; Chapters 7 and 8 describe the work on a VDM support tool (VST); and Chapter 9 describes a novel approach to the animation of specifications. Chapters 10 and 11 are again relevant to all components of *mural*: the former describes some applications and the latter draws some conclusions and sets out further research goals.

A glossary of VDM notation is given in Appendix A and one of terms is included in Appendix B; Appendices C and D contain VDM specifications. Appendix E looks far beyond the current project to a vision of a possible future.

The *mural* system is available for both research and commercial use; it is written in Smalltalk'80 and requires a large workstation to run. Details of how to obtain *mural* are available from Dr. Richard Moore, PEVE Group, Department of Computer Science, Manchester University, M13 9PL, U.K. In addition to this book, an introductory video and a 'User Guide' are available.

The specific contributions to this book are given in the following table. In addition, the four main authors took responsibility for editing the whole work and all authors read other parts of the book in various drafts.

Preface	C. B. Jones
Chapter 1	C. B. Jones
Chapter 2	R. Moore
Chapter 3	P. A. Lindsay
Chapter 4	P. A. Lindsay
Chapter 5	R. E. Fields
Chapter 6	K. D. Jones
Chapter 7	J. Bicarregui and B. Ritchie
Chapter 8	J. Bicarregui and B. Ritchie
Chapter 9	R. Kneuper
Chapter 10	M. Elvang and R. E. Fields
Chapter 11	C. B. Jones
Appendix A	C. B. Jones
Appendix B	*omnes*
Appendix C	P. A. Lindsay and R. Moore
Appendix D	R. Kneuper
Appendix E	A. C. Wills

Acknowledgements

We should like to express our gratitude to John Fitzgerald, who contributed to the instantiation of the *mural* proof assistant and who also provided many valuable comments on the various drafts of this book. Thanks are also due to Lockwood Morris, a senior visiting fellow involved with the project for one year, who contributed to the development of the proof model ('boxes-and-lines') for an early prototype of *mural*, and to Michel Sintzoff, who provided invaluable external criticism of our evolving ideas.

We are grateful to SERC and the Alvey Directorate for providing funding for the *IPSE 2.5* project. In addition, CBJ would like to thank SERC for support under the Senior Fellowship Grant and the Wolfson Foundation for its grant, and MEG acknowledges partial support of a grant from the Danish Technical Research Council (STVF).

The authors also wish to acknowledge the support and encouragement of the staff at Springer-Verlag's London office and the valuable feedback from the reviewers of an earlier draft of this material.

Contents

APPENDICES

Chapter 1

General introduction

This chapter describes the context in which the scientific work reported in later chapters was undertaken. After a general description of formal methods, VDM is used as an example to make the sort of tasks involved in formal development more precise. Section 1.3 outlines the overall project in which the work on formal methods was undertaken. The last section in this chapter deduces a number of requirements for the support of the theorem proving process. Chapter 2 offers an introduction to the *mural* system itself.

1.1 Formal methods

Before focusing on formal methods for the development of computer systems, it is worth looking at what the adjective 'formal' indicates when applied to notations and proofs. To be called formal, a notation must have some understood meaning or semantics. For example, in the logic of propositions, the expression $A \wedge (B \vee C)$ depends in a precise way on what the identifiers A etc. denote. Exactly how such meaning can be defined need not be discussed here. The important fact is that a claim that the expressions $A \wedge (B \vee C)$ and $A \wedge B \vee A \wedge C$ have the same meaning is, in any given logic, either true or false.[1] Unlike in what computer scientists call 'natural languages', expressions in a formal language have a formal semantics which can settle disputes about their intended interpretation.

One might then expect that a formal specification language for computer systems should be such that the precise meaning of any particular specification can only be disputed through ignorance. This expectation can be fulfilled. But, without the additional bonus of being able to reason about such specifications, the cost of their construction might be hard to justify. Fortunately, formal specification languages, at least for sequential computer systems, are also tractable in the same way as logic notation: proofs can be constructed.

The essence of what makes a proof formal is that its steps rely only on symbol manipulation. Consider the claim made above about the two propositional expressions. One half of what needs to be proved is that the second expression can be deduced from the first. This can be written as a sequent $A \wedge (B \vee C) \vdash A \wedge B \vee A \wedge C$. One rule of deduction about $\wedge$ is that from a conjunction either of its conjuncts can be deduced. Thus both $A \wedge (B \vee C) \vdash A$ and $A \wedge (B \vee C) \vdash B \vee C$ are valid steps in a proof. An entire proof of the required result can be built from such simple steps. More remarkably, any

---

[1]Of course, in classical logic it is true; as it is in VDM's LPF – see below; but the symbols like $\wedge$ could be used for totally different purposes in other languages.

true statement in propositional logic can be proved using a small repertoire of basic rules.

Rather than imbed proofs in text, it is possible to make them more readable by displaying them. In the style known as 'natural deduction' the required proof is

---

from $A \wedge (B \vee C)$

1	A	$\wedge\text{-}E(\text{h})$
2	$B \vee C$	$\wedge\text{-}E(\text{h})$
3	from B	
3.1	$\quad A \wedge B$	$\wedge\text{-}I(1,\text{h}3)$
	infer $A \wedge B \vee A \wedge C$	$\vee\text{-}I(3.1)$
4	from C	
4.1	$\quad A \wedge C$	$\wedge\text{-}I(1,\text{h}4)$
	infer $A \wedge B \vee A \wedge C$	$\vee\text{-}I(4.1)$
	infer $A \wedge B \vee A \wedge C$	$\vee\text{-}E(2,3,4)$

Proof that and distributes over or (one
direction)

In this proof, steps 1 and 2 are shown as being justified by a rule known as 'and elimination' ($\wedge\text{-}E$). It can be expressed by a deduction rule

$$\boxed{\wedge\text{-}E}\ \frac{E_1 \wedge E_2}{E_i}\ 1 \leq i \leq 2$$

Such rules are really schema for an infinite set of possible deductions. If known (proven) expressions can be found to match the hypotheses above the line, then a conclusion which matches what is written below the line is valid. The matching process in this instance links E_1 with A and E_2 with $B \vee C$. Thus line 2 of the proof is justified by eliminating the left conjunct from the overall hypothesis of the proof.

A more interesting rule is that which facilitates the elimination of disjunctions. This can be thought of as providing a way of reasoning by cases. The rule is

$$\boxed{\vee\text{-}E}\ \frac{E_1 \vee E_2;\ E_1 \vdash E;\ E_2 \vdash E}{E}$$

The final conclusion of the boxed proof above uses this rule with E_1 substituted by B, E_2 by C, and E by $A \wedge B \vee A \wedge C$. Notice here that, as well as an expression $B \vee C$ which is needed as a hypothesis, two subsidiary proofs are required. To apply the or-elimination rule, the facts that $B \vdash A \wedge B \vee A \wedge C$ and $C \vdash A \wedge B \vee A \wedge C$ are required. In the given proof, these are shown by the inner boxes 3 and 4. The required proofs for these two boxes are easy to complete. Step 3.1 follows from the hypothesis of box 3 and the already proven line 1 by the and-introduction rule ($\wedge\text{-}I$).

$$\boxed{\wedge\text{-}I}\ \frac{E_1;\ E_2}{E_1 \wedge E_2}$$

The conclusion of box 3 follows from the rule of or-introduction

$$\boxed{\vee\text{-}I}\ \frac{E_i}{E_1 \vee E_2}\ 1 \leq i \leq 2$$

The key point about the proof is that each step is mediated by a rule whose application can be completely checked by symbol manipulation. There is no room for debate about whether a formal proof does or does not follow the rules.

In passing, it is also worth mentioning that the steps of such a proof can be understood either forwards from the hypotheses to the conclusion or backwards from the goal to subgoals. In fact, it is frequently useful to attempt both directions when trying to discover a proof. It is explained below that the freedom to work in any order was a major design goal of the *mural* proof assistant.

Having established a benchmark of 'formality', the topic of formal methods can be explored more carefully. It is claimed above – and the claim is illustrated in the next section – that specification languages exist which deserve the adjective 'formal'. Is it then possible to prove that a program satisfies a specification? Under certain assumptions the answer is yes. The programming language itself can be regarded as a formal language because it has a precise semantics. In an ideal world, this semantics is given by something like the definition of ALGOL 60 in [BJ82]; at the other extreme it can be given by the code of the compiler. In practice, neither of these texts would be usable in a proof and what is needed is a series of proof rules for program constructs which are designed in the same spirit as those for logics. The strongest assumption then – under which programs are proven to satisfy a specification – is that the implementation (compiler[2] and machine) reflect the proof rules used in such proofs. There is also an assumption of practicability: the size of programs for which *post facto* proof is practical is severely limited. Methods like VDM respond to this observation by offering ways of decomposing a design into stages which can be separately justified. This has the additional advantage that errors made early in design are detected long before running code is created. In traditional software development, such errors might well be detected only when the code is available for testing. Since 'scrap and rework' is a major cause of lost time in software development, carefully applied formal methods such as VDM can actually improve the productivity of the development process. One further caveat about proving facts about programs is in order: what is (theoretically) possible is to show that one formal text – the program – satisfies another – the specification; this can never *prove* that the specification describes the system desired by some user.

There are, within the formal approach to system development, three more-or-less distinct[3] paradigms; implementations can be developed by:

- iterative specification, design, and verification;

- program transformation; or

- constructive mathematics.

VDM [Jon90a] is taken as the principal example of the first paradigm in this book. The early Floyd/King style of verification condition generation leads to proof obligations called 'verification conditions'. These are, however, open to the criticism [Cra85] – when applied *post-facto* – that it is often hard to relate the verification conditions to the program. Methods of 'data reification' and 'operation decomposition' in VDM provide

---

[2]The unavoidable reliance on a compiler is the reason that so much of the early work on formalization focussed on defining programming languages – see [MP66, JL71, Jon79b].

[3]Of course these paradigms overlap, and it could be argued that the first and the third are different aspects of the same paradigm, but such arguments do not concern us here – the point is that they all involve formal reasoning. Proof obligations arise in each of these paradigms.

many instances of proof obligations which are made intelligible to the user by having the steps of development convey the structure of the correctness argument.

The 'program transformation' approach is typified by CIP [CIP85, B⁺87]. The basic idea is to transform inefficient – but clearly correct – 'implementations' into runnable programs. A transition from recursive functions to iterative procedures is an example of such transformations. But many transformations have associated applicability conditions which give rise to proof obligations when used.

The most direct use of formal reasoning is in the 'constructive mathematics' paradigm. Specifications are recast as statements that an implementation exists; and a 'program' is extracted directly from a constructive proof of the claim. NuPRL [C⁺86] is an example of a system supporting this paradigm.

1.2 VDM development

In order to provide more specific examples of the sort of proofs which are required in the formal development of software, an outline of parts of VDM is given. Appendix A provides a glossary to VDM notation. For a fuller, and more pedagogic description of VDM the reader is referred to [Jon90a].

1.2.1 Specification

A VDM specification describes the behaviour of a system in terms of the operations which can be performed by the system. The meaning of these operations is specified by pre- and post-conditions. Pre-conditions describe under what circumstances the system is required to perform and post-conditions describe what function is to be performed. In very simple systems, it is sometimes possible to describe the behaviour by considering only inputs and outputs; most interesting systems also have a state which reflects the effect of earlier operations. In VDM, pre-conditions define which input and initial state combinations must be handled by an operation while post-conditions relate inputs and initial states to outputs and final states. In general, post-conditions are shorter than constructive algorithms to achieve the desired result. Moreover, the use of abstract objects makes even more dramatic abbreviation possible by allowing a specification to be written in terms of objects which match the application rather than the intricacies of the final implementation machine.

The notion of *state* is then central to a specification in VDM. If one were to be describing a system[4] which handled a collection of signals (*Sig* is the name of the set of these objects), one might define the (abstract) state (*Abs*) as

$$Abs :: poss : Sig\text{-set}$$
$$curr : Sig\text{-set}$$
$$\text{inv } (mk\text{-}Abs(p, c)) \triangleq c \subseteq p$$

Here the sets of possible (*poss*) and current (*curr*) signals are stored as fields of the composite object *Abs*; furthermore, the data type invariant constrains any valid object $mk\text{-}Abs(p, c) \in Abs$ to have its c set contained in its p set.

As has been claimed, VDM offers a formal language (sometimes known – in order to distinguish it from the method – as 'Meta-IV'): its expressions can be expanded into

---

[4]This system is a simplified view of the reactor protection example which is studied in Chapter 10.

standard mathematical ones. It is convenient here to present a partial expansion since this is necessary to present specifications to the *mural* system. The state *Abs* can then be defined via *Abs0* as follows

Abs0 :: *poss* : *Sig*-set
curr : *Sig*-set

Abs = {*a* ∈ *Abs0* | *inv-Abs*(*a*)}

inv-Abs : *Abs0* → B
inv-Abs(*a*) △ *curr*(*a*) ⊆ *poss*(*a*)

For most systems that are specified in VDM, there are many operations affecting the same state. These operations represent the external interface of the system. They are gathered together with the state into a module. The state itself is considered to be hidden within the module and can only be manipulated by the operations. Here, only one operation is given. Furthermore, in order to minimize the discussion of VDM's module construct, its specification is given in a way which ignores some of the sophistication of VDM.[5] An operation (*ADD*) which adds a new signal to the field *curr* within the state could be specified

ADD (*new*: *Sig*)
ext wr *a* : *Abs*
pre *new* ∈ *poss*(*a*)
post *curr*(*a*) = *curr*($\overleftarrow{a}$) ∪ {*new*} ∧ *poss*(*a*) = *poss*($\overleftarrow{a}$)

The post-condition relates the fields of the initial state $\overleftarrow{a}$ to those of the final state *a*; the pre-condition invites the developer to ignore cases where the *new* signal is not in the *poss* field of the initial state (*a* here).

Paradoxically, one test of a specification language is whether it can be used to write nonsense! VDM's pre- and post-conditions can be used to specify operations which cannot be built. But one can make mathematically precise the claim that this has not happened. An operation is *satisfiable* if for any possible starting condition (as given by the pre-condition) there is a possible state and result which satisfies the post-condition. For the current example, this can be written in the predicate calculus as

∀*new* ∈ *Sig*, $\overleftarrow{a}$ ∈ *Abs* ·
    pre-*ADD*(*new*, $\overleftarrow{a}$) ⇒ ∃*a* ∈ *Abs* · post-*ADD*(*new*, $\overleftarrow{a}$, *a*)

This is the first example of a *proof obligation* from VDM. Its proof is straightforward and is not pursued here but it is worth noticing the way in which the data type invariant (*inv-Abs*) expands for the differing quantifiers

---

[5]The *ADD* operation could be specified as follows

ADD (*new*: *Sig*)
ext rd *poss*: *Sig*-set,
    wr *curr*: *Sig*-set
pre *new* ∈ *poss*
post *curr* = $\overleftarrow{curr}$ ∪ {*new*}

$$\forall new \in Sig, \overleftarrow{a} \in Abs0 \cdot$$
$$inv\text{-}Abs(\overleftarrow{a}) \wedge pre\text{-}ADD(new, \overleftarrow{a}) \Rightarrow$$
$$\exists a \in Abs0 \cdot inv\text{-}Abs(a) \wedge post\text{-}ADD(new, \overleftarrow{a}, a)$$

Satisfiability proof obligations are a check on the internal consistency of a specification. For complex systems, a user might use the *mural* proof assistant to provide proofs for those proof obligations which are automatically generated by the VST. Another sort of proof which might be undertaken before the process of design begins is to prove properties about combinations of operations. This can, to some extent, ameliorate doubts as to whether the formal specification does describe a system whose behaviour will be accepted by users. Chapter 9 of this book describes an alternative approach to the animation of specifications.

1.2.2 Reification

Development in VDM proceeds by data reification (making more concrete) and/or operation decomposition. In order to illustrate the sort of proof obligation which arises during developments, a simple step of reification of the *Abs* state is considered. The *poss* set is represented by a sequence (without duplicates) *posl*; the *curr* set is represented by a list *curl*, of the same length as *posl*, which contains Boolean values – a true value in *curl* indicates that the corresponding element of *posl* is considered to be in the set [6]

$$Rep0 :: posl : Sig^*$$
$$\quad\quad curl : B^*$$

$$Rep = \{r \in Rep0 \mid inv\text{-}Rep(r)\}$$

$$inv\text{-}Rep : Rep0 \to B$$
$$inv\text{-}Rep(r) \;\;\triangle\;\; \text{len}\, posl(r) = \text{len}\, curl(r) \wedge is\text{-}uniquel(posl(r))$$

$$is\text{-}uniquel : X^* \to B$$
$$is\text{-}uniquel(l) \;\;\triangle\;\; \forall i,j \in \text{inds}\, l \cdot i \neq j \;\Rightarrow\; l(i) \neq l(j)$$

In VDM, the precise relationship between *Abs* and *Rep* is normally[7] documented by a 'retrieve function' which maps elements of the latter to elements of the former. For the simple example in hand this is

$$retr\text{-}Abs : Rep \to Abs$$
$$retr\text{-}Abs(r) \;\;\triangle$$
$$\quad mk\text{-}Abs0(\text{elems}\, posl(r), \{posl(r)(i) \mid i \in \text{inds}\, posl(r) \wedge curl(r)(i)\})$$

---

[6]Again VDM offers the more compact notation

$$Rep :: posl: Sig^*$$
$$\quad\quad curl: B^*$$

inv $(mk\text{-}Rep(pl, cl)) \triangle \text{len}\, pl = \text{len}\, cl \wedge is\text{-}uniquel(pl)$

[7]Chapter 9 of [Jon90a] does, however, describe the use of the more general rules presented in [Nip86, Nip87]

The direction of this function is important. As can be seen in this case, there can be more than one representation for each element of the set of abstract states. This is typical of steps of reification where representations become more intricate and redundant as the constraints of the target machine and goals of efficiency are considered.

There is a need to check that the retrieve function is defined over all elements of its domain. Showing the totality (over *Rep*) of *retr-Abs* is not difficult but the reader should note the way in which the definedness of the expression $\{posl(r)(i) \mid i \in \text{inds} \, posl(r) \wedge curl(r)(i)\}$ depends on the invariant *inv-Rep*.

Experience in large scale applications of VDM has shown that the *adequacy* proof obligation is a cost-effective check on design steps of reification. It is observed above that there can be more than one element of *Rep* for each element of *Abs*; adequacy requires that there must be – at least – one! Formally, for the step of reification considered here

$$\forall a \in Abs \cdot \exists r \in Rep \cdot a = retr\text{-}Abs(r)$$

Here again, expansion showing the invariants explicitly is revealing

$$\forall a \in Abs0 \cdot inv\text{-}Abs(a) \; \Rightarrow \; \exists r \in Rep0 \cdot inv\text{-}Rep(r) \wedge a = retr\text{-}Abs(r)$$

Only because $a(\in Abs0)$ is restricted by *inv-Abs* can representations be found (consider *mk-Abs0*$(\{a\}, \{a, b\})$). Whereas *inv-Abs* being the antecedent of an implication makes the task easier, *inv-Rep* is conjoined to the consequent and therefore checks that the designer has not inadvertently ruled out needed representations. The adequacy proof obligation corresponds to one's intuition; experience shows that in non-trivial steps of reification it identifies mistakes early in the design process; it is inexpensive in the sense that only one proof is required for a complete reification step.

Once this overall check on a design step has been performed, it is time to consider each of the operations. In this illustrative example there is only one operation (*ADD*) shown on the abstract state and an operation which should exhibit the same behaviour on *Rep* can be specified.

ADDR (*new*: *Sig*)
ext wr *r* : *Rep*
pre $\exists i \in \text{inds} \, posl(r) \cdot posl(r)(i) = new$
post $\exists i \in \text{inds} \, posl(r) \cdot$
$\qquad posl(r)(i) = new \wedge posl(r) = posl(\overleftarrow{r}) \wedge curl(r) = modl(curl(\overleftarrow{r}), i, \text{true})$

modl (l: $\mathbf{B}^*$, i: $\mathbb{N}_1$, v: $\mathbf{B}$) r: $\mathbf{B}^*$
pre $i \leq \text{len} \, l$
post $\text{len} \, r = \text{len} \, l \wedge r(i) = v \wedge \forall j: \mathbb{N}_1 \cdot j \leq \text{len} \, l \wedge j \neq i \; \Rightarrow \; r(j) = l(j)$

For each such pair of abstract/representation operations there are *domain* and *result* proof obligations. The former checks that the pre-condition of the reified operation does not rule out any states which were required to be handled on the abstract level; formally

$$\forall new \in Sig, r \in Rep \cdot pre\text{-}ADD(new, retr\text{-}Abs(r)) \; \Rightarrow \; pre\text{-}ADDR(new, r)$$

At a level of detail which would be used in [Jon90a], the proof might be written

---

from *new* ∈ *Sig*, *r* ∈ *Rep*
1   from *pre-ADD(new, retr-Abs(r))*
1.1   *new* ∈ *poss(retr-Abs(r))*   h1,*pre-ADD*
1.2   *new* ∈ elems *(posl(r))*   1.1,*retr-Abs*
1.3   ∃*i* ∈ inds *(posl(r))* · *posl(r)(i)* = *new*   *LIST*, 1.2
         infer *pre-ADDR(new, r)*   1.3, *pre-ADD*
2   δ(*pre-ADD(new, retr-Abs(r))*)   *pre-ADD*
infer *pre-ADD(new, retr-Abs(r))* ⇒ *pre-ADDR(new, r)*   ⇒-*I*(1,2)

                        Domain proof obligation for *ADDR*

In this proof there is only one step which is justified by an inference rule of logic: the final step uses

$$\boxed{\Rightarrow\text{-}I}\quad \frac{E_1 \vdash E_2;\ \delta(E_1)}{E_1 \Rightarrow E_2}$$

In classical logic, the 'Deduction Theorem' only needs the first hypothesis. VDM uses a 'logic of partial functions' (LPF) – see [BCJ84, CJ91]. This variant of classical logic was developed because of the preponderance of partial terms in proofs about computer systems. For example, the term *retr-Abs(r)* in the consequent of the expanded adequacy condition could be undefined when the antecedent is false. The rule for implication-introduction in LPF requires that the antecedent be proved to be defined. Most of the other steps rely on the folding or unfolding of definitions. Step 1.3 uses a lemma which would be proved in the *LIST* theory. This proof actually hides some of the detail of the proof and should be regarded as 'rigorous' rather than completely formal. The *mural* proof assistant can be used to create fully formal proofs – such a proof of this result is about the right size to squeeze screen dumps of *mural* onto the pages of this book (cf. Chapter 2).

Although it is not pursued below, the result proof obligation for *ADDR* is

∀*new* ∈ *Sig*, $\overleftarrow{r}$, *r* ∈ *Rep* ·
    pre-ADD(new, retr-Abs($\overleftarrow{r}$*))* ∧ *post-ADDR(new,* $\overleftarrow{r}$ *, r)* ⇒
                                post-ADD(new, retr-Abs($\overleftarrow{r}$*), retr-Abs(r))*

1.3   The *IPSE 2.5* project

The work described in this book was part of the *IPSE 2.5* project which was funded by the UK Alvey directorate. The project ran from October 1985 to March 1990. The overall list of collaborators in the project was STC, ICL, Dowty, Plessey, British Gas, Manchester University and SERC (RAL). Of these, Manchester University and Rutherford Appleton Laboratory were the 'academic partners' responsible for the work described in this book. The people involved included Juan Bicarregui, Jen Cheng, Ian Cottam, David Duce, Neil Dyer, Bob Fields, John Fitzgerald, Julie Haworth, Jane Gray, Cliff Jones, Kevin Jones, Ralf Kneuper, Peter Lindsay, Richard Moore, Lockwood Morris, Tobias Nipkow, Brian Ritchie, Michel Sintzoff, Mark van Harmelen, Chris Wadsworth, and Alan Wills.

The overall *IPSE 2.5* project set out very ambitious objectives (see [DDJ⁺85] for the project proposal) to integrate formal methods support with tools which covered familiar industrial objectives for a project support environment like version control and project management. The project stalled on this level of ambition and it was decided to split it into a series of 'themes' two of which were to support formal reasoning. The academic partners in the project concentrated on the formal reasoning support. The industrial partners worked on providing support for the processes involved in the commercial development of software systems. The principle means underlying such provision was the development of an approach described as 'process modelling'. An overview of this aspect of the project is given in [Sno89, War90].

The main effort of the academic partners has been on the construction of a generic proof assistant. It became clear during the project that the industrial partners were not going to provide a formal methods environment which would exercise the proof assistant and it was decided that the academic partners had to create an example specification support tool which would make it possible to input specifications and generate proof obligations. Since the main purpose was to create useful (software engineering) tasks for the proof assistant, it was considered acceptable to generate a tool which was specific in a number of ways. For example, an obvious decision was to support only VDM. The specification support tool is therefore known as the VDM Support Tool (VST): it is far less generic than the proof assistant. In fact, because the whole *mural* project has been built on Smalltalk'80, much of the VST code would be re-used if another specification language were to be supported.

1.4   Proof assistant requirements

Based on the original project proposal [DDJ⁺85], a series of 'concept papers' were written which set out the requirements for different aspects of the *IPSE 2.5* project. The concept paper for formal reasoning [JLW86] contains a detailed rationale for the research which led to *mural*; a published overview of this material with an intermediate project report is given in [JL88]; this section provides only a sketch of the main requirements. It must be realized that, because of various pressures, not all of the project objectives were met (cf. Chapter 11).

The VDM proof obligations in Section 1.2 are specific to the development in hand. It is also desirable to develop 'theories' (see below) which can be re-used across many developments. Such theorems are more general than those for a specific program. Furthermore there is sometimes a need for even more general results such as justifying (against a denotational semantics) the rules which generate proof obligations. If a very high degree of confidence is required in the correctness of proofs they ought to be checked by a computer program. As is obvious from the discussion of formality in Section 1.1, it is not difficult to write a program which checks that all steps of a formal proof are justified by stated inference rules. The snag is that completely formal proofs are at such an excruciating level of detail that they take enormous effort to prepare. The natural question to ask is whether a computer can be programmed to assist the process of *constructing* such proofs. There have been attempts to build automatic theorem provers. In general, automatic discovery of proofs is theoretically impossible; in practice, systems like that described in [BM79] have proved very difficult to steer. The obvious compromise is to find a balance where human intuition guides an interactive program which performs mechanical tasks smoothly. To maximise this synergy, the system must offer a more inviting environment than pencil and paper. One might think that this was not difficult, but a

survey at the beginning of the project[8] showed that users viewed most systems as something to wrestle with once a proof had been planned by hand. Even recently, the authors
of [RvH89] describe their use of EHDM thus

> One of us broke the published proof of Lamport and Melliar-Smith down
> into elementary steps, while the other encoded these in EHDM and persuaded
> the theorem prover to accept the proofs. ...All this work was done by hand,
> and only cast into EHDM and mechanically verified towards the end.

A large part of the problem results from the fact that, in existing systems, the machine
usually dictates (to greater or lesser extent) how the proof proceeds, and when – as often
occurs – it leads down an obscure path, the user is left to work out what is happening and
how to get back on the right track.

It is currently the case that very few proofs are written completely formally. There
are a number of reasons for this. It must be clear that a comparison between proofs in
mathematics – where what is provided is no more than a plan for a proof – and computing
can be confusing. Many proofs required in program development are basically long and
somewhat tedious. Rather than recording a brilliant insight, the proof is intended to
cross-check that no details have been overlooked in a design. The sheer amount of detail
involved renders machine support and formal verification essential.

Given this view of the sort of proof to be created, *mural* has to genuinely help with
proof construction. A synergy of man and machine is required in which each performs
the tasks to which it is best suited. The human guides the proof (based on insight into the
reasons for belief in its truth); the machine makes faultless mechanical steps together with
(constrained) searches. A proof assistant has to be designed so that the human, rather than
the program, is in control of the proof creation. The key requirement is that the formal
reasoning tools of *IPSE 2.5* facilitate proof 'at the workstation' rather than the machine
being a challenge one faces after having planned a proof.

If proving that programs satisfy specifications is hark work, one is naturally prompted
to see if the work can be re-used. An obvious example of the reuse of work is to employ
the same module in more than one system. An overall project support environment can
facilitate such reuse and there is here a clear need for formal methods because of the
central role of specifications in such re-use. There are, however, severe limitations to the
impact of the reuse of modules in standard programming languages: most modules are
so specific that they are of use in *at most* one system.

A requirement which we considered crucial was to support the gathering of results
into 'theories'. As seen in [Dah77, Jon79a, Hay89, Möl90], the development of 'theories'
presents one of the major hopes for getting formal reasoning more widely used. Such
theories become one way of establishing 'levels' in proofs: a detailed proof at one level
becomes a simple inference rule at another. The use of such derived rules was seen as
one of the essential ways of obtaining higher-level proofs in *mural*.

The need for generic formal reasoning tools has been alluded to above. A key area
where the need for genericity was recognised from the beginning was that of logics.

---

[8]One of the first steps taken towards writing a set of requirements for the proof assistant was to experiment with theorem proving systems developed by others. To a large extent, we were able to obtain copies
of such systems and import them to run on our own machines (e.g. work with Iota is reported in [All86]).
The overall conclusions of the survey were published as [Lin88]. (See also [Kem86] – which has only
recently become available to us – in which two of the key goals for 'next generation verification systems'
are the use of graphics interfaces and the development of reusable theories.) The impression gained was
that machines were not being used well in the support of formal reasoning.

The framework provided enables users to instantiate *mural* for a wide range of logics. The process of going from generator to generated system should be one of parameter instantiation, in contrast to writing (procedural) programs. There is, however, a further requirement: the generated systems should not be significantly more difficult to use than hand-constructed ones.

We decided to stop short of the sort of searching implied in automatic theorem proving. We did not believe, in any case, that automatic theorem proving is what was needed in *IPSE 2.5*. In particular, it seemed clear that the paradigm 'write code plus assertions then do verification condition generation' is unworkable even for quite small programs – see [Cra85]. At the same time, conducting proofs interactively very soon becomes impossibly tedious without some automated aids. There is a need to capture and import relevant automated tools. Some data types have decision procedures which, although often very costly (exponential), are worth implementing. Certainly, it has proved worthwhile to have a simple checker for propositional calculus; other examples might include finite lists and, possibly, Presburger arithmetic.

The aim to create a system in which the insight of the user as to why a result holds is used to steer proof construction puts the emphasis on interaction. It is important to realize that an incomplete proof is an object of interest. In fact, a proof is of interest while it is incomplete; once proved, only the statement of the theorem is needed for most purposes. The user might pursue different avenues until a proof is found. Keeping track of these threads and facilitating movement between them is essential. When the proof is finally completed there is the problem of 'garbage collecting' in a sophisticated way. Many interaction styles were considered (see [CJNW83, CJN+85, CJN+86, JM88])[9] before that implemented in *mural* was finally chosen.

In a useful instantiation of *mural*, there are likely to be very many applicable inference rules and tactics. Derived rules for the logic and underlying data types will also be present and, along with tactics and basic inference rules, will often be specific to certain theories. This leads to the problem of displaying such rules and tactics, since users cannot be expected to hold them all in their minds. Another (major) challenge is how help can be provided which displays only the applicable rules at the current (sub-)goal.

It should be clear from the above that UI considerations (of generated systems) are crucial to the success of the formal reasoning. A distinction can be made between surface and deep UI issues. The UI is designed so that the (generated) system is more like a helper than a master. It must, on request, show what needs to be done rather than try to dictate the order in which the user must work. There must also be alternative ways for a user (or different users) to view the status of an ongoing proof. Multiple views of different parts of proofs must be possible consistently and naturally across the whole of the UI.

It is essential that it be possible to project different – orthogonal – views of formal objects. The Veritas proof trees [Han83] are a nice test case for what should be possible. In general, it must be possible to view objects at different levels of detail.

It is clear that the user of any complex system will make mistakes. The effect of erroneous input and the control of its removal required serious study. A related need is the ability to invoke any system subroutines from the UI (e.g. substitution). We should even accept that it might be worth simplifying a formula with some (test-case) values before trying to prove that it holds.

The requirements for *mural* reflect the training of the people who are likely to be using

---

[9]Even at the stage of the Muffin prototype [JM88] has a formal specification of the system – cf. Chapter 6.

the formal reasoning tools. Such users are likely to be expert programmers who have received training in formal methods: users cannot be assumed to be mathematicians by training. The tools *mural* provides are intended to expedite the proof process and, together with more education in formal reasoning, will help introduce these harder concepts to 'typical' users.

Chapter 2

Introduction to *mural*

This chapter attempts to give a general overview of the whole of the *mural* system by working through the development described in Chapter 1. It should be noted, however, that, whilst most of what's contained herein is the truth (and where it's not the appropriate confession appears), it is by no means the whole truth – not only has much detail been omitted but the example development has been specifically chosen to make it possible to skip over, or even ignore completely, some of the more esoteric features of the system. These are largely covered in the more detailed descriptions of the separate components of *mural* to be found in Chapters 3 to 8.

2.1 General introduction

The *mural* system consists of two parts, a VDM support tool and a proof assistant. Both components were themselves specified in VDM (see Appendix C for the specification of the proof assistant) and together they provide support for the construction and refinement of VDM specifications and for the proof of the associated proof obligations. In addition, some research work was done on the symbolic execution of specifications, seen as a means of increasing the specification writer's confidence in the initial formal specification by providing a way of 'animating' that specification, and on the basis of this a prototype system was built (see Chapter 9). This prototype was never developed sufficiently for integration with the other components of *mural*, however.

The *mural* interface is based around a series of *tools*. Each tool occupies a separate window and provides a means of creating, inspecting and interacting with the different types of object within the system. Use of a tool generally proceeds via a series of operations like selecting an item from a list of possible items, selecting an action from a menu of possible actions, pressing a "button" to indicate a choice between two alternatives, etc. etc. Most of the interaction is performed with the mouse, though some facilities (e.g. naming of identifiers, use of parsers) clearly require keyboard input[1]. The system tries to be as free as possible both by placing no restriction on the number of tools that can be active at any time and by allowing a task started in one tool to be set aside while still incomplete and the focus of attention to be switched to another task in a different tool. The basic philosophy of the system is that it enforces consistency constraints but permits and records incompletenesses. Thus, for example, it is possible to prove a given result using some lemma without first being forced to prove the lemma, and the result is then

---

[1]Further details of the design of the UI can be found in Chapter 6.

proven modulo the lemma being eventually proven.

The top-level access to both the proof assistant and the VDM support tool is provided by the *store tool* (Figure 2.1). Access to the proof assistant is via the right-hand side of this tool, whilst its left-hand side provides access to the VDM support tool.

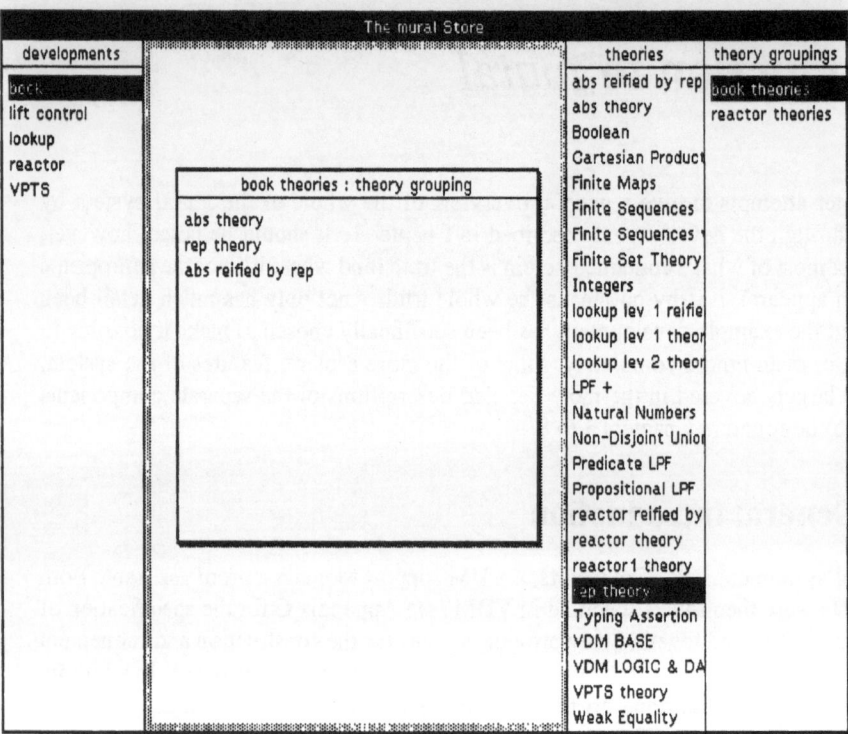

Figure 2.1: The Store Tool

2.2   The proof assistant

The proof assistant essentially provides a way of creating and storing mathematical *theories* hierarchically such that information stored in one theory can be inherited by other theories. A list of (the names of) all the theories currently stored is displayed in the store tool, and new theories can be added or existing ones displayed, renamed or removed from there.

A theory is built or edited with the help of the *theory tool*. This lists the components of the theory around the edge and provides a central area for displaying and editing these components. Figure 2.2 shows the theory tool for propositional LPF[2] which will be used for illustration throughout the beginning of this chapter.

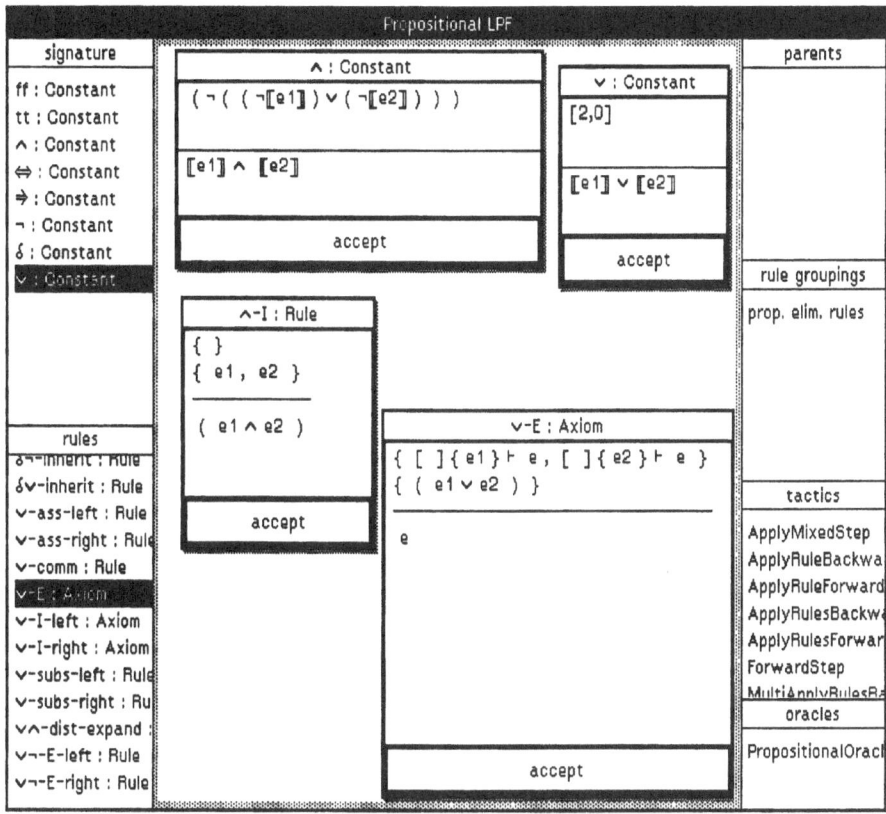

Figure 2.2: The Theory Tool for Propositional LPF

A theory has three main components: a *signature*, a set of *axioms* and a set of *rules*. The signature records the declarations of the symbols which can be used to construct valid formulae in the theory, whilst the axioms record the 'primitive' properties of these symbols, that is those properties which are accepted as being true without proof. Additional properties of the symbols which do require proof are represented by the theory's rules. Rules having a complete proof can be thought of as *derived* rules, those having an incomplete proof as *conjectures*.

Symbols can be declared as 'primitive', in which case their declaration simply records their *arity* (the number of arguments they expect), or they can be defined in terms of

---

[2]Logic of Partial Functions. See [BCJ84].

other symbols by giving the formula representing that definition. Thus, for example, the constants ¬ (not) and ∨ (or) are primitive constants in propositional LPF, having declarations $(1, 0)^3$ and $(2, 0)$ respectively. The constant ∧ (and), on the other hand, is defined in terms of ¬ and ∨ via:

$$\wedge \mapsto \neg(\neg \,[\![e1]\!] \vee \neg \,[\![e2]\!])$$

The *expression placeholder* $[\![ei]\!]$, $i = 1, 2$ represents the ith (expression) argument of the defined symbol ∧ (you can think of the definition as $a \wedge b \triangleq \neg(\neg a \vee \neg b)$ if you prefer – the placeholders simply represent arbitrary values of a and b). The symbol ∧ thus expects two (expression) arguments according to this definition.

Axioms and rules represent valid logical deductions in *mural*. In general they consist of a set of *hypotheses* and a *conclusion* and are to be interpreted as a statement that their conclusion is a direct logical consequence of their hypotheses, alternatively that if all their hypotheses are, or can be proved to be, true then their conclusion is, or can be proved to be, true also.

In *mural* axioms and rules are written with their hypotheses and conclusion respectively above and below a horizontal line. Thus, for example, the axiom ∨-*I-right* ('or introduction on the right') of propositional LPF is written as:

$$\boxed{\vee\text{-}I\text{-}right} \quad \frac{A}{A \vee B}$$

and effectively states that $A \vee B$ is true if A is true.

Axioms and rules can also have *sequents* as well as expressions[4] amongst their hypotheses. A sequent consists of a set of *premises*, each of which is an expression, and an *upshot*, which is also an expression, and is generally written

premises ⊢ *upshot*

The axiom ∨-*E* ('or elimination') in propositional LPF contains sequent hypotheses:

$$\boxed{\vee\text{-}E} \quad \frac{A \vee B, \ A \vdash C, \ B \vdash C}{C}$$

Here the interpretation is that the conclusion C is true if $A \vee B$ is true and if C can be shown to be true by assuming first that A is true and second that B is true. The premises of each sequent thus represent additional local hypotheses which can be assumed to be true when attempting to show that the sequent's upshot is true.

Actually, axioms and rules are considerably more powerful than the above might have implied as the symbols A, B and C appearing in the examples don't stand for *specific* objects but instead represent *any* object, that is they can themselves be complex expressions. In *mural*-speak they're *metavariables*[5] and the axioms ∨-*I-right* and ∨-*E* in fact represent valid deductions for any expressions A, B and C.

Generally axioms are only needed to express the primitive properties of primitive symbols – all properties of defined symbols are usually provable and thus appear as rules. Thus, for example, the standard introduction and elimination properties for the symbol ∧

---

[3]The 1 represents the number of *expression* arguments, the 0 the number of *type* arguments. More about expressions and types later, but for the moment just ignore types.

[4]For a full description of how to construct expressions in *mural* see Section 4.2 or the full formal specification in Appendix C.

[5]There are also *type metavariables* which stand for any type, but we'll ignore those for now. They'll crop up soon enough anyway in Chapters 3 and 4.

appear as (derived) rules in *mural* when ∧ is defined in terms of ¬ and ∨ as above:

$$\boxed{\wedge\text{-}E\text{-}left}\;\frac{A\wedge B}{B}$$

$$\boxed{\wedge\text{-}E\text{-}right}\;\frac{A\wedge B}{A}$$

$$\boxed{\wedge\text{-}I}\;\frac{A,\;B}{A\wedge B}$$

These are proved from the definition of ∧ and the axioms for the primitive constants ¬ and ∨. As an example, the proof of the rule ∧-*I* is shown in Figure 2.3.

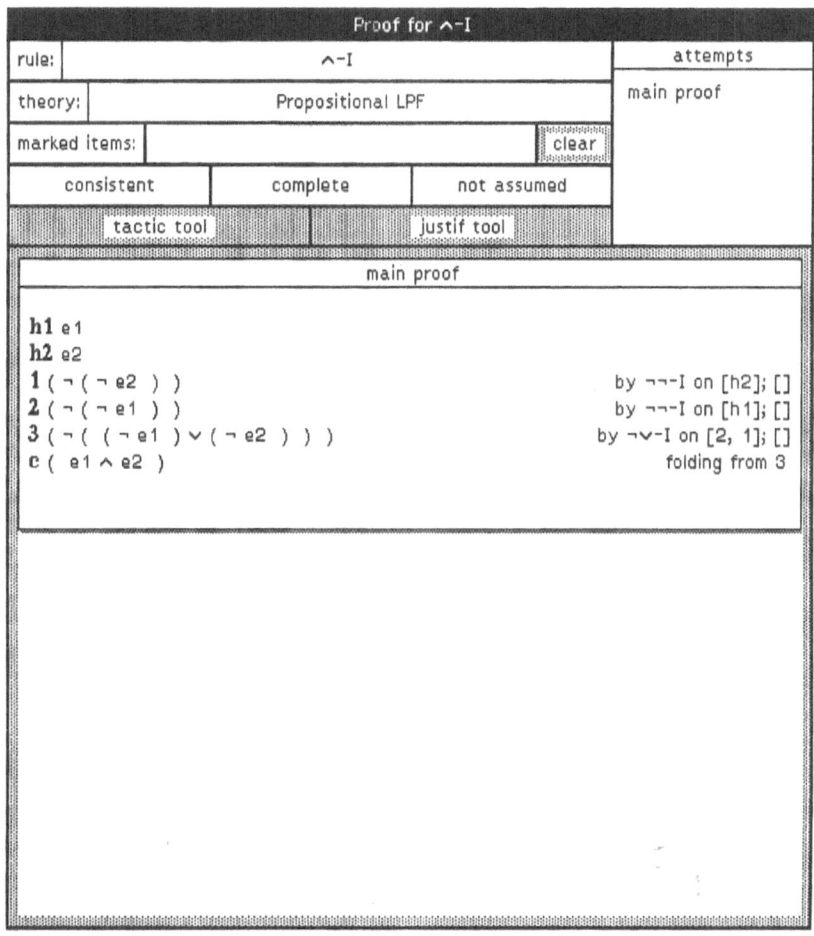

Figure 2.3: The Proof of ∧-*I*

The proof assistant is extensible in that a user can at any stage add new theories to the store using the store tool or new symbol declarations, axioms and rules to an existing theory using the appropriate theory tool. This latter is particularly important as it means that the reasoning power of the system can be increased by adding (and hopefully proving!) more and more powerful rules. These can then be used in attempting to prove yet more powerful rules, and so on.

One rule that might be added to the theory of propositional LPF is the $\wedge\vee$-*dist* rule we've already met in Chapter 1:

$$\boxed{\wedge\vee\text{-}dist}\ \frac{A \wedge (B \vee C)}{(A \wedge B) \vee (A \wedge C)}$$

This can be added to the theory either by structure editing a template rule or by simply typing the required expressions into the template and invoking the parser. Its proof can then be attempted with the help of the *proof tool*.

A proof consists of a set of *hypotheses*, which can include both sequents and expressions, a list of *lines* and *boxes*, and a *conclusion* which is also a line. A line consists of an expression and a *justification* of that expression in terms of some deduction applied to preceding lines, boxes and hypotheses. A box has the same components as a proof except that its hypotheses must all be expressions. The hypotheses and conclusion of a proof should be the same as those of the rule it purports to prove, and the proof is said to be complete if and only if its conclusion has been shown to be a direct logical consequence of its hypotheses.

The proof tool supports five different kinds of justification, though justification by the application of a rule is by far the most commonly used. It also supports three distinct modes of reasoning, namely *forward*, *backward* and *mixed* reasoning. These are best illustrated by returning to the example and showing how the proof of $\wedge\vee$-*dist* might be constructed in *mural*.

When the $\wedge\vee$-*dist* rule is added to the theory of propositional LPF a template proof is automatically attached to it. This is shown in Figure 2.4. The hypotheses and conclusion of this proof are the same as those of the rule, and it has no lines or boxes.

The bold-face (null!) justification **<Justif>** indicates that the justification of the conclusion line is incomplete[6]. Bold-face line numbers, on the other hand, indicate *knowns* of the proof, that is lines which have been shown to be direct logical consequences of the proof's hypotheses. Currently the only known is the hypothesis $h1$ itself!

The first step in the construction of the proof might be to apply the $\wedge$-*E-left* rule to the hypothesis $h1$. This can be done using the *justification tool*, a sub-tool of the proof tool which essentially supports the construction of a single justification at a time.

The justification tool allows the user to designate some subset of the lines, boxes and hypotheses of the proof as *local assumptions* and some line of the proof as a *local goal* and to attempt to justify the local goal by some valid deduction applied to a set of lines, boxes and hypotheses including all the local assumptions. Additional lines and boxes which don't appear amongst the local assumptions but which are needed as assumptions in order to make the deduction valid will be called *ancillary assumptions*. Cases where a local goal is designated but where the set of local assumptions is empty are instances of backward reasoning and correspond to the reduction of the local goal to subgoals. Cases in which no local goal is given and in which no ancillary assumptions are necessary constitute forward reasoning. All other cases are instances of mixed reasoning.

---

[6]A bold-face justification might also indicate that the validity of the justification has not been checked.

```
┌─────────────────────────────────────────────────────────────────┐
│                        Proof for ∧∨-dist                          │
├──────────┬──────────────────────────────────────┬───────────────┤
│  rule:   │              ∧∨-dist                  │   attempts    │
├──────────┼──────────────────────────────────────┼───────────────┤
│ theory:  │         Propositional LPF             │  main proof   │
├──────────┼──────────────────────────────┬────────┤               │
│ marked items: │                          │ clear  │               │
├───────────────┴──────────────┬──────────┴────────┤               │
│   consistent    │ incomplete  │    not assumed    │               │
├─────────────────┴─────────────┴───────────────────┤               │
│      tactic tool          │       justif tool     │               │
└───────────────────────────┴───────────────────────┘               
```

main proof

h1 (A ∧ (B ∨ C))
c ((A ∧ B) ∨ (A ∧ C))   ⟨Justif⟩

Figure 2.4: The Template Proof for ∧∨-*dist*

Justifications built using the justification tool are only actually incorporated into the proof when the user presses an 'update proof' button within it. The justification tool thus provides a means of exploring the consequences of different sequences of actions before the actions are actually performed. In this way, the user might investigate the effect of changing the local assumptions, the local goal, the rule being applied, or indeed try to use a different type of justification altogether before selecting which seems to be the 'best' combination. In each case the tool will show both any necessary ancillary assumptions and, in cases where no local goal is designated, a *new conclusion*. When the user chooses to update the proof, the ancillary assumptions will be added to the proof as new unjustified lines and boxes. In addition, either the local goal will be justified by the justification just constructed or the new conclusion will be added to the proof justified by that justification, whichever is appropriate.

In our simple example the user will select the hypothesis $h1$ as the single local assumption and no local goal will be designated. Selecting the ∧-*E-left* rule from the list of available rules will then cause the justification tool to display the expression $B \vee C$ as a new conclusion. This will be added to the proof as line 1, justified by applying the ∧-*E-left* rule to the hypothesis $h1$, when the proof is updated (see Figure 2.5). Note that the line has a bold-face line number, indicating that it is a known of the proof.

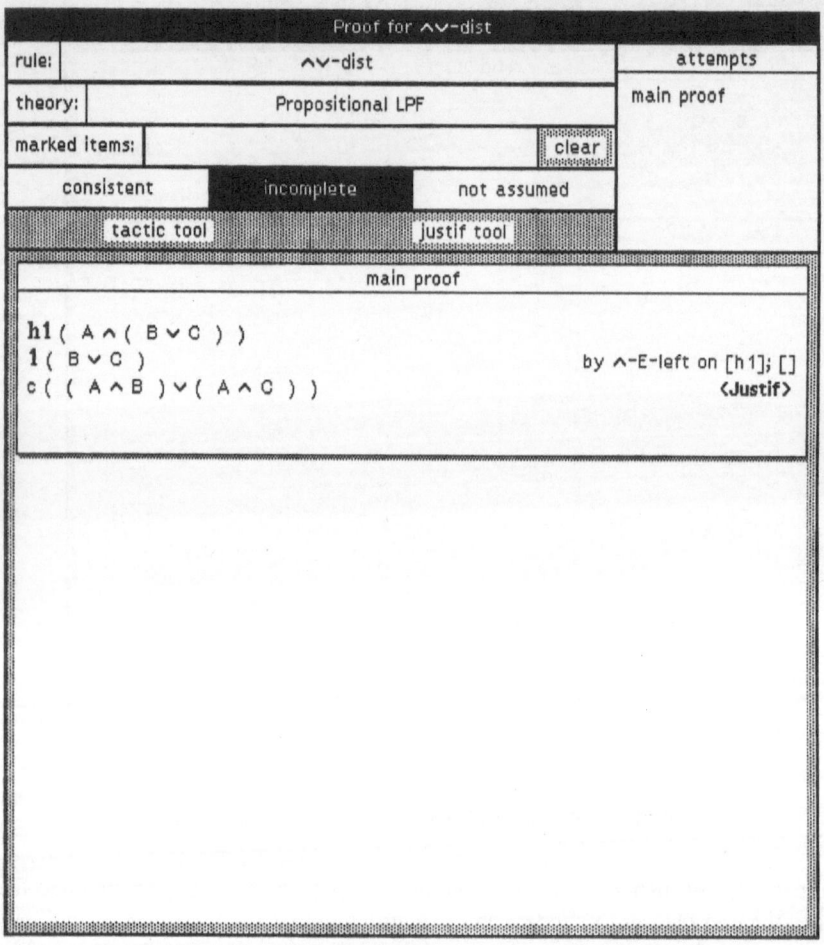

Figure 2.5: The Proof for ∧∨-*dist* after first step

This sort of procedure is fine in simple cases where we already know which rule we want to try to apply, but if we have no idea then trying all possibilities could be somewhat time-consuming. To help with this case, the justification tool has a built-in pattern-matching facility which the user can invoke. This causes the tool to search a user-controlled subset of all potentially applicable rules to find ones which have hypotheses matching each of the local assumptions and whose conclusion similarly matches the local goal, if any. Selecting the new line 1 as the single local assumption and the conclusion of the proof, line *c*, as the local goal and invoking this facility shows that there is only one rule which could possibly be used to try to justify the conclusion line from a set of assumptions including line 1, namely the ∨-*E* rule[7].

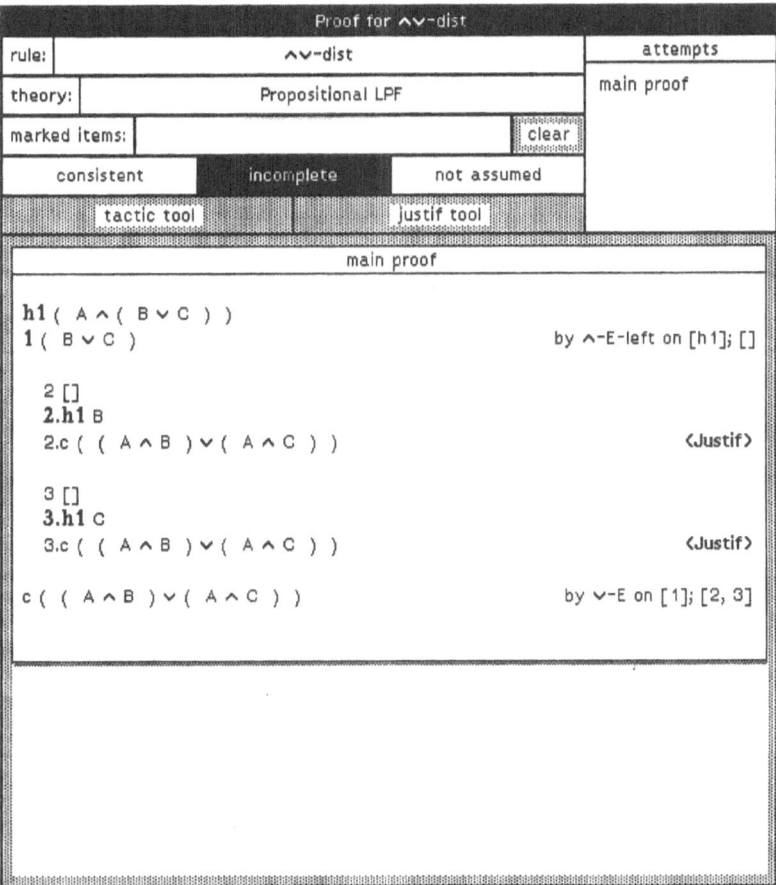

Figure 2.6: The Proof for ∧∨-*dist* after second step

Selecting this causes the justification tool to display two ancillary assumptions, in fact the two sequents

$$B \vdash (A \wedge B) \vee (A \wedge C)$$

$$C \vdash (A \wedge B) \vee (A \wedge C)$$

These appear as boxes when the proof is updated, the premises of the sequent forming

---

[7]Assuming that the theory of propositional LPF only contains its axioms and the introduction and elimination rules for ∧, that is!

the hypotheses of the box and the upshot of the sequent the conclusion of the box. The proof after this step is shown in Figure 2.6. Note that the conclusion line does not have a bold-face line number as its justification depends on unproven assumptions, namely the two boxes 2 and 3 just added[8].

A series of similar manipulations results in the complete proof shown in Figure 2.7.

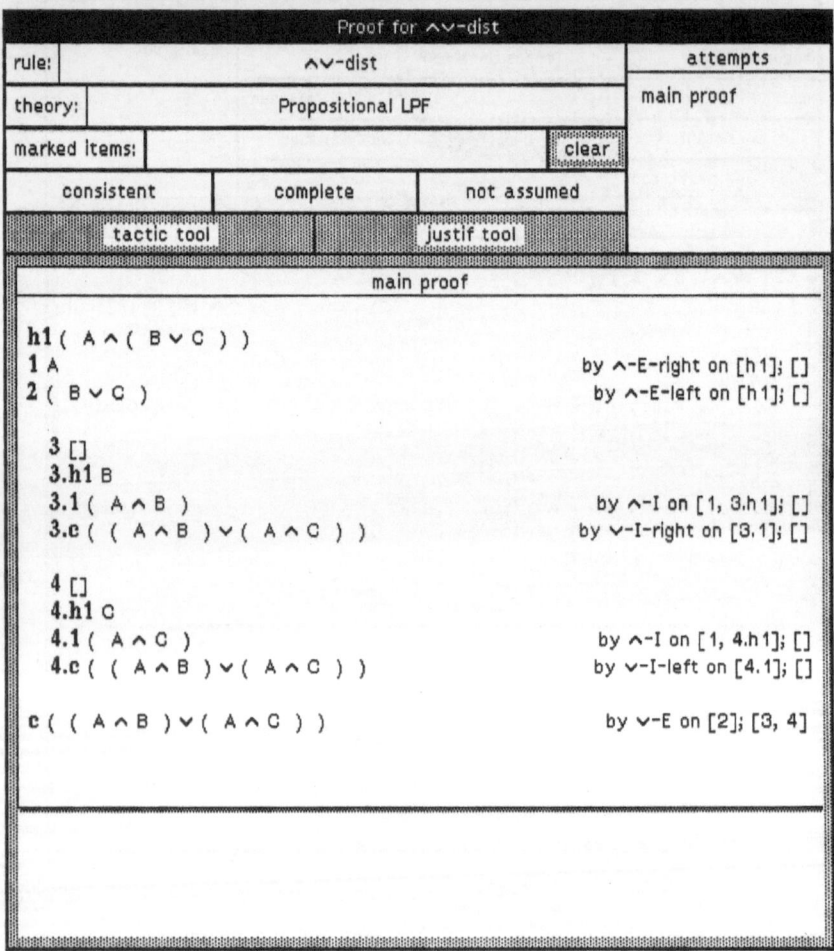

Figure 2.7: The Complete Proof for ∧∨-*dist*

2.2.1 Advanced topics

So far we've only considered building a simple proof by a series of applications of rules. In fact the proof assistant is much more powerful than this in many ways.

---

[8]A box is known when its conclusion is known.

Other kinds of justification

The proof assistant supports four other types of justification in addition to justification by the application of a rule:

justification by application of a sequent hypothesis

Sequent hypotheses can be used in justifications in a similar way to rules except that no substitution for their metavariables is allowed. Thus, for example, the sequent hypothesis $A \vdash B$ may be used as a valid justification of the line B from the line A as in

n	A	
$n+1$	B	by seq hyp $A \vdash B$ on n

but would not be a valid justification in any other case.

justification by unfolding a definition

When a line in a proof contains an expression in which defined symbols occur, the definitions of those symbols may be expanded. The line with the expanded definition is justified by unfolding the definition on the other line, as in the expansion of the definition of $\wedge$ in

n	$A \wedge (B \vee C)$	
$n+1$	$\neg(\neg A \vee \neg(B \vee C))$	by unfolding from n

justification by folding a definition

The reverse of the above, that is the replacement of an expanded definition by its contracted form. Note that the system helps with the construction of both this and the previous kind of justification by highlighting the subterms of the expression which are foldable or unfoldable, whichever is appropriate.

justification by oracle

An oracle is essentially a piece of raw Smalltalk code which is attached to a theory and which can decide whether or not a particular deduction is valid in that theory. Oracles are based on the axioms of the theory but don't make use of them in any real sense, so care has to be taken to ensure that oracles remain in step with changes to the axioms[9]. There's actually not much we can do to enforce this automatically, just as there's no way of enforcing that you don't build a theory with an inconsistent set of axioms, unfortunately. However, there's currently no interface to allow general users to add oracles to the system so you have to make do with the one that's there. By an amazing coincidence, this is one for propositional LPF! Using this, all the hard work expended on that wretched proof of $\wedge\vee$-*dist* could have been avoided and the proof could have been done in a single step! (see Figure 2.8).

Multiple proof attempts

If you get stuck whilst trying to do a proof you might like to set it aside and try a different approach. The proof tool supports this by allowing multiple attempts at a proof to coexist. One attempt is designated the *main attempt* and this is the

---

[9]In principle there would be nothing to stop one writing an oracle which simply returned 'true' for all possible inputs. This would, of course, make all proofs fairly straightforward, but could be said to compromise the soundness of the system somewhat!

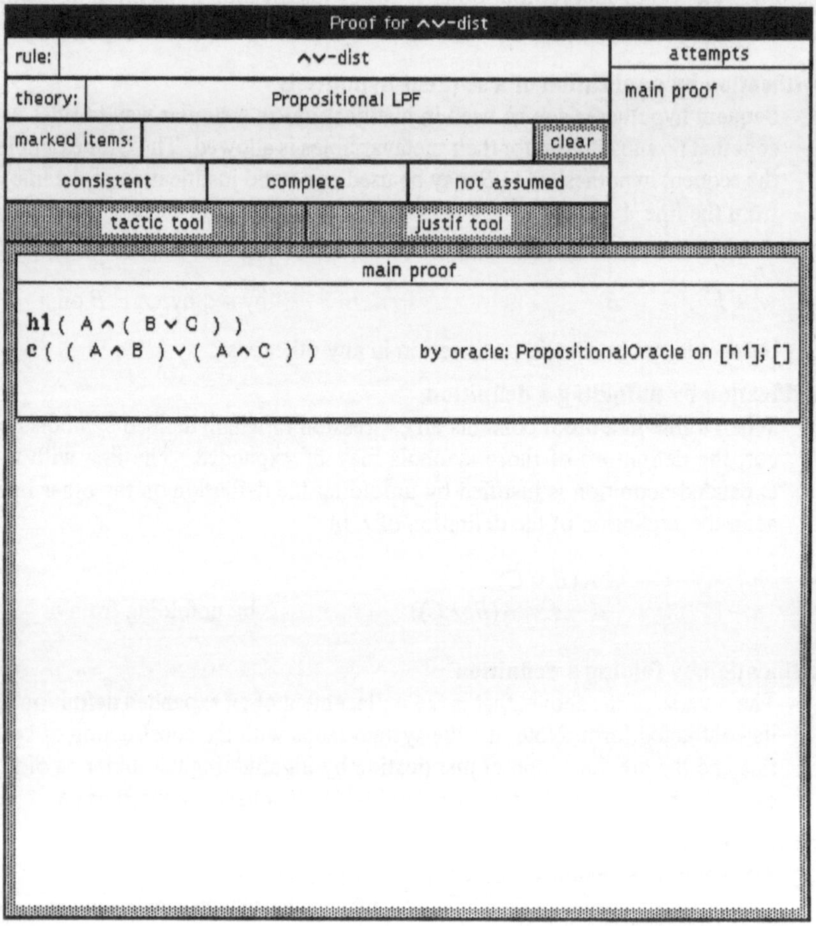

```
                        Proof for ∧∨-dist
 rule:                     ∧∨-dist                          attempts

 theory:               Propositional LPF               main proof

 marked items:                              clear

      consistent         complete         not assumed
           tactic tool               justif tool

                          main proof

 h1 ( A ∧ ( B ∨ C ) )
 c ( ( A ∧ B ) ∨ ( A ∧ C ) )          by oracle: PropositionalOracle on [h1]; []
```

Figure 2.8: The Proof for ∧∨-*dist* using the Oracle

one with which the proof tool interacts. However, you can at any stage make new attempts, either as copies of existing attempts or as new template proofs, and you can switch the designation of the main attempt at will.

In-line lemma creation

If you're in the middle of a proof and feel that some inference would be best separated off as a lemma you can do this in-line by simply designating which lines, boxes and hypotheses are to form the hypotheses of your new lemma and which line its conclusion. You can then use the newly-created lemma immediately to build the justification you want in your current proof without having to go off and prove the lemma first. The proof assistant thus supports a notion of *rigorous*, as opposed to fully formal, proof – rules are only fully formally proved if none of the justifications in the proof appeal to unproven lemmas[10].

Naturally, the proof tool also provides a facility whereby all unproven lemmas on which a proof depends can be found. It also keeps track of the dependency relationship between rules induced by this facility and doesn't allow circularities in this dependency relationship to develop.

Tactics

So far we've only considered the process of building a single justification at a time. However, *mural* also provides a *tactic language*, which allows users to write *tactics* and attach them to theories, and a *tactic tool*, another sub-tool of the proof tool, for running them.

Tactics effectively provide a means of encoding and parametrizing commonly used proof strategies; for instance, a tactic might be written which steps through a list of rules and attempts to apply each rule in turn somewhere in the proof. In this way it is possible for a tactic to perform many steps of a proof. However, it is also possible to make a complete mess of a proof with tactics, for instance by asking a tactic to apply a rule that is always applicable as often as it can[11]. For this reason the tactic tool copies the current main proof attempt before it runs the tactic and then works on the copy. It also displays some information as the tactic executes. If things do go awry you can always stop the execution and throw the copied attempt away.

Removal of garbage

When (the main attempt of) a proof is complete, the proof tool offers a *garbage collection* facility which goes through the proof and throws out any redundant lines and boxes, that is lines and boxes which are not crucial to the logical completeness of the proof. It also throws out all other proof attempts.

2.3 The VDM support tool

The VDM support tool provides facilities for creating and storing specifications and reifications between specifications in VDM[12]. Related[13] specifications and their associated reifications are grouped together as *developments*, which are added, accessed, renamed and removed via the store tool (see Figure 2.1). The left-hand column of the store tool displays a list of (the names of) all the developments currently stored in the system.

A development is built using the *development tool*, which lists the specifications and reifications making up a particular development and allows new ones to be added and old ones to be displayed, renamed or removed. Figure 2.9 shows the development tool for the development described in Section 1.2, which will be taken as the example development throughout the remainder of this chapter.

A general VDM specification consists of a set of *type definitions*, a set of *constant definitions*, a set of *function definitions*, a *state definition* (optional), and a set of *operations*. These are built or edited with the help of the *spec tool* (see Figure 2.10). The various

---

[10]Note that this appeal might be direct or indirect, e.g. all lemmas used in the justifcations in the proof itself might have complete proofs but these proofs might appeal to unproven lemmas, etc.

[11]I once created a line in a proof with 14 ¬'s in it by applying the ¬¬-*I* rule in exactly this way!

[12]Actually a subset of BSI standard VDM.

[13]If only in the mind of the user!

(Abstract) specifications	Reifications	(Concrete) specifications
abs	abs -> rep	abs
rep		rep
abs -> rep aux. spec.		abs -> rep aux. spec.

Figure 2.9: The Development Tool

components of the specification are listed down the left-hand side of the tool under the appropriate headings, whilst the right-hand side of the tool provides an area for displaying and editing them. The various components are constructed by structure editing a template object of the appropriate kind.

The abstract specification in our example development contains three[14] type definitions (*Abs0*, *Abs* and *Sig*) and one operation (*ADD*). These are shown displayed in the spec tool in Figure 2.10. Note that there is no need for a separate function definition describing the invariant *inv-Abs* on *Abs* as this is included as part of the definition of *Abs*. If the form of the other declarations contains the least element of surprise, however, you are advised to go back and read Section 1.2 before continuing. On the basis of this, you should be able to work out for yourself what the components of the corresponding concrete specification look like[15].

Having built the two specifications, you have to return to the development tool to designate the concrete specification as a refinement of the abstract specification. This is done by selecting the two specifications in the left and right portions of the tool as appropriate and adding a reification. You can then use the *reif tool* and the *op model tool* to build the retrieve function[16] and to designate the operation *ADDR* in the concrete specification as the concrete form of the abstract specification's operation *ADD*.

---

[14]Note that an alternative formulation would have been to make *Abs* the state and not a type definition.
[15]If not you might as well give up now!
[16]Again, depressingly similar to that given in Section 1.2.

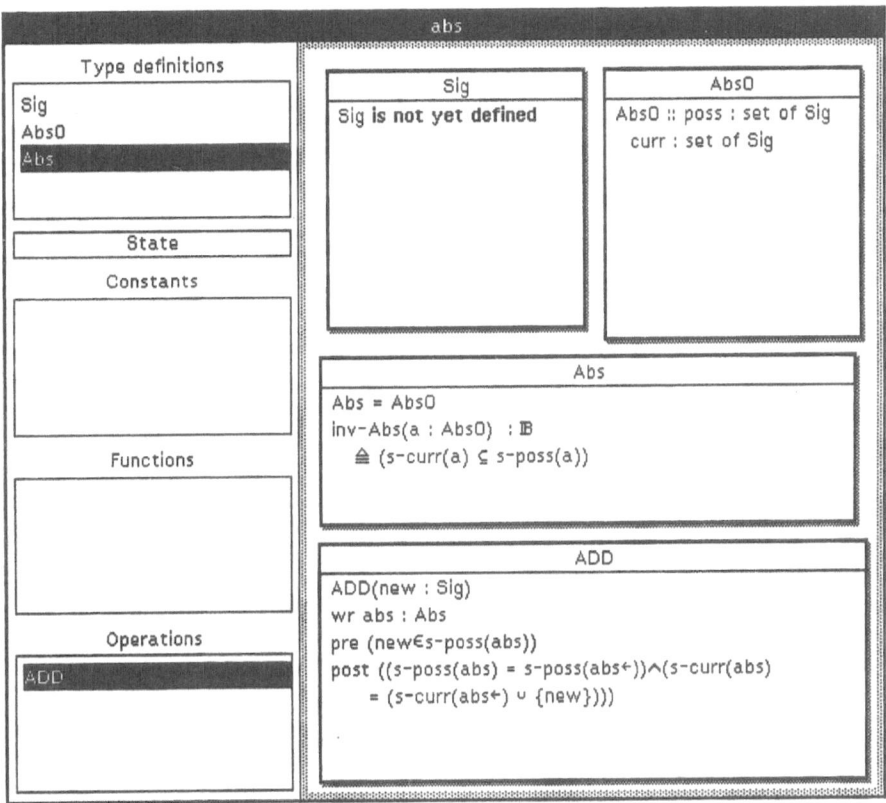

Figure 2.10: The Spec Tool

2.4 Reasoning about developments

It is, of course, perfectly feasible to reason informally about a development as it stands simply by using your knowledge of what its various components 'mean'. Indeed, you probably do so, even though you might not think of it in those terms, when you're writing each specification and reification, at least to the extent of trying to convince yourself that the whole thing hangs together properly. On the other hand, it is very difficult to reason formally about it in its current form as we have no formal language in which to do so. We thus have to somehow extract the 'meaning' we use in our informal reasoning in a form which does admit formal reasoning. This facility is provided in *mural* in the form of a mechanism whereby a specification or a reification in the VDM support tool can be 'translated' automatically into a theory supporting reasoning about it in the proof assistant[17].

One thing we have to consider here is that the components of a particular development

---

[17]But a reification can only be translated if the specifications it reifies have already been translated.

are built up not only out of user-defined type, constant and function definitions but also out of the 'primitive' constructors of the specification language itself. Thus, for example, in order to be able to reason about a VDM development we need to be able to reason about things like sets, sequences, integers, etc. which are part of the VDM language. Of course, these objects are common to all VDM developments and can thus be factored out. This is done in *mural* by making use of the proof assistant's inheritance hierarchy on theories and introducing the notion of an *instantiation* of the proof assistant to a particular specification language: theories describing the properties of the primitive data types of the specification are built and one theory, which will inherit from all these, is designated as the theory of the specification language. Theories generated by translation from a specification support tool[18] are then placed in the theory hierarchy so that they inherit from the theory of the appropriate specification language. Theories of specifications are currently placed so that they inherit directly from this theory, theories of reifications so that they inherit directly from the theories of the specifications they reify.

Returning to our example, translation of the abstract specification gives rise to a theory called *abs theory* in (a VDM instantiation of) the proof assistant. This is shown in Figure 2.11. Its signature contains declarations of symbols representing the types and invariants defined in the specification (*Abs0*, *Abs*, *Sig* and *inv-Abs*) and of symbols representing auxiliary functions implicitly associated with the composite type *Abs0*, that is a symbol *mk-Abs0* representing the *mk*-function and symbols *s-poss* and *s-curr*[19] representing the selector functions for its fields. With the exception of *Abs* and *inv-Abs*, which are translated to a defined type constant and a defined constant respectively (see Figure 2.11), all these symbols are translated to primitive symbols in the signature. Thus, *Sig* and *Abs0* both have arity (0,0), *s-poss* and *s-curr* both have arity (1,0), and *mk-Abs0* has arity (2,0).

The translation process also generates axioms describing the properties of these symbols. There are two axioms for each of the selector functions (*s-poss* and *s-curr*) of *Abs0*, a *formation* axiom and a *definition* axiom. The former states the typing information associated with the particular selector function, whilst the latter defines which component of the composite object it selects. For the *s-poss* selector function their explicit forms are:

$$\boxed{poss\text{-}formation} \quad \frac{a\colon Abs0}{s\text{-}poss(a)\colon Sig\text{-}set}$$

$$\boxed{poss\text{-}definition} \quad \frac{mk\text{-}Abs0(p, c)\colon Abs0}{s\text{-}poss(mk\text{-}Abs0(p, c)) = p}$$

Note that the colon ':' represents type assignment – the expression $a\colon Abs0$ is thus to be read '*a* is of type *Abs0*' or '*a* is an *Abs0*'. In words, the formation axiom states that if *a* is an *Abs0* then *s-poss* applied to *a* is a set of *Sig*s, whilst the definition axiom states that *s-poss* selects the first component of any composite object of type *Abs0* (in this axiom $mk\text{-}Abs0(p, c)$ simply represents the most general form of an object of type *Abs0*). The axioms describing *s-curr* are unremarkably similar.

---

[18]Although the current version of *mural* only supports developments in VDM, the proof assistant is sufficiently generic that it could be used in conjunction with tools supporting a wide range of other specification languages in exactly the same way.

[19]Since the BSI standard for VDM hadn't been fixed as we neared the end of the project, we were forced to adopt what seemed to be the most stable part of what passed for it around the end of 1989 when building our VDM support tool. Inevitably, this turned out to be not as stable as we had hoped, and this notation has now been changed. When the standard finally settles down it's fairly easy to change these names, but until then it seems a bit futile. In the meantime, our apologies for the anachronism.

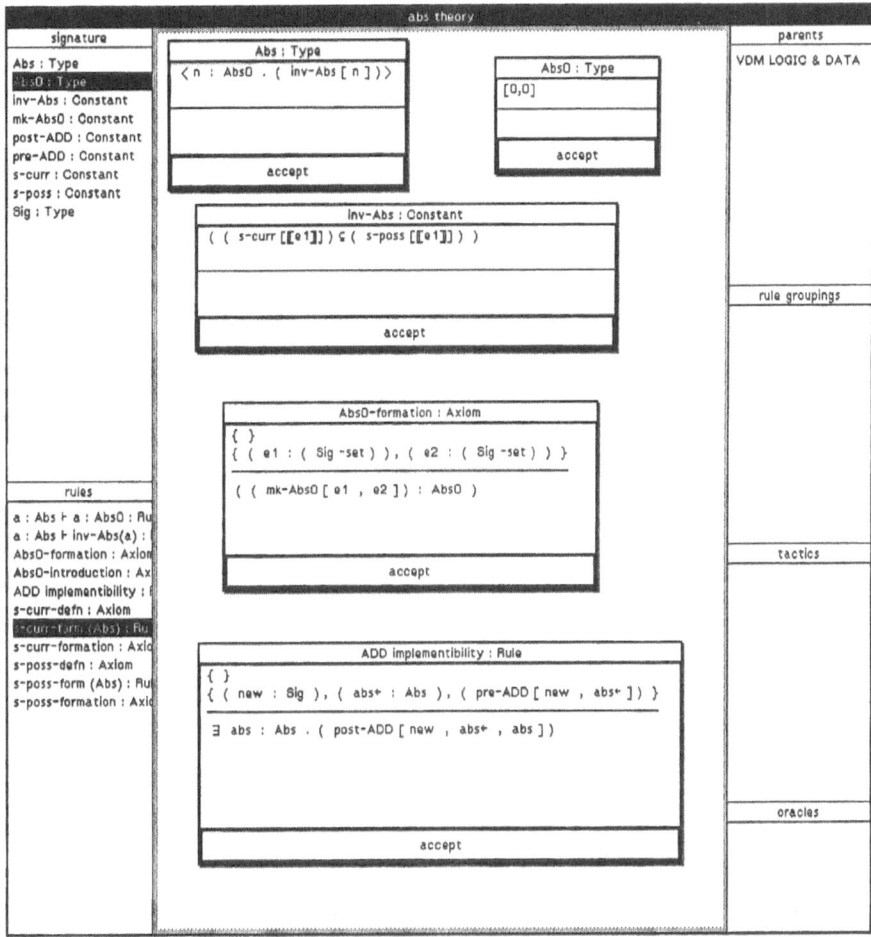

Figure 2.11: The Theory Tool for the Abstract Specification

The properties of the composite type *Abs0* are similarly described by two axioms, a *formation* axiom and an *introduction* axiom. This time, the formation axiom states that you can build an object of type *Abs0* by applying the *mk*-function to component objects of the appropriate type (i.e. two sets of *Sig*s):

$$\text{Abs0-formation}\ \frac{p\colon Sig\text{-set},\ c\colon Sig\text{-set}}{mk\text{-}Abs0(p,c)\colon Abs0}$$

whilst the introduction axiom states that the selector functions and the *mk*-function are inverse, in the sense that if we smash an object of type *Abs0* to pieces using the selector functions then combine the pieces using the *mk*-function we get back the original object:

$$mk\text{-}Abs0\text{-introduction}\ \frac{a\colon Abs0}{mk\text{-}Abs0(s\text{-}poss(a),s\text{-}curr(a))=a}$$

There are no axioms describing *Abs* and *inv-Abs* since these are translated to defined symbols[20].

Other components of the theory arise from translating the operation *ADD*. This process adds defined symbols *pre-ADD* and *post-ADD* to the signature[21] and additionally generates the *satisfiability proof obligation*[22] associated with the operation (see Section 1.2) as a *rule*[23]. This rule has the form:

$$\boxed{\textit{ADD-satisfiability}} \quad \frac{\textit{new}\colon \textit{Sig},\ \overleftarrow{a}\colon \textit{Abs}0,\ \textit{pre-ADD}(\textit{new},\ \overleftarrow{a}\,)}{\exists a\colon \textit{Abs} \cdot \textit{post-ADD}(\textit{new},\ \overleftarrow{a}\,,\,a)}$$

The proof assistant can then be used to attempt to prove this rule via a series of steps like those outlined in Section 2.2.

By a similar process we can generate the theory corresponding to the concrete specification and discharge the proof obligation stating the satisfiability of the operation *ADDR*.

Having constructed the theories of our two specifications we are now in a position to try to prove that our reification is valid. The relevant theory can again be constructed automatically and is placed in the theory hierarchy so that it inherits directly from the theories of the two specifications that we've just created. This theory has a signature which contains only one symbol, the defined symbol *retr-Abs* corresponding to the retrieve function in the reification, and it has no axioms[24]. It does contain three rules, however, namely those stating the proof obligations associated with the reification (that is the adequacy, domain and result obligations. See Section 1.2). Again, the proofs of these can be attempted using the proof assistant. As an example, the rule stating the domain obligation has the form

$$\boxed{\textit{ADDR-domain-obl}} \quad \frac{\textit{new}\colon \textit{Sig},\ r\colon \textit{Rep},\ \textit{pre-ADD}(\textit{new},\ \textit{retr-Abs}(r))}{\textit{pre-ADDR}(\textit{new},\ r)}$$

Its proof is shown in Figure 2.12. Note that this proof is somewhat longer than the 'text-book style' version given in Section 1.2. This is because it shows *all* the formal manipulations performed – some 'obvious' steps are elided in Section 1.2.

---

[20]Actually, at the time of writing this is a lie! *Abs* is indeed translated to a defined symbol but axioms are generated to describe the properties of *inv-Abs*. Work on the translation process is still being carried out, however, and it is expected that *inv-Abs* will be translated to a defined symbol by the time you read this. We'll assume so here anyway, if only because it makes the proof appearing at the end of the chapter shorter! (Translating to a defined symbol means that the definition can be expanded or contracted in a single step using the justifications by folding and unfolding definitions – with the axiomatic approach currently adopted each of these processes requires two steps.)

[21]Again a lie! But the same applies here as to the invariant (see above).

[22]Aka the *implementability proof obligation, ADD-implementability*!

[23]We are (deliberately!) ignoring the generation of 'well-formedness rules' stating that preconditions, etc. are correctly typed here. See Section 8.2 for a discussion of these.

[24]More lies! But again the same applies to the retrieve function as to the invariant (see above).

Proof for ADDR domain obl

rule:	ADDR domain obl	attempts
theory:	abs reified by rep	main proof
marked items:		clear

consistent	complete	not assumed

tactic tool   justif tool

main proof

h1 (new : Sig)
h2 (r : Rep)
h3 (pre-ADD [new , (retr-Abs [r])])
1 ((retr-Abs [r]) : Abs)   by retr-Abs formation on [h2]; []
2 ((retr-Abs [r]) : Abs0)   by a : Abs ⊢ a : Abs0 on [1]; []
3 ((mk-Abs0 [(elems [(s-posi [r])]) , those s : Sig .
∃ i : N_i . ((i ∈ (inds [(s-posi [r])])) ∧ (((s-curl [r
]) @ i) ∧ (s = ((s-posi [r]) @ i))))]) : Abs0)   unfolding from 2
4
((s-poss [(mk-Abs0 [(elems [(s-posi [r])]) , those s :
Sig . ∃ i : N_i . ((i ∈ (inds [(s-posi [r])])) ∧ (((
s-curl [r]) @ i) ∧ (s = ((s-posi [r]) @ i))))])]) = (
elems [(s-posi [r])]))   by s-poss-defn on [3]; []
5 ((s-poss [(retr-Abs [r])]) = (elems [(s-posi [r])]))   folding from 4
6 (new ∈ (s-poss [(retr-Abs [r])]))   unfolding from h3
7 (new ∈ (elems [(s-posi [r])]))   by =-subs-right on [6, 5]; []
8 ∃ i : N_i .
((i ∈ (inds [(s-posi [r])])) ∧ (((s-posi [r]) @ i) =
new))   by elems expand on [7, h1, s-posi-form (Rep) on [h2]; []]; []
c (pre-ADDR [new , r])   folding from 8

Figure 2.12: The Proof of the *ADDR* Domain Obligation

Chapter 3

Instantiation

The *mural* proof assistant is generic in that it can be instantiated with many different logics and theories. The user is provided with a *logical frame* which can be configured to support reasoning in any number of different logics. The purpose of this chapter is to illustrate how to instantiate *mural* for some common logics. It can be used to gain familiarity with the proof assistant or as a kind of cookbook for people intending to configure *mural* for formalisms of their own interest.

3.1   Symbolic logic in *mural*

The two main logics illustrated are classical predicate calculus and a logic of partial functions (LPF). For both logics, many different theories are axiomatized, including the theories of commonly used mathematical constructs such as sets and lists, and along the way many subtle points and potential pitfalls are noted. The theory of VDM is given in some detail, providing an interesting case study of what can realistically be achieved using *mural*. Later sections are devoted to other powerful logics.

The chapter is addressed to all *mural* users, but for convenience we shall distinguish two different kinds of user:

1. 'the instantiator', who configures the system so that it can be used for reasoning in a particular formalism – by axiomatizing the basic concepts and instantiating the underlying logic, etc.

2. 'the verifier', who wants assistance reasoning in a particular problem domain – say, to validate a particular VDM specification, or to derive new properties of an abstract data type.

The main difference between these two kinds of user is that the first is concerned with setting up the right axiom system, perhaps from scratch, while the second is more interested in proving theorems. (In fact, the two activities cannot be separated quite so easily: the instantiator chooses axioms at least partly on the basis of their ease of use, and the verifier has to understand the theories provided by the instantiator.) This chapter will be of interest to both kinds of user, but many remarks will be addressed to one over the other.

For any particular theory there are often many different possible formulations, depending for example on which concepts are taken as primitive and which derived, or even on the order in which concepts are introduced. Such distinctions may be important, especially on a philosophical or methodological level, or simply for pedagogical reasons.

In what follows, however, the primary motivation is to illustrate properties of the *mural* logical frame; concepts are often introduced simply to make a point, to illustrate a subtlety or to show alternative approaches to formalization.

This chapter is not supposed to be an introduction to symbolic logic: the reader is assumed to have at least a passing familiarity with the notions being formalized. Intuitions about the correctness of axioms can only be gained by careful study of the semantics of the mathematical objects involved, and understanding the problem domain well is the only way to achieve simple, manageable proofs. The other vital consideration is choice of formalism, but this chapter can offer only general words of advice and illustration by example.

3.1.1   Terminology and notation

Only a brief informal introduction to the terminology and notation used in this chapter will be given here. Formal details of the *mural* logical frame are presented in the 'Foundations' chapter, Chapter 4 below.

Theories

A *theory* is a grouping of results that have something in common. A *mural* theory consists of:

- a *signature*, indicating which symbols are available;

- a set of *inference rules*, some of which are *axioms* (self evident truths or assumptions), some of which are *derived* from axioms using proofs, and some of which are merely *conjectures* which the user may or may not prove at some later date;

- a set of *tactics*, which are strategies for building proofs in this theory;

- a set of *oracles*, which are hand-coded decision procedures.

A *logic* is just a theory of special significance: logics and theories are not distinguished in *mural*.

mural theories are stored in an inheritance hierarchy. Theories have a (possibly empty) set of 'parent' theories from which they inherit symbols, rules, tactics and oracles. Thus for example, a theory of lists might inherit results from the theory of natural numbers which would be used when it comes to reasoning about the length function on lists, say. Turning it around the other way, we sometimes say the child theory *extends* its parents. Theories inherit from their parents, their parents' parents, and so on. Thus in fact a theory inherits from all of its 'ancestor' theories.

Signatures

Four different kinds of symbol (*atoms*) can be declared in a signature:

- constants, such as 'true', '∧', '∈', '='

- binders, such as '∀', '∃', 'λ'

- type constructors, such as 'ℕ', '×', '-set'

- type binders, such as dependent products

By 'constant' we mean functions, operators, predicates, relations, metavariables and so on. Similarly, 'type constructors' covers type constants, type functions, type metavariables, etc. The syntax is considerably simplified by grouping things in these ways.

As well as declaring symbols, signatures perform several other roles. Information about how the symbol is to be displayed on the screen is stored there. The *arity* of constants and type constructors (how many arguments they expect) is also declared there. (Note that arities are fixed in *mural*.) And signatures can store definitions, such as

$$P \wedge Q \;\triangleq\; \neg(\neg P \vee \neg Q)$$

which defines $\wedge$ in terms of $\vee$ and $\neg$, and

$$\exists x{:}A \cdot P[x] \;\triangleq\; \neg \forall x{:}A \cdot \neg P[x]$$

which defines $\exists$ in terms of $\forall$ and $\neg$.

Formulae

Symbols from signatures and variables are put together to form *terms*, the abstract syntax of which can be defined in Extended BNF (Backus-Naur Form) roughly as follows:

```
Term =  Exp | Type
 Exp =  VSymb
        | CESymb{Exp}{Type}
        | DESymb VSymb':'Type'·'Exp
Type =  CTSymb {Exp}{Type}
        | DTSymb VSymb':'Type'·'Type
        | '<'VSymb':'Type'·'Exp'>'
```

where {} means zero or more occurrences and symbols in inverted commas are concrete syntax, introduced to enhance legibility.

In more detail, there are two different kinds of term: *expressions* (Exps) and *Types* (Types). All mathematical formulae are Exps in *mural* syntax. Expressions are built up from variables (VSymbs) using two kinds of combinators:

- *compound* (or *ordinary*) *expressions*, whereby a constant (CESymb) is 'applied' to (possibly empty) lists of expressions and types, called its operands or *arguments*;[1]

- *binder expressions*, whereby a binder (DESymb) is supplied with a dummy variable (the variable it binds), a type (the universe of the bound variable) and an expression (the body of the binder expression).

Types are built up using three kinds of combinator:

- *compound* (or *ordinary*) *types*, whereby a type constructor (CTSymb) is applied to expression and type argument lists;

---

[1] What mathematicians would normally call constants are compound expressions with empty argument lists, in this syntax.

- *dependent types*, whereby a dependent-type symbol (DTSymb) is supplied with a dummy variable and two types (the universe of the bound variable and the body of the dependent type, respectively);

- *subtypes* of given types, specified by giving a dummy variable, the universe over which it ranges (a Type) and a defining predicate (an Exp).

Collectively, constants and type constructors will be called *constructors*. Binder expressions, dependent types and subtypes will be called *variable binding constructs* since they bind occurrences of their dummy variables in their bodies.

The arity of a constructor is a pair of natural numbers, the first indicating how many Exp arguments it expects and the second indicating the number of Type arguments. So for example, $\wedge$ is a CESymb of arity (2, 0) and -set is a CTSymb of arity (0, 1).

The full syntax also allows indexed *placeholders* (called *expression holes* and *type holes*) which act as formal parameters in definitions, instantiations, and so on. Thus for example, the definition of $\wedge$ above must actually be given to *mural* in the form

$$\neg(\neg \llbracket e1 \rrbracket \vee \neg \llbracket e2 \rrbracket)$$

where $\llbracket ei \rrbracket$ stands for the ith Exp placeholder.

That finishes our brief summary of the *mural* syntax for expressions and types: for formal details see Section 4.2. Note that although *mural* provides a syntax for writing types, it does not impose a type discipline: that is the instantiator's job.

Some examples

Here are some examples from VDM to illustrate the *mural* approach:

- $P \wedge Q$ and cons(a, l) are compound expressions, with CESymbs $\wedge$ and cons respectively;

- $\forall x: \mathbf{Z} \cdot 0 \leq x^2$ and $\lambda y: \mathbf{R} \cdot y^2 + 1$ are binder expressions, with DESymbs $\forall$ and λ; and

- $\mathbf{N}$-set and $A \xrightarrow{m} B$ are compound types, with CTSymbs set and map.

Note that the name and the display form of a symbol are not necessarily the same thing.

In VDM, subtypes are defined by specifying an invariant on a constructed or pre-existing type. VDM subtypes must be given names, but our syntax provides for direct construction, such as

$$EvenNumbers \triangleq\ < n: \mathbf{N} \cdot n \bmod 2 = 0 >$$

VDM doesn't have dependent types, but most readers will have come across dependent products such as

$$\prod_{n:\mathbf{N}} < m: \mathbf{N} \cdot n^2 \leq m >$$

consisting of functions $f: \mathbf{N} \to \mathbf{N}$ such that $n^2 \leq f(n)$ for all $n: \mathbf{N}$, and dependent sums such as

$$\sum_{n:\mathbf{N}_1} < s: A^* \cdot \operatorname{len} s = n^2 >$$

consisting of pairs (n, s) from $\mathbf{N}_1 \times A^*$ such that $\operatorname{len} s = n^2$.

Rules

Inference rules are the primary unit of reasoning in *mural*, covering axioms, theorems, lemmas, conjectures and so on. An inference rule consists of:

1. a set of zero or more *ordinary hypotheses*

2. a set of zero or more *sequent hypotheses*

3. a *conclusion*

In Extended BNF this can be defined roughly as:

$$
\begin{aligned}
\texttt{Rule} &= \texttt{\{Ohyp\}\{SHyp\}Concl} \\
\texttt{OHyp} &= \texttt{Concl = Exp} \\
\texttt{SHyp} &= \texttt{\{VSymb\}\{Premise\}Upshot} \\
\texttt{Premise} &= \texttt{Upshot = Exp}
\end{aligned}
$$

For example, the law of induction over natural numbers can be expressed as

$$
\frac{P[0],\quad \{n\colon \mathsf{N},\ P[n]\} \vdash_n P[n+1]}{\forall m\colon \mathsf{N}\cdot P[m]}
$$

This has a single hypothesis of each kind. The ordinary hypothesis is $P[0]$, which corresponds to the base case of the induction. The sequent hypothesis is

$$
\{n\colon \mathsf{N},\ P[n]\} \vdash_n P[n+1]
$$

corresponding to the induction step. (Since subscripting is not available in the *mural* screen format, such a sequent is displayed on the screen as

$$
[n]\{n\colon \mathsf{N},\ P[n]\} \vdash P[n+1]
$$

Sequents are explained in detail in Section 4.3. In brief: a sequent consists of a set of premises and an upshot, and a sequent can 'bind' variables, e.g. n in the above case.) Finally, the conclusion of the rule is written below the horizontal line. The notation

$$
\frac{P}{\overline{Q}}
$$

stands for the pair of rules $\frac{P}{Q}$ and $\frac{Q}{P}$.

Metavariables

As the induction example above shows, *mural* rules can in fact represent whole schemas of inference rules. For example, $P[x]$ might be instantiated by

$$
P[x] \;\longmapsto\; \forall y\colon \mathsf{N}\cdot x+y=y+x
$$

to give a rule instance with conclusion

$$
\forall m\colon \mathsf{N}\cdot \forall y\colon \mathsf{N}\cdot m+y=y+m
$$

new base case $\forall y\colon \mathsf{N}\cdot 0+y=y+0$, and so on. P is called a *metavariable*, and it is a parameter to the rule. (In fact, it is the only parameter to the rule above.) Ordinary free variables are not allowed in rules.

Simple proofs

New inference rules are derived from old inference rules by building a *proof*. Essentially, a proof is simply a chaining together of instances of rules. For example,

$$\frac{A \wedge B}{B \wedge A}$$

can be derived by putting together appropriate instances of the rules

$$\frac{P \wedge Q}{P} \qquad \frac{P \wedge Q}{Q} \qquad \frac{P,\ Q}{P \wedge Q}$$

in the following way:

$$\frac{\dfrac{A \wedge B}{B} \qquad \dfrac{A \wedge B}{A}}{B \wedge A}$$

For larger derivations it is more convenient to express the proof in the flattened form

    from $A \wedge B$

1	A	rule 1 (h1)
2	B	rule 2 (h1)
infer $B \wedge A$		rule 3 (2,1)

which is roughly how it is displayed in *mural*.

Let's look a little more closely at the components of the above proof. It consists of:

- a single hypothesis ($A \wedge B$ – implicitly labelled h1),

- a sequence of lines (labelled 1, 2), and

- a conclusion ($B \wedge A$).

Non-hypothesis lines are *justified* by rule instances: e.g. line 1 follows from h1 by an appropriate instance of the first rule. The justification – on the right-hand side of each non-hypothesis line – notes which rule is used and on which lines the justification depends (its *antecedents*). The actual instantiation used is not displayed in the proof, but is stored by *mural* to speed correctness checking.

Other forms of justification are possible, such as by unfolding a definition, or by making appeal to an oracle: see Section 4.7.5 for more details. Antecedents are always noted, by listing them in parentheses at the end of the line. There are restrictions on which lines can be used to justify other lines, mainly to do with precluding circular reasoning: see Section 4.7.4 for details. Roughly, justifications should only appeal to lines appearing earlier in the proof.

Proofs with subproofs

Things are a bit more complicated when justifications involve sequents. Consider a proof by induction for example: the induction step involves making some temporary, 'local' assumptions (the so-called induction hypotheses) – so we must allow for subproofs which have their own additional hypotheses. Such subproofs are called *boxes* in *mural*. A box consists of a set of hypotheses, a sequence of lines and boxes, and a conclusion. Boxes can be nested within boxes to any degree. Boxes may also introduce their own local variables, corresponding to variables bound in sequents. In fact, a sequent is just a 'squashed' box.

These ideas are illustrated in the following simple proof, involving induction over natural numbers:

from
1    $0 + 0 = 0$ + axiom 1 ()
2_n from $n: \mathbb{N},\ 0 + n = n$
2.1 $0 + (n + 1) = (0 + n) + 1$ + axiom 2 (2.h1)
       infer $0 + (n + 1) = n + 1$ substitution (2.h2,2.1)
infer $\forall m: \mathbb{N} \cdot 0 + m = m$ $\mathbb{N}$ induction (1,2)

The box structure of the proof is indicated by indenting and using from and infer keywords. At the outermost level, this proof has zero hypotheses, a single line (1) and a single box (2). Box 2 is the subproof corresponding to the induction step: it introduces a new variable n – shown here as a subscript on the box's label – such that n is a natural number (hypothesis 2.h1) and $0 + n = n$ (hypothesis 2.h2). No other assumptions can be made about n, and its scope is restricted to box 2 and its subboxes, if it had any; in other words, n cannot be used elsewhere in the proof outside box 2. (Similarly, lines outside the box cannot make appeal to lines within the box.) Finally, as a notational convention, all lines within the box are labelled with prefix '2.', including hypothesis lines and subboxes, if any.

The rule extracted from the above proof is

$$\frac{}{\forall m: \mathbb{N} \cdot 0 + m = m}$$

Note that the main proof itself is a box, but it is not allowed to introduce variables since rules cannot have free variables.

Figure 3.1 shows a proof of the – not very deep – fact that sets can be represented by non-repeating lists; in symbols:

$$\frac{s: Set}{\exists l: List \cdot elems\ l = s}$$

Tactics

The interactive approach to verification can call for a considerable amount of work on the user's part. LCF [GMW79] and its descendants [C⁺86, Gor85, Pau86] showed how that burden can be lessened by providing the user with a simple imperative language for expressing certain commonly-used proof strategies, called *tactics*. In technical terms, LCF tactics are functions which reduce 'goals' to lists of 'subgoals', together with a validation function which is supposed to build an 'achievement' of the goal from achievements of the subgoals. Tactics in *mural*, on the other hand, operate directly on proofs, extending them non-destructively. The *mural* tactic language gives the same access to basic *mural* operations as is available from the user interface, in addition to imperative constructs such as sequencing, branching and backtracking. Tactics can be parameterized, can call other tactics – including themselves – and can even poll the user for additional information at runtime.

from s: *Set*

1	elems $[\,] = \{\,\}$	elems axiom1 ()
2	$[\,]$: *List*	$[\,]$-formation ()
3	$\exists l$: *List* $\cdot$ elems $l = \{\,\}$	$\exists$-introduction (1,2)
$4_{a,w}$	from $a \notin w$, $\exists l$: *List* $\cdot$ elems $l = w$	
4.1_{l_0}	from l_0: *List*, elems $l_0 = w$	
4.1.1	$a \notin$ elems l_0	substitution (4.1.h2,4.h1)
4.1.2	cons(a, l_0): *List*	cons-formation (4.1.h1,4.1.1)
4.1.3	elems cons$(a, l_0) =$ elems $l_0 \cup \{a\}$	elems axiom2 ()
4.1.4	elems cons$(a, l_0) = w \cup \{a\}$	substitution (4.1.h2,4.1.3)
	infer $\exists l$: *List* $\cdot$ elems $l = w \cup \{a\}$	$\exists$-introduction (4.1.4,4.1.2)
	infer $\exists l$: *List* $\cdot$ elems $l = w \cup \{a\}$	$\exists$-elimination (4.h2,4.1)
5	$\forall u$: *Set* $\cdot$ $\exists l$: *List* $\cdot$ elems $l = u$	set induction (3,4)
	infer $\exists l$: *List* $\cdot$ elems $l = s$	$\forall$-elimination (h1,5)

Figure 3.1: An example proof.

Oracles

It would be impossibly tedious to perform all reasoning at the level of inference rules, even with the aid of tactics. There are large classes of problems for which fully automated solutions are feasible: decision procedures exist for classical propositional calculus (via truth-tables), simple arithmetic, linear algebra, naive set theory, and many other theories. Such decision procedures can be incorporated into *mural* as oracles.

Basically, an oracle is a procedure which, when invoked on a proof line, checks the validity of that line in terms of its antecedents. Oracles must be hand-coded and so require some knowledge of the internal workings of the *mural* software. Oracles are axiomatic, in as much as their truth is never questioned. Their validity is entirely the responsibility of the person instantiating the logic, and it is obviously important they be logically consistent with the axioms of the theory in which they are placed. Instantiators are thus advised to use this facility with great care.

Morphisms

Theory morphisms were proposed as the *mural* solution to inheritance with renaming and after-the-fact inheritance (cf. Section 3.4.4) but are not currently implemented in *mural*.

3.1.2   Chapter outline

For the most part, the present chapter is concerned with theories, inference rules and proofs; tactics (see Chapter 5) and oracles are only briefly touched upon.

First order predicate calculus

As its name indicates, Section 3.2 develops predicate calculus – the logic of propositions, properties, variables and quantifiers – from a 'classical' point of view. 'First order' means quantifiers range over sets of values and functions have fixed arities. As is well known, first order predicate calculus is sufficiently expressive to formalize all of mathematics. The reader needn't know much symbolic logic to commence reading this section, although obviously some familiarity with the underlying concepts would help. The development consists of a series of smaller theories introducing equality, propositional connectives, quantifiers and conditionals (if-then-else) step by step.

Data types

Section 3.3 explores the formalization of some commonly used data types: lists, finite sets, subtypes, cartesian products, records, etc. This is all pretty straightforward and should be easily accessible to anyone who has completed a first course in discrete mathematics. Section 3.4 is an optional section which can easily be skipped on first reading. It looks at some slightly less straightforward techniques, such as

- extending a theory of *finite* sets with a notation $\{x : A \cdot P[x]\}$ for set comprehension

- defining maps (finite partial functions) as sets of pairs

- defining lists as maps whose domains are initial segments of the natural numbers

- forming a theory of 'abstract collections' which generalizes the notions of sets, lists, bags, etc.

The topics are chosen fairly much at random, and are intended to broaden the reader's strengths in formal reasoning.

VDM

An axiomatization of the formal software development method known as *VDM* [Jon86] is outlined in Section 3.5. Since VDM uses a non-classical logic (LPF), the beginner will get a first taste for the genericity (logic independence) of *mural*. We go on to discuss how the 'data model' of a VDM specification gives rise to a theory in which proof obligations must be discharged. To illustrate the ideas involved, a couple of little 'scenarios' are given, namely:

- a small reification

- a validation of part of the *mural* specification itself

The abstract *mural* specification is introduced in Chapter 4, but enough of the details are summarized here that the example should easily be understandable.

Other logics

Section 3.6 deals with some other kinds of logics, including:

- Lambda Calculus
  or more precisely, the dependently typed lambda calculus

- Higher Order Logic

- Modal Logic (**S4**)

• Hoare Logic

It also discusses the propositions-as-types analogy which underlies certain other logical frames.

3.2 Classical first order predicate calculus

In this section we build a few simple theories ('calculi') about different forms of reasoning, and then put them together to form First Order Predicate Calculus (FOPC) – a theory in which all of mathematics can be formulated. This is not to say that FOPC is always the most elegant or practical way of formulating *all* mathematical reasoning, but it has certainly proven to be the simplest and most versatile. Almost any good book on mathematical logic[2] will explain FOPC and its semantics (model theory). Here we are primarily interested in having a useful set of axioms from which we can easily build the kinds of inference rules we'll need for later applications.

3.2.1 Equality

As a first, very simple, example we develop a theory of equality. The essential properties we wish to capture are the symmetry, reflexivity and transitivity of '=', together with its properties as a congruence relation (viz. that equal values can be substituted for each other in any expression without changing that expression's meaning). To define the theory of equality – which we shall simply call 'Equality' – we shall first describe its signature and its axioms, and then give some example derived rules; the same pattern is followed throughout the chapter.

Signature

Because it is such a basic theory, 'Equality' requires no parents. Its signature can consist simply of the primitive constant '=' of arity $(2, 0)$. The symbol will be displayed infixed between its arguments, which can be achieved simply by declaring it to have display form

$$[\![e1]\!] = [\![e2]\!]$$

In *mural*, $[\![ei]\!]$ stands for the ith *expression placeholder*; thus if the arguments to = are a and b then the whole will be displayed as $a = b$.

Axioms

The properties of equality as a congruence relation can be deduced from two axioms:

1. The axiom of 'reflexivity'

$$\overline{a = a}$$

   which says that any value is equal to itself (equality is reflexive). This rule has no hypotheses.

---

[2]e.g. [Bar77, End72, GG83, Kle52].

2. The axiom of 'substitution'

$$\frac{a = b, \quad P[a]}{P[b]}$$

which says that if $a = b$ then b can be substituted for a in P.

Here a and b are metavariables of arity $(0, 0)$ and P is a metavariable of arity $(1, 0)$. In future we won't explicitly note metavariables and arities, since they are usually clear from context.

A brief note about the *mural* substitution mechanism is in order here (see Section 4.2.2 for more discussion): P can be instantiated in ways which will result in b being substituted for zero, one, or more occurrences of a in an expression. For example, four different conclusions can be deduced from '$0 = 0+0$' and '$0*1 = 0$' by using different instantiations of the Substitution rule: namely,

$$(0+0)*1 = 0+0, \quad (0+0)*1 = 0, \quad 0*1 = 0+0, \quad 0*1 = 0$$

The instantiations in question send a to 0, b to $0 + 0$ and $P[x]$ to $x * 1 = x$, $x * 1 = 0$, $0 * 1 = x$ and $0 * 1 = 0$ respectively. (In fact, there are even more possibilities if we don't assume $a = b$ is matched against '$0 = 0 + 0$'.)

Example derivations

Here are a couple of simple derivations. As you can probably imagine, there aren't many mind-blowingly deep rules about '$=$' on its own.

(1) The symmetry rule

$$\frac{a = b}{b = a}$$

can be derived from the axioms as follows:

```
from a = b
1    a = a                              reflexivity ()
infer b = a                             substitution (h1,1)
```

The proof has a single box comprising two ordinary lines (the 'intermediate' line 1 and the main conclusion) and a single hypothesis line ($h1$). Line 1 has no antecedents since 'reflexivity' has no hypotheses.

As usual, instantiations are suppressed from display, but can be inferred by pattern-matching: e.g. the instantiation for 'substitution' in the above proof is

$$\{a \mapsto a, \quad b \mapsto b, \quad P[x] \mapsto x = a\}$$

and the rule instance in question is

$$\frac{a = b, \quad a = a}{b = a}$$

The *mural* justification tool can find this instantiation for you by pattern matching.

(2) As a second example, the transitivity rule

$$\frac{a = b, \quad b = c}{a = c}$$

can be derived as follows:

> from $a = b$, $b = c$
> infer $a = c$ substitution (h2,h1)

The reader is invited to uncover the relevant instantiation.

3.2.2   Classical propositional calculus

Let's turn to a more expressive theory – the so-called *Propositional Calculus*. This is the theory in which basic logical reasoning is formalized in terms of the so-called propositional connectives: 'and', 'or', 'not', 'implies', etc. Propositional Calculus is often given as the first example of a simple algebra, since all propositional statements ('formulae') are built up from

- 'true' and 'false' and

- primitive propositions ('sentence symbols')

using

- unary connective '$\neg$' and

- binary connectives '$\wedge$', '$\vee$', ' $\Rightarrow$ ', etc.

The algebraic properties of these connectives were originally studied by Boole in the mid-nineteenth century.

Various interpretations

The reader is probably aware that Boole's interpretation of the 'laws' of propositional connectives is not the only possible one. In fact, for some applications other interpretations are sometimes more appropriate. For example:

- If the 'constructive content' of a proof or theorem is important, an *intuitionistic* (or 'constructive') logic [Pra65, C⁺86] should be employed – one in which the law of excluded middle, for example, is not valid. (See Section 3.6.3 for more discussion.)

- When reasoning about partial functions or non-terminating computations, on the other hand, it becomes important to know how to deal with 'non-denoting' terms, and a *three-valued* logic such as LPF [BCJ84, Jon86, CJ91] might be more appropriate. LPF is explored in Section 3.5.1.

In this section we'll stick to Boole's original formulation – the so-called *classical* propositional calculus – since it is the most straightforward and probably the most familiar of them all.

Signature

Let 'Propositional Calculus' be the base theory (i.e., without parents) with the following primitive constants in its signature:

- 'true' for truth

- '¬' for negation ('not')

- '∨' for disjunction ('or')

Their display forms are

$$\text{true}, \quad \neg \, [\![e1]\!], \quad [\![e1]\!] \vee [\![e2]\!]$$

respectively. The following definitions will also be added to the signature:

$$
\begin{aligned}
\text{false} &\triangleq \neg\,\text{true} \\
P \wedge Q &\triangleq \neg(\neg P \vee \neg Q) \\
P \Rightarrow Q &\triangleq \neg P \vee Q \\
P \Leftrightarrow Q &\triangleq (P \Rightarrow Q) \wedge (Q \Rightarrow P)
\end{aligned}
$$

They stand for falsehood, conjunction ('and'), implication ('implies'), and logical equivalence ('iff'), respectively. The usual operator precedences will be used: i.e. from highest to lowest:

$$\neg \quad \wedge \quad \vee \quad \Rightarrow \quad \Leftrightarrow$$

Henceforth precedence priorities will not be given explicitly. (They will be clear enough from context.)

Axioms

The following rules will be taken as the axioms of classical propositional calculus:

1. truth introduction:

$$\frac{}{\text{true}}$$

2. ∨ introduction (right):

$$\frac{P}{P \vee Q}$$

3. ∨ introduction (left):

$$\frac{Q}{P \vee Q}$$

4. ∨ elimination:

$$\frac{P \vee Q, \quad \{P\} \vdash R, \quad \{Q\} \vdash R}{R}$$

5. excluded middle:

$$\frac{}{P \vee \neg P}$$

6. contradiction:

$$\frac{P, \quad \neg P}{Q}$$

The reader should consider himself/herself privileged, since the writer has graciously provided names for the rules. Don't get used to it – it won't last; there's not enough space for such a luxury. (And to tell the truth, it's very time consuming coming up with good names – as you'll find when you start to use *mural* yourself.)

Example derivations

From the axioms and definitions we can build up a large collection of useful derived rules. In what follows we shall derive the following rules from the axioms above:

$$\frac{\text{false}}{Q} \quad \frac{P \vee Q}{Q \vee P} \quad \frac{P,\ P \Rightarrow Q}{Q} \quad \frac{\{\neg P\} \vdash \text{false}}{P}$$

The reader may care to try to prove each of these before looking at the solutions given below.

(1) The rule we'll call 'false elimination'

$$\frac{\text{false}}{Q}$$

can be derived as follows:

```
from false
1    ¬ true                                             unfolding (h1)
2    true                                          truth introduction ()
infer Q                                             contradiction (1,2)
```

It's our first example of a proof involving unfolding a definition – in this case 'false'. We'll denote the appropriate justification by `unfolding`, with the line containing the term to be unfolded given as antecedent. In *mural* the index of the term being unfolded must also be given as part of the justification; it has been 'suppressed from display' here (just as instantiations are suppressed from display throughout these examples).

(2) The rule '∨ commutes'

$$\frac{P \vee Q}{Q \vee P}$$

can be derived as follows:

```
from P ∨ Q
1    from P
     infer Q ∨ P                                ∨ introduction (left) (1.h1)
2    from Q
     infer Q ∨ P                                ∨ introduction (right) (2.h1)
infer Q ∨ P                                          ∨ elimination (h1,1,2)
```

The proof has two subboxes

$$\text{from } P \text{ infer } Q \vee P, \quad \text{from } Q \text{ infer } Q \vee P$$

which are used to justify the sequent hypotheses of the relevant instantiation of '∨ elimination':

$$\frac{P \vee Q,\ \{P\} \vdash Q \vee P,\ \{Q\} \vdash Q \vee P}{Q \vee P}$$

(3) The rule '*modus ponens*'

$$\frac{P, \; P \Rightarrow Q}{Q}$$

can be derived as follows:

    from $P, \; P \Rightarrow Q$
1    $\neg P \vee Q$ unfolding (h2)
2   from $\neg P$
       infer Q contradiction (h1,2.h1)
   infer Q $\vee$ elimination (1,2)

Line 1 follows from the second hypothesis by unfolding $P \Rightarrow Q$. Box 2 (or rather, its conclusion Q) follows from the first hypothesis and the box's local assumption by contradiction. As for the main conclusion, note that the second sequent of the relevant instance of '$\vee$ elimination'

$$\{Q\} \vdash Q$$

holds trivially and so has no corresponding antecedent in the proof.

(4) The next example involves a new kind of justification: *justification by sequent hypothesis*. The rule to be derived is

$$\frac{\{\neg P\} \vdash \text{false}}{P}$$

For future reference we'll call the rule 'otherwise contradictory'. It's our first example of a derived rule having a sequent hypothesis. Here's its proof:

    from $\{\neg P\} \vdash$ false
1    $P \vee \neg P$ excluded middle ()
2   from $\neg P$
2.1   false   sequent hyp 1 (2.h1)
       infer P false elimination (2.1)
   infer P $\vee$ elimination (1,2)

The sequent hypothesis is used to justify line 2.1 in the following way: when all the premises of the sequent have been established then its upshot can be deduced.[3] Unlike justifications by rules, metavariables must be used unchanged: they *cannot* be instantiated. Note also that the sequent hypothesis is not formally a line in the proof. Finally, on a different point, note that one of the sequent hypotheses of (the relevant instantiation of) '$\vee$ elimination' holds trivially.

---

[3]As an informal explanation of justification by sequent hypotheses, think about how 'otherwise contradictory' will be used in other proofs: The proof will have a box, b say, which establishes the upshot from the premises. We could replace the use of 'otherwise contradictory' by a copy of the above proof, with the contents of b interpolated into box 2 before line 2.1 (so line 2.1 corresponds to the conclusion of b) and with the sequent hypothesis deleted. Full details of this procedure are beyond the scope of this chapter.

Other derivable rules

The reader might care to try deriving the following rules:

$$\frac{P}{\neg\neg P}$$

$$\frac{\{P\} \vdash Q, \quad \{\neg P\} \vdash Q}{Q}$$

$$\frac{P, \ Q}{P \wedge Q} \qquad \frac{\{P\} \vdash Q}{P \Rightarrow Q} \qquad \frac{\{P\} \vdash \text{false}}{\neg P}$$

$$\frac{P, \ P \Leftrightarrow Q}{Q} \qquad \frac{P \Rightarrow Q, \ Q \Rightarrow R}{P \Rightarrow R}$$

Many more examples can be found in the sections below.

Remarks:

(1) Note that by the time we get to 'otherwise contradictory' we're actually starting to use some of our derived rules – in this case 'false elimination'.

(2) (This is a slightly esoteric remark.) One of the limitations of the *mural* system is that only 'directly derivable' rules can be derived: viz. rules which are built by fitting other rules together.[4] For an example of an *indirectly* derivable rule, consider

$$\frac{P \Leftrightarrow Q}{R[P] \ \Leftrightarrow \ R[Q]}$$

which asserts the substitutivity of equivalents. If we were working in a 'closed system' – one in which no further extensions could be made to the signature of the theory – the rule could be derived by induction over the structure of possible instantiations of $R[x]$.[5] Of course, such a proof only remains valid as long as there are no new ways of forming propositions; each time a new predicate is introduced (with its own axioms) the proof must be redone. But it is implicit in the requirements that *mural* is to be an 'open' system (cf. [JL88]), whereby users can add new theories without invalidating any of the proofs that went before; hence the restriction to directly derivable rules. In practice, the

---

[4]Kleene calls these '[derived] rules of the direct type': cf. p.94 of [Kle52].

[5]For possible instantiands of $R[x]$ it's enough to consider expressions formed from primitives and the formal parameter x. (The definitions in this theory are non-recursive and hence reducible to primitives.) The base cases of the induction would thus be

$$R[x] \mapsto \text{true}, \quad R[x] \mapsto x$$

and the induction steps would correspond to

$$R[x] \mapsto \neg R'[x], \quad R[x] \mapsto R'[x] \vee R''[x]$$

The proof follows easily from the following (directly derivable) lemmas:

$$\frac{}{\text{true} \Leftrightarrow \text{true}} \qquad \frac{P \Leftrightarrow Q}{\neg P \Leftrightarrow \neg Q} \qquad \frac{P \Leftrightarrow Q, \ R \Leftrightarrow S}{P \vee R \Leftrightarrow Q \vee S}$$

restriction to directly derivable rules does not seem to be much of a hindrance: the odd exception only proves the rule, if you'll excuse the dreadful pun (and mangled reasoning).

Rules which cannot be derived directly must be added as axioms.

(3) As it happens, the rule

$$\frac{P \Leftrightarrow Q}{R[P] \Leftrightarrow R[Q]}$$

would *not* be a good axiom to add, since it allows complete nonsense to be deduced in descendant theories. For example, there is nothing to stop us instantiating $R[x]$ by '$2+2$' to derive

$$2+2 \Leftrightarrow 2+2$$

from a trivially true equivalence such as 'true $\Leftrightarrow$ true'.[6]

A much better formulation of the rule would be

$$\frac{P \Leftrightarrow Q, \ R[P]}{R[Q]}$$

since it 'conserves sense'. That is, the conclusion $R[Q]$ could only be nonsense (ill-formed) if $R[P]$ is already nonsense – assuming of course, that $P \Leftrightarrow Q$ is not non-sense. To infer '$2+2 \Leftrightarrow 2+2$' from 'true $\Leftrightarrow$ true' we would already have to know '$2+2 \Leftrightarrow 2+2$'.

Note that, with the exception of 'contradiction', the axioms given above all conserve sense. It follows that any rules derived from them similarly conserve sense. ('Contradiction' only gets used in arguments by contradiction, at which times it is sometimes necessary to introduce nonsense.[7]) For people using this logic, this is a very reassuring property of our formulation, since no-one wants to derive nonsense. But of course it goes further than this: it also means that when we come to formulate new conjectures we should be careful that they in turn conserve sense, since otherwise there will be no way of proving them.

(4) The rule in the previous remark is a relatively innocuous example of an ill-advised axiom. In Section 3.5.2 we give an example where a careless formulation of an axiom leads to outright inconsistency.

(5) Readers familiar with other logical frames – such as ELF [AHM87] – might wonder

---

[6]In some textbooks (e.g. [End72]) such problems are circumvented by defining an appropriate notion of 'well-formed formula' (*wff*) and only allowing rule instances whose components are wffs. Thus e.g. $P \wedge Q$ is a wff but '$2+2$' isn't. See Section 4.3.2 for a brief discussion of the decision not to follow such an approach.

[7]e.g. in the following proof the law of contradiction is used to infer the nonsensical expression $0 < 1/n$ when $n = 0$:

```
from ¬ (0 = n² + 2n)
1      n = 0 ∨ n ≠ 0                                    ...
2      from n = 0
2.1        0 = n² + 2n                                      ...
           infer 0 < 1/n              contradiction (2.1,h1)
3      from n ≠ 0
           infer 0 < 1/n                                  ...
       infer 0 < 1/n                     ∨ elimination (1,2,3)
```

why we didn't introduce a type *Prop* and write e.g.

$$\vee: Prop \times Prop \to Prop$$

This would require first formulating a type system, to give some meaning to such a 'declaration'. (See Section 3.6.2 for a way of doing this.) But as we've seen, there is no need for a typing mechanism in order to build up such a basic theory of reasoning as Propositional Calculus. Our reasoning capabilities are being developed independently of any particular assumptions about typing, and will be reused in many different situations.[8]

3.2.3   Conditionals

This section introduces a small theory which combines the theories of propositional calculus and equality. Such a theory is the appropriate place to define inequality ($\neq$), for example, and to introduce the notion of the *conditional constructor* (if then else) for definition by cases.

Signature

'Conditionals' will be the theory with 'Propositional Calculus' and 'Equality' as parents, and with signature – or 'extension signature', to give its full name – consisting of

- primitive constant '*ITE*' with display form

$$\text{if } [\![e1]\!] \text{ then } [\![e2]\!] \text{ else } [\![e3]\!]$$

- the definition

$$a \neq b \;\triangleq\; \neg(a = b)$$

Axioms

The axioms of the theory are:

$$\frac{P}{(\text{if } P \text{ then } a \text{ else } b) = a} \qquad \frac{\neg P}{(\text{if } P \text{ then } a \text{ else } b) = b}$$

Derived rules

The reader is invited to derive the following rules:

$$\frac{}{\neg(a \neq b) \;\Leftrightarrow\; a = b}$$

$$\frac{}{a \neq a \;\Rightarrow\; Q}$$

$$\frac{}{(\text{if } (P \Rightarrow Q) \text{ then } a \text{ else } b) = (\text{if } P \text{ then } (\text{if } Q \text{ then } a \text{ else } b) \text{ else } a)}$$

(Hint: do case analysis on P and Q.)

---

[8]A closely related – but rather more esoteric – objection is that we want a 'predicative' system: this is discussed further in Section 3.2.4.

Remarks:

In some ways, adding the definition of $\neq$ actually causes more work than it saves, at least initially. The *mural* pattern-matcher does not unfold definitions, so it becomes necessary to 'double up' on many rules: e.g. we'll need a new form of the contradiction rule

$$\frac{a = b, \quad a \neq b}{Q}$$

In fact, for almost every rule of propositional calculus involving negation, a corresponding rule would need to be written in terms of inequality. Although such rules can be easily deduced, it's annoying to have to spend time putting them into *mural* (thinking of good names for them, which theory to put them into, etc.). If a definition is used often this is a small price to pay, but it's worth bearing in mind when considering less frequently used definitions.

3.2.4 Classical predicate calculus

Before we look at the theories of various data types it will be useful to build up some machinery for reasoning about types and quantifiers. In this section we axiomatize *many-sorted classical predicate calculus*.

Signature

The theory 'Predicate Calculus' will have 'Propositional Calculus' as parent, and its signature will contain

- a primitive binder '$\forall$' for universal quantification ('for all')

- a primitive constant ':' for typing assertions, with display form [9] $[\![e1]\!]{:}\,[\![t1]\!]$

- a defined binder '$\exists$' for existential quantification ('there exists'), with definition

$$\exists x{:}\, A \cdot P[x] \;\triangleq\; \neg\, \forall x{:}\, A \cdot \neg P[x]$$

Intuitively,

- $a{:}\,A$ means that a is a value of type A,

- $\forall x{:}\, A \cdot P[x]$ means that P holds for *all* elements of A, and

- $\exists x{:}\, A \cdot P[x]$ means that P holds for *some* element of A.

Scoping of binders

In *mural*, quantifier scopes are 'as long as possible', so that for example

$$\forall x{:}\, A \cdot P \Rightarrow Q$$

should be parsed as

$$\forall x{:}\, A \cdot (P \Rightarrow Q)$$

---

[9] In *mural*, $[\![ti]\!]$ is used as a placeholder for the ith Type argument (cf. the use of $[\![ei]\!]$ in Section 3.2.1). Note also that the CESymb ':' should not be confused with the colon used as separator in the display form of binder terms such as $\forall x{:}\, A \cdot \ldots$ (although the similarity is obviously intended).

Axioms

The following two rules can be taken as the axioms of classical predicate calculus (as an extension of propositional calculus):

1. '∀ introduction'

$$\frac{\{x\!:\!A\} \vdash_x P[x]}{\forall x\!:\!A \cdot P[x]}$$

   which says that, if $P[x]$ holds for an arbitrary term x of type A, then it holds for all terms of that type.

2. '∀ elimination'

$$\frac{a\!:\!A, \quad \forall x\!:\!A \cdot P[x]}{P[a]}$$

   which says that, if P holds for all elements of type A, then it holds for any particular term a which can be shown to be of type A.

The usual 'variable occurrence side-condition' on '∀ introduction' – viz. that x does not occur free in any assumption on which $P[x]$ depends, other than $x\!:\!A$ – is handled by the treatment of variable bindings in *mural*. (See Section 4.3.3 for details.) Roughly, if we suppose the sequent hypothesis is established by a box b in a proof, then x must be introduced by box b and no other box; and *mural* ensures the conclusion of box b can depend only on lines from b or enclosing boxes.

Example derivations

(1) The rule '∃ introduction'

$$\frac{a\!:\!A, \quad P[a]}{\exists x\!:\!A \cdot P[x]}$$

can be derived as follows:

from $a\!:\!A, \quad P[a]$
1   from $\neg\, \exists x\!:\!A \cdot P[x]$
1.1 $\neg\neg\, \forall x\!:\!A \cdot \neg\, P[x]$ unfolding (1.h1)
1.2 $\forall x\!:\!A \cdot \neg\, P[x]$ $\neg\neg$ elimination (1.1)
1.3 $\neg\, P[a]$ ∀ elimination (h1,1.2)
       infer false   contradiction (h1,1.3)
infer $\exists x\!:\!A \cdot P[x]$ otherwise contradictory (1)

(2) Perhaps of more interest is the proof of the rule '∃ elimination'

$$\frac{\exists x\!:\!A \cdot P[x], \quad \{y\!:\!A, \ P[y]\} \vdash_y Q}{Q}$$

which can be derived as follows:

from $\exists x: A \cdot P[x]$, $\{y: A, \; P[y]\} \vdash_y Q$
1    $\neg \forall x: A \cdot \neg P[x]$ unfolding (h1)
2   from $\neg Q$
2.1$_x$ from $x: A$
2.1.1   from $P[x]$
2.1.1.1 Q sequent hyp 1 (2.1.h1,2.1.1.h1)
               infer false   contradiction (2.1.1.1,2.h1)
             infer $\neg P[x]$ otherwise contradictory (2.1.1)
2.2 $\forall x: A \cdot \neg P[x]$ $\forall$ introduction (2.1)
        infer false   contradiction (2.2,1)
   infer Q otherwise contradictory (2)

Line 2.1.1.1 is justified by a sequent hypothesis which binds a variable (y). In such justifications the variable can be renamed (in this case to x): see Section 4.7.5 for full details.

Variants of rules

A useful variant of '$\forall$ elimination' is the following:

$$\frac{a: A, \quad \{x: A\} \vdash_x P[x]}{P[a]}$$

In classical logic this can be proven as follows:

from $a: A$, $\{x: A\} \vdash_x P[x]$
1    $\forall x: A \cdot P[x]$ $\forall$ introduction (seq hyp 1)
infer $P[a]$ $\forall$ elimination (h1,1)

In essence, $\forall x: A \cdot P$ and $\{x: A\} \vdash_x P$ are different ways of saying the same thing, at least in classical logic. (In fact, the same derivation works equally well for appropriate formulations of many other logics: e.g. intuitionistic logic and LPF.)

To see why the variant of '$\forall$ elimination' given in example 3 above can be useful, imagine the following scenario:

When trying to establish goal G suppose you recognise that it would be easier to prove a more general statement, G' say. More often than not, G' will be the result of replacing (one or more occurrences of) a subterm t in G by a variable, x say. There's no need to prove a separate rule, however; we can use the variant as follows:

- write down – or find a line which gives – the type of t, say $t: T$

- use the justification tool to generate the relevant instance of the above rule (by matching $a: A$ against $t: T$ and $P[a]$ against G)

- apply the rule.

This will have the effect of opening a new subproof

from $x: T$
infer G'

(with box variable x) which will be used to establish G.

Since this kind of procedure is fairly common, it could be streamlined by writing it as a tactic. By using the facility for user input, the tactic could be designed to

- ask the user which subterm is to replaced, then

- ask which particular occurrences of the subterm are to replaced (using the 'select subterm' facility), and

- if it can't find a line in the proof which already asserts the subterm's type, ask the user for the type

and then do all the rest itself.

Other derivable rules

The reader is invited to derive the following rules:

$$\frac{\forall x: A \cdot \forall y: B \cdot P[x, y]}{\forall y: B \cdot \forall x: A \cdot P[x, y]}$$

$$\frac{\exists x: A \cdot \forall y: B \cdot P[x, y]}{\forall y: B \cdot \exists x: A \cdot P[x, y]}$$

(Hint: try justifying the conclusion by '∃ elimination'.)

$$\frac{\forall x: A \cdot (P[x] \wedge Q[x])}{(\forall y: A \cdot P[y]) \wedge (\forall z: A \cdot Q[z])}$$

$$\frac{\forall x: A \cdot (R \Rightarrow P[x])}{R \Rightarrow \forall x: A \cdot P[x]}$$

$$\frac{\forall x: A \cdot (P[x] \Rightarrow R)}{(\exists x: A \cdot P[x]) \Rightarrow R}$$

Note that there is no need for a side-condition saying that x does not occur free in R since it is enforced by the *mural* frame.

Remarks:

(1) Note that these axioms say nothing about whether types can be empty or not. This question must however be resolved (say by adding an axiom $\exists x: A \cdot x = x$) before rules such as

$$\frac{(\exists x: A \cdot P[x]) \Rightarrow R}{\forall x: A \cdot (P[x] \Rightarrow R)}$$

can be derived.

(2) The syntax does not allow for multiple simultaneous bindings such as

$$\forall x: A, y: B \cdot P(x, y)$$

In most cases such bindings can be expressed by equivalent sequential single bindings: viz.

$$\forall x\!: A \cdot \forall y\!: B \cdot P(x, y)$$

An alternative is to use pairing: viz.

$$\forall z\!: A \times B \cdot P(\mathsf{fst}\ z, \mathsf{snd}\ z)$$

(3) Although multiple simultaneous bindings do not present a serious problem from the theoretical point of view, it is rather awkward to have to write e.g.

$$\forall x, y, z\!: A \cdot \ldots$$

in the verbose form

$$\forall x\!: A \cdot \forall y\!: A \cdot \forall z\!: A \cdot \ldots$$

Unfortunately the *mural* concrete syntax mechanism does not help with this problem.

(4) Note that we now have two new primitives – ':' and '∀' – for forming propositions. We hinted that the meaning 'for all elements x of A ...' can be assigned to $\forall x\!: A \cdot \ldots$, polymorphic in A. Continuing one of the remarks from Section 3.2.2, here is another reason for not introducing a type *Prop* for propositions: if A is instantiated by *Prop* the meaning assignment becomes circular; $\forall x\!: Prop\cdot$ means 'for all propositions x' – *including this one*. There are foundational difficulties with such 'impredicative' definitions and, since it is difficult to give them a semantics while avoiding self-reference, they are felt by logicians to be rather unpalatable. (See Hazen's chapter on Predicative Logics in [GG83] for a good discussion.)

For software engineers the upshot is, you can introduce 'Booleans' as a type – although if you're careful you often won't need to – but try to keep the distinction between Boolean values (*true* and *false*, or 0 and 1 if you prefer) and propositions in mind. Sometimes it's OK to mix the two with care (cf. Sections 3.5.2 and 3.6.5).

3.2.5 First order predicate calculus

'FOPC' is formed by combining the theories of 'Equality' and 'Predicate Calculus'. In fact, we'll go slightly further than this and also include the theory 'Conditionals' and the following new binder symbols:

1. The quantifier 'there exists a unique' can be defined by

$$\exists!\, x\!: A \cdot P[x] \;\triangleq\; \exists x\!: A \cdot P[x] \wedge (\forall y\!: A \cdot P[y] \;\Rightarrow\; y = x)$$

2. The 'unique choice' operator 'ι' (iota) is a primitive binder with defining axioms

$$\frac{\exists!\, x\!: A \cdot P[x]}{P[\iota x\!: A \cdot P[x]]} \qquad \frac{\exists!\, x\!: A \cdot P[x]}{(\iota x\!: A \cdot P[x])\!: A}$$

3. The Hilbert choice operator ε (for arbitrary choice) can be defined similarly, but with $\exists$ replacing $\exists!$:

$$\frac{\exists x\!: A \cdot P[x]}{P[\varepsilon x\!: A \cdot P[x]]} \qquad \frac{\exists x\!: A \cdot P[x]}{(\varepsilon x\!: A \cdot P[x])\!: A}$$

(Many standard logic textbooks have explanations of these concepts.) The resulting theory would be an appropriate place to store derived results such as

$$(\exists x\colon A \cdot x = a \wedge P[x]) \;\Leftrightarrow\; a\colon A \wedge P[a]$$

This finishes our formulation of FOPC. As explained in for example [Kle52], FOPC is a sufficiently rich theory to formulate all of mathematics.

3.2.6   Rigorous proofs

In Section 3.3 a number of mathematical theories are formulated as extensions to FOPC. We finish the current section by making a temporary diversion to explore a minor liberalization of the definition of proof.

Fully formal proofs give absolute assurance that derived rules are logical consequences of the axioms from which they are derived. In practice however, it is often not feasible to fully derive *every* inference rule one would like to use. For example, in following through the consequences of a design decision in the development of a piece of software, one would like to leave the more 'obvious' truths unproven and concentrate instead on the 'dubious' or 'convoluted' (purported) truths. Candidates for 'obvious' truths would include arithmetic results ('$2+2=4$'), simple algebraic identities ($(x+1)^2 = x^2+2*x+1$), simple properties of basic data types ($\text{elems}\,(s1 \curvearrowright s2) = \text{elems}\,s1 \cup \text{elems}\,s2$), and so on.

Several mechanisms for dealing with such truths are provided in *mural*. Oracles can be written to handle large classes of problems such as the above, and tactics can automate common patterns of inference. (Of course, both these approaches still lead to fully formal proofs.) Here we shall present a simple but effective way of breaking out of the shackles of fully formal proof.

The solution is simply to add an 'and-then-a-miracle-occurred' rule of the form

$$\frac{}{Q}$$

where Q is a metavariable which can be instantiated by *any* expression. Now, it would be pretty stupid to suggest adding this rule as an axiom – obviously it would make a mockery of theorem proving altogether! But it *is* useful to add it as a defined rule. (With any luck) it should never be derivable.[10] Obviously the 'miracle rule' should be used with some caution, and only in places where you're very confident it is valid – that is to say, at places where you believe you could supply a complete proof but don't feel it is worth your effort. The exact circumstances are a matter for the user to decide.

Rules proven using instances of the above rule will be said to be proven *rigorously*. You can find out which proofs are rigorous – as opposed to being fully formal – by asking *mural* for the list of unproven rules on which this rule depends (cf. Section 4.5.2). If the 'miracle rule' appears in the list you'll know your rule is (at best) only rigorously established. Finally, by declaring the 'miracle rule' to be 'assumed', the *mural* facility for reporting the status of a rule – as proposed in Section 4.5.2 – can be used to full advantage.

---

[10]It's certainly not derivable in FOPC, since the latter is provably consistent. (You might ask what logic is used to prove FOPC is consistent, but this is not the place to go into all that – see instead any good book on mathematical logic, such as [End72].)

Remark:

In fact, it would be better to introduce a whole set of different 'miraculous' rules, each with a different number of hypotheses: viz.

$$\frac{H1, \ H2, \ ..., \ Hn}{Q}$$

The user would choose the rule with the number of hypotheses corresponding to the number of lines in the proof on which the desired conclusion depends (its so-called antecedents). Hypotheses would get bound to antecedents one-to-one. In this way antecedent information is maintained by *mural*, and any changes to the lines on which the conclusion depends would cause the 'miraculous' line to be flagged as no longer being justified, not even 'rigorously'.

3.3 Some common data types

This section explores the theories of some commonly used (generic) data types, such as lists, finite sets, subtypes, cartesian products and records. All the theories will build upon 'FOPC' as defined in the previous section: so, unless otherwise stated, it can be assumed they have 'FOPC' among their parents.

3.3.1 List theory

The generic 'list' data type consists of finite sequences of elements from a given type. Thus we want a theory which is equally good for lists of natural numbers as for lists of trees, or booleans, or whatever. On the other hand, let's suppose we don't want to allow lists with mixed types of elements. (This will show how naturally polymorphism can be handled in *mural*.)

Signature

The signature of 'List Theory' will consist of

- a primitive type constructor 'list of' with display form $[\![t1]\!]^*$

- a primitive constant '[ ]' for the empty list

- a primitive constant for adding an element onto the front of a list, with display form cons($[\![e1]\!]$, $[\![e2]\!]$)

- primitive constants for list destructors 'head' and 'tail', with display forms hd $[\![e1]\!]$ and tl $[\![e1]\!]$ respectively

and definitions

$$
\begin{array}{rcl}
[a] & \triangleq & \mathsf{cons}(a, [\,]) \\
a \ in \ s & \triangleq & a = \mathsf{hd}\,s \vee a \ in \ \mathsf{tl}\,s \\
s \frown t & \triangleq & \text{if } s = [\,] \text{ then } t \text{ else } \mathsf{cons}(\mathsf{hd}\,s, (\mathsf{tl}\,s) \frown t)
\end{array}
$$

for singleton lists, list membership and concatenation of lists, respectively. (The last two are examples of recursive definitions in *mural*.)

from $s: A^*$, $s \neq [\,]$

1     $[\,] \neq [\,] \Rightarrow \text{hd}\,[\,]: A$ =reflex lemma ()

2$_{h,t}$ from $h: A$

2.1 $\text{hd cons}(h, t) = h$ hd -axiom ()

2.2 $\text{hd cons}(h, t): A$ substitution (2.1,2.h1)

        infer $\text{cons}(h, t) \neq [\,] \Rightarrow \text{hd cons}(h, t): A$ conseq true (2.2)

3     $\forall w: A^* \cdot w \neq [\,] \Rightarrow \text{hd}\, w: A$ list induction (1,2)

4     $s \neq [\,] \Rightarrow \text{hd}\, s: A$ $\forall$-elimination (h1,3)

infer hd $s: A$ modus ponens (h2,4)

Figure 3.2: A proof of the formation rule for the 'head of a list' function.

Axioms

We shall take the following as axioms for 'List Theory':

$$\overline{[\,]: A^*} \qquad \frac{a: A, \quad s: A^*}{\text{cons}(a, s): A^*}$$

$$\frac{}{\text{cons}(a, s) \neq [\,]}$$

$$\overline{\text{hd cons}(a, s) = a} \qquad \overline{\text{tl cons}(a, s) = s}$$

$$\frac{P[[\,]], \quad \{h: A, \ t: A^*, \ P[t]\} \vdash_{h,t} P[\text{cons}(h, t)]}{\forall s: A^* \cdot P[s]}$$

Of course, the last one is the induction rule for lists.

Derived rules

A proof for the 'formation rule' for head

$$\frac{s: A^*, \quad s \neq [\,]}{\text{hd}\, s: A}$$

is given in Figure 3.2. Note that the pattern of using induction, then $\forall$-elimination and *modus ponens* is a very common one, and is a good candidate for a tactic. Likewise, use of the induction rule itself could be usefully semi-automated, by writing a tactic 'SetUpListInduction' which polls the user for the subterm t and for the particular occurrences of t in the conclusion, and then sets up P from this information. This is a good illustration of the usefulness of an interactive tactic language, and how it can be used to customize the user interface of *mural*.

Other example derivable rules are

$$\frac{s: A^*, \quad s \neq [\,]}{s = \text{cons}(\text{hd}\, s, \text{tl}\, s)}$$

$$\frac{s: A^*, \quad t: A^*}{s \frown t: A^*}$$

$$\frac{a\!:\!A, \quad s\!:\!A^*, \quad t\!:\!A^*}{a \; in \; s \frown t \;\Leftrightarrow\; a \; in \; s \lor a \; in \; t}$$

$$\frac{s_1\!:\!A^*, \quad s_2\!:\!A^*, \quad s_3\!:\!A^*}{(s_1 \frown s_2) \frown s_3 = s_1 \frown (s_2 \frown s_3)}$$

Remarks:

(1) Note how the typing hypotheses of the formation rule for 'cons' ensure that only elements of the correct type are appended to lists. The cons function needs no type argument – unlike its counterpart in strongly typed logical frames such as ELF – and thus is truly polymorphic. Of course, there is a cost associated with such flexibility: *mural* does not automatically type-check expressions. There are (at least) two good reasons for this:

- One of the goals of *mural* (cf. [JL88]) is to support different type structures for different applications.

- For some applications type-checking is not even decidable.

Generally speaking, the *mural* approach to automated type-checking is to write a domain-specific tactic to do as much as possible. Early experience suggests that this is quite effective, although it adds considerably to the length of proofs. A viable alternative might be to use an oracle.

(2) The role of typing assertions in the above formulation of list theory is roughly to 'filter out nonsense'. An unstated principle is at work in the above axiomatization: a term is typable if and only if it is meaningful. For example, there is nothing to stop someone writing 'hd [ ]' in *mural*, but it's not possible to deduce a type for it using the rules above. In fact, because of the way the axioms are formulated, the only 'facts' that can be deduced about 'hd [ ]' are essentially trivial, such as 'hd [ ] = hd [ ]'. (In Section 3.5.1 we look at a logic in which not even this equation can be deduced.)

(3) Note that, as formulated above, '[ ] $\frown t = t$' holds for *any* expression t, not just for lists. If instead the theory called for a stronger typing on $\frown$, the symbol should instead be introduced as a primitive constant with its properties defined axiomatically – with due care to add the relevant typing hypotheses: viz.

$$\frac{t\!:\!A^*}{[\,] \frown t = t} \qquad \frac{a\!:\!A, \quad s\!:\!A^*, \quad t\!:\!A^*}{\mathrm{cons}(a,s) \frown t = \mathrm{cons}(a, s \frown t)}$$

(4) An alternative form of the induction rule is

$$\frac{\begin{array}{c} t\!:\!A^*, \\ P[[\,]], \\ \{a\!:\!A, \; s\!:\!A^*, \; P[s]\} \vdash_{a,s} P[\mathrm{cons}(a,s)] \end{array}}{P[t]}$$

Formally, the two rules are equivalent (at least, in the presence of FOPC) but there are certain practical reasons for preferring the original version.

To see this, note that '*P*[*t*]' matches *any* expression and does so in many different ways (cf. the examples in Section 3.2.1). Thus the *mural* justification tool will return many different matches for the conclusion of the rule above. On the other hand, the conclusion

$$\forall s: A^* \cdot P[s]$$

is much more constrained in the matching it allows, and if the user is prepared to first state the appropriate generalization of the assertion – going from '*rev*(*rev x*) = *x*' to '$\forall x: A^* \cdot rev(rev\ x) = x$' for example – the justification tool would find a unique match against the conclusion of the original rule, and in a much shorter time. With practice, such 'tricks' become almost second nature.

(5) As a final point in this section, note that the above formulation essentially treats lists as an algebra, with generators '[ ]' and 'cons'. But lists can also be viewed, for example, as a special kind of map (finite partial function) with domain an initial segment of the natural numbers. Such an approach can be reconciled with the above: see Section 3.4.2 for further discussion.

3.3.2   Basic set theory

The basic generic 'set' data type – consisting of *finite* sets over a given type – can be formalized in a similar fashion to 'List Theory' above. We'll go through an axiomatization here (even though it contains few surprises) since there are deeper questions about finite sets to be explored later.

Signature

As usual, 'Basic Set Theory' will have 'FOPC' as a parent. Its signature will consist of

- a primitive type constructor 'set of', with display form '⟦*t*1⟧-set'

- a primitive constant '{ }' for the empty set

- a primitive constant for the function which adds an element to a set, with display form '⟦*e*1⟧ ∪ {⟦*e*2⟧}'

- a primitive constant '∈' for the set membership relation (infixed)

- a defined constant defining the singleton set as the addition of an element to the empty set ({*a*} ≙ { }∪{*a*} – note that the right-hand side of this definition is simply the concrete syntax for the function which adds an element to a set and has nothing to do with the normal union operator which will be discussed in Section 3.4.1)

- a defined constant for the anti-membership function, defined in the obvious way ($a \notin s \triangleq \neg (a \in s)$)

Axioms

The axioms of this theory are:

$$\frac{}{\{\ \}: A\text{-set}} \qquad \frac{a: A, \quad s: A\text{-set}}{s \cup \{a\}: A\text{-set}}$$

$$\overline{a \notin \{\}} \quad \overline{a \in s \cup \{b\} \iff a \in s \vee a = b}$$

$$\frac{s: A\text{-set}, \quad t: A\text{-set},}{\forall x: A \cdot (x \in s \iff x \in t)}$$
$$\frac{}{s = t}$$

$$\frac{P[\{\}], \quad \{x: A, \ s: A\text{-set}, \ x \notin s, \ P[s]\} \vdash_{x,s} P[s \cup \{x\}]}{\forall s: A\text{-set} \cdot P[s]}$$

Example derived rules

(1) Consider the following proof of the fact that '$a \in s \cup \{a\}$':

from

1	$a \in s \cup \{a\} \iff a \in s \vee a = a$	$\in$-axiom2 ()
2	$a \in s \vee a = a \iff a \in s \cup \{a\}$	$\iff$ symmetry (1)
3	$a = a$	=-reflexivity ()
4	$a \in s \vee a = a$	$\vee$ introduction (left) (3)
infer $a \in s \cup \{a\}$		$\iff$ -elimination (2,4)

This is an example of how even quite simple reasoning can be awkward at times. Note that the reasoning here is almost purely propositional, having almost nothing in particular to do with sets. The desired conclusion could thus be simply justified using lines 1 and 3 and an oracle for propositional logic.

(2) The fact that '$s \cup \{a\} \neq \{\}$' can be derived as follows:

from

1	from $s \cup \{a\} = \{\}$	
1.1	$a \in s \cup \{a\}$	lemma ()
1.2	$a \in \{\}$	substitution (1.h1,1.1)
1.3	$a \notin \{\}$	$\in$-axiom1 ()
infer false		$\in$ contradiction (1.2,1.3)
infer $s \cup \{a\} \neq \{\}$		otherwise contradictory (1)

(3) The reader is invited to derive the following rules:

$$\frac{a: A, \quad b: A, \quad s: A\text{-set}}{(s \cup \{a\}) \cup \{b\} = (s \cup \{b\}) \cup \{a\}}$$

(Hint: use extensionality and the associativity of $\vee$, for example.)

$$\frac{a \in s, \quad s: A\text{-set}}{a: A}$$

(Hint: first prove $\forall t: A\text{-set} \cdot (a \in t \implies a: A)$ by induction.)

3.3.3 Subtypes

Recall that the *mural* syntax makes provision for a 'subtype' constructor, displayed as '$< x{:}A \cdot P >$'. The following pair of axioms capture the notion that '$< x{:}A \cdot P[x] >$' represents those elements a of A that satisfy $P[a]$:

$$\frac{a{:}A \wedge P[a]}{a{:} < x{:}A \cdot P[x] >}$$

The subtyping syntax was 'hard-wired' into *mural* because of its peculiar form (a type binder with an expression body). That is not to say that subtyping is mandatory; rather that it is the choice of the person configuring *mural* whether or not the above axioms should be included. In fact, there are times when it definitely should *not* be used (cf. Section 3.6.1).

Remarks:

Subtyping (or 'inclusion polymorphism') is a very powerful technique, and gives *mural* a distinct advantage over logical frames based on strong typing in which any term has at most one type. For example, '2' is both an even number and a prime number, which can be represented as the following two statements:

$$2 : \ < n{:}\mathsf{N} \cdot (n \bmod 2 = 0) >$$

$$2 : \ < n{:}\mathsf{N} \cdot \forall m{:}\mathsf{N}^+ \cdot (n \bmod m = 0 \ \Rightarrow \ m = 1 \vee m = n) >$$

In many formalisms based on set theory (e.g. VDM, Z) it is important to be able to regard types as sets, and consequently to allow types to overlap. In particular, subtyping is vital for a natural axiomatization of VDM's data type invariants – coercion functions are far too awkward; cf. Section 3.5.3. Strong typing systems just don't allow such flexibility.

3.3.4 Other common type constructors

In this section we look at a number of other common ways of constructing types, including intervals of numbers, enumerated types, type unions, and type products.

Signature

Let's assume we're working in a theory which has 'Basic Set Theory' and an appropriate theory of integer arithmetic as parents. We'll add the following primitives:

- a type constructor '*Interval*' – with display form '$[[e1]]..[[e2]]$' – for constructing intervals of natural numbers

- a type constructor '*EnumType*' for coercing finite sets into 'enumerated types'; in what follows we'll often write 's' as the display form of '*EnumType(s)*' although *mural* doesn't actually allow superscripts

- type constructors '|' and '×' for type union and type product, respectively (both infixed)

- constant ',' for pairing (infixed)

- constants 'fst' and 'snd' for projection functions

Axioms

The axioms of the theory are:

$$\frac{m \leq j \wedge j \leq n}{j: [m..n]} \qquad \frac{a \in s}{a: \hat{s}} \qquad \frac{a: A \vee a: B}{a: A \mid B}$$

$$\frac{a: A, \quad b: B}{(a, b): A \times B} \qquad \frac{p: A \times B}{\text{fst } p: A} \qquad \frac{p: A \times B}{\text{snd } p: B}$$

$$\frac{p: A \times B}{(\text{fst } p, \text{snd } p) = p}$$

$$\frac{}{\text{fst } (a, b) = a} \qquad \frac{}{\text{snd } (a, b) = b}$$

3.3.5 Record types

Another useful way of constructing types is the *record type* (or 'tagged tuple'). Unfortunately there seems to be no simple way of axiomatizing this concept all in one go in *mural*, although individual examples are easy enough.

For example, consider the VDM-like record type

> *Record* :: *sel1* : *Field1*
>   *sel2* : *Field2*
>   *sel3* : *Field3*

where *Field1*, *Field2* and *Field3* are assumed to have been defined in some ancestor theory of the theory in which the particular record type is needed. We simply extend the signature by new primitive constants *sel1*, *sel2*, *sel3* and *mk-Record* and new primitive type constructor *Record*, and add the following axioms:

$$\frac{a1: Field1, \quad a2: Field2, \quad a3: Field3}{mk\text{-}Record(a1, a2, a3): Record}$$

$$\frac{r: Record}{sel1(r): Field1} \qquad \frac{r: Record}{sel2(r): Field2} \qquad \frac{r: Record}{sel3(r): Field3}$$

$$\frac{}{sel1(mk\text{-}Record(a1, a2, a3)) = a1}$$

$$\frac{}{sel2(mk\text{-}Record(a1, a2, a3)) = a2}$$

$$\frac{}{sel3(mk\text{-}Record(a1, a2, a3)) = a3}$$

$$\frac{r: Record}{mk\text{-}Record(sel1(r), sel2(r), sel3(r)) = r}$$

3.4 More complicated formulations

This section discusses a number of more advanced techniques, including

- extending a theory of *finite* sets with a set constructor '$\{x: A \cdot P[x]\}$'

- defining maps (finite partial functions) as sets of pairs

- defining lists as maps whose domains are initial segments of the natural numbers

- forming a theory of 'abstract collections' which generalizes the notions of sets, lists, bags, etc.

This section can easily be skipped on first reading.

3.4.1   Set comprehension

Defining a theory of set comprehension (formation of sets according to a defining predicate, as in '$\{x:A \cdot P\}$') is complicated if we only want to allow finite sets. If we're to use the basic set theory we built up in Section 3.3.2 above, we can't suddenly say that we'll allow infinite sets: the induction axiom commits us to finite sets. So how do we restrict P so that only finitely many elements of A satisfy it?

If A is countably infinite, one solution would be to assert the existence of a natural number n and a one-to-one function f mapping A to N such that

$$\forall x:A \cdot (P[x] \ \Rightarrow \ f(x) < n)$$

Since f is 1-1, less than n elements of A must satisfy P. But this is far too complicated! For a start, it would require us to formulate higher order logic (to express the existence of f) and that's a lot of work: cf. Section 3.6.1 and [Gor85]. Fortunately, a much simpler solution is possible, based on the well-known Zermelo-Frankel (**ZF**) approach [Bar77].

Signature

First of all, it's easy enough to add a set comprehension constructor to the theory. 'Set Comprehension' will be the theory which extends 'Basic Set Theory' by a primitive binder '*those*', with display form

$$\{[\![e1]\!] \cdot [\![e2]\!]\}$$

Axioms

There will be three axioms in our formulation. The fundamental axiom of set comprehension is

$$\overline{a \in \{x:A \cdot P[x]\} \ \Leftrightarrow \ a:A \wedge P[a]}$$

This is very similar to the formulation of subtyping in Section 3.3.3 above, except that subtypes are types whereas subsets are values, which makes them different kinds of term as far as *mural* is concerned.

The other two axioms are 'formation rules' for sets: rules which tell us how to form new sets from existing sets. In **ZF** there are two basic methods:

1. The first is called 'Separation' and simply forms subsets of existing sets:

$$\frac{s:A\text{-set},}{\{x:A \cdot (P[x] \ \Rightarrow \ x \in s)}{\{x:A \cdot P[x]\}:A\text{-set}}$$

   Since only subsets of existing sets can be created this way, only finite sets result.

2. The second method is called 'Replacement' and forms images of existing sets under a given mapping F:

$$\frac{s:A\text{-set},}{\forall x:A \cdot (x \in s \ \Rightarrow \ F[x]:B)}{\{y:B \cdot \exists x:A \cdot (x \in s \wedge y = F[x])\}:B\text{-set}}$$

   Again, the resulting set has at most as many elements as s and so must be finite, assuming s is.

If A has a constant, a_0 say, which is known to satisfy P then the first form becomes a special case of the second upon instantiating

$$\{B \mapsto A, \ F[x] \mapsto \ \text{if } P[x] \text{ then } x \text{ else } a_0\}$$

Remarks:

(1) To keep the *mural* syntax simple, only *Types* were allowed as the universes of bindings. As a consequence we must write

$$\{x \colon A \cdot x \in s \wedge R[x]\}$$

instead of

$$\{x \in s \cdot R[x]\},$$

although the awkwardness can be circumvented to some extent by making use of enumerated types (cf. Section 3.3.4) to write

$$\{x \colon s \cdot R[x]\}.$$

(2) Given a fixed type X, we can define the intersection and difference operations on sets of X by

$$s \cap t \ \triangleq \ \{x \colon X \cdot x \in s \wedge x \in t\}$$
$$s - t \ \triangleq \ \{x \colon X \cdot x \in s \wedge x \notin t\}$$

and derive rules such as

$$\frac{s \colon X\text{-set}, \quad t \colon X\text{-set}}{s \cap t \colon X\text{-set}}$$

Alternatively, we could define them polymorphically by making use of enumerated types: e.g.

$$s \cap t \ \triangleq \ \{x \colon s \cdot x \in t\}$$

It is left as an exercise for the reader to show that, given the definition

$$s \cup t \ \triangleq \ \{x \colon X \cdot x \in s \vee x \in t\}$$

one can derive

$$\frac{s \colon X\text{-set}, \quad t \colon X\text{-set}}{s \cup t \colon X\text{-set}}$$

(Hint: use induction on s and the Separation axiom.) There would seem to be no way, however, of defining '$\cup$' polymorphically with the machinery developed up to this point. By analogy with **ZF**, a full formulation of set theory would need to introduce the union, powerset and distributed union operators and the subset relation as primitives, with their properties defined axiomatically. (Left as an exercise for the reader.)

(3) The set

$$\{y \colon B \cdot \exists x \colon A \cdot (x \in s \wedge y = f(x))\}$$

resulting from replacement is more usually written in the form

$$\{f(x) \cdot x \in s\}$$

but our simple syntax does not support such expressions. As a compromise, we could introduce a new binder '*replace*' with display form

$$\{[\![e2]\!] \cdot [\![e1]\!]\}$$

and write $\{f(x) \cdot x: \mathcal{S}\}$. More generally, we would like to be able to define

$$\{F[x] \cdot x: A\} \quad \underline{\triangle} \quad \{y: B \cdot \exists x: A \cdot y = F[x]\}$$

but, because of restrictions on the use of formal parameters in definitions, B must have a fixed value. Thus, the new binder must instead be added as a primitive, with its properties formalized axiomatically: viz.[11]

$$\frac{\{x: A\} \vdash_x F[x] : B}{\{F[x] \cdot x: A\} = \{y: B \cdot \exists x: A \cdot y = F[x]\}}$$

3.4.2 Map theory

In this section we show how the theory of maps (finite partial functions) can be defined in terms of set theory. For illustrative purposes, we develop the theory of the data type '$X \xrightarrow{m} Y$', consisting of maps from X to Y, for *fixed* (but arbitrary) types X and Y.

Signature

The theory will have as parents 'Common Type Constructors' (see Section 3.3.4) and the extension of 'Set Comprehension' by an appropriate formulation of the set-union function '$\cup$'. Maps will be represented as sets of pairs of elements from X and Y. This leads to the the following definitions:

$$
\begin{aligned}
\textit{is-maplike}(s) &\;\underline{\triangle}\; \forall e_1: \mathcal{S} \cdot \forall e_2: \mathcal{S} \cdot (\text{fst } e_1 = \text{fst } e_2 \cdot \Rightarrow\ e_1 = e_2) \\
X \xrightarrow{m} Y &\;\underline{\triangle}\; < s: (X \times Y)\text{-set} \cdot \textit{is-maplike}(s) > \\
\text{dom } m &\;\underline{\triangle}\; \{x: X \cdot \exists y: Y \cdot (x, y) \in m\} \\
\text{rng } m &\;\underline{\triangle}\; \{y: Y \cdot \exists x: X \cdot (x, y) \in m\} \\
\{x \mapsto y\} &\;\underline{\triangle}\; \{(x, y)\} \\
m \text{ at } x &\;\underline{\triangle}\; \iota y: Y \cdot (x, y) \in m \\
m_1 \dagger m_2 &\;\underline{\triangle}\; \{e: X \times Y \cdot e \in m_1 \wedge \text{fst } e \notin \text{dom } m_2\} \cup m_2 \\
s \triangleleft m &\;\underline{\triangle}\; \{e: X \times Y \cdot e \in m \wedge \text{fst } e \notin s\}
\end{aligned}
$$

and so on. (ι is the unique choice operator introduced in Section 3.2.5 and '$\mathcal{S}$' is the enumerated type introduced in Section 3.3.4.)

---

[11]The sequent hypothesis might be thought of as asserting that F represents a function from A to B. More generally however, $F[x]$ can be any expression involving x: e.g.

$$\frac{\{x: \mathsf{N}\} \vdash_x x^2 + 1 : \mathsf{N}}{\{x^2 + 1 \cdot x: \mathsf{N}\} = \{y: \mathsf{N} \cdot \exists x: \mathsf{N} \cdot y = x^2 + 1\}}$$

is a legitimate instantiation of this rule.

Derived rules

The usual axioms for maps can be deduced from the rules for set theory: e.g.

$$\frac{m: X \xrightarrow{m} Y}{\mathrm{dom}\, m : X\text{-set}} \qquad \frac{x: X, \quad y: Y}{\{x \mapsto y\} : X \xrightarrow{m} Y}$$

$$\frac{m: X \xrightarrow{m} Y, \quad x \in \mathrm{dom}\, m}{(m\ \mathrm{at}\ x) : Y} \qquad \frac{m_1: X \xrightarrow{m} Y, \quad m_2: X \xrightarrow{m} Y}{m_1 \dagger m_2 : X \xrightarrow{m} Y}$$

(Hints: for the first use 'Replacement' and for the last use 'Separation'.)

The rule 'map induction'

$$\frac{P[\{\,\}], \quad \{m: X \xrightarrow{m} Y,\ x{:}X,\ y{:}Y,\ x \notin \mathrm{dom}\, m,\ P[m]\} \vdash_{m,x,y} P[m \dagger \{x \mapsto y\}]}{\forall m: X \xrightarrow{m} Y \cdot P[m]}$$

can be derived from set induction.

Remarks:

(1) Here's a hint of how to prove 'map induction'. First prove

$$\forall s: (X \times Y)\text{-set} \cdot is\text{-}maplike(s) \ \Rightarrow\ P[s]$$

by induction over sets. The sequent hypothesis of 'map induction' is used in the induction step. Unfortunately it cannot be used directly and instead must be converted into an equivalent formula: viz.

$$\forall m: X \xrightarrow{m} Y \cdot \forall x: X \cdot \forall y: Y \cdot ((x \notin \mathrm{dom}\, m \wedge P[m]) \ \Rightarrow\ P[m \dagger \{x \mapsto y\}])$$

The following lemma is also useful

$$\frac{is\text{-}maplike(m \cup \{e\}),\quad e \notin m}{\mathrm{fst}\ e \notin \mathrm{dom}\, m\ \wedge m \cup \{e\} = m \dagger \{\mathrm{fst}\ e \mapsto \mathrm{snd}\ e\}}$$

in the induction step.

(2) Note that the definitions given in the signature are specific to the type '$X \xrightarrow{m} Y$' for the given (fixed) types X and Y. A generic theory is possible, of course, but most of the constants would have to be introduced instead as primitives, with their properties defined axiomatically (cf. the comments on $\cup$ in Section 3.4.1 above).

3.4.3 Lists as maps

In Section 3.3.1 above we remarked that an alternative way of formulating list theory would be to regard lists of X as a special case of maps from natural numbers to X. In *mural* there are (at least) two different ways this observation can be exploited:

(1) The first way is to construct a theory morphism from 'List Theory' to (a polymorphic formulation of) 'Map Theory', where the latter has been extended by arithmetic concepts,

including a notion of cardinality. (See Section 4.8 for an explanation of morphisms.) The following signature morphism is one candidate

$$
\begin{aligned}
A^* &\mapsto N \xrightarrow{m} A' \\
[] &\mapsto \{\} \\
\mathrm{cons}(a, s) &\mapsto s' \cup \{\mathrm{card}\, s' \mapsto a'\} \\
\mathrm{hd}\, s &\mapsto s' \text{ at } (\mathrm{card}\, s' - 1) \\
\mathrm{tl}\, s &\mapsto (\mathrm{card}\, s' - 1) \triangleleft s'
\end{aligned}
$$

where A' is the appropriate translation of A, etc. The effect of this morphism is to translate

$$\mathrm{cons}(x_1, \mathrm{cons}(x_2, \dots \mathrm{cons}(x_n, \mathrm{nil}) \dots))$$

to

$$\{0 \mapsto x_n, 1 \mapsto x_{n\text{-}1}, \dots, n - 1 \mapsto x_1\}$$

This gives a way of viewing lists as maps and lets us translate results about lists into results about the corresponding maps. Unfortunately, it doesn't help us translate results about maps back to results about lists, even though the morphism is 'almost' an isomorphism. (It's not an isomorphism because it translates the unprovable equation 'tl nil = nil' to a provable statement.) It seems that the reverse 'morphism' is well beyond the expressive capabilities of the simple 'syntactic' (homo-) morphisms described in Section 4.8. It would be an interesting research topic to see whether there is a suitable generalization of morphisms which will handle cases like this while still being easy to apply.

(2) A second – more profitable – way to bring the two different formulations of lists together is to define a new subtheory of 'List Theory' and 'Map Theory' in which one representation is 'coerced' into another via an inference rule. For example, assuming the subtheory also inherits a theory of arithmetic and the definition

$$is\text{-}initial(ns) \triangleq \exists n{:}\, N \cdot ns = \{m{:}\, N \cdot m \leq n\}$$

then the following axiom pair

$$\frac{s{:}\, A^*}{(s{:}\, N \xrightarrow{m} A) \wedge is\text{-}initial(\mathrm{dom}\, s)}$$

lets us move freely back and forth between the two different views of lists.

3.4.4   Abstract collections

Next we illustrate how morphisms can be used for 'after-the-fact abstraction' by considering a theory which extracts the properties common to various forms of finite collections.

Let the 'Theory of Abstract Collections' be the theory which extends the FOPC with the following primitives:

- a type constructor 'coll of'

- constants

    - ○ (for the empty collection)
    - ⋆ (for adding an element to a collection)

- ∈ (for the membership predicate) and
- ⊕ (for combining two collections)

and the following axioms:

$$\frac{}{\bigcirc: \text{coll of } A} \qquad \frac{a: A}{\neg\, (a \in \bigcirc)} \qquad \frac{a, b: A, \quad c: \text{coll of } A}{a \in (b \star c) \;\Leftrightarrow\; a = b \lor a \in c}$$

$$\frac{c: \text{coll of } A}{\bigcirc \oplus c = c} \qquad \frac{a: A, \quad c, c': \text{coll of } A}{(a \star c') \oplus c = a \star (c' \oplus c)}$$

$$\frac{P[\bigcirc], \quad \{a: A, \quad c: \text{coll of } A, \quad P[c]\} \vdash_{a,c} P[a \star c]}{\forall c: \text{coll of } A \cdot P[c]}$$

In this theory one can show, for example, that ⊕ is associative, that ○ is a right identity for ⊕, and that ⋆ never yields ○. In addition a group of rewrite rules can be identified which will reduce terms to 'normal form', and these could be used as input to a general simplification tactic.

There are morphisms from the above theory into theories of various different kinds of collection: e.g.

- sets, with

  - coll of $A \mapsto A'$-set
  - $\bigcirc \mapsto \{\}$
  - $a \star c \mapsto c' \cup \{a'\}$
  - $a \in c \mapsto a' \in c'$
  - $c_1 \oplus c_2 \mapsto c_1' \cup c_2'$

- lists, with

  - coll of $A \mapsto A'^*$
  - $\bigcirc \mapsto [\,]$
  - $a \star c \mapsto \text{cons}(a', c')$
  - $a \in c \mapsto a' \in \text{elems}\, c'$
  - $c_1 \oplus c_2 \mapsto c_1' \frown c_2'$

bags, and so on. (In the above, A' stands for the translation of A under the morphism, and so on.)

Remarks:

(1) One of the advantages of morphisms is that they allow symbols to be renamed: e.g. from '○' to '{ }'. To a certain degree the same effect could be achieved (much more simply) by adding renaming to the inheritance mechanism. More generally however, morphisms can rename symbols to expressions: e.g. from '_ ∈ _' to '_ ∈ elems _'. How much of an advantage over simple renaming this represents remains to be seen.

(2) Perhaps the singular advantage of morphisms is that they allow 'after-the-fact abstraction', in as much as generalizations such as 'Abstract Collections' can be made without

disturbing the existing theory hierarchy and without the risk that the generalization actually changes the target theory. Thus, in terms of the above example, before the morphism can be used – say to deduce that list concatenation is associative – it must be shown that all the axioms of abstract collections (appropriately translated) hold in List Theory. But if the Theory of Abstract Collections were merely to be added to the parents of List Theory there would be no such guarantee that it is not fundamentally changing what can be deduced about lists.

3.5 The theory of VDM

In this section we outline how the formal development method VDM can be axiomatized, based on the presentation given in [Jon86].[12]

- We start by describing in Section 3.5.1 the underlying logic LPF [BCJ84], a three-valued logic which differs from the classical logic of Section 3.2 in subtle ways.

- Section 3.5.2 discusses the theory of VDM primitives: sets, lists, maps, Booleans, 'let' clauses, etc.

- Section 3.5.3 describes how a theory can be extracted from the 'data model' of a VDM specification module (roughly, its data types and auxiliary functions). This theory then serves as the context in which reasoning about the specification takes place.

- Section 3.5.5 deals with the 'reification' of one specification module by another, and what is involved in proving it correct. A (very simple) reification – sets implemented as nonrepeating lists – is used to illustrate the main points.

- Finally, in Section 3.5.6 we illustrate the ideas on a more substantial example, by validating part of the abstract specification of *mural* itself.

Many of the techniques and issues discussed are not restricted to VDM, but are relevant to all model-oriented specification methods and (to a lesser extent) to algebraic methods.

3.5.1 LPF

This section describes the predicate calculus underlying VDM. A three-valued logic, *LPF* (for 'Logic of Partial Functions') was chosen as the basis for VDM since it is well suited to reasoning about partial functions. LPF is broadly similar to the classical predicate calculus developed in Section 3.2 above, the main differences being in the propositional part and in the treatment of equality. Here we formulate a *many-sorted* version of LPF by modifying the single-sorted version presented in [BCJ84].

---

[12]The axiomatization given here is largely the same as that given on-line in the standard release of *mural*, although the exact set of axioms and the names given to rules differ at some points.

Propositional part

LPF has all the propositional connectives (primitive and defined) from Section 3.2.2 above, but a different set of axioms. The new axioms are:

$$\overline{\text{true}}$$

$$\frac{P}{P \vee Q} \qquad \frac{Q}{P \vee Q}$$

$$\frac{P \vee Q, \quad \{P\} \vdash R, \quad \{Q\} \vdash R}{R}$$

$$\frac{P, \ Q}{P \wedge Q} \qquad \frac{P \wedge Q}{P} \qquad \frac{P \wedge Q}{Q}$$

$$\frac{P}{\neg \neg P} \qquad \frac{\neg \neg P}{P} \qquad \frac{P, \ \neg P}{Q}$$

These are paraphrased from [BCJ84].[13]

Note that LPF is in some sense a subset of classical logic, in that all the above axioms are valid classically and thus so too are any rules that can be derived from them. The converse is definitely *not* true however. For example, as explained in [BCJ84], the law of excluded middle does not hold in LPF since '$P \vee \neg P$' might be undefined (e.g. if computation of 'P' does not terminate).[14]

Although not all of the rules of classical logic are valid in LPF, they can often be modified – by adding 'definedness' hypotheses – to do so. For example, the LPF counterpart of ' $\Rightarrow$ -introduction' is

$$\frac{\delta P, \ \{P\} \vdash Q}{P \Rightarrow Q}$$

where $\delta P \triangleq P \vee \neg P$. In essence, the assertion 'δP' says that P denotes a meaningful proposition (or *well-formed formula*). Of course, δ is not needed in classical logic, since 'δP' simply evaluates to 'true'.

The reader is referred to [BCJ84] for more discussion.

A many-sorted version of LPF

When formulating a typed version of LPF we are faced with two choices:

- assign types to all terms, including non-denoting terms such as 'hd [ ]';

- type only denoting terms.

The first approach is explored in [Mon87], where it is used for what is sometimes called 'static analysis' (or 'syntactic type-checking') of VDM specifications. Invariants are ignored and pre-conditions of functions are not checked, in a kind of rough first pass through

---

[13]The undefined ('bottom') element 'undef' and corresponding axioms (such as $\frac{\text{undef}}{Q}$) have been omitted since they never seem to be used in practice. They were included in [BCJ84] as part of the basis of a semantic explanation (model theory) and the corresponding completeness theorem.

[14]LPF also differs from intuitionistic logic (cf. Section 3.6.3) in that it admits the rule of $\neg\neg$-elimination.

the specification looking for type clashes. Such reasoning will detect certain forms of error at an early stage in a specification's life and can be fully automated, which makes it a very useful tool. But it is too coarse-grained for general verification purposes.

Here we shall follow the second alternative, arranging things so that the typing predicate bears a direct relationship to typing in the data model – so that '$a\colon A$' means the value of expression a is an element of type A and satisfies any invariants associated with A. As a consequence, the typing relation is only semi-decidable, since arbitrarily complicated predicates can be used as invariants in VDM.

Implicit in our decision is the intention to only assign types to expressions which denote actual values. Thus for example we shall be careful *not* to assign a type to 'hd [ ]'. The axiom defining 'hd' (for the head of a list) will be stated as

$$\frac{a\colon A, \quad s\colon A^*}{\mathsf{hd\,cons}(a, s) = a}$$

From this can be derived rules such as

$$\frac{s\colon A^*, \quad s \neq [\,]}{\mathsf{hd}\,s\colon A}$$

but no type can be deduced for the head of an empty list. Apart from having good theoretical reasons for making such restrictions there are strong practical reasons: many LPF rules become much simpler to state.

For reasons which will become apparent below, we shall also restrict type assignment to *first order* terms.[15] In particular, functions cannot be typed. As it happens, this is not a terribly inconvenient restriction: it's just a matter of getting used to using formation rules such as

$$\frac{x\colon X, \quad s\colon X^*}{\mathsf{cons}(x, s)\colon X^*}$$

instead of declarations such as

$$\mathsf{cons}\colon X \times X^* \to X^*$$

Equality

In LPF, equality is *strict*: that is, it is defined only on denoting terms. Thus for example 'hd [ ] = hd [ ]' is undefined. In particular, equality does not satisfy the usual law of reflexivity

$$\frac{}{a = a}$$

when a is nondenoting. As a consequence, the axioms for equality are a little more complicated than the classical laws given in Section 3.2.1. The solution takes advantage of our typing restrictions, making use of the fact that '$a\colon A$' only if a denotes an actual (first order) value. In particular, the rule of reflexivity for equality will be stated as

$$\frac{a\colon A}{a = a}$$

---

[15]This is also the reason we haven't introduced the 'function space' constructor → before now. See Section 3.6.1 for the treatment of higher order concepts such as →.

So this is the reason for restricting to first order terms: weak equality is not defined on higher order terms (such as functions).

We shall take the following as the main axioms of equality in LPF:

$$\frac{a:A, \quad b:B}{\delta(a=b)} \qquad \frac{a=b, \quad P[a]}{P[b]} \qquad \frac{a=b}{b=a}$$

The first says equality is a total predicate across all types; note the use of typing hypotheses to ensure that a and b are denoting terms. The second axiom says that equal terms can be substituted for each other. The third axiom says that equality is symmetric. From these we can deduce

$$\frac{a=b}{a=a} \qquad \frac{a=b}{b=b}$$

and the transitivity of equality, but not its reflexivity.

For completeness, the following three axioms also seem to be required:

$$\frac{a \neq b}{a=a} \qquad \frac{a \neq b}{b=b} \qquad \frac{a \neq a}{\text{false}}$$

however they rarely seem to get used in practice – at least, beyond establishing early, basic properties of equality (such as reflexivity).

Remarks:

It is important that user-supplied axioms respect the principle that equality is defined only on denoting terms. In practice this means that whenever an axiom is introduced which has '=' or '≠' in its conclusion, enough hypotheses should be included to ensure that subterms are semantically well-formed. Thus for example the typing hypotheses in

$$\frac{a:A, \quad s:A^*}{\text{hd cons}(a, s) = a}$$

ensure that the conclusion 'hd cons$(a, s) = a$' is defined.

By using typing hypotheses systematically it is easy to adhere to the above principle (although rules now need more hypotheses than their presentation in [Jon86] might suggest). If all axioms respect the principle then any rules derived from them will automatically also respect the principle; this is of course good news from a consistency point of view, but the flipside of the observation is that users should remember the principle when formulating conjectures to be proven.

Quantifiers

The quantifiers '∀' and '∃' from Section 3.2.4 above will be used again here, with the same axioms for '∀-introduction' and '∀-elimination'.[16] Unlike the classical case how-

---

[16]Apart from a few small terminological differences, the formulation of quantifiers given here is almost the same as that in [BCJ84]. The main difference is that here we use the typing assertion to distinguish denoting terms, whereas the treatment given in [BCJ84] is based around the use of equality. Thus e.g. the rule for ∃-introduction in [BCJ84]

$$\frac{s = s, \quad P[s]}{\exists x \cdot P[x]}$$

has as its counterpart

$$\frac{a:A, \quad P[a]}{\exists x:A \cdot P[x]}$$

in the current formulation.

ever, these two axioms are not enough on their own: the rules for '∃-introduction' and '∃-elimination' must also be given as axioms. (Classical proofs of these rules essentially depend on the law of excluded middle.)

Since it will sometimes be necessary to say when a quantified expression is semantically well-formed, we also add

$$\frac{\{x{:}A\} \vdash_x \delta P[x]}{\delta(\forall x{:}A \cdot P[x])}$$

as an axiom: i.e., '$\forall x{:}A \cdot P[x]$' denotes a truth value provided '$P[x]$' denotes a truth value for each element x of A. (The corresponding rule for ∃ can be deduced from this.)

It will also be useful to add a definition which says that a type is non-empty:

$$A \text{ is-nonempty} \; \triangleq \; \exists x{:}A \cdot \text{true}$$

Conditionals

The axioms for conditionals are:

$$\frac{a{:}A, \quad P}{(\text{if } P \text{ then } a \text{ else } b) = a} \qquad \frac{b{:}A, \quad \neg P}{(\text{if } P \text{ then } a \text{ else } b) = b}$$

Note that, if 'P' is true then the value of 'if P then a else b' is 'a' irrespective of whether or not 'b' denotes a value: the conditional constructor is said to be *non-strict*. Similarly, if '$\neg P$' is true, then it doesn't matter if 'a' is undefined, provided 'b' is denoting.

3.5.2   The theory of VDM primitives

The next step in our axiomatization of VDM is to treat the VDM primitives – its primitive data types, type constructors, predicates and destructors, and so on. We'll define a 'Theory of VDM Primitives' which pulls together all the facts about predicate calculus, equality, set theory, and so on, which might be used in any VDM specification. This would be done by extending the predicate calculus by

- a theory of arithmetic,

- theories of data type primitives (sets, sequences, maps, etc.),

- theories of type constructors (unions, products, enumerated types, etc.),

and so on. It should be clear by now how this could be done, at least for most VDM primitives. Some things – such as record types (cf. Section 3.3.5) and case statements – are better introduced on an as-required basis, since it is awkward to give schema which cover the general case.

In the rest of this section we will discuss some of the subtleties involved. The reader with no particular interest in the finer details of VDM can easily skip this section.

The Boolean type

In VDM, propositions and Boolean-valued terms are used interchangeably. Let us thus introduce a primitive type '**B**' to stand for Boolean values. To relate the two views we can add the axiom pair

$$\frac{b{:}\mathbf{B}}{\delta b}$$

to our formulation.

Rules such as

$$\frac{P: \mathbf{B}, \quad \{P\} \vdash Q: \mathbf{B}}{(P \wedge Q): \mathbf{B}}$$

can be easily derived. Paraphrased, this rule says that '$P \wedge Q$' is a well-formed formula (*wff*) if

- 'P' is a wff, and

- 'Q' is a wff under the assumption that P is true.

This explains why it is alright to write something like '$x \neq 0 \wedge x/x = 1$' in VDM.

For many purposes $\Leftrightarrow$ can be used as equality on Booleans. For completeness however we should add the axiom

$$\frac{P \Leftrightarrow Q}{P = Q}$$

From this we can derive rules such as

$$\frac{b: \mathbf{B}}{b = \text{true} \vee b = \text{false}}$$

which says that there are only two possible Boolean values. It also now becomes possible to give a direct derivation of the rule for substitutivity of equivalents (cf. Section 3.2.2):

$$\frac{P \Leftrightarrow Q, \quad R[P]}{R[Q]}$$

Remarks:

Note that the axioms given above 'conserve sense' (in the sense of Section 3.2.2). It would be fatal to the consistency of the theory to use an axiom of the form

$$(b: \mathbf{B}) \Leftrightarrow \delta b$$

since for example from the (perfectly reasonable) assertion that the numeral 0 is not a Boolean we could derive a contradiction as follows:

from $\neg (0: \mathbf{B})$
     $\neg \delta 0$ $\Leftrightarrow$ -substitution
     $\neg (0 \vee \neg 0)$ unfolding
     $\neg 0 \wedge \neg \neg 0$ de Morgan's law
     $\neg 0$ $\wedge$-elimination (left)
     $\neg \neg 0$ $\wedge$-elimination (right)
infer false   contradiction

Our formulation avoids this fate because it is not possible to infer '$\neg \delta 0$' from '$\neg (0: \mathbf{B})$'.[17]

---

[17]For example the law of contraposition

$$\frac{\delta P, \quad \neg Q, \quad \{P\} \vdash Q}{\neg P}$$

would require us to first establish the – perfectly unreasonable – definedness hypothesis '$\delta \delta 0$'.

Disjoint types

Elementary types (such as B and N) are non-overlapping and are disjoint from composite types (such as 'set' types, record types, etc). For most applications it's not necessary to make such assumptions explicit: it's usually simply enough to note that such overlaps cannot be derived (provided the specification is type-consistent, of course). Every now and then, however, such assumptions must be made explicit, and the easiest way to do this is probably by adding an axiom of the form

$$\frac{a:A, \quad b:B}{a \neq b}$$

for the relevant types A and B.

Definitions

When making definitions care should be taken that non-denoting cases are not inadvertently overlooked. For example, the definition of the list membership predicate used in Section 3.3.1 above

$$a \; in \; s \; \triangleq \; a = \mathsf{hd}\,s \vee a \; in \; \mathsf{tl}\,s$$

should *not* be used here, since it leaves '$a \; in \; [\,]$' undefined (non-denoting). The solution would be to use

$$a \; in \; s \; \triangleq \; s \neq [\,] \wedge (a = \mathsf{hd}\,s \vee a \; in \; \mathsf{tl}\,s)$$

instead.

Note that it is not necessary for the *definiendum* (rhs) of a definition to denote a value, since the definition symbol ($\triangleq$) is interpreted as strong equality (cf. [CJ91]): in other words, $a \triangleq b$ does not imply $a = b$.

Predicates

In the VDM view, predicates are functions which return Boolean values. Thus for each user-supplied predicate symbol Q – with domain A say – an axiom of the form

$$\frac{a:A}{\delta Q(a)}$$

should be added. Such rules are called δ-*rules*. For example, the δ-rule for set membership is

$$\frac{a:A, \quad s:A\text{-set}}{\delta(a \in s)}$$

In the discussion of equality in Section 3.5.1 above we remarked that user-supplied axioms should ensure that equality is defined only on denoting terms, but similar care should be taken with axioms for (other) predicates. For example, the expression '$\{x:A \cdot P[x]\}$' may not denote a finite set (e.g. if there are infinitely many values of A that satisfy $P[x]$), so '$a \in \{x:A \cdot P[x]\}$' may be undefined in LPF. The classical law of set comprehension (cf. Section 3.4.1)

$$\frac{}{a \in \{x:A \cdot P[x]\} \; \Leftrightarrow \; a:A \wedge P[a]}$$

is thus not valid in LPF, and must be replaced by

$$\frac{\{x:A \cdot P[x]\} : A\text{-set}}{a \in \{x:A \cdot P[x]\} \; \Leftrightarrow \; a:A \wedge P[a]}$$

'Let' clauses

VDM has two forms of 'let' clause:

- one for introducing named expressions

- the other for selecting an arbitrary element of a type

Although they appear very similar, they are in fact quite different kinds of operator, and they both cause problems: the first because it is a binder whose natural 'universe' is an *Exp* rather than a *Type*; the second because it is non-deterministic, and LPF does not handle non-determinism. We'll look at the two cases separately:

(1) An example use of named expressions is

$$\text{let } x = (a + b) \text{ in } t = x^2 + x + 1$$

which is a shorthand for '$t = (a + b)^2 + (a + b) + 1$'. The 'let' clause is used to break up long expressions by factoring out recurring subterms, thereby making the expression easier to read. It was intended that the definition facility in *mural* would give similar benefits but the mechanism was only implemented at the level of *Theory*s and not at the level of individual expressions. Thus it becomes necessary to describe how 'let' clauses might be simulated in the 'Theory of VDM Primitives'.

A particularly bombastic solution would be to simply 'expand out' all uses of named expressions when translating a VDM specification to a theory. This would be counter-productive in the extreme – quite out of step with *mural*'s stated goal of providing *useful* support for reasoning about specifications.

Instead, we'll meet the problem head-on by introducing a new (primitive) binder with display form 'let $[\![e1]\!]$ in $[\![e2]\!]$'. In the above example x is the bound variable and the 'universe' of the binding consists of the single value '$a + b$'. Since binder universes must be *Type*s in *mural*, it's necessary to introduce a mock type constructor for coercing an *Exp* into a *Type*. By declaring its display form to be '$= [\![e1]\!]$', the above expression would be displayed as

$$\text{let } x := (a + b) \text{ in } t = x^2 + x + 1$$

which is almost identical to the original.

The properties of the new binder are defined by the axiom pair:

$$\frac{E[t]}{\text{let } x := t \text{ in } E[x]}$$

Note that this deals with abbreviations at the level of assertions only – that is, the body '$E[x]$' must be an assertion (such as $t = x^2 + x + 1$) rather than simply a term (such as $x^2 + 1$). While this is a significant improvement in granularity from *Theory* level, it is still not as fine-grained as is needed in VDM use. The problem can be overcome by adding new (more complicated) axioms. (Left as an exercise for the reader.)

(2) The other form of the VDM 'let' clause is the *choice operator*, used for selecting an arbitrary element from a type, similar to Hilbert's ε-operator (cf. Section 3.2.5). The main difficulty is that it must be interpreted deterministically if we are to reason about it in LPF. (In fact, this restriction will apply only to uses of the operator in the *data model* of

a specification, and not to specifications of operations: see the discussion in Section 3.5.3 below.)

To illustrate the problems involved, let us consider the following definition of a function for converting a set into a list:

$convert : X\text{-set} \to X^*$
$convert(s) \quad \triangle \quad$ if $s = \{\,\}$
$\qquad\qquad\qquad$ then $[\,]$
$\qquad\qquad\qquad$ else let $x \in s$ in $cons(x, convert(s - \{x\}))$

Suppose we took this to mean that *convert* is non-deterministic, so that e.g. '$convert\{x, y\}$' might be '$[x, y]$' at some times and '$[y, x]$' at others. But this would mean that

$$convert\{x, y\} = convert\{x, y\}$$

is not valid (at least, not when $x \neq y$), violating one of the basic tenets of LPF – that equality is reflexive on denoting terms.

To keep our formulation consistent we must insist that uses of the choice operator be considered not to be non-deterministic, but rather *under-determined*. In other words, given the same input, the operator always makes the same choice. Any choice from the set will do – the smallest element, the largest, or whatever – just as long as it is always the same. If the choice operator is used in a specification, part of the subsequent design process should be concerned with replacing it by something more determined.

When it makes sense (i.e., when A is non-empty), the only thing we can say about the term

$$\text{let } x\!:\! A \text{ in } F[x]$$

is that it has property P, provided $F[x]$ satisfies P for *any* possible choice of x from A. The appropriate axiom is thus

$$\frac{A \text{ is-nonempty,} \quad \{x\!:\!A\} \vdash_x P[F[x]]}{P[\,(\text{let } x\!:\! A \text{ in } F[x])\,]}$$

The second hypothesis ensures that no inadvertent bias is associated with the choice of x from A. Using the above axiom it is possible to prove e.g.

$$\frac{l\!:\! \mathsf{N}^*}{(\text{let } x\!:\! \mathsf{N} \text{ in } cons(x, l))\!:\! \mathsf{N}^*}$$

Remarks:

(1) Note that the treatment of the first form of 'let' clause actually reduces to a special case of the second form. In particular, its axioms can be derived from those for the choice operator.

(2) Expressions of the form

$$\text{let } x\!:\! A \text{ be such that } P[x] \text{ in } Q[x]$$

should be translated to

$$\text{let } x\!:\! < z\!:\! A \cdot P[z] > \text{ in } Q[x]$$

(3) Recursive 'let' clauses ('letrec') are more of a problem, since *mural* does not allow multiple simultaneous bindings (cf. Section 4.11).

3.5.3 Translating specifications into theories

In this section we outline how to construct a theory in which to reason about a given VDM specification module. The theory will be extracted from the 'data model' of the specification (roughly, its data types and auxiliary functions). A more precise definition of the data model will be given below; for the moment it's enough to know that it defines the abstract data types on which the 'operations' of the specification take place.

For reasons of economy of space, the operational side of VDM will not be treated in any detail here. A full treatment would cover

- properties of *chains* of operations

- operation decomposition and other refinement techniques

- techniques for verifying that programs correctly implement operations

and more, and a full formalization of these topics would require a complete book in itself. The reader is referred instead to other sections of this book where such topics are treated: e.g.

- Chapter 9 for symbolic execution of (chains of) operations

- Chapter 7 for operation decomposition

- Section 3.6.5 for Hoare's logic of program correctness

The only 'operational' reasoning covered here is the 'implementability proof obligation' for showing that operations can be implemented *in principle*. Such obligations can be stated in terms of the pre- and post-conditions on the operations, without actually making reference to the operations themselves. In Section 3.5.5 we also consider the proof obligations arising when a specification is 'reified' by another: these include obligations corresponding to the operations of the specifications, but once again they can be stated in terms of pre- and post-conditions.

The theory extracted from the data model establishes the 'context' in which to reason about a specification. It can be used to validate the data model, by showing that (formally stated) requirements are logical consequences of the model. In particular, internal consistency checks (such as the claims scattered through the abstract specification in Chapter 4) can be shown to hold. These ideas are illustrated in Section 3.5.6 by validating part of the abstract specification of *mural* itself.

After defining what is meant by the data model of a VDM specification module, much of the rest of this section is devoted to describing a 'cookbook' approach to building the theory corresponding to a given VDM data model. First, so as to inherit all the basic facts about VDM, the theory will have the 'Theory of VDM Primitives' as parent. Next we translate the specification module component by component. (No attempt will be made to capture VDM naming conventions, etc.) The translation process – and how to automate it – is discussed further in Chapter 7. The main obstacle to making the process fully automatic would seem to be the difficulty of producing induction axioms for recursive domain equations (especially those defined by mutual recursion).

Some terminology

In Section 3.5.2 we saw that LPF does not handle non-deterministic operators. It should also be clear that operators with 'side effects' cannot be allowed. This leads us to divide each VDM specification module into two parts:

1. a data model, in which all functions are 'applicative' (side-effect free) and deterministic (although possibly undetermined);

2. an operational part, containing operations on a global state and non-deterministic operators.

The VDM syntax does not distinguish between the different kinds of function/operation so we need to introduce some new terminology.

Definition: In this chapter, the notions *auxiliary function* and *operation* will be used with the following meanings:

- VDM definitions which have recourse to a global state ('external variables') will be called operations.

- Definitions which are intended to be non-deterministic – in that they may return different values on the same arguments – will also be called operations.

- Explicit defined functions – in which the definition is given directly and does not involve external variables, post-conditions, or uses of the choice operator – will be called auxiliary functions.

- Implicitly defined functions – given in terms of post-conditions, or using the choice operator, but not involving external variables – will be called auxiliary functions, *provided* the choice operator is interpreted deterministically. Such functions are regarded as being underspecified, and part of the subsequent design task will be to specify them more fully.

Definition: The *data model* of a VDM specification module consists of:

- elementary types, including type parameters and primitive types

    – e.g. N and B, but also types such as *VSymb* in Section 4.2

- type definitions and record type declarations, possibly with invariants

- elementary (or 'atomic') values

    – e.g. AXIOM in Section 4.5

- primitive (or 'black box') functions, representing e.g.

    – user input
    – system-wide functions which are more naturally specified at a different level (e.g. '*has-manag-priv*' and '*is-logged-in*' on pp.71-2 of [CHJ86])

- auxiliary functions (defined explicitly or implicitly)

On the other hand, the *operational part* of a VDM specification module consists of:

- operations (as defined above)

- initial state declarations

Of course, *we are implicitly assuming that the VDM module can be neatly separated into these two components*, so that the data model can be defined completely independently of the operational part. (The converse is certainly not true: the operational part is defined in terms of the data model.) This assumption underlies the use of VDM as a model-oriented specification language.

Data types

In Section 3.5.2 we saw how the data types for VDM primitives can be axiomatized on top of LPF. In this section we describe how user-defined data types are axiomatized. There are basically three ways a specification writer can form new data types:

1. as primitive types

2. via type definitions

3. as record types ('tagged definitions')

Defined types can also have associated 'data type invariants'; we'll return to these below. Finally, note that definitions by mutual recursion are possible. These are the main problems we must address.

Translation proceeds as follows:

1. For each primitive type in the specification we add a corresponding primitive type to the theory.

2. For each type definition we simply add a corresponding defined type. In most cases this just involves a straightforward translation from VDM syntax to *mural* syntax, as the examples below will show. For simple (non-recursive) definitions no additional axioms are required.

3. The axioms for simple (invariant-free) record types are almost exactly as presented in Section 3.3.5 above, except that those defining selectors require typing hypotheses: e.g.

$$\frac{mk\text{-}REC(a1, a2, a3)\colon Rec}{sel1(mk\text{-}Rec(a1, a2, a3)) = a1}$$

(cf. the remarks on equality and denoting terms in Section 3.5.1).

To reason about recursive type definitions we'll also need *induction axioms*. For example, given the definition

$$Tree \;\triangleq\; (Tree \times \mathsf{N} \times Tree) \mid \mathsf{N}$$

the relevant induction axiom is

$$\frac{\{n\colon \mathsf{N}\} \vdash_n P[n],\quad \{t_1\colon Tree,\; m\colon \mathsf{N},\; t_2\colon Tree,\; P[t_1],\; P[t_2]\} \vdash_{t_1,m,t_2} P[(t_1, m, t_2)]}{\forall t\colon Tree \cdot P[t]}$$

In general such axioms must be added on an *ad hoc* basis. For simple shapes of definition it should be possible to generate induction axioms mechanically from the specification, but the question won't be treated here.

Data type invariants

When an invariant is associated with a defined data type, subtyping should be employed: e.g.

$Longlist = X^*$

where

$inv\text{-}Longlist(s) \triangleq \text{len } s \geq 2$

becomes

$$Longlist \triangleq \; < s\text{:} X^* \cdot (\text{len } s \geq 2) >$$

In fact, to aid legibility it is often better to introduce the invariant as a separate definition.

When a record type is defined with an invariant, e.g.

$Record' :: \; s1 \; : \; T1,$
$\qquad\qquad s2 \; : \; T2$

where

$inv\text{-}Record'(mk\text{-}Record'(x, y)) \triangleq inv ar(x, y)$

there are two possible approaches:

1. the direct approach, where the invariant is directly incorporated into the axioms: e.g.
$$\frac{x\text{:} T1, \quad y\text{:} T2, \quad invar(x, y)}{mk\text{-}Record'(x, y)\text{:} Record'} \qquad \frac{r\text{:} Record'}{invar(s1(r), s2(r))}$$

2. the indirect approach, whereby an intermediate type – say *ProtoRecord'* – is introduced and *Record'* is defined via subtyping:

$ProtoRecord' :: \; s1 \; : \; T1,$
$\qquad\qquad\qquad s2 \; : \; T2$

$$Record' \triangleq \; < r\text{:} ProtoRecord' \cdot invar(s1(r), s2(r)) >$$

In small examples the direct approach is usually more convenient, but in larger examples – particularly where *Record'* is recursively defined or where there are many associated auxiliary functions – the indirect approach is better (cf. the use of *ProtoTerm* in Section 4.2).

Remarks:

(1) This is a good place to point out one of the advantages of the *mural* approach over strongly typed logical frames such as ELF: viz. ones in which every value has at most one type. In the latter *Longlist* would be introduced as a primitive type, with coercion functions

$$coerc_{ls} \; : Longlist \rightarrow X^*$$
$$coerc_{sl} \; : X^* \rightarrow Longlist$$

say, where *coerc*$_{sl}$ is a partial function. Now consider how functions over *Longlist* must be defined: e.g. the function for concatenating two *Longlist*s would be

$$concat(l_1, l_2) \triangleq coerc_{sl}(coerc_{ls}(l_1) \frown coerc_{ls}(l_2))$$

Contrast this with the 'inclusion polymorphism' available in a type system with sub-typing: the ordinary list concatenation function '$\frown$' can be used directly to concatenate *Longlist*s without having to define a new function. Clearly inclusion polymorphism is vastly preferable!

As a matter of fact, it would be extremely awkward to have to axiomatize VDM specifications in a strongly typed system, since data type invariants are used so frequently. The same could be said for any specification method based on set theory.

(2) Note how the typing principle – that only denoting terms can be typed – extends to data types with invariants: a term is denoting only if it satisfies the invariant. Thus for example '*l: Longlist*' asserts not only that *l* denotes a list of *X*'s, but also that the list has at least two elements. The typing relation thus captures the 'meaning' behind invariants, which gives many benefits. For a start, it makes VDM proof obligations much easier to state.

Elementary values and auxiliary functions

For each elementary value used in the specification a corresponding primitive constant should be added to the theory. Similarly, each primitive function should have a corresponding primitive constant of the appropriate arity; if available, typing information can be added as axioms (e.g. *maxnum*: $\mathbb{N}$). Defined constants we can treat simply as defined functions without arguments. That leaves only defined functions, which we treat as two subcases:

(1) For each *explicitly defined* function we add a corresponding function definition to the theory: e.g. the body of

$$last : X^* \to X$$
$$last(s) \quad \triangleq \quad \text{if } tl\, s = [\,] $$
$$\text{then } hd\, s$$
$$\text{else } last(tl\, s)$$
$$\text{pre } s \neq [\,]$$

can be used as a function definition more-or-less as it stands. The information in the signature can then be stated as a rule

$$\frac{s: X^*, \quad s \neq [\,]}{last(s): X}$$

and derived by induction over sequences. Note that the pre-condition is not included in the definition, but should be included in any rule involving the function.

(2) For each *implicitly defined* function a new primitive constant should be introduced, together with an axiom stating the function's defining property. Thus for example, given the specification

$$sort\ (s: \mathbb{N}^*)\ s': \mathbb{N}^*$$
$$\text{post } is\text{-}increasing(s') \wedge \text{elems } s' = \text{elems } s$$

we would add a new constant *sort* to the theory, with axiom

$$\frac{s: \mathsf{N}^*}{\textit{is-increasing}(\textit{sort}(s)) \wedge \mathsf{elems}\, s = \mathsf{elems}\, \textit{sort}(s)}$$

Since type information cannot generally be inferred from an implicit definition, it must also be added axiomatically; in this case:

$$\frac{s: \mathsf{N}^*}{\textit{sort}(s): \mathsf{N}^*}$$

Finally, recall that although an implicit definition may have several different solutions, it is assumed that the function defined is deterministic (cf. the discussion in Section 3.5.2 above on 'let' clauses).

Operations' pre- and post-conditions

We said that operations will not have direct counterparts in the theory of the data model of a specification. It is useful however to add definitions of their pre- and post-conditions, so that we can at least state implementability proof obligations. Thus for example, given an operation

ADD (*n*: *Name*)
ext wr *s* : *Name*˙
pre *n* ∉ elems *s*
post elems *s* = elems $\overleftarrow{s} \cup \{n\}$

we shall add defined constants

$$pre\text{-}ADD(n, s) \quad \triangleq \quad n \notin \mathsf{elems}\, s$$
$$post\text{-}ADD(n, \overleftarrow{s}, s) \quad \triangleq \quad \mathsf{elems}\, s = \mathsf{elems}\, \overleftarrow{s} \cup \{n\}$$

The implementability proof obligation for this operation can simply be stated as

$$\frac{n: Name, \quad s: Name^*, \quad pre\text{-}ADD(n, s)}{\exists s': Name^* \cdot post\text{-}ADD(n, s, s')}$$

(See Section 3.5.5 for more details.)

3.5.4   Validating the specification

As already mentioned, the theory extracted from the data model can be used to validate the model by showing that (formally stated) requirements are logical consequences of the model. There is also an obligation to show that the data model is internally consistent in some sense; in particular, it should be shown that:

- initial state declarations are of the appropriate types

- pre-conditions and data type invariants are well-formed formulae (denote Boolean values)

- post-conditions are well-formed formulae, under the assumption that their corresponding pre-conditions hold

- function definitions agree with their signatures

as well as the usual context conditions and 'syntactic correctness' criteria (such as absence of free variables, and so on). Many of these checks can – and should – be performed fully automatically, possibly by external tools.

Implementability

Another important way of validating a specification is to show that its operations are implementable in principle. Actual implementation concerns – such as efficiency, target language, and so on – are questions for the design phase; here we 'merely' want to establish whether an operation can be realized at all. Thus, given an operation specification

OP *(arg: ArgType) res: ResType*
ext rd r : *Type*1,
    wr w : *Type*2
pre *pre-OP(arg, r, w)*
post *post-OP(arg, r, $\overleftarrow{w}$, w, res)*

the implementability proof obligation is

$$\frac{arg : ArgType, \quad r : Type1, \quad \overleftarrow{w} : Type2, \\ pre\text{-}OP(arg, r, \overleftarrow{w})}{\exists w : Type2 \cdot \exists res : ResType \cdot post\text{-}OP(arg, r, \overleftarrow{w}, w, res)}$$

Note that this form of the proof obligation subsumes the need to check state invariants, since they have been incorporated into the definitions of *Type*1 and *Type*2. In other words, in addition to showing that there exist w and *res* such that '*post-OP(arg, r, $\overleftarrow{w}$, w, res)*' holds, the demonstration must show that w and *res* satisfy the appropriate invariants on *Type*1 and *Type*2, respectively.

Note also that, having proven implementability in principle, there is absolutely no obligation to actually implement the operation in any way related to the methods used in the proof. The only requirement on the implementor is that the operation satisfy its post-condition whenever it is invoked in a situation where its pre-condition is true. (When the pre-condition is false the operation is totally unconstrained.) The importance of separating analysis and implementation phases of the software development cycle cannot be over-emphasized.

For implicit function definitions there is also an implementability proof obligation. Thus for example given a function definition

ImplicitFn (arg: ArgType) res: ResType
pre *pre-ImplicitFn(arg)*
post *post-ImplicitFn(arg, res)*

the associated proof obligation is

$$\frac{arg : ArgType, \quad pre\text{-}ImplicitFn(arg)}{\exists res : ResType \cdot post\text{-}ImplicitFn(arg, res)}$$

In fact, this result must be proven in an impoverished theory, namely one in which '*ImplicitFn*' has not been introduced, since otherwise the obligation is trivially true upon setting *res* equal to *ImplicitFn(arg)*.

Layered data models

If two or more functions are implicitly defined, the situation becomes even more complicated: they should be put in some order, with the first shown to be implementable only in terms of primitive and explicitly defined functions, and the rest shown to be implementable in terms of primitive functions, explicitly defined functions and preceding implicitly defined functions. To formalize all this we would need to define a sequence of theories, one built on top of another, corresponding to the sequence of implicitly defined functions. This in turn would require that a VDM specification be defined in layers, to indicate the sequence of implicitly defined functions.

But all this is moving well beyond the realms of *mural* and into questions about VDM itself. Let's leave the problem there and move on.

3.5.5   Data type reifications

In the standard text on VDM [Jon86], a *reification* is defined to consist of two specifications – let's call them an abstract and a concrete specification – plus a 'retrieve function', which maps elements of the concrete state to elements of the abstract state. (Where the state is distributed between several data types there will of course be a retrieve function corresponding to each state.) In this section we start by defining the theory associated with a reification, and then illustrate the ideas on a small example.

The theory given by a reification

The theory corresponding to a reification – the context in which reasoning about the reification takes place – is formed simply by combining the theories of the individual specifications, together with a definition of the retrieve function. If name clashes occur, where the same name has been used to mean different things in the two specifications, one or both the names must be changed. (This is where a renaming mechanism is sadly lacking from the *mural* theory structure.) Of course, sometimes the two names are meant to represent the same thing (e.g. the primitive type X is common to both specifications in the example given below) in which case no change is required.

To verify that the reification is correct, certain proof obligations must be discharged. To illustrate, let's suppose we have an abstract state $State_0$, a concrete state $State_1$ and a retrieve function *retr*. There are four different kinds of proof obligation:

1. The first obligation is to show that the retrieve function is of the correct type: viz.

$$\frac{s: State_1}{retr(s): State_0}$$

2. Next, it must be shown that there are sufficiently many concrete states to represent all the abstract states (the 'adequacy obligation'):

$$\frac{\sigma_0: State_0}{\exists \sigma_1: State_1 \cdot retr(\sigma_1) = \sigma_0}$$

3. If the abstract specification defines an initial value $init_0$ for the state, the concrete specification should likewise define an initial state $init_1$, and the retrieve function

should map the concrete value to the abstract value:

$$retr(init_1) = init_0$$

There are also obligations to show that the initial values have the required types.

4. Corresponding to each pair of operations $OP_0(x: X)$ and $OP_1(x: X)$ – where the latter is the 'concrete' version of the former – there are two proof obligations:

   (a) The pre-condition of the concrete operation is weaker than that of the abstract operation (the 'domain obligation'):

$$\frac{x\colon X, \quad \sigma\colon State_1,}{pre\text{-}OP_0(x, retr(\sigma))}$$
$$\overline{pre\text{-}OP_1(x, \sigma)}$$

   (b) The post-condition of the concrete operation is stronger than that of the abstract operation, at least when the latter's pre-condition is true (the 'result obligation'):

$$x\colon X, \quad \overleftarrow{\sigma}\colon State_1, \quad \sigma\colon State_1,$$
$$pre\text{-}OP_0(x, retr(\overleftarrow{\sigma})),$$
$$\frac{post\text{-}OP_1(x, \overleftarrow{\sigma}, \sigma)}{post\text{-}OP_0(x, retr(\overleftarrow{\sigma}), retr(\sigma))}$$

Note that auxiliary functions of the concrete specification might have nothing to do with the auxiliary functions of the abstract specification, although in practice the retrieve function will involve a mixture of both.

An example abstract specification

Consider the following (almost trivial) VDM specification of an operation which takes an element and, as a side-effect, adds it to the state, where the latter is modelled as a set of elements.

$State_0 = X$-set

$ADD_0 \ (x: X)$
ext wr s : $State_0$
pre $x \notin s$
post $s = \overleftarrow{s} \cup \{x\}$

The operation has as a pre-condition that the element added is not already in the state. This is the kind of primitive operation that might arise after some more complicated operations have been decomposed, for example.

Now let's consider the corresponding theory. The only new constructors it needs are a new primitive type X and defined type

$$State_0 \triangleq X\text{-set}$$

for the state. In this (very simple) case no additional axioms are required – all the relevant axioms are inherited from the 'Theory of VDM Primitives'.

A reification of the example

Now let's consider a reification of the previous specification in which sets are represented as non-repeating lists:

$$State_1 = X^*$$

where

$$inv\text{-}State_1(l) \quad \triangleq \quad is\text{-}non\text{-}repeating(l)$$

$$is\text{-}non\text{-}repeating : X^* \to \mathbb{B}$$
$$is\text{-}non\text{-}repeating(l) \quad \triangleq \quad \forall i, j \in \text{dom}\, l \cdot i \neq j \;\Rightarrow\; l(i) \neq l(j)$$

$$ADD_1\ (x\colon X)$$
$$\text{ext wr } l \,:\, State_1$$
$$\text{pre } x \notin \text{elems}\, l$$
$$\text{post } l = \text{cons}(x, \overleftarrow{l}\,)$$

Note that the reification is itself another specification. It is very similar to the first, but with a couple of extra design decisions: viz.

- sets are represented as non-repeating lists

- the *ADD* operation puts its argument onto the *front* of the list

The corresponding theory has primitive type X, defined type

$$State_1 \quad \triangleq \quad <\, l\colon X^* \cdot is\text{-}non\text{-}repeating(l)\, >$$

and defined constant

$$is\text{-}non\text{-}repeating(l) \quad \triangleq \quad \forall i\colon \widehat{\text{dom}\, l} \cdot \forall j\colon \widehat{\text{dom}\, l} \cdot i \neq j \;\Rightarrow\; l \text{ at } i \neq l \text{ at } j$$

(The awkwardness of writing '$\widehat{\text{dom}\, l}$' could be overcome by introducing a new type constructor which works directly on lists.) The implementability proof obligation is

$$\frac{x\colon X, \quad \overleftarrow{l} : State_1,}{\exists l\colon State_1 \cdot l = \text{cons}(x, \overleftarrow{l}\,)}$$
$$x \notin \text{elems}\, \overleftarrow{l}$$

It would be useful to build up a collection of derived rules about the new specification – as validation exercises for example, or as lemmas to aid in later proofs. Promising candidates might include the following:

$$\frac{}{[\,]\colon State_1} \qquad \frac{x\colon X, \quad l\colon State_1,}{\text{cons}(x, l)\colon State_1} \qquad \frac{s\colon X^*,}{s\colon State_1}$$
$$x \notin \text{elems}\, l \qquad\qquad \text{card elems}\, s = \text{len}\, s$$

The proof obligations for our example

To show that the second specification is a valid reification of the first we must provide a *retrieve function* taking elements of the concrete representation to their counterparts in the abstract representation. In this case the choice is obvious; we simply map lists to the set having the same elements:

$retr : State_1 \rightarrow State_0$
$retr(\sigma)$ $\triangleq$ elems σ

To build a theory corresponding to the reification we simply take the theories corresponding to the abstract and concrete specifications as parents and add a defined constant for the retrieve function: viz.

$$retr(\sigma) \triangleq \text{elems } \sigma$$

No additional axioms are required. The definition should be validated by 'deriving its signature': viz. showing that

$$\frac{\sigma : State_1}{retr(\sigma) : State_0}$$

The 'adequacy' proof obligation is

$$\frac{\sigma_0 : State_0}{\exists \sigma_1 : State_1 \cdot retr(\sigma_1) = \sigma_0}$$

The 'domain' and 'result' obligations are

$$\frac{\dots, \quad x \notin \text{elems } l}{x \notin \text{elems } l}$$

and

$$\frac{\dots, \quad x \notin \text{elems } l, \quad l = \text{cons}(x, \overleftarrow{l})}{\text{elems } l = \text{elems } \overleftarrow{l} \cup \{x\}}$$

respectively.

An example proof

Here's a sketch proof of the adequacy proof obligation for this reification:

from σ_0: $State_0$
1   elems $[\,] = \{\,\}$ elems axiom1 ()
2      $[\,]$: $State_1$ lemma0 ()
3      $\exists\sigma$: $State_1 \cdot$ elems $\sigma = \{\,\}$ $\exists$-introduction (1,2)
$4_{x,s}$ from x: X, s: X-set, $x \notin s$, $\exists\sigma$: $State_1 \cdot$ elems $\sigma = s$
4.1_l from l: $State_1$, elems $l = s$
4.1.1 $x \notin$ elems l substitution (4.1.h2,4.h3)
4.1.2   cons(x, l): $State_1$ lemma1 (4.h1,4.1.h1,4.1.1)
4.1.3   elems cons(x, l) = elems $l \cup \{x\}$ elems axiom2 ()
4.1.4   elems cons(x, l) = $s \cup \{x\}$ substitution (4.1.h2,4.1.3)
                infer $\exists\sigma$: $State_1 \cdot$ elems $\sigma = s \cup \{x\}$ $\exists$-introduction (4.1.4,4.1.2)
            infer $\exists\sigma$: $State_1 \cdot$ elems $\sigma = s \cup \{x\}$ $\exists$-elimination (4.h4,4.1)
5      $\forall s$: X-set $\cdot \exists\sigma$: $State_1 \cdot$ elems $\sigma = s$ set induction (3,4)
infer $\exists\sigma_1$: $State_1 \cdot retr(\sigma_1) = \sigma_0$ $\forall$-elimination (h1,5)

The other two proof obligations are left as exercises for the reader.

3.5.6   An example validation

To illustrate the ideas on a more substantial example, let's see what would be involved
in translating part of the abstract specification of *mural* itself; we can even try proving
one of the assertions made about it. We'll look at the abstract syntax (*ProtoTerm*s, etc.)
defined in Section 4.2.3 and prove that the variables which occur among the subterms of
a *ProtoTerm*, z say, form a subset of *allVars(z)*.

The specification

First let's pull out the definition of the abstract syntax from Section 4.2.3:

   ProtoTerm = ProtoExp | ProtoType

   ProtoExp = VSymb | ProtoCompExp | ProtoBindExp

   ProtoType = ProtoCompType | ProtoSubType | ProtoDepType

   ProtoCompExp :: *symb* : *CESymb*
                         eArgs : *ProtoExp**
                         tArgs : *ProtoType**

   ProtoBindExp :: *symb* : *DESymb*
                         var   : *VSymb*
                         univ   : *ProtoType*
                         body   : *ProtoExp*

etc...

$Subterms : ProtoTerm \rightarrow ProtoTerm\text{-set}$
$Subterms(z) \quad \triangle$
    cases z **of**
    $VSymb \qquad\qquad\qquad \rightarrow \{z\}$
    $mk\text{-}ProtoCompExp(c, el, tl) \rightarrow \{z\} \cup \bigcup \{Subterms(x) \mid x \in \text{elems } el \cup \text{elems } tl\}$
    $mk\text{-}ProtoBindExp(q, v, t, e) \rightarrow \{z\} \cup Subterms(t) \cup Subterms(e)$
    $\vdots$
    end

etc...

The assertion we shall try to prove is

$$\forall z{:}\,ProtoTerm \cdot \{v{:}\,VSymb \mid v \in Subterms(z)\} \subseteq allVars(z)$$

The corresponding theory

Rather than trying to axiomatize the whole specification in one go, let's just give axioms for the functions involved in the statement of the conjecture, then jump straight into a proof attempt and see what additional axioms will be needed as we go along.

Let's first consider the *Subterms* function. To define *Subterms* directly we would need to formulate case statements, but as we've said before this is too much like hard work. Instead, it's much simpler to define *Subterms* axiomatically by cases: viz.

$$\frac{z{:}\,VSymb}{Subterms(z) = \{z\}}$$

$$\frac{z{:}\,ProtoCompExp}{Subterms(z) = \{z\} \cup \bigcup \{Subterms(x) \mid x \in \text{elems } eArgs(z) \cup \text{elems } tArgs(z)\}}$$

$$\frac{z{:}\,ProtoBindExp}{Subterms(z) = \{z\} \cup Subterms(univ(z)) \cup Subterms(body(z))}$$

$$\vdots$$

Remembering the difficulties with set comprehension (cf. Section 3.4.1), however, it would seem to be better to introduce a type abbreviation

$$ArgsOf(z) \quad \triangle \quad EnumType(\text{elems } eArgs(z) \cup \text{elems } tArgs(z))$$

and to rewrite the second of the axioms above as

$$\frac{z{:}\,ProtoCompExp}{Subterms(z) = \{z\} \cup \{Subterms(x) \mid x{:}\,ArgsOf(z)\}}$$

The axiom for *ProtoCompType* would be treated similarly. We claim that such axioms can be extracted mechanically from the specification, thereby reducing the possibility of 'transcription errors'.

Axioms for the functions *bndVars* and *freeVars* would be given similarly, and *allVars* would be defined as

$$allVars(z) \quad \triangle \quad freeVars(z) \cup bndVars(z)$$

An induction rule

The other main axiom we'll need at this stage is an induction rule for *ProtoTerm*s. The axiom will have as it conclusion

$$\forall z\colon ProtoTerm \cdot P[z]$$

The base case – when z is a *VSymb* – is given by the sequent hypothesis

$$\{v\colon VSymb\} \vdash_v P[v]$$

There will be five induction cases, corresponding to the other five kinds of *ProtoTerm*:

$$ProtoCompExp, ProtoBindExp, \text{etc.}$$

As a first attempt to state the *ProtoCompExp* case we might write

$$\{c\colon CESymb,\ el\colon ProtoExp^*,\ tl\colon ProtoType^*,\ \forall x \in \text{elems } el \cup \text{elems } tl \cdot P[x]\}$$
$$\vdash_{c,el,tl} P[mk\text{-}ProtoCompExp(c, el, tl)]$$

but upon reflection

$$\{z\colon ProtoCompExp,\ \forall x\colon ArgsOf(z) \cdot P[x]\} \vdash_z P[z]$$

is much better. The second induction case could be stated as

$$\{z\colon ProtoBindExp,\ P[univ(z)],\ P[body(z)]\} \vdash_z P[z]$$

The other cases are analogous to these two.

  With regard to automatic extraction of axioms from specifications, although the above example is quite straightforward, it's harder to accept that there might be an algorithm that finds the most useful form of an induction axiom in every case. More research is needed here.

The proof

Recall that our aim is to show that

$$\forall z\colon ProtoTerm \cdot \{v\colon VSymb \cdot v \in Subterms(z)\} \subseteq allVars(z)$$

To make the proof easier to understand let's introduce the following abbreviation for the variables *occurring* in z:

$$occVars(z) \triangleq \{v\colon VSymb \cdot v \in Subterms(z)\}$$

Before going any further with the formalization it would be well worth deriving a few typing rules, to check what's been given so far: e.g.

$$\frac{z\colon ProtoTerm}{occVars(z)\colon VSymb\text{-set}} \qquad \frac{z\colon ProtoTerm}{allVars(z)\colon VSymb\text{-set}}$$

Details are left to the reader. (Hint: a good place to start would be to prove

$$\frac{z\colon ProtoTerm}{Subterms(z)\colon ProtoTerm\text{-set}}$$

by induction on z. A useful lemma from Set Theory is

$$\frac{s: A\text{-set}}{\{x: B \cdot x \in s\}: B\text{-set}}$$

After that, it's pretty straightforward.)

Now we're ready to embark on a proof by induction that

$$\forall z: Proto\,Term \cdot occVars(z) \subseteq allVars(z)$$

The base case:

For the base case we're required to prove '$occVars(v) \subseteq allVars(v)$' for '$v: VSymb$'. A couple of useful lemmas immediately spring to mind:

$$\frac{v: VSymb}{allVars(v) = \{v\}} \qquad \frac{v: VSymb}{occVars(v) = \{v\}}$$

The first of these follows easily from the definition of *allVars* and the relevant axioms for *freeVars* and *bndVars*. The second follows upon unfolding the definition of *occVars* and using the relevant axiom for *Subterms*, plus a lemma from set theory:

$$\frac{s: A\text{-set}}{\{x: A \cdot x \in s\} = s}$$

(Note that the local hypothesis '$v: VSymb$' is needed in order to establish the result that '$\{v\}: VSymb$-set'.) The base case follows from these lemmas and elementary properties of sets, such as

$$\frac{s: A\text{-set}}{s \subseteq s}$$

In the time-honoured tradition, details are left to the reader.

The induction step for *ProtoCompExp***:**

Assuming '$z: ProtoCompExp$' and

$$\forall x: ArgsOf(z) \cdot occVars(x) \subseteq allVars(x)$$

we're require to prove '$occVars(z) \subseteq allVars(z)$'. A useful first lemma would be

$$\frac{z: ProtoCompExp}{allVars(z) = \bigcup\{allVars(x) \cdot x: ArgsOf(z)\}}$$

which follows by unfolding definitions and using a lemma of the form

$$\frac{\cdots}{\bigcup\{f(x) \cup g(x) \cdot x: A\} = \bigcup\{f(x) \cdot x: A\} \cup \bigcup\{g(x) \cdot x: A\}}$$

from Set Theory (with appropriate hypotheses to ensure the sets involved are finite).

For the other part, upon unfolding the definition and using the defining property of *Subterms(z)* we arrive at

$$occVars(z) = \{v: VSymb \cdot v \in \{z\} \cup \bigcup\{Subterms(x) \cdot x: ArgsOf(z)\}\}$$

To eliminate the possibility that $v \in \{z\}$ we'll need an axiom to say that *VSymb* and *ProtoCompExp* are disjoint types: e.g.

$$\frac{v\colon VSymb, \quad z\colon ProtoCompExp}{v \neq z}$$

Some more set theoretic manipulations will then simplify the equation to

$$occVars(z) = \{v\colon VSymb \cdot v \in \bigcup\{Subterms(x) \cdot x\colon ArgsOf(z)\}\}$$

At this stage it might be tempting to search through Set Theory for a rule with conclusion of the form

$$\{x\colon A \cdot x \in \bigcup ss\} = \bigcup\{\{x\colon A \cdot x \in s\} \cdot s \in ss\}$$

but remembering the awkwardness of set comprehension (cf. Section 3.4.1) there's unlikely to be a rule in precisely this form. Let's suppose instead that a search for rules with conclusion matching

$$\{v\colon VSymb \cdot v \in \bigcup\{Subterms(x) \cdot x\colon A\}\} \subseteq allVars(z)$$

yields a rule of the form

$$\frac{\cdots, \quad \{s \in ss\} \vdash_s \{x\colon A \cdot x \in s\} \subseteq t}{\{x\colon A \cdot x \in \bigcup ss\} \subseteq t}$$

This seems promising, since it will generate a new subproof (*Box*) with box variable s and local hypothesis

$$s \in \{Subterms(x) \cdot x\colon ArgsOf(z)\}$$

from which we are required to show

$$\{v\colon VSymb \cdot v \in s\} \subseteq allVars(z)$$

Now s must equal $Subterms(x)$ for some $x\colon ArgsOf(z)$, and

$$\{v\colon VSymb \cdot v \in Subterms(x)\} = occVars(x) \subseteq allVars(x) \subseteq allVars(z)$$

so let's try this rule. Later on we'll review this decision to see if we couldn't do better.

Following the sketch above, to start off the subproof we would use the lemma

$$\frac{\cdots, \quad b \in \{f(x) \cdot x\colon A\}}{\exists x\colon A \cdot b = f(x)}$$

and '∃-elimination' to generate a new subproof with box variable x, local hypotheses

$$x\colon ArgsOf(z), \quad s = Subterms(x)$$

and goal '$\{v\colon VSymb \cdot v \in s\} \subseteq allVars(z)$'. Now we can apply '∀-elimination' to the induction hypothesis to get

$$occVars(x) \subseteq allVars(x)$$

All that's required to finish off the subproof would be some manipulations using the lemma on *allVars(z)* above plus a lemma

$$\frac{ss\colon (A\text{-set})\text{-set},\ \ s \in ss}{s \subseteq \bigcup ss}$$

This finishes this particular induction step.

It's interesting to go back and review the step where we gave up the simplification of *occVars(z)*. If we had been able to get

$$occVars(z) = \bigcup\{occVars(x) \cdot x\colon ArgsOf(z)\}$$

then we could have used a lemma such as

$$\frac{\cdots,\quad \forall x\colon A \cdot f(x) \subseteq g(x)}{\bigcup\{f(x) \cdot x\colon A\} \subseteq \bigcup\{g(x) \cdot x\colon A\}}$$

to finish the proof more directly.[18] A little reflection shows that the appropriate simplification lemma would have conclusion of the form

$$\{u\colon A \cdot u \in \bigcup\{f(v) \cdot v\colon B\}\} = \bigcup\{\{u\colon A \cdot u \in f(v)\} \cdot v\colon B\}$$

The appropriate typing hypotheses are left as an exercise for the reader.

The other induction cases

... are similar. In fact, they are so similar that the person verifying the original assertion, having completed the case for *ProtoBindExp*, can have a fair degree of faith that the conjecture is true. If necessary, tactics could be extracted from the first two induction cases and applied to the other three.

3.6   Some other logics

In this section we turn briefly to some logics which try to overcome some of the perceived limitations of First Order Predicate Calculus. We start by formulating the dependently-typed Lambda Calculus, which is then extended to full higher order logic (including quantification over functions). There is a brief digression into the fascinating correspondence between propositions in Intuitionistic logic and types, whereby proofs are thought of as values of the propositions they establish. The section finishes with discussions of Modal Logic and Hoare Logic.

---

[18]In fact, the typing hypotheses of such a lemma are quite horrendous. A simpler – but slightly less direct – formulation would be

$$\frac{s\colon B\text{-set},\ \ \forall x\colon A \cdot f(x) \subseteq s}{\bigcup\{f(x) \cdot x\colon A\} \subseteq s}$$

with *s* instantiated by *allVars(z)*.

3.6.1   Lambda calculus

To show that higher order concepts can be formalized in *mural* we present an axiomatization of the *dependently-typed lambda calculus*. This is an extension of Church's
Simply Typed Lambda Calculus [Chu40] by the notion of dependent products, which are
a richer way of expressing types of functions than the usual function space constructor '
→'.[19]

Signature

Let 'Lambda Calculus' be the theory with 'Equality' (cf. Section 3.2.1) as parent, and
signature consisting of the following primitives:

- constant ':' for the typing relation (infixed)

- dependent type symbol 'Π' for dependent products

- constant '.' for function application (infixed)[20]

- binder 'λ' for lambda abstraction

and definition

$$A \to B \triangleq \Pi x{:}A \cdot B$$

for the function space constructor.

Informally:

- '$f.a$' represents the result of applying function f to value a

- '$\lambda x{:}A \cdot F[x]$' stands for the function which maps elements x of A to $F[x]$

- '$\Pi x{:}A \cdot B[x]$' consists of all (total) functions from A to $B[x]$

- '$A \to B$' consists of all (total) functions from A to B

Dependent products are more expressive than the usual function space constructor '→'
since the type of the range may depend on x; thus for example

$$\Pi n{:}\,\mathsf{N} \cdot\, < m{:}\,\mathsf{N} \cdot (m \geq n) >$$

consists of functions f such that $f(n) \geq n$ for all $n{:}\,\mathsf{N}$.

---

[19]Dependent products are sometimes known as general (Cartesian) products or dependent function
spaces. Confusingly enough, in NuPRL [C⁺86] they are called dependent function spaces, while dependent
product means something quite different (dependent sum).

[20]The more usual concrete syntax declaration for function application would be '[[e1]]([[e2]])': i.e., '$f.a$'
would usually be displayed as '$f(a)$'. The dot notation is used here to make it more obvious when a function
is being applied to a value; in particular it avoids any ambiguity about the arity of f. Free use will be made
of currying.

Axioms

The axioms of the dependently-typed λ-calculus can be stated as follows:

1. abstraction formation:

$$\frac{\{x:A\} \vdash_x F[x]: B[x]}{(\lambda u: A \cdot F[u]): (\Pi v: A \cdot B[v])}$$

2. application formation:

$$\frac{\begin{array}{c} a: A, \\ f: (\Pi x: A \cdot B[x]) \end{array}}{f.a : B[a]}$$

3. extensionality:

$$\frac{\{x:A\} \vdash_x F[x] = G[x]}{(\lambda u: A \cdot F[u]) = (\lambda v: A \cdot G[v])}$$

4. β-conversion:

$$\frac{a: A}{(\lambda x: A \cdot F[x]).a = F[a]}$$

5. η-conversion:

$$\frac{f: (\Pi x: A \cdot B[x])}{(\lambda x: A \cdot f.x) = f}$$

There are usually side-conditions on the last two rules, but they are handled by the treatment of variable binding in *mural*. Thus for example: in the rule for β-conversion, the requirement that variables free in F do not get captured by λx is automatically ensured by the instantiation mechanism (since the dummy variable x will get renamed appropriately). The rule for η-conversion usually has two side-conditions: namely, that f is a function and x does not occur free in f. The first of these is ensured by the hypothesis; the second is similar to the case for β-conversion.

We won't go into examples of the use of the lambda calculus as there are plenty of good textbooks around (e.g. [Jon87c]). When this theory is extended by appropriate primitives for arithmetic, say, we can derive typings such as

$$(\lambda x: N \cdot x^2 + x + 1): N \to N$$

Remarks:

Great care must be taken if extending the dependently-typed lambda calculus with subtyping, as there are many traps for the unwary. For example, if A is a subtype of C and $f: C \to B$ then at first sight it might seem reasonable that $f: A \to B$. This would however be inconsistent with η-conversion and the axioms of equality, since one could infer e.g.

$$id_A = (\lambda x: A \cdot id_A.x) = (\lambda x: A \cdot id_C.x) = id_C$$

yet id_A cannot be applied wherever id_C can and hence cannot be said to be truly equal to it.

3.6.2 Higher order logic

Higher order logic differs from first order logic in that it allows quantification over functions, functions of functions, and so on. As a logic it is problematic however, since it is not even recursively axiomatizable. (See the chapter by van Benthem and Doets in [GG83] for a summary of most of what is known about higher order logic and its problems.)

We can nevertheless give a useful partial formulation by adding a primitive type *Prop* (of 'propositions') and appropriate logical constants to the lambda calculus. Then e.g. $\land$ and $\forall$ can be constants with types

$$\land : Prop \to (Prop \to Prop)$$

$$\forall : (A \to Prop) \to Prop$$

where '$\forall(\lambda x{:}A \cdot P)$' stands for '$\forall x{:}A \cdot P$'. (Note that $\forall$ is a primitive constant, not a primitive binder, in this formulation.)

A suitable axiomatization of these 'constants' would allow us to state and prove 'higher order' results such as

$$\forall f{:}\mathsf{N} \to \mathsf{N} \cdot \exists n{:}\mathsf{N} \cdot f(n+1) \geq f(n)$$

$$\forall f{:}A \to B \cdot (\forall x, y{:}A \cdot x \neq y \ \Rightarrow \ f(x) \neq f(y)) \ \Rightarrow \ \exists g{:}B \to A \cdot g \circ f = id_A$$

This is the approach taken in HOL [Gor85]. (See §D4 of [Bar77] for a similar approach.)

3.6.3 Propositions as types

Church introduced the Lambda Calculus to describe function application (.) and function abstraction (λ). Types were added to avoid problems associated with self-application, so that '$f.a$' is well-formed (typable) only if f is an expression of type $A \to B$ and a is an expression of type A (for some A and B); thus e.g. '$E.E$' is not well-formed. Finally, dependent products were introduced when the 'propositions-as-types' analogy was discovered (by Curry and others), as will be explained below.

Under the propositions-as-types analogy, proofs are thought of as values of the propositions they establish. (Here we are talking about proofs abstractly, not as *mural Proof* objects.) When appropriately extended with pairing, type union, etc, the dependently-typed lambda calculus provides a formalization of *intuitionistic* ('constructive') predicate calculus. The interested reader is referred to [Mar75] or [C+86] for more details: only the main ideas will be sketched here.

To start with an easy example, suppose that $p1$ is a proof of '$P1$' and $p2$ is a proof of '$P2$'; then taken together $p1$ and $p2$ constitute a proof of '$P1 \land P2$', and we can write

$$\frac{p1{:}P1, \quad p2{:}P2}{(p1, p2){:}P1 \land P2}$$

But this is looks just like the law for pairing (cf. Section 3.3.4) if '$P1 \land P2$' is thought of as '$P1 \times P2$'. Similarly, we can identify '$P1 \lor P2$' with the type union '$P1 \mid P2$'. From here it takes only a small conceptual leap to identify '$P1 \Rightarrow P2$' with '$P1 \to P2$'. That is, a proof of '$P1 \Rightarrow P2$' is a function taking a (hypothetical) proof of '$P1$' to a proof of '$P2$'; or in other words, it's a way of showing that '$P2$' holds, given the assumption that '$P1$' holds. The Deduction Theorem

$$\frac{\{P\} \vdash Q}{P \Rightarrow Q}$$

corresponds exactly to the rule for simple function abstraction:

$$\frac{\{p\colon P\} \vdash q\colon Q}{(\lambda p\colon P \cdot q)\colon P \to Q}$$

To get the rest of the propositional connectives we can identify 'false' (contradiction) with the empty type (since after all, 'false' has no proofs) and define

$$\neg\, P \triangleq P \Rightarrow \text{false}$$

(since under the intuitionistic interpretation of negation, '$\neg\, P$' amounts to saying that 'P' leads to a contradiction).

The analogy gives a very natural interpretation of intuitionistic propositional calculus. The obvious next question is whether it can be extended to the predicate calculus. What would be the analogue of '$\forall x\colon A \cdot P$' for example? Now, proving '$\forall x\colon A \cdot P[x]$' amounts to showing that $P[x]$ can be proven for all x in A. To the intuitionists this means supplying a function which, given $x\colon A$, yields a proof of $P[x]$.

Dependent products are just the solution required! We simply identify the proposition '$\forall x\colon A \cdot P[x]$' with the type '$\Pi x\colon A \cdot P[x]$'. (Note that ordinary function spaces aren't good enough since they don't capture the fact that the type $P[x]$ depends on x.) Under this analogy, the axioms for $\forall$

$$\frac{\{x\colon A\} \vdash_x P[x]}{\forall x\colon A \cdot P[x]} \qquad \frac{a\colon A, \quad \forall x\colon A \cdot P[x]}{P[a]}$$

become exactly the laws for function abstraction and function application given above.

Dependent types and the propositions-as-types analogy were used to implement intuitionistic logic in the AUTOMATH system [dB80]. The analogy has been studied intensively by Per Martin-Löf and his followers, and has been extended to a full *Intuitionistic Type Theory* [Mar75, Mar85, NPS90]. Related type theories serve as the basis of NuPRL and ELF.

In a programming context, a further extension of the analogy is possible, whereby program specifications are identified with types (or propositions) and programs are identified with values. In this way, Intuitionistic Type Theory can be regarded as a full programming language (with β-reduction corresponding to evaluation). This allows e.g. programs to be extracted directly from proofs that their specifications are implementable. The interested reader is referred to [C+86] for more details.

3.6.4 Modal logic

Let's now turn to a Natural Deduction formulation of a logic in which the modalities 'necessarily' and 'possibly' are formalized. Following the usual convention, we shall write '$\Box p$' for 'p is necessary' and '$\Diamond p$' for 'p is possible'.

As an example of the use of such modalities, given an expression e of propositional calculus, '$\Box e$' might be interpreted as saying e is a tautology ('e is necessarily true'). Thus e.g. '$p \Rightarrow p \vee q$' is necessarily true, in that it holds for all values of p and q, whereas '$p \Rightarrow q$' is only contingently true, since there are cases when it is true and others when it is false.

Another example use of modalities is to interpret them in a temporal sense: viz. $\Box p$ means that p is true at *all* times in the future, and $\Diamond p$ means that p is true at *some* time in the future. Modal logics are also useful for reasoning about knowledge and actions: cf. [Ram88].

The axiomatization

In [Pra65] Prawitz gives two different formulations of modal logic. In this section we'll study the simpler of the two (S4), although the other can be treated very similarly. We first extend Propositional Calculus by primitive constant '$\Box$' and defined constant

$$\Diamond p \triangleq \neg\Box\neg p$$

A formula of the form '$\Box q$' will be called a *modal formula*; these are in some sense the necessary truths.

The axioms defining $\Box$ are:

1. '$\Box$ introduction'

$$\frac{p}{\Box p}$$

   where *the assumptions on which p depends are modal formulae*[21]

2. '$\Box$ elimination'

$$\frac{\Box p}{p}$$

Note the side condition on '$\Box$ introduction': clearly some kind of condition is required, since otherwise from the truth of any specific p could be derived the necessity that p always holds – which is patently not the intended interpretation of $\Box$. Roughly, if p follows from necessary truths only, then there is nothing contingent about p, and $\Box p$ can legitimately be inferred. Of course, other interpretations of modal logic are possible and lead to different side conditions.[22]

In *mural*, side-conditions could be written as extra pieces of code to be evaluated by the proof checker. In terms of Section 4.7.5 this would mean adding a clause to the *Is-properly-justified* predicate on the relevant *RuleJustif*s. Formally, the condition

$$\forall fmla \in Assumptions(l, pf) \cdot fmla\colon CompExp_0 \wedge symb(fmla) = \lceil\Box\rceil$$

would be added to the test *Is-properly-justified*(l, pf) for each line l in proof pf which is justified by an instance of '$\Box$ introduction', where $\lceil x \rceil$ is the CESymb spelt x.

Example derivations

(1) Here's an example proof:

```
from □p, □q
1    p                              □ elimination (h1)
2    q                              □ elimination (h2)
3    p ∧ q                          ∧ introduction (1,2)
infer □(p ∧ q)                      □ introduction (3)
```

---

[21]The assumptions on which a line depends are all those undischarged hypotheses and unjustified lines in the transitive closure of the antecedent relation: see Section 4.7.7 for full details.

[22]e.g. in the other formulation (S5) of modal logic in [Pra65], the side condition is relaxed to allow also negations of modal formulae. [AHM87] contains an alternative formalization of S4 – which translates easily into the *mural* setting – in which the side-condition is formulated directly in the theory, rather than being coded into the proof checker. The main advantage of such an approach is that is does not require extra code to be written for the proof-checker, which lessens the risk of corruption of the latter; the main disadvantage· is that proofs are much longer and far less intuitive.

The use of '□ introduction' is valid since the assumptions on which the conclusion ultimately depends – namely, □p and □q – are modal formulae.

As an aside, it's interesting to note the 'shape' of the proof, consisting of applications of elimination rules followed by applications of introduction rules. This basic shape arises surprisingly often and so is a prime candidate for turning into a tactic. The interested reader is referred to [Pra65] for an explanation of this phenomenon, plus general 'normal form' results for proof shapes.

(2) A more interesting proof is that of '◇ elimination':

from □($p \Rightarrow q$), ◇p
1    $p \Rightarrow q$ □ elimination (h1)
2   ¬□¬p unfolding (h2)
3   from □¬q
3.1   ¬q □ elimination (3.h1)
3.2   ¬p contraposition (1,3.1)
3.3   □¬p □ introduction (3.2)
        infer false   contradiction (3.3,2)
4   ¬□¬q otherwise contradictory (3)
infer ◇q folding (4)

Note that line 3.3 is valid since the assumptions on which it depends – namely □($p \Rightarrow q$) and □¬q – are modal formulae. Line 3.3 does not depend on hypothesis h2.

(3) The reader might like to try to derive the following rules:

$$\frac{□p}{□□p} \qquad \frac{□(p \wedge □q)}{□(q \wedge □p)}$$

$$\frac{p}{◇p} \qquad \frac{□(p \vee q), \ □(p \Rightarrow q)}{□q} \qquad \frac{◇p \vee ◇q}{◇(p \vee q)}$$

(Hint for the last one: first prove □($p \Rightarrow p \vee q$).)

3.6.5 Hoare logic

This section briefly outlines how a 'Hoare logic' of program triples could be formulated in *mural*. We form a new theory by extending Predicate Calculus and appropriate data type theories by primitive constants as follows:

- '{_}_{_}' for Hoare triples

- 'skip' for the trivial program (do nothing)

- '_ ; _' for sequential composition of programs

- 'if _ then _ else' for 'if-statements'

- 'while _ do _' for 'while-statements'

- '_ : = _' for assignment of values to program variables

Intuitively, '$\{p\}\ S\ \{q\}$' means that, if 'p' holds before program S is executed, then 'q' holds afterwards.

The Hoare axioms for skip, composition and weakening are:

$$\overline{\{p\}\ \text{skip}\ \{p\}}$$

$$\frac{\{p\}\ S_1\ \{q\},\ \{q\}\ S_2\ \{r\}}{\{p\}\ S_1;S_2\ \{r\}}$$

$$\frac{p' \Rightarrow p,\ \{p\}\ S\ \{q\},\ q \Rightarrow q'}{\{p'\}\ S\ \{q'\}}$$

If- and while-statements

The axioms for if- and while-statements are:

$$\frac{\{p \wedge g\}\ S_1\ \{q\},\ \ \{p \wedge \neg g\}\ S_2\ \{q\}}{\{p\}\ \text{if } g \text{ then } S_1 \text{ else } S_2\ \{q\}}$$

$$\frac{\{p \wedge g\}\ S\ \{p\}}{\{p\}\ \text{while } g \text{ do } S\ \{p \wedge \neg g\}}$$

Of course, only partial correctness can be guaranteed by the latter rule: i.e., the rule does not guarantee that the program loop 'while g do S' terminates in a finite number of steps. If instead the reasoning is to be about total correctness, appropriate well-founded relations should be added to the triples: cf. [Gri81, Jon86].

Of course, guards in if- and while-statements should be 'executable', and so should not involve quantifiers, for example. One way of precluding nonsensical instantiations of g in the above rules would be to introduce a new primitive type 'B^e' (standing for executable boolean expressions) and to add axioms

$$\overline{\text{true}: \mathsf{B}^e} \qquad \frac{p: \mathsf{B}^e}{(\neg p): \mathsf{B}^e} \qquad \frac{p: \mathsf{B}^e,\ q: \mathsf{B}^e}{(p \vee q): \mathsf{B}^e} \qquad \frac{a: A,\ b: A}{(a = b): \mathsf{B}^e} \qquad \frac{m: \mathsf{N},\ n: \mathsf{N}}{(m \leq n): \mathsf{B}^e}$$

and so on – one for each primitive constant representing an executable predicate. Corresponding rules for defined logical connectives ($\wedge$, $\Rightarrow$, etc) and defined predicates ($\neq$, etc) can be deduced from the above. The axioms for if- and while-statements then become:

$$\frac{g: \mathsf{B}^e,\ \{p \wedge g\}\ S_1\ \{q\},\ \ \{p \wedge \neg g\}\ S_2\ \{q\}}{\{p\}\ \text{if } g \text{ then } S_1 \text{ else } S_2\ \{q\}}$$

$$\frac{g: \mathsf{B}^e,\ \{p \wedge g\}\ S\ \{p\}}{\{p\}\ \text{while } g \text{ do } S\ \{p \wedge \neg g\}}$$

For brevity of proof, however, the unrestricted forms of these rules will be employed in the example below.

Program variables and the assignment statement

But how shall program variables be represented?

It's not appropriate to use logical variables, since for example program variables do not α-convert. In this simple formulation we shall only consider global (program) variables, so it is generally safe to represent them as logical *constants*. Certainly their values change during execution of a program, but Hoare reasoning deals with 'snapshots' of a program's execution, and in each such snapshot the value of a program variable is fixed. The example below should convince the reader that this is a reasonably natural solution. For reasons which will become apparent below, however, program variables should never be used in definitions.

The axiom for assignment to program variable x is

$$\overline{\{P[e]\}\ x := e\ \{P[x]\}}$$

where x *does not occur in* (the instantiand of) P.

For example,

$$\{e \mapsto 0,\quad P[y] \mapsto x \neq y\}$$

is not a valid instantiation for this rule: it would lead to the patently false conclusion

$$\{x \neq 0\}\ x := 0\ \{x \neq x\}$$

As usual, the proof-checker must be modified to meet this side-condition. In terms of Section 4.7.5 the clause

$$\lceil x \rceil \notin Subterms(eInst(instn(justif(l)))(\lceil P \rceil))$$

should be added to the definition of *Is-properly-justified*(l, pf) for any line l in proof pf which is justified by the above rule. Note that this formulation assumes that program variables are always used explicitly and never implicitly (such as in a definition) – otherwise the restriction could be circumvented by defining say $c(y) \triangleq x \neq y$ and instantiating $P[y]$ by $c(y)$.[23]

The assignment axiom extends easily to multiple assignments: e.g.

$$\overline{\{P[e,f]\}\ x,y := e,f\ \{P[x,y]\}}$$

where x and y do not occur in P.[24] A separate axiom must be introduced for each pair (x, y) of distinct program variables. An alternative approach would be to introduce a predicate for recognizing program variables, and to condense all the various axioms into a single scheme

$$\frac{Is\text{-}prog\text{-}var(a),\quad Is\text{-}prog\text{-}var(b),\quad a \neq b}{\{P[e,f]\}\ a,b := e,f\ \{P[a,b]\}}$$

(where a and b are metavariables) with an appropriately redefined side-condition. Of course, it is then necessary to introduce axioms to the effect that *Is-prog-var*(x), $x \neq y$, etc. If only a handful of program variables will be needed it doesn't seem worth going to this much bother.

Finally, if program variables have declared types, the assignment axioms can be modified appropriately: e.g. if $x:\mathsf{N}$ then

$$\frac{e:\mathsf{N}}{\{P[e]\}\ x := e\ \{P[x]\}}$$

---

[23]An alternative approach is to formulate the side condition directly in the theory by introducing a predicate which confirms that a given program variable is not used in a given term: cf. [AHM87].

[24]The comma ',' is being used in two ways in this rule: as the (object level) pairing operation in the assignment statement (twice); and as the (metalevel) separator for the arguments to the metavariable P. Hopefully no confusion will result.

Some derived rules

We'll make use of the following derived rules in the example below

$$\frac{p \Rightarrow q}{\{p\} \text{ skip } \{q\}}$$

$$\frac{\{p\}\, S\, \{q\}, \quad q \Rightarrow p', \quad \{p'\}\, S'\, \{q'\}}{\{p\}\, S;\, S'\, \{q'\}}$$

$$\frac{p \Rightarrow p', \quad \{p'\}\, S\, \{q\}}{\{p\}\, S\, \{q\}}$$

where they are called 'lemma1', 'lemma2' and 'lemma3' respectively.

An example program

As an example, consider the following program P:

$m, j := a(1), 1;$
while $j \neq N$ do $(j := j + 1;$ if $m < a(j)$ then $m := a(j)$ else skip$)$

We show below that P finds the largest element in an array a of natural numbers, indexed from 1 to N; formally:

$$\frac{0 < N}{\{\text{true}\}\, P\, \{m = \max i: [1..N] \cdot a(i)\}}$$

We first form a theory of this program. Array a is represented as a primitive constant taking a single argument. The constant N and program variables m, j are similarly represented as primitive constants (without arguments). All we need to know about these 'constants' is given in the following axioms:

$$\frac{1 \leq i, \quad i \leq N}{a(i): \mathsf{N}} \qquad \overline{N: \mathsf{N}} \qquad \overline{m: \mathsf{N}} \qquad \overline{j: \mathsf{N}}$$

We'll define a binder max to represent the maximum value generated by expression $f[i]$ as i ranges over a type A; formally:

$$\max i: A \cdot f[i] \;\triangleq\; \iota x: \mathsf{N} \cdot (\exists i: A \cdot x = f[i] \wedge \forall j: A \cdot f[j] \leq x)$$

where ι is the 'unique choice' operator introduced in Section 3.2.5. As used below, A will be a finite type and $f[i]$ will be an expression which yields a natural number for each i in A, so max denotes a finite value.

Finally, to make the proof go through we'll need a loop invariant:

$$I(x, y) \;\triangleq\; 1 \leq y \leq N \wedge x = \max i: [1..y] \cdot a(i)$$

It's also convenient to have an abbreviation for the loop body:

$$S(x, y) \;\triangleq\; y := y + 1;\; \text{if } x < a(y) \text{ then } x := a(y) \text{ else skip}$$

Note that x and y are formal parameters in these definitions.

Figure 3.3 is a (rigorous) proof that, for $0 < N$, program P finds the largest element in array a and assigns it to m.

from $0 < N$

1	$\text{true} \Rightarrow I(a(1), 1)$	obvious (h1)
2	$\{I(a(1), 1)\}$	
	$m, j := a(1), 1$	
	$\{I(m, j)\}$	assignment$_{m,j}$ ()
3	$I(m, j) \land j \neq N \Rightarrow I(m, (j + 1) - 1) \land j \leq N$	obvious ()
4	$\{I(m, (j + 1) - 1) \land j + 1 \leq N\}$	
	$j := j + 1$	
	$\{I(m, j - 1) \land j \leq N\}$	assignment$_j$ ()
5	$\{I(m, j) \land j \neq N\}$	
	$j := j + 1$	
	$\{I(m, j - 1) \land j \leq N\}$	lemma3 (3,4)
6	$I(m, j - 1) \land j \leq N \land m < a(j) \Rightarrow I(a(j), j)$	obvious ()
7	$\{I(a(j), j)\}\ m := a(j)\ \{I(m, j)\}$	assignment$_m$ ()
8	$\{I(m, j - 1) \land j \leq N \land m < a(j)\}$	
	$m := a(j)$	
	$\{I(m, j)\}$	lemma3 (6,7)
9	$I(m, j - 1) \land j \leq N \land \neg (m < a(j)) \Rightarrow I(m, j)$	obvious ()
10	$\{I(m, j - 1) \land j \leq N \land \neg (m < a(j))\}$	
	skip	
	$\{I(m, j)\}$	lemma1 (9)
11	$\{I(m, j - 1) \land j \leq N\}$	
	if $m < a(j)$ then $m := a(j)$ else skip	
	$\{I(m, j)\}$	if-rule (8,10)
12	$\{I(m, j) \land j \neq N\}\ S(m, j)\ \{I(m, j)\}$	sequential composition (4,11)
13	$\{I(m, j)\}$	
	while $j \neq N$ do $S(m, j)$	
	$\{I(m, j) \land \neg (j \neq N)\}$	while-rule (12)
14	$\neg (j \neq N) \Leftrightarrow j = N$	$\neg \neq$-rule ()
15	$\{I(m, j)\}$	
	while $j \neq N$ do $S(m, j)$	
	$\{I(m, j) \land j = N\}$	substit of equivs (14,13)
16	$\{I(a(1), 1)\}\ P\ \{I(m, j) \land j = N\}$	sequential composition (2,15)
17	$I(m, j) \land j = N \Rightarrow m = \max i : [1..N] \cdot a(i)$	obvious ()
infer	$\{\text{true}\}\ P\ \{m = \max i : [1..N] \cdot a(i)\}$	weakening (1,16,17)

Figure 3.3: Verification of program P

Remarks:

1. To be honest, throughout the proof liberal use has been made of folding of definitions without stating the justification.

2. It is vital to the validity of lines 3 and 6 that j and m do not occur in the definition of I.

3. Lines 6 and 9 would be a good ones to check in more detail.

Chapter 4

Foundation

This chapter presents the formal foundations of the *mural* proof assistant, in the form of a 'walk' into the *mural* specification (Appendix C). To understand the need for a separate chapter, a little of the history of the development of *mural* should be explained. As would be expected, our concept of *mural* evolved as the project progressed and as we experimented with different styles of user interface and different logical frames. The VDM specification was used as the repository for our ideas, and as the vehicle for any major changes to the functionality of the system; at any time we had clearly stated objectives for what we wanted to build. But as a result, the full specification is large, poorly structured and virtually impossible for a newcomer to come to grips with easily. This chapter (hereafter called *the Walk*) attempts to redress the problem. The chapter 'Instantiation' (Chapter 3) was written as an accompanying paper, containing plenty of examples illustrating various points raised during the Walk.

4.1 Preamble

The Walk is an attempt to write an informal development of the *mural* specification from a very abstract level, through a number of steps introducing essentially orthogonal concepts, down to the level of version 2.2 of the full specification (Appendix C). It was done as a way of explaining the formal underpinnings of the system, by having something reasonably formal on which to hang the explanation. It's not supposed to be a formal development, nor is it an historical development. It does however include many internal consistency checks – in the form of facts which should be deducible from the information provided – to clarify the specification-writers' intentions; some of these facts are especially useful in later sections. And of course, it's written in VDM. The need to simplify and unify concepts has meant that this chapter differs from the full specification in certain details, and in its levels of abstraction, although the spirit has been zealously guarded. Differences between the Walk and the full specification are summarized briefly in Section 4.10.

The reader is expected to be familiar with VDM. The Walk differs from many other VDM specifications in that it is not a single monolithic whole with clearly distinguished levels of abstraction. No attempt is made to refine data representations, nor to decompose operations. As more concepts are introduced the further we walk into the specification, some data types need to be extended. In particular, record types will sometimes be extended by extra fields and invariants. Auxiliary functions on such types have been carefully defined in terms of destructors (field selectors), so that they carry through unchanged. To keep track of where new concepts are introduced, types will sometimes be given numeric subscripts. When no subscript is present, the 'latest' definition is the relevant one – so the definition changes the further one walks into the specification. (These rather *ad hoc* extensions to the language seemed to be the easiest way to modularize the specification, in the absence of any more appropriate modularization mechanism in VDM – or most other specification languages for that matter.)

In fact, most extensions are *conservative*, in the sense that nothing essentially new can be deduced about the extended type – other than properties which explicitly involve the new fields, of course. Such extensions do not change the 'semantics' of anything that came before; in this sense we are trying to capture something far more structured than *Z* schemas, for example. In its way, the result is a kind of formal development, with 'forgetful' retrieve functions.

Sections 4.2 to 4.4 describe the *mural* syntax up to and including inference rule schemas and instantiation. Section 4.5 describes how the collection of rules is organized into a theory hierarchy, how rules can have different status (from 'conjecture', through 'rigorously established', to 'established from first principles'), and how rules depend on one another. Section 4.6 introduces theory signatures and defines the well-formed terms over a syntactic context. The next section explains the *mural* proof model and shows that it correctly captures the notion of Natural Deduction proof. Section 4.8 treats an advanced topic (theory morphisms) and can easily be skipped on first reading.

Section 4.9 specifies and develops a pattern-matching operation for the *mural* syntax; an (informal) verification shows that the development is correct and that the resulting algorithm is in some sense complete. Section 4.10 explains briefly how the Walk differs from the full specification in Appendix C, both in terminology and content. Finally, the last section explores the limitations of the *mural* approach and suggests where further work could profitably be done.

The author would like to thank the rest of the *mural* team for the many useful discussions and comments which helped shape this document. Special thanks are due to Richard Moore for co-writing the full specification on which this is based. Michel Sintzoff, Lockwood Morris and Tim Clement also made significant contributions (by way of questions and comments) for which the author is very grateful.

4.2   Syntax

4.2.1   Informal treatment

The *mural* abstract syntax was explained informally in Chapter 3, but it is summarized here for convenience.

Atomic symbols

The atomic symbols in our syntax are taken from the following classes:

- *VSymb* – for *variables*.

- *CESymb* – for constants, functions, operators, predicates, relations and metavariables, all at 'expression' level; we'll call them *expression constructors* or more simply *constants*.

- *DESymb* – for quantifiers and other symbols (at expression level) that bind variables; we'll call them *dependent expression symbols* or more simply *binders*.

- *CTSymb* – for constants, functions, operators and metavariables at 'type' level; we'll simply call them *type constructors*.

- *DTSymb* – for symbols (at type level) that bind variables; we'll simply call them *dependent type symbols*.

Abstract syntax

In Extended BNF (Backus-Naur Form), the syntax is roughly:

```
Term =  Exp | Type
 Exp =  VSymb
        | CESymb{Exp}{Type}
        | DESymb VSymb':'Type'·'Exp
Type =  CTSymb{Exp}{Type}
        | DTSymb VSymb':'Type'·'Type
        | '<'VSymb':'Type'·'Exp'>'
```

In other words, *expressions* are built up from variables using two kinds of combinators:

- *compound expressions*, whereby a constant is 'applied' to (possibly empty) lists of expressions and types (called its operands, or 'arguments');[1]

- *binder expressions*, whereby a binder is supplied with a dummy variable (the 'variable it binds'), a type (the 'universe' of the bound variable) and an expression (the 'body' of the binder expression).

Types are built up using three kinds of combinator:

- *compound types*, whereby a type constructor is applied to expression and type argument lists;

- *dependent types*, whereby a dependent-type symbol is supplied with a dummy variable and two types (the 'universe' of the bound variable, and the 'body' of the dependent type, respectively);

- *subtypes* of given types, specified by giving a dummy variable, the 'universe' over which it ranges (a *Type*), and a predicate (an *Exp*).

(Certain context conditions will be imposed on the syntax at later stages.) No distinction is drawn between formulae and terms in *mural*.

---

[1]Compound expressions are called *OExps* in the *mural* system. Different names were used here to avoid potential confusion with the full specification: see Section 4.10 for more details.

Concrete syntax

In *mural*, the user can specify the display form of symbols by supplying a simple 'template'. For example, it's easy to tell the system that an expression which would be written as *ITE P a b* in our abstract syntax, should be displayed as

$$\text{if } P \text{ then } a \text{ else } b$$

This makes it possible to closely approximate the concrete syntax used by many formalisms, which in turn makes formulae much easier to read. At the same time, formulae are structured objects for which an (abstract-) syntax-directed editor is provided. We shall make no attempt here to specify the concrete syntax facility, although all the examples given below make use of it (for legibility). Likewise, no attempt is made to formalize precedence, associativity, etc.

4.2.2   Substitution

The ability to substitute one term for another is an important feature of most logical calculi, and is thus a facility a logical frame must provide. It is also where *mural* differs from most other logical frames, so some words of explanation are necessary.

In logic textbooks, substitution is traditionally handled by having an explicit substitution operator [./.]. But substitution problems generally fall into one of two fundamentally distinct categories, as illustrated by the following two laws of inference:

- substitutivity of equals, whereby Q is deduced from $a = b$ and P, where Q is the result of replacing one or more occurrences of a in P by b;

- specialization, whereby Q is deduced from $a : A$ and $\forall x : A \cdot P$, where Q results from P by replacing all free occurrences of x by a.

The first 'law' is actually too vague to be formalized directly – it hides information (namely, exactly which occurrences are to be replaced) which the user would typically have to supply in a 'rule-driven' proof editor as envisaged for *mural*. The second law does not suffer the same ambiguity, however, and is often expressed simply by writing (something like) $P[a/x]$ for Q.

The main disadvantage with having an explicit substitution operator is that it obscures syntactic equivalence. For example, for any expression P, $\neg(P[x/y])$ is exactly the same as $(\neg P)[x/y]$ (where the parentheses are used simply to show order of 'application'). Similarly, $P[x/y][y/x]$ is syntactically equivalent to P, provided x does not occur free in P. As a result, it is very difficult to specify – let alone implement – pattern-matching and other algorithms which work on expressions when the latter can contain uses of [./.].

The approach adopted by AUTOMATH [dB80] and several modern proof assistants (e.g. HOL [Gor85], ELF [HHP87], Isabelle [Pau86]) is to base the syntax on (variants of) λ-calculus and to treat substitution as function application. In such an approach, the above rules would be expressed as

$$\frac{a = b, \ \ P(a)}{P(b)} \qquad \frac{a : A, \ \ \forall x : A \cdot P(x)}{P(a)}$$

where P can be instantiated by a 'boolean-valued' function. For example, when instantiated by

$$\{a \mapsto [7, 3, 4], \ A \mapsto \mathbf{N}^*, \ P \mapsto \lambda z : \mathbf{N}^* \cdot rev(rev(z)) = z\}$$

the second law becomes

$$\frac{[7, 3, 4]: \mathsf{N}^*, \quad \forall x: \mathsf{N}^* \cdot rev(rev(x)) = x}{rev(rev([7, 3, 4])) = [7, 3, 4]}$$

upon β-reducing. (Syntactic equivalence is thus $\alpha\beta\eta$-equivalence.) This makes for a very elegant solution, and even allows binders to be treated as (higher order) functions: e.g.

$$\forall: (A \rightarrow Proposition) \rightarrow Proposition$$

where $\forall(\lambda x: A \cdot P)$ stands for $\forall x: A \cdot P$.

The λ-calculus approach is an excellent way of formalizing substitution, and is good for formalizing mathematical syntax generally, hence its use for Logical Frames.[2] From *mural*'s point of view, however, this approach has a major drawback: pattern-matching and unification are difficult, if not impossible. (Higher order unification is undecidable in general. Indeed, most general unifiers are not even guaranteed to exist, even when unification is possible; in some cases infinitely many essentially-different unifiers result. The decidability of h.o. matching seems to still be an open question.) Despite these problems, Larry Paulson has implemented a theorem prover – Isabelle [Pau86] – based around a lazy version of Huet's h.o. unification algorithm.

The designers of *mural* were well aware of the λ-calculus approach from an early stage in the project. Upon inspecting the formulation of the target logics[3] in λ-calculus, we soon recognised that only very limited use is made of the full h.o. capabilities on offer. Upon further investigation it became apparent that an intermediate solution was feasible – essentially one that uses the principle of substitution as function application, but which restricts how (meta-level) functions can be formed. Complete pattern-matching then became possible, and even a (limited form of) unification could be given.[4]

The *mural* approach to substitution uses the fact that, in our syntax, metavariables can take arguments. Full details are deferred until the discussion of instantiation in Section 4.4, but to illustrate briefly: the law of specialization would be written

$$\frac{a: A, \quad \forall x: A \cdot P[x]}{P[a]}$$

and the relevant instantiation would be expressed as

$$\{a \mapsto [7, 3, 4], \ A \mapsto \mathsf{N}^*, \ P[z] \mapsto rev(rev(z)) = z\}$$

The instantiation mechanism is specified in such a way as to preclude capture of free variables. It's important to note that it is still possible to express (and reason about) higher order logics in *mural* (cf. Section 3.6.1). The main difference is that β- and η-conversion are not done automatically in *mural*, although it would be feasible to write a tactic to do such things.

It soon becomes obvious to the user that pattern-matching is an extremely important component of the *mural modus operandi*. At any stage in a proof the user can typically

---

[2]See [AHM87] for a large collection of logics that have been formalized in ELF using this approach. The report [Lin87c] compares various logical frames and notes some other limitations of the λ-calculus approach, such as the need for strong typing and a fixed type structure.

[3]The class of logics targeted for *mural* support is described in [Lin87c]. These include first order predicate calculi (classical, constructive and LPF), many sorted equational logic and Hoare logics.

[4]A complete matching algorithm is specified, developed and proven correct in Section 4.9. At the time of writing we haven't yet explored whether provision of a full algorithm is possible for our syntax.

ask to see a complete, *finite* set of rule instances from which to choose. In this author's opinion, this is one of the factors which makes *mural* very much easier to understand and use than other existing logical frames.

4.2.3 Formal treatment

Now for a more formal definition of the syntax.

Primitive types

In this specification *VSymb*, *CESymb*, *DESymb*, *CTSymb* and *DTSymb* are taken to be primitive types: viz. mutually disjoint infinite sets of structureless tokens. (In the full specification some of these are further split up: e.g. within *CESymb*, metavariables are distinguished from ordinary constants.)

The proto-syntax

As already indicated, we intend to impose certain context conditions on the abstract syntax. In the meantime we can translate the 'proto-syntax' directly into VDM as follows:

$ProtoTerm = ProtoExp \mid ProtoType$

$ProtoExp = VSymb \mid ProtoCompExp \mid ProtoBindExp$

$ProtoType = ProtoCompType \mid ProtoSubType \mid ProtoDepType$

$ProtoCompExp$ :: $symb$: $CESymb$
$\qquad\qquad\qquad\ eArgs$: $ProtoExp^*$
$\qquad\qquad\qquad\ tArgs$: $ProtoType^*$

$ProtoBindExp$ :: $symb$: $DESymb$
$\qquad\qquad\qquad var$: $VSymb$
$\qquad\qquad\qquad univ$: $ProtoType$
$\qquad\qquad\qquad body$: $ProtoExp$

$ProtoCompType$ :: $symb$: $CESymb$
$\qquad\qquad\qquad\ eArgs$: $ProtoExp^*$
$\qquad\qquad\qquad\ tArgs$: $ProtoType^*$

$ProtoDepType$ :: $symb$: $DTSymb$
$\qquad\qquad\qquad var$: $VSymb$
$\qquad\qquad\qquad univ$: $ProtoType$
$\qquad\qquad\qquad body$: $ProtoType$

$ProtoSubType$ :: var : $VSymb$
$\qquad\qquad\qquad univ$: $ProtoType$
$\qquad\qquad\qquad body$: $ProtoExp$

Auxiliary functions

Next we define some useful auxiliary functions for accessing various components of terms. The subterms of a given term – including the term itself – are given by:

Subterms : *ProtoTerm* → *ProtoTerm*-set
Subterms(z) ≜
    cases z of
      VSymb → {z}
      mk-ProtoCompExp(c, el, tl) → {z} ∪ ⋃{*Subterms*(x) | x ∈ elems el ∪ elems tl}
      mk-ProtoBindExp(q, v, t, e) → {z} ∪ *Subterms*(t) ∪ *Subterms*(e)
      mk-ProtoCompType(ct, el, tl) → {z} ∪ ⋃{*Subterms*(x) | x ∈ elems el ∪ elems tl}
      mk-ProtoDepType(dt, v, u, b) → {z} ∪ *Subterms*(u) ∪ *Subterms*(b)
      mk-ProtoSubType(v, t, e) → {z} ∪ *Subterms*(t) ∪ *Subterms*(e)
    end

Henceforth, we won't bother to state definitions when the compound type (dependent type and subtype) case is exactly analogous to the compound expression (resp. binder expression) case.

The *bound variables* of a term are those which are bound by a variable binding construct in some subterm:

bndVars : *ProtoTerm* → *VSymb*-set
bndVars(z) ≜
    cases z of
      VSymb → {}
      mk-ProtoCompExp(c, el, tl) → ⋃{*bndVars*(y) | y ∈ elems el ∪ elems tl}
      mk-ProtoBindExp(q, v, t, e) → {v} ∪ *bndVars*(t) ∪ *bndVars*(e)
      ⋮
    end

The *free variables* of a term are those which occur in the term without getting bound:

freeVars : *ProtoTerm* → *VSymb*-set
freeVars(z) ≜
    cases z of
      VSymb → {z}
      mk-ProtoCompExp(c, el, tl) → ⋃{*freeVars*(y) | y ∈ elems el ∪ elems tl}
      mk-ProtoBindExp(q, v, t, e) → *freeVars*(t) ∪ (*freeVars*(e) − {v})
      ⋮
    end

A term with no free variables is said to be *closed*.

allVars : *ProtoTerm* → *VSymb*-set
allVars(z) ≜ *freeVars*(z) ∪ *bndVars*(z)

Claim: For any prototerm z, *allVars*(z) includes all those variables which occur as subterms of z:

$$\{v\text{:}\, VSymb \mid v \in Subterms(z)\} \subseteq allVars(z)$$

The inclusion is proper when vacuous bindings are present: e.g. when z is $\forall x\text{:}\, A \cdot$ true.

4.2.4   Context conditions

As given so far, the syntax is a bit *too* flexible. What would it mean for a variable being bound to occur free in the universe over which it is being bound, for example? What does it mean if nested bindings refer to the same dummy variable? There are many different solutions to these problems, but most are intended for parsing by humans and so can be considered primarily to be addressing concrete syntax issues. Although often ingenious and elegant, such solutions are usually quite long and involved when formalized (i.e., in the present case, when written in VDM).

We decided instead to adopt a strong convention whereby

Convention:

Logically different variables will be represented by different *VSymb*s.

For example, expressions like

$$\forall x\text{:}\, A \cdot \exists x\text{:}\, B \cdot P, \quad \lambda x\text{:}\, A[x] \cdot P, \quad (\forall x\text{:}\, A \cdot P) \wedge (\forall x\text{:}\, B \cdot Q), \quad \forall x\text{:}\, A[y] \cdot \exists y\text{:}\, B \cdot P$$

will be considered to be ill-formed. Initially it was intended that this restriction would apply only to the abstract syntax at the specification level, and that the final concrete syntax would be more liberal. As it turns out, at least some of the spirit of the restriction has carried over, fortunate or unfortunate as this may be.

The main reason for introducing the restriction is that it makes later functions much easier to specify. In particular, we won't continually be dogged by the problems of variable renaming to avoid capture which arise in most attempts to specify syntaxes having variable binding constructs and substitution.[5] This in turn does away with most of the variable occurrence side-conditions on inference rules.

We define a subclass $Term_0$ of *ProtoTerm* consisting of just those terms which respect the above principle:

$Term_0 = Exp_0 \mid Type_0$

$Exp_0 = VSymb \mid CompExp_0 \mid BindExp_0$

$Type_0 = CompType_0 \mid SubType_0 \mid DepType_0$

To respect our principle, the arguments of a compound expression should use different bound variables, and variables free in one argument should not be bound in another argument. Arguments may however share free variables. The restriction can be captured

---

[5] An alternative approach would have been to do away with the names of bound variables altogether and use de Bruijn indices instead (cf. [dB80]). We felt that, while such an approach is perhaps more concise, it would make the specification far less intuitive and too difficult to read.

succinctly by saying that the *allVars* of one argument must not overlap the *bndVars* of any other. Formally:

$$
\begin{aligned}
CompExp_0 \ &::\ symb\ :\ CESymb \\
&\quad\ eArgs\ :\ Exp_0^* \\
&\quad\ tArgs\ :\ Type_0^*
\end{aligned}
$$

where

$inv\text{-}CompExp_0(e) \triangleq Is\text{-}valid\text{-}arglist(eArgs(e) \frown tArgs(e))$

$Is\text{-}valid\text{-}arglist : Term_0^* \to \mathbb{B}$
$Is\text{-}valid\text{-}arglist(xl) \triangleq$
$\qquad \forall i,j \in \mathsf{inds}\, xl \cdot i \neq j \Rightarrow allVars(xl(i)) \cap bndVars(xl(j)) = \{\ \}$

Again, to respect our principle, the dummy variable of a variable binding construct must not already be bound in the body of the construct, and it must not occur at all in the universe. Also, variables bound in the universe should not occur in the body, and vice-versa. Formally:

$$
\begin{aligned}
BindExp_0 \ &::\ symb\ :\ DESymb \\
&\quad\ var\ \ \ :\ VSymb \\
&\quad\ univ\ \ :\ Type_0 \\
&\quad\ body\ :\ Exp_0
\end{aligned}
$$

where

$inv\text{-}BindExp_0(mk\text{-}BindExp_0(q, v, t, e)) \triangleq Is\text{-}valid\text{-}binding(v, t, e)$

$Is\text{-}valid\text{-}binding : VSymb \times Type_0 \times Term_0 \to \mathbb{B}$
$Is\text{-}valid\text{-}binding(v, t, e) \triangleq v \notin allVars(t) \cup bndVars(e)$
$\qquad \wedge allVars(t) \cap bndVars(e) = \{\ \} = allVars(e) \cap bndVars(t)$

The other definitions are very similar:

$$
\begin{aligned}
CompType_0 \ &::\ symb\ :\ CESymb \\
&\quad\ eArgs\ :\ Exp_0^* \\
&\quad\ tArgs\ :\ Type_0^*
\end{aligned}
$$

where

$inv\text{-}CompType_0(t) \triangleq Is\text{-}valid\text{-}arglist(eArgs(e) \frown tArgs(e))$

$$
\begin{aligned}
DepType_0 \ &::\ symb\ :\ DTSymb \\
&\quad\ var\ \ \ :\ VSymb \\
&\quad\ univ\ \ :\ Type_0 \\
&\quad\ body\ :\ Type_0
\end{aligned}
$$

where

$inv\text{-}DepType_0(mk\text{-}DepType_0(dt, v, u, b)) \triangleq Is\text{-}valid\text{-}binding(v, u, b)$

$$
\begin{aligned}
SubType_0 \ &::\ var\ \ \ :\ VSymb \\
&\quad\ univ\ \ :\ Type_0 \\
&\quad\ body\ :\ Exp_0
\end{aligned}
$$

where

$$inv\text{-}SubType_0(mk\text{-}SubType_0(v, t, e)) \quad \triangle \quad Is\text{-}valid\text{-}binding(v, t, e)$$

Henceforth, when we say term, expression, type, etc. we mean an element of *Term*, *Exp*, *Type* or whatever.

Claim: No variable occurs both free and bound in the same term: i.e.

$$\forall x\colon Term_0 \cdot freeVars(x) \cap bndVars(x) = \{\,\}$$

(Of course, this is not generally true of *ProtoTerm*s.)

Claim: If a prototerm satisfies the context conditions then so do all its subterms: viz.

$$Subterms\colon Term_0 \to Term_0\text{-set}$$

4.2.5   Equivalence

The informal treatment above referred to 'dummy' variables. The idea is that the name of the variable is not really important – the term would have just the same 'meaning' if a different name were used throughout (provided no ambiguities arose of course). This idea is captured by defining an equivalence relation on terms.

First we'll need a function which renames variables according to a given mapping. Variables not in the domain of the mapping will be left unchanged.

$$RenameVars : ProtoTerm \times (VSymb \xrightarrow{m} VSymb) \to ProtoTerm$$
$$RenameVars(x, vm) \quad \triangle$$

```
        cases x of
        VSymb                       → if x ∈ dom vm then vm(x) else x
        mk-ProtoCompExp(c, el, tl) → let el' = [RenameVars(el(i), vm) | i ∈ inds el],
                                          tl' = [RenameVars(tl(j), vm) | j ∈ inds tl] in
                                          mk-ProtoCompExp(c, el', tl')
        mk-ProtoBindExp(q, v, t, e) → let v' = RenameVars(v, vm),
                                          t' = RenameVars(t, vm),
                                          e' = RenameVars(e, vm) in
                                          mk-ProtoBindExp(q, v', t', e')
            ⋮
        end
```

Note that this form of renaming is extremely simplistic and certainly does not preserve invariants such as *inv-CompExp_0*. In particular, it is manifestly *not* true that

$$RenameVars\colon Term_0 \times (VSymb \xrightarrow{m} VSymb) \to Term_0$$

Definition: Two terms x and y are $(\alpha\text{-})equivalent$ (written $x \equiv y$) if one can be obtained from the other simply by renaming bound variables, provided the logical distinction between different variables is preserved:[6]

---

[6]In VDM, $D \xrightarrow{m} R$ stands for the collection of 1-1 maps (finite functions) from D to R.

$$\equiv : Proto\,Term \times Proto\,Term \to \mathbb{B}$$
$$x \equiv y \;\triangleq\; \exists f \colon VSymb \xleftarrow{m} VSymb \cdot$$
$$\mathsf{dom}\, f = allVars(x)$$
$$\wedge\; \forall v \in freeVars(x) \cdot f(v) = v$$
$$\wedge\; RenameVars(x, f) = y$$

Thus for example, the term $\forall x \colon A \cdot x = y$ is α-equivalent to $\forall z \colon A \cdot z = y$ but not to $\forall y \colon A \cdot y = y$.

The definition of $\equiv$ makes essential use of our principle regarding bound variables. Together, the principle and the 1-1-ness of f ensure that logical distinctions between variables are preserved. (This is a good example of how the principle makes some functions much easier to define.)

Here are some useful corollaries of the above definition:

$$
\begin{aligned}
freeVars(Rename(x, f)) &= \mathsf{rng}\,(freeVars(x) \lhd f) \\
bndVars(Rename(x, f)) &= \mathsf{rng}\,(bndVars(x) \lhd f) \\
Rename(Rename(x, f), f^{-1}) &= x
\end{aligned}
$$

when f is 1-1 and $allVars(x) \subseteq \mathsf{dom}\, f$. Using these facts we can prove the following:

Claim: $x \equiv y \;\Rightarrow\; freeVars(x) = freeVars(y)$

Claim: $\equiv$ is an equivalence relation on $Term_0$.

Claim: $\equiv$ respects syntactic classes: e.g.

$$x \equiv y \wedge x \colon CompExp_0 \;\Rightarrow\; y \colon CompExp_0$$

In particular, $x \equiv y \wedge x \colon Term_0 \;\Rightarrow\; y \colon Term_0$.

4.2.6   Some useful auxiliary functions

Now that the notion of equivalence has been introduced, it is possible to define functions which will allow us to forget about the complicated invariants almost entirely. For example, consider the following specification of a function for building compound expressions from constant symbols and lists of expressions and types:

$build\text{-}CompExp_0$ $(c \colon CESymb, el \colon Exp_0^*, tl \colon Type_0^*)$ $ce \colon CompExp_0$
post let $mk\text{-}CompExp_0(c', el', tl') = ce$ in
 $c = c'$
 $\wedge\; \mathsf{len}\, el = \mathsf{len}\, el' \wedge \forall i \in \mathsf{inds}\, el \cdot el(i) \equiv el'(i)$
 $\wedge\; \mathsf{len}\, tl = \mathsf{len}\, tl' \wedge \forall i \in \mathsf{inds}\, tl \cdot tl(i) \equiv tl'(i)$

At first sight this function might appear innocent enough and easy to implement, but remember there is an an invariant associated with $CompExp_0$ which says that logically distinct variables must be named apart. Thus it might well be necessary to rename bound variables in el and/or tl in order to preserve the invariant. Just exactly which variables get renamed, and to what, is left up to the implementor's discretion (the function is said to be underspecified).[7]

A '*build*-function' for binder expressions can be defined similarly:

$build\text{-}BindExp_0$ (q: $DESymb$, v: $VSymb$, t: $Type_0$, e: Exp_0) be: $BindExp_0$
post let $mk\text{-}BindExp_0(q', v', t', e') = be$ in
$\quad q' = q \wedge t' \equiv t \wedge RenameFreeVars(e', \{v' \mapsto v\}) \equiv e$

Note that v indicates which variable in e to bind. If $v \in freeVars(t)$ then a new symbol must be used as be's dummy variable (in order to satisfy the invariant), hence the use of v' in the above.

RenameFreeVars is a function which renames free variables in a given term x according to a given mapping vm. Only that part of vm which acts on free variables from x will be relevant. Free variables may get 'collapsed' together by vm, but they should not be captured by binders (etc.) in x. Of course this may mean that variables bound in x must be renamed, to respect our principle about variable names. The easiest way to define this formally is to use an intermediate term x' in which x's dummy variables have been renamed so that binders (etc.) in x' cannot possibly capture free variables, even if they get renamed. Formally:

$RenameFreeVars$ (x: $Term_0$, vm: $VSymb \xrightarrow{m} VSymb$) y: $Term_0$
post let $vm' = freeVars(x) \lhd vm$ in
$\quad \exists x'$: $Term_0 \cdot$
$\qquad x \equiv x' \wedge bndVars(x') \cap rng\ vm' = \{\ \} \wedge y = RenameVars(x', vm')$

Note that

$$bndVars(x') \cap dom\ vm' \quad \subseteq bndVars(x') \cap freeVars(x)$$
$$= bndVars(x') \cap freeVars(x')$$
$$= \{\ \}$$

thus $bndVars(y) = bndVars(x')$. The restriction that

$$bndVars(x') \cap rng\ vm' = \{\ \}$$

ensures that renamed free variables don't get captured by binders in y. On the other hand, free variables which aren't renamed under vm also won't get captured since, from above,

$$bndVars(y) \cap freeVars(x) = bndVars(x') \cap freeVars(x) = \{\ \}$$

Note also that the 'function' is well-defined in the same sense that $build\text{-}CompExp_0$ is well-defined (viz. all possible results are equivalent).

4.2.7 Definitions

The *mural* proof assistant provides the ability to make abbreviations and definitions, including recursive definitions. Constants and functions, binders, types and type constructors can all be defined. (We anticipated little or no use for defined dependent types, so they were omitted to keep the specification simpler.)

---

[7]Note however that for given arguments, all possible results are equivalent. Thus (at an abstract level) the underspecification is almost illusory. In fact, if VDM had a quotient-type construct we could consider equivalent terms to be equal, and the specification of *build-CompExp_0* above would be a fully well-defined function specification.

For constants and functions, a definition consists of two expressions: a *definiens* and a *definiendum,* or more simply put, a left hand side (*LHS*) and a right hand side (*RHS*). A simple example is

$$P \Leftrightarrow Q \triangleq (P \Rightarrow Q) \wedge (Q \Rightarrow P)$$

which defines bi-implication ($\Leftrightarrow$) in terms of ordinary implication ($\Rightarrow$) and conjunction ($\wedge$). The LHS is a *CompExp*$_0$ whose *symb* is the symbol being defined; its arguments are formal parameters (with no repetitions). The RHS is an *Exp*$_0$ which is well-formed in the 'context' in which the definition is being made (cf. Section 4.6.3).[8] Every formal parameter introduced on the LHS should be used at least once on the RHS, so that no extra information will ever be required for the folding (RHS $\rightarrow$ LHS) or unfolding (LHS $\rightarrow$ RHS) operations.

Recursive definitions – in which the symbol being defined appears on the RHS – can also be made. For example, the factorial function can be defined recursively by

$$fact(n) \triangleq \text{ if } n = 0 \text{ then } 1 \text{ else } n * fact(n-1)$$

Definitions by mutual recursion are also possible. It is the user's responsibility to ensure that such definitions make sense. Because termination cannot be guaranteed in the presence of arbitrary recursive definitions, *mural* does not provide an operation for 'unfolding to ground terms'.

The definition facility for types and type constructors is exactly analogous to that for constants and functions (with *CompType*$_0$ and *Type*$_0$ replacing *CompExp*$_0$ and *Exp*$_0$, respectively). Binder definitions are slightly different however. In the above, formal parameters were essentially *CESymb*s and *CTSymb*s with arity $(0, 0)$, and were unrestricted in number. We shall insist however that defined binders use at most two formal parameters: a *CTSymb* of arity $(0, 0)$ for the universe and a *CESymb* of arity $(1, 0)$ for the body.[9] For example, in classical logic existential quantification ($\exists$) can be defined in terms of $\forall$ and $\neg$ by

$$\exists x{:}A \cdot P[x] \triangleq \neg \forall y{:}A \cdot \neg P[y]$$

A and *P* are parameters to this definition. Instances of this definition are obtained by instantiating *A* and *P* (cf. Section 4.4).

Precise details of the definition facility and the corresponding folding and unfolding operations can be found in the full specification (Appendix C). The details are straightforward but lengthy, and weren't felt to be sufficiently interesting for a high level specification.

4.2.8 Concluding remarks

In many ways, the syntax could have been more elegant as a single level syntax of the form:

```
Term = VSymb | CSymb {Term} | DSymb VSymb ':' Term '.' Term
```

---

[8]As described in Appendix C, the definition facility is only available at the level of theory signatures. In such a case the well-formedness criterion is that the RHS is closed (no free variables) and uses only symbols available in the theory's signature. More generally it would be much better to be able to make abbreviations at various different levels: theories, proofs, even expressions themselves (cf. VDM's 'let' clause).

[9]The universe parameter should perhaps not be compulsory.

If nothing else, the specification would have been a lot shorter and not so many auxiliary functions would be necessary. Some of the awkwardness (cf. Section 4.11) of the present syntax would also have been avoided. We felt however that having two distinct levels (values and types) reflected more closely the way the syntax would be used in the target logics, and that as a result the support we offered the user would be that little bit higher. Only time will tell if this was the right decision.

4.3 Natural Deduction rules

The *mural* proof assistant supports *Natural Deduction* proofs. This section explains the reasons for this choice and describes the *mural* syntax for *inference rules*, or more precisely, for inference rule *schemas*. Section 4.4 describes how schemas get instantiated to form *instances* of inference rules and Section 4.7 describes how proofs are constructed from instances of inference rules.

4.3.1   Proof systems

The literature contains many different formulations of the notion of 'proof'. The particular proof formalism used in *mural* is based on Gentzen's Natural Deduction System **ND**. Alternative formalisms include Hilbert Style, Sequent Calculus and Semantic Tableaux.[10]

The different approaches offer different advantages, but this is not the place to go into a lengthy comparison. Basically:

- Hilbert Style is the simplest possible, and is the best suited to metareasoning: i.e., for proving results *about* particular theories (such as consistency). Because it is such a simple system, however, it is not very well suited to deriving new rules of inference *within* a theory.

- The Sequent Calculus is good for exploring patterns of reasoning and for proving results about patterns of reasoning (e.g. the existence of 'normal forms' for proofs). It is more general than the other systems, in that the other systems can be expressed very naturally in Sequent Calculus.

- Semantic Tableaux are based around the notion of proof by contradiction, which can be a good way for novices to explore proofs and is good for constructing counterexamples. On the other hand, proof by contradiction is considered 'poor style' by many practitioners and it can be confusing to work with the negation of the result you are trying to prove. For such reasons semantic tableaux have not caught on very well in software engineering.

---

[10]The best exposition of Natural Deduction is in [Pra65], but sadly this is long out of print. See also Sundholm's chapter on Systems Of Deduction in [GG83]. Ramsay gives a good, though brief, introduction to the three alternative systems in §2 of [Ram88]. (Sundholm ib.cit. also treats Hilbert Style and Sequent Calculus.) Note that Gentzen invented both **ND** and the Sequent Calculus, and that in much of the literature the distinction between the two is blurred or glossed over; confusingly, the latter is often called natural deduction – even in [Ram88]. Although the two systems are very similar, they *are* different representations, and such differences are vital when it comes to designing a proof assistant. Another point to note is that there is a school of thought which says that an **ND** logic is one for which every propositional function has an 'introduction' and an 'elimination' rule, and that the two should be related in a particular way (cf. [Pra65]). Perhaps there is some deeper truth in such a belief, but we certainly do not intend to impose such restrictions here.

- **ND** has a great advantage over other deduction systems in that it bears a very close resemblance to intuitive, informal proofs of the kind found in mathematics and (formal) software engineering textbooks (cf. [Gri81, Jon86]). In particular, the main structure of informal arguments can often be preserved when the reasoning is formalized within **ND**. There is also evidence [Dyb82] that **ND** proofs closely reflect spoken proofs.

It is widely recognised that the cost of *fully formal* proof outweighs many of the benefits of mathematical reasoning; so it seemed to us wisest to aim to support *rigorous* reasoning, with the potential to go fully formal by simply supplying enough details: hence the choice of **ND**.[11]

4.3.2   Rule statements

The laws of reasoning are captured in *inference rules*; here are three typical examples:

$$\frac{P}{(\text{if } P \text{ then } a \text{ else } b) = a} \qquad \frac{x \in s, \quad s \cap t = \{\}}{x \notin t} \qquad \frac{a{:}A, \quad l{:}A^*}{\text{cons}(a, l){:}A^*}$$

The formulae above the line are called *hypotheses* and the one below the line the *conclusion*. The conclusion is said to follow from the hypotheses according to the given rule of inference.

Perhaps the most distinguishing feature of **ND** is that hypotheses can have 'local assumptions' which can be used – in addition to any other assumptions in force – when establishing the hypothesis. For example, the classical law for introducing the symbol $\Rightarrow$ is

$$\frac{\{P\} \vdash Q}{P \Rightarrow Q}$$

which means that in order to infer $P \Rightarrow Q$ it is sufficient to show that Q follows from assumption P. (The 'turnstile' $\vdash$ is a special symbol of **ND**.)

Hypotheses with such local assumptions are called *sequents*. We'll look more closely at sequents below; for the moment we can say that the *statement* of a rule (as opposed to its proof, etc.) consists of ordinary hypotheses, sequent hypotheses and a conclusion:

$$
\begin{aligned}
RuleStmt :: \quad &ordHyps \;:\; Exp_0\text{-set} \\
&seqHyps \;:\; Sequent\text{-set} \\
&concl \quad\;:\; Exp_0
\end{aligned}
$$

Remarks:

In many textbooks (e.g. [End72] p.73) there is a clear separation between the class of '(ordinary) terms' (called *Exp* here) and the class of 'well-formed formulae' (*wffs*), and only the latter can appear as the hypotheses or conclusions of rules. But such a separation seems to us to sacrifice more than it gains. For example, it makes it hard to identify Boolean-valued terms with propositions; yet this is a quite common practice (cf. Section 3.5.2). It also limits the freedom to use the system as a *transformation system*:

---

[11]One of the main negative consequences of the decision to support **ND** is that non-monotonic logics cannot be directly supported: cf. the discussion in the section on the limitations of the *mural* approach in Section 4.11. All of the target logics (cf. the glossary in the appendix) can however be expressed in **ND**.

e.g. for rewriting numerical expressions

$$\frac{m + succ(n)}{succ(m + n)} \qquad \frac{\{a\} \vdash b, \quad P[a]}{P[b]}$$

Thus it was felt to make the system more flexible if any term (or Exp_0, rather) could appear in a rule. There are of course certain disadvantages to such an approach: cf. the discussion in Section 3.2.2.

4.3.3 Sequents

A *sequent* consists of a set of *premises* and an *upshot*. Sequents can also bind variables, which we'll call *sequent variables* and show as subscripts on the turnstile. For example, the law of induction over natural numbers can be expressed as

$$\frac{P[0], \quad \{n: \mathsf{N}, \ P[n]\} \vdash_n P[n+1]}{\forall m: \mathsf{N} \cdot P[m]}$$

This has two hypotheses: an ordinary hypothesis $P[0]$ (for the base case), and a sequent hypothesis $\{n: \mathsf{N}, \ P[n]\} \vdash_n P[n+1]$ (for the induction step). In the induction step, a new parameter, n say, is introduced and it is assumed (for the purposes of the subproof only) that $n: \mathsf{N}$ and $P[n]$ hold; one is then obliged to show that $P[n+1]$ holds. Once both the base case and the induction step are established, we can infer $\forall m: \mathsf{N} \cdot P[m]$.

Note that because it lacks a subscript facility, sequent variables are displayed at the start of a sequent in *mural* instead of being subscripts on the turnstile.

By paying special attention to the way sequents bind variables (and here we are indebted to the ELF work [HHP87] on expressing logics), some of the nasty 'side conditions' on inference rules can be avoided. For example, the usual $\forall$-introduction rule says that $\forall x: A \cdot P$ follows from P provided x does not occur free in any assumption on which P depends, other than $x: A$. This rule would be expressed as

$$\frac{\{x: A\} \vdash_x P[x]}{\forall x: A \cdot P[x]}$$

in *mural*. (The fact that x may appear in P is implicit in the informal statement of the rule, but must be stated explicitly in *mural*.)

This leads to the following definition:

    Sequent :: *seqVars* : *VSymb*-set
                  premises : Exp_0-set
                  upshot : Exp_0

where

    inv-Sequent(s) $\triangle$ $\forall e \in Constituents(s) \cdot bndVars(e) \cap seqVars(s) = \{\ \}$

where

    Constituents : *Sequent* $\rightarrow$ Exp_0-set
    Constituents(s) $\triangle$ *premises*(s) $\cup$ {*upshot*(s)}

The invariant ensures there is no ambiguity between sequent variables and variables bound within the constituents of the sequent. In practice, sequent variables will usually occur free in at least one constituent of the sequent, but not all variables free in constituents need be sequent variables.

Note that we haven't carried our principle about variable naming through to sequents. To do so would mean tightening the invariant *inv-Sequent* so that different constituents use different bound variables (cf. *Is-valid-arglist*). At this stage the usefulness of our principle has just about run its course, and it's becoming a liability instead.

To return to the specification, variables which appear unbound in a sequent will be said to be *free* in that sequent:

$$freeVars : Sequent \rightarrow VSymb\text{-set}$$
$$freeVars(s) \quad \underline{\Delta} \quad \bigcup\{freeVars(e) \mid e \in Constituents(s)\} - seqVars(s)$$

A sequent is *(syntactically) equivalent* to another if its sequent variables can be renamed – in a 1-1 fashion – to give an equivalent set of premises and an equivalent upshot. More formally,

$$\equiv : Sequent \times Sequent \rightarrow \mathbf{B}$$
$$s \equiv s' \quad \underline{\Delta} \quad \exists vm: VSymb \xleftarrow{m} VSymb \cdot$$
$$\qquad \text{dom } vm = seqVars(s) \wedge \text{rng } vm = seqVars(s')$$
$$\qquad \wedge RenameFreeVars(upshot(s), vm) \equiv upshot(s')$$
$$\qquad \wedge \exists em: Exp_0 \xleftarrow{m} Exp_0 \cdot$$
$$\qquad\qquad \text{dom } em = premises(s) \wedge \text{rng } em = premises(s')$$
$$\qquad\qquad \wedge \forall e \in \text{dom } em \cdot RenameFreeVars(e, vm) \equiv em(e)$$

As its name suggests, $\equiv$ is an equivalence relation on *Sequents*.

Remarks:

A couple of remarks of a technical nature can be made concerning the above definition:

1. Although the variables in dom *vm* are not bound in *upshot(s)*,

$$RenameVars(upshot(s), vm)$$

   might result in the capture of variables from rng *vm*; thus *RenameFreeVars* cannot be replaced by *RenameVars* in the third subconjunct of the definition.

2. The restriction that *em* be 1-1 was made for the convenience of the definition, but could be replaced by a weaker condition to the effect that the two sets of premises are equivalent under the renaming: e.g. $\{\forall x: A \cdot \text{true}, \forall y: A \cdot \text{true}\}$ is equivalent to $\{\forall z: A \cdot \text{true}\}$.

4.3.4 Establishing sequents

But what is a sequent? Intuitively,

$$prems \vdash_{x_1,\ldots,x_n} up$$

means that – for arbitrary variables $x_1, \ldots, x_n$ – from *prems* one can infer *up*.

A sequent is *trivially true* if its upshot is equivalent to one of its premises:

Is-trivially-true : *Sequent* → **B**
Is-trivially-true(s) $\triangleq$ $\exists e \in premises(s) \cdot e \equiv upshot(s)$

In fact, we can get even more mileage (kilometrage?) out of our interpretation of sequents, independent of any particular logic. For example, if u can be inferred from H_1 – with no 'arbitrary variables' – then clearly u can be inferred from any set extending H_1, or more generally from any set containing expressions syntactically equivalent to those in H_1. Thus, if $H_1 \vdash u$ and

$$\forall e \in H_1 \cdot \exists e' \in H_2 \cdot e \equiv e'$$

then $H_2 \vdash u$. We say $H_1 \vdash u$ *establishes* $H_2 \vdash u$.

The presence of sequent variables complicates the situation a little. For example, $\{\ \} \vdash x = $ nil does *not* establish $\{x\!:\!A^*\} \vdash_x x = $ nil because x in the first sequent has a fixed interpretation (determined by context) and is by no means arbitrary. The difference between the two sequents becomes even clearer when the second sequent is replaced by its syntactic equivalent $\{y\!:\!A^*\} \vdash_y y = $ nil.

Leaving such ambiguities aside for the moment – as they're easily dealt with by judicious renaming of variables – it's clear that a sequent which 'resolves more variables' than another, but otherwise looks much the same, is somehow stronger: e.g.

$$\{x\!:\!\mathsf{N}, y\!:\!\mathsf{N}\} \vdash_{x,y} x + y = y + x$$

is stronger than

$$\{z\!:\!\mathsf{N}\} \vdash_z z + z = z + z$$

Putting all this together we arrive at the following definition:

Establishes : *Sequent* × *Sequent* → **B**
Establishes(s, s') $\triangleq$ $\exists s'' \equiv s' \cdot$
$\qquad seqVars(s'') \cap freeVars(s) = \{\ \} \wedge$
$\qquad \exists vm\!: VSymb \xrightarrow{m} VSymb \cdot$
$\qquad\qquad \text{dom } vm = seqVars(s) \wedge \text{rng } vm \subseteq seqVars(s'') \wedge$
$\qquad\qquad RenameFreeVars(upshot(s), vm) \equiv upshot(s'') \wedge$
$\qquad\qquad \forall e \in premises(s) \cdot \exists e' \in premises(s'') \cdot RenameFreeVars(e, vm) \equiv e'$

(It might be necessary to rename sequent variables in s' to avoid confusing them with variables actually free in s – hence the introduction of an equivalent sequent s''.)

Claim: *Establishes* is transitive and reflexive on sequents, and refines syntactic equivalence.

Remarks:

(1) In many logics the interpretation of sequents can be further liberalized to allow replacement of sequent variables by *terms* rather than simply variables. Thus for example it might be considered valid to deduce

$$\{0 + 1\!:\!\mathsf{N}, 2\!:\!\mathsf{N}\} \vdash (0 + 1) + 2 = 2 + (0 + 1)$$

from the sequent

$$\{x\!:\!\mathsf{N}, y\!:\!\mathsf{N}\} \vdash_{x,y} x + y = y + x$$

In *mural* we resisted this interpretation for two reasons:

1. It was felt to be moving too far away from the 'pure' Natural Deduction interpretation: *viz.* that the x_i's are arbitrary *variables* in $\vdash_{x_1,\dots,x_n}$. We take the approach that it is the instantiator's responsibility to induce the extended interpretation, for example by adding axioms like

$$\frac{a\!:\!A, \quad \{x\!:\!A\} \vdash_x P[x]}{P[a]}$$

2. Pattern matching and other operations on sequents are much harder to specify and implement under the broader interpretation.

Perhaps this will be shown to be an overly cautious approach (cf. ELF [HHP87] where the extended interpretation is used).

(2) An even richer proof system than **ND** can be obtained by allowing 'nested sequents' – sequents with sequents as premises, and so on. This is explored further in [Sch84]. Again, we stuck with the simpler formulation, which is quite adequate for the target logics.

4.3.5 Side conditions and oracles

A reader with any familiarity with formal proof systems will know that many rules are stated with *side conditions* – conditions which must be met for an instance of a rule to be valid. By far the most common kind are those which refer to substitution instances (e.g. from $a = b$ and P deduce Q, where Q is the result of replacing one or more occurrences of a by b in P); we saw how such rules are expressed in *mural* in Section 4.2.1 above. The next most common are those which place restrictions on what free variables can occur in assumptions on which an assertion depends, and we saw in Section 4.3.3 how sequents handle these.

In [AHM87] it is shown how many other kinds of side condition can be handled by expressing restrictions as additional hypotheses on rules. Most of the techniques used there easily translate to the *mural* setting. There may however be side conditions which cannot be handled within the logical frame, or for which a fully formal treatment is inappropriate or 'expensive' in terms of user effort. (For example, the formulations of Modal Logic and Hoare Logic in [AHM87] make for much longer, less intelligible proofs than those given in Sections 3.6.4 and 3.6.5.) The *mural* solution is to allow appeal to 'oracles' – tests written in the implementation language of the proof assistant (in our case, *Smalltalk-80*) which are run when justifications are checked for correctness.

Oracles are in fact a general mechanism for allowing appeal to external agents, be they side-conditions, decision procedures, or even other theorem provers. This can be a particularly effective way of combining tools for specific problem domains in a generic environment. Thus for example, the user might wish to use the Boyer-Moore theorem prover to do inductive proofs about Lisp-like data structures, but still be free to guide the proof assistant in the cases where Boyer-Moore fails.

Because they are potentially so powerful (and because they call for some intimate knowledge of *mural*'s implementation), the general user will not be allowed to write his or her own oracles.

4.4 Rule schemas and instantiation

In this section we explain how rule instances are formed from rule schemas.

4.4.1 Metavariables

A rule statement such as

$$\frac{P}{(\text{if } P \text{ then } a \text{ else } b) = a}$$

actually represents a whole *schema* of rule instances: P, a and b are *metavariables* which get instantiated when the rule is used. For example,

$$\frac{x = 0}{(\text{if } x = 0 \text{ then } \bot \text{ else } 1/x) = \bot}$$

and

$$\frac{\{a, b\} \subseteq s}{(\text{if } \{a, b\} \subseteq s \text{ then } s - \{a\} \text{ else } s \cup \{b\}) = s - \{a\}}$$

are both instances of the above rule.

In *mural*, metavariables are represented by *CESymb*s and *CTSymb*s. In particular, they can take arguments: e.g. the law of substitutivity of equals can be expressed as

$$\frac{a = b, \ P[a]}{P[b]}$$

In what follows, a compound expression (*CompExp$_0$*) whose *CESymb* is a metavariable will be written as $P[...]$ instead of $P(...)$ to make it easier to recognize metavariables. (Similarly for *CTSymb*s.)

Instantiations are then expressed using the appropriate number of formal parameters: e.g. the instantiation

$$\{a \mapsto n^2, b \mapsto 16, P[x] \mapsto x * (n + 1) \leq f(x)\}$$

if applied to the above rule would yield the following rule instance:

$$\frac{n^2 = 16, \ \ n^2 * (n + 1) \leq f(n^2)}{16 * (n + 1) \leq f(16)}$$

The operation of instantiation renames bound variables (if necessary) to avoid capture: e.g. if applied to $\forall n: \mathbb{N} \cdot P[n+b]$ the above instantiation would yield (something equivalent to)

$$\forall m: \mathbb{N} \cdot (m + 16) * (n + 1) \leq f(m + 16)$$

These issues are discussed further below.

Because the syntax is essentially untyped, the *Exp/Type* distinction is the only restriction on what can instantiate metavariables. Thus for example,

$$\frac{1 + \{\}}{(\text{if } 1 + \{\} \text{ then } \text{cons}(3, 2) \text{ else } [\,]) = \text{cons}(3, 2)}$$

is a legal instance of the above rule. Of course, in any reasonable logic it won't be possible to establish $1 + \{\}$, so this rule instance will never be used. The lesson to be learnt here is that it is necessary to take care when postulating rules and axioms: this is discussed in Section 3.2.2 above.

4.4.2   Extending the syntax by formal parameters

Before we can formalize the notion of an instantiation we'll need some kind of notation for formal parameters. In fact, formal parameters are used in several other places below and in the full specification – namely for expressing various kinds of definitions and morphisms.

Placeholders

The simplest way to bring formal parameters into the syntax is to introduce two new classes consisting of *placeholders* – one for expressions and one for types. Placeholders will be numbered by an 'index'; the nth placeholder stands for the nth formal parameter (of the appropriate kind).

OPH :: *index* : N_1

TPH :: *index* : N_1

We'll write $[\![e1]\!]$ for *mk-OPH*(1) and $[\![t1]\!]$ for *mk-TPH*(1), etc. Intuitively, an instantiation which would be written informally as

$$P[x] \mapsto x * (n+1) \leq f(x)$$

will be written as

$$P \mapsto [\![e1]\!] * (n+1) \leq f([\![e1]\!])$$

in our abstract syntax. The former is to be preferred for legibility, but the latter is much easier to manipulate in the formal specification.

The extended syntax

The extended syntax is defined by

$Term_1 = Exp_1 \mid Type_1$

$Exp_1 = VSymb \mid CompExp_1 \mid BindExp_1 \mid OPH$

$Type_1 = CompType_1 \mid SubType_1 \mid DepType_1 \mid TPH$

$CompExp_1$ :: *symb* : *CESymb*
          eArgs : Exp_1^*
          tArgs : $Type_1^*$

where

$inv\text{-}CompExp_1(e) \quad \triangleq \quad Is\text{-}valid\text{-}arglist(eArgs(e) \frown tArgs(e))$

and so on, as before *mutatis mutandis* throughout Section 4.2. Auxiliary functions are defined in the obvious way: e.g.

$$Subterms([\![e1]\!]) = \{[\![e1]\!]\}$$

$$freeVars([\![e1]\!]) = bndVars([\![e1]\!]) = \{\}$$

The results from Section 4.2 carry through.

Note: Section 4.3 does *not* change: in particular, placeholders are *not* allowed in rule statements.

The arity of a term

It will be useful to have a function which counts the number of parameters (of each kind) in a $Term_1$:

$Arity : Term_1 \to N \times N$
$Arity(x) \quad \triangleq$
  let $m = \max \{i \mid i = 0 \vee mk\text{-}OPH(i) \in Subterms(x)\}$,
     $n = \max \{i \mid i = 0 \vee mk\text{-}TPH(i) \in Subterms(x)\}$ in
  (m, n)

In particular, a term with no placeholders has arity $(0, 0)$. Henceforth we shall identify $Term_0$ with the subtype

$$< x\colon Term_1 \mid Arity(x) = (0, 0) >$$

since the two are clearly isomorphic.

4.4.3   Instantiation

An *instantiation* is a mapping from metavariables to our extended syntax. Formally:

$Instantiation :: eInst : CESymb \xrightarrow{m} Exp_1$
             $tInst : CTSymb \xrightarrow{m} Type_1$

Elements of rng $eInst$ and rng $tInst$ are called *instantiands*.

To *instantiate* a term by an instantiation, we replace the term's metavariables by their instantiands, with placeholders 'filled in' appropriately. (As noted above, bound variables may need to be renamed to avoid capture, but all other symbols are left unaffected.) For example, the result of instantiating $P[\text{cons}(h, t)]$ by the instantiation

$$\{h \mapsto 3, t \mapsto [7, 5], P \mapsto rev(rev(\llbracket e1 \rrbracket)) = \llbracket e1 \rrbracket\}$$

is $rev(rev(\text{cons}(3, [7, 5]))) = \text{cons}(3, [7, 5])$.

We can now sketch the definition of the operation for applying an instantiation to a term. There is a precondition: namely that each occurrence of a metavariable in the term has enough arguments to fill the placeholders in its instantiand. As usual, we only give the definition in a few cases since the other cases are exactly analogous (and the reader is referred to the full specification for details).

$Instantiate : Term_1 \times Instantiation \rightarrow Term_1$
$Instantiate(x, inst) \quad \triangle$

    let $mk\text{-}Instantiation(om, tm) = inst$ in
    cases x of
    $VSymb \qquad\qquad\qquad \rightarrow x$
    $mk\text{-}CompExp_1(c, el, tl) \rightarrow$ let $el' = [Instantiate(el(n), inst) \mid n \in$ inds $el]$,
                                   $tl' = [Instantiate(tl(n), inst) \mid n \in$ inds $tl]$ in
                          if $c \in$ dom om
                          then $FillPHs(om(c), el', tl')$
                          else $build\text{-}CompExp_1(c, el', tl')$
    $mk\text{-}BindExp_1(q, v, t, e) \rightarrow$ let $t' = Instantiate(t, inst)$,
                           $e' = Instantiate(e, inst)$ in
                         $build\text{-}BindExp_1(q, v, t', e')$
    $OPH \qquad\qquad\qquad\quad \rightarrow x$
    $\vdots$
    end

  pre ... (see above)
where

  $FillPHs : Term_1 \times Exp_1^* \times Type_1^* \rightarrow Term_1$
  $FillPHs(x, el, tl) \quad \triangle$
    cases x of
    $VSymb \qquad\qquad\qquad \rightarrow x$
    $mk\text{-}CompExp_1(c, el', tl') \rightarrow$ let $el' = [FillPHs(el'(n), el, tl) \mid n \in$ inds $el']$,
                                  $tl' = [FillPHs(tl'(n), el, tl) \mid n \in$ inds $tl']$ in
                            $build\text{-}CompExp_1(c, el', tl')$

    $\vdots$
    $mk\text{-}OPH(n) \qquad\qquad \rightarrow el(n)$
    $\vdots$
    $mk\text{-}TPH(n) \qquad\qquad \rightarrow tl(n)$
    end

  pre $Arity(x) \leq ($len $el,$ len $tl)$
and

$$(i, j) \leq (k, l) \quad \triangle \quad i \leq k \wedge j \leq l$$

In other words, $FillPHs(x, el, tl)$ simply fills placeholders in x by the appropriate element of el or tl, renaming bound variables – if necessary – to preserve invariants and to avoid capture. $FillPHs$ may need to rename dummy variables in variable binding constructs so that variables free in instantiands do not get captured.

We'll need similar functions for instantiating sequents and rule statements:

  $Instantiate : Sequent \times Instantiation \rightarrow Sequent$
  $Instantiate(s, inst) \quad \triangle \quad ...$
  pre $\forall e \in Constituents(s) \cdot pre\text{-}Instantiate(e, inst)$

Instantiate : *RuleStmt* × *Instantiation* → *RuleStmt*
Instantiate(*rs*, *inst*) ≜ ...
pre ...

These functions may need to rename sequent variables so that variables free in instan-tiands do not get captured. Again, the reader is referred to the full specification (Appendix C) for details.

In Section 4.9 an algorithm for pattern-matching ('anti-instantiation') is specified and developed.

4.5 The *mural* store

At a very abstract level, the 'state' of a proof assistant consists of a set of inference rules, together with their proofs, if any. Proofs in turn are built from rules, which gives rise to the notion that rules may depend on other rules. We want to exclude circular arguments. We also want to distinguish between 'rigorous' and 'fully formal' proofs, which gives rise to a notion of the status of a rule. Finally, we want to group rules into theories. These are the considerations explored in this section.

4.5.1 Rules, axioms and dependencies

For simplicity, in this specification we won't distinguish between inference rules, theorems, propositions, lemmas, corollaries, conjectures and so on. The only distinction we draw is between rules which are *axiomatic* (self-evident) and those which require proof. Thus, at least to a first approximation, a rule consists of its statement and a proof (if appropriate). Formally:

$Rule_0$ :: *stmt* : *RuleStmt*
        proof : *Proof* | {AXIOM}

where *Proof* is defined in Section 4.7. Let us assume *Proof* comes with a function (again, to be specified later) which says which rules were used to establish the proof:

Rules-used: *Proof* → *Rule*-set

This is enough to define a *dependency relation* on rules as follows:

≺ : *Rule* × *Rule* → B
$r_1 ≺ r_2$ ≜ let *p* = *proof*(r_2), *S* = *Rules-used*(*p*) in
            p: *Proof* ∧ (r_1 ∈ *S* ∨ ∃*r'* ∈ *S* · r_1 ≺ *r'*)

Clearly ≺ is transitive. We define

a ≼ *b* ≜ *a* = *b* ∨ *a* ≺ *b*

Later we'll overload the symbol ≺ but we mean this definition to carry through.

At this level of abstraction, the *mural* store is simply a non-circular set of rules downwards closed under the dependency relation:

$Store_0$ = $Rule_0$-set

where

$inv\text{-}Store_0(S) \quad \triangleq \quad \forall r \in S \cdot r \not\prec r \wedge \forall r' : Rule \cdot r' \prec r \Rightarrow r' \in S$

Hence $\preceq$ is a partial ordering on the store.

4.5.2 The status of a rule

In many applications it is hard to justify the effort of providing fully formal proofs: e.g. a proof from first principles that $2 + 2 = 4$ might take many lines. One of the goals of *mural* is to support forms of *rigorous* reasoning – as opposed to fully formal reasoning – in the belief that many users will want to use the proof assistant to help with difficult or convoluted arguments, but will be content to leave gaps in the reasoning when assertions are 'obviously true'. Thus *mural* provides ways of simply asserting that rules are valid, without further justification.

For the purposes of this specification, let's assume there is a primitive function

$Is\text{-}assumed : Rule \rightarrow \mathbb{B}$

which determines whether a rule is assumed. The function is actually defined (interactively) by the user of the system, so no more detail need be given in this specification. Note that assumed rules are qualitatively different from axioms: axioms are self-evident truths upon which a whole theory is based, whereas assumed rules are believed to be derivable from axioms, given 'sufficient effort'. Note also that assumed rules may have partial (or sketch) proofs and may depend on other rules.

In Section 4.7.6 we define a function

$Is\text{-}complete : Proof \rightarrow \mathbb{B}$

which determines whether a proof is complete. Putting the various concepts together we can distinguish different levels of rules:

- axiomatic – in which the rule is an axiom

- fully derived – in which the rule has been demonstrated to follow from axioms

- rigorously derived – in which the rule has been demonstrated to follow from axioms and assumed rules

- proven – in which the rule has a complete proof, but some of the rules on which it depends may be as yet unproven

- unproven – in which the rule's proof is not yet complete

More formally, we introduce a enumerated type

$RuleStatus = \{$AXIOMATIC, FULLYDERIVED, RIGDERIVED, PROVEN, UNPROVEN$\}$

together with a linear ordering

$$\text{UNPROVEN} < \text{PROVEN} < \text{RIGDERIVED} < \text{FULLYDERIVED} < \text{AXIOMATIC}$$

The *status* of a rule is then defined by:

$Status : Rule \rightarrow RuleStatus$
$Status(r) \quad \triangleq \quad$ let $p = proof(r), rs = Rules\text{-}used(p)$ in
    if $p = $ AXIOM
    then AXIOMATIC
    else if $Is\text{-}complete(p)$
        then if $\forall r' \in rs \cdot Status(r') \geq$ FULLYDERIVED
            then FULLYDERIVED
            else if $Is\text{-}assumed(r) \vee \forall r' \in rs \cdot Status(r') \geq$ RIGDERIVED
                then RIGDERIVED
                else PROVEN
        else UNPROVEN

Given a rule, the next function tells the user what rules must be established in order for the given rule to be (rigorously) derived:

$Rules\text{-}yet\text{-}to\text{-}be\text{-}proven : Rule \rightarrow Rule\text{-}set$
$Rules\text{-}yet\text{-}to\text{-}be\text{-}proven(r) \quad \triangleq \quad$ let $p = proof(r)$ in
    if $Is\text{-}assumed(r) \vee p = $ AXIOM
    then $\{\,\}$
    else if $Is\text{-}complete(p)$
        then $\bigcup\{Rules\text{-}yet\text{-}to\text{-}be\text{-}proven(r') \mid r' \in Rules\text{-}used(p)\}$
        else $\{r\}$

Claim: $Status(r) \geq$ RIGDERIVED $\Leftrightarrow Rules\text{-}yet\text{-}to\text{-}be\text{-}proven(r) = \{\,\}$

The other extreme is to disregard all assumed rules. The following function gathers together the rules which must be established in order for a rule to be derived from first principles:

$Rules\text{-}ytbp\text{-}ffp : Rule \rightarrow Rule\text{-}set$
$Rules\text{-}ytbp\text{-}ffp(r) \quad \triangleq \quad$ let $p = proof(r)$ in
    if $p = $ AXIOM
    then $\{\,\}$
    else if $Is\text{-}complete(p)$
        then $\bigcup\{Rules\text{-}ytbp\text{-}ffp(r') \mid r' \in Rules\text{-}used(p)\}$
        else $\{r\}$

Claim: $Rules\text{-}yet\text{-}to\text{-}be\text{-}proven(r) \subseteq Rules\text{-}ytbp\text{-}ffp(r)$

Claim: $Status(r) \geq$ FULLYDERIVED $\Leftrightarrow Rules\text{-}ytbp\text{-}ffp(r) = \{\,\}$

4.5.3 Theories

Rules are arranged into *theories* in *mural*. For example, the rules about the logical connectives $\wedge, \vee, \Rightarrow$, etc. might be collected together in a single theory, called Propositional Calculus. Other candidates for theories would be Arithmetic, Set Theory, List Theory, the theory of VDM primitives, the theory of a design method, and so on. The length function on lists – for example – involves numbers and lists, so results about it could usefully be stored in a theory which combines Arithmetic and List Theory. Many more examples are given in Chapter 3.

Experience shows that it is very useful to structure the theory collection as a hierarchy with 'inheritance'. For example, all the above theories build on Propositional Calculus, and the Theory of VDM Primitives builds on Arithmetic, Set Theory and so on. This notion is captured in the following definitions:

$$Rule_1 :: \begin{array}{ll} theory & : Theory_0 \\ stmt & : RuleStmt \\ proof & : Proof \mid \{\text{AXIOM}\} \end{array}$$

where

$$Theory_0 :: parents : Theory_0\text{-set}$$

As it stands, the definition of $Theory_0$ is virtually trivial. For example, the least fixed point of this definition is

$$Theory_0 = \{\{\,\}, \{\{\,\}\}, \{\{\,\}, \{\{\,\}\}\}, \ldots\}$$

In the next section another field will be added, making for a less trivial definition; in the meantime the above is enough to explore the concept of a hierarchy of theories.

The transitive closure of the *parents* relation is defined by

$$\prec : Theory \times Theory \to \mathbf{B}$$
$$T_1 \prec T_2 \;\triangleq\; T_1 \in parents(T_2) \vee \exists T \in parents(T_2) \cdot T_1 \prec T$$

The *ancestors* of a theory are itself, its parents, its parents' parents, and so on:

$$Ancestors : Theory \to Theory\text{-set}$$
$$Ancestors(T) \;\triangleq\; \{T': Theory \mid T' \preceq T\}$$

Another useful auxiliary function collects the ancestor theories of a set of rules:

$$TheoriesOf : Rule\text{-set} \to Theory\text{-set}$$
$$TheoriesOf(S) \;\triangleq\; \bigcup\{Ancestors(theory(r)) \mid r \in S\}$$

We shall add a clause to the invariant on the store to ensure that the theory hierarchy admits no circularities:[12]

$$Store_1 = Rule_1\text{-set}$$

---

[12]Some remarks about VDM are in order here:

According to some schools of VDM thought, the non-circularity condition on the theory hierarchy is not strictly necessary, since it is enforced by a least fixed point semantics of recursively defined data types. We've chosen to include the condition here anyway, in the belief that it is only fair to point out to the reader that such a condition applies, and that it makes it easier to reason about the specification.

Of course, nothing should be inferred about the order in which theories can be defined in *mural*: e.g. the user should be free to add a 'higher' theory before introducing its parents; to think otherwise would be to read too much into the specification. In some sense, the data model being described here is a 'perfect world' model in that it describes the state of a complete collection of theories and rules. In practice, *mural* will almost always be in an incomplete state.

In the full specification, theories (and rules, and many other objects) are given *names* – or references, if you prefer – which goes some way towards modelling the *mural* state the user sees. The overhead with using references is that mappings from names to objects must be passed to functions, which makes the specification (even more) tedious to write and read. Some of these problems would be alleviated if VDM had 'pointers'. (Note that the non-circularity condition must be stated explicitly when references are employed.)

where

$inv\text{-}Store_1(S) \quad \triangleq \quad inv\text{-}Store_0(S) \wedge \forall T \in TheoriesOf(S) \cdot T \not\prec T$

Thus $\preceq$ is a partial ordering on the theories of the store.

Finally, a theory inherits all the rules of its ancestor theories:

$RulesOf$ $(T: Theory)$ rs: $Rule$-set
ext rd S : $Store_1$
post $rs = \{r \in S \mid theory(r) \in Ancestors(T)\}$

4.6 Syntactic contexts and well-formedness

4.6.1 Theories and their signatures

So how is the syntax introduced in Section 4.2 related to the theories introduced in Section 4.5? To take some examples: the theory of arithmetic talks about symbols like

$$0, 1, =, +, \times, \mathsf{N}, \ldots$$

and list theory talks about things like

$$[\,], \text{cons}, \text{hd}, \curvearrowright, \text{seq of}, \ldots$$

Note that 0 and [ ] expect no arguments, whereas '=' expects exactly two *Exp* arguments and seq of expects exactly one *Type* argument. It's useful to capture such information; in fact, we've found it so useful that we're going to go a little overboard and insist that theories not only record what symbols they talk about but also how many arguments those symbols expect.

Such information is stored in a *signature*:

$Signature$ :: $constrs$: $ArityMap$
$\qquad\qquad\quad binders$: $(DESymb \mid DTSymb)$-set

$ArityMap = (CESymb \mid CTSymb) \xrightarrow{m} (\mathsf{N} \times \mathsf{N})$

The numbers of arguments a symbol expects is called its *arity* and is recorded as a pair of natural numbers (the first for the number of *Exp*s and the second for the number of *Type*s). For later convenience, elements of dom *constrs* (i.e., the *CESymb*s and *CTSymb*s) will be called *constructors*.

A theory inherits the constructors and binders from all its parent theories, and may introduce new ones of its own (via a *local signature*):

$Theory_1$ :: $parents$: $Theory_1$-set
$\qquad\qquad\ localSig$: $Signature$

where

$inv\text{-}Theory_1(T) \quad \triangleq$
$\qquad \forall T_1, T_2 \in Ancestors(T) \cdot Are\text{-}nonclashing(localSig(T_1), localSig(T_2))$

where

$Are\text{-}nonclashing : Signature \times Signature \rightarrow \mathbb{B}$
$Are\text{-}nonclashing(\Sigma, \Sigma') \quad \triangle \quad$ let $cm = constrs(\Sigma), cm' = constrs(\Sigma')$ in
$\quad \forall x \in \text{dom } cm \cap \text{dom } cm' \cdot cm(x) = cm'(x)$

The invariant says that there should be no clashing declarations: i.e., any shared constructors should have the same arities.

The rest of this section defines some auxiliary functions which will be needed later on. The first one merges two signatures together, provided they have no clashing declarations:

$Merge\text{-}sigs : Signature \times Signature \rightarrow Signature$
$Merge\text{-}sigs(\Sigma, \Sigma') \quad \triangle$
$\quad mk\text{-}Signature(constrs(\Sigma) \dagger constrs(\Sigma'), binders(\Sigma) \cup binders(\Sigma'))$
pre $Are\text{-}nonclashing(\Sigma, \Sigma')$

Note that (when it is defined) *Merge-sigs* is an associative-commutative (AC) function. The next function merges a set of non-clashing signatures:

$Merge\text{-}sig\text{-}set : Signature\text{-set} \rightarrow Signature$
$Merge\text{-}sig\text{-}set(SS) \quad \triangle \quad$ if $SS = \{\,\}$
$\qquad\qquad\qquad\qquad$ then $mk\text{-}Signature(\{\,\}, \{\,\})$
$\qquad\qquad\qquad\qquad$ else let $\Sigma \in SS$ in
$\qquad\qquad\qquad\qquad\qquad Merge\text{-}sigs(\Sigma, Merge\text{-}sig\text{-}set(SS - \{\Sigma\}))$
pre $\forall \Sigma, \Sigma' \in SS \cdot Are\text{-}nonclashing(\Sigma, \Sigma')$

The order in which the signatures are merged is irrelevant since *Merge-sigs* is AC. Finally, the last of the current batch of auxiliary functions collects the 'full signature' of a theory by merging the local signatures of all its ancestors (including itself):

$FullSigOf : Theory \rightarrow Signature$
$FullSigOf(T) \quad \triangle \quad Merge\text{-}sig\text{-}set(\{localSig(T') \mid T' \in Ancestors(T)\})$

Note that symbols which occur in more than one ancestor theory get 'coalesced' – i.e., they enjoy *all* the properties they have in the various separate defining theories. This calls for some care on the user's part since it can easily result in inconsistent theories. In Section 4.8.4 we describe a mechanism for renaming symbols before combining theories, so that such coalescing is circumvented.

4.6.2 Rules and their metavariables

In essence, metavariables are constructors 'local' to a rule, and not exported to a theory. To make it clear exactly which things in a rule are metavariables, and how many arguments they expect, we'll add a new field to *Rules* recording its metavariables (and their arities):

$Rule_2 ::$ *theory*   : $Theory_1$
$\qquad\quad$ *stmt*   : $RuleStmt$
$\qquad\quad$ *metavars* : $ArityMap$
$\qquad\quad$ *proof*   : $Proof \mid \{\text{AXIOM}\}$

where

$inv\text{-}Rule_2(r) \quad \triangle \quad \text{let } \Sigma = FullSigOf(theory(r)) \text{ in}$
$\qquad \text{dom } metavars(r) \cap \text{dom } constrs(\Sigma) = \{\,\}$

The invariant says that metavariables must be symbols not already declared in the theory of the rule, which will prevent any ambiguity about whether a constructor is a constant or a metavariable. Finally, it will be useful to have a function which extracts the signature of a rule, which consists of all the symbols available in the rule's theory plus any new metavariables introduced by the rule:

$SigOf : Rule \rightarrow Signature$
$SigOf(r) \quad \triangle \quad \text{let } \Sigma = FullSigOf(theory(r)) \text{ in}$
$\qquad \mu(\Sigma, constrs \mapsto constrs \dagger metavars(r))$

4.6.3 Well-formedness

Just as when using a programming language, all symbols in a proof must make some kind of sense, even if they're only temporary (local) variables. The next definition captures the notion of a *syntactic context*:

$Context :: \ vars : VSymb\text{-set}$
$\qquad\qquad\ \ sig \ : Signature$

A term is well-formed in a syntactic context if – apart from its own bound variables – it only uses symbols from that context, and it uses them in a manner consistent with their arities:

$Is\text{-}wfd : Term_1 \times Context \rightarrow \mathbf{B}$
$Is\text{-}wfd(x, \Gamma) \quad \triangle \quad \text{let } mk\text{-}Context(vs, mk\text{-}Signature(cm, bs)) = \Gamma \text{ in}$
$\quad \text{cases } x \text{ of}$
$\quad VSymb \qquad\qquad\qquad \rightarrow x \in vs$
$\quad mk\text{-}CompExp(c, el, tl) \rightarrow c \in \text{dom } cm$
$\qquad\qquad\qquad\qquad\qquad \wedge (\text{len } el, \text{len } tl) = cm(c)$
$\qquad\qquad\qquad\qquad\qquad \wedge \forall y \in \text{elems } el \cup \text{elems } tl \cdot Is\text{-}wfd(y, \Gamma)$
$\quad mk\text{-}BindExp(q, v, t, e) \rightarrow q \in bs \wedge v \notin vs$
$\qquad\qquad\qquad\qquad\qquad \wedge Is\text{-}wfd(t, \Gamma)$
$\qquad\qquad\qquad\qquad\qquad \wedge Is\text{-}wfd(e, \mu(\Gamma, vars \mapsto vs \cup \{v\}))$
$\quad mk\text{-}OPH(n) \qquad\qquad\ \rightarrow \text{true}$
$\quad \vdots$
$\quad \text{end}$

Claim: The only variables which occur free in a well-formed term are those given by the context: i.e.

$$Is\text{-}wfd(x, \Gamma) \ \Rightarrow \ freeVars(x) \subseteq vars(\Gamma)$$

Claim: Well-formedness is monotonic: e.g.

$Is\text{-}wfd(x, mk\text{-}Context(vs, \Sigma))$
$\wedge vs \subseteq vs' \wedge Are\text{-}nonclashing(\Sigma, \Sigma')$
$\Rightarrow Is\text{-}wfd(x, mk\text{-}Context(vs', Merge\text{-}sigs(\Sigma, \Sigma')))$

Claim: The subterms of a well-formed term are well-formed in the appropriately extended context: e.g.

$$\text{Is-wfd}(x, \Gamma) \;\Rightarrow\; \forall y \in \text{Subterms}(x) \cdot \text{Is-wfd}(y, \mu(\Gamma, \text{vars} \mapsto \text{freeVars}(y)))$$

Here are some other useful definitions. The first says that a sequent is well-formed provided its (sequent) variables are new and its constituents are well-formed in the appropriately extended context:

Is-wfd : *Sequent* × *Context* → **B**
Is-wfd(*s*, Γ) △ let *mk-Sequent*(*vs, prems, up*) = *s* in
  $vs \cap \text{vars}(\Gamma) = \{\,\}$
  $\wedge\; \forall e \in \text{prems} \cup \{up\} \cdot \text{Is-wfd}(e, \mu(\Gamma, \text{vars} \mapsto \text{vars} \cup vs))$

In particular, for a sequent to be well-formed in a context without free variables, its constituents must have only sequent variables as their free variables: viz.

$$\forall e \in \text{Constituents}(s) \cdot \text{freeVars}(e) \subseteq \text{vars}(s)$$

The notion extends to rule statements in the obvious way:

Is-wfd : *RuleStmt* × *Context* → **B**
Is-wfd(*mk-RuleStmt*(*hyps, seqs, c*), Γ) △ $\forall x \in \text{hyps} \cup \text{seqs} \cup \{c\} \cdot \text{Is-wfd}(x, \Gamma)$

Well-formed instantiations are defined similarly.

Finally, rules should not have variables floating around freely: this reflects the desire to 'wrap up' rules so that they can be freely moved between contexts. In technical terms, the invariant on rules must be extended to say that the rule statement contains no free variables:

Rule₃ :: *theory*   : *Theory₁*
     stmt   : *RuleStmt*
     metavars : *ArityMap*
     proof   : *Proof* | {AXIOM}

where

inv-Rule₃(*r*) △ *inv-Rule₂*(*r*) ∧
  let Γ = *mk-Context*({ }, *SigOf*(*r*)) in
  Is-wfd(*stmt*(*r*), Γ)

4.7 Proofs

The following sections formalize the notion of proof which was introduced informally in Chapter 3. For the most part, the formal model is very close to the informal model illustrated above, although of course it contains information that is not explicitly displayed above, such as instantiations. (Line- and box-numbers will however not be used, since they complicate the specification of editing operations and are not really needed in an abstract specification – although circularities must of course be precluded somehow.)

In Section 4.7.7 we show that our model correctly captures the notion of **ND** proof.

4.7.1 Scoping of assumptions

The first notion to be formalized will be that of the subordinate proof, or *box*. Boxes can introduce new (local) hypotheses and new (local) parameters. Because the new parameters correspond to sequent variables, we represent them using *VSymb*s and will call them *box variables*. Neither the new parameters nor the new hypotheses are available for use outside the box, but they can be used within subboxes of their defining box. This leads to the following definition:

$$Box_0 :: boxVars : VSymb\text{-set}$$
$$subBoxes : Box_0\text{-set}$$

Here we are only concerned about the use of boxes as a scoping mechanism: at this level of abstraction we are not concerned about the ordering of subboxes and variables in a box, nor with the lines in a box. The transitive closure of the subbox relationship is given by:

$$\prec : Box \times Box \to \mathbf{B}$$
$$b_1 \prec b_2 \triangleq b_1 \in subBoxes(b_2) \lor \exists b \in subBoxes(b_2) \cdot b_1 \prec b$$

To relate this to the usual (linear) textual display of **ND** proofs, $b_1 \prec b_2$ if and only if b_1 is contained in b_2.

Our first attempt to specify *Proof* simply considers the box structure of a proof. The whole proof will be contained in a box called the *root*. Since we have insisted that rules have no free variables, the root box should have empty *boxVars* field. Also, since boxes represent scopes of assumptions and box variables, the nesting of boxes in a proof should be block-structured, in the sense that boxes may be nested but may not otherwise overlap. In keeping with the principle that logically different variables should be spelt differently, we'll also insist that different *VSymb*s must be used for the box variables of different boxes. This leads to the following definition:

$$Proof_0 :: root : Box_0$$

where

$$inv\text{-}Proof_0(p) \triangleq \text{ let } bs = BoxesOf(p) \text{ in}$$
$$boxVars(root(p)) = \{ \}$$
$$\land \forall b \in bs \cdot b \not\prec b$$
$$\land \forall b_1, b_2 \in bs \cdot$$
$$b_1 \neq b_2$$
$$\Rightarrow subBoxes(b_1) \cap subBoxes(b_2) = boxVars(b_1) \cap boxVars(b_2) = \{ \}$$

where

$$BoxesOf : Proof \to Box\text{-set}$$
$$BoxesOf(p) \triangleq \{b : Box \mid b \preceq root(p)\}$$

Part of the invariant says that box nesting is non-circular and another part that boxes do not share immediate subboxes; together these conditions imply that the box structure is tree-like (or 'block-structured').

4.7.2 Lines in a proof

This section describes how *lines* are assigned to boxes. There are many ways this could be specified but the following seems to work out easiest. But first of all, lines are labelled by *assertions* and come in two varieties: *hypothesis* lines and *ordinary* (or justified) lines.

Line = Hypline | Ordline

Hypline :: *assertion* : Exp_0

Ordline :: *assertion* : Exp_0
    justif   : *Justification*

Each proof will have a mapping which assigns lines to boxes, but for each box one of its (ordinary) lines must be distinguished as its *conclusion*. This leads to the following definitions:

*Box*₁ :: *boxVars* : *VSymb*-set
    subBoxes : *Box*₁-set
    boxConcl : *Ordline*

*Proof*₁ :: *root*   : *Box*₁
    lbMap : *Line* $\xrightarrow{m}$ *Box*₁

where

$inv\text{-}Proof_1(p) \triangleq inv\text{-}Proof_0(p) \wedge$
    let *lm* = *lbMap*(p) in
    rng *lm* $\subseteq$ *BoxesOf*(p) $\wedge \forall b \in$ rng *lm* $\cdot$ *lm*(*boxConcl*(b)) = b

The last part of the invariant simply says that a box's conclusion is assigned to the box itself.

Note that (at this stage) we're not concerned about the order in which lines appear in a box. In fact, there are good reasons – such as ease of specification and orthogonality of concerns – for delaying such a design decision as long as possible. Instead, we'll introduce (later) a notion of how a line depends on other lines, and use this to exclude circularities in proofs. In the meantime, here are a couple of useful auxiliary functions for collecting the lines of a proof:

LinesOf : *Proof* → *Line*-set
LinesOf(p) $\triangleq$ dom *lbMap*(p)

OrdlinesOf : *Proof* → *Ordline*-set
OrdlinesOf(p) $\triangleq$ {*l*: *Ordline* | *l* ∈ *LinesOf*(p)}

A line will be said *to belong to* a box if it is assigned to the box, or to one of its subboxes, or to one of its sub-subboxes (and so on):

is-in : *Line* × *Box* × *Proof* → **B**
is-in(*l*, *b*, *p*) $\triangleq$ *lbMap*(p)(*l*) $\preceq$ *b*
pre *l* ∈ *LinesOf*(p) ∧ *b* ∈ *BoxesOf*(p)

We'll write *is-in*(l, b, p) as $l \in_p b$, or simply as $l \in b$ when p is clear from context.

Claim: $\preceq$ acts like the subset relation on lines in boxes – viz.

$$\forall b_1, b_2 \in BoxesOf(p) \cdot l \in b_1 \wedge b_1 \preceq b_2 \Rightarrow l \in b_2$$

Claim: The only box to which a proof's conclusion may belong is the root: i.e.,

$$\forall b \in BoxesOf(p) - \{root(p)\} \cdot boxConcl(root(p)) \notin b$$

(This follows from the non-circularity of $\prec$.)

It will be useful to have functions which extract the (assertions labelling the) conclusion and hypotheses of a box:

Conclusion : *Box* → *Exp*$_0$
Conclusion(b) ≜ *assertion*(*boxConcl*(b))

Hyps-of : *Box* × *Proof* → *Exp*$_0$-set
Hyps-of(b, p) ≜ {*assertion*(h) | h: *Hypline* ∧ *lbMap*(p)(h) = b}

As remarked above, a sequent is like a 'squashed' box: sequent variables correspond to box variables, premises correspond to hypotheses, and the upshot corresponds to the box's conclusion. Thus we can extract a sequent from a box as follows:

Extract-sequent : *Box* × *Proof* → *Sequent*
Extract-sequent(b, p) ≜
    mk-Sequent(*boxVars*(b), *Hyps-of*(b, p), *Conclusion*(b))

4.7.3 Well-formedness of assertions on lines

The syntactic 'context' of a line in a proof consists of the signature of the rule being proven (namely, its metavariables and the full signature of its theory) and the box variables of the boxes which enclose the line. The latter will be called the line's 'available variables' and are given by:

availVars : *Line* × *Proof* → *VSymb*-set
availVars(l, p) ≜ {*boxVars*(b) | b ∈ *BoxesOf*(p) ∧ l ∈ b}

The next function defines what it means for the assertion on a line to be well-formed:

Has-wfd-assertion : *Line* × *Rule* → B
Has-wfd-assertion(l, r) ≜
    let p = *proof*(r),
        Γ = *mk-Context*(*availVars*(l, p), *SigOf*(r)) in
    Is-wfd(*assertion*(l), Γ)
pre p: *Proof* ∧ l ∈ *LinesOf*(p)

We'll now strengthen the invariant on rules so that their proofs and statements are related, and proof lines are well-formed. In particular, the only variables that may occur free in assertions in a proof are box variables from enclosing boxes:

$$\forall l \in LinesOf(p) \cdot freeVars(assertion(l)) \subseteq availVars(l, p)$$

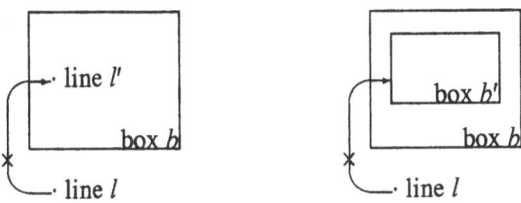

Figure 4.1: Invalid dependencies from line *l*.

In fact, *mural* is rather more liberal than the above specification suggests. For example, sometimes it is particularly useful to be able to leave 'uninstantiated metavariables' in proofs when not enough information is at hand at the time an inference rule is invoked. This lets the user continue with construction of a proof without committing to certain decisions: e.g. a proof by induction can be set up without deciding on a particular induction hypothesis. Another example would be to deliberately leave *P* uninstantiated in

$$\forall x{:}\, \mathsf{N} \cdot P[x] \;\Rightarrow\; (x-1)^2 \le \textit{factorial}(x)$$

until the proof is explored further and requirements on *P* become more apparent. The full specification allows for many other kinds of 'ill-formedness' and syntactic inconsistency.

$Rule_4$ :: *theory* : $Theory_1$
  stmt   : *RuleStmt*
  metavars : *ArityMap*
  proof   : $Proof_1$ | {AXIOM}

where

$inv\text{-}Rule_4(r) \;\triangleq\; inv\text{-}Rule_3(r) \land$
  let $p = proof(r)$ in
  $(p \ne$ AXIOM
  $\Rightarrow (ordHyps(rs) = Hyps\text{-}of(root(p), p)$
    $\land\; concl(rs) \equiv Conclusion(root(p))$
    $\land\; \forall l \in LinesOf(p) \cdot Has\text{-}wfd\text{-}assertion(l, r)))$

Note that, apart from the sequent hypotheses, a rule's statement can be extracted from its proof (if it has one).

4.7.4 Dependencies within proofs

This section considers (in abstract) how lines can depend on other lines and boxes, and strengthens the invariant on proofs to respect scoping and to exclude circular arguments. With each ordinary line we'll associate a set of lines, boxes and sequents called its *antecedents*. Typically, antecedent lines are the lines on which the justification of the line depends, and similarly for boxes and sequents.

There are of course restrictions on which lines and boxes can be antecedents of any given line. As remarked above it is not valid, for example, to appeal to a line (or box) *inside* a box from a line outside that box, as illustrated in Figure 4.1. This leads to the following first definition of the lines 'accessible' from a given line:

$Accessible\text{-}lines_0 : Line \times Proof \to Line\text{-set}$
$Accessible\text{-}lines_0(l, p) \;\;\underline{\triangle}\;\; \{l' \in LinesOf(p) \mid \nexists b \in BoxesOf(p) \cdot l \notin b \wedge l' \in b\}$

It may help to note that the defining predicate can be written equivalently as

$$\forall b \in BoxesOf(p) \cdot l' \in b \;\Rightarrow\; l \in b$$

The boxes accessible from a given line are defined analogously:

$Accessible\text{-}boxes_0 : Box \times Proof \to Box\text{-set}$
$Accessible\text{-}boxes_0(l, p) \;\;\underline{\triangle}\;\;$
$\qquad \{b' \in BoxesOf(p) \mid \nexists b \in BoxesOf(p) \cdot l \notin b \wedge b' \prec b\}$

These definitions are over-generous in that they allow for example a line to appeal to itself or to an enclosing box, which would not be valid logical reasoning. Later we'll tighten these definitions somewhat; in the meantime, it's interesting to see how far we can get with such weak restrictions.

Claim: The lines accessible from l are those which are assigned to boxes containing l: i.e.

$$l' \in Accessible\text{-}lines_0(l, p) \;\Leftrightarrow\; l \in lbMap(p)(l')$$

It follows that the variables available at accessible lines are a subset of those available at the line: i.e.,

$$\forall l' \in Accessible\text{-}lines_0(l, p) \cdot availVars(l', p) \subseteq availVars(l, p)$$

Claim: The boxes accessible from l are the immediate subboxes of boxes which enclose l: i.e.,

$$Accessible\text{-}boxes_0(l, p) = \bigcup\{subBoxes(b) \mid l \in_p b\}$$

(The proof uses the tree-like nature of boxing.)

For the purposes of this specification, the antecedent relations will be stored as extra fields of a proof. To prevent circular arguments it is necessary to place additional restrictions on the antecedent relations: e.g. we do not allow a situation whereby line a is justified by appeal to line b, line b by appeal to line c and line c by appeal to line a. We do this by defining

$Proof_2 ::$ $root$: Box
            $lbMap$: $Line \xrightarrow{m} Box_1$
            $antLines$: $Ordline \xrightarrow{m} Line\text{-set}$
            $antBoxes$: $Ordline \xrightarrow{m} Box\text{-set}$
            $antSeqs$: $Ordline \xrightarrow{m} Sequent\text{-set}$

where

$inv\text{-}Proof_2(p) \;\;\underline{\triangle}\;\; inv\text{-}Proof_1(p) \wedge$
    let $lm = antLines(p), bm = antBoxes(p), sm = antSeqs(p)$ in
    dom lm = dom bm = dom sm = $OrdlinesOf(p)$
    $\wedge \; \forall l \in Ordlines(p) \cdot$
        $l \not\prec_p l$
        $\wedge \; lm(l) \subseteq Accessible\text{-}lines_0(l, p)$
        $\wedge \; bm(l) \subseteq Accessible\text{-}boxes_0(l, p)$

where $l_1 \prec_p l_2$ stands for *Depends-on*(l_1, l_2, p) and

> *Depends-on* : *Line* × *Ordline* × *Proof* → **B**
> *Depends-on*(l_1, l_2, p) $\triangleq$
>   let *cons* = {*boxConcl*(*b*) | *b* ∈ *antBoxes*(*p*)(l_2)},
>   *ls* = *antLines*(*p*)(l_2) ∪ *cons* in
> l_1 ∈ *ls* ∨ ∃*l* ∈ *ls* · *Depends-on*(l_1, l, p)

The dependency relation is roughly the transitive closure of the antecedent relation(s), where boxes 'export' their conclusions only. We'll simply write $l_1 \prec l_2$ when *p* is clear from context.

In Section 4.7.7 it is shown that this invariant correctly captures the notion of **ND** proof. In the meantime we explore the consequences of our definitions, which leads to a useful strengthening of the invariant on *Proof*.

The next function extracts the set of lines on which the conclusion of a proof depends:

> *Lines-used* : *Proof* → *Line*-set
> *Lines-used*(*p*) $\triangleq$ {*l* ∈ *LinesOf*(*p*) | *l* $\preceq$ *boxConcl*(*root*(*p*))}

If all the individual justifications of 'used lines' are correct, then any other line in the proof is redundant (in the sense that it's not actually needed to establish the result). Boxes which don't contain 'used lines' are also extraneous to the proof. A 'garbage collector' – to be invoked by the user – is provided in *mural* which cleans up a proof by removing redundant lines and boxes, but such an operation is awkward to specify at this level.[13]

It's convenient to make the following abbreviation:

> *Ordlines-used* : *Proof* → *Ordline*-set
> *Ordlines-used*(*p*) $\triangleq$ {*l*: *Ordline* | *l* ∈ *Lines-used*(*p*)}

Claim: Ordinary lines used to establish the conclusion of a proof cannot appeal to boxes to which they belong: i.e.

$$\forall l \in \textit{Ordlines-used}(p) \cdot \forall b \in \textit{antBoxes}(p)(l) \cdot l \notin b$$

(Hint: the proof uses the following lemma

$$l_1 \prec l_2 \implies \forall b \in \textit{BoxesOf}(p) \cdot (l_1 \in b \wedge l_2 \notin b \implies l_1 \preceq \textit{boxConcl}(b) \prec l_2)$$

which can be proven by a straightforward induction. Let's suppose

$$b \in \textit{antBoxes}(p)(l)$$

and *l* ∈ *b* and derive a contradiction. First note that

$$\textit{boxConcl}(b) \prec l$$

---

[13]For example,

GarbageCollect
ext wr *p*: *Proof*
post *LinesOf*(*p*) = *Lines-used*($\overleftarrow{p}$)
  ∧ *Extract-sequent*(*root*(*p*), *p*) = *Extract-sequent*(*root*($\overleftarrow{p}$), $\overleftarrow{p}$)

is too loose a specification for what we have in mind because it says too little about the box structure. This is not the place to go into a lengthy discussion; suffice it to say that it is much easier to specify the operation at a level in which lines and boxes are given names (or 'references', if you prefer).

by definition. We can thus rule out the case $b = root(p)$ since

$$l \preceq boxConcl(root(p))$$

and $\prec$ is non-circular. It follows from an earlier result that

$$boxConcl(root(p)) \notin b$$

and hence from the lemma that $l \preceq boxConcl(b)$. But this contradicts the observation above that $boxConcl(b) \prec l$.)

It's also clear that it would contradict the non-circularity of $\prec$ for a line to make appeal to itself. Thus we can strengthen the definitions above:

$Accessible\text{-}lines_1 : Line \times Proof \rightarrow Line\text{-set}$
$Accessible\text{-}lines_1(l, p) \quad \triangleq$
  let $bs = BoxesOf(p)$ in
  $\{l' \in LinesOf(p) \mid l \nprec l' \wedge \nexists b \in bs \cdot (l \notin b \wedge l' \in b) \vee l = boxConcl(b)\}$

$Accessible\text{-}boxes_1 : Box \times Proof \rightarrow Box\text{-set}$
$Accessible\text{-}boxes_1(l, p) \quad \triangleq$
  $\{b' \in BoxesOf(p) \mid l \notin b' \wedge \nexists b \in BoxesOf(p) \cdot l \notin b \wedge b' \prec b\}$

$Proof_3$ is defined exactly as $Proof_2$ above but with the new definitions $Accessible\text{-}lines_1$ and $Accessible\text{-}boxes_1$.

We've said nothing about antecedent sequents yet. They will be taken from among the sequent hypotheses of the rule being proven:

$Rule_5 :: theory$ $: Theory_1$
            $stmt$ $: RuleStmt$
            $metavars : ArityMap$
            $proof$ $: Proof_3 \mid \{\text{AXIOM}\}$

where

$inv\text{-}Rule_5(r) \quad \triangleq \quad inv\text{-}Rule_4(r) \wedge$
  let $p = proof(r)$ in
  $(p \neq \text{AXIOM} \Rightarrow rng\, antSeqs(p) \subseteq seqHyps(stmt(r)))$

4.7.5   Justifications

In formal proofs, new 'facts' are deduced from existing facts and hypotheses by rules of inference. In our terminology, ordinary lines in a proof are justified by (instances of) rules, making reference to other lines, boxes and sequents; this notion is captured in *RuleJustif* below.

For various reasons, however, we find it convenient to introduce other kinds of justification – justifications which could be considered 'shorthand' for certain kinds of justification by rules, such as

- folding and unfolding definitions

- appealing to sequent hypotheses

- nested justifications

- appeal to an 'oracle' (for example, an external decision procedure)

and more. After introducing *RuleJustif*, we'll look briefly at one of these 'shorthands' – namely justification by appeal to a sequent hypothesis. In Section 4.8.5 we look at justifications by rules which are translated over theory morphisms. The other kinds of justification are dealt with in the full specification.

Putting all this together gives us:

Justification = RuleJustif | SeqHypJustif | ...

For each kind of justification we shall define a predicate

Is-properly-justified: *Ordline* × *Proof* → B

which checks the correctness of a line's justification.

Justification by rules

The most common way of justifying a line is by appeal to an instance of an inference rule:[14]

$RuleJustif :: rule : Rule_5$
$\qquad\qquad\quad instn : Instantiation$

where

$inv\text{-}RuleJustif(rj) \quad \triangle \quad$ let $m = metavars(rule(rj)),$
$\qquad\qquad\qquad\qquad\qquad mk\text{-}Instantiation(om, tm) = instn(rj)$ in
$\text{dom } m = \text{dom } om \cup \text{dom } tm$
$\land \; \forall c \in \text{dom } om \cdot Arity(om(c)) \leq m(c)$
$\land \; \forall c \in \text{dom } tm \cdot Arity(tm(c)) \leq m(c)$

where $(i, j) \leq (k, l) \;\triangle\; i \leq k \land j \leq l$.

Part of the invariant says that the instantiation instantiates the metavariables of the rule and no more. The rest of the invariant gives a sufficient condition for the instantiation to be possible – namely, that each occurrence of a metavariable c in (the statement of) r has enough arguments to fill the placeholders in the instantiand of c. This, together with the well-formedness invariant on rules, ensures the precondition on instantiation is satisfied: i.e.

$$\forall rj: RuleJustif \cdot pre\text{-}Instantiate(stmt(rule(rj)), instn(rj))$$

The following predicate says what it means for a *RuleJustif* to be correct: [15]

---

[14]Once again (cf. the footnote in Section 4.5.3), it would be better to make the *RULE*-field a *pointer* to a rule, rather than the actual rule itself. Strictly, the noncircularity condition on rules in Section 4.5 follows as a consequence of (VDM semantics and) the definition of *RuleJustif* given here, but that was not the specification writer's intention, nor will the fact be exploited here.

[15]Rules which have side conditions (cf. Section 4.3.5), should be checked as part of the *Is-properly-justified* relation.

$\textit{Is-properly-justified} : Ordline \times Proof \rightarrow \mathbf{B}$

$\textit{Is-properly-justified}(l, p) \;\triangleq$

    let $mk\text{-}RuleJustif(r, inst) = justif(l),$

      $rs = Instantiate(stmt(r), inst), p = proof(r),$

      $ls = antLines(p)(l), bs = antBoxes(p)(l), ss = antSeqs(p)(l)$ in

   $assertion(l) \equiv concl(rs)$

   $\wedge\; \forall oh \in ordHyps(rs) \cdot \exists l' \in ls \cdot assertion(l') \equiv oh$

   $\wedge\; \forall sh \in seqHyps(rs) \cdot$

      $\textit{Is-trivially-true}(sh)$

      $\vee\; \exists l' \in ls \cdot Establishes(\textit{Extract-sequent}(l'), sh)$

      $\vee\; \exists b \in bs \cdot Establishes(\textit{Extract-sequent}(b, p), sh)$

      $\vee\; \exists s \in ss \cdot Establishes(s, sh)$

  pre $justif(l): RuleJustif$

where

$\textit{Extract-sequent} : Line \rightarrow Sequent$

$\textit{Extract-sequent}(l) \;\triangleq\; mk\text{-}Sequent(\{ \}, \{ \}, assertion(l))$

$\textit{Extract-sequent} : Box \times Proof \rightarrow Sequent$

$\textit{Extract-sequent}(b, p) \;\triangleq$

    $mk\text{-}Sequent(boxVars(b), Hyps\text{-}of(b, p), Conclusion(b))$

In other words, the assertion on the line in question should be equivalent to the conclusion of the rule instance, and all hypotheses of the rule instance should be established by antecedents of the line. Only a line can establish an ordinary hypothesis, but lines, boxes and sequents can establish sequent hypotheses. Sometimes a sequent hypothesis even becomes trivially true upon instantiation. (In practice however, sequent hypotheses are usually established by boxes.) There are a number of examples in Chapter 3 above (e.g. in Section 3.2.2).

We note in passing that the above definition leaves room for plenty of redundancy. For example, there may be antecedent lines and/or boxes which are not actually needed as far as establishing hypotheses of the rule instance. Such redundancy needn't bother us at this stage, but it would be useful (in a subsequent development of the specification) to introduce an 'garbage collector' for removing it from a proof.

Of course, only rules which are in, or inherited by, the theory of the rule being proven can be used in a *RuleJustif*. This restriction is enforced by strengthening the invariant on *Rule*:[16]

$Rule_6$ ::   *theory*   : $Theory_1$

        stmt   : $RuleStmt$

        metavars : $ArityMap$

        proof   : $Proof_3 \mid \{\text{AXIOM}\}$

  where

---

[16]A note about the definition of *inv-Rule₆*: as defined, the function *RulesOf* depends on the store (or 'state') and so strictly should not be used here. The problem can be overcome by writing instead

$$theory(rule(rj)) \preceq theory(r)$$

but although this is formally better it was felt to be less evocative for the reader.

$inv\text{-}Rule_6(r) \quad \triangleq \quad inv\text{-}Rule_5(r) \wedge$
    $\text{let } p = proof(r) \text{ in}$
    $(p \neq \text{AXIOM} \implies \forall l \in Ordlines\text{-}used(p) \cdot$
        $\text{let } rj = justif(l) \text{ in}$
        $rj: RuleJustif \implies rule(rj) \in RulesOf(theory(r)))$

Justification by sequent hypotheses

There are a whole class of rules to do with sequents which can legitimately be considered to be general rules of Natural Deduction: e.g.

$$\frac{P, \; \{P\} \vdash Q}{Q} \qquad \frac{P, \; Q, \; \{P,Q\} \vdash R}{R}$$

When sequent variables are present the situation is slightly more complicated: e.g.

$$\frac{P[a], \; \{P[x]\} \vdash_x Q[x]}{Q[a]}$$

provided a is instantiated by a *VSymb*.[17] Because such rules are common to all **ND** logics (i.e. logics whose inference rules are expressible in **ND** form), it was decided to 'hard-wire' them into the system, by providing a special kind of justification: namely, *justification by sequent hypothesis*. The relevant notions are captured in the following definitions:

$SeqHypJustif \; :: \; sequent \; : \; Sequent$
                      $varMap \; : \; VSymb \xrightarrow{m} VSymb$

where

$inv\text{-}SeqHypJustif(mk\text{-}SeqHypJustif(seq, vm)) \quad \triangleq \quad \text{dom } vm = seqVars(seq)$

For a line to be properly justified by a sequent hypothesis, its assertion should be equivalent to the sequent's upshot, and each of the sequent's premises should be established at antecendent lines. Of course, this is subject to sequent variables being renamed according to *varMap*:

$Is\text{-}properly\text{-}justified : Ordline \times Proof \rightarrow \mathbb{B}$
$Is\text{-}properly\text{-}justified(l, p) \quad \triangleq \quad \text{let } mk\text{-}SeqHypJustif(seq, vm) = justif(l) \text{ in}$
    $assertion(l) \equiv RenameFreeVars(upshot(seq), vm)$
    $\wedge \; \forall e \in premises(seq) \cdot \exists l' \in antLines(p)(l) \cdot$
        $assertion(l') \equiv RenameFreeVars(e, vm)$
$\text{pre } justif(l): SeqHypJustif$

---

[17]cf. the discussion of our interpretation of 'arbitrary variable' in a footnote in Section 4.3.3. To take account of the more general interpretation, the *varMap*-field of *SeqHypJustif* should be replaced by

$$varMap: VSymb \xrightarrow{m} Exp_0$$

in what follows. In the definition of *Is-properly-justified*, *RenameFreeVars* would also have to be suitably generalized to allow free variables to be replaced by expressions.

In practice, to meet well-formedness criteria it will almost always be the case that

$$\text{rng } vm \subseteq availVars(l, p)$$

if the line is to be properly justified (because sequent variables usually occur free in at least one of the constituents of a sequent hypothesis).

Once again, some of the antecedent lines may be redundant and could be 'garbage collected away' (along with all of the antecedent boxes, if any).

4.7.6   The status of a proof

A line in a proof is *known* if every line on which it depends is properly justified:

> *Is-known* : *Ordline* × *Proof* → **B**
> *Is-known*(*l*, *p*) $\triangle$ $\forall l' \preceq l \cdot l'$: *Ordline* $\Rightarrow$ *Is-properly-justified*(*l'*, *p*)

A proof is *complete* if every ordinary line used to establish its conclusion is properly justified (or equivalently, if its conclusion is known):

> *Is-complete* : *Proof* → **B**
> *Is-complete*(*p*) $\triangle$ $\forall l \in$ *Ordlines-used*(*p*) · *Is-properly-justified*(*l*, *p*)

The rules which are used in a proof are just those used in the *RuleJustif*s of relevant lines:

> *Rules-used* : *Proof* → *Rule*-set
> *Rules-used*(*p*) $\triangle$ {*rule*(*justif*(*l*)) | *l* $\in$ *Ordlines-used*(*p*) $\land$ *justif*(*l*): *RuleJustif*}

This completes the definitions missing from Section 4.5 above.

4.7.7   ND proof trees

The second half of *inv-Proof₃* defines what it means for the dependency graph underlying a proof to be well-formed. It seems like a reasonable definition, but how do we know that it faithfully captures the notion of **ND** proof? After all, it has probably never even been written down in a textbook in quite this form (the closest description seems to be that of Jáskowski discussed in [Pra65]) – obviously some validation is called for. Fortunately this can be done by showing how our proof graphs are related to the widely-accepted notion of a Natural Deduction *proof tree* (cf. [Pra65]).

Without loss of generality, let's assume all justifications in a proof are *RuleJustif*s (cf. the discussion at the start of Section 4.7.5). Informally, a Natural Deduction proof tree can be obtained by 'unfolding' the proof graph from the proof's conclusion, following antecedents and copying nodes. More precisely, nodes of the tree correspond to (copies of) lines in the proof, labelled by their assertions. When an antecedent is a box, its conclusion is used as the new node and the unfolding continues from there. Clearly the unfolding process terminates since the dependency relation is noncircular (and VDM values are finite).

Hypothesis lines and lines which are not properly justified will be called *assumptions*. The next function extracts the assumptions upon which a line depends:

$Assumptions : Line \times Proof \rightarrow Exp_0$-set
$Assumptions(l, p)$ $\triangleq$
      if $l: Hypline \lor \neg\ Is\text{-}properly\text{-}justified(l, p)$
      then $\{assertion(l)\}$
      else let $S_1 = \bigcup\{Assumptions(l', p) \mid l' \in antLines(p)(l)\}$,
            $S_2 = \bigcup\{Assumptions(boxConcl(b'), p) - Hyps\text{-}of(b', p) \mid b' \in bs\}$,
            $bs = antBoxes(p)(l)$ in
            $S_1 \cup S_2$
      pre $l \in LinesOf(p)$

Notice how the hypotheses of a box are 'discharged' from the assumption set when a line appeals to a box. That's because they were temporary assumptions, relevant only to lines inside the box.

Claim: Clearly the assumptions on which a line depends are a subset of the assertions on lines on which the line depends: i.e.,

$$Assumptions(l, p) \subseteq \{assertion(l') \mid l' \preceq l\}$$

Claim: The *Assumptions* function is monotonic with respect to the antecedents relation: i.e.

$$l' \in antLines(p)(l) \ \Rightarrow\ Assumptions(l', p) \subseteq Assumptions(l, p)$$

A similar result holds for antecedent boxes:

$$b' \in antBoxes(p)(l) \ \Rightarrow$$
$$Assumptions(boxConcl(b'), p) - Hyps\text{-}of(b', p) \subseteq Assumptions(l, p)$$

Claim: If a line is 'known', its only assumptions are hypotheses of enclosing boxes: i.e.

$$Is\text{-}known(l, p) \ \Rightarrow\ Assumptions(l, p) \subseteq \bigcup\{Hyps\text{-}of(b, p) \mid b \in BoxesOf(p) \land l \in b\}$$

(The proof uses two of the lemmas in Section 4.7.4.)

Claim: If the conclusion c of a box b is 'known', then the box variables of b do not occur free in any assumption on which c depends, other than the hypotheses of b: i.e.

$\forall b \in BoxesOf(p) \cdot$
      let $c = boxConcl(b)$, $ass = Assumptions(c, p) - Hyps\text{-}of(b, p)$ in
      $Is\text{-}known(c, p) \ \Rightarrow\ \forall e \in ass \cdot freeVars(e) \cap boxVars(b) = \{\ \}$

This fact embodies a common 'variable occurrence' side-condition (cf. Section 4.3.3 above and the discussion in the section on Predicate Calculus in Section 3.2.4). The proof relies on the scoping and well-formedness invariants, and follows easily from earlier lemmas.

Claim: Given a rule R and a line l in the proof pf of R, $assertion(l)$ follows from $Assumptions(l, pf)$ and the sequent hypotheses of $stmt(R)$ according to the laws of Natural Deduction.

Sketch proof: The proof is by induction on the number of lines on which l depends in pf. Let $n = card\ \{l': LinesOf(pf) \mid l' \prec l\}$. Without loss of generality we can assume

$$Is\text{-}properly\text{-}justified(l, pf)$$

Base case: If $n = 0$ then $antLines(pf)(l) = \{\} = antBoxes(pf)(l)$, and $assertion(l)$ is simply established by $justif(l)$ and the sequent hypotheses of R (if any).

Induction step: For convenience, let's abbreviate $Assumptions(l, pf)$ by A.

Consider the justification $justif(l)$. To each ordinary hypothesis $ohyp$ of the relevant rule instance there corresponds a line $l' \in antLines(pf)(l)$. By the induction hypothesis, $ohyp$ follows from $Assumptions(l', pf)$, and thus from the superset A. Similar considerations apply to sequent hypotheses (of the rule instance) which are established by lines or sequent hypotheses. That just leaves the case when a sequent hypothesis $shyp$ is established by a box b'. Now, after appropriate renaming of sequent variables, the upshot of $shyp$ is equivalent to $Conclusion(b')$. The latter follows from $Assumptions(boxConcl(b'), pf)$, and thus from $A \cup Hyps\text{-}of(b', pf)$, by the induction hypothesis. Of course, according to the (meta-)laws of Natural Deduction, the premises of $shyp$ – in our case $Hyps\text{-}of(b', pf)$ – are 'discharged' by the rule in $justif(l)$. Thus, since $justif(l)$ is a proper justification, we get $assertion(l)$ follows from A, as required. $\square$

Since any tree-like **ND** proof can clearly be put into linear form, we have:

Corollary The *mural* proof model faithfully captures the notion of **ND** proof.

In particular, unless the axioms of a theory are inconsistent, only valid consequences of the theory can be proven in *mural*.

4.8 Morphisms

This section treats an advanced topic. Due to time constraints, the facilities described in this section were not included in early releases of the *mural* system. The reader can thus safely skip this section on first reading.

4.8.1 Motivation

In Sections 4.5.3 and 4.6.1 a simple theory structure was described, amounting to an acyclic directed graph of theories with simple inheritance. Although this is good enough for many purposes, there are times when it is too simple: e.g.

- When the same symbol is used for different purposes in different parent theories, it inherits both sets of properties. In some cases this is precisely what is intended. In other cases the symbol can safely be considered to be 'overloaded' with different meanings. But there are also cases when such coalescing makes for inconsistencies.

- Sometimes it is desirable to be able to simply rename some of the symbols in the theory. For example, the theory might be being used in an application domain with different notation to that in which it was originally developed (e.g. list concatenation might be written as '@' instead of '$\frown$'). Renaming can also be used to avoid symbol clashes when combining theories.

- Descending the theory hierarchy from the root often means moving from abstract, general theories to more specific theories. For example, a simple way to form a theory of AC operators would be to develop theories of associative and commutative operators separately and then to make them parents of the new theory. Once a theory hierarchy is constructed however it's difficult to insert further abstractions without redoing a whole part of the hierarchy.

- Sometimes it is desirable to construct two different but equivalent versions of a theory: e.g. propositional calculus formulated in terms of '∧' and '¬' versus a formulation in terms of '∨' and '¬'. Wherever one theory is used the other should be equally available: but this is clearly not possible in an acyclic directed graph.

Our proposed solution to these problems is to augment the simple structure by extra links, called *morphisms*.[18] Essentially, morphisms define 'faithful interpretations' of one theory in another – simple translations which preserve meaning (in the sense of 'provability').

A simple example of a morphism, taken from Abstract Algebra, would be to interpret the integers as a group under + (with identity 0). Let's suppose the Theory of Groups is formulated in terms of primitive constants $\otimes$, *id* and *inv* of arities $(2, 0)$, $(0, 0)$ and $(1, 0)$ respectively (with $\otimes$ displayed infixed). We'll also assume the integers are formulated in an appropriate Theory of Arithmetic, and that both theories inherit the appropriate Theory of Equality. The axioms of Group Theory are

$$a \otimes (b \otimes c) = (a \otimes b) \otimes c$$
$$a \otimes id = a = id \otimes a$$
$$a \otimes inv(a) = id = inv(a) \otimes a$$

(universally quantified over a, b and c).

The translation from group theory to arithmetic is induced by

$$a \otimes b \mapsto a' + b'$$
$$id \mapsto 0$$
$$inv(a) \mapsto 0 - a'$$

where a and b are formal parameters and a' and b' are their translations. Symbols from the shared parent Equality Theory are translated unchanged, as are variables and metavariables. Thus for example, the term $inv(id \otimes inv(x)) = x$ translates to $0 - (0 + (0 - x)) = x$.

Clearly, all the axioms of group theory remain true under this interpretation. And since proofs can be translated in a similar way, it follows that the translation of any derived rule of Group Theory will hold in the Theory of Arithmetic.

In the remainder of this section we lay down the basic foundations for morphisms in *mural*. Unfortunately, time may not permit a full implementation of the supporting operations.

4.8.2 Signature morphisms

A *morphism* is defined by its action on the primitive symbols of a theory:

$$
\begin{aligned}
Morph :: \quad &CEMap &:\ &CESymb \xrightarrow{m} Exp_1 \\
&CTMap &:\ &CTSymb \xrightarrow{m} Type_1 \\
&DEMap &:\ &DESymb \xrightarrow{m} DESymb \\
&DTMap &:\ &DTSymb \xrightarrow{m} DTSymb
\end{aligned}
$$

---

[18]This solution was initially inspired by Burstall and Goguen's modular approach to building mathematical models in *Institutions* [GB84].

In this definition, constructors can be replaced by more complicated expressions (of the correct kind). The expressions may contain placeholders, which get filled in by (translations of) the constructor's arguments upon translation (cf. Section 4.8.3.) Variable binding symbols can only be replaced by other variable binding symbols (of the correct kind).

The definition uses the 'placeholders' mechanism – introduced in Section 4.4.2 – to deal with the formal parameters in instantiations. Thus instead of writing

$$a \otimes b \mapsto a' + b'$$

formally we would write

$$\otimes \mapsto [\![e1]\!] + [\![e2]\!]$$

where $[\![ei]\!]$ stands for *mk-OPH(i)*. In fact, the definition of translation will be almost exactly the same as for instantiation of metavariables (cf. Section 4.4) except that now variable binding symbols may also be affected.

A *signature morphism* is a morphism together with a pair of signatures such that symbols from one signature get translated to expressions/symbols in the other signature in a consistent way. In particular, constructors should be translated to well-formed, closed expressions with at most as many formal parameters as the symbol expects arguments.

> *SigMorph* :: *from* : *Signature*
>   *to*   : *Signature*
>   *via*   : *Morph*

where

> *inv-SigMorph*(σ) $\triangleq$ let *mk-Signature(m, bs)* = *from*(σ),
>   *mk-Morph(cm, ctm, bm, dtm)* = *via*(σ),
> Γ = *mk-Context*({ }, *to*(σ)) in
> dom *cm* $\cup$ dom *ctm* $\subseteq$ dom *m*
> $\wedge$ dom *bm* $\cup$ dom *dtm* = *bs*
> $\wedge$ $\forall c \in$ dom *cm* · *Is-wfd(cm(c)*, $\Gamma) \wedge$ *Arity(cm(c))* $\leq$ *m(c)*
> $\wedge$ $\forall ct \in$ dom *ctm* · *Is-wfd(ctm(ct)*, $\Gamma) \wedge$ *Arity(ctm(ct))* $\leq$ *m(ct)*

(This definition leaves room in dom *m* – (dom *cm* $\cup$ dom *ctm*) for metavariables, which would normally simply be translated identically under a morphism.)

Note in particular that terms in the 'range' of a signature morphism are closed: i.e.

$$\forall x \in \text{rng } cm \cup \text{rng } ctm \cdot freeVars(x) = \{\,\}$$

4.8.3 Translation under morphisms

The *translation* induced by a signature morphism is defined by applying the morphism to the leaves of the syntax tree and propagating the result back up the tree, renaming bound variables (if necessary) to avoid capture and to preserve invariants.

Translate : $Term_1 \times SigMorph \rightarrow Term_1$

Translate(x, σ) $\triangleq$ let *mk-Morph*$(cm, ctm, bm, dtm) = via(\sigma)$ in

    cases x of

    VSymb $\rightarrow x$

    mk-CompExp$_1(c, el, tl) \rightarrow$ let $el' = [\,Translate(el(i), \sigma) \mid i \in$ dom $el\,]$,

                           $tl' = [\,Translate(tl(i), \sigma) \mid i \in$ dom $tl\,]$ in

                         if $c \in$ dom cm

                         then *FillPHs*$(cm(c), el', tl')$

                         else *build-CompExp*$_1(c, el', tl')$

    mk-BindExp$_1(b, v, t, e) \rightarrow$ let $b' = bm(b)$,

                            $t' = Translate(t, \sigma)$,

                            $e' = Translate(e, \sigma)$ in

                         build-BindExp$_1(b', v, t', e')$

    OHP $\rightarrow x$

    $\vdots$

    end

pre *Is-wfd*$(x, mk\text{-}Context(freeVars(x), from(\sigma)))$

The precondition *pre-Translate* ensures that, if a constructor in x is to be morphed, then it has enough arguments to fill all the placeholders of its image.

Claim: Signature morphisms do not introduce new free variables: i.e.

$$freeVars(Translate(x, \sigma)) \subseteq freeVars(x)$$

Claim: Signature morphisms take well-formed terms to well-formed terms; more precisely

let $\Gamma_f = mk\text{-}Context(vs, from(\sigma))$,

    $\Gamma_t = mk\text{-}Context(vs, to(\sigma))$ in

Is-wfd$(x, \Gamma_f) \Rightarrow$ *Is-wfd*$(Translate(x, \sigma), \Gamma_t)$

4.8.4 Theory morphisms

A *theory morphism* is a morphism which translates axioms of one theory into (not necessarily proven) rules of another:

ThMorph :: *from* : $Theory_1$

         to   : $Theory_1$

         via   : *SigMorph*

         justif : $Rule_3 \xrightarrow{m} Rule_3$

where

inv-ThMorph(*mk-ThMorph*$(T_f, T_t, \sigma, J))$ $\triangleq$

    FullSigOf$(T_f) = from(\sigma) \land$ *FullSigOf*$(T_t) = to(\sigma)$

    $\land$ dom $J = \{r \in RulesOf(T_f) \mid proof(r) = \text{AXIOM}\}$

    $\land$ rng $J \subseteq RulesOf(T_t)$

    $\land \forall r \in$ dom $J \cdot Translate(stmt(r), \sigma) \equiv stmt(J(r))$

where *Translate* and $\equiv$ are extended to *RuleStmt* appropriately.[19]

---

[19]For rule statements, $\equiv$ should also take simple renaming of metavariables into account.

A theory morphism is *valid* (or a *faithful* interpretation) if it translates axioms into established rules:

Is-valid : *ThMorph* → B
Is-valid(τ) $\triangleq$ ∀*r* ∈ rng *justif*(τ) · *Status*(*r*) ≥ RIGDERIVED

Claim: Given a valid theory morphism from theory *T* to theory *T'*, the appropriate translation of any derived rule in *T* must be derivable in *T'*.
(This follows from the obvious fact that complete proofs translate to complete proofs.)

The reader is referred to Sections 3.4.3 and 3.4.4 for examples of valid theory morphisms.

4.8.5   Theory morphisms in rule justifications

It's possible to take advantage of the last fact in the previous section to save the user a lot of work repeating proofs which are simple translations of existing proofs. This will be done by extending the notion of *RuleJustif* to allow appeal to (translations of) rules across theory morphisms.

The new kind of justification is defined by

MorphedRuleJustif :: *rule* : *Rule₃*
                                      via   : *ThMorph*
                                      instn : *Instantiation*

where

inv-MorphedRuleJustif(*rj*) $\triangleq$
      let *mk-MorphedRuleJustif*(*r*, τ, *inst*) = *rj* in
      r ∈ *RulesOf*(*from*(τ)) ∧ *pre-Instantiate*(*Translate*(*stmt*(*r*), *via*(τ)), *inst*)

The test for whether a *MorphedRuleJustif* is valid is exactly analogous to that for ordinary *Rulejustif*s upon translating the rule across the morphism:

Is-properly-justified : *Ordline* × *Proof* → B
Is-properly-justified(*l*, *p*) $\triangleq$
      let *mk-MorphedRuleJustif*(*r*, τ, *inst*) = *justif*(*l*),
          rs = *Instantiate*(*Translate*(*stmt*(*r*), *via*(τ)), *inst*),
          etc in
      ... as for *RuleJustif*
   pre *justif*(*l*): *MorphedRuleJustif*

Finally, the invariant on *Rule₆* should be strengthened to say that any theory morphisms used are morphisms to ancestor theories of the rule being proven: viz.

$$rj: MorphedRuleJustif \;\Rightarrow\; to(via(rj)) \in Ancestors(theory(r))$$

Rules-used should be redefined to include not just *rule*(*rj*) but also all the rules to validate the theory morphism (i.e. all rules in rng *justif*(*via*(*rj*))).

4.9   Pattern matching

The *mural* proof assistant provides a *pattern-matching* (or 'anti-instantiation') algorithm for its syntax. This is particularly useful for matching conclusions of rules against proof lines, in order to determine exactly which rules are candidates for justifications. If in addition the user can identify a line or lines on which the justification depends, hypotheses of rules can simultaneously be matched against them, which further narrows the choice of applicable rules. As well as determining whether a match is possible, the algorithm returns a set of (partial) instantiations, which is particularly useful when filling in the justification of a line. (The instantiations are partial for example when the rule has metavariables which do not appear in the conclusion, and hence which play no part in the matching.) This has all been incorporated into the *mural* search tool.

In this section we specify, develop and informally verify an algorithm for matching *Term*$_0$s against *Term*$_0$s. In the worst case, matching is of exponential complexity: e.g. when P and a are metavariables and $P[a]$ is matched against $c(d, d, \ldots, d)$, the result is the set of all instantiations of the form

$$\{a \mapsto d, \; P[x] \mapsto c(\mathbf{d'})\}$$

where $\mathbf{d'}$ is $(d, d, \ldots, d)$ with some d's replaced by the formal parameter x. The complexity of matching is the price we pay for allowing metavariables to take arguments (cf. Section 4.2.2). With due care to the form of inference rules, however, matching is often linear in practice (cf. the discussion in Section 3.3.1 above).

In fact, very significant improvements can be made to the algorithm given here, for example by passing sets of (partial) candidate instantiations around the syntax tree in a depth-first manner. Such improvements are left as exercises for the reader.

4.9.1 The specification of pattern matching

Before we give the formal specification, it will be convenient to define a type to hold the set of metavariables to be matched:

$$MVS = (CESymb \mid CTSymb)\text{-set}$$

An instantiation will be said to be *ok* with respect to a set *mvs* of metavariables and a set *vs* of variables if it only instantiates metavariables from *mvs* and it only introduces free variables from *vs*; more formally:

$Is\text{-}ok\text{-}inst : Instantiation \times MVS \times VSymb\text{-set} \rightarrow \mathbb{B}$
$Is\text{-}ok\text{-}inst(mk\text{-}Instantiation(cm, ctm), mvs, vs) \quad \triangle$
    $\mathrm{dom}\, cm \cup \mathrm{dom}\, ctm \subseteq mvs$
    $\wedge \; \forall x \in \mathrm{rng}\, cm \cup \mathrm{rng}\, ctm \cdot freeVars(x) \subseteq vs$

The set *mvs* will usually consist of the metavariables of the rule being matched. (It's necessary to make it explicit just exactly which metavariables *can* be instantiated since there may be metavariables which definitely can *not* be instantiated: e.g. the metavariables in the statement of the rule being proven.) The set *vs* will usually consist of the free variables available in the 'context' in which the matching is being done (e.g. the box variables of boxes enclosing the line to be matched against).

We say *x can be matched against y* over (*mvs, vs*) if there is an instantiation *inst* which is ok with respect to (*mvs, vs*) such that

$$Instantiate(x, inst) \equiv y$$

Here's a first specification of pattern-matching:[20]

> *Match-against* $(x, y: Term_0, mvs: MVS, vs: VSymb$-set$)$ *insts*: *Instantiation*-set
> post $\forall inst \in insts \cdot$
>
> $$Is\text{-}ok\text{-}inst(inst, mvs, vs) \wedge Instantiate(x, inst) \equiv y$$

It's not a terribly satisfactory specification, however, since it has a trivial implementation (viz. *insts* = { }). You might think that a more appropriate specification would require that *insts* contain *all* relevant instantiations. Unfortunately, this would be asking too much since there might be infinitely many possibilities: e.g. one can α-convert to one's heart's content; and any extension of a possibility is another possibility. One way around this would be to define an appropriate partial ordering on *Instantiation* and insist that *Match-against* return a 'maximal set' satisfying the above condition; on the other hand, it doesn't seem worth the overhead of specifying this formally. Instead, in Section 4.9.5 we give an informal argument that the algorithm presented gives a complete solution, in the sense that, for any *inst*: *Instantiation* satisfying

$$Is\text{-}ok\text{-}inst(inst, mvs, vs) \wedge Instantiate(x, inst) \equiv y$$

there is an instantiation in *Match-against*(x, y, mvs, vs) which is somehow equivalent to *inst* on x.

4.9.2 Some pre-processing

In this section we sketch a first step which takes care of the trivial cases, thereby allowing us to assume a stronger precondition. For example, the only thing that a *VSymb* matches is itself (in which case any instantiation works). The empty set of instantiations is returned if no match is possible.

---

[20]Strictly, the postcondition of *Match-against* should be a total predicate. This could be achieved by adding the conjunct *pre-Instantiate*$(x, inst)$ to the body of the formula.

Match-against : $Term_0 \times Term_0 \times MVS \times VSymb$-set $\rightarrow$ *Instantiation*-set
Match-against(x, y, mvs, vs) $\triangleq$
    cases x of
    VSymb $\rightarrow$ if $x = y$ then $\{Trivial\text{-}inst\}$ else $\{\,\}$
    CompExp$_0$ $\rightarrow$ let *mk-CompExp$_0$*$(c, el, tl) = x$ in
            if $c \in mvs$
            then if y: Exp_0
                then $AUX_E(x, y, mvs, vs)$
                else $\{\,\}$
            else if y: $CompExp_0 \wedge symb(y) = c \wedge$
                  len el = len $eArgs(y) \wedge$ len tl = len $tArgs(y)$
                then let $eis = AUX_L(el, eArgs(y), mvs, vs)$,
                         $tis = AUX_L(tl, tArgs(y), mvs, vs)$ in
                  Combine-inst-sets(eis, tis)
                else $\{\,\}$
    BindExp$_0$ $\rightarrow$ let *mk-BindExp$_0$*$(b, v, t, e) = x$ in
            if y: $BindExp_0 \wedge symb(y) = b$
            then let *newvar*: $VSymb$ be s.t.
                newvar $\notin vs \cup freeVars(x) \cup freeVars(y)$ in
                let $xe = RenameFreeVars(e, \{v \mapsto newvar\})$,
                    $ye = RenameFreeVars(body(y), \{var(y) \mapsto newvar\})$,
                    $univ = Match\text{-}against(t, univ(y), mvs, vs)$,
                    $body = Match\text{-}against(xe, ye, mvs, vs)$ in
                Combine-inst-sets$(univ, body)$
            else $\{\,\}$
    CompType$_0$ $\rightarrow$ let *mk-CompType$_0$*$(ct, el, tl) = x$ in
            if $ct \in mvs$
            then if y: $Type_0$
                then $AUX_T(x, y, mvs, vs)$
                else $\{\,\}$
            else if y: $CompType_0 \wedge symb(y) = ct \wedge$
                  len el = len $eArgs(y) \wedge$ len tl = len $tArgs(y)$
                then $\ldots$
                else $\{\,\}$
    $\vdots$
    end

where

    Trivial-inst : *Instantiation*
    Trivial-inst $\triangleq$ *mk-Instantiation*$(\{\,\}, \{\,\})$

    Merge-insts : *Instantiation* $\times$ *Instantiation* $\rightarrow$ *Instantiation*
    Merge-insts(*mk-Instantiation*(cm, ctm), *mk-Instantiation*$(cm', ctm'))$ $\triangleq$
        mk-Instantiation$(cm \dagger cm', ctm \dagger ctm')$
    pre $\forall c \in$ dom $cm \cap$ dom $cm' \cdot cm(c) \equiv cm'(c)$
        $\wedge \, \forall ct \in$ dom $ctm \cap$ dom $ctm' \cdot ctm(ct) \equiv ctm'(ct)$

Combine-inst-sets : *Instantiation*-set × *Instantiation*-set → *Instantiation*-set
Combine-inst-sets(*is*, *is'*) △
    {*Merge-insts*(*i*, *i'*) | *i* ∈ *is* ∧ *i'* ∈ *is'* ∧ *pre-Merge-insts*(*i*, *i'*)}

This function is well-defined since *Merge-insts* is associative-commutative (up to '≡')
when defined.

AUX_L : $Term_0^*$ × $Term_0^*$ × *MVS* × *VSymb*-set → *Instantiation*-set
$AUX_L(xl, yl, mvs, vs)$ △   if *xl* = [ ]
                                    then {*Trivial-inst*}
                                    else let *head* = *Match-against*(hd *xl*, hd *yl*, *mvs*, *vs*),
                                            rest = AUX_L(tl *x*, tl *y*, *mvs*, *vs*) in
                                        Combine-inst-sets(*head*, *rest*)

pre len *xl* = len *yl*

The auxiliary operations are specified as follows:

AUX_E (*x*: $CompExp_0$, *y*: Exp_0, *mvs*: *MVS*, *vs*: *VSymb*-set) *insts*: *Instantiation*-set
pre *symb*(*x*) ∈ *mvs*
post *post-Match-against*(*x*, *y*, *mvs*, *vs*, *insts*)

AUX_T (*x*: $CompType_0$, *y*: $Type_0$, *mvs*: *MVS*, *vs*: *VSymb*-set) *insts*: *Instantiation*-set
pre *symb*(*x*) ∈ *mvs*
post *post-Match-against*(*x*, *y*, *mvs*, *vs*, *insts*)

where the postconditions are as given in the previous section. The operation AUX_E is
refined further in the following section; AUX_T is very similar.

4.9.3   The main algorithm

This section presents an 'implementation' of AUX_E. One of the subsidiary functions
involved is given by an implicit specification, with its implementation deferred to the
next section.

We first sketch how the algorithm proceeds. Let's suppose

$$x = mk\text{-}CompExp_0(c, el, tl)$$

and suppose *inst* is a candidate element of $AUX_E(x, y, mvs, vs)$ with *c* ∈ *mvs*, where

$$inst = mk\text{-}Instantiation(om, tm)$$

Now

$$Instantiate(x, inst) = FillPHs(om(c), el', tl')$$

where *el'* △ [*Instantiate*(*el*(*n*), *inst*) | *n* ∈ dom *el*], etc. In other words, *y* should result
from filling placeholders in *om*(*c*). (Let's ignore renaming of bound variables for the
moment.) Thus *om*(*c*) must correspond to a 'pruned' version of the syntax tree for *y*,
where certain subterms have been replaced by placeholders. If a subterm *z* of *y* is replaced by *mk-OPH*(*n*), say, then from the definition of *FillPHs* we would require that
Instantiate(*el*(*n*), *inst*) ≡ *z*.

Now, there might be many different ways of pruning the tree while satisfying this last
condition, so let's introduce a subsidiary function AUX_M for collecting the possibilities:

AUX_M (y: $Term_0$, el: Exp_0^*, tl: $Type_0^*$, mvs: MVS, vs: $VSymb$-set) m: $IndexMap$
post dom $m \subseteq Indices\text{-}of(y) \land \{ \} \notin$ rng m
   $\land \forall i \in$ dom $m \cdot \forall(ph, inst) \in m(i) \cdot$
      $Is\text{-}ok\text{-}inst(inst, mvs, vs)$
      $\land$ let $n = index(ph)$ in
      $(ph: OPH \Rightarrow Instantiate(el(n), inst) \equiv Term\text{-}at\text{-}index(y, i)) \land$
      $(ph: TPH \Rightarrow Instantiate(tl(n), inst) \equiv Term\text{-}at\text{-}index(y, i))$

where[21]

$IndexMap = Index \xrightarrow{m} ((OPH \mid TPH) \times Instantiation)\text{-set}$

We won't go into details of the definition of *Index* and its auxiliary functions[22], except to say that they are used to 'get hold of' *particular* subterms, even if there are other subterms with the same structure. As usual, the reader is referred to the full specification for details.

Again, as specified, AUX_M has a trivial implementation, but in the next section we present an algorithm which gives a complete solution (in the same sense as discussed above).

To return to our candidate for *om(c)*, let's prune *y* at some set of subterms given by AUX_M; of course, it's enough to consider 'fringe-like' sets of subterms, since it would be wasteful to prune the same branch twice. If the candidate has all its free variables among *vs* then we can try merging all the relevant instantiations returned by AUX_M to get *inst*. (The individual instantiations might not be broad enough on their own, or might be mutually incompatible – hence the need to merge them if possible.) And that's all there is to the algorithm.

So here it is in more formal notation. The programming constructs

for each $< var > \in < set\text{-}expr >$ do $< stmt >$ odef

if $< bool\text{-}expr >$ do $< stmt >$ odif

are self-explanatory.

---

[21]It's implicit in *Instantiate(el(n), inst)* $\equiv$ ... that $n \leq$ len *el* and *pre-Instantiate(el(n), inst)*, etc.
[22]Signatures and preconditions of the auxiliary functions are as follows:

Indices-of : *ProtoTerm* $\rightarrow$ *Index*-set

Term-at-index : *ProtoTerm* $\times$ *Index* $\rightarrow$ *ProtoTerm*
Term-at-index(z, i) $\triangleq$ ...
pre $i \in Indices\text{-}of(z)$

Replace-subterms : *ProtoTerm* $\times$ *Index* $\xrightarrow{m}$ *ProtoTerm* $\rightarrow$ *ProtoTerm*
Replace-subterms(z, m) $\triangleq$ ...
   pre $\forall i \in$ dom $m \cap Indices\text{-}of(z) \cdot m(i)$: *ProtoExp* $\Leftrightarrow$ *Term-at-index(z, i)*: *ProtoExp*
Finally, $i \prec j$ iff *Term-at-index(z, j)* is a proper subterm of *Term-at-index(z, i)* in *z*.

$AUX_E : CompExp_0 \times Exp_0 \times MVS \times VSymb\text{-set} \to Instantiation\text{-set}$

$AUX_E(mk\text{-}CompExp_0(c, el, tl), y, mvs, vs) \quad \triangle$

       local program variables: $insts\colon Instantiation\text{-set}$

                                 $m\colon IndexMap$

                                 $s\colon (Index\text{-set})\text{-set}$

                                 $inst\colon Instantiation \mid \{nil\}$

   1.% *Initialize insts* %

     $insts\colon = \{\,\};$

   2. $m\colon = AUX_M(y, el, tl, mvs, vs);$

   3. $s\colon = \{is \subseteq \operatorname{dom} m \mid \nexists i, j \in is \cdot i \prec j\};$

     % *s consists of fringe-like subsets of* dom m %

   4. for each $is \in s$

     do for each $m' \in Distribute\text{-}setmap(is \lhd m)$

       % $m'\colon Index \xrightarrow{m} ((OPH \mid TPH) \times Instantiation)$ %

       do $candidate\colon = Replace\text{-}subterms(y, Project_1(m'));$

         if $freeVars(candidate) \subseteq vs$

         do let $inst_0 = mk\text{-}Instantiation(\{c \mapsto candidate\}, \{\,\})$ in

           $inst\colon = Merge\text{-}inst\text{-}set(\{inst_0\} \cup \operatorname{rng} Project_2(m'));$

           if $inst \neq nil$

           do $insts\colon = insts \cup \{inst\}$

           odfi

         odfi

       odef

     odef;

   5. return *insts*

 pre $c \in mvs$

(The value nil is used when the instantiations cannot be merged.) Before defining the auxiliary functions used above, note that if y contains only free variables from vs, then $c \mapsto y$ is a candidate instantiation: i.e.

$$freeVars(y) \subseteq vs \;\Rightarrow\; mk\text{-}Instantiation(\{c \mapsto y\}, \{\,\}) \in AUX_E(x, y, mvs, vs)$$

Three of the auxiliary functions are defined polymorphically, in terms of arbitrary types X, Y and Z:

$Project_1 : X \xrightarrow{m} (Y \times Z) \to X \xrightarrow{m} Y$

$Project_1(m) \quad \triangle \quad \{x \mapsto fst(m(x)) \mid x \in \operatorname{dom} m\}$

$Project_2 : X \xrightarrow{m} (Y \times Z) \to X \xrightarrow{m} Z$

$Project_2(m) \quad \triangle \quad \{x \mapsto snd(m(x)) \mid x \in \operatorname{dom} m\}$

$Distribute\text{-}setmap : X \xrightarrow{m} (Y\text{-set}) \to (X \xrightarrow{m} Y)\text{-set}$

$Distribute\text{-}setmap(m_0) \quad \triangle$

    $\{m\colon X \xrightarrow{m} Y \mid \operatorname{dom} m = \operatorname{dom} m_0 \wedge \forall x \in \operatorname{dom} m \cdot m(x) \in m_0(x)\}$

(Of course, the set returned by this function is likely to be very large in practice. Some data reification might be desirable at this point.)

    Finally,

$Merge\text{-}inst\text{-}set : Instantiation\text{-}\mathsf{set} \to Instantiation \mid \{\mathsf{nil}\}$
$Merge\text{-}inst\text{-}set(is) \quad \triangleq \quad$ if $is = \{\,\}$
  then $\{Trivial\text{-}inst\}$
  else let $i \in is,$
    $i' = Merge\text{-}inst\text{-}set(is - \{i\})$ in
    if $i' \ne$ nil $\land pre\text{-}Merge\text{-}insts(i, i')$
    then $Merge\text{-}insts(i, i')$
    else nil

4.9.4 The subsidiary algorithm

The algorithm for AUX_M simply runs through all subterms z of y trying to match elements of elems $el \cup$ elems tl against z. (Thus it calls *Match-against* recursively.)

$AUX_M : Term_0 \times Exp_0^* \times Type_0^* \times MVS \times VSymb\text{-}\mathsf{set} \to IndexMap$
$AUX_M(y, el, tl, mvs, vs) \quad \triangleq$
  local program variables: $m: IndexMap$
    $z: Term_0$
  1. $m := \{\,\};$
  2. for each $i \in Indices\text{-}of(y)$
    do $z := Term\text{-}at\text{-}index(y, i);$
      if $z : Exp_0$
      do for each $n \in$ dom el
        do for each $inst \in Match\text{-}against(el(n), z, mvs, vs)$
          do $m := Aux\text{-}add\text{-}el(m, i, (mk\text{-}OPH(n), inst))$
          odef
        odef
      odif;
      if $z : Type_0$
      do for each $n \in$ dom tl
        do for each $inst \in Match\text{-}against(tl(n), z, mvs, vs)$
          do $m := Aux\text{-}add\text{-}el(m, i, (mk\text{-}TPH(n), inst))$
          odef
        odef
      odif
    odef;
  3. return m

where

$Aux\text{-}add\text{-}el : (X \xrightarrow{m} Y\text{-}\mathsf{set}) \times X \times Y \to X \xrightarrow{m} Y\text{-}\mathsf{set}$
$Aux\text{-}add\text{-}el(m, x, y) \quad \triangleq \quad$ if $x \in$ dom m
  then $m \dagger \{x \mapsto m(x) \cup \{y\}\}$
  else $m \dagger \{x \mapsto \{y\}\}$

4.9.5 Verification of the algorithm

The algorithm clearly terminates, because it is called recursively on *proper* subterms of its first argument. The verification of correctness will be done in pieces, with each algorithm verified individually against its specification. (AUX_M is clearly correct by construction.)

Verification of *Match-against*

We are required to show that, for each $inst \in Match\text{-}against(x, y, mvs, vs)$

$$Is\text{-}ok\text{-}inst(inst, mvs, vs) \wedge Instantiate(x, inst) \equiv y$$

The first part follows easily from the following facts

1. $Is\text{-}ok\text{-}inst(Trivial\text{-}inst, mvs, vs)$

2. *Merge-insts* preserves $Is\text{-}ok\text{-}inst(\_, mvs, vs)$

3. *Combine-inst-sets* preserves $\forall inst \in \_ \cdot Is\text{-}ok\text{-}inst(inst, mvs, vs)$

and the post-conditions on AUX_E and AUX_T. (Of course, the definition of AUX_L must also be unfolded.)

The second part follows almost directly from the definition of $Instantiate(x, inst)$ by case analysis on x. We won't go into the details as they are straightforward but messy; instead we just note the following useful facts:

- $Instantiate(x, Trivial\text{-}inst) \equiv x$

- $Instantiate(x, \_)$ is monotonic: viz.
  $pre\text{-}Merge\text{-}insts(i, i') \Rightarrow Instantiate(x, i) \equiv Instantiate(x, Merge\text{-}insts(i, i'))$

The rest of the details are left to the dedicated reader. □

Verification of AUX_E

Let *inst* be one of the instantiations returned by $AUX_E(x, y, mvs, vs)$ – if any – and let $is \in s$ and $m' \in Distribute\text{-}setmap(is \lhd m)$ be the corresponding choices. We use the same notation as in the algorithm itself, so for example $x = mk\text{-}CompExp_0(c, el, tl)$, etc. In particular,

$$inst = Merge\text{-}inst\text{-}set(\{inst_0\} \cup rng\ Project_2(m'))$$

where $inst_0 = mk\text{-}Instantiation(\{c \mapsto candidate\}, \{\ \})$.

We must show that

$$Is\text{-}ok\text{-}inst(inst, mvs, vs) \wedge Instantiate(x, inst) \equiv y$$

The first part is easy. Since $c \in mvs$ and $freeVars(candidate) \subseteq vs$, we have:

$$Is\text{-}ok\text{-}inst(inst_0, mvs, vs)$$

When non-nil, *Merge-inst-sets* preserves *Is-ok-inst*, so $Is\text{-}ok\text{-}inst(inst, mvs, vs)$ will follow once it is shown that

$$Is\text{-}ok\text{-}inst(inst', mvs, vs) \text{ for each } inst' \in rng\ Project_2(m').$$

But this is clear from $post\text{-}AUX_M(y, el, tl, mvs, vs)$.

For the second part, note that

$z: Term_0 \wedge i \in Indices\text{-}of(z) \wedge el_0(n) \equiv Term\text{-}at\text{-}index(z, i)$
$\wedge z' = Replace\text{-}subterms(z, \{i \mapsto mk\text{-}OPH(n)\})$
$\Rightarrow FillPHs(z', el_0, tl_0) \equiv z$

Using the monotonicity of *Instantiate* with respect to *Merge-insts*, and the fact that *is* is fringe-like, it is straightforward (but messy) to extend this result to show that

$$FillPHs(Replace\text{-}subterms(y, Project_1(m')), el', tl') \equiv y$$

(where $el'(n) \triangleq Instantiate(el(n), inst)$, etc.), since by *post-AUX$_M$*

$$el'(n) = Instantiate(el(n), inst') \equiv Term\text{-}at\text{-}index(y, i)$$

when $\{i \mapsto (mk\text{-}OPH(n), inst')\} \in m'$. Hence

$$\begin{aligned} Instantiate(x, inst) \ &= Instantiate(mk\text{-}CompExp_0(c, el, tl)) \\ &= FillPHs(candidate, el', tl') \\ &= FillPHs(Replace\text{-}subterms(y, Project_1(m')), el', tl') \\ &\equiv y \end{aligned}$$

as required. $\square$

The algorithm is complete

Let's call an instantiation a *sub-instantiation* of another if each metavariable of the first maps to something equivalent under both instantiations. (Of course, the second may instantiate more metavariables than the first.) In this section we argue that, if *inst* satisfies

$$Is\text{-}ok\text{-}inst(inst, mvs, vs) \wedge Instantiate(x, inst) \equiv y$$

then the algorithm for *Match-against*(x, y, mvs, vs) returns some sub-instantiation of *inst*. In this sense the algorithm yields a complete solution; moreover the solution is the 'cleanest' possible, in that it does not instantiate more metavariables than it needs to. The proof is by induction on the size of x as a syntax tree (or equivalently, by structural induction on x).

The base case is trivial. For the induction step, note first that it is clear from the definition of *Instantiate* that the syntax trees for x and y must agree at least down as far as compound terms with symbols from *mvs*. So without loss of generality, let's assume $x = mk\text{-}CompExp_0(c, el, tl)$ with $c \in mvs$, the case x: *CompType$_0$* being exactly analogous. As discussed earlier, $eInst(inst)(c)$ must be a pruned version of y, with the pruning corresponding to some choice of fringe-like subset of the domain of the map returned by $AUX_M(y, el, tl, mvs, vs)$; the induction hypothesis is used to justify the fact that AUX_M returns a complete solution. It also follows from the induction hypothesis that each relevant instantiation returned by AUX_M is a sub-instantiation of *inst*, in the above sense. The result of merging the relevant instantiations is again a sub-instantiation of *inst*, and the proof is complete. $\square$

4.10 Reading the full specification

As remarked in the introduction, the Walk is an abstraction of the full *mural* specification given in Appendix C (simply called *the FullSpec* hereafter). Because it is a simplification, the Walk naturally differs from the FullSpec in several fundamental aspects. For a start, the latter covers more topics, including:

- other kinds of justification

- multiple proof attempts

- folding and unfolding of definitions

- incomplete and null terms

- editing operations and subterm access functions

- other user interface (UI) operations

It also gives some flavour of the intended UI by distinguishing whether for example functions are

- exported (available to the user)

- auxiliary (introduced simply for purposes of definition)

- background (constraints maintained by the system)

In order to specify many of the UI operations, the FullSpec deals with *references* (names) for individual theories, rules, proof lines, and so on. The mapping from names to the objects they represent is stored as part of the 'state' of the *mural* proof assistant in the FullSpec (the *Store*). To have a UI which was unmoded as far as possible, it was necessary for the FullSpec to allow for 'temporary inconsistencies' in the state, such as the statement of a rule getting out of step with its proof, or the use of a symbol before its declaration. As a result, invariants in the FullSpec are much looser, with more use being made of 'consistency checks' instead. (For example, the invariant on rule statements does not insist that hypotheses have no free variables; instead, a predicate *is-OK-RuleStmt* is introduced.) These are the main stylistic differences between the two specifications.

There are also important terminological differences, explained below. Unless otherwise stated below, classes and functions with the same name – give or take case distinctions – can be assumed to correspond more or less exactly in the two specifications.

Syntax

Table 4.1 summarizes the correspondence between classes of symbols in the two specifications. Selector names also differ, but the correspondence should be obvious enough. There is also a slightly different factoring of the abstract syntax, but on the whole the correspondence is quite close. The exception is the class *Term* in the FullSpec, which is much more general than *Term*$_1$, in that the former includes subcomponents – such as individual symbols and lists of arguments – which are not considered to be terms in their own right in the Walk. This difference is reflected in the *Subterms* function; but for the most part, all the other basic functions (e.g. *freeVars* and *RenameFreeVars*) have the same meanings in the two specifications. Of course, $\equiv$ corresponds to *isEquivalentTo* in the FullSpec.

The correspondence extends to sequents and rule statements in a fairly straightforward manner. For example, the definition of *RuleStmt* in the Walk is

$$RuleStmt :: \quad ordHyps \; : \; Exp_0\text{-set}$$
$$seqHyps \; : \; Sequent\text{-set}$$
$$concl \quad : \; Exp_0$$

Walk	FullSpec	Walk	FullSpec
CESymb	*OESymb*	*CTSymb*	*OTSymb*
CompExp$_1$	*OExp*	*CompType$_1$*	*OType*
DESymb	*QESymb*	*DTSymb*	*QTSymb*
BindExp$_1$	*QExp*	*BindType$_1$*	*QType*
OPH	*EPHole*	*TPH*	*TPHole*
Exp$_1$	*Exp*	*Type$_1$*	*Type*

Table 4.1: Syntax classes.

Walk	Section	FullSpec	Appendix
AXIOM	4.5.1	nil	C.3.2
$\prec$		*dependsOnRule*	C.9.1
inv-Store$_0$		*isNoncircular*	C.9.1
$\succ$	4.5.3	*inheritsFrom*	C.6.2
Ancestors		*ancestors*	C.6.2
RulesOf		*rules*	C.6.1
localSig	4.6.1	*EXSIG*	C.6.2
Are-nonclashing		*areNonclashingSigs*	C.5.4
Merge-sig-set		*mergeSigs*	C.5.4
Is-wfd	4.6.3	*isReasonableWRTSig*	C.5.2
inv-Rule$_3$		*isReasonableWRTTheory*	C.6.2

Table 4.2: Functions and predicates.

while in the FullSpec it is

$$RuleStmt :: \begin{array}{ll} SEQHYPS & : Sequent\text{-set} \\ ORDHYPS & : Exp\text{-set} \\ CONCL & : Exp \end{array}$$

For sequents (Section 4.3.3), *seqVars* corresponds to *NFV* and *Constituents* to *exps* (Appendix C.3.1). The reader should note that the *freeVars* function on sequents is defined differently in the two specifications: in the Walk sequent variables are considered to be 'bound' by the turnstile.

Rules, theories, signatures and well-formedness

Table 4.2 shows the rough correspondence between definitions of the main functions from Sections 4.5 to 4.6 and their counterparts in the FullSpec. The status of a rule (Section 4.5.2) is not discussed in the FullSpec, and neither specification treats the classification of rules as theorems or lemmas. Similarly, there is no exact equivalent to contexts (Section 4.6.3) in the FullSpec, nor are metavariables explicitly listed in *Rule*s (cf. *Rule$_2$* in Section 4.6.2).

Proofs

The two specifications take different approaches to the definitions of lines and boxes in proofs, quite apart from the fact that the FullSpec manipulates references (pointers). In

Walk	Section	FullSpec	Appendix
boxVars	4.7.1	*newFreeVarsOfBox*	C.8.2
$\prec$		*isSubbox*	C.8.1
inv-Proof$_0$		*inv-Boxmap*	C.8.1
inv-Proof$_1$	4.7.2	*hasClosedJustifs*	C.8.2
$l \in_p b$		$l \in linesOfBox(p, b)$	C.8.2
Hyps-of		*hypsOfBox*	C.8.2
Has-wfd-assertion	4.7.3	*isReasonableAtLine*	C.8.7
inv-Rule$_4$		*is-OK-Rule* $\wedge$ *isComplete* (part)	C.3.2,C.8.9
inv-Proof$_2$	4.7.4	*isWfdProof*	C.8.5
$\prec$		*dependsOnLine*	C.8.5
inv-RuleJustif	4.7.5	*hasInstantiableRule*	C.8.3
Is-properly-justified		*isJustifiedLine*	C.8.9
inv-Rule$_6$		$\forall ol \cdot isOK(justif(ol))$	C.8.3
Is-known(l)	4.7.6	$assumptionsOfLine(l) = \{\,\}$	C.8.6
Is-complete		*isComplete*	C.8.9
Rules-used		*antecedents*	C.9.1
Assumptions	4.7.7	*assumptionsOfLine*	C.8.6

Table 4.3: Functions and predicates on proofs.

the Walk, lines are assigned to boxes by a mapping

$$lbMap: Proof \rightarrow (VSymb \xrightarrow{m} Box_1)$$

whereas in the FullSpec, lines are a direct attribute of boxes – viz.

$$LINES: Box \rightarrow (Ordline\text{-}ref \xrightarrow{m} Ordline)$$

A second difference is that box variables are an attribute of boxes in the Walk

$$boxVars: Box_1 \rightarrow VSymb\text{-set}$$

but are instead assigned to boxes by a mapping

$$NFV: Proof \rightarrow (VSymb \xrightarrow{m} Box\text{-}ref)$$

in the FullSpec.

With these differences in mind, Table 4.3 gives the rough correspondence between definitions in the Walk and their counterparts in the FullSpec. Note that there is no exact equivalent to *inv-Proof$_3$* in the FullSpec, and the definition of rule justifications (Section 4.7.5) is considerably simplified by ignoring theory morphisms (cf. Appendix C.8.3).

4.11 Limitations of the *mural* approach

In this section we summarize the main theoretical limitations of the *mural* approach and look at what might be done to overcome them in future incarnations.

4.11.1 Syntax

Aside from constraints on the concrete syntax, the following seem to us to be the main areas where the *mural* syntax is more restrictive than common 'pencil and paper' practice:

1. Certain syntactic conventions can't be supported, especially those which elide information and rely on the reader's implicit understanding: e.g. throughout Section 4.7.4 it was much more convenient to write $l_1 \prec l_2$ instead of $l_1 \prec_p l_2$, since p could always be inferred from context.

2. Essentially only one form of variable binding is supplied. This means that 'letrec-expressions' which involve mutually recursive bindings cannot generally be supported. It is also not really expressive enough to accurately capture the binding of program variables in Hoare triples.

3. Simultaneous multiple bindings such as $\forall x, y, z: \mathsf{N} \cdot \ldots$ are not supported. The restriction to single bindings was considered acceptable for our target applications, since multiple bindings could be achieved as nested single bindings (cf. Section 3.2.4). The resulting notation

$$\forall x: \mathsf{N} \cdot \forall y: \mathsf{N} \cdot \forall z: \mathsf{N} \cdot \ldots$$

   is somewhat cumbersome however; a more flexible display mechanism might help here, but would involve rethinking a number of our design decisions.[23]

4. The constraint that the 'universe' of a binding be a *Type* can also be awkward at times: cf. set comprehension (Section 3.4.1), 'let' clauses (Section 3.5.2).

5. In *mural*, defined binders take formal parameters for both universe and body: i.e. the left-hand side of a binder definition is always essentially of the form

$$\mho x: A \cdot G[x] \triangleq \ldots$$

   (although of course different concrete syntax declarations are possible). The 'two parameter' principle was adopted since it covers the most common defined binders while respecting the 'conservation of information' principle for folding/unfolding operations (i.e. the same formal parameters are used on both sides of a definition).

   Unfortunately, there are times when it would be better to use a fixed universe. Consider e.g. the operator

$$\mu n: \mathsf{N} \cdot P[n] \triangleq \iota x: \mathsf{N} \cdot (P[x] \wedge \forall y: \mathsf{N} \cdot y < x \Rightarrow \neg\, P[y])$$

   which finds the least number n (if any) satisfying $P[n]$. Under the existing mechanism the definition must be given in terms of an arbitrary type A, which carries the danger that A might be instantiated by a type for which '$<$' is not defined.

---

[23]Note that simultaneous bindings are not the whole answer anyway: e.g. branching bindings such as

$$\begin{pmatrix} \forall x \exists y \\ \forall u \exists v \end{pmatrix} \cdot P[x, y, u, v]$$

cannot be expressed in terms of simultaneous bindings; Skolem functions are even more general.

6. Defined dependent types are not supported at all. This was an 'economy of design' decision (read: laziness on our part) rather than because of any theoretical problems: defined binders gave us enough headaches, and we couldn't think of any defined dependent types that weren't rather contrived.

7. It's sometimes rather restrictive to insist on fixed arities for function symbols and type constructors. The first example that springs to mind is the use of function names on their own (without arguments) in higher order logics: e.g.

$$OneOneFunctions \triangleq \ <f\colon \mathsf{N} \to \mathsf{N} \mid \forall x\colon \mathsf{N} \cdot \forall y\colon \mathsf{N} \cdot x \neq y \ \Rightarrow \ f(x) \neq f(y) >$$

But, as shown in Section 3.6.1, the problem is illusory, at least in this case: the solution is to introduce an explicit 'function application' operator; the concrete syntax facility can even be used to display $apply(f, x)$ as $f(x)$.

8. A more serious problem arises with (for example) associative-commutative (AC) operators, where it would be convenient to allow arbitrary numbers (≥ 2) of arguments. An example would be a summation operator *sum*, with $sum(x_1, x_2, \ldots, x_n)$ displayed as

$$x_1 + x_2 + \ldots + x_n$$

say. Other candidates for operators with non-fixed arity would be associative operators, case statements and guarded conditionals. Note that what is being proposed here is a significant extension to the *abstract* syntax – not simply a new way of displaying $sum(cons(x_1, \ldots))$. In particular, new unification and matching algorithms would have to be written, and many of the *mural* design decisions would have to be rethought. It is an extension which is thought to merit serious research effort.

9. It would also be very useful to extend the syntax to cover indexing, such as

$$\text{let } rk_i = mk\text{-}RKey(nm_i, fs_i, ts_i) \text{ in } \ldots rk_1 \ldots rk_2 \ldots$$

4.11.2   Rules

A frequent comment we receive is that it would be useful to allow rules to have multiple conclusions. Unfortunately, the proponents of this view cannot agree on an interpretation: should conclusion set $\{P, Q, R\}$ be regarded as meaning that *all* of P, Q and R hold, or as meaning that (at least) one of P, Q and R holds? There are good reasons for both interpretations. We resisted joining the argument since an extension to multiple conclusions would undoubtedly have made the *mural* User Interface (even) more complicated.

A less frequently received comment was that it would be useful to allow 'arbitrary nesting' of sequents – so that e.g. a sequent could have another sequent as its premise. Such an approach is explored for example in [Sch84]. No great practical benefit seems to accrue beyond one level of nesting, however; in fact, for the *mural* target logics there is demonstrably *no* increase in expressive power, since a sequent

$$\{p_1, \ldots, p_n\} \vdash_{x_1, \ldots, x_m} \text{ upshot}$$

is essentially equivalent to the formula

$$\forall x_1, \ldots, x_m \cdot (p_1 \wedge \ldots \wedge p_n \ \Rightarrow \ \text{upshot})$$

This is not to say that sequents should be done away with altogether, of course, since they are essential to the efficacy of Natural Deduction as a proof system, leading to 'block-structured' proofs: cf. the discussion in Section 4.3.1.

A broader interpretation of 'sequent' – whereby 'sequent variables' stand for (or are 'instantiable' by) arbitrary terms (from *Exp*) rather than simply arbitrary variables (from *VSymb*) – was discussed in Section 4.3.4. Again, in the case of the *mural* target logics, the narrower interpretation does not sacrifice any expressive power; on the other hand, it quite considerably simplifies certain algorithms (such as checking whether a subproof establishes a sequent hypothesis) and certain aspects of the User Interface (such as rule instantiations).

4.11.3 Logics

In essence, *mural* provides support for those many-sorted predicate calculi which can be expressed in Natural Deduction format. As we have seen, this is a large class covering by far the most commonly used logics in software engineering. There are certain logics which can *not* however be expressed in Natural Deduction format, particularly the so-called *non-monotonic logics* – logics in which the addition of new assumptions can invalidate existing deductions (as for example in a logic of evidence in jurisprudence). To date, the contribution of such logics to software engineering has been negligible.

A more serious limitation of *mural* is that it only supports *direct* derivations of rules: that is, new rules are built essentially by fitting together (instantiations of) other rules; see the discussion in Section 3.2.2. This excludes a large class of rules that could be deduced by more sophisticated 'meta-reasoning'. Apart from the obvious methodological advantages of direct derivation – it's hard to imagine a User Interface for general meta-reasoning for a start – it was felt to be important to make *mural* an 'open' system whereby the user could build new theories by extending existing theories, simply inheriting results from the latter. No extension will ever invalidate a direct derivation of a rule, whereas most indirect (meta-) results assume a fixed ('closed') theory.

Paraphrasing, we could say that *mural* is a *generic* proof assistant rather than a 'full worldview' system. Without attempting to define these terms, the latter would support reasoning *about* itself, so that for example its meta-theory could be formalized within itself and used to derive meta-theorems, which could subsequently be applied to its object logics. This is true to a certain extent of logical frames with formalized meta-theories, such as ELF.[24] By contrast, the *mural* tactic mechanism – like that of its predecessor LCF [GMW79] – supports meta-reasoning by allowing the user to form 'proof templates' which can be rerun in different situations.

---

[24]In an interesting departure from the usual meta-theory/object theory dichotomy, Weyhrauch [Wey80] explores the use of 'reflection principles' to allow a theory to reason about itself.

Chapter 5

The tactic language

5.1 Mechanising proof in *mural*

It is perfectly possible to conduct all proofs in the *mural* proof assistant using only the single-step-at-a-time strategy provided by the justification tool; this can, however, become tedious. It was therefore felt advantageous to provide an additional layer of functionality whereby the user can interact with the system using 'large scale' operations.

The method by which *mural* (and indeed most other comparable systems) achieves this higher level interaction is to provide a *tactic language*. The tactic language is essentially a kind of programming language which has access to the same functions (or a superset thereof) which are visible at the user interface level, and some control constructs or *tacticals* for composing sequences of these functions into *tactics*. Tactics and the tactic language, therefore, present the user with a language flexible enough to express the equivalent of arbitrary sequences of (UI level) interactions and, more importantly, to 'code up' algorithms or strategies which can search for things (e.g. rules to apply, definitions to unfold), possibly using backtracking to try alternative approaches, thus providing the user with facilities for a limited (but customisable) mechanical theorem proving capability.

The approaches to tactics taken in other interactive theorem proving systems have been quite diverse, with LCF and its derivatives being among the best known. In the LCF (see [Sok83]) and Isabelle [Nip89] systems, tactics are effectively written in the functional language ML; tactics are ML functions and are written using the provided tacticals and built in tactics, which implement operations like resolution, sequencing, repetition, depth- and breadth-first searching and so on. All this provides the LCF and Isabelle systems with a fairly rich and powerful tactic language. In the ωp Logic Environment (developed at Imperial College, London) [Daw88] the only means of interacting with proofs is by writing *strategies* – a very simple form of tactics somewhat akin to regular expressions[1]. Strategies can repeatedly apply a set (or sequence) of rules to a proof, try applying a set of rules until one succeeds, or try applying a rule once. The only 'tactical-like' feature is that strategies can be sequentially composed and repeatedly applied. Additional constraints can be applied like 'first try using inference rules with only one hypothesis' (to reduce branching in the proof tree). The strategy mechanism, impoverished as it is, seems to be quite successful in the context of ωp; in *mural*, however, tactics of this kind would not really be powerful enough since the structure of proofs (and the possible modes of interaction with them) is rather more complicated.

---

[1] A similar approach is taken in the **B-tool** – the sole purpose of the 'theory structure' in **B** is to partition conjectures so that the same set of tactics is likely to be applicable to each proof in the theory.

This chapter describes the *mural* tactic system, both from the point of view of the syntax and semantics of the tactic language itself and of how this language is used to write tactics. Some user-interface issues, such as how to operate the tools provided for editing and invoking tactics are covered.

Tactics provide the *mural* user with a method of encoding commonly used strategies for doing proofs as procedures in a procedural programming language – the *tactic language*. These strategies can either be very domain specific (such as setting up a particular kind of induction step) or more general (such as 'given a set of inference rules, try applying them backwards to all unproved lines in the proof').

A *mural* user will see the tactics as being closely integrated with the rest of the system even though the formal model of the 'core' (see Chapter 4) makes no reference to tactics. Tactics seem to be valid only in certain theories (e.g. equational reasoning tactics will only be useful in theories where equality has been defined), so a possible implementation (**the** implementation!) would attach tactics to the theory hierarchy in a similar way to rules; a tactic is therefore inherited by descendents of the theory to which it is attached[2]. This is, of course, not the only way tactics could be attached to the theory hierarchy[3], but it seems a flexible enough approach to cope with most situations which actually arise.

5.2   The language

A tactic is rather like a procedure in a (imperative) programming language; it has a *name* (a string), some *parameters*, a *body* and it may return a result[4]. The formal parameters of a tactic are pairs consisting of a variable and a type. The type is a symbol from the set { SEQOFPROOFOBJECT, SEQOFRULE, ARBITRARY }, and is simply there so that the user interface can correctly enforce the types of arguments when a tactic is invoked. Some run-time type checking is performed for some language constructs (e.g. the primitive operations and operators), but not for whole tactics. The body of a tactic is a sequence of statements (the various kinds of which are described below). The variables used in tactic language constructs are not typed, nor are they declared, and the scope of a variable is the entire tactic in which it is used (with *holes* in the scope whenever other tactics are called). The parameter variables to a tactic and the loop variable of the iterative constructs (for-some, for-each statements and binder expressions) are considered *bound* (for the duration of the tactic and construct respectively), which means any attempt to re-assign the variable's value (by explicit assignment or by another iterative construct) will result in a run-time error. The set of values which can be passed as arguments to tactics, or assigned to variables, or returned as a result of evaluating tactics or tactic language expressions includes mural objects (rules, expressions, etc.) the Boolean values (true and false), nil, integers, sets and lists of these, maps containing these objects in their domain and range, and indices for accessing and manipulating *mural* subterms[5].

---

[2]Although tactics are inherited via the theory hierarchy, the notion of translating tactics over theory morphisms was not considered useful, and has not been developed.

[3]For instance the *mural* store could contain a collection of tactics alongside the theories it already contains, and each tactic could have stored with it the arbitrary collection of theories in which it can be used.

[4]In fact all tactics return a result – the value of *result variable* of that tactic at the time the tactic finishes execution. If no result need be returned, then the result variable is left unassigned

[5]Note that tactics are not themselves included in this class of values – this means that the tactic language is not *higher order* in the way that ML tactics (cf. LCF, Isabelle, etc.) are. The examples which have been

5.2.1 Abstract syntax

In this section we define the abstract syntax of the tactic language, from the level of tactics and tacticals (called statements in the terminology of *mural* tactics) right down to the level of expressions. In several places the language requires conditionals (Boolean valued expressions), but here everything on this level is lumped together into one class of *TacticExpression*s, and it will be left to the semantic functions to check things have the correct value or type at 'run time'.

Hopefully the meanings of most of the language constructs introduced should be fairly intuitively clear. Further description and a specification of an interpreter for the language are presented in Section 5.2.2.

Tactics

$$
\begin{aligned}
Tactic :: \quad &ARGS \quad : Variable^* \\
&RESULT : Variable \\
&BODY \quad : TacticBody
\end{aligned}
$$

A tactic has a list of argument variables (where *Variable* is just some class of structureless tokens or spellings or something), a result variable – rather like the heading of an operation in VDM – and a *TacticBody*, which is simply a sequence of statements forming the 'code' of the tactic. Additionally, each tactic will be associated with a name, so that tactics can refer to (and call) each other. The name is not considered to be a property of the tactic itself, but of the environment in which it is executed, and is thus reflected in the specification of the interpreter in Section 5.2.2 rather than at the level of tactics.

$$TacticBody = Statement^*$$

Statements

Statement forms the (fixed) class of tacticals supported by the system. It is hoped that this set of tacticals is sufficiently rich that the user will not feel the need to define new ones. This partially removes the need to make tactics 'higher order'.

$$
\begin{aligned}
Statement = &Assignment \mid IfStatement \mid WhileStatement \mid ForEachStatement \mid \\
&ForSomeStatement \mid TryStatement \mid Call \mid \\
&RepeatUntilNothingChanges
\end{aligned}
$$

A *SKIP* statement is not really needed (for instance, in a situation where the *Else* part of an *If* statement is absent), since an empty *TacticBody* will do the same thing (i.e. nothing).

$$
\begin{aligned}
Assignment :: \quad &VAR \quad : Variable \\
&VALUE : TacticExpression
\end{aligned}
$$

$$
\begin{aligned}
IfStatement :: \quad &IF \quad : TacticExpression \\
&THEN : TacticBody \\
&ELSE : TacticBody
\end{aligned}
$$

$$
\begin{aligned}
WhileStatement :: \quad &WHILE : TacticExpression \\
&DO \quad : TacticBody
\end{aligned}
$$

---

tried suggest that this is not a serious restriction.

The meaning of *If*, *While* and *Assignment* statements should be intuitively fairly clear, since such things exist in many programming languages. The other kinds of statements, however, may be less familiar. The *ForEach* and *ForSome* statements are iterative constructs corresponding more-or-less to the existential and universal quantifiers of predicate logic.

ForEachStatement :: *BOUND*   : *Variable*
                      UNIVERSE : *TacticExpression*
                      DO   : *TacticBody*

ForSomeStatement :: *BOUND*   : *Variable*
                       UNIVERSE   : *TacticExpression*
                       DO   : *TacticBody*
                       OTHERWISE : *TacticBody*

TryStatement :: *TRY*   : *TacticBody*
                   COND : *TacticExpression*

The *Try* statement is a backtracking construct which allows *mural* tactics to try alternative strategies for constructing proofs. Once a strategy has been tried, the proof reverts to its previous state if the given condition is not satisfied.

Call = *TacticCall* | *MuralCall*

TacticCall :: *FUNC* : *TacticName*
                 ARGS : *TacticExpression**

MuralCall :: *FUNC* : *MuralOperationName*
               ARGS : *TacticExpression**

These *Call* statements correspond roughly to procedure calls, and come in two varieties: *TacticCalls*, which are calls to other (user-defined) tactics, and *MuralCalls*, which cause the execution of functions which are built into the tactic language. *MuralOperationName* refers here to the set of operations and functions which are available for use by tactics – see Section 5.2.3.

RepeatUntilNothingChanges :: *BODY* : *TacticBody*

Expressions

TacticExpression = *Variable* | *Constant* | *Unary* | *Binary* | *Pair* | *Call* |
                      MuralObject | *Comprehension* | *Make* | *Universal* | *Existential*

The meaning of variables, constants, unaries, binaries and pairs is fairly straightforward; *Calls* are calls to *mural* functions or to other tactics (which when executed as expressions return a value); *Comprehension*, *Universal* and *Existential* represent set comprehension, universal and existential quantification respectively and *Make* is intended to be similar to the VDM *mk-* function (useful mainly for building justifications). *MuralObject* allows the user to reference *mural* objects directly from within the tactic language (particularly expressions and types).

Constant = {{ }, [ ], true, false, nil}

The class of constants includes the empty set and the empty list, the Boolean values true and false, and the literal nil.

Unary :: *OPERATOR* : *UnarySymbol*
        ARG   : *TacticExpression*

UnarySymbol = {¬, hd, tl, last, { }, [ ], fst, snd, IsEmpty, NotEmpty, OneOf}

The unary symbols are negation, head, tail, last (operators on lists), unit sets and lists[6], first and second projection functions for pairs, tests for whether a collection is empty, and a *OneOf* operator which non-deterministically returns an element of a collection.

Binary :: *OPERATOR* : *BinarySymbol*
         *ARG*1   : *TacticExpression*
         *ARG*2   : *TacticExpression*

BinarySymbol = {∪, ∩, ∈, ∉, ⊂, ⊆, =, ≠, ∧, ∨, +, −, *, /}

The binary symbols include a variety of operators on sets, lists and numbers. The elements of *Constant*, *UnarySymbol* and *BinarySymbol* are just tokens or spellings, rather than operators of the VDM language. The intention is that unary and binary expressions are those which operate on the basic tactic language types (sets, lists etc.,) whereas the *MuralCalls* operate on *mural* objects, or, more generally, on the *mural* proof state.

Pair :: *FST* : *TacticExpression*
        SND : *TacticExpression*

MuralObject = *Rule* | *RuleStmt* | *Exp* | *Type* | *Justification* | *Symb* ...

The type *MuralObject* is provided so that tactics can directly refer to and manipulate the expressions, types, symbols, rules and so on, of the *mural* language as defined in Appendix C.

Comprehension :: *VAR*   : *Variable*
               UNIVERSE : *TacticExpression*
               PRED   : *TacticExpression*

Make :: *CLASS* : *MuralType*
        FIELDS : *TacticExpression**

MuralType = *RuleJustif, SeqHypJustif, FoldDefJustif* ...

Universal :: *VAR*   : *Variable*
           UNIVERSE : *TacticExpression*
           PRED   : *TacticExpression*

Existential :: *VAR*   : *Variable*
            UNIVERSE : *TacticExpression*
            PRED   : *TacticExpression*

---

[6]The unary symbols { } and [ ] are used to mean the symbols occurring in expressions like {*X*} and [*X*] – kind of 'out-fix' unary operators.

5.2.2   The tactic interpreter

The semantics of the language are defined by a set of evaluation operations which effectively execute language terms, inducing a change in the state (e.g. the proof and the tactic language variable bindings), and in some cases returning a result. These operations could form the basis for a specification of a tactic language interpreter.

A couple of extra data types will be needed to keep track of variable bindings and the proof state. First, the *Environment* keeps both a mapping from variables to their (assigned) values and a set of 'bound' variables (i.e. those variables which cannot be assigned to, including variables bound by *ForSome/ForEach* constructs and the parameter variables to tactics).

$$Environment :: VALUES : Variable \xrightarrow{m} Value$$
$$BOUND : Variable\text{-set}$$

where *Value* is the set of values returned by evaluating *TacticExpressions* – see below. Secondly, the *State* holds (references to[7]) the proof, theory and *mural* store[8] on which the tactic execution is invoked, together with a map containing all tactics which are 'accessible' from that theory. From the point of view of this specification, *TacticName* needs only to be an infinite set of tokens, much the same as the *Symb* thingies in the *mural* specification. In an implementation they could be the actual names a user sees.

$$
\begin{aligned}
State :: \ &PROOF &&: Proof \\
&THEORY &&: Theory \\
&MURALSTORE &&: Store \\
&TACTICSTORE &&: TacticName \xrightarrow{m} Tactic
\end{aligned}
$$

Two new types must be introduced to represent the objects returned when expressions are evaluated by the interpreter. The type *Value* includes the evaluations of all tactic expressions, and *ValuePair* contains the evaluations of *Pair* expressions.

$$Value = MuralObject \mid \mathbb{B} \mid Value\text{-set} \mid Value^* \mid ValuePair \mid \{nil\} \mid Index$$

$$ValuePair :: FST : Value$$
$$SND : Value$$

Many of the evaluation operations have preconditions which either do some form of type checking or test whether certain variables are bound; they need not, however, be preconditions in the usual VDM sense, but simply specify the 'run time error checker' (described in Section 5.3.1). This is an important point since it means that the evaluation function will not in general be satisfiable in the formal sense of [Jon90a]. The reason for this kind of presentation is partly that it is a shorthand, and partly that it neatly encapsulates the execution and error checking functions for each term of the language.

Tactics

---

[7]If it was necessary for this specification to resemble the *mural* specification more closely, the *State* would have a *Proof-ref* etc.

[8]The store is probably only needed to fit in with the way many *mural* operations and functions are specified.

TacEvaluate (*t*: *Tactic*) *r*: *Value*
ext rd E : *Environment*
   wr S : *State*
pre rng $ARGS(t) \subseteq$ dom $VALUES(E)$
post let *env* =
        $mk\text{-}Environment(((\text{rng } ARGS(t) \lhd VALUES(\overleftarrow{E})) \dagger \{RESULT(t) \mapsto \text{nil}\}),$
                                      $(\text{rng } ARGS(t)))$ in
   $\exists newenv\text{: } Environment \cdot$
      $post\text{-}BlockEvaluate(BODY(t), env, \overleftarrow{S}, newenv, S) \wedge$
      $r = VALUES(newenv)(RESULT(t))$

Note that the assumption here is that there can be no non-local accessing of variables –
variables are local to one tactic (hence the domain restriction of the environment), and
values can only be shared by passing parameters. If it were considered necessary, a change
to this postcondition could allow global or other non-local variables.

BlockEvaluate (*b*: *TacticBody*)
ext wr E : *Environment*
   wr S : *State*
post if $b = [\,]$
   then $E = \overleftarrow{E} \wedge S = \overleftarrow{S}$
   else $\exists E'\text{: } Environment, S'\text{: } State \cdot$
         $post\text{-}StatEvaluate(\text{hd } b, \overleftarrow{E}, \overleftarrow{S}, E', S') \wedge$
         $post\text{-}BlockEvaluate(\text{tl } b, E', S', E, S)$

Statements

StatEvaluate (*s*: *Statement*)
ext wr E : *Environment*
   wr S : *State*
post cases *s* of

IfStatement	$\rightarrow post\text{-}IfEvaluate(s, \overleftarrow{E}, \overleftarrow{S}, E, S)$
WhileStatement	$\rightarrow post\text{-}WhileEvaluate(s, \overleftarrow{E}, \overleftarrow{S}, E, S)$
ForSomeStatement	$\rightarrow post\text{-}ForSomeEvaluate(s, \overleftarrow{E}, \overleftarrow{S}, E, S)$
TryStatement	$\rightarrow post\text{-}TryEvaluate(s, \overleftarrow{E}, \overleftarrow{S}, E, S)$
Assignment	$\rightarrow post\text{-}AssignmentEvaluate(s, \overleftarrow{E}, \overleftarrow{S}, E, S)$
Call	$\rightarrow post\text{-}CallEvaluate(s, \overleftarrow{E}, \overleftarrow{S}, E, S)$
ForEachStatement	$\rightarrow post\text{-}ForEachEvaluate((s, \overleftarrow{E}, \overleftarrow{S}, E, S)$
RepeatUntilNothingChanges	$\rightarrow post\text{-}RepeatEvaluate((s, \overleftarrow{E}, \overleftarrow{S}, E, S)$

end

AssignmentEvaluate (*a*: *Assignment*)
ext wr E : *Environment*
   wr S : *State*
pre $VAR(a) \notin BOUND(E)$

post $\exists v\colon Value \cdot$

$\qquad$ $post\text{-}ExpEvaluate(VALUE(a),\overleftarrow{E},\overleftarrow{S},S,v) \wedge$

$\qquad$ $E = mk\text{-}Environment((VALUES(\overleftarrow{E}) \dagger \{VAR(a) \mapsto v\}), BOUND(\overleftarrow{E}))$

IfEvaluate (i: IfStatement)
ext wr E : *Environment*
$\quad$ wr S : *State*
pre $\exists S'\colon State, v\colon \mathsf{B} \cdot post\text{-}ExpEvaluate(IF(i), E, S, S', v)$
post $\exists S'\colon State, v\colon \mathsf{B} \cdot$

$\qquad$ $post\text{-}ExpEvaluate(IF(i),\overleftarrow{E},\overleftarrow{S},S',v) \wedge$
$\qquad$ if v
$\qquad$ then $post\text{-}BlockEvaluate(THEN(i),\overleftarrow{E},S',E,S)$
$\qquad$ else $post\text{-}BlockEvaluate(ELSE(i),\overleftarrow{E},S',E,S)$

WhileEvaluate (w: WhileStatement)
ext wr E : *Environment*
$\quad$ wr S : *State*
pre $\exists S'\colon State, v\colon \mathsf{B} \cdot post\text{-}ExpEvaluate(WHILE(w), E, S, S', v)$
post $\exists S'\colon State, v\colon \mathsf{B} \cdot post\text{-}ExpEvaluate(WHILE(w),\overleftarrow{E},\overleftarrow{S},S',v) \wedge$

$\qquad$ if v
$\qquad$ then $\exists E''\colon Environment, S''\colon State \cdot$

$\qquad\qquad$ $post\text{-}BlockEvaluate(DO(w),\overleftarrow{E},S',E'',S'') \wedge$
$\qquad\qquad$ $post\text{-}WhileEvaluate(w, E'', S'', E, S)$

$\qquad$ else $(E = \overleftarrow{E} \wedge S = S')$

ForEachEvaluate (f: ForEachStatement)
ext wr E : *Environment*
$\quad$ wr S : *State*
pre $\exists S'\colon State, v\colon Value\text{-set} \mid Value^* \cdot post\text{-}ExpEvaluate(UNIVERSE(f), E, S, S', v) \wedge$
$\quad$ $BOUND(f) \notin BOUND(E)$
post $\exists S'\colon State, v\colon Value\text{-set} \mid Value^* \cdot$

$\qquad$ $post\text{-}ExpEvaluate(UNIVERSE(f),\overleftarrow{E},\overleftarrow{S},S',v) \wedge$
$\qquad$ let $v' = $ if $v\colon Value^*$ then v else $asList(v)$
$\qquad\quad$ in
$\qquad$ if $v' = \{\}$
$\qquad$ then $E = \overleftarrow{E} \wedge S = S'$
$\qquad$ else $post\text{-}SequenceEvaluate(v', BOUND(f), DO(f),\overleftarrow{E},S',E,S)$

The following two functions convert a set into a list, and repeatedly evaluate a block of statements with a different assignment of values to a variable respectively.

asList (s: Value-set) l: seqofValue
post rng $l = s \wedge$ card $s = $ len l

SequenceEvaluate (seq: Value*, var: Variable, block: TacticBody)

ext wr E : *Environment*
    wr S : *State*

post let *env* = *mk-Environment*($VALUES(\overleftarrow{E})$ † {*var* ↦ hd *seq*},

$$BOUND(\overleftarrow{E}) \cup \{var\}) \text{ in}$$

if *seq* = [ ]
then $E = \overleftarrow{E} \wedge S = \overleftarrow{S}$
else ∃E': *Environment*, S': *State* ·

post-*BlockEvaluate*(*block*, *env*, $\overleftarrow{S}$, E', S') ∧
post-*SequenceEvaluate*(tl *seq*, *var*, *block*, E', S', E, S)

ForSomeEvaluate (*f*: *ForSomeStatement*)
ext wr E : *Environment*
    wr S : *State*

pre ∃S': *State*, v: *Value*-set | *Value** · post-*ExpEvaluate*($UNIVERSE(f)$, E, S, S', v) ∧
    $BOUND(f) \notin BOUND(E)$

post ∃S': *State*, v: *Value*-set | *Value** ·

post-*ExpEvaluate*($UNIVERSE(f)$, $\overleftarrow{E}$, $\overleftarrow{S}$, S', v) ∧
let v' = if v: *Value*-set then v else rng v
    in

if v' = { }
then post-*BlockEvaluate*($OTHERWISE(f)$, $\overleftarrow{E}$, S', E, S)
else ∃$e \in v'$, E'': *Environment* ·

let *newE* = *mk-Environment*(($VALUES(\overleftarrow{E})$†{$BOUND(f) \mapsto e$}),

$$(BOUND(\overleftarrow{E}) \cup \{BOUND(f)\})) \text{ in}$$
post-*BlockEvaluate*($DO(f)$, *newE*, S', E'', S) ∧
$E = $ *mk-Environment*(($BOUND(f) \triangleleft VALUES(E'')$), $BOUND(\overleftarrow{E})$)

TryEvaluate (*t*: *TryStatement*)
ext wr E : *Environment*
    wr S : *State*

post ∃E': *Environment*, S': *State* · post-*BlockEvaluate*($TRY(t)$, $\overleftarrow{E}$, $\overleftarrow{S}$, E', S') ∧
    ∃S'': *State*, v: *Value* ·
        post-*ExpEvaluate*($COND(t)$, E', S', S'', v)
        if v = true
        then $E = E' \wedge S = S''$
        else $E = \overleftarrow{E} \wedge S = \overleftarrow{S}$

In the evaluation of a *TryStatement* the type of the condition is not checked in the pre-condition − unlike most of the other cases where tests, sets and other expression sub-components must evaluate to the correct type. This is for simplicity since the condition must be evaluated *after* the block of statements. Thus if the condition part evaluates to true then execution continues normally; otherwise (if the condition evaluates to *anything* other than true) backtracking occurs, in which case the proof reverts to the state it was in before execution of the statement began.

CallEvaluate (*c*: *Call*) *r*: *Value*
ext wr E : *Environment*
   wr S : *State*
post cases *c* of

    MuralCall → *MuralCallEvaluate*(*c*, $\overleftarrow{E}$, $\overleftarrow{S}$, *E*, *S*, *r*)
    TacticCall → *post-TacticCallEvaluate*(*c*, $\overleftarrow{E}$, $\overleftarrow{S}$, *E*, *S*, *r*)
    Make   → *post-MakeEvaluate*(*c*, $\overleftarrow{E}$, $\overleftarrow{S}$, *E*, *S*, *r*)
    end

Plenty of checks could be put in the precondition for call evaluation (arity checks, making sure the name in a *TacticCall* is actually in the *TACTICSTORE*, etc.). Note that the operation *CallEvaluate* is the only one in this section which returns a result. What happens to this result in an actual execution will depend on the context in which the call occurs – if the call is 'acting as an expression' (e.g. if it occurs as the *VALUE* part of an assignment statement) then its result will be used by the surrounding statement or expression; if it is acting as a statement then the result is ignored. *MuralCallEvaluate* does exactly what the name suggests – executes (or asserts the postcondition of) a function/operation in *mural* (see Section 5.2.3). *MakeEvaluate* is not specified, but it simply constructs a new element of a particular *mural* type. *TacticCallEvaluate* allows a named tactic to be called from within another tactic.

TacticCallEvaluate (*c*: *TacticCall*) *r*: *Value*
ext rd E : *Environment*
   wr S : *State*
pre ∃*tac*: *Tactic* ·

       TACTICSTORE($\overleftarrow{S}$)(*FUNC*(*c*)) = *tac* ∧ len *ARGS*(*c*) = len *ARGS*(*tac*)

post let *tac* = *TACTICSTORE*($\overleftarrow{S}$)(*FUNC*(*c*)) in
    ∃*S'*: *State* ·
       post-ExpListEvaluate(*ARGS*(*c*), *E*, $\overleftarrow{S}$, *S*, *argList*) ∧
       ∃*env*: *Environment* ·
          rng *ARGS*(*tac*) ⊆ dom *VALUES*(*env*) ∧
          ∀*i* ∈ dom *argList* · *VALUES*(*env*)(*ARGS*(*tac*)[*i*]) = *argList*[*i*] ∧
          ∃*newenv*: *Environment* ·
             post-TacEvaluate(*tac*, *env*, *S'*, *newenv*, *S*, *r*)

ExpListEvaluate (*seq*: *TacticExpression**) *r*: *Value**
ext rd E : *Environment*
   wr S : *State*
post if *seq* = [ ]
   then *r* = [ ]
   else ∃*S'*: *State*, *h*: *Value*, *t*: *Value** ·

       post-ExpEvaluate(hd *seq*, *E*, $\overleftarrow{S}$, *S'*, *h*) ∧
       post-ExpListEvaluate(tl *seq*, *E*, *S'*, *S*, *t*) ∧
       r = cons(*h*, *t*)

RepeatEvaluate (*r*: *RepeatUntilNothingChanges*)

ext wr E : *Environment*
    wr S : *State*
post $\exists S'$: *State, E': Environment* ·

      post-BlockEvaluate(BODY(r), $\overleftarrow{E}$, $\overleftarrow{S}$, E', S') $\wedge$
      if *AreEquivalentStates($\overleftarrow{S}$, S')*
      then $E = E' \wedge S = S'$
      else *post-RepeatEvaluate(r, E', S', E, S)*

AreEquivalentStates is not specified, but is essentially a function with signature *State* ×
State → B which decides if the proofs of the two states are 'the same'.

Expressions

Most of the evaluation operations for expressions are fairly simple, so here's a couple
of examples (mostly with the the preconditions missing). Note that all the evaluation
functions for expressions have read-only access to the environment (since they cannot
assign to variables) but require both read and write access to the state (since they can
change the proof by means of *mural* calls).

ExpEvaluate (e: TacticExpression) r: Value
ext rd E : *Environment*
    wr S : *State*
post cases e of
    $\vdots$
    Pair   → *post-PairEvaluate(e, E, $\overleftarrow{S}$, S, r)*
    Binary   → *post-BinaryEvaluate(e, E, $\overleftarrow{S}$, S, r)*
    MuralObject → *post-MuralObjectEvaluate(e, E, $\overleftarrow{S}$, S, r)*
    $\vdots$
    end

PairEvaluate (p: Pair) r: Value
ext rd E : *Environment*
    wr S : *State*
pre true
post $\exists S'$: *State, f, s: Value* ·

      post-ExpEvaluate(FST(p), E, $\overleftarrow{S}$, S', f) $\wedge$
      post-ExpEvaluate(SND(p), E, $\overleftarrow{S}$, S', s) $\wedge$
      $r = $ *mk-ValuePair(f, s)*

BinaryEvaluate (b: Binary) r: Value
ext rd E : *Environment*
    wr S : *State*

post cases *OPERATOR*(*b*) of

⋮

∪ → *post-UnionEvaluate*(*ARG*1(*b*), *ARG*2(*b*), *E*, $\overleftarrow{S}$, *S*, *r*)

⋮

end

UnionEvaluate (*a*, *b*: *TacticExpression*) *r*: *Value*-set
ext rd *E* : *Environment*
   wr *S* : *State*
pre ∃*S'*: *State*, *f*, *s*: *Value*-set ·

    post-ExpEvaluate(*a*, $\overleftarrow{E}$, $\overleftarrow{S}$, *E'*, *S'*, *f*) ∧
    post-ExpEvaluate(*b*, *E'*, *S'*, *E*, *S*, *s*)
post ∃*S'*: *State*, *f*, *s*: *Value*-set ·

    post-ExpEvaluate(*a*, $\overleftarrow{E}$, $\overleftarrow{S}$, *E'*, *S'*, *f*) ∧
    post-ExpEvaluate(*b*, *E'*, *S'*, *E*, *S*, *s*) ∧
    r = *f* ∪ *s*

Notice that the precondition enforces the run-time typechecking constraint that the union operator can only be applied to sets of objects.

MuralObjectEvaluate (*f*: *MuralObject*) *r*: *MuralObject*
ext rd *E* : *Environment*
   rd *S* : *State*
post *r* = *f*

5.2.3   Built-in *mural* operations

The *mural* procedures to which tactics have access are divided into two categories: *operations* and *functions*. The only difference is that executing an operation may change the state of the proof (possibly returning a result) whereas a function may only interrogate the state and return a value.

The calls which are provided perform a wide range of functions, varying from reasonably high-level manipulation of proofs (such as adding new lines or finding the set of goal lines) down to functions concerned with low-level manipulation of expressions. Decisions as to which operations were to be provided were driven by requests from users of the system working in several application areas, so the hope is that the facility is comprehensive enough to cover most needs.

In addition to the descriptive text for each function, a signature is also given specifying the types of the arguments and the result. At run time, a check is done to ensure that the correct number of arguments has been supplied, that they are of the correct types, and that performing the operation will not corrupt the proof or return a nonsensical result[9]. If one of these conditions fails, then a run-time error is signalled.

Syntactically a *MuralCall* is a name followed be a sequence of arguments separated by commas and enclosed in parentheses (e.g. *Unifier*(*a*, *b*)) just like an ordinary procedure or function call.

---

[9]For example, **SetJustif** must not create dependency circularities in the lines of the proof and **InstantiateProof** must only try to instantiate the proof with a *permissible* instantiation.

Operations

InsertNewBoxAfter *(Line | Box) × Exp*-set × *Exp → Box*
builds a new box whose hypotheses and conclusion are the expressions supplied in the second and third arguments respectively. Adds this box to the proof after the first argument (a line or box occurring in the proof). The value returned is the new box.

InsertNewBoxBefore *(Line | Box) × Exp*-set × *Exp → Box*
as above except that the new box is added to the proof before the first argument.

InsertNewLineAfter *(Line | Box) × Exp → OrdLine*
builds a new ordinary line with the second argument as its body and with a null justification. Adds this line to the proof after the first argument (a line or box occurring in the proof). The value returned is the new line.

InsertNewLineBefore *(Line | Box) × Exp → OrdLine*
as above except that the new line is added to the proof before the first argument.

InstantiateProof *Instantiation →* {nil}
instantiates the current proof by the argument (an instantiation). The argument must be permissible. Not only are the expressions on all lines instantiated, but also the instantiations in rule justifications.

SetJustif *OrdLine × Justification →* {nil}
the justification field of the first argument (an *OrdLine*) is set to be the second argument (a *Justification*).

CollapseLines *Line × Line →* {nil}
this operation expects as arguments two lines from the proof which have identical (or equivalent) expressions as their bodies. These two lines are to be 'collapsed' – the second is to be deleted from the proof and all references to it should be replaced by references to the first line. A special case occurs if the second line is the conclusion of a box (i.e. it cannot be deleted). In this case the justification of the first line is copied onto the second line.

Functions

ArgsList *Term → Term**
returns a list containing all the expression and type parameters of the argument.

ArgsMap
(CESymb | CTSymb | QESymb | QTSymb) → Index $\xrightarrow{m}$ Index-set
see Section 5.3.3 for more on indices.

BoxCon *Box → OrdLine*
takes a box as argument and returns its conclusion.

Boxes *→ Box*-set
returns the set of all boxes in the proof.

BoxesAccessibleFrom   *OrdLine* → *Box*-set
the argument is a line. Returns all boxes *accessible* from that line.

BoxesKnownAt   *OrdLine* → *Box*-set
the argument is a line. Returns all boxes which are accessible from that line and which are *known* (i.e. whose conclusion line is known).

BoxHyps   *Box* → *HypLine*-set
takes a box as the argument and returns its hypothesis lines.

EstablishesSeq   (*Box* | *Justification* | *Line*) × *Sequent* → B
returns true if and only if the first argument (a *Box*, a *Justification* or a *Line*) *Establishes* the second (a *Sequent*) .

FillOutInstantiation   *Rule* × *Instantiation* → *Instantiation*
the arguments are a rule statement and an instantiation. Returns a new instantiation which is the second argument plus a map element for each (exp or type) metavariable in the rule statement not in the argument mapping to a brand new metavariable.

FreeVars   (*Term* | *Sequent*) → *VSymb*-set
returns all the free variables of the argument.

GOALS   → *OrdLines*-set
returns the goals (those lines with a null justification) of the current proof.

IndexOfTerm   *Term* × *Term* → *Index* | {nil}
see Section 5.3.3.

IndicesOfEquivalents   *Term* × *Term* → *Index*-set
see Section 5.3.3.

Instantiate   *Term* × *Instantiation* → *Term*
takes a term and an instantiation and returns the result of instantiating the first argument by the second.

InstAtPut   *Instantiation* × (*MESymb* | *MTSymb*) × *Term* → *Instantiation*
a function for building instantiations. Adds to the relevant mapping (exp or type) of the first argument (an instantiation) an element mapping the second argument (an exp or type metavariable symbol) to the third argument (an exp or type).

IsDefined   *Symb* → B
true if and only if the argument (a symbol) is a *defined* (rather than a primitive) constant, type, binder, etc.

IsEquivalentTo   *Term* × *Term* → B
takes a pair of terms and tests whether they are equivalent (as defined in the *mural* specification).

IsInstantiableBy   *Term* × *Instantiation* → B
tests the precondition for instantiating the first argument (a term) by the second (an instantiation).

IsKnown   *Line* → B
tests whether the argument is one of the known lines of the proof.

IsPermissible *Instantiation* → B
> tests whether the argument is a *permissible* instantiation (i.e. only instantiates metavariables which do not occur in the proof's statement).

IsTriviallyTrue *Sequent* → B
> true if and only if the argument is a trivially-true sequent (one whose upshot is included among its premises).

IsValidIndex *Term* × *Index* → B
> see Section 5.3.3.

KNOWNS → *Line*-set
> returns the set of known lines in the current proof.

KnownsAt *Line* → *Line*-set
> returns the set of lines in the current proof which are known and which are accessible from the argument (a line).

LeftOp *Term* → *Term*
> the argument is an ordinary expression or type with at least one argument. Returns the first of these.

LineBody *Line* → *Exp*
> given a proof line, returns the expression on it.

Lines → *Line*-set
> returns all the lines in the current proof.

LinesAccessibleFrom *Line* → *Line*-set
> returns all the lines in the proof accessible from the argument (a line).

MapAt $A \xrightarrow{m} B \times A \to B$
> takes a map and an object. Returns the object's image under the map if it is in the domain, nil otherwise (map application).

MapAtPut $(A \xrightarrow{m} B) \times A \times B \to A \xrightarrow{m} B$
> adds a map element to the first argument (a map) mapping the second argument to the third.

MatchAgainst *Term* × *Term* → *Instantiation*-set
> performs pattern matching with the two args. Both arguments are terms, the first is to be instantiated.

MatchesLine *Exp* × *Line* → B
> matches the first argument (an exp) with the body of the second (a line). Returns true if and only if the set of permissible instantiations returned is non-empty.

MatchLineAgainstLine *Line* × *Line* → *Instantiation*-set
> matches the bodies of the two arguments (lines). Tries to make the resulting instantiations permissible by throwing out of each instantiation those elements which instantiate 'fixed metavariables'.

MergeableWith *Instantiation* × *Instantiation* → B
> tests the precondition for merging two instantiations (i.e. that they are consistent).

MergeWith *Instantiation* × *Instantiation* → *Instantiation*
> merges two instantiations.

NewMVar → *MESymb*
> return a 'brand-new' metavariable (i.e. a completely new spelling).

NewTMVar → *MTSymb*
> returns a 'brand-new' type metavariable (i.e. one with a completely new spelling).

NewVar → *VSymb*
> returns a 'brand-new' variable (i.e. one with a completely new spelling).

ProofConcl → *OrdLine*
> returns the current proof's conclusion line.

ProofOrdHyps → *HypLine*-set
> returns the current proof's ordinary hypotheses.

ProofSeqHyps → *SeqHypLine*-set
> returns the current proof's sequent hypotheses.

ReDrawProof → {nil}
> causes the view of the main proof attempt to be re-drawn

RenameFreeVars *Term* × *VSymb* $\xrightarrow{m}$ *VSymb* → *Term*
> replaces free variables in the first argument (a term) according to the second (a map from (*mural*) variables to variables)

ReplaceEquivTerm *Term* × *Term* × *Term* → *Term*
> returns the term which is like the first term, but with all subterms *equivalent to* the second argument replaced by the third argument (all three arguments are terms).

ReplaceTerm *Term* × *Term* × *Term* → *Term*
> returns a term which is the first argument with all (*exact*) occurrences of the second argument replaced by the third argument (all three arguments are terms).

RightOp *Term* → *Term*
> the argument is an ordinary expression or type with at least one argument. Returns the last of these.

RuleConcl *RuleStmt* → *Exp*
> returns the conclusion of the argument (a rule statement).

RuleOrdHyps *RuleStmt* → *Exp*-set
> returns the ordinary hypotheses of the argument (a rule statement).

RuleSeqHyps *RuleStmt* → *Sequent*-set
> returns the sequent hypotheses of the argument (a rule statement).

RuleStmt *Rule* → *RuleStmt*
> returns the statement of the argument (a rule).

SequentPremises *Sequent* → *Exp*-set
> returns the premises of the argument (a sequent).

SequentUpshot *Sequent* → *Exp*
> returns the upshot of the argument (a sequent).

SubTerms *Term* → *Term*-set
> returns all subterms of the argument (a term).

Symb *Term → Symb*

the argument is an ordinary expression or type, a binder expression or a dependent type. This function returns the argument's symbol.

TermAtIndex *Term × Index → Term* | {nil}

see Section 5.3.3.

Unfold *Term × Symb → Term*

returns the result of unfolding the definition of the second argument (a symbol) in the first argument (a term).

UnifierOf *Term × Term → Instantiation × Instantiation*

runs the unification algorithm on the two (term) arguments. Returns a pair of instantiations, one to instantiate each of the arguments. Both of these will be permissible. Names of metavariables in the first argument take precedence over those in the second. If the algorithm fails to find a unifier, the pair < nil, nil > is returned. The 'occurs check' often used as a precondition in unification algorithms is not needed, since any 'clashing' metavariables are renamed internally[10].

User interaction with tactics

Two *MuralCalls* exist which allow the tactic writer to ask the user for some assistance while a tactic is running. They both cause the execution to stop and wait for the user to take some action before continuing with the tactic. The intention is to allow the user to guide searches and so on.

UserSelection $X^* → X \cup$ {nil}

the argument is a collection of objects. The user is presented with a menu with an option for each of these objects (e.g. if a collection of rules is passed in, then a menu of their names will appear). The function returns the object which is selected, or nil if the user selects outside the menu.

UserSelectionOfSubterm *Term → Term* $\cup$ {nil}

this is similar to **UserSelection**, but the argument is a term, and one of its subterms can be selected. Instead of a menu, this function first prompts the user for the size and position of a window in which to display a structured presentation of the given term. A menu item allows the designation of a particular subterm.

Make constructs

The *Make* construct which is provided for building composite objects is much the same as the VDM '*mk-*' function. The types of objects which can be formed with this construction are limited to those listed below. For each type which can be 'made' the signature of the corresponding *mk-* function is given. For each type, the make function has a precondition which ensures that the resulting object will be sensible; if the precondition is false then a run-time error occurs.

---

[10]In fact, the problem of finding a most general unifier for terms of the *mural* language is not decidable. What has been implemented is a partial algorithm (which always terminates!) based on [Hue75].

RuleJustif   *Rule × Instantiation × VSymb* $\xrightarrow{m}$ *VSymb × OrdDeps*-set[11] *× SeqDeps*-set[12]
  → *RuleJustif*

FoldDefJustif   *Line × Term → FoldDefJustif*

UnfoldDefJustif   *Line × Term → UnfoldDefJustif*

SeqHypJustif   *SeqHypLine × VSymb* $\xrightarrow{m}$ *VSymb × OrdDeps*-set → *SeqHypJustif*

Justification   → *NullJustification*

Ordinary Expression   *(CESymb | MESymb) × Term* → OExp*

Ordinary Type   *(CTSymb | MTSymb) × Term* → OType*

Binder   *QESymb × VSymb × Type × Exp → QExp*

Dependent Type   *QTSymb × VSymb × Type × Type → QType*

5.3   The implementation of tactics

This section describes the implementation of tactics which exists in the *mural* system;
the facilities provided by the tactics system and the user's view of them are discussed,
but no mention is made of the methods and techniques actually used in implementing the
tactics subsystem.

5.3.1   Note on error checking

All error checking is done at run-time (indeed, since the language is not statically typed,
it is impossible to decide prior to the execution of a tactic whether errors would occur
as the result of incorrectly typed parts of the tactic language (for example, the condition
part of an *If* statement must be a Boolean) or calls to *mural* functions and operations. It
would, however, be possible to do some checking at the time a tactic is written – such
as ensuring that all *mural* calls have the correct number of arguments (though this was
not done in the implementation of *mural*). The tactic system could be further enhanced
by the addition of an exception handling mechanism (such as exists in ML or Eiffel, for
example) to deal in a clean way with failures and abnormal conditions which occur at run
time. Errors can occur in several ways:

- calls (to tactics or the *mural* core) are given the wrong number of arguments.

- type check failure. Some typechecking is performed – for instance the '∧' operator
  must have Booleans as its arguments and 'hd' expects a non-empty collection as
  its argument.

- the name supplied to a tactic call doesn't refer to any tactic available in the theory
  where the execution is taking place.

---

[11]*OrdDeps* at present include only Lines, so no facilities are provided for constructing nested justifications from within tactics.

[12]*SeqDeps* are *SeqHypLines* or *Boxes*.

- certain operations or functions have preconditions (which include a test that the arguments are correctly typed); an error will occur is one is violated.

- the execution of a *Stop* statement, while not strictly erroneous, will halt the execution and behave in just the same way as an error.

When any of these error conditions arises a run-time error notifier, similar in style to the Smalltalk-80 source-level debugger, will be displayed, showing the code of the tactic which was executing, with the particular statement in which the error occurred highlighted and some diagnostic text explaining the reason for the failure. Clicking with a mouse button will remove the error notification, stop the execution of the tactic and return control to the user interface[13].

5.3.2 Note on pattern matching and unification

The *mural* system provides algorithms for both *pattern matching* and *unification* of terms, although the unification algorithm cannot be invoked directly form the user interface in the way that the pattern matcher can – it is only visible from the tactic system. The provision of these two algorithms can sometimes lead to confusion when writing tactics.

Why is unification necessary?

When rules are applied backwards to goals in proofs, pattern matching (or unification for that matter) will not always be able to find the complete instantiation which will be required, so some metavariables will be mapped to arbitrary new values and the relevant new lines added to the proof (e.g. applying $\frac{a \wedge b}{a}$ to a line x the instantiation for b is not known, so a new metavariable $\hat{b}$ (actually just a unique number) is introduced and the line $x \wedge \hat{b}$ is added to the proof. Before the proof can ever be considered complete, all occurrences of $\hat{b}$ must be 'filled in' using a call to *InstantiateProof*). Later on, when these new lines are themselves being treated as goals, more information may be found and these new metavariables can be 'filled in'. Pattern matching is not enough since it will only instantiate metavariables on *one* of its arguments (typically an expression from an uninstantiated rule); here we need to instantiate metavariables in both a proof line and a rule.

When to use unification and when to use pattern matching

When applying a rule backwards (or indeed doing anything involving matching or unification) to justify a goal line in a proof, which may itself have been the result of an earlier backward step, use unification – for most other things pattern matching will do (pattern matching is somewhat more efficient, therefore preferable).

5.3.3 Indexing terms

The tactic language provides primitives for accessing and manipulating subterms of a term by means of *indices*. Indices are sequences of non-zero natural numbers. Full details of indexing are given in the specification in Appendix C, but here is an example.

---

[13]The disadvantage of this kind of error notification is that the notifier window 'grabs control', which means that the user cannot go off and do anything else (like look in another window to try and track down

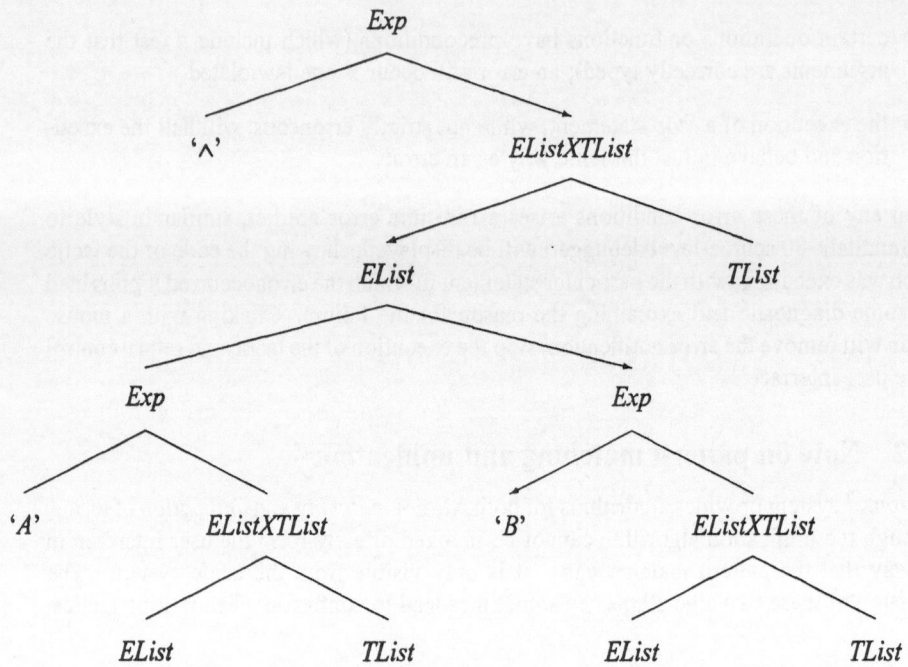

Figure 5.1: Structure of a *mural* Expression

Figure 5.1 shows the structure of the expression $A \wedge B$. The nodes of the tree labelled *EListXTList*, *EList* and *TList* are parts of the abstract syntax of the *mural* language which are hidden from the user in ordinary circumstances (i.e. normal structure editing), but which must be understood in order to write tactics which manipulate terms at this level of detail[14]. In Figure 5.1 it can be seen (by following the branches of the tree which are drawn as arrows) that the symbol B[15] has the index $[2, 1, 2, 1]$. For most applications indices and the detailed structure of terms can be completely ignored, but the interested reader (or one who is forced to write such perverse tactics) is referred to the specification (in Appendix C.2.2) which defines the syntax of terms, explains indices, and specifies the functions *IsValidIndex* and *TermAtIndex* as mentioned in Section 5.2.3. *IndexOfTerm* takes a pair of terms, a and b, and returns the index of a subterm of a which is *identical* to b[16] (or nil if no such subterm exists). *IndicesOfEquivalents* is similar, but returns the set of indices of those subterms of a which are α-equivalent to b.

The *MuralCall ArgsMap* is slightly more complicated. It takes a defined expression or type symbol and returns a map from *Index* to set of *Index*. Each index in the domain of the map is a singleton list representing one of the arguments to the definition (e.g. [3] indicates the third argument) and its image under the map is the set of indices corresponding to the occurrences of that argument in the definition. (Slightly) more formally this can be specified as follows:

---

the problem) while the error message is displayed.

[14]Thankfully, such tactics seem to be fairly esoteric.

[15]Note: the *symbol B*, rather than the *expression* with the symbol *B*.

[16]i.e. the same Smalltalk object as *b*.

ArgsMap (*s*: *ExpOrTypeSymbol*) *r*: *Index* $\xrightarrow{m}$ *Index*-set
pre *isDefined*(*s*)
post ∀*h* ∈ *Holes*(*Defn*(*s*)) · *r*([*number*(*h*)]) = *IndicesOfEquivalents*(*Defn*(*s*), *h*)

where *Holes* returns all the expression and type placeholders in a term, and *Defn* returns the definition of a defined expression or type symbol[17]. The function *number* returns the index of a placeholder[18], with the quirk that it 'adds type placeholders after expression placeholders'. For example, if a definition had three expression arguments and two type arguments the *number*s of the type placeholders would be [4] and [5].

Well that's enough of indexing. Now for something completely different.

5.3.4 Interacting with tactics

Editing

Inside a Tactic Notice (in a theory tool) a structured presentation can be displayed to allow one of the theory's tactics to be edited. When a new tactic is added to the theory it is completely 'empty' – that is, it has no arguments, its result variable is set to a default value (result) and the body of the tactic contains no statements. Middle-button menu options are available when the whole tactic is selected to add arguments and to change the name. Null statements can be added to the body, and can subsequently be refined into one of the types listed in Section 5.2.1. When such a refinement is performed, a template form of the new statement will be displayed, which will typically contain null expressions and empty bodies (further blocks or sequences of statements) which can themselves be edited. The editing options on expressions are similar to those for statements, and an expression can be refined into any of the kinds listed in Section 5.2.1.

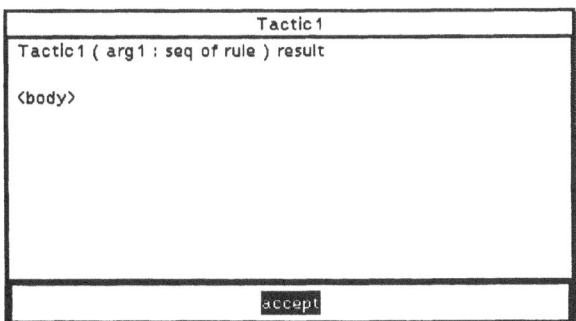

Figure 5.2: a Nearly-new Tactic

After a couple of editing steps, a tactic might look like Figure 5.2. The word body is not strictly part of the tactic; it is simply a piece of concrete syntax which delimits the

---

[17]To be fully formal, the symbol's definition would have to be looked up in the signature of the theory where it is introduced.

[18]In this case, 'index' refers to the numeric identifier of the placeholder (an element of N_1), not to be confused with the indices we're mainly concerned with in this section.

beginning of a tactic's block of statements so that the whole block can be selected when structure editing, rather than just single statements.

Although there are some differences between the structure editor for tactics and that for the rest of *mural* the general principles are much the same and anyone acquainted with the other *mural* editors should have no trouble editing tactics.

A parser has been written for the tactic language, and works in much the same way as the standard *mural* parser: left button to select and place the insertion point; middle button menu option on text to copy and paste text and restore the previous state; middle button menu option on the whole tactic to parse unparsed text[19].

Invoking tactics

Tactics can (only) be invoked from a tactic tool inside a proof tool. A new tactic tool (obtained by clicking on the 'tactic tool' button on a proof tool) initially has on its right-hand side a list of the names of all the tactics which can be run in the current context (i.e. all those in the current theory or its ancestors which have no ARBITRARY arguments). The list of tactics can be filtered by selecting a theory from the left-hand list, causing the right-hand list to show only the tactics in the selected theory.

When the user has selected an item from the list of applicable tactics the arguments may be instantiated to appropriate things, and the tactic set to run. When the arguments to a tactic are being 'set up' (prior to execution) a list appears, on the left-hand side, of all the arguments, and when one is selected a list appears in the middle of the tool containing all the things which can be added to the sequence corresponding to that argument (this will either be all the rules in the current theory and its ancestors, or all the lines, boxes and sequent hypotheses in the current proof, depending on the type of the argument). When one of the items in this central list is selected a menu option allows it to be added to the argument sequence (shown in the right hand column). A menu option allows items to be removed from the argument sequence.

It is often desirable to write tactics which are invokable from the user interface (i.e. which have only sequences of rules or proof objects among their arguments), but which actually require only a single object (for example the 'goal' line on which the tactic is to operate). The simplest way of achieving this kind of effect is to pass in a unit list, and only use the head of this list in the following way.

> *Tactic*1 (*arg*1: SEQ OF PROOFOBJECT, $\cdots$) *result*
> body *goalLine* ← hd *arg*1
> $\vdots$

A couple of other things should be noted about the tactic invocation tool. Firstly, when a tactic is running (after the start button has been clicked), the main section of the tactic tool is replaced by a 'trace' of the tactic's execution. A line is displayed in this trace each time a mural call is executed, and when various other events occur. The purpose of this is to give the user some idea of what is going on at any instant in time (and

---

[19]*Caveat*: in the current version this sometimes behaves rather unpredictably, particularly when something fails to parse.

also to prove that *something* is going on!). When a tactic is running the start button changes to be labelled stop and can be used to interrupt an executing tactic. Secondly, each time the start button is pressed to run a tactic, a copy is made of the main attempt of the proof and is added to the list of existing proof attempts. This is a 'back up' facility so that the effects of running a tactic can be undone – by simply switching back to the copied version.

5.4 Examples

In this section a few simple example tactics are presented.

5.4.1 Backwards rule application

The first example is of a tactic which takes as an argument a sequence of rules and tries applying them in a backwards way to all the goal lines[20] in the proof. The important part of the tactic is the line where the tactic ApplyRulesBackwards is called and passed the rule list and one of the goals which is subsequently removed from the goals set. ApplyRulesBackwards returns a pair of values, the first of which is a Boolean flag indicating whether or not the tactic was successful in applying one of the rules to the given line. The second element of the result is a set containing the new lines and boxes which have been added to the proof. In general these lines correspond to a subset of the instantiated hypotheses of the rule which was applied – a subset since some of the rule's hypotheses may already exist as *known* lines in the proof. These new lines are added to the current set of goals, so that a similar attempt will be made to justify them. The MultiApplyRulesBackwards tactic will terminate when there no goals left to try and justify.

> *MultiApplyRulesBackwards* (*RL*: SEQOFRULE) *result*
> body *goals* ← *GOALS*.
>   while *goals* ≠ [ ]
>   do *g* ← OneOf(*goals*).
>   *res* ← *ApplyRulesBackwards*([*g*], *RL*).
>   *goals*: ← *goals* − {*g*}.
>   *goals* ← *goals* ∪ snd(*res*)

Of course, care must be taken not to supply a tactic like MultiApplyRulesBackwards with sets of rules which are 'circular'. For example, either of $\frac{\neg\neg\phi}{\phi}$ or $\frac{\phi\wedge\psi}{\phi}$ individually or $\frac{a:\mathbf{B}}{\delta(a)}$ and $\frac{\delta(a)}{a:\mathbf{B}}$ together as arguments will cause the tactic not to terminate.

5.4.2 Forward rule application

Whereas the example tactic shown in the previous section applies inference rules to goal lines in a proof, generating new sub-goals, the one shown below (ForwardStep) applies

---

[20]All lines in the main proof attempt which have null justifications are considered to be goal lines.

single rules in a forward direction to generate new known lines from existing ones. It could be used as the basis of a `MultiApplyRulesForwards`, which would make repeated calls to `ForwardStep` from within a *While* loop. The arguments to `ForwardStep` are a line (l_0) to indicate the position at which new lines should be added to the proof, the rule to be applied (R), a sequence of lines (ls) and a sequence of boxes (bs) which the tactic will work forward from, and an instantiation ($inst$) which will be applied to the rule. The return value is a pair, the first element of which is the new proof line corresponding to the conclusion of the rule, and the second is the set of new lines added to the proof corresponding to hypotheses of the rule.

ForwardStep (l_0: ARBITRARY, *R*: ARBITRARY, *ls*: SEQOFPROOFOBJECT,
$\qquad\qquad\qquad\qquad$ *bs*: SEQOFPROOFOBJECT, *inst*: ARBITRARY) *S*

body *rs* ← *RuleStmt(R)*.
$\qquad$ *inst'* ← *FillOutInstantiation(rs, inst)*.
$\qquad$ *new* ← *InsertNewLineAfter(l_0, Instantiate(RuleConcl(rs), inst'))*.
$\qquad$ *newHyps* ← *ApplyMixedStep(new, R, ls, bs, inst')*.
$\qquad$ *S* ← < *new, newHyps* >

5.4.3 User interaction

As was mentioned in Section 5.2.3, tactics can be written which 'poll' the user for extra information; the tactic shown below makes use of this facility. The purpose of this tactic is to help the user set up a proof by induction over sequences. The rule for sequence induction is built into the tactic (its name is enclosed in 'Strachey' brackets, [[*Seq-Ind*]] – like this), but a variation could easily be written in which the particular induction needed was passed as a parameter, so that the tactic would be applicable in a larger set of theories. Additionally, some checks should be put is to detect nil being returned from the user selection calls, but have been omitted for the sake of simplicity. Both this tactic and the next one (`BasicEqualsSubstitution`) operate at a fairly low level by manipulating terms using the *Symb*, *RightOp* and *LeftOp MuralCalls*, and by constructing instantiations for use in justifications. Subsequent tactics which rely on these can operate at a higher level, so some of the gory detail is hidden.

SetUpInduction (*gl*: SEQOFPROOFOBJECT) *result*

```
body  g ← hd gl.
      b ← LineBody(g).
      l ← UserSelectionOfSubterm(b).
      P ← ReplaceEquivTerm(b, l, [[e1]]).
      r ← [[Seq-Ind]].
      con ← RuleConcl(RuleStmt(r)).
      ts ← Symb(LeftOp(con)).
      Ps ← Symb(con).
      inst ← InstAtPut(InstAtPut(mk-Instantiation({ }, { }), ts, l), Ps, P).
      inst ← FillOutInstantiation(RuleStmt(r), inst).
      ApplyRuleBackwards(g, r, inst)
```

The conclusion of the rule for induction over sequences (*Seq-Ind*) is of the form $Q[x]$, where Q is some predicate and x is the 'induction variable'. The above tactic builds an instantiation for the metavariables Q and x based on the line given as input to the tactic, and the user's selection, l. In building this instantiation, the subterm selected by the user is replaced in (a copy of) the original l by an expression hole, $[[e1]]$. This is often necessary in tactics which construct instantiations (such as `BasicEqualsSubstitution` below).

5.4.4 Equational reasoning

Basic rewriting tactic

The tactic shown here forms the basis of a range of others which use equations (or rather inference rules with equations as their conclusion) to rewrite lines in a proof, substituting equals for equals. `BasicEqualsSubstitution` takes three arguments: a line in the proof, l, a subexpression of the expression on the proof line, *term*, and a rule (with an equation as its conclusion), r. The idea is to add a new line to the proof which has the expression of l with *term* rewritten using the equation of r. This involves applying the rule of equals substitution:

$$\boxed{\text{=-subs}} \; \frac{s1 = s2, \, E[s1]}{E[s2]}$$

The tactic `ForwardStep` is used twice, first with the rule r to add the equation as a line in the proof, and secondly with the =-*subs* rule applied to this equation and the original line which is to be rewritten (l).

Not only is the name of the equals substitution rule 'hard-wired' into this tactic (for simplicity), also the tactic contains information about the form of the rule, in the lines containing *MuralSymb*(...) close to the end of the tactic. These are quoted *mural* metavariable symbols which correspond directly to the metavariables in the statement of the equals substitution rule.

BasicEqualsSubstitution (*l*: ARBITRARY, *term*: ARBITRARY, *r*: ARBITRARY) *lp*
body *left* ← *LeftOp(RuleConcl(RuleStmt(r)))*.
      insts ← *MatchAgainst(left, term)*.
      if IsEmpty(*insts*)
      then
      else *kl* ← KnownsAt(*l*).
           if IsEmpty(*RuleSeqHyps(RuleStmt(r))*)
           then *kb* ← { }
           else *kb* ← *BoxesKnownAt(l)*
           inst ← OneOf(*insts*).
           eqn ← fst(ForwardStep(*l, r, kl, kb, inst*)).
           term' ← *RightOp(LineBody(eqn))*.
           newBody ← *ReplaceTerm(LineBody(l), term, term')*.
           pterm ← *ReplaceTerm(LineBody(l), term, [[e1]])*.
           s1s ← *MuralSymb(s1)*.
           s2s ← *MuralSymb(s2)*.
           Es ← *MuralSymb(E)*.
           inst2 ← *InstAtPut(InstAtPut(InstAtPut(mk-Instantiation({ }, { }),*
                                                  s1s, term), s2s, term'), Es, pterm).
           lppair ← *ForwardStep(eqn, [[=-subs]], {l} ∪ {eqn}, { }, inst2)*.
           lp ← fst(*lppair*)

Interactive rewrite

The previous tactic is rather unwieldy, and in any case cannot be invoked by the user since
it has arguments which are of type ARBITRARY. Consequently, a more 'user-friendly' variant is required. InteractiveFR (or interactive forward rewrite) is a tactic which hides the
functionality of BasicEqualsSubstitution behind a user interface similar in style to
the induction tactic. The tactic takes a sequence of lines *ll* (containing the line to be rewritten), and a list of rules *RL* providing the rewriting equations. The user is prompted for a
subterm to rewrite and a rule to apply, then a call is made to BasicEqualsSubstitution
to actually perform the rewrite.

InteractiveFR (*ll*: SEQOFPROOFOBJECT, *RL*: SEQOFRULE) *newLine*
body *l* ← hd *ll*.
      term ← *UserSelectionOfSubterm(LineBody(l))*.
      if *term* = nil
      then *newLine* ← nil
      else *rule* ← *UserSelection(RL)*.
           if *rule* = nil
           then *newLine* ← nil
           else *newLine* ← *BasicEqualsSubstitution(l, term, rule)*

Multiple rewriting

A common strategy employed in proofs is to use chains of equalities to rewrite or simplify terms over a number of steps, and further extensions can easily be made to the interface of the term rewriting tactics which support this. MultInteractiveFR repeatedly calls InteractiveFR until the user makes a nil selection (for example by clicking outside a menu), thus creating a sequence of lines related by applications of the equals substitution rule.

MultiInteractiveFR(startLine: SEQOFPROOFOBJECT, *RL*: SEQOFRULE)*result*
body *line* ← hd *startLine*.
    while *line* ≠ nil
    do *line* ← *InteractiveFR([line], RL)*

Multiple sequences

Chapter 6

Implementing the *mural* proof assistant

Previous chapters describe the *mural* proof assistant, both at the abstract level and in terms of the specification of the system. We should not forget that this abstraction has been realized as a working piece of software. This chapter discusses the process of implementation and points out some of the things we learned along the way that we believe may be of interest or significance to others. This is not the place to attempt to give full detail of the implementation, rather we attempt to illustrate the general structure and to focus on some of the interesting issues in its development. It is written more for the curious than for those who would like to implement their own version of the system[1]. This chapter deals specifically with the implementation of the *mural* proof assistant, but much of it applies to the entire *mural* system.

Background

As with any system of more than trivial size, much of the eventual form and style of the *mural* proof assistant was due to an evolutionary process involving a large number of design decisions. To understand the reasoning behind such design decisions without having been present at these discussions is a difficult task. A lot can be deduced from the scene setting given in Section 1.4. Here we offer a little more background to give you a picture of our thinking and perspective during the design.

Things uppermost in our minds

There were many possible routes we could have taken in the development of the *mural* proof assistant, even after things had been fixed at the specification level. To give you a flavour of the things that led us in the direction we chose, the points that were uppermost in our minds at the time were:

- The VDM specification was the Bible of current information. It was the sole repository for decisions already made.

- Any decision that had been made in the abstract *had to be reflected in the code*. If we discovered the need during implementation to alter something recorded in the specification, then the *only* permitted mechanism for doing so was to amend

---

[1] If there are any such people, and if going and sitting in a dark room for a while doesn't cause you to think better of it, then we suggest you get in touch with us directly. We should be able to give more useful information in higher bandwidth communication than anything we could provide in a book of this kind.

the specification and then to implement from the revised specification. Given the lack of a system offering the functionality of a full *mural*, it was not reasonable to attempt a formal development of the *mural* proof assistant. However, the relationship between the specification and the code was monitored informally as if the retrieve functions had been written. In a few cases where the correspondence of the implementation was not obvious, some formal proof was done. The specification also contained some validation properties of the operations that were used as a confidence check on some parts of the implementation.

- The initial implementation had to be a fully functional prototype. It was considered acceptable to compromise on performance to a reasonable extent to expedite the development, but we had to provide all of the functionality necessary to use the *mural* proof assistant on realistic examples.

- We viewed the system as broadly divided into two parts:

  1. the kernel functionality covered by the specification;
  2. the user interface that permits access to this kernel.

  The specification had addressed many of the design issues involved in 1, but we had no way of conveniently discussing 2 without constructing prototypes. We needed a great deal of flexibility in constructing interfaces since we were sure to get it wrong the first time.

These points should be kept firmly in mind when reading the following sections.

The implementation language: Smalltalk-80

We have been asked on many occasions: 'Why Smalltalk?'[2], as this would seem to distance ourselves from most of the other work that was being done in the area of supporting formal reasoning. Traditionally, theorem provers and their brethren have been implemented in either ML [Pau85a] or one of the LISP dialects. It is generally believed that these languages are particularly suitable for supporting the symbolic manipulation involved in this class of application. As was discussed in Chapter 1 and above, we had different priorities as far as the *mural* proof assistant was concerned.

As we have said, we believed that one of the key requirements of the *mural* system was to provide an interface that was helpful in constructing proofs. Since we had no clear picture of precisely what this entailed when starting out, we needed to be able to try a number of different approaches to the UI. This led us to pick an environment where the basic facilities necessary for building an interface, such as windows, selection mechanisms and so forth, were available and could be easily combined in a variety of ways. From the literature and simple experiments, we thought Smalltalk to be more suitable in this regard than any of the other options we had available since it offered the necessary primitives and allowed rapid experimentation without a high rebuilding overhead for a large application. We were also of the opinion that Smalltalk lost nothing on the symbolic manipulation front since it supported abstract data types, such as sets and lists, that matched the way we had specified the kernel operations. This would allow a

---

[2]The *mural* system was developed in Objectworks for Smalltalk 80, Version 2.5, ParcPlace Systems, using Sun 3 and 4 as our development systems.

very direct implementation of the specification. Early experiments to convince ourselves (and others) of the suitability of Smalltalk and the conclusions we reached are discussed in [Jon87a]. Section 6.3.4 gives our opinion on this matter at the end of the project.

As is often the case, our choice of implementation language had some effect on the style of the eventual implementation. It is obvious to anyone familiar with Smalltalk that *mural* is a Smalltalk application. It is equally obvious that it is not a standard application. This is discussed later.

6.1 The process of implementation

One of the interesting aspects of the *mural* project was that it combined the approaches of formal specification and prototyping in a complementary way. In this section, we discuss this relationship and explain why we feel that this proved to be a very successful approach to building our system.

As we mentioned above, the starting point for the implementation *per se* was the VDM specification (Appendix C). This document recorded a complete description of the core of the system at a behavioural level.

The process by which we arrived at the final version of the specification is of interest in itself. We will describe it here, even though it is a precursor to what would normally be considered part of the implementation.

'Ground Zero' was a mathematical presentation of the functionality of the kernel. This was written as a description of the logical frame the *mural* proof assistant was to support [Lin87a]. This document allowed many of the discussions and decisions to be taken at a very abstract level where the issues were clearer. This allowed a separation of concerns, since we could concentrate solely on the issues of importance at that level of abstraction.

Once we were happy at this level, the mathematical description was then translated into a VDM specification [Jon87b] which gave the base for the system specification. From this point, the specification was expanded to be a complete functional specification for the kernel [Moo88].

At this point, we realized that we needed some feedback on aspects of our design, such as the level of user interaction involved, that could not be examined very well in abstract. To get this feedback, we built a prototype by 'translating' the specification into Smalltalk[3] and executing it. As expected, this led to our realizing the need for some changes in the primitives and a revision of the structure of the kernel.

At this point it would have been too easy to just make what we felt were the necessary changes at the implementation level, ignore the specification hereafter, and plough on regardless – especially since we now had a working prototype to play with. This is not the model that use of a formal method suggests and we forced ourselves to take our own medicine. It should be noted that this was easier for some than for others and any project using these techniques can expect some problems with programmers who don't see that this discipline is necessary for their work. It's also easy to predict which people have responsibility for the parts of the system that cause problems further down the track!

The changes were documented by producing a revised version of the specification and this document ([LM89]) served as the gospel during the construction of the *mural*

---

[3]This translation was not exactly a mechanical process since in general the specification was not directly executable. However, this sentence gives the flavour of what we were trying to achieve.

proof assistant. The prototype was notionally thrown away and the implementation began cleanly. In retrospect, we feel that this was one of the key points in the process and the reason that the combination of techniques worked well for us. If we had not been prepared to incorporate the feedback from the prototype at the specification level, rather than at the code level, then this is the stage where we would have lost our precise specification and would have been reduced to a 'hack it and see' strategy. Given the number of times an appeal to the specification solved a problem, or resolved an ambiguity, or cleared up a misunderstanding, in the weeks that followed, this would have been a high price to pay for the instant gratification of being able to carry on playing with our prototype.

Just to complete this historical perspective, the system kernel was then implemented from the specification, exploiting the obvious relationship between the types in the specification and the objects that could be constructed in Smalltalk[4]. A user interface was designed and built on top of this, and the system was released to the group for feedback. The final step in the process was modifying the system according to user feedback, via the specification where this was relevant, and by improving efficiency where this was shown to be important.

Now that you know some of the reasons the *mural* proof assistant looks the way it does, we can look at some detail of the implementation.

6.2   The implementation

6.2.1   The implementation of the kernel

The kernel of the *mural* proof assistant was implemented as a class hierarchy with *MuralObject* as its root. Fig. 6.1 shows an outline of this hierarchy. Items followed by ... have further subclasses. Those marked with * are pragmatic rather than semantic entities. Since there is a natural correspondence between a VDM type and a Smalltalk class (particularly when the type is a record, as most of the types in the *mural* specification are), the derivation of the classes in this hierarchy was quite straightforward.

Since there is no notion of inheritance in VDM, we were somewhat surprised how inconvenient it was to be limited to Smalltalk-80's single inheritance model when translating the types. All of the kernel classes needed to be subclasses of *MuralObject*, to inherit the basic properties of any *mural* type, but we often would have liked to be able to inherit functionality from a pre-existing Smalltalk class as well. An obvious example of this is the *ArgList* type. As well as being a *Construct*, it is also an obvious subclass of *OrderedCollection*.

To illustrate the correspondence between the code and the specification, Fig. 6.2 shows both the specification and the implementation for *Rule*.

Each field of the record was represented as an instance variable of the class. In addition extra variables were used to hold information that was not relevant at the level of

---

[4]During this part of the implementation, we evolved a style of working that was remarkable successful for us, involving two people at one workstation. This is now referred to as the 'spare feet on the desk' programming paradigm, so named because of the working position usually adopted by the person not driving the keyboard. The combination of this style, which avoided many errors of both omission and commission that would have been harder to track down after the fact, together with the use of the formal specification in an environment that provided powerful programming abstractions, gave us high productivity during this phase. How well this would translate to other teams, on other projects, is left as an exercise for the interested manager.

```
MuralObject *
  MICollector ... *
  Store
  Theory
  Signature
  ThMorph
  Proof
  Box
  HypLine ...
  Rule
  Sequent
  Term
    Construct
      ArgList ...
      BTerm ...
      Exp ...
      Type ...
    Symb ...
  Zilch *
```

Figure 6.1: An outline of the *mural* class hierarchy

abstraction at which the specification was written, such as a comment associated with the rule.

The rest of the kernel types were implemented in a similar fashion. In some cases, we had to resort to tricks to simulate multiple inheritance. This was usually done in one of two ways, although in some cases of sheer desperation we had to resort to copying code.

1. For the cases where we wished to inherit the functional behaviour of an existing class, the trick was to encode an object of the desired second superclass in an instance variable of the class. For example, *ArgList* is a subclass of *MuralObject* and has an instance variable, *list*, which contains an *OrderedCollection*.

2. When we were actually interested in subtyping (i.e. not in method inheritance), we made use of a separate hierarchy rooted by *MICollector*, the subclasses of which were used to represent second parents for *mural* classes. For example, *Leaf* has one instance variable that contains a list of all the classes that would be considered subclasses of *Leaf*, such as *Atom, Vsymb*, etc. We could then test if something was a subtype by checking if it was in this list.

This lacked the elegance of true multiple inheritance but was sufficient to allow us to write the operations we were interested in.

Most of the operations given in the specification were implemented as methods on the obvious class. Sometimes, the class structure of Smalltalk allowed a number of possibilities for the 'right' place to attach a method. In such cases, 'obvious' was decided by the toss of a coin. If the specification was sufficiently explicit, the code was usually written by simply translating the VDM, since most of the operations used in the specification (such as $\cup, \dagger$ etc.) were also available in Smalltalk (Fig. 6.3).

For the cases where the specification was implicit, some non-trivial design was necessary. The problem usually involved searching thorough a fairly small domain of possibilities, taking advantage of some meta-knowledge of the situation. In these cases, a proof of consistency with the specification was done in an informal manner. The correctness of the relationship shown in Fig. 6.4 is less obvious than for the case above.

The security of the *mural* proof assistant depends only on the security of this kernel, since all operations available to the user through the user interface interact with the state only through the kernel functions.

6.2.2   The implementation of the user interface

Our aim for the user interface was to take advantage of the sophisticated interaction possible on a workstation to make the process of constructing a proof as convenient as possible for the user. We had a number of broad principles in mind:

- No arbitrary restrictions on the order of actions or on the layout of information. We assumed that the user was more intelligent than the machine and if he or she wanted to do things in a particular order, or lay out windows in a particular way, then, provided there were no semantic restrictions, we should allow this. We should support the user, not enforce a style.

- Wherever possible, the interface should follow the direct manipulation principle, i.e. you should be able to edit the representation of the object that you see.

- Notation and layout etc. should be as close to what the user actually wants as we were able to achieve. Mathematical founts make a large difference to the readability of the texts.

- In contrast to the previous item, we should not slavishly follow what one would do on paper, but should take advantage of the processing power of the machine and the interactive nature of the medium to do better than paper.

This led us to create two basic interactors which underlie most of the the *mural* proof assistant user interface:

- *Structured presentations* are representations of an object that allow the binding of menu actions to subcomponents. Using this mechanism, the *mural* proof assistant presents a structure editing interface to the underlying objects. This mechanism is used for the construction and editing of most small objects within the system.

- *Noticeboards* allow the grouping of *notices*, which can be regarded as sub-windows, in arbitrary ways. This technology allows the user to decide on the layout and organization of information within a view of a larger structure. For example, the presentation of components within a theory uses a noticeboard to allow the special grouping of related rules and signature items for convenient navigation. This is in keeping with the principle of allowing the user complete freedom when there are no semantic constraints.

Both of these components are visible in a number of forms in the picture in Fig. 6.7 on page 213.

User interaction with small-scale objects

The basic user interface component necessary for the majority of kernel objects was some mechanism for constructing such objects. We chose to use *structured presentations* which permit the editing of the objects. As an efficiency improvement, a parser was added later.

The basic interactor for a simple kernel object is presented as a notice containing the syntactic definition of the object, plus a definition of its concrete syntax. A *RuleNotice* is shown in Fig. 6.5.

User interaction with complex objects

For objects of more involved structure, one structured presentation would not be a very good interaction mechanism. In fact, a *Rule* is the largest structure we approached in such a fashion. For objects of greater complexity, such as a *Theory* or a *Proof*, we used the notion of a *Tool* as a structuring mechanism, together with a *ToolView* which handles the physical layout on the screen.

Tools can be considered as part of the user interface even though they have nothing to do with the screen interaction as such. The basic idea behind a tool (we shall take *ProofTool* (Fig. 6.6) as an example) is that there is information that is not part of the state, in the sense the specification describes the state, but that needs to be stored somewhere. For example, in the *ProofTool*, there are a number of instance variables. Some contain kernel information, such as the proof itself. Others hold selection or caching information, such as the selected attempt. It is the tool that provides the functionality the user actually sees. Since the tool only changes the state via the kernel operations, the security of the system depends only on the security of the kernel functions. Tools should be viewed solely as pragmatic constructs.

ToolViews describe the layout of the interface to an object in terms of the panes, buttons, lists and so on that the user sees on the screen. Most views are built of a number of common interactors, such as buttons, menus, selection from lists and so forth. There is little point in discussing these here since the best way of getting a feel for what's in a *ToolView* is to look at some of the example screens in this book, such as Figs. 2.1 to 2.12 in Chapter 2.

6.3 Lessons learnt and advice to the young

The *mural* project has two things to offer: the system itself and the experience of the use of formal methods gained by building this system. To benefit from the former, you need a large workstation and a copy of *mural*. The benefit from the latter is more cheaply obtained and perhaps of more general interest. Many of the points are made piecemeal and by implication in the preceding sections. This final section tries to bring them together and make some definite comments. Much of it is repetition of what's above, but being brought together makes it a stronger statement of what we believe. This is probably even less of a consensus view than most of the preceding comments. Comments in bold should be surrounded by a *<Mounts soapbox>* bracketing.

6.3.1   The use of formal specification with prototyping

Since *mural* is a support system for formal methods, we obviously had to make use of such technology in its development[5]. We are convinced that this made the development much easier and more successful than it would have been otherwise. It was a number of months before the first line of code was written and by the time it was, many of the contentious and difficult problems had already been resolved. This is evidence of one of the classic arguments for the use of formal specifications: problems are picked up earlier in the lifecycle. The initial implementation was quite straightforward and went much more quickly than we had hoped. Had we had more suitable tools, this would have been done more formally. Given what was available, this was not feasible; the actual development can at best be described as rigorous. Some of the code was verified, using the *claims* in Chapter 4 as validation conditions. A bold statement: **formal specification has benefit even without formal verification**. Also, **formal verification increases the benefit but at higher cost**.

We feel that the interaction between the specification and the prototypes contributed significantly to the development of the system. The early feedback from a running system allowed us to validate our specification at a pragmatic level and helped us to improve the system at a number of levels of abstraction. This worked only because we made sure all of the feedback was reflected in the specification. **Prototypes enhance a development provided they feed back into the specification, not replace it**. This was a difficult discipline to maintain at first, but we are convinced that this is one of the most important points we learned: **the specification should be the 'Truth' at all stages of the project lifecycle**. Also, **the specification should lead the code, not track it**.

6.3.2   Naive implementation

Our approach to writing the code was perhaps atypical. Where possible we took advantage of Smalltalk's sophisticated abstractions and simply translated the VDM into an executable form. Generally, this would have been decried as sure to produce a grossly inefficient system. And, surely enough, it did. However, we would argue that this was not a problem and actually saved us much wasted effort. One of the benefits of a language like Smalltalk is the ease with which things can be changed. There were large portions of the code for which optimization was completely unnecessary since the significance of these sections to the overall performance of the system was small. The chances are that if we'd tried to write optimal code from the start we would have wasted time and effort in these areas. For the places where the system did need tuning, and there were quite a number of these, Smalltalk allowed us to do so in an incremental fashion. Eventually, we ended up with a system that has acceptably efficient code, without much wasted effort. It's not clear how much more we could have gained if we'd been prepared to do a more complex development from the specification and benefited from optimization at a more global level. I can't think of a nice pithy one-liner that sums up this point, so I'll use a quote that I first heard from Richard Bird in a slightly different context: **premature optimization is the root of most evils**.

---

[5]Would you trust a BMW salesman who drives a Mercedes?

6.3.3 User interface experimentation

Formal techniques were not much help to us in designing the user interface. Actually, that's not entirely true. The specification ensured that we knew precisely what functionality the interface had access to, so the underlying structure of the interface was determined by the specification. The actual combination of buttons and texts and what-nots that represent the system as far as the user is concerned was designed by scribbles on a whiteboard and experimentation. We followed the guiding principles mentioned above and tried to give an interface that permitted as much freedom as possible. This made the task of building the interface much harder. It is much easier to develop an interface to a proof, for example, that only allows you to construct new lines from existing lines (forward reasoning) than one which allows you to go forwards, backwards or from the middle. The other thing that became obvious was that to design an interface that allows total flexibility without significantly increasing the user's workload, is a *very* hard task. The *mural* proof assistant allows a lot of freedom but it has its price: the user often has to do a lot of the positioning of windows by hand, such as in noticeboards. This is often inconvenient if you really don't care where they go and just want a quick look at the contents. Perhaps this could be summarized as **freedom has its price**?

The first interfaces we tried on the *mural* proof assistant were more simplistic than the current version. Such interfaces were quickly shown to lack some functionality that users needed. The current interface is the end point of a number of experiments and seems to offer most of the facilities one would look for. However, using some of these features is more complicated than we would have wished. Further development would now concentrate on packaging some of the more common features to make them easier to use. **Interfaces are not right the 1st (or n^{th}) time, no matter how hard you try, and need to evolve with feedback**.

6.3.4 Smalltalk as an implementation language

We should state here that we doubt that we could have built *mural* to the level of sophistication we did, in the time that we had, in any other language that was available to us at the time. It's important to mention this since most of the rest of this section is griping about various features of Smalltalk that we were unhappy with. We'll try to remember to point out the positive features, but it's always easier to take what you're happy with for granted and complain noisily about the bits you'd like to change.

The abstractions provided as standard in Smalltalk, such as sets, lists and dictionaries, make it very easy to program the complex structures the *mural* proof assistant depends upon. However, it was not as easy to take full advantage of these as we had hoped. We often found ourselves in the situation of wanting to make a subclass of a system container class to add functionality specific to the element type, as in, say, *ArgList*. We also usually wanted these classes to have the functionality of any other *mural* class in the same category. Usually the only way to achieve this was to copy code from one or other of the possible parents which seemed contrary to the reuse philosophy of Smalltalk. **Inheritance is nice but nothing more complex than an amoeba is really born from a single parent**.

We made much use of some features of the environment that are not provided in many languages. The most important of these was the dependency mechanism. Smalltalk provides a class, *Model*, which gives mechanisms for attaching dependents to an object, and notifying these dependents whenever certain events take place with respect to the object. The obvious use of such a mechanism is within the interface to notify a view that its underlying object has changed state. We use this mechanism heavily in our interface code. However, we also make use of dependencies in other ways. For example, a *Line* is dependent on its *Justification*, which in turn is dependent on the lines it refers to and the rules it uses. If one of these rules is changed in any way, then the dependency mechanism is used to inform the proof that, say, it is no longer complete and should unset the relevant flag. Use of this mechanism was one of the main modifications we made when improving the efficiency of the implementation. To have had to either build such a mechanism, or manage without it, would have made life a lot harder for us.

We managed to build prototype interfaces very quickly and easily making use of Smalltalk's MVC[6] mechanism and using the provided window classes. Unfortunately, this only gave a loose approximation to the interface we actually wanted. Once we moved away from the standard Smalltalk kind of interface, the cost seemed to go up exponentially. Eventually, the *mural* interface code required the redevelopment of the interface components from a very low level. **Smalltalk makes building interfaces easy, but only provided you stick within the bounds of its standard philosophy.**

Smalltalk works best as a single person environment[7]. We found that it was often quite difficult to successfully hive off chunks of the development to different people and then recombine the code. The problem was usually caused by needing to modify an existing class in both branches of the development, with each developer needing to add an instance variable to the class, say. There is then no automatic way of combining these classes into a single image. We often ended up reading through the code manually, trying to work out what could be read in, what needed modifications to be done by hand and so forth. Smalltalk needs to provide a mechanism for multi-person change management.

The final, and perhaps largest, complaint we had about Smalltalk was that after the development was finished we had no way of doing the equivalent of shipping a binary. In a conventional compiled language, we could have compiled to a client's machine and shipped the binary. With Smalltalk, we could only give the system to those people who had a license for the Smalltalk runtime system, and then we had to be careful to ensure that the sources were not visible in the circumstances where we didn't want them to be. The opposite of this complaint is the benefit that the *mural* system runs on any system that supports Smalltalk-80 without any porting whatsoever.

Our final word on Smalltalk would be that there was much we were unhappy with, but *for a prototyping project* we could not have done as much without it.

6.4   The future

At the end of any project, you can see how you could have done better. This section[8] tells some of the truth about what we believe could be better in *mural*.

One of the things we would like to do, now that we have a complete system, is to reimplement in a language that would avoid the problems mentioned in the final point of the preceding section. This would give us easier distribution and probably more effi-

---

[6]Model-View-Controller.

[7]Actually, it works even better as a two person environment – provided they adopt the 'spare feet on the desk' paradigm mentioned earlier.

[8]Subtitled, a better *mural* would have been...

ciency. The drawback is that we would have to target to some generally available window system, such as X. The porting exercise would be non-trivial, to say the least.

Some of the features of the interface, and the *justification tool* springs immediately to mind as an example, are general enough to permit all the desired functionality, but are overly complex for most simple interactions. The system would be better from the user's perspective if these general tools were replaced (or more probably augmented) by a number of simpler mechanisms for those simple cases. We have some ideas about ways in which this could be achieved by extending certain basic selection mechanisms to allow, for example, selecting a set of lines in a proof.

It would also be nice to increase the power of the prover in a number of ways to remove some of the burden of proof construction from the user. Extending the system to incorporate rewrite rule technology, in a way consistent with the fundamental belief that things should always be under the user's control, would make certain kinds of proof less tedious to construct. In a similar vein, the tactic language did not get as much attention as other aspects of the *mural* proof assistant, and was considered more of an existence proof than the ideal language. The system should have a powerful tactic language together with a basic library of tactics. These should be easy to invoke from the interface with a minimum of interaction to make their use in proof more seamless.

6.5 The final word

The best way to truly understand any system is to use it! So just to pique your interest, Fig. 6.7 presents a picture of the *mural* proof assistant in action.

specification

> *rule* :: *STMT*   : *RuleStmt*
>   *THEORY* : *Theory-ref*
>   *PROOF*   : [*Proof*]

implementation

```
MuralObject subclass: Rule
instanceVariableNames: 'STMT THEORY PROOF comment lemmaStatus metaVars'
classVariableNames: 'RuleActions'
poolDictionaries: '
category: 'mural-Kernel'
```

Figure 6.2: The specification and implementation of Rule

specification

> *subterms* : *Exp* → *Term*-set
> *subterms*(*e*) ≜ cases *e* of
>   *mk-QExp*(*qet*, *be*) → {*e*, *qet*} ∪ *subterms*(*be*)
>   *mk-OExp*(*oet*, *elxtl*)→ {*e*, *oet*} ∪ *subterms*(*elxtl*)
>   others {*e*}
>   end

implementation

(This method is on the class *OExp*. Something similar is on the class *QExp*)

```
subterms
        | s |
        s ← Set with: self with: self symbol.
        ↑s union: self args subterms
```

Figure 6.3: The subterms function

specification

> $establishesSequent : Sequent \times Sequent \to \mathbb{B}$
> $establishesSequent(s, s') \quad \triangle \quad \exists m \in VSymb \xrightarrow{m} VSymb \cdot$
> $\quad\quad \operatorname{dom} m = NFV(s) \wedge \operatorname{rng} m \subseteq NFV(s')$
> $\quad\quad \wedge (freeVars(s) - NFV(s)) \cap NFV(s') = \{\,\}$
> $\quad\quad \wedge isEquivalentTo(renameFreeVars(UPSHOT(s), m), UPSHOT(s'))$
> $\quad\quad \wedge \forall e \in PREMISES(s) \cdot \exists e' \in PREMISES(s') \cdot$
> $\quad\quad\quad\quad isEquivalentTo(renameFreeVars(e, m), e')$

implementation

```
establishesSequent:  seq
"One sequent establishes another 'weaker' sequent
(i.e.  one with more hypotheses and less collapsing of freevars).
This kind of enumeration is believed to be acceptable
since there are unlikely to be many premises or many free vars"
| mSeemsOK equivfound testExp |
self nfv size < seq nfv size ifTrue:  [↑false].
((self freeVars diff:  self nfv) intersect:  seq nfv) isEmpty
ifFalse:  [↑false].
"Try all possible renamings to find an equivalent"
(Map makeAllMapsFrom:  self nfv to:  seq nfv)
do:  [:map |
     "first check upshots - if they're not equivalent, forget this map"
     ((self upshot deepCopy renameFreeVars:  map)
     isEquivalentTo:  seq upshot)
     ifTrue:
     [mSeemsOK ← true.
     'Now try to find an equivalent premise'
     self premises do:  [:exp |
         "if the map's not already junked, keep trying"
         mSeemsOK ifTrue:
         [equivfound ← false.
         "so far we don't have an equivalent"
         testExp ← exp deepCopy renameFreeVars:  map.
         "try all premises of seq"
         seq premises do:  [:expprime |
                          (testExp isEquivalentTo:  expprime)
                          ifTrue:  [equivfound ← true.]
                          "Ah ha we've found one"]].
         equivfound ifFalse:  [mSeemsOK ← false]]].
     "if m still seems good then we've found a map that works,
     so seq is established"
     mSeemsOK ifTrue:  [↑true]]].
↑false
```

Figure 6.4: The establishesSequent function

```
∃∨-dist-expand : Rule
{ }
{ ∃ x : X .
( ( E1 [ x ] ) ∨ ( E2 [ x ] ) ) }
_____

( ∃ x : X . ( E1 [ x ] ) ∨ ∃ x :
X . ( E2 [ x ] ) )
                                    Rule
                            add sequent hypothesis
                accept         add  hypothesis
                                    show proof
```

Figure 6.5: A Rule Notice

```
Tool subclass:  ProofTool
    instanceVariableNames:  'proof markedBuffer selectedAttempt'
    classVariableNames:  '
    poolDictionaries:  '
    category:  'mural-Interface'
```

Figure 6.6: ProofTool

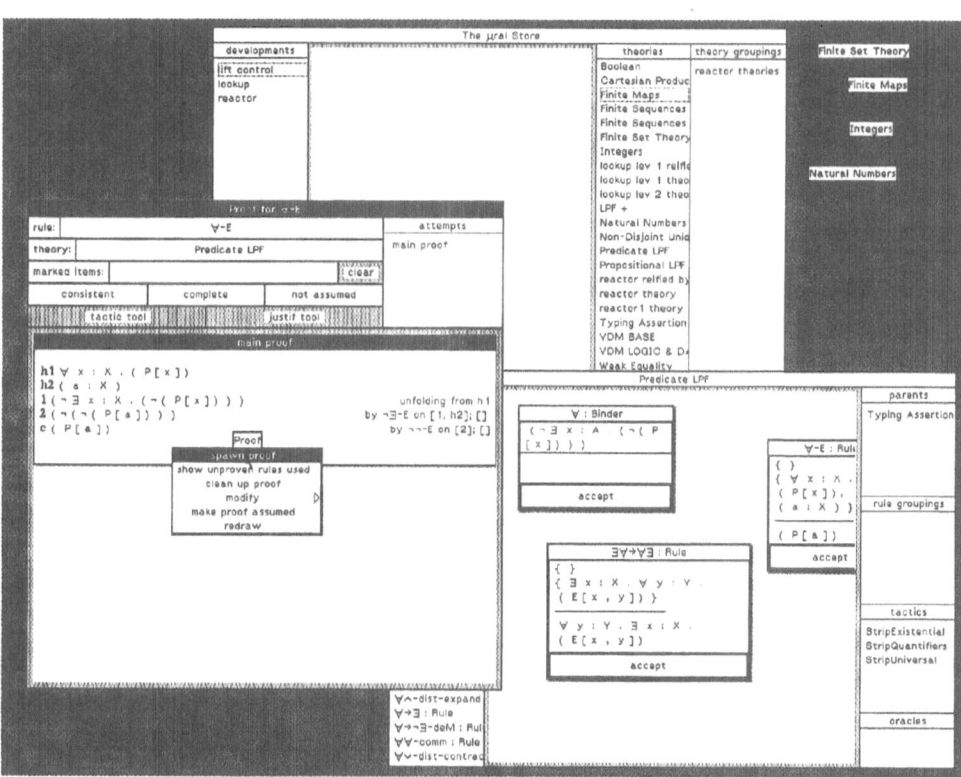

Figure 6.7: The *mural* proof assistant in action

Chapter 7

Supporting formal software development

This chapter presents the concepts of formal software development as a basis for the description of the VDM Support Tool in the following chapter.

The primary aim of formal methods of software development is to produce software systems that are formally verified with respect to their specifications. It is important that the specification should be at a high, 'human-oriented' level of description, devoid of machine-dependent or implementation-specific representations. Most formal development methods incorporate an abstract specification language designed for this purpose. To determine that an implementation formally satisfies its specification often involves the generation and discharge of *proof obligations*; the foundation of a formal method is that the proof of these is sufficient to ensure the correctness of the implementation. Discharging a proof obligation involves the construction of a proof; ensuring the correctness of the reasoning in this proof is of central importance. The development method should also be compositional, so that the process of moving from an abstract specification towards a particular implementation can be performed in small, manageable steps. Even with compositionality, the management of a fully formal design is non-trivial. Machine support for the processes involved is essential in order to maximise the degree of formality. This applies not only to the construction of proofs as described in Chapter 1, but also to the roles that these proofs play in the design process.

7.1 Abstract specification

7.1.1 Aims

An abstract specification of a system should concentrate upon *what* a system should do, rather than *how* it should do it. The intention in the design of the abstract specification should be to describe the properties the system should exhibit, rather than to attempt to describe a particular way to produce such a system. Thus, the specification should avoid making decisions about the data representations or algorithms to be used in the final system. This is not merely an exercise in the joys of abstraction; the separation of implementation decisions from the description of the system has many benefits. For example:

- The specification provides a precise description of the system earlier in its development and thus may expose faults in design that would otherwise not have emerged until after implementation.

- Discussion and correction of any weaknesses in a design is easier by reference to a specification than an implementation, (for example, there is no need to 'back-translate' from program-language constructs to what they are intended to represent or achieve).

- A specification makes it possible to consider alternative implementations (using different data representations, algorithms, or implementation languages).

There are two main 'flavours' of formal specification language: model-oriented and property-oriented (or 'algebraic'). In each case, the specification describes the class of those mathematical models which can be considered to satisfy the specification. The making of implementation decisions can be viewed as narrowing this class of models.

Both kinds of specification language typically have high-level data type constructors: model-oriented data type definitions correspond to set constructions, while algebraic type constructions define algebras (which may be modelled in a variety of ways, not necessarily set-theoretically). In the model-oriented approach, functions are specified by giving mathematical predicates that describe the relationship between the result and the arguments. An algebraic specification language uses *axioms* (often equations) which define properties of (combinations of) functions over data types.

Each of the two approaches has advantages and disadvantages. We will not go into these here. In the following, we will adopt the model-oriented approach, and work with the Vienna Development Method (VDM) as our example, but it should be noted that much of what follows can also be applied to the algebraic approach.

7.1.2　Specifications in VDM

We will give only a brief outline of specifications in VDM; further details may be found in [Jon90a].

A VDM specification typically consists of a set of data type definitions and a set of function and operation definitions upon these data types. The type definitions are abstract in the sense that they are built from mathematical type constructors (sets, maps, sequences). Of particular importance is the use of data type *invariants*: in a type definition, an invariant is a property that must always hold for members of that type. The use of invariants gives a richer (more expressive) type language than type constructors alone.

Unlike algebraic specifications, VDM specifications have a notion of state. The state is described as a particular type; often this is a composite type whose components can then be referred to separately. Operations can be defined in terms of their effects upon the state (i.e. operations can have side effects). Functions cannot have side effects.

Both functions and operations may be implicitly specified by giving *pre-* and *post-conditions* which stipulate criteria that are to hold before and after their 'execution'. The pre-condition of a function is a predicate on its 'arguments' whilst the post-condition is a predicate on it's 'arguments' and 'result'. For an operation these predicates may in addition describe how the operation must effect the state. Thus functions and operations may be defined in terms of their effects rather than the means by which they are to achieve them.

VDM permits specification at varying levels of abstraction. Through the use of abstract data types and implicit function and operation definitions, specifications can be written which capture what a system should do, rather than how it should be done. However, other specifications can capture particular design decisions through the use of type definitions with more implementation bias or through more explicit function and operation definitions. How one verifies that such a specification implements a more abstract specification will be discussed in more detail later.

7.1.3 Validation and verification of specifications

The construction of a formal specification is motivated by an informal notion of the behaviour of the final system. It is important to satisfy ourselves (or our clients) that the formal specification agrees with this informal idea. For example, we should check that no unexpected behaviour arises, and that every eventuality is catered for. The name given to this process of relating a formal specification to informal requirements is *validation*. We can formally prove that an implementation is correct with respect to a formal specification, but since validation concerns the interface between formality and informality, we can never conclusively prove that a formal specification agrees with an informal one: we can only increase our confidence that this is so. In a sense, validation is to specifications as testing is to programs. However, it can be carried out at a higher level of reasoning, using terminology suited to the particular application, rather than implementation-biased representations. The use of a formal development method increases confidence in a design by minimising the informal aspects, and by restricting the informal/formal interface to an early stage in the design process.

In the VDM Support Tool, our main concern is in reasoning about formal specifications and developments: the *verification* side of the design process. Some techniques for validation of formal specifications are addressed in Chapter 9.

A major advantage of a formal specification over an informal specification is that it can be mathematically analysed for flaws and weaknesses. There are several kinds of checks that will reveal inconsistencies in a formal specification.

One possible check is to determine whether or not a particular data type in a specification is actually inhabited (whether or not it will be possible to construct an object of that type). 'Simple' type-checking, as is performed in most programming languages, can be used to detect blatant type errors. However, the use of invariants can lead to subtler type errors, whereby one can construct objects that have the correct 'type shape', but which fail to satisfy the invariant. In general, this cannot be decided automatically, and thus type checking becomes a theorem proving exercise.

Another check, given an implicit specification of a function, is to consider whether or not there are indeed functions that satisfy this specification. The *implementibility* or *satisfiability* obligation states that for any valid inputs, there is at least one possible valid output. A proof of this assures us that so long as we implement the data types correctly, then there will be some way to implement the function[1]. The statement of the implementibility proof obligation is wholly determined by the function specification (and the type definitions), and so it can be automatically generated in a support environment.

---

[1] In fact this is not quite true, as it is possible to implicitly specify a non-computable function that could not then be implemented. Thus a satisfiability proof is to be seen as eliminating one kind of non-implementability.

The major role of verification, however, arises when relating one formal specification to another, as we will see in the next section.

7.2   Relating specifications

Once we have a formal specification, the remainder of the development process towards an implementation can be made fully formal. Note that this does not mean that the process is automatic, for the design decisions often involve a degree of intuition, but that each design step can be formally verified. Indeed, the need for proof obligations is partly due to the presence of intuitive steps. Each time we introduce intuition into a formal development, we must back it up by verification.

We can view the development process as the production of successive layers of specifications, where each layer adds some implementation bias to the previous layer. Thus we move from an abstract specification that describes the task to be performed towards one particular solution to the problem.

7.2.1   Data reification

In *data reification*, the designer chooses new representations of data types in the abstract specification. The new representations will typically be suited to data types available in the final implementation language of the design. A particular choice may be made to ensure that some operations can be efficiently implemented. In a multi-layered design, each layer might encapsulate a single small design decision. For example, we may choose to represent sets by lists of non-repeating elements in one reification, and then represent lists in turn by arrays. By breaking the reification into several steps we can isolate the issues involved in each form of representation.

When a new data representation is made on an intuitive basis, we must then justify the choice formally. In VDM, when we claim that one data type is a reification of another, we must give a *retrieve function* which for any element of the more 'concrete' type will give the corresponding element of the more 'abstract' one. We can then prove the *adequacy obligation*, which insists that every element of the abstract type is represented by some element of the concrete type (via the retrieve function). Note that two or more elements of the concrete type could be retrieved to the same abstract value; in other words, redundancy is permitted in the concrete representation.

7.2.2   Function/operation modelling

As well as relating the data structures of the two specifications via data reification, we must also relate the functions and operations in the 'concrete' specification to their counterparts in the 'abstract' specification. Roughly speaking, the concrete version of a function or operation must behave 'no worse than' the abstract version in analogous circumstances. That is, there must be an increase in definedness and a decrease in non-determinism.

In VDM, these conditions are captured in the *domain* and *result* proof obligations. The domain obligation states the increase in definedness: that is, whenever the abstract specification can be invoked, then so can the concrete counterpart. The result obligation encapsulates the decrease in non-determinism: that is, when invoking the abstract specification could lead to one of a range of behaviours, then the possibilities for its concrete counterpart will be a subset of these. The precise formulation of these obligations is detailed in Section 8.2.3; for further explanation and justification, see [Jon90a].

7.2.3 Operation decomposition

In a VDM specification, it is also possible to define an operation as a *composition* of other operations, for example as the invocation of one operation followed by another. The constructs for composing operations are very much like some of those found for composing statements in many programming languages. Though such a definition may be thought of as an *explicit* definition of the operation, it should not be forgotten that the individual 'statements' may consist of *implicit* operations, or even pre- and post-assertions. Similarly, a function may be explicitly defined by an expression in its arguments, but that expression may contain applications of other implicit functions.

The above description details 'bottom-up' design. Often, it is desired to build the operation in the opposite direction: that is, given its pre- and post-conditions, we wish to *de*compose it into simpler operations, such that their composition satisfies the original conditions. Associated with the composition constructs are a set of rules in the style of Hoare logic which relate the pre- and post-annotations of a composition to those of its components and thus provide a means for the verification of decomposition steps.

Thus, development of a specification can proceed in two directions: by *data* refinement through reification and function/operation modelling, and *algorithm* refinement through function definition and operation decomposition.

7.3 Support for reasoning about formal developments

A method such as VDM prescribes the proof obligations whose discharge ensures validity of design decisions. Thus such formal software development processes are suitable for automated support, not only in generating proof obligations from designs and in assisting in their proof, but also for maintaining the relationships between the proof obligations and the particular design steps from which they arise.

Clearly, we want our support tool for VDM to use the proof assistant for the discharging of proof obligations. In this section we discuss some of the issues involved in achieving this. (A more detailed description of the VDM Support Tool will be given in the next chapter.) Though our description will be based upon a support tool for VDM, there is much that will apply to the design of any specification support system that intends to use *mural's* proof assistant for its formal reasoning.

7.3.1 Instantiating the theory store for VDM

Before we can reason about VDM proof obligations, we must instantiate the proof assistant to provide the logic, types, constants, axioms and rules which form the 'reasoning kernel' for VDM, and which will be used in every single development. In addition to the LPF predicate calculus, this includes definitions of integers, sets, maps and so on, axioms which define the properties of them and functions on these types such as set membership and addition that VDM specifications assume are available. Note that this instantiation need only be carried out once, by the designers of the specification support tool: users of the tool need only know how to browse through the resultant body of knowledge[2].   In Section 3.5 it is shown how such an instantiation can be carried out in detail; here, we merely note that every development in our support tool for VDM can take advantage of this large, structured body of knowledge.

7.3.2   Translation of specifications and reifications

The foregoing is not the end of the theory-building story. Each VDM specification can be thought of as an extension of the base theory: it may define new types; and its function (and operation) specifications define properties of functions upon these data types (and its state). When attempting to discharge the proof obligations arising from a specification, the proof assistant (or the user thereof) must have access to this new information, otherwise the statement of the proof obligation will be meaningless. Where proof obligations concern the reification of one specification by another, then the information from both specifications should be available. This can be done by placing reification obligations in a theory which inherits information from the theories of its abstract and concrete specifications.

The VDM Support Tool provides a means for extracting the relevant information from a specification to form a theory (or hierarchy of theories) in the proof assistant; this then becomes the theory within which the proof obligations connected with that specification can be discharged. It also constructs suitable theories within which to reason about reifications. Thus the generation of proof obligations is part of a much larger translation process. Ideally, the writer of a VDM specification could be 'sheltered' from the theory construction. Perhaps the support system should even go so far as to never let the writer see the resultant theory, but to always 'unparse' it as a VDM specification. (Of course, this could only be done for theories that arose from translated VDM specifications.)

In our case, we are interested in showing that it is possible to use *mural* to support a particular development method; we are not so concerned with the niceties of converting specifications into theories. Our solutions are therefore crude, and fail to make the best use of the sharing and reuse of information that is possible using the full power of *mural*'s hierarchical theory store. Instead of directly translating a specification (or indeed, a development) into a *mural* theory, we shall have a separate VDM store which contains specifications and reifications as structured objects in their own right[3]; these are then translated to create *mural* theories containing the appropriate definitions and proof obligations. The translation process is defined in greater detail in the next chapter.

---

[2]Of course, this 'core of knowledge' about VDM constructs need not be static. In order to simplify proofs of obligations, users are likely to want to prove new theorems about the basic types and functions of VDM which would then be available for use in subsequent proofs.

[3]At first thought, it may seem that this is the *only* sensible approach, on the basis that specifications etc. contain extra information in addition to theoretical content (their display format, semantic relationships between certain components, and so on). However, there is no reason to prevent such extra information from being associated with the generated *mural* theory; this could even be done by providing an extension to the implementation of *mural* theories. (Readers who have an understanding of Smalltalk may best appreciate this point.)

Chapter 8

The *mural* VDM Support Tool

This chapter describes the support tool for VDM which has been built to integrate with the proof assistant. Through reference to the formal specification of the tool, it introduces the notions of specification, reification and development, and describes some of the operations upon the components of a development, including the generation of proof obligations.

As will be seen, there are many respects in which the support offered is incomplete. The VDM Support Tool was never intended to be a complete support environment for VDM, its main purpose being to demonstrate that *mural* could be extended by such tools. The tool only caters for a subset of the VDM specification language, and only permits limited kinds of reifications. In particular, operation decomposition is not addressed at all. Finally, the tool makes little effort to 'track' dependencies between specifications or reifications and their counterparts in the *mural* theory store.

The first section describes the support offered for building specifications in VDM and the second how theories can be built in the proof assistant to reason about them. In the third section we focus on some particular areas where the level of support provided could be improved.

8.1 Specifying VDM developments in VDM

From an early stage of its design, the VDM Support Tool (or VST) was envisaged as a structure editor within which specifications (and indeed reification relationships between specifications) could be built. Thus far it is a separate tool from the *mural* proof assistant and its theory store. In order to reason about specifications and reifications constructed in the VST, it would be necessary to construct corresponding *mural* theories about them. Originally considered to be a separate process, this 'translation' stage later became a function of the structure editor itself.

In developing the VST as a structure editor, we had to determine at least the 'abstract' syntax of the structures to be constructed. We chose to do this by specifying it in VDM, using type structures for the various syntactic classes.

For the specification language, this had already been done, as part of the BSI standardisation effort for VDM. From the (then current version of the) draft standard, we chose what we considered to be an 'interesting' subset of the language's abstract syntax definition. Here, 'interesting' means, 'neither too hard, nor too dull'! Some parts of the language were not considered because they introduced too much syntactic complexity, others because they were too similar to constructs that had already been introduced[1]. In practice, many constructs from the draft standard's syntax for expressions were added on a 'need to use' basis (as in, 'I need a set comprehension expression for this example').

As mentioned above, one of the main interests in constructing a support tool for VDM was in the generation of proof obligations that would 'exercise' the proof assistant. The most interesting proof obligations in VDM arise not from the need to check that an individual specification is well-formed and implementible, but from the need to justify the intuition behind design decisions in reification of one specification (or even of a single type definition) by another. In order to get to the stage of producing such interesting proof obligations, we chose to provide structure editing support for the construction and maintenance of reifications as objects in their own right. This led us to the model of a structure for *developments*, which record a formal development leading from an abstract specification towards a concrete implementation by reification. Such a model for developments is not provided in BSI/VDM.

It is important to note that for most of its lifespan, a development is incomplete, in that one or more levels of specification will be unfinished, or a reification of one specification by another will be incomplete, or incompletely justified.

Another important point to note is that the process of constructing different levels of specifications and reifications between them should have the same degrees of freedom as the construction of theories and proofs in the proof assistant. It should be possible to 'expand' a development in any direction, leaving some aspects incomplete whilst exploring others. For example, a developer may wish to concentrate upon reifying the type definitions in an abstract specification, perhaps for several levels, before considering the functions and operations in detail. In preference to imposing a process model of developments that insists (for example) that the abstract specification should be syntactically complete and semantically well-formed before work can begin on a more concrete specification, it should be possible to construct partial versions of both. Though this freedom in construction order could lead to misfortune (a mis-managed development could end up with countless 'loose threads' to be tied up), we consider it preferable to the imposition of unnecessary order[2]. It is not for us to decide what is 'the' correct manner in which to proceed with a development. What matters is that, regardless of the route taken, the final development is verified (as ever, with respect to its most abstract specification). Our structure for developments does not record the order of construction, but only the relationships between the parts constructed thus far.

8.1.1 Developments

In its most abstract sense, a development is a directed graph, whose nodes are specifications, with an edge from a specification A to a specification B when B is a reification of A. We might expect that a completed development will have a single 'most abstract' specification (which does not reify any other specification) and one or more 'implementations', and that for each implementation we can trace a path from the abstract specification to it. However, during construction, a development may look quite unlike this. There may

---

[1]The above is not intended as a criticism of BSI/VDM, but is merely the result of our intention to develop a prototype which examined some interesting issues, rather than a marketable support tool.

[2]It must be recognised that there is also a degree of *necessary* order in the design process. For instance, it is not possible to determine whether or not a function definition is well-formed if the types it refers to have not yet been defined.

be multiple attempts at the most abstract specification; there may be incomplete specifications and reifications even in the middle of a development path; or there may be
specifications which have not yet been related to any others. In short, there is very little structure that we can impose upon developments in mid-construction that would not
restrict the developer's style of working.

In preference to defining a general notion of directed graphs in VDM, and then using
this to define our 'syntax' for developments, we chose to model a development as a
collection of (named) specifications, and a collection of (named) reifications between
them:

$$Development :: SPECM : SpecName \xrightarrow{m} SpecDef$$
$$REIFM : ReifName \xrightarrow{m} ReifDef$$

8.1.2 Specifications

The abstract syntax of the specifications we support closely follows that of (part of) the
draft BSI standard for VDM.

In a *SpecDef*, we associate the body of a specification with a theory in a *mural* theory
store; the intention is that the associated theory will contain or inherit all of the information
necessary to reason about the specification.

$$SpecDef :: Spec : VdmBody$$
$$Theory : MuralTheoryName$$

A VDM specification may define new types, constants, functions and operations. We
model this by a collection of maps from names to these different kinds of definitions. It
may also define a state model.

$$VdmBody :: typem : TypeName \xrightarrow{m} TypeDef$$
$$state : [StateInfo]$$
$$constm : ConstName \xrightarrow{m} ConstDef$$
$$fnm : FnName \xrightarrow{m} FnDef$$
$$opm : OpName \xrightarrow{m} OpDef$$

The VDM Support Tool does not support modular specification as, at the time of writing, both the syntax and semantics of modularity in the draft standard are in a state of
flux, and we considered that to provide such support would require a considerable amount
of research into reification of modular specifications. As a result, each specification in a
development is both 'flat' and isolated from every other specification. If the same definition is required in two different specifications, then it must be duplicated in each. This
could lead to confusion if the two specifications define the same name in different ways.
It was a sad but necessary decision that we did not have the effort to consider modularity
issues, especially as the hierarchical nature of the *mural* theory store encourages reuse
of definitions. We will return to this subject when we consider the generation of *mural*
theories from developments in Section 8.2.

Type definitions

A type definition in a specification has a 'type shape' and possibly an invariant, which is described as an explicit function definition.

> *TypeDef* :: *shape* : *Type*
>   *inv*   : [*ExplFnDef*]

The type shape part is made up from a number of type constructors:

> *Type* = *BasicType* | *CompositeType* | *UnionType* | *SetType* |
>   *SeqType* | *MapType* | *FnType*[3] | *TypeName* | *OptionalType*

We shall not give the formal definitions of the various type constructors here: a full definition of *Type* can be found in [BSI90]. To give two examples, *BasicType* includes the types N, N_1, B, etc., whilst *CompositeTypes* are Cartesian products with named components, such as:

> *Date* :: *day*   : *Day*
>   *month* : *Month*
>   *year*   : *Year*

(Note: this is actually a named type definition. Unlike other *Types*, *CompositeType* shapes are not used except in type definitions.)

Notice that invariants are only associated with type definitions, and cannot appear within type shapes. However, a type shape can of course be the *name* of a type whose definition includes an invariant.)

Describing the invariant as a function definition raises the question of what type it should have. The approach we take is that the invariant is a function from values of the type shape part of the type definition to B; the type being defined can then be described as comprising those values of the type shape part for which the invariant holds. For example, in the type definition:

> *Evens* = N

> **where**
> *inv-Evens*$(n) \triangleq \exists m: N \cdot n = m \times 2$

the invariant function *inv-Evens* has the type $N \to B$.

This interpretation fits in well with *mural*'s subtyping construction. However, it leads to problems with composite type definitions: though *CompositeType* is indeed a *Type*, it is not properly a 'type expression' in that it can only be used in type definitions, and not in other places where a type expression is expected. In particular, a *CompositeType* cannot appear as an argument type of a function definition. One solution would be to introduce an 'intermediate' type name to represent the composite type without the invariant's restriction, but we feel that these 'in between' types are usually irrelevant. Instead, we prefer to treat the invariant as a function from the Cartesian product of the field types to B. For example in:

---

[3]*FnType* is included only to simplify the specification of explicit function definitions; it is not available as a 'first class' type in our model.

Date :: *day*   : *Day*
       month : *Month*
       year : *Year*

where
$inv\text{-}Date(d, m, y) \triangleq (m = \text{JAN} \implies d \le 31) \wedge \ldots$
the invariant is considered to have type *Day* × *Month* × *Year* → **B**.[4]

State definitions

The state of a specification is defined to be a special type definition whose shape is a *CompositeType*. This defines the 'state variables' of the specification as the components of the record, with the appropriate types. In addition to an invariant, the state may also have an *initialisation condition*, which specifies properties of the initial state.

StateInfo :: *name* : *Name*
          tp   : *CompositeType*
          inv   : *[ExplFnDef]*
          init   : *[ExplFnDef]*

Constant definitions

Constant definitions declare constants of particular types, which may or may not be given explicit values:

ConstDef :: *type* : *Type*
          val : *[Expr]*

As with the type shapes, we will not describe the various forms of expression here – a full definition of expressions can be found in [BSI90]. It will suffice for the moment to say that there are a large number of them and that the support tool does not cater for them all.

Function definitions

Functions may be defined explicitly or implicitly:

FnDef = *ImplFnDef* | *ExplFnDef*

ImplFnDef :: *dom* : *PatternTypePair**
           rng : *IdTypePair*
           pre : *Expr*
           post : *Expr*

---

[4]Since this decision was made, the abstract syntax of BSI/VDM type definitions has changed, so that an invariant is recorded as an expression and an 'argument pattern', where the free variables in the expression should also occur in the pattern.

ExplFnDef :: *type*   : [*FnType*]
             pre   : [*ExplFnDef*]
             parms : *Pattern**
             clause : *Expr*

An implicit function definition has a precondition and a postcondition. The precondition should be a predicate in the arguments to the function; the postcondition can additionally refer to the result (whose name is given by the *Id* in the *rng*). An explicit function has no postcondition; instead it has an explicit clause expression. In both cases, the arguments are given as *Patterns* (either a single variable, or an expression containing variables, such as *mk-Date(d, m, y)*).

Operation definitions

Operation specifications are similar to functions, but with an additional list of 'read and write' state access descriptions:

OpDef = *ImplOpDef* | *ExplOpDef*

ImplOpDef :: *dom* : *PatternTypePair**
               rng : [*IdTypePair*]
               exts : *ExtVarInf**
               pre : *Expr*
               post : *Expr*

ExtVarInf :: *mode* : (READ | READWRITE)
               rest : *IdTypePair*

ExplOpDef :: *dom*   : *Type**
               rng   : [*Type*]
               pre   : [*ExplFnDef*]
               parms : *Pattern**
               clause : *Stmt*

The above gives a brief overview of the components of specifications in the VDM Support Tool. More detail will be introduced when we describe the generation of proof obligations and the kinds of consistency checks to be made upon specifications.

8.1.3 Reifications

The above abstract syntax definition of a VDM specification has followed, more or less, that given in [BSI90]. However, that definition does not give a model for the reification process. The basis for the following model of reification is the description given in [Jon90a].

The main information to be recorded in the reification of one specification by another is recorded in a *ReifDef*. It gives the names of the specs, the definition of the initial state reification obligation, and the operation and function models:

$ReifDef$ :: $Reifier$: $SpecName$
$Reifiee$: $SpecName$
$StateReif$: $StateReif$
$OpModels$: $OpModel$-set

We could also have added a set of data reifications at this level, to match the type definitions of the specifications. However, as we shall see, the required data reifications are 'driven' by the operation and function models, rather than by the type definitions themselves. Therefore, we have encapsulated the data reifications within the operation and function modelling components.

State reifications

Reification of the state model of one specification by another involves showing that the more concrete specification's state type reifies that of the more abstract specification. In addition, there is an obligation to show that the concrete invariant initial state condition satisfies their abstract counterparts under retrieval:

$StateReif$ :: $DataReif$: $DataReif$
$InvStateObl$: $OblPacket$
$InitStateObl$: $OblPacket$

This is the first place where we have introduced a proof obligation into our model. (Strictly speaking, we should have done so earlier, and associated an implementibility proof obligation with each implicit function definition.) We model proof obligations as *OblPackets*, which simply record the (VDM) form of the obligation and possibly a reference to the corresponding theorem in the *mural* theory store:

$OblPacket$ :: $ProofObl$: $Expr$
$Place$: $[ThmRef]$

(In the implementation the need for *OblPackets* has been circumvented: proof obligations, in the form of unproven rules, are generated directly as part of the translation of the specification.)

Operation modelling

Each operation model records a modelling relationship between an abstract and a concrete operation. Though we refer to them as abstract and concrete operations, 'concrete' in this case does not mean 'explicit'. Both operations should be implicit. Relationships between implicit and explicit operations fall within the remit of operation decomposition, which is not catered for in our support tool.

$$OpModel :: \begin{array}{ll} AbstractOpn & : \; OpName \\ ConcreteOpn & : \; OpName \\ DomReifs & : \; DataReif^* \\ RngReif & : \; [DataReif] \\ ExtReifs & : \; DataReif^* \\ DomainObl & : \; OblPacket \\ ResultObl & : \; OblPacket \end{array}$$

We associate a data reification with each argument (*DomReifs*) and each state designator (*ExtReifs*), and with the result (*RngReif*). (The two operations must have the same number of arguments and state designators for this to be possible.) This is done because it is possible that each argument of the abstract operation could be reified in a different way in the concrete operation (even if they are of the same abstract type, although this would be somewhat unorthodox.) Furthermore, the arguments of an operation may have type shapes that are not just the names of types given in the type definitions of the specification. (Consider an operation which takes an argument $x: X$-set.) This is why it is not sufficient to have data reifications only for the type definitions of a specification.

The insistence that the abstract and concrete operations must have the same number of state designators imposes restrictions upon the ways in which the state model can be reified. If an operation refers to state components rather than to the state as a whole, this forces us to treat the reification of the state as a composition of the reifications of the components, whereas in general, data reification of the state model of a specification is performed on the state as a whole.

To see this in more detail, suppose that the abstract state model AS contains two components, $a_1: A_1$ and $a_2: A_2$, and that an abstract operation OP_A reads a_1 and writes a_2. In order for a concrete operation OP_C to be a candidate to model OP_C, the concrete state CS must have components $c_1: C_1$ and $c_2: C_2$ which are the concrete counterparts of a_1 and a_2 under retrieval. In other words, there should be retrieve functions

$$retr\text{-}A_1: C_1 \rightarrow A_1, \quad retr\text{-}A_2: C_2 \rightarrow A_2$$

such that these components are independent of each other when the entire state is retrieved, thus forcing the definition of the state retrieval as:

$$retr\text{-}AS : CS \rightarrow AS$$
$$retr\text{-}AS(mk\text{-}CS(c_1, c_2)) \quad \triangleq \quad mk\text{-}AS(retr\text{-}A_1(c_1), retr\text{-}A_2(c_2))$$

(i.e. forcing *retr-AS* to satisfy a homomorphism property). Furthermore, the abstract and concrete operations must mention the corresponding components in the same order in the externals list.

The alternative to the above treatment would be to 'expand out' the externals of an operation, replacing their occurrences in the pre and postconditions by references to the entire state. For example, suppose our abstract state model is as above and we have the abstract operation:

$OP_A \, ()$
ext rd $a_1 \; : \; A_1$
    wr $a_2 \; : \; A_2$
pre $P(a_1, a_2)$
post $Q(a_1, \overleftarrow{a_2}, a_2)$

then the externals information would be expanded to give the operation:

$OP_A' \ ()$
ext wr as : AS
pre $P(s\text{-}a_1(as), s\text{-}a_2(as))$
post $Q(s\text{-}a_1(as), s\text{-}a_2(\overleftarrow{as}), s\text{-}a_2(as)) \wedge s\text{-}a_1(as) = s\text{-}a_1(\overleftarrow{as})$

Each instance of a component in the pre and postcondition has been replaced by an application of the corresponding selector function upon the whole state. Note in particular how the 'before' state has to be handled in the postcondition, and the need to explicitly state that the a_1 component remains unchanged. The situation is more complex when there are state components that are neither read nor written by the operation.

Ideally, rather than build a new data reification for each argument of each operation we model, we would want to refer to some existing body of data reifications. This can be modelled by having a 'library' of named *DataReifs* within each *ReifDef*, and by giving these names in the operation models instead. However, at the moment we want to avoid introducing such 'referential clutter' as much as possible (it is a form of implementation bias, after all), in order to concentrate upon the relationships between data reifications and operation models. Therefore we choose our abstract specification as above[5].

Domain and result proof obligations are associated with the operation model. Details of how this is done will be given in Section 8.2.3.

Data reifications

A data reification is between an abstract type and a concrete type. It requires a retrieve function from the concrete type to the abstract type, and has an associated adequacy proof obligation (as described in Chapter 7.)

$$
\begin{array}{lll}
DataReif :: & concr\_type & : \ Type \\
& abstr\_type & : \ Type \\
& retrieve\_fn & : \ ReifFn \\
& adequacy\_obl & : \ OblPacket
\end{array}
$$

8.1.4   Well-formedness checks: an apology

As stated in the introduction to this chapter, it was never intended that the VDM Support Tool should be 'complete'. Effort in its design has concentrated upon the generation of proof obligations together with sufficient information to permit the use of the proof assistant in discharging them. As a consequence, many of the checks that one might expect such a tool to perform (without resort to the proof assistant) have been omitted: static patent type-checking, checks on arities of function calls against their definitions, use of undefined names, and so forth. Some such checks are described in earlier project

---

[5]In this case, it is easy to see how the transition towards a more referential implementation may be made. It is more problematic to consider how one might alter our model to allow the *composition* of data reifications, that would for example allow us to use the information in a reification of *WeekDays* by $\mathbb{N}$ in the construction of a reification of *WeekDay*-set by $\mathbb{N}^*$.

documents. In the main, these checks would not be difficult to perform. However, errors of these kinds in specifications will be revealed either during the translation into the theory store (see next section), or in attempting to reason about the translated specification.

8.2   Theories from specifications

In this section we outline how specifications and reifications are translated into a *mural* store to yield new theories complete with relevant proof obligations.

Recall from the previous chapter that the *mural* store to which we translate should be instantiated for VDM, so that it contains a 'VDM Primitives' theory. This theory should be an ancestor of every theory generated from a specification or reification in the VDM Support Tool.

8.2.1   Translation of specifications

How best to divide the objects corresponding to specifications into theories is largely a matter of taste. For example, we could try to place each type definition in a theory of its own; this would allow reuse of the type definition when reasoning about other specifications. However, we would then have to make the theory structure reflect the inter-dependency of type definitions, in particular, mutually recursive type definitions would present some difficulties. We choose a simpler approach where each specification becomes a single *mural* theory. If a 'finer-grained' structure is required, then the theories must be rebuilt by hand.

Thus, the result of translation of a specification is a single *mural* theory, with the VDM Primitives theory as its (sole) parent. The theory contains:

- *mural* type definitions, type formation and checking axioms corresponding to the type definitions of the specification;

- definitions of any constants and explicit functions;

- definitions of the pre- and postconditions of implicit functions and operations;

- (initially unproven) rules corresponding to proof obligations and type-checking (including invariant checking) of functions and operations

Translation of types and type definitions

Generally, a type definition in a specification will be translated to a similar type definition in *mural*. Most of the type constructors of VDM can be described in 'general' theories which form part of the VDM Primitives theory. Sets, maps, sequences, (binary) type unions and optional types are in this category. Type definitions using these constructors can be translated as *mural* definitions using instances of the generic constructors. N-ary type unions can be translated as a composition of binary unions.

Invariants

For a definition of type T with an invariant where the type shape uses the above constructors, translation is straightforward. First, the definition of the invariant $inv\text{-}T$ is translated as an explicit function definition (as will be described later), then the type definition is translated to a *SubType* definition. For example, the type definition:

$$T = Texp$$

where

$$inv\text{-}T(v) \triangleq P(v)$$

is translated to

$$T \mapsto <v\!: Texp' \mid inv\text{-}T(v)>$$

where *Texp'* is the translation of the type shape *Texp* and *inv-T* is the defined constant corresponding to the invariant function.

Composite types

Composite type definitions require a different treatment. It is not a simple matter to define a generic 'composite type constructor' in *mural*. Therefore composite type shapes cannot be translated into *mural* type expressions directly. Furthermore, a greater amount of information is associated with composite types than with other type constructions, in that a composite type definition also defines constructor and destructor functions. Instead, we create an axiomatic definition, with formation and typing rules for expressions involving the constructor and destructors.

For example, the composite type definition

$$T :: f1 : A$$
$$ f2 : B$$

should be translated to a type constant *T* and a declaration of the constructor and destructor functions as expression constants with expression arity two and one:

$$mk\text{-}T \mapsto [2, 0]; s\text{-}f1, s\text{-}f2 \mapsto [1, 0]$$

with the appropriate typing axioms:

$$\boxed{\text{mk-T formn}}\ \frac{a\!: A, b\!: B}{mk\text{-}T(a, b)\!: T}$$

$$\boxed{\text{s-f1 formn}}\ \frac{t\!: T}{s\text{-}f1(t)\!: A}$$

$$\boxed{\text{s-f2 formn}}\ \frac{t\!: T}{s\text{-}f2(t)\!: B}$$

and axioms defining *mk-T*, *s-f1* and *s-f2*:

$$\boxed{\text{mk-T intro}}\ \frac{t\!: T}{mk\text{-}T(s\text{-}f1(t), s\text{-}f2(t)) = t}$$

$$\boxed{\text{s-f1 intro}}\ \frac{mk\text{-}T(a, b)\!: T}{s\text{-}f1(mk\text{-}T(a, b)) = a}$$

$$\boxed{\text{s-f2 intro}}\ \frac{mk\text{-}T(a, b)\colon T}{s\text{-}f2(mk\text{-}T(a, b)) = b}$$

(note the use of typing assertions to ensure that $mk\text{-}T(a, b)$ is well-formed)

When a composite type definition has an associated invariant, this must also be declared and mentioned in the $mk\text{-}T$ formation axiom, e.g.:

$$\boxed{\text{mk-T formn}}\ \frac{a\colon A, b\colon B, inv\text{-}T(a, b)}{mk\text{-}T(a, b)\colon T}$$

and we must also provide an axiom for asserting the invariant:

$$\boxed{\text{inv-T intro}}\ \frac{mk\text{-}T(a, b)\colon T}{inv\text{-}T(a, b)}$$

Translation of functions and operations

A VDM definition of a function, f, declares a new function name for use in expressions. Therefore the process of translation creates a declaration in the corresponding theory of a constant symbol f of the appropriate arity. To help the readability of any expressions involving them, it is also useful to create declarations for the precondition and postcondition of the function where appropriate. Operations do not form part of the expression syntax and therefore have no direct counterpart in the theory of the specification; rather we create, in the translation of operations, unproven rules whose proof corresponds to the demonstration of desired properties of the operation such as satisfiability or well-formedness.

There are various different approaches that can be taken to 'interpretation' of functions and operations in the theory store. In this section we describe just one possible approach and give some discussion of its advantages and disadvantages over some possible alternatives. In particular, the approach described here differs somewhat from that described in Chapter 3.

Translation of preconditions and postconditions

The most natural way in which to interpret preconditions and postconditions is as defined constants in the proof assistant. Thus, for example, the implicit function:

$f\ (a\colon A, b\colon B)\ r\colon R$
pre $P(a, b)$
post $Q(a, b, r)$

Would give rise to two defined constants:

$pre\text{-}f \triangleq P(\llbracket 1 \rrbracket, \llbracket 2 \rrbracket)$
$post\text{-}f \triangleq Q(\llbracket 1 \rrbracket, \llbracket 2 \rrbracket, \llbracket 3 \rrbracket)$

Here, $P(\llbracket e1 \rrbracket, \llbracket e2 \rrbracket)$ is the translation of $P(a, b)$ with instances of a and b replaced by the placeholders $\llbracket e1 \rrbracket$ and $\llbracket e2 \rrbracket$ respectively.

These are then available in the theory of the specification. For example, one might wish to show that the function is implementable by proving the rule:

$$\boxed{\text{f-implementibility}}\ \frac{a\colon A, b\colon B, pre\text{-}f(a, b)}{\exists r\colon R \cdot post\text{-}f(a, b, r)}$$

During this proof, *pre-f* and *post-f* could be unfolded and folded simply as required.

There are, however, a few consequences of this approach that are worthy of elaboration. One difficulty arises when the expressions P and Q do not mention all of their possible free variables. If the expression P say, does not involve variable a, then the translation is complicated for it is impossible simply to construct the definition[6]:

$$pre\text{-}f \triangleq P(\llbracket 2 \rrbracket)$$

A possible solution would be to simply add some clause to the translated form of P that mentioned the absent variable but did not alter the semantic content. One such possibility would be to add '$\wedge\ a = a$' to the body of the definition. This would have the additional consequence of making the precondition strict in all the arguments of the function which may or may not be desirable. In either case, it is certainly not an elegant solution.

Another approach, indeed that which is favoured here, is to translate such predicates to definitions of smaller arities and for the translation mechanism to 'remember' which arguments are to be used in the translation other things that use them. For example, in the above case, the precondition translates to the definition:

$$pre\text{-}f \triangleq P(\llbracket 1 \rrbracket)$$

but then the mechanism that constructs the satisfiability obligation must 'know' to insert the second of the possible arguments into the precondition, thus:

$$\boxed{\text{f-implementibility}} \frac{a\colon A,\, b\colon B,\, pre\text{-}f(b)}{\exists r\colon R \cdot post\text{-}f(a, b, r)}$$

A third alternative is to translate the preconditions and postconditions to primitive constants and give their semantics via axioms added to the theory. This was considered to complicate their manipulation unnecessarily and is not discussed here, though the approach will be described in the treatment of the function bodies in the next section.

Another source of possible debate regards whether preconditions should be denoting for all values of the types of the function's arguments. One viewpoint is that we are only interested in those properties of a function that hold when its precondition is true, and therefore the precondition need not be defined for all possible values of the function's argument types. It does not matter whether the precondition is false or undefined for some values, because in either case we will not be able to prove anything about the result of applying the function. However, this does become relevant if we want to be able to determine for which values the function is *not* defined. This may happen in validation, for example. Furthermore, a prototype implementation may include tests to check whether or not preconditions hold before functions and operations are invoked (providing one form of specification testing). This could run into problems if such tests were derived from non-total preconditions.

The insistence that the precondition should be total can be captured by the proof obligation:

$$\boxed{\text{wf-pre-f}} \frac{a\colon A,\, b\colon B}{pre\text{-}f(a, b)\colon \mathbb{B}}$$

---

[6]The proof assistant does not allow this kind of defined constant as the ensuing complication of the folding and unfolding of definitions would work against their intended purpose. Technically, definitional equality corresponds to strong equality and so is non-strict. Consider $pre\text{-}f(a, b) = P(b)$ where a is non-denoting.

A similar requirement can be made of the postcondition: that is, that it should always be denoting, or at least whenever the precondition holds. Formally, this is captured by the rule:

$$\boxed{\text{wf-post-f}}\ \frac{a\colon A,\ b\colon B,\ \textit{pre-f}(a,b)}{\textit{post-f}(a,b,r)\colon \mathbb{B}}$$

These two well-formedness rules can be thought of as describing points of style rather than being essential to the validation of the specification. Instead of regarding them as proof obligations, they could be thought of as 'proof opportunities'.

Translation of explicit function definitions

It is possible to use defined constants for the translation of the body of explicit functions definitions. This approach is described in 3.5. Thus the explicit function definition

$$f : A \times B \to R$$
$$f(a,b) \;\triangleq\; Q(a,b)$$
$$\text{pre } P(a,b)$$

could be translated to the two defined constants

$$f \triangleq Q(\llbracket e1 \rrbracket, \llbracket e2 \rrbracket)$$
$$\textit{pre-f} \triangleq P(\llbracket e1 \rrbracket, \llbracket e2 \rrbracket)$$

The information in the signature can be captured by the rule:

$$\boxed{\text{f-form'n}}\ \frac{a\colon A,\ b\colon B,\ P(a,b)}{f(a,b)\colon R}$$

and this can be proven by using the typing rules for the constructs in Q. This rule plays a similar role to that which implementibility plays for implicit functions.

Again, however, we have the problem of unmentioned arguments, this time additionally in the function body. However, the translation of a binary function to a unary definition is not really acceptable as some of the intended meaning of the function definition would be lost. Equally the addition of a dummy clause to mention the dummy argument is not very attractive: if the function is Boolean valued, we could use '$\wedge\, a = a$' again; however, if it is not, then a different 'trick' needs to be found. One possibility would be to use a let expression; thus:

$$f : A \times B \to R$$
$$f(a,b) \;\triangleq\; Q(b)$$
$$\text{pre } P(a,b)$$

would give:

$$f \triangleq \text{let } a\colon A = \llbracket 1 \rrbracket \text{ in } Q(\llbracket 2 \rrbracket)$$

but this is not at all natural[7].

Therefore we have chosen to translate explicit functions into primitive constants and to give their meaning via axioms rather than directly via definitions. This has the further advantage of making the translation of explicit functions similar to that for implicit functions. In this way:

---

[7]Of course, we could consider defining a new binder λ, and translating f to a nullary defined constant: $\lambda a\colon A.\lambda b\colon B.Q(b)$ but this is departing too far from the style of VDM.

$$f : A \times B \to R$$
$$f(a\colon A, b\colon B) \;\triangleq\; Q(a, b)$$
$$\text{pre } P(a, b)$$

yields a primitive constant with expression arity two (and, as described above, a defined constant for the precondition). The semantic content is given via the axiom:

$$\boxed{\text{f-def'n}}\ \frac{a\colon A, b\colon B, \textit{pre-f}(a, b), Q(a, b)\colon R}{f(a, b) = Q(a, b)}$$

Note that we encode the fact that the body should be well formed as a hypothesis in the axiom. This precaution prevents reasoning about ill-formed functions; however, it is likely to cause some inconvenience in use. Thus it may be advisable to discharge a general well-formedness requirement:

$$\boxed{\text{wf-f}}\ \frac{a_2\colon A_2, \textit{pre-f}(a_2)}{Q(a_2)\colon R}$$

Then we could prove a lemma corresponding to the axiom without the last hypothesis.

With this mechanism for translating explicit functions it becomes a simple matter to handle unmentioned arguments. For example:

$$f : A \times B \to R$$
$$f(a\colon A, b\colon B) \;\triangleq\; Q(b)$$
$$\text{pre } P(a)$$

would still yield a primitive constant with expression arity two and the axiom:

$$\boxed{\text{f-def'n}}\ \frac{a\colon A, b\colon B, \textit{pre-f}(a), Q(b)\colon R}{f(a, b) = Q(b)}$$

Translation of implicit function definitions

Using the above mechanism for the translation of explicit functions has the aesthetic advantage of making it possible to handle implicit functions in a similar manner. Consider the similar example:

$$f \ (a\colon A, b\colon B) \ r\colon R$$
$$\text{pre } P(a, b)$$
$$\text{post } Q(a, b, r)$$

This again yields one new primitive constant f of expression arity two. In this case we have two defined constants, the extra one being for the postcondition:

$$f \mapsto [2, 0]$$
$$\textit{pre-f} \triangleq P(\llbracket 1 \rrbracket, \llbracket 1 \rrbracket)$$
$$\textit{post-f} \triangleq Q(\llbracket 1 \rrbracket, \llbracket 2 \rrbracket, \llbracket 3 \rrbracket)$$

The definition axiom is also similar to the implicit case except that now we do not know the value of the application of f, rather only that the postcondition holds for this value:

$$\boxed{\text{f-def'n}}\ \frac{a\colon A, b\colon B, \textit{pre-f}(a, b), \exists r\colon R \cdot \textit{post-f}(a, b, r)}{\textit{post-f}(a, b, f(a))}$$

This time the typing information must be given via an additional axiom:

$$\boxed{\text{f-form'n}} \frac{a\!:\!A,\, pre\text{-}f(a),\, \exists r\!:\!R \cdot post\text{-}f(a,r)}{f(a)\!:\!R}$$

As before, general implementability is then a rule that can, but need not, be discharged:

$$\boxed{\text{f-impl'y}} \frac{a\!:\!A,\, pre\text{-}f(a)}{\exists r\!:\!R \cdot post\text{-}f(a,r)}$$

In this case it is crucial to have the last hypothesis to the definition and formation axioms. Without it one could prove the implementability obligation directly from the formation axiom (see the discussion in Section 3.5.3). More generally, one would also be able to introduce inconsistencies into the theory – even when the function is not implementable. To see how this might happen, consider the function specification:

$f\ (a\!:\!A, b\!:\!B)\ r\!:\!R$
pre true
post false

The definition axiom (without the extra hypothesis) would become:

$$\boxed{\text{f-def'n}} \frac{a\!:\!A,\, b\!:\!B}{\text{false}}$$

This is certainly not desirable!

Translation of operation definitions

As operation decomposition is not supported, only implicit operation definitions are translated.

Preconditions and postconditions are translated in a similar manner to that for function definitions except that their translation is slightly more complicated because they can additionally refer to the 'before' and 'after' states of the operation. The externals construct makes it possible to refer to subcomponents of the state and these are added to the list of parameter variables in the predicates. The order in which these variables are arranged is unimportant but, of course, the same order must be used in all cases.

The implementibility obligation for an operation

$OP\ (x\!:\!X)\ r\!:\!R$
ext rd rd : Rd
   wr wr : Wr
pre $P(x, rd, wr)$
post $Q(x, r, rd, \overleftarrow{wr}, wr)$

is translated as an unproven rule:

$$\boxed{\text{OP implementibility}} \frac{x\!:\!X,\, rd\!:\!Rd,\, \overleftarrow{wr}\!:\!Wr,\, pre\text{-}OP[x, r, rd, \overleftarrow{wr}]}{\exists r\!:\!R \cdot \exists wr\!:\!Wr \cdot post\text{-}OP[x, r, rd, \overleftarrow{wr}, wr]}$$

8.2.2 Translation of reifications

In order to reason about a reification of one specification by another, we need the information contained in the two specifications. Therefore, the theory within which we reason about the reification inherits from the theories associated with both specifications. This is achieved by making the theories of the two specifications parents of the reification theory.

Roughly, the theory of a reification contains definitions of the retrieve functions used in the data reifications, together with all the concomitant proof obligations of data reification and operation modelling. It also contains definitions of any auxiliary types and functions used.

Translation of data reifications

Within a reification, a particular data reification from concrete type C to abstract type A via a retrieve function *retr-A* translates to:

- a definition or declaration of the retrieve function (in the same manner as for explicit function definitions), as a function from C to A:

  $retr\text{-}A \longmapsto [1, 0];$

- and an unproven rule expressing the adequacy obligation for the data reification:

$$\boxed{\text{retr-A adequacy}}\ \frac{a \colon A}{\exists c \colon C \cdot retr\text{-}A[c] = a}$$

Both of these are situated in the theory of the overall reification.

8.2.3 Translation of operation models

Recall that an operation modelling refers to the abstract and concrete operations and a number of *DataReifs*. Translation of the *OpModel* amounts to the translation of each of these along with the creation of two unproven rules in the reification theory: one expressing the domain obligation, and another expressing the result obligation.

Suppose an abstract operation OP_A is modelled by a concrete operation OP_C and that a_c, r_c, rd_c, wr_c are names of the argument, result, reads and writes of OP_C and that *retr-a*,...,*retr-wr* are their associated retrieve functions. Then the proof obligations generated are of the form:

$$\boxed{OP_C \text{ domain obligation}}\ \frac{\begin{array}{c} a_c \colon A_c,\ rd_c \colon RD_c,\ wr_c \colon WR_c, \\ pre\text{-}OP_A[retr\text{-}a(a_c),\ retr\text{-}rd(rd_c),\ retr\text{-}wr(wr_c)] \end{array}}{pre\text{-}OP_C[a_c,\ rd_c,\ wr_c]}$$

which says that the concrete precondition should hold whenever the abstract precondition holds for the retrieved values, and

$$\boxed{OP_C \text{ result obligation}}\ \frac{\begin{array}{c} a_c \colon A_C,\ r_c \colon R_C,\ rd_c \colon RD_C,\ \overleftarrow{wr_c} \colon WR_C,\ wr_c \colon WR_C, \\ pre\text{-}OP_A[retr\text{-}a(a_c),\ retr\text{-}rd(rd_c),\ retr\text{-}wr(\overleftarrow{wr_c})], \\ post\text{-}OP_C[a_c,\ r_c,\ rd_c,\ \overleftarrow{wr_c},\ wr_c] \end{array}}{\begin{array}{c} post\text{-}OP_A[retr\text{-}a(a_c),\ retr\text{-}r(r_c),\ retr\text{-}rd(rd_c), \\ retr\text{-}wr(\overleftarrow{wr_c}),\ retr\text{-}wr(wr_c)] \end{array}}$$

that is that the abstract postcondition should hold on the retrieved values whenever both the abstract precondition and the concrete postcondition hold. The generalisation to multiple arguments and state references is straightforward.

Note that this definition supports operation modelling where the types of the arguments and results are reified. It could be argued that these are the 'visible' types of the specification and as such should not be subjected to refinement. We choose the more general formulation here, but notice that a simpler form of the obligations could be given in the restricted case.

8.3   Scope for growth

As we have frequently pointed out, our VDM Support Tool is not a fully-fledged environment, but was developed to demonstrate some of the interesting issues arising from reasoning about VDM specifications and developments. In this section we describe some of the ways in which the tool could be improved or extended, both in itself and with respect to its interface with the proof assistant.

8.3.1   Theory structuring for greater reuse

At present, each specification is translated into a single theory which is a direct descendant of the 'VDM Primitives' theory. In practice, this proves very restrictive: for example, it is not possible to re-use the type definitions etc. of one specification in other specifications. From the proof assistant's point of view, there is no reason why this cannot be done. However, our tool would then have to support modular VDM specifications, or extend its VDM with some form of non-standard 'use the definitions from this theory' construct. The latter approach is unacceptable in the face of current attempts to standardise the VDM notation; the former awaits the outcome of further research in modularisation.

Reification is also limited in practice by the present approach of making the reification theory a direct descendant of the theories of its abstract and concrete specifications. Just as it would be useful to be able to reuse type definitions, etc., it would be useful to be able to draw data reifications from a library, and to compose new data reifications from them.

This suggests a far more complex theory structure for developments. Commonly used type definitions would reside in their own theories, creating a hierarchy of type definition theories. Data reifications between particular types would belong in theories which are descendants of the theories of those types, or possibly of other data reifications. Specification theories would then inherit information from the theories of the types (and possibly other specifications) to which they refer. Finally, reification theories would inherit from the theories of their abstract and concrete specifications, and from the theories of the data reifications that they use.

8.3.2   Determining a correct order for translation

Ideally, when asked to translate a specification, the VDM Support Tool should determine the dependencies between the components of the specification, and translate them in the correct order. At present, this is not done, and 'blind' translation can cause problems;

frequently, the user must translate the components individually in the correct order. Furthermore, it is not possible at present to translate recursive type definitions or mutually recursive function definitions. At the time of writing, some work is planned to improve this situation.

8.3.3 Tracking of proof obligations

At present, the VDM Support Tool does not keep track of the translations of specifications and reifications. This has two main disadvantages: firstly, changes to a specification or reification are not carried through to any existing translation; and secondly, there is no way of knowing from the VDM Support Tool whether or not all the obligations pertaining to a specification or reification have been discharged. The latter problem would be easy to solve, modulo the first problem, which would be more difficult.

8.3.4 Consistency checks

As mentioned earlier, the VDM Support Tool performs very few consistency checks. Many errors in specifications that are left to be discovered when using the proof assistant (or during translation) could be detected much earlier, for example:

static (patent) type-checking: in the presence of invariants, it is not possible to be certain that an expression is correctly typed without resorting to proof; however, it would be perfectly possible to detect and inform the user of 'blatant' type errors.

consistency of usage: it would be easy to check that function calls have the correct number of arguments, etc.

consistency of definition: for example: at present, it is possible to change the arity of the retrieve function, and to give it the wrong type signature. It would not be difficult to make it impossible for the user to do this, thus limiting the damage.

undefined names: would be easy to detect.

unfilled templates: in some cases an incomplete definition in a specification will yield an incomplete translation in the proof assistant. (The user is warned, but the translation is still performed.) In other cases (for example, an uncompleted operation model), an attempt to translate will fail. It would be better if unfilled templates could be checked for in advance of translation.

8.3.5 Data reification and patterns

In BSI VDM, the formal arguments to operations can take the form of *patterns* such as $mk\text{-}T(a, b)$: T; then the pre- and postconditions can refer to a and b. However, if this were the argument to the concrete operation OP_C in an operation model, we would want to retrieve $mk\text{-}T(a, b)$ as a single value, rather than retrieve a and b separately. At present, this is not possible in our support tool, and patterns are not supported.

Unfortunately, the same problem arises when an operation accesses subcomponents of the state rather than the state as a whole. An abstract operation can only be modelled by a concrete one if both refer to the state as a whole, or if, when retrieving T_a from T_c, we have:

$$retr\text{-}T_a(mk\text{-}T_c(a_c, b_c)) = mk\text{-}T_a(retr\text{-}A_a(a_c), retr\text{-}B_c(b_c))$$

This greatly limits the possibilities for state reification.

One solution in the state case is to consider a and $\overleftarrow{a}$ in the above as abbreviations for $s\text{-}a(t)$ and $s\text{-}a(\overleftarrow{t})$, where t and $\overleftarrow{t}$ are names representing the initial and final states and to replace occurrences of a and $\overleftarrow{a}$ by the latter expressions in translation of proof obligations. Suppose that the abstract operation OP_A in an operation model as above writes a component c of the abstract state, and that OP_C only writes state component a. Then the result obligation might look like:

$$t\colon T,\ \overleftarrow{t}\colon T$$
$$pre\text{-}OP_A[s\text{-}c[retr\text{-}T[\overleftarrow{t}\,]]],$$
$$post\text{-}OP_C[s\text{-}a[t], s\text{-}a[\overleftarrow{t}\,]]$$

$$\boxed{OP_C \text{ result obligation}}\ \overline{\ post\text{-}OP_A[s\text{-}c[retr\text{-}T[t]], s\text{-}c[retr\text{-}T[\overleftarrow{t}\,]]]\ }$$

A similar solution may be possible for patterns.

8.3.6 Support for operation decomposition

This would require a considerable amount of work. One possible approach would be to construct a theory of a Hoare-like logic for operation decomposition within the *mural* theory store, and to then translate 'explicit' operations into this (in an analogous fashion to explicit functions). Another approach would be to construct a specific tool for operation decomposition, which would encapsulate the Hoare-like logic. In order to show that a particular composition satisfies certain assertions (for example, the pre- and postconditions of an implicit operation) this tool could produce proof obligations (in 'ordinary' predicate logic rather than as Hoare triples) for the proof assistant to discharge. Certainly, our model would have to be significantly extended to accommodate operation decomposition.

Chapter 9

Foundations of specification animation

One major problem in producing software (both using formal and informal methods) is the capture of the user's requirements. Although one can (at least in theory) prove the correctness of an implementation with respect to a specification, this is no help at all if the specification itself is not correct, i.e. does not match the user's requirements.

It was therefore decided to include in *mural* some support for the validation of *specifications* against their informal requirements, in order to allow validation early on in the development process while it is still comparatively cheap to correct any mistakes. The best method for doing this was considered to be *animation* of the specification, where animation is taken to mean any method for making the specification 'move' or 'behave' in some way in order to derive some consequences or properties of the specified software system before it is actually implemented. The following discussion will only be concerned with animation and not with other validation techniques, such as static checks, including for example checking of syntax and static semantics, even though their use should obviously also form part of the validation process. It will always be assumed that syntax checks have already been done and the specifications handled are syntactically correct.

9.1 Approaches to animation

Animation can be done on different levels, for example:

Actual execution (Testing or prototyping) Interpreting the specification on given input values. This approach obviously requires that one uses an executable specification language, which is a severe restriction on the expressiveness of the language (cf. [HJ89]). Actual execution is discussed in more detail in Section 9.1.1 below.

Symbolic execution Running the specification on symbolic input, i.e. variables over the input domain or, more generally, predicates on such variables, which we will call 'description values'. This approach is discussed in more detail in the following.

Formal reasoning Deriving properties of the specification using theorem proving techniques. This can be a useful technique in some cases but in general it is often not clear what should be proven about a specification (although formal methods such as VDM do give rise to a number of proof obligations). Possible properties to derive include implementability, security with respect to some security model, or correct treatment of certain border cases.

Formal reasoning is a very general technique and can be said to include both actual and symbolic execution: execution can be viewed as deriving theorems of the form $input = ... \Rightarrow output = ...$

User interface prototyping User interface (UI) ideas can be used for animating a specification in two different contexts. First, they can be used to animate and validate the UI, as opposed to the *functionality* of the system. This usually involves building a prototype that displays only some of the functionality of the system, but basically the same UI as is intended for the final system, or at least a good graphical description of it. Such a graphical description might be most adequate for computer systems that regulate or control some other equipment and which require the user to enter some data, for example by pressing buttons.

Second, graphics can be used to help understand the functionality of a specified system. In this case, they just provide a different front-end to (or view of) the output of animation. Consider for example a specification of a lift system. Rather than describing with formulae and/or text that the lift moves from one floor to another, one might display a picture of a lift moving on the screen.

This second approach seems very difficult to generalise: any one system can probably only support graphical animation of a small group of similar applications.

For a survey of different approaches to user interface prototyping see [HI88, §3.2].

Each of the methods described has got a number of drawbacks if used on its own as a tool for ensuring the correctness of a program. To a certain extent, these can be overcome by combining the different methods and using each to check a particular aspect of the program's correctness. Since *mural* is intended to support non-executable specification languages, it was decided to use symbolic execution as the main approach to animation, thus complementing the support for formal reasoning provided by the proof assistant. In this chapter, we will therefore discuss some of the theoretical questions that had to be solved in order to support symbolic execution for a range of different languages. Appendix D will then describe the specification animation tool SYMBEX developed as part of *mural*. Chapter 9 and Appendix D are based heavily on [Kne89].

9.1.1   Actual execution and prototyping

For some languages, actual execution of specifications will be possible directly (this is often referred to as *prototyping*). As described in [Flo84], a prototype is a system that displays some, but not all, of the features of the final product. This way, one can try out some ideas without investing the effort to build a complete system. Which features are left out depends on the particular application; a common approach is to ignore efficiency and UI questions and build a prototype which only displays (some of) the functionality of the final system. Often this can be done in a language that is higher-level than the implementation language of the final system, because the prototype does not have to be as efficient.

[Flo84] distinguishes three main classes of prototyping:

exploratory prototyping puts the emphasis on clarifying requirements and on helping communication between software developer and user. Used for discussing various alternative solutions.

experimental prototyping puts the emphasis on determining the adequacy of a proposed solution before implementing it.

evolutionary prototyping puts the emphasis on adapting the system gradually to changing or evolving requirements. In this case, the prototype gradually develops into the final product.

The following is mainly concerned with experimental prototyping, since it is assumed that a specification (and hence a 'proposed solution') already exists, or at least a high-level rudimentary version of it.

In general, prototyping is different from animation of specifications since a prototype is not usually derived directly from the specification. It usually has to be implemented separately and, since it is executable, the prototyping language cannot be as rich as a specification language might be, an aspect that is often ignored in the prototyping literature. Strictly speaking, prototyping can only be regarded as animation if the prototype itself is (part of) the specification of the final system, or at least can be derived directly from it. Languages suitable for this are often referred to as *executable specification languages*. [HJ89] gives a detailed account why it is not advisable to restrict oneself to *executable* specification languages.

Examples of executable specification languages that are used for prototyping are me too [Hen84, HM85] and EPROL [HI88]. They are both based on the executable part of VDM, expressed in a functional style. In particular, this implies that implicit definitions and operations (functions with side effects) cannot be handled. In me too, specifications written in this restricted subset of VDM are then translated into a version of LISP called Lispkit. EPROL is interpreted in the EPROS prototyping system.

In general, however, a specification may contain non-executable constructs, so that testing or prototyping will not be possible directly. In this case, one has to translate (manually, semi-automatically or automatically) the specification into a suitable (programming) language. This requires a major refinement of the specification before it can be animated. Note here that the specification and programming language are not necessarily separate languages: wide-spectrum languages combine the two into a single language (e.g. CIP, see [B⁺87]) to allow for a gradual refinement from a specification including non-executable terms to an executable program.

A different approach to prototyping is based on algebraic specification or programming languages, where systems are described in terms of (conditional) equations on terms. Functions are defined implicitly by giving equations describing their effects, for example $pop(push(e, st)) = st$. These equations are then directed to turn them into rewrite rules. The specification is animated by applying the resulting rewrite system. Example systems of this approach are OBJ (see [GM82]) and RAP (see [Hus85, GH85]).

Prototyping can be very useful for providing some early 'hands-on' experience of a system and helping to clarify the requirements on the system. The benefits that can be gained from prototyping are discussed in some detail in [HI88, §2.5]. However, prototyping as a method for validating specifications also has a number of disadvantages, including all the usual disadvantages of testing. In particular, it is very unreliable as a tool for validation, since testing only provides results for a fairly small set of input values. Furthermore, it loses at a very early stage in the development process all the under-determinedness[1] that a good specification usually allows, since a prototype will al-

---

[1]A specification $[\![spec]\!]$ is non-deterministic, if, given any input values, the output value of executing

ways have to choose one out of several possible output values. Additionally, any possible non-determinacy will often not be visible to the user.

9.1.2 Symbolic execution

The problems described above were the reason why it was decided to use *symbolic execution* as the main technique for animation of specifications in *mural*. The work done on this is described in detail in [Kne89].

Symbolic execution is a concept that was first introduced by King (see [Kin76]). It is based on the idea of executing a program without providing values for its input variables. The output will then in general be a term depending on these input variables, rather than an actual[2] value. This is usually described as supplying a *symbolic* input value and returning a symbolic output value.

Symbolic execution has been used for a number of different purposes, such as program verification, validation, and test case generation. See [Kne89, §2.1] for a summary of these different approaches and a survey of systems implementing symbolic execution, including in particular those mentioned below.

In the work described here, the original concept of symbolic execution has been extended in order to handle specifications as well as programs. This is done by introducing so-called *description values*, in addition to the usual actual and symbolic values. Description values of (program) variables are formulae that describe (usually implicitly) the value associated with this variable.

Symbolic execution can be considered as a technique for 'executing' programs when some of the information normally needed is not available. In this sense, symbolic execution allows one to handle partial information about

- input data: the input values are not determined (or at least not uniquely); this means one has to handle a whole range of input values, rather than a single value.

- algorithm: the algorithm for computing the output value for any given input value is not provided (or at least is incomplete). In this case one usually talks about a *specification* rather than a program. So far, symbolic execution has usually only been applied to programs; only in the GIST system [Coh83] and the system developed by Kemmerer [Kem85] has the concept of symbolic execution been extended to specifications.

- output data: the output values are not determined uniquely by the input values and the algorithm, i.e. the program or specification is non-deterministic or under-determined.

The symbolic execution system described here (called SYMBEX) is intended to be used as a tool to validate a (formal) specification against its (informal) requirements, and thus to support the first step in formal software development. SYMBEX should help the user

---

(an implementation of) $[\![spec]\!]$ is not uniquely defined and may be different in different executions. $[\![spec]\!]$ is under-determined if, given any input values, the output value of executing an implementation of $[\![spec]\!]$ is not uniquely defined, but for any given implementation the value is always the same. Under-determinedness is thus a property of *specifications* only, while non-determinism may be a property both of specifications and of programs, see [Wie89].

[2]I shall call values in the usual sense 'actual values', in order to distinguish them from 'symbolic values'. Similarly, I shall call the usual form of execution of programs 'actual execution'.

to analyse and understand a specification *before* it is implemented, by providing suitable feedback about the specified behaviour. Therefore, symbolic execution as described here is intended to be used during and after the development of a specification. Symbolic execution can indeed be a useful tool even *during* the specification phase, since it can be applied to incomplete specifications. This is possible since symbolic execution can deal with *names* (symbols) of functions instead of their definitions.

A problem with using symbolic execution for checking the correctness of a specification or a program is the danger that, even though the system might *show* a mistake, such as referencing a wrong variable, the user might not *notice* it. This can happen in particular when the results of symbolic execution look too similar to the original specification. Since the user overlooked the error there, he will probably do the same again when looking at the results of symbolically executing the specification. This puts special importance on the UI of SYMBEX, since it has to present the information in such a way that it helps the user understand a specification. The UI of SYMBEX is discussed in more detail in [Kne89, §6.2].

Providing a *useful* symbolic execution system is made more difficult by the fact that users are different from one another and therefore find different kinds of expressions easy to understand. Thus, a 'simplification' for one user, perhaps by folding a function definition, will make the output considerably more difficult to understand for another user, who might not know the new function introduced. This implies that the system has to be highly interactive and give the user a lot of control about the information presentation, for example what simplification to apply. For this reason, 'simplification' in the following will always mean 'simplification with respect to a certain user'. Section 9.3.3 will describe simplification in more detail.

The remainder of this chapter will discuss the theoretical foundations of SYMBEX. First, the denotational and operational semantics of symbolic execution are discussed. These will be used to achieve language genericity of SYMBEX. The denotational semantics of symbolic execution, expressed in terms of the denotational semantics of the specification language, provide a correctness notion for symbolic execution. A description of the operational semantics of the language is used as a parameter to tailor symbolic execution to that language. The operational semantics of a specification language will be expressed as a collection of theories in *mural*. These theories are introduced in Section 9.4. (For more detail on the semantics of symbolic execution see [Kne89, Kne91].) Additionally, Appendix D describes the specification of the SYMBEX system. This specification builds on the theoretical basis given here by using the theories describing the semantics of the relevant language.

Using this approach, language-genericity was achieved in the sense that SYMBEX supports all languages whose semantics can be expressed in terms of states and state transitions. This includes in particular specification languages such as VDM or Z, and all imperative programming languages. The language-genericity of SYMBEX is discussed in detail in [Kne89, §4.3].

9.2 Denotational semantics of symbolic execution

Given a set *Name* of identifiers (names) and a set *Val* of values, a state is a map of type

$$\Sigma = Name \xrightarrow{m} Val_{\perp}$$

Define

$$\Sigma_\perp = \Sigma \cup \{\perp\}$$

where $\perp$ denotes abortion or non-termination.
Pred is the type of predicates (over states) whose valuation function is some function

$$\mathcal{M}_{Pred}: Pred \rightarrow \Sigma_\perp \rightarrow \mathsf{B}$$

such that

$$\forall f: \{\text{partial recursive functions } \Sigma_\perp \rightarrow \mathsf{B}\} \cdot \exists [\![\varphi]\!]: Pred \cdot \mathcal{M}_{Pred}[\![\varphi]\!] = f$$

This condition is introduced in order to ensure that the language of predicates as used later is 'sufficiently expressive', i.e. that all recursive predicates can be expressed.

A specification denotes a binary relation on states. A valuation function on specifications *Spec* therefore is some function that satisfies

$$\mathcal{M}_{Spec} ([\![spec]\!]: Spec) \, R: (\Sigma_\perp \times \Sigma_\perp) \rightarrow \mathsf{B}$$
$$\text{post } \forall \sigma: \Sigma_\perp \cdot [R(\perp, \sigma) \;\Rightarrow\; \sigma = \perp] \wedge \exists \sigma': \Sigma_\perp \cdot R(\sigma, \sigma')$$

and

$$\forall f: \{\text{partial recursive functions } \Sigma_\perp \times \Sigma_\perp \rightarrow \mathsf{B}\} \cdot \exists [\![spec]\!]: Spec \cdot \mathcal{M}_{Spec}[\![spec]\!] = f$$

We now can define the denotational semantics of symbolic execution in terms of the denotational semantics of the specification being executed. This definition should satisfy the following requirements:

- The input should model a set of input states to a specification. Originally, this set will often be the universe of all states, but may be restricted by the user to a subset, usually because the result expressions would otherwise get too complicated. For example, when symbolically executing a conditional statement, the user may assume that the condition is true, after which symbolic execution only needs consider the true-case.

- The semantic model should describe the relationship between individual input and output states (and not just the relationship between the set of *all* input states and the set of *all* output states). Otherwise, given for example the specification $x = 0 \vee x = \overleftarrow{x} + 1$, symbolic execution would only map N to N and thus not really provide sufficient information. To get more useful information, one would have to restrict the input set S, in this case $\{\sigma \mid \sigma(x) \in \mathsf{N}\}$, to a small subset, which would be contrary to the ideas of symbolic execution and lead towards 'testing' of specifications.

- It should allow composition of two (or more) symbolic execution steps. This implies in particular that input and output must be of the same type.

- Furthermore, it should be possible to make assumptions on the set of input states (as described above) not only at the beginning of a sequence of symbolic execution steps but also at an intermediate stage. In this case, assumptions may be expressed in terms of the values of variables in earlier states.

The model of symbolic execution that we are going to use is based on a 'symbolic execution state' called *SEStateDen* which contains sets of *sequences* of states. The definition of *SEStateDen* is given in Figure 9.1. The name *SEStateDen* is a shorthand for *Symbolic Execution State* as used for *Denotational* semantics. Similarly, Section 9.3 will introduce *SEStateOp* for states in operational semantics.

In addition to the set of sequences of states, *SEStateDen* contains a field *LEN* which stores the number of symbolic execution steps performed, plus 1 for the initial state (see Figure 9.1). At the same time, this is the number of *actual* execution steps modelled in any sequence of states in the field *SEQS* plus 1, which leads to the first conjunct in the invariant. In this model, user-introduced restrictions on the set of states allowed are modelled by 'cutting off' as much as necessary from the end of all sequences of states until the condition is satisfied. This intuition explains the second conjunct on the invariant on *SEStateDen*, which demands that no sequence in *SEStateDen* is an initial segment of another such sequence.

A state as used in symbolic execution is given by

$$SEStateDen :: \begin{array}{ll} SEQS &: \mathcal{P}(\Sigma_{\perp}^*) \\ LEN &: \mathbb{N} \end{array}$$

where

$inv\text{-}SEStateDen(mk\text{-}SEStateDen(set, l)) \quad \triangle$
$\qquad \forall \sigma\text{-}seq \in set \cdot \text{len } \sigma\text{-}seq \leq l$
$\qquad \wedge \forall \sigma\text{-}seq_1, \sigma\text{-}seq_2 \in set \cdot \forall \sigma\text{-}seq: \Sigma_{\perp}^* \cdot$
$\qquad\qquad \sigma\text{-}seq_1 = \sigma\text{-}seq_2 \curvearrowright \sigma\text{-}seq \implies \sigma\text{-}seq = [\,]$

Figure 9.1: Denotational semantics of symbolic execution – State

---

As a convention, τ will be used to denote elements of *SEStateDen*, while σ denotes elements of $\Sigma_{\perp}$, as before.

Symbolic execution of a specification is modelled by adding another state to all those sequences that have not been 'cut off', see Figure 9.2. Just as interpretation or execution, given a specification, maps states to states, so symbolic execution, given a specification, maps *SEStateDen*s to *SEStateDen*s.

Doing symbolic execution in the way described here and storing *all* possible sequences of states allowed by a sequence of specifications requires a fairly rich language for expressing the results of symbolic execution, which might not always be available. For example, the result of executing a while-loop will often not be expressible in the language available. Therefore, in addition to such *full* symbolic execution Figure 9.2 also defines *weak* symbolic execution, where the result includes the set of *all* possible sequences of states. This ensures that the properties one gets as a result of weak symbolic execution still hold for the denotation of the full result; they just do not in general give a complete description.

Note that there is a distinction between symbolic execution of the composition of specifications and the composition of symbolic executions. They give rise to *SEStateDen*s that describe the same relationship between initial and final states, but the *SEStateDen*s themselves are different. They lead to *SEStateDen*s of different lengths, since symbolic execution of the composition of specifications is considered as a single step, while a sequence of symbolic executions in general consists of several steps (Lemma 4.1.7 of

(Full) symbolic execution is given by the functions

$symbolic\text{-}ex : Spec \rightarrow SEStateDen \rightarrow SEStateDen$

$symbolic\text{-}ex[\![spec]\!]\tau \quad \underline{\triangle}$

    $mk\text{-}SEStateDen($

        $\{\sigma\text{-}seq \mid \text{len } \sigma\text{-}seq = LEN(\tau) + 1 \wedge \text{front } \sigma\text{-}seq \in SEQS(\tau)$

                $\wedge \, \mathcal{M}_{Spec}[\![spec]\!](\text{last front } \sigma\text{-}seq, \text{ last } \sigma\text{-}seq)$

                $\vee \text{ len } \sigma\text{-}seq < LEN(\tau) \wedge \sigma\text{-}seq \in SEQS(\tau)\},$

        $LEN(\tau) + 1)$

and

$symbolic\text{-}ex\text{-}s : Spec^{*} \rightarrow SEStateDen \rightarrow SEStateDen$

$symbolic\text{-}ex\text{-}s[\![spec\text{-}seq]\!]\tau \quad \underline{\triangle}$

    if $spec\text{-}seq = [\,]$

    then τ

    else $symbolic\text{-}ex\text{-}s[\![\text{tl } spec\text{-}seq]\!](symbolic\text{-}ex[\![\text{hd } spec\text{-}seq]\!]\tau)$

Weak symbolic execution is a function

$w\text{-}symbolic\text{-}ex \, ([\![spec]\!]: Spec, \tau_1: SEStateDen) \; \tau_2: SEStateDen$

$\text{post } SEQS(\tau_2) \supseteq SEQS(symbolic\text{-}ex[\![spec]\!]\tau_1)$

    $\wedge \, LEN(\tau_2) = LEN(symbolic\text{-}ex[\![spec]\!]\tau_1)$

with a similar function for sequences of specifications.

Figure 9.2: Denotational semantics of symbolic execution – Functions

[Kne89]).

It is not immediately obvious that *symbolic-ex* as defined is a *total* function. Although a result is constructed for any input values, this result might not satisfy the invariant and thus might not be of type *SEStateDen*. The following lemma shows that this case does not arise.

Lemma 9.2.1 *The function symbolic-ex is total, i.e. symbolic-ex$[\![spec]\!]\tau$ satisfies the invariant inv-SEStateDen for all $[\![spec]\!]$ and all τ.*

Proof See Lemma 4.1.1 of [Kne89]. $\square$

Example 9.2.2 Let *Name* = $\{x, y\}$. We want to symbolically execute the operation

OP_1
ext wr x : $\mathbf{Z}$
    wr y : $\mathbf{Z}$
pre $x \geq 0$
post $y^2 \leq \overleftarrow{x} \wedge x = \overleftarrow{x} + 1$

Then

$\mathcal{M}_{Spec}[\![OP_1]\!](\sigma, \sigma_1) \; \Leftrightarrow \;$ if $\sigma(x) \geq 0$ then $\sigma_1(y)^2 \leq \sigma(x) \wedge \sigma_1(x) = \sigma(x) + 1$ else true

Now the user **assumes** that the pre-condition of OP_1 is true. This means that OP_1 is to be symbolically executed in the *SEStateDen* τ_1 which represents the predicate $x \geq 0$:

$\tau_1 \; = \; mk\text{-}SEStateDen(\{[\sigma] \mid \mathcal{M}_{Pred}[\![x \geq 0]\!]\sigma\}, 1)$

$$= mk\text{-}SEStateDen(\{[\sigma] \mid \sigma(x) \geq 0\}, 1)$$

Then symbolic execution of the specification OP_1 starting in the *SEStateDen* τ_1 results in the *SEStateDen*

$$symbolic\text{-}ex[\![OP_1]\!]\tau_1$$
$$= mk\text{-}SEStateDen(\{\sigma\text{-}seq \mid \text{len }\sigma\text{-}seq = LEN(\tau_1) + 1 \wedge \text{front }\sigma\text{-}seq \in SEQS(\tau_1)$$
$$\wedge \mathcal{M}_{Spec}[\![OP_1]\!](\text{lastfront }\sigma\text{-}seq, \text{last }\sigma\text{-}seq)$$
$$\vee \text{len }\sigma\text{-}seq < LEN(\tau_1) \wedge \sigma\text{-}seq \in SEQS(\tau_1)\}, LEN(\tau_1) + 1)$$
$$= mk\text{-}SEStateDen(\{\sigma\text{-}seq \mid \text{len }\sigma\text{-}seq = 2 \wedge \sigma\text{-}seq[1](x) \geq 0$$
$$\wedge \mathcal{M}_{Spec}[\![OP_1]\!](\sigma\text{-}seq[1], \sigma\text{-}seq[2])\}, 2)$$
$$= mk\text{-}SEStateDen(\{\sigma\text{-}seq \mid \text{len }\sigma\text{-}seq = 2 \wedge \sigma\text{-}seq[1](x) \geq 0$$
$$\wedge \sigma\text{-}seq[2](y)^2 \leq \sigma\text{-}seq[1](x)$$
$$\wedge \sigma\text{-}seq[2](x) = \sigma\text{-}seq[1](x) + 1\}, 2)$$

9.3 Operational semantics of symbolic execution

This section describes a model of symbolic execution based on the operational semantics approach. The style of operational semantics used is based on that of Plotkin's 'Structured Operational Semantics' [Plo81], but of course many of the transitions themselves are rather different since they describe *symbolic* rather than actual execution. However, if there is no danger of confusion, I shall in future not explicitly mention that I am dealing with the particular version of operational semantics used for symbolic execution, but just talk about operational semantics.

The following discussion starts off with the underlying data structure used, then shows a number of transitions and rules for various language constructs.

There is an important difference between the descriptions of the denotational and operational semantics of symbolic execution. While it is possible to explicitly define the denotational semantics of symbolic execution itself by expressing them in terms of the denotational semantics of the language used, this is not feasible for the operational semantics. Instead, one here has to provide a different version of the operational semantics of the language, specifically for symbolic execution. This chapter does not try to provide the complete operational semantics for any language, but shows the rules for a number of important language constructs instead.

9.3.1 The data structure

States as used on the operational level will be called *SEStateOps* – Symbolic Execution *States* as used for *Operational* semantics. In *SEStateOps*, the information derived by symbolic execution should get associated with those identifiers whose values are described by it. For this reason, *SEStateOps* use maps from *Name* to the relevant information. This information will be modelled by predicates. These predicates must be predicates on *sequences* of states rather than single states, since they should model the relationship between different states. Such predicates are introduced as *PredS* below. These are the predicates the user should actually get to see as description values of variables at any stage in the symbolic execution. A *PredS* then is any expression whose semantics can be given as

$$\mathcal{M}_{PredS}: PredS \rightarrow StateSeq \rightarrow \mathbb{B}$$

where *StateSeq* is defined as

$$StateSeq = (\Sigma_\perp \mid StateSeq)^*$$

StateSeq is defined recursively rather than just as a sequence of states in order to be able to handle blocks and loops, as described below. This decision does not seriously affect the definition of *PredS*. The language of *PredS* has to include constant symbols true and false, and operator symbols for $\wedge$, $\Rightarrow$, $\Leftrightarrow$ (all with their standard interpretation), and a conditional provided-then (as defined in Section 9.3.3).

The only condition on the internal structure of *PredS* is that it must be possible to define a function

mentions: *PredS* $\rightarrow$ *Name*-set

which collects the identifiers mentioned in a given *PredS* into a set. No other conditions are needed since symbolic execution itself makes almost no use of the information contained in the *PredS*; only *simplification* needs to know about the syntax and semantics of *PredS* (in particular, it needs to know when two *PredS* are equivalent.). The definitions of the syntax and semantics of *PredS* are therefore given in a theory which is used to instantiate symbolic execution for a particular specification language (and thus for a particular language of *PredS*), but they are not used in the model of symbolic execution itself. These simplification theories will be described in Section 9.4.2.

Since allowing *sets of PredS* rather than only individual *PredS* as description values makes it easier to combine different *PredS* and, when needed (for example for simplification), split the result again to get its components, *SEStateOps* are modelled using maps from *Name* to *PredS*-set.

An additional complication arises because each symbolic execution step gives rise to a new predicate on sequences of states, and obviously each such predicate may provide valuable information that should be associated with the appropriate identifier and the appropriate execution step. Therefore, *SEStateOps* will be defined as *sequences* of maps from identifiers to sets of predicates on sequences of states. An *SEStateOp* thus stores a *history* of the results of symbolic execution.

In this history a loop should be considered as a single step, even though it may really consist of any number of steps (including 0). Therefore, the result of the loop is modelled as an *SEStateOp* itself, which is then considered as one step in the original *SEStateOp*. Similarly, blocks should be considered as a single step and are therefore also modelled as an *SEStateOp* themselves. This leads to the recursive definition of *SEStateOp* given below. One might thus consider an *SEStateOp* as a tree, where the leaves of the tree are maps and the inner nodes are *SEStateOps*. Pre-order traversal of this tree describes the execution sequence modelled by the (root) *SEStateOp*.

In addition to the sequence described above, *SEStateOp* contains a field *INDEX* which stores the index or position of this *SEStateOp* in the recursive definition – this will be needed to get the right description values in the *SEStateOp*. Since these express properties of sequences of states, they need to know which sequence of states they should refer to. This issue should become clearer in the discussion of simplification in Section 9.3.3. Compare also the example transition for VDM-operations given in [Kne89, §4.2.6], where *INDEX* is actually needed.

Definition 9.3.1 (SEStateOp) *Define*

$Index = \mathbb{N}_1^*$

A state as used for describing the operational semantics of a language as used for symbolic execution is defined recursively as

$SE\text{-}map = Name \xrightarrow{m} PredS\text{-}set$

$SE\text{-}elem = SE\text{-}map \mid SEStateOp$

$SEStateOp :: SEQ \quad : SE\text{-}elem^*$
$\qquad\qquad\qquad INDEX : Index$

where

$inv\text{-}SEStateOp(mk\text{-}SEStateOp(Seq, ix)) \quad \triangle$
$\qquad Seq \neq [\,]$
$\qquad \wedge \text{hd } Seq: SE\text{-}map$
$\qquad \wedge \forall k \leq \text{len } Seq \cdot Seq[k]: SEStateOp \implies INDEX(Seq[k]) = cons(k, ix)$

The invariant on *SEStateOp* ensures that every *SEQ(S)* has a first element which defines the allowed parameter states. An *SEStateOp* itself would not be allowed as first element because it should only arise *as a result of* symbolically executing a specification (usually a loop or block). Additionally, the invariant ensures that *SEStateOp* describes the intuition behind *INDEX* as described above – the *INDEX* of any *SEStateOp* which is the k-th element of *SEQ* of the *SEStateOp* S is the *INDEX* ix of S with k added at the front, or $cons(k, ix)$.

A valuation function $\mathcal{M}_{SEStateOp}$ has also been defined, see [Kne89, Figure 4.3]. It maps an *SEStateOp* to an *SEStateDen*, where the *SEStateDen* contains those sequences of states that satisfy all the predicates in the *SEStateOp*.

In Figure 9.1 we described how an *SEStateDen* can represent a predicate on states (expressed there as a set of states). Similarly, one can represent such predicates by *SEStateOp*s. Given φ: *Pred*, let Φ be the *PredS*

$\mathcal{M}_{Pred}[\![\varphi]\!]\{n \mapsto \eth([1], n) \mid n: Name\}$

and let

$S(\varphi) \quad \triangle \quad mk\text{-}SEStateOp([\{n \mapsto \{\Phi\} \mid n: Name\}], [\,])$

Then $\mathcal{M}_{SEStateOp}[\![S(\varphi)]\!]$ is the *SEStateDen* that represents φ, and we say that $S(\varphi)$ is the *SEStateOp* that represents φ. Of course, Φ does not have to be associated with each *Name* n; one could alternatively only associate it with those n that are mentioned in Φ, or even only with one arbitrary n.

The valuation function of *SEStateOp*, like the others defined before, could also be considered as a *retrieve* function [Jon90a, pages 204ff]. In this case, it has an adequacy proof obligation associated with it.[3] If *Val* is finite, then it depends on the expressiveness of *PredS* whether $\mathcal{M}_{SEStateOp}$ satisfies this obligation. For infinite *Val*, however, there are uncountably many sets of state sequences and therefore uncountably many *SEStateDen*. On the other hand, there are only countably many *SEStateOp*, and therefore *SEStateOp* cannot be adequate w.r.t. $\mathcal{M}_{SEStateOp}$.

---

[3] A representation *Rep* is *adequate* with respect to a retrieve function *retr*: *Rep* $\rightarrow$ *Abs* iff $\forall a \in Abs \cdot \exists r \in Rep \cdot retr(r) = a$

9.3.2   Transitions and rules

In the following I am going to define the kind of transitions and rules used for describing the operational semantics of language constructs in general, and then give the appropriate transitions and rules for various constructs. In many cases (e.g. the rule for if-then-else), the transitions and rules of the operational semantics of various language constructs are defined by translating them into an equivalent construct in the language used for describing the results, then simplifying the result whenever possible. This simplification will hopefully help to eliminate the construct from the description.

From the point of view of their purpose, one can therefore distinguish three different kinds of transitions:

- Transitions describing (state-changing) specifications. Since such operations actually lead to a new state, they are described by transitions that extend an S: $SEStateOp$ by adding another element to the sequence $SEQ(S)$.

- Transitions that eliminate combinators such as if-then-else for specifications by translating them into equivalent constructs used inside $PredS$ expressions.

- Simplification transitions derived from the theory for $PredS$, as discussed in Section 9.3.3. The transition $S_1 \hookrightarrow S_2$ is allowed if S_2 can be derived from S_1 by simplification of $PredS$ only.

We now define the various components that will be needed to express transitions. $SpecName$ is the type of specification names, and $SpecMap$ associates specification names with specifications:

$$SpecMap = SpecName \xrightarrow{m} Spec$$

A configuration consists of a sequence of $SpecName$s (which may be empty) and an $SEStateOp$:

$$
\begin{aligned}
Conf :: \quad & SNSEQ \ : \ SpecName^* \\
& STATE \ : \ SEStateOp
\end{aligned}
$$

A configuration $mk\text{-}Conf(sn\text{-}seq, S)$ will be written as $\langle sn\text{-}seq, S \rangle$. The configuration $\langle sn\text{-}seq, S \rangle$: $Conf$ describes the fact that the sequence of specifications given by $sn\text{-}seq$ is to be applied to S. Given some sm: $SpecMap$, the denotation of a configuration is therefore defined as (using the auxiliary function $evalseq$ which applies sm to every element of the sequence $sn\text{-}seq$)

$$M_{Conf} : Conf \to SEStateDen$$
$$M_{Conf}[\![\langle sn\text{-}seq, S \rangle]\!] \triangleq symbolic\text{-}ex\text{-}s[\![evalseq(sn\text{-}seq, sm)]\!](M_{SEStateOp}[\![S]\!])$$

Transitions are defined as

$$Trans = \biguplus_E E \times E$$

where $\uplus$ denotes disjoint union, and E ranges over $Conf$ and the different syntactic categories of the specification language, such as $Expr$. A transition $mk\text{-}Trans(e_1, e_2)$ will be written as $e_1 \hookrightarrow e_2$.
$\langle Op_1, S_1 \rangle \hookrightarrow \langle Op_2, S_2 \rangle$ denotes the fact that one interpretation step transforms $\langle Op_1, S_1 \rangle$ into $\langle Op_2, S_2 \rangle$, but $\hookrightarrow$ will also be used to denote its transitive-reflexive closure.
Rules take the form

$$Rule :: ordhyps : (Trans \mid PredS)\text{-set}$$
$$conc \quad : Trans$$

This is a simplified version of the definition of rules (or rule statements, to be exact) in *mural*, since both *Trans* and *PredS* are special forms of *Exps*. Sequent hypotheses are not needed here.

An important general rule that shows how symbolic execution of a sequence of specifications can be split up into symbolic execution of its elements is the following:

Rule 9.3.2

$$\frac{\langle [sn], S \rangle \hookrightarrow \langle [\,], S' \rangle}{\langle cons(sn, sn\text{-}seq), S \rangle \hookrightarrow \langle sn\text{-}seq, S' \rangle}$$

Lemma 9.3.3 *Rule 9.3.2 preserves faithfulness: if the hypothesis transition is faithful[4], then so is the conclusion.*

Proof See Lemma 4.2.6 of [Kne89]. □

9.3.3 Simplification

Now assume we are given a fixed specification language $\mathcal{L}$. To reason about *PredS*, for example to decide whether a *PredS* ps_1 can be simplified to ps_2, one needs a suitable theory of *PredS*. This theory, which will be called $\widetilde{Th}(\mathcal{L})$, needs to be based on the theory used to reason about terms in $\mathcal{L}$, but additionally an indexing mechanism is needed to differentiate between the values of program variables (identifiers or names) at different stages in an execution sequence. To do so, sequences $(\sigma_i)_i$ of states are introduced, where $\sigma_i : \Sigma_\perp$. Since the definition of *SEStateOp* is recursive, simple sequences are not enough – we actually need iterated sequences where σ_i might be a sequence of states itself. This is modelled by introducing a function $\check{\sigma}$, which returns the name of the value of the identifier n at a given stage in the execution, with the signature

$$\check{\sigma} : Index \times Name \to Val\text{-}ref$$

For simplicity, we shall in the following identify the element $i : \mathbb{N}_1$ with the index $[i]$. Now a *PredS* is a predicate that contains names of values of identifiers *at some stage*, instead of the identifiers themselves. See Section 9.4.2 for a more detailed explanation of *PredS*. The resulting theory of *PredS* is the theory used for simplification: $ps_1 : PredS$ inside some *SEStateOp* can be simplified to $ps_2 : PredS$ if they are equivalent in $\widetilde{Th}(\mathcal{L})$. Weak simplification, as used in weak symbolic execution, requires that ps_1 implies ps_2 in $\widetilde{Th}(\mathcal{L})$.

The language of $\widetilde{Th}(\mathcal{L})$ has to include the provided-then construct on *PredS*, which is used for expressing predicates with pre-conditions. The following should hold

$$(\text{provided true then } \varphi) \Leftrightarrow \varphi$$

and

$$(\text{provided false then } \varphi) \Leftrightarrow \text{true}$$

---

[4]A transition $c_1 \hookrightarrow c_2$ is faithful with respect to $\mathcal{M}$, if it implies $\mathcal{M}[\![c_1]\!] = \mathcal{M}[\![c_2]\!]$, or $\mathcal{M}[\![c_1]\!] \supseteq \mathcal{M}[\![c_2]\!]$ if $\mathcal{M}$ returns a *set* of valuations. See [Sch86, §10.7]

The reason for not expressing provided φ then ψ as if φ then ψ else true is that one may want to treat unsatisfied pre-conditions differently and for example provide a warning message. The *denotational* semantics of both expressions are the same.

9.3.4   Block structures and local variables

We start off the description of operational semantics of language constructs with some rules describing block structures. The approach taken, for example, by Plotkin [Plo81] for operational semantics of *actual* execution of blocks and local variable declarations is not adequate here, since it discards information about earlier states, only the current values of variables being stored. In symbolic execution, this is not sufficient since the predicates describing a current value of a variable in general refer to earlier values, therefore the whole history needs to be preserved.

Therefore, as mentioned before, blocks will be modelled by *SEStateOp*s that are *elements* of the sequence *SEQ* of the original *SEStateOp*. In order to be able to describe how this is done, the following auxiliary functions will be needed:

$$current\text{-}names : SEStateOp \rightarrow Name\text{-set}$$
$$current\text{-}names(S) \quad \triangleq \quad \text{if last } SEQ(S)\text{: } SE\text{-map}$$
$$\text{then dom last } SEQ(S)$$
$$\text{else dom hd } SEQ(\text{last } SEQ(S))$$

and

$$add\text{-}to\text{-}SEStateOp : SEStateOp \times SE\text{-elem} \rightarrow SEStateOp$$
$$add\text{-}to\text{-}SEStateOp(S, e) \quad \triangleq \quad mk\text{-}SEStateOp(SEQ(S) \oplus e, INDEX(S))$$

Here $\oplus$ denotes addition of a single element to the end of a sequence.

The function *start-block* starts a new block by creating a new *SEStateOp* which is then added as a new element to the sequence *SEQ* of the current one. *SEQ* of the new *SEStateOp* only consists of one element which describes that 'nothing changes' – all identifiers keep the same value that they had before.

$$start\text{-}block : SEStateOp \rightarrow SEStateOp$$
$$start\text{-}block(S) \quad \triangleq$$
$$\text{let } S' = mk\text{-}SEStateOp\big([\{n \mapsto \{\check{\sigma}([1, \text{len } SEQ(S) + 1] \frown INDEX(S), n) =$$
$$\check{\sigma}([\text{len } SEQ(S)] \frown INDEX(S), n)\}$$
$$\mid n \in current\text{-}names(S)\}],$$
$$\text{cons(len } SEQ(S) + 1, INDEX(S))\big) \text{ in}$$
$$add\text{-}to\text{-}SEStateOp(S, S')$$

$$finish\text{-}block : SEStateOp \rightarrow SEStateOp$$
$$finish\text{-}block(S) \quad \triangleq$$
$$\text{let } m = \{n \mapsto \{\check{\sigma}([\text{len } SEQ(S)] \frown INDEX(S), n) = \check{\sigma}(INDEX(S), n)\}$$
$$\mid n \in \text{dom hd } (SEQ(S))\} \text{ in}$$
$$add\text{-}to\text{-}SEStateOp(S, m)$$

The rule for describing the operational semantics of a block is then given by

Rule 9.3.4

$$\frac{\langle \textit{sn-seq}, \textsf{last } SEQ(\textit{start-block}(S)) \rangle \hookrightarrow \langle [\,], S' \rangle}{\langle \texttt{begin } \textit{sn-seq} \texttt{ end}, S \rangle \hookrightarrow \langle [\,], \textit{add-to-SEStateOp}(S, \textit{finish-block}(S')) \rangle}$$

where begin *sn-seq* end is used as the *name* of the appropriate sequence of specifications. A similar convention will be used for other constructs below.

The functions *start-block* and *finish-block* are not just auxiliary functions for expressing these rules, but will also be used in the specification of the UI of SYMBEXin order to
be able to display the newly-started *SEStateOp*, which represents the block (or, similarly,
a loop), as an element of *SEQ* of the old one. As long as discharging the hypotheses
in a rule such as Rule 9.3.4 above can be done automatically, one does not need such a
special mechanism, but if user interaction is required then one needs to display *some* of
the results *before* the hypothesis has been fully discharged. In this case, the functions
start-block and *finish-block* should be used to 'tell the system' that it is dealing with a
block which should be displayed accordingly.

9.3.5 Example: A VDM-operation

Given the specification OP_1 from Example 9.2.2. As before, we assume that the pre-
condition holds. Since x and y are the only identifiers used, we therefore start with the
SEStateOp

$$S = mk\text{-}SEStateOp([\{x \mapsto \{\check{\sigma}([1], x) \geq 0\}, y \mapsto \{\check{\sigma}([1], x) \geq 0\}\}], [\,])$$

The appropriate instantiation of the rule giving the operational semantics of VDM-
operations is then given by (after some simplification)

$$\textsf{let } m = \left\{ \begin{array}{l} x \mapsto \{\check{\sigma}([2], y)^2 \leq \check{\sigma}([1], x), \\ \qquad \check{\sigma}([2], x) = \check{\sigma}([1], x) + 1\} \\ y \mapsto \{\check{\sigma}([2], y) \leq \check{\sigma}([1], x)\} \end{array} \right\} \textsf{ in}$$
$$\vdash \langle [OP_1], S \rangle \hookrightarrow \langle [\,], \textit{add-to-SEStateOp}(S, m) \rangle$$

In the resulting state we then have

$$\begin{aligned} \textsf{value of } x \;:\; & y_2^2 \leq x_1 \\ & x_2 = x_1 + 1 \\ \textsf{value of } y \;:\; & y_2^2 \leq x_1 \end{aligned}$$

The full rule describing the operational semantics of VDM-operations is given in [Kne89,
§4.2.6].

9.3.6 Applying the Operational Semantics

Assume we are given some configuration $\langle \textit{sn-seq}, S \rangle$, plus the operational semantics of
the relevant language. Such a configuration, as defined in Section 9.3.2, consists of a
sequence *sn-seq*: *SpecName** of specification names and an *SEStateOp* S, and denotes an
interpreter configuration in which the sequence of specifications referred to by *sn-seq* is
to be applied to S. The operational semantics will be expressed as a collection of theories,
as described below in Section 9.4.

One now wants to transform the configuration $\langle \textit{sn-seq}, S \rangle$ into an equivalent configuration (under the equivalence relation induced by $\mathcal{M}_{Conf}$) of the form $\langle [\,], S' \rangle$, since this

provides the resulting *SEStateOp S'*. This transformation is done by repeatedly applying transitions from the operational semantics to the configuration until it has the right form.

Considered as an object handled by *mural*, a transition is an expression of type *Prop* (proposition). The rules of the operational semantics correspond to axioms or rules as defined in the specification of *mural*, and thus consist of zero or more assertions (possibly themselves transitions) and sequents as hypotheses and an assertion which is its conclusion, and, in the case of (derived) rules, a justification.

So what exactly happens if one has a configuration $\langle sn\text{-}seq, S \rangle$ and wants to evaluate it? The relevant theory should contain (an instantiation of) a rule that has as its conclusion the transition $\langle sn\text{-}seq, S \rangle \hookrightarrow conf$ for some configuration *conf*. The hypotheses of such a rule consist of a (possibly empty) set of transitions and *PredS* (predicates on sequences of states). Before a rule can be used, its hypotheses would have to be discharged. For each *PredS* this is done by trying to prove it using the *PredS* known to hold in *S* as hypotheses. A transition is therefore discharged by recursively running the same algorithm on this transition as on $\langle sn\text{-}seq, S \rangle \hookrightarrow conf$:

transform(trans) $\triangle$
    1. Try to find a rule *r* with (instantiated) conclusion *trans*
    cases *Number of such rules* of
    0 → answer NO and stop
    1 → make the appropriate substitution and store it
    ≥ 2→ let user decide which one to use
    end

    2. for every *preds* in *hyps(r)*
    do try to decide – is it the conclusion of a provable rule,
           where all hypotheses are known to hold?
    cases *result* of
    true → nothing needs to be done
    false → ignore the rule *r* and go back to 1.
    others keep it as a condition on future results
    end

    3. for every *trans* in *hyps(r)*
    do *transform(trans)*
    4. If you get this far, the collected substitution applied to *trans* gives
           the provable instantiation

This recursive algorithm will be expressed as a proof tactic, which can then be used to find a proof of the relevant transition. Alternatively, it could be expressed as a program procedure or an oracle.

If *conf* has the form $\langle [\,], S' \rangle$ then symbolic execution of *sn-seq* on *SEStateOp S* is finished with the resulting *SEStateOp S'*. If not, then *conf* must itself have the form $\langle sn\text{-}seq', S' \rangle$. In this case there should be (an instantiation of) a rule that has as its conclusion the transition $\langle sn\text{-}seq', S' \rangle \hookrightarrow conf'$ for some configuration *conf'*. Now one needs a rule that says: if the transitions $a \hookrightarrow b$ and $b \hookrightarrow c$ are (instances of) conclusions of rules, then one can derive a rule with conclusion $a \hookrightarrow c$, i.e. transitions are transitive. In the example, this leads to a rule with conclusion $\langle sn\text{-}seq, S \rangle \hookrightarrow conf'$, and the same cycle starts again. If *conf'* has the right form, symbolic execution is finished, otherwise there should be a transition starting with *conf'*. This cycle is repeated until one gets to a configuration of the form $\langle [\,], S'' \rangle$.

Effectively, in symbolic execution one tries to prove a theorem but, in contrast to the usual way of doing so, one does not know the conclusion of the theorem when starting to prove it. Instead, one knows that it should take the form $\langle sn\text{-}seq, s \rangle \hookrightarrow S'$, and that at any stage either there is only one rule that applies, or the user gets the choice which one to apply.

9.4 Theories to support symbolic execution

The theory of the operational semantics of a particular language $\mathcal{L}$ is split up into two separate theories

- *ThOpSem* is common to all such theories

- *ThOpSem*($\mathcal{L}$) contains the part specific to language $\mathcal{L}$

Simplification is based on a theory $\widetilde{Th(\mathcal{L})}$ which includes the logic used for describing $\mathcal{L}$ (for VDM, this would be LPF [BCJ84]), plus the theories of its basic data types. Additionally, every specification module has a theory *ThModule*(*Mod*) of its own containing, among other things, the type and function definitions of the module.

So far, only 'full' theories were mentioned, i.e. theories that describe the operational semantics of full symbolic execution (as defined in Figure 9.2). Additionally the 'weak' theories *WThOpSem*($\mathcal{L}$) and *WThModule*(*Mod*) are needed that describe weak symbolic execution where some of the restrictions on the result state are 'lost', leading to non-faithful transitions in the operational semantics.

These theories are all based on the same logic, a common 'logic of operational semantics', rather than having a collection of different language-dependent logics. Here one has to distinguish between the logic of a specification language, which is included in $Th(\mathcal{L})$ and used for reasoning about terms of the language, and the logic used for reasoning within the various theories about transitions etc., which is independent of the language used. LPF was chosen as this common logic.

Before describing these theories in more detail, the following diagram shows the *parent* $\rightarrow$ *child* relationships existing between them. ($\overset{*}{\rightarrow}$ denotes the fact that the parent theory is inherited by the child theory via a *morphism*.)

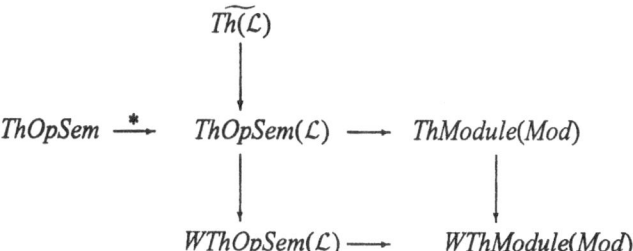

Several of the definitions in the following were already introduced earlier. The new definitions are given because they now define objects in the various theories of operational semantics, used by SYMBEX, while before they defined general data structures.

9.4.1   The common theory *ThOpSem*

Sorts

The theory *ThOpSem* should have the sort symbols *name*, *preds* and *SEStateOp*. Here one has to distinguish between the *primitive* sort symbols *name* and *preds* as introduced in *ThOpSem*, and the defined sorts *Name* and *PredS* which are language-dependent and will therefore be introduced in *ThOpSem(L)*. *ThOpSem(L)* will inherit *ThOpSem* via a morphism translating *name* to *Name* and *preds* to *PredS*.

ThOpSem also has the sort constructors A^* for sequences, with type parameter A, and $A \xrightarrow{m} B$ for maps and $A \mid B$ for type union, both with type parameters A and B. All these sort constructors have their appropriate theory associated, either as part of *ThOpSem* itself, or, more likely, as a parent theory. Also needed is the sort *Prop* of propositions. Among other things, this includes equations and transitions.

Transitions

ThOpSem has the primitive (polymorphic) constant

$$\hookrightarrow : A \times A \to Prop$$

which denotes transitions, and the constants *from* and *to* denoting the inverses of $\hookrightarrow$. Since $\hookrightarrow$ is polymorphic, *from* and *to* cannot be declared as having a certain type. Transitions are reflexive and transitive:

$$\vdash E \hookrightarrow E \qquad\qquad \frac{E_1 \hookrightarrow E_2 \qquad E_2 \hookrightarrow E_3}{E_1 \hookrightarrow E_3}$$

and *from*, *to* are the inverses of $\hookrightarrow$:

$$\vdash from(E_1 \hookrightarrow E_2) = E_1 \qquad\qquad \vdash to(E_1 \hookrightarrow E_2) = E_2 \qquad\qquad \frac{from(t):A}{to(t):A}$$

SEStateOps

SEStateOps are defined as in Definition 9.3.1, except that we here use *name* and *preds* instead of *Name* and *PredS*. Note that an *SEStateOp* as defined here is an object in the theory *ThOpSem* rather than a general data structure.

9.4.2   The simplification theories $Th(L)$ and $\widetilde{Th}(L)$

Now assume that a fixed specification language L is given. Let $Th(L)$ be the theory used to reason about terms in L. For example, $Th(VDM) = LPF+$ theories of data types. $Th(L)$ should not be considered as denoting one *parameterised* theory, but rather a collection of different theories, one for each language L.

$Th(L)$ is based on the logic of L, with type $Prop_{Simp}$ of propositions, and additionally contains the theories of the basic data types of L such as sets, sequences, etc. It is thus the theory needed for reasoning about L in general, independent of symbolic execution.

Let *Name* be the type of identifiers or program variables of L, as before. For a typed language L, this would actually have to be a collection of types, but for simplicity this fact is ignored here. Let *Val* be the type of values that an identifier may take. Again, for a typed language L this would have to be a collection of types.

We require that the language of $Prop_{Simp}$ includes the constants true and false, and operators $\wedge$, provided-then, $\Rightarrow$ and $\Leftrightarrow$. Also needed are the functions *start-block* and *finish-block*, as defined in Section 9.3.4. These are needed in order to be able to describe the operational semantics of blocks (cf. Section 9.3.4) or loops (cf. [Kne89, §4.2.8]). Furthermore, the language should be 'reasonably expressive' in the sense that the transitions of the operational semantics of $\mathcal{L}$, as will be discussed in Section 9.4.3, can be expressed.

One needs to introduce an indexing mechanism to differentiate between the values of program variables (identifiers or names) at different stages in an execution sequence. To do so, we introduce sequences $(\sigma_i)_i$ of states, where $\sigma_i\colon \Sigma_\perp$. Since the definition of *SEStateOp* is recursive, simple sequences are not enough – we actually need iterated sequences where σ_i might be a sequence of states itself. This is modelled by introducing a constant symbol $\eth$ with arity (2,0), which is the name of the value of the identifier n at a given stage in the execution, with the only axiom

$$\frac{i\text{-}seq\colon \mathsf{N}_1^* \qquad i\text{-}seq \neq [\,] \qquad n\colon Name}{\eth(i\text{-}seq, n)\colon Val\text{-}ref}$$

For simplicity, the element $i\colon \mathsf{N}$ will in the following sometimes be identified with the sequence $i\text{-}seq = [i]$.

Now define a *PredS* as a proposition of $Th(\mathcal{L})$ where each *Name* n has been replaced by $\eth(i\text{-}seq, n)$ for some $i\text{-}seq$.

$$\frac{\Phi\colon Prop_{Spec} \qquad i\text{-}seq\colon \mathsf{N}_1^*}{\Phi[n/\eth(i\text{-}seq, n) \mid n\colon Name]\colon PredS}$$

These are the predicates the user actually gets to see as description values of variables at any stage in the symbolic execution. The resulting new theory with *PredS* instead of $Prop_{Simp}$ will be called $\widetilde{Th(\mathcal{L})}$. Effectively, this new theory then contains multiple copies of $Prop_{Spec}$, one for each value of $i\text{-}seq$. Note that, in the example of LPF, if n gets replaced by $\eth(i, n)$ then $\overleftarrow{n}$ gets replaced by $\eth(i-1, n)$.

Also needed is the following auxiliary function:

mentions: $PredS \rightarrow Name$-set

which collects the identifiers n mentioned in a given $ps\colon PredS$, i.e. those n for which ps contains $\eth(i, n)$ for any i. This function has to be defined recursively over the syntax of *PredS* (or $Prop_{Simp}$).

The theory $\widetilde{Th(\mathcal{L})}$ is used for simplification: $ps_1\colon PredS$ inside some *SEStateOp* can be simplified to (i.e. replaced by) $ps_2\colon PredS$ if they are equivalent in $\widetilde{Th(\mathcal{L})}$, given that all *PredS* that occur in the *SEStateOp* at an earlier stage hold. Note that, in symbolic execution, one is not directly interested in the theorems of $\widetilde{Th(\mathcal{L})}$ as such, but indirectly in them providing a justification of those theorems of $ThOpSem(\mathcal{L})$ which describe simplification steps.

9.4.3   The language-dependent theories $ThOpSem(\mathcal{L})$

Again assume one is given some fixed language $\mathcal{L}$ and wants to describe the theory $ThOpSem(\mathcal{L})$ of its operational semantics. As before, $ThOpSem(\mathcal{L})$ does not denote one *parameterised* theory, but a collection of different theories. $ThOpSem(\mathcal{L})$ is the theory that describes the operational semantics of symbolic execution of a particular language $\mathcal{L}$.

It inherits as parent theories the theory *ThOpSem* of operational semantics in general (via a morphism translating *name* to *Name* and *preds* to *PredS*), independent of the language $\mathcal{L}$, and $\widetilde{Th}(\mathcal{L})$, the simplification theory of $\mathcal{L}$.

Let *Spec* be the type of all specifications and programs, i.e. all terms in $\mathcal{L}$ denoting a binary relation on states. *SpecName* is the type of specification names, and *SpecMap* associates specification names with specifications:

$$SpecMap = SpecName \xrightarrow{m} Spec$$

Configurations consist of a sequence of *SpecName*s and an *SEStateOp*:

$$Conf :: \begin{array}{ll} SNSEQ & : SpecName^* \\ STATE & : SEStateOp \end{array}$$

One can now introduce the transitions and transition rules describing the language $\mathcal{L}$ as axioms or rules of *ThOpSem($\mathcal{L}$)*, as described in Section 9.3, and derive the wanted transitions from them.

9.4.4 The theories *ThModule(Mod)* of specification modules

A specification module *Mod*[5] consists of

- type definitions

- function definitions

- definitions of specifications. Here specifications are terms denoting a relation on states. In VDM, these would be called operations.

The theory *ThModule(Mod)* of a specification module *Mod* then inherits the theory *ThOpSem($\mathcal{L}$)* of the language used and additionally contains

- symbols for all the defined types of the module, plus their definitions

- symbols for all the functions of the module, plus their definitions (axiomatic or otherwise)

- a constant *specmap*: *SpecMap*

- transitions found by symbolic execution, expressed as rules.

However, in *ThModule(Mod)* all these definitions have to be expressed in the language of *mural* rather than the specification language, since they are to be part of a *mural* theory. Since they are originally expressed in the specification language (and stored in the specification support tool described in Chapter 7), they will have to be translated first.

---

[5]Note that a specification module is similar to, but not the same as, a *Module* in the BSI-Protostandard for VDM [And88, BSI90].

The constant *specmap*

The function *specs* takes a reference to a theory (it will be applied to theories of speci-fication modules) and returns the names of specifications in the domain of the constant *specmap*, i.e. the names of specifications in the module. From now on, *specmap* will be a *fixed* constant symbol of type *CESymb*.

> *specs* (*thr: Theory-ref*) *r: SpecName*-set
> ext rd *mural* : *Store*
> pre *thr* ∈ dom *THS(mural)*
>   ∧ *specmap* ∈ *atoms(thr, THS(mural))*
>   ∧ ⊢*THS(mural)(thr)* *specmap: SpecMap*
> post ∀*sn: SpecName* · *sn* ∈ *r* ⟺ ⊢*THS(mural)(thr)* *sn* ∈ dom *specmap*

We require for any theory *ThModule(Mod)* that the axioms provided about *specmap* en-sure that *specs* is implementable. This will usually be achieved by defining the map *specmap* explicitly.

9.4.5   The weak theories *WThOpSem(L)* and *WThModule(Mod)*

The theory *WThOpSem(L)* includes those rules of the operational semantics of *L* which are not faithful (and therefore do not describe *full* symbolic execution) but which do describe *weak* symbolic execution. It has *ThOpSem(L)* as a parent theory. The *PredS*-information contained in an *SEStateOp* after *weak* symbolic execution is also correct under *full* symbolic execution, but it may be incomplete and not fully describe the results of actual execution.

The theory *WThModule(Mod)* merges information about the module *Mod* and infor-mation about weak symbolic execution. Therefore it is defined as a theory that does not contain any constants or axioms itself, but only the two parent theories *ThModule(Mod)* and *WThOpSem(L)*.

One can see that from the point of view of the theories involved, *weak* symbolic execution is not essentially different from *full* symbolic execution. The rules used take the same form, and they will be applied in the same way. The essential difference between the two is that the rules for weak symbolic execution convey less information in the sense that the sets of *PredS* one gets as values for the different *Names* may be smaller, and the individual *PredS* may only be consequences of rather than equivalent to those one gets from full symbolic execution. However, this does not affect the structure of these rules; indeed a rule describing weak symbolic execution of one operation may at the same time describe full symbolic execution of some other operation: let *SORT1* be an operation that sorts a list of *Persons* by their age. If several *Persons* have the same age then they may be put in some arbitrary order. Alternatively, *SORT2* requires that in this case they should be ordered alphabetically on their names. Then in *weak* symbolic execution of *SORT2* the additional requirement might be dropped and thus lead to the same result as *full* symbolic execution of *SORT1*.

9.5   Conclusions

This chapter described the theoretical foundations for a component of *mural* called SYM-BEX. SYMBEX supports the symbolic execution of specifications in order to validate them against the informal user requirements. In order to achieve language-genericity for SYM-BEX, it is based on a variation of the operational semantics of the language concerned. These are expressed as a collection of theories in the TPA. A notion of correctness of symbolic execution is added by defining the denotational semantics of symbolic execution. As a result of this approach, symbolic execution as described here is applicable for a large class of specification (and programming) languages, namely all those that are based on a notion of states and state transformations.

A specification of SYMBEX is given in Appendix D. This specification only deals with the functional aspects of the system; the user's view of the system is not covered here but is described in [Kne89, §6.2].

Because of time pressure, only a very basic prototype of SYMBEX was eventually implemented, and it is therefore not included in the version of *mural* distributed. At the time, the tactics language was still under development; there was only a small number of tactics available, and the pattern matching/unification algorithms were fairly naïve and slow. As a result the system at that stage was very slow, and only a few small experiments with it were possible.

Chapter 10

Case Studies

The PA ('proof assistant') has been instantiated with a hierarchy of theories with rules for VDM. These cover rules for inferring the well-definedness and the dynamic properties of VDM specifications. This chapter contains two case studies highlighting some of the capabilities of this special instantiation of the *mural* system. To prepare for the case studies, we first give a description of VDM specifications, and then describe how a few VDM constructs can be transformed into *mural*.

The first case study is a watchdog for a reactor system[1]. This case is nice, since it is small and fairly simple without being trivial. The second case study is an algorithm for topological sorting[2]. The algorithm is interesting, because its formal specification involves an abstract data structure that is not trivial. This 'TopSort' example is so far the largest example that has been processed on *mural*. The case studies are presented in turn. In the presentation we show most of the *mural* constants and rules directly representing the specification, but have skipped most of the additional rules (and constants) created as lemmas during proof construction.

When doing the case studies, the VST was still at a rather prototypal level, which meant that it was necessary to create the PA theories for the VDM specifications 'by hand' in order to come through. However, with the later additions to the VST both case studies could have been carried out using the direct transformation from specifications in the VST to theories in the PA.

The basis for these case studies is the VDM instantiation of *mural*. The theory for VDM entered into *mural* is a form of LPF [BCJ84] extended also to handle types[3], where conservative extensions are added to handle sets, sequences, mappings, etc. The work on the VDM instantiation has been done independently of – and does not correspond to – any established proof theory for VDM apart from what is described here. The VDM theory store consists of a huge number of rules. We only present a few of these rules, namely the ones that have been applied in the small examples we are giving of proofs. The style of the proofs and proof rules is similar to that in Cliff Jones' book [Jon90a], so that is the place for the hungry reader to collect more information.

---

[1]The reactor example originates from Bloomfield and Froome [BF86]. The VDM formulation given here has been extracted from [FE91].

[2]The algorithm for topological sorting has previously been given a VDM formulation in [EB89], which includes a complete VDM development from an abstract specification over several design stages to an implementation in VAX-11 Pascal. The VDM development in this chapter is extracted from [Elv90].

[3]There is no magic in this. We are referring to expressions of the form $s: T$, saying that s has type T. Such typing expressions are not part of the original definition of LPF.

10.1   Specifications in VDM

A VDM development – in its purest form – consists of a sequence of less and less abstract specifications and of reifications between succeeding abstract/concrete specifications. The first specification in the sequence is referred to as the abstract specification. The succeeding specifications are referred to as design step one, two, etc.

VDM specifications automatically give rise to some proof obligations that have to be discharged in order for the specification to be consistent. Similarly for steps of development. There are also a number of proof obligations that arise less automatically, namely those we regard as validation conditions. Thus proof obligations for a VDM development divide into three classes: validation conditions for the specifications, consistency proof obligations for the specifications, and proof obligations for the reifications.

To validate an abstract specification means to increase your own confidence that it is really a model of the problem you want to solve. To validate design steps means to assure yourself that the new features/properties added to the design do not affect the validity of the specification.

Each of the specifications must be internally consistent. Functions must be total over their specified domains and operations must be satisfiable[4].

Concrete specifications must be proper refinements of more abstract ones. The concrete data structures must be adequate to represent the abstract ones. The concrete functions and operations must be proper models of the abstract ones, which can be ensured by discharging the domain and result proof obligations.

The two latter classes of proof obligations can easily be extracted from the specifications. The obligation to validate a specification is more difficult to formalize: you can never undertake a formal proof that guarantees you a contented customer. It is only necessary to validate the extensions added to the design steps, since validity of the core part of the specification, originating from the refinement of the previous step (initially the abstract specification), is inherited.

Discharging a proof obligation is performed through a formal proof. The preparation for carrying out such formal proofs is usually to represent the specification or development as logical formulae in some theorem prover or proof assistant. This is exactly the approach that we take in the two case studies, where the properties expressed by the proof obligations must be logical consequences of (the representation of) the specification: that is they must be derivable from the specification by the rules in the VDM instantiation of *mural*.

10.2   Transformation of VDM into *mural*-theories

This section describes the transformation of a few VDM constructs into constants and rules in the VDM theory store. We are only giving a few very specific examples, which have all explicitly been used as central parts of the transformation of the case studies. A more complete set of transformation rules for VDM constructs has been developed in connection with the description of the VST – see Chapter 8. This section is not comple-

---

[4]Satisfiability was in the first edition of [Jon90a] called implementability. Satisfiability means that an operation satisfies the satisfiability proof obligation. If some function ensures this property, then this function is denoted as the implementation of the operation. We use the sloppy convention, that an operation is an 'implicitly defined function', and that a function is 'an explicitly defined operation'.

menting, but rather illuminating, other aspects of that work. The transformation schemes in this section have been developed solely as an aid to carry the case studies through. Better schemes could perhaps be found.

10.2.1 Data types

The VDM instantiation takes a number of types as primitive, such as natural numbers, sets, sequences, and maps. These will not be described here. Instead we propose a way of providing new composite data types with induction rules. The technique is based on the algebraic principle of generator induction.

In VDM a new data type is introduced by a (set of) domain equation(s). The valid objects are pointed out by an invariant. To prove properties of such defined data types we often need an induction rule.

One way to derive an induction rule can be found in the algebraic principle of generator induction over finitely generated domains. Consider the following example:

Example 10.2.1 (Generator Induction) *Let the domain L be non-empty lists of elements from the VDM domain P, with the partial ordering* $\preceq: P \times P \to B$.

$$L = P^+$$

where

$inv\text{-}L : L \to B$
$inv\text{-}L(l) \quad \triangleq \quad (\text{len } l \geq 2) \ \Rightarrow \ (\text{hd tl } l \preceq \text{hd } l)$

L is finitely generated by the single generator function

$gen\text{-}L : P \times L \to L$
$gen\text{-}L(p, l) \quad \triangleq \quad \text{if hd } l \preceq p$
$\qquad\qquad\qquad\quad \text{then } [p] \frown l$
$\qquad\qquad\qquad\quad \text{else } [\text{hd } l] \frown [p] \frown \text{tl } l$

from the basic set[5] of objects $\{[p] \mid p : P\}$ *of singleton lists over P. To prove that objects in L have some property* $Q: L \to B$, *the following generator induction scheme can be applied:*

$$\boxed{\text{L ind}} \frac{[p]\{p : P\} \vdash Q[[p]],}{\quad [p, l]\{p : P, l : L, Q[l]\} \vdash Q[gen(p, l)]}{\forall l : L \cdot Q[l]}$$

Example 10.2.1 is easy to generalize for other finitely generated domains, and we will see another example of how this works for the TopSort case study.

The principle of generator induction is in particular applicable in VDM, where all objects of any domain must be of finite size, and therefore are very likely to be finitely generable in some sense.

Remark: In [Elv90] we tried to formulate a general scheme for how to formulate induction rules, where the soundness of the resulting rules should be provable in the PA. This turned out to be very indigestible. It seems that such induction rules are best formulated *ad*

---

[5]This set is not a VDM set.

hoc and then added as axioms to the PA. Whether their formulation in practice can be automated is still an open question, even though there are no deep foundational questions involved in this.

10.2.2   Functions

We use a loose abstract notation – borrowed from *mural* – to express how function definitions look in general. Thus a function defined in VDM as

$$f : A_1 \times \ldots \times A_n \to D$$
$$f(a_1, \ldots, a_n) \; \triangleq \; E[a_1, \ldots, a_n], n \geq 0$$
$$\text{pre } P[a_1, \ldots, a_n]$$

transforms in *mural* to

$$f[n, 0] \triangleq E[[[e1]], \ldots, [[en]]] \qquad\qquad\qquad \text{pre-}f[n, 0] \triangleq P[a_1, \ldots, a_n]$$

Here we have used E to denote an arbitrary expression and P an arbitrary predicate, both with free variables among $a_1, \ldots, a_n$. Note that it is possible also to define recursive functions in this way. Examples of recursive functions can be seen in the TopSort case study. The typing information of the precondition and the function are expressed in definedness rules, which need to be proved, i.e. they are consistency proof obligations:

$$\boxed{\text{def } f} \; \frac{a_1 : A_1, \ldots, a_n : A_n, \; \text{pre-}f[a_1, \ldots, a_n]}{f[a_1, \ldots, a_n] : D}$$

$$\boxed{\text{def pre-}f} \; \frac{a_1 : A_1, \ldots, a_n : A_n}{\text{pre-}f[a_1, \ldots, a_n] : \mathbb{B}}$$

For proving properties about recursive functions defined over some abstract data type, we have defined a rule for well-founded induction, which could also have been called induction 'on the size of the argument':

$$\boxed{\text{WF Induction}} \; \frac{\begin{array}{c} par : PAR, \\ \forall pp : PAR \cdot ord[pp] : \mathbb{N} \\ [q]\{q : PAR, (\forall p : PAR \cdot (ord[p] < ord[q]) \;\Rightarrow\; F[p])\} \vdash F[q] \end{array}}{F[par]}$$

The function *ord* is a function that decides the 'size' of a given argument. It is always possible to define such a function for objects in a finitely generated domain, since the size can be defined as the number of generator function applications that is necessary in order to generate the object. Thus *ord* is not a bijection, but an injection from *PAR* to $\mathbb{N}$, defining a well-founded ordering on *PAR* (of course *PAR* must be finitely generated).

Refer to Chapter 8 for a description of how to transform operations.

10.2.3   Let expressions

The let-expressions used in the case studies generalize to expressions of the form

$$\text{let } P[x] \text{ in } E[x],$$

which can be translated to an expression of the form

$$E[(\varepsilon\ x{:}A.P[x])]\ \textit{iff}\ \exists x{:}A \cdot P[x],$$

where ε is the usual choice operator from first order logic. Since variables can only be primitive, there is no way to define things like (recursive) functions in let constructs.

The ε-operator is defined as a primitive binder, together with the following axioms:

$$\boxed{\varepsilon\ \text{def}}\ \dfrac{\exists x{:}A \cdot P[x]}{P[\varepsilon\ x{:}A \cdot P[x]]}\qquad\qquad\boxed{\varepsilon\ \text{form}}\ \dfrac{\exists x{:}A \cdot P[x]}{\varepsilon\ x{:}A \cdot P[x]{:}A}$$

There are no problems with non-determinism of choice. To see that choice is deterministic, one can easily prove:

$$\boxed{\varepsilon\ \text{deterministic}}\ \dfrac{\exists x{:}A \cdot P[x]}{\varepsilon\ x{:}A \cdot P[x] = \varepsilon\ x{:}A \cdot P[x]}$$

This follows since a rule in the VDM instantiation requires that all well-defined expressions are equal to themselves.

10.3 A watchdog for a reactor system

The system – a part of which we are going to specify – is illustrated in Figure 10.1. It consists essentially of four units: a reactor, its controller, a watchdog, and a display. Trip, veto, and indicator signals are transmitted between these units. We shall specify the functionality of the watchdog unit, whose responsibility it is to set the indicator signals and the mode (a special 'error' or 'danger' indicator) on the basis of the trip and veto information it receives from the other units.

The presence of a trip signifies an abnormal situation (for example, the output of some sensor in the reactor rising above a threshold level) which may require intervention by the user (the 'user' could either be a human operator or another part of the system). The display board, therefore, must be notified (by setting indicators) if a trip occurs. A veto is a signal indicating that a particular trip signal has either been properly handled or that the controller unit has decided to ignore or override the trip. An indicator signal is a notification of the occurrence of a particular trip (the indicator signals could drive warning lights on the display board). There are only a finite number of different signals. The mode (or overall safety indicator of the reactor) can take one of two values: OK or TRIP, representing, respectively, the normal operating state and some emergency state.

The function of the watchdog – specified as an operation called *watch* – is to control the reactor by setting (i.e. updating) indicators and the mode depending on how trips and vetoes have been altered since the last update. The (mode of the) reactor is OK if (and only if) the set of all trips is equal to the set of all vetoes and the reactor was not previously in TRIP-mode, otherwise the reactor is in TRIP-mode. Problems of initialization and so on are not being considered. It is envisaged that something periodically causes the watchdog to execute the *watch* operation. We are mainly concerned with the internals of the watchdog. A specification of the whole reactor would have to ensure that *watch* was, for example, executed sufficiently frequently or immediately following certain other events.

The watchdog's *watch* operation must satisfy the following conditions in order to operate safely:

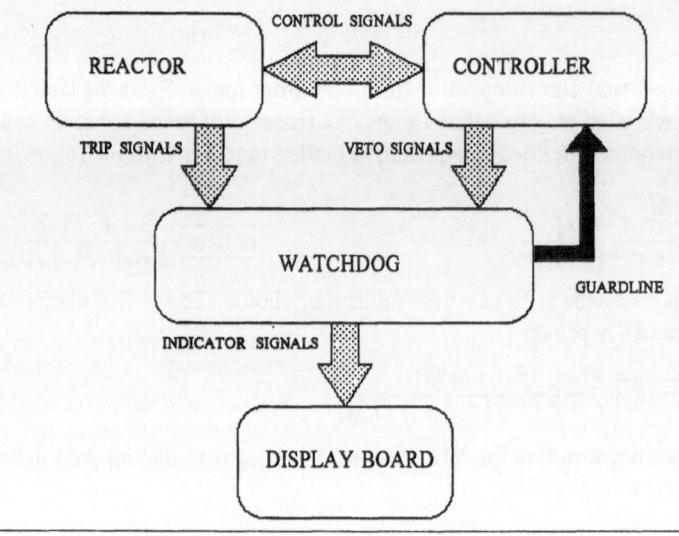

Figure 10.1: The Reactor Control System

- signals (indicators, trips, and vetoes) must latch – that is, once on, *watch* must not turn them off,

- a signal can never be indicated before it has been tripped,

- a signal can never be vetoed before it has been tripped,

- once the reactor is in TRIP-mode we must rely on some external agent to cancel the TRIP (that is, *watch* must never take the system from a TRIP state to an OK state),

- if there is an un-vetoed trip, then *watch* must set the state to TRIP-mode, and

- any tripped signal must be indicated by the watchdog.

The condition described in the third item is a requirement on parts of the reactor system external to the watchdog. In the validation of the abstract specification in Section 10.3.2 we discuss this in more depth.

10.3.1 Design guidelines

We model signals as a type with finitely many objects. The state of the watchdog is then modelled as consisting of four parts: vetoes, trips, and indicators, which are sets of signals, and a reactor mode, which is either OK or TRIP. With access to this state the operation watch operates. In the first design stage signals are changed to be natural numbers from some index set, and the sets of signals are changed to be lists of Booleans with a fixed length equal to the maximum of the index set. Each number then indexes a position in the list, and that position's Boolean value indicates whether the signal represented by that number has been registered. It is not decided how the watchdog interacts with the other units. We are mainly interested in the functionality of the *watch* operation[6].

10.3.2 Formal development

Abstract specification

We model signals as a type with finitely many objects. This type is described by an index set of natural numbers, where *max* denotes some fixed but arbitrary natural number. The state of the watchdog is then modelled as consisting of four parts: vetoes, trips, and indicators, which are sets of signals, and a reactor mode, which is either OK or TRIP. With access to this state the operation *watch* operates.

$$Signal = \{1, .., max\}$$

$$Mode = \{TRIP, OK\}$$

$$
\begin{aligned}
State :: \ &tr \ : Signal\text{-set} \\
&vt \ : Signal\text{-set} \\
&md : Mode \\
&ind : Signal\text{-set}
\end{aligned}
$$

The fields of *State* are *trips*, *vetoes*, a *mode* and some *indicators*. The state of the watchdog is formalized as a subtype of *State*. Note how the requirements that no signal can ever be indicated before it has been tripped and that no signal can ever be vetoed before it has been tripped are built into the state through the invariant.

$$WDstate = State$$

where

$$inv\text{-}WDstate(s) \ \triangleq \ (ind(s) \subseteq tr(s)) \ \wedge \ (vt(s) \subseteq tr(s))$$

watch
ext wr s : *WDstate*
post $((md(s) = TRIP) \ \Leftrightarrow \ ((\neg (tr(\overleftarrow{s}) \subseteq vt(\overleftarrow{s}))) \vee (md(\overleftarrow{s}) = TRIP))) \wedge$
$\qquad ind(s) = ind(\overleftarrow{s}) \cup tr(\overleftarrow{s}) \wedge$
$\qquad tr(s) = tr(\overleftarrow{s}) \wedge$
$\qquad vt(s) = vt(\overleftarrow{s})$

Strictly speaking it is not necessary to model the change in the indicators as the union of the trips and the indicators in the old state. It would be sufficient just to assign the trips to the indicators, since a trip can only be removed by some reset operation.

First design stage

The design decision guiding the data reification from the abstract to the concrete level uses the information that only finitely many different signals exist. The three sets of signals

---

[6]It is very convenient to limit our concern to pure functionality, since there is no standard way of handling interaction, that is concurrency, in VDM, and in particular not in the VDM logic implemented in *mural*. (Such extensions have been seen. Refer for instance to the work of Woodcock and Dickinson [WD88] or Ketil Stølen [Stø90]).

in the abstract state can then be modelled as sequences of Booleans of length equal to the number of different signals; the state still includes a mode.

$Mode = \{\text{TRIP}, \text{OK}\}$

$State2 :: \; tr2 \quad : \; \mathbf{B}^*$
$\qquad\qquad vf2 \quad : \; \mathbf{B}^*$
$\qquad\qquad md2 \; : \; Mode$
$\qquad\qquad ind2 \; : \; \mathbf{B}^*$

$WDstate2 = State2$

where

$inv\text{-}WDstate2(mk\text{-}State2(tr, vt, md, ind)) \quad \triangle$
$\qquad \text{len } tr = \text{len } vt \wedge$
$\qquad \text{len } ind = \text{len } vt \wedge$
$\qquad ptwImpliedBy(tr, ind) \wedge$
$\qquad ptwImpliedBy(tr, vt)$

All the lists of Booleans must have the same length, and still no signal can be indicated or vetoed before it has been tripped. The auxiliary function *ptwImpliedBy* ('pointwise implied by') models the $\subseteq$-relation on sets.

$ptwImpliedBy : \mathbf{B}^* \times \mathbf{B}^* \to \mathbf{B}$
$ptwImpliedBy(l, m) \quad \triangle \quad \forall i : \mathbf{N}_1 \cdot (i \in \text{inds } l \wedge i \in \text{inds } m) \Rightarrow (m[i] \Rightarrow l[i])$

In the initial state all items in the lists are false. We insist that *watch* must not take the system from a TRIP state back to an OK state. The refined version of *watch* is called *watch2*. Note that the predicate *restUnchanged* makes sure that the lengths of the lists in the old and the new states are the same. This property is not ensured by the invariant, since we did not give fixed length to the lists – we simply stated that they should all have the same length. Now we have also made sure that this length is fixed over time.

$watch2$
$\text{ext wr } s \; : \; WDstate2$
$\text{post } ((md2(s) = \text{TRIP}) \;\Leftrightarrow\; (sigNotVetoed(s) \vee (md2(\overleftarrow{s}) = \text{TRIP}))) \wedge$
$\qquad indsCorrect(\overleftarrow{s}, s) \wedge$
$\qquad restUnchanged(\overleftarrow{s}, s)$

The auxiliary functions are self-explanatory:

$sigNotVetoed : WDstate2 \to \mathbf{B}$
$sigNotVetoed(s) \quad \triangle \quad \exists i : \mathbf{N}_1 \cdot (i \in \text{inds } ind2(s)) \wedge tr2(s)[i] \wedge \neg (vf2(s)[i])$

$indsCorrect : WDstate2 \times WDstate2 \to \mathbf{B}$
$indsCorrect(s, ss) \quad \triangle \quad \forall i : \mathbf{N}_1 \cdot (i \in (\text{inds } ind2(s) \cap \text{inds } ind2(ss)))$
$\qquad \Rightarrow \; ind2(ss)[i] = (ind2(s)[i] \vee tr2(s)[i])$

$restUnchanged : WDstate2 \times WDstate2 \rightarrow \mathsf{B}$
$restUnchanged(s, ss) \quad \underline{\triangle}$
$\quad tr2(s) = tr2(ss) \wedge$
$\quad vf2(s) = vf2(ss)$

Proof obligations

Consistency of the abstract specification
The following two formulae express 'sensibleness' conditions (i.e. well-formedness proof obligations) to ensure that the definitions are total and correctly typed. The reason it is necessary to show that the invariant and postcondition are of type B (a type with two elements: {true, false}) is that VDM is based on logic for partial functions, where you are only allowed to reason about terms that have a well-defined[7] value (refer to [BCJ84]).

$$\forall s: State \cdot inv\text{-}WDstate(s): \mathsf{B}$$

$$\forall s: WDstate, \; ss: WDstate \cdot post\text{-}watch(s, ss): \mathsf{B}$$

The following formula is the standard *satisfiability* proof obligation[8]:

$$\forall s: WDstate \cdot \exists ss: WDstate \cdot post\text{-}watch(s, ss)$$

Validation of the abstract specification
We now express formally the validation conditions stated informally at the beginning of this section. Indicator, trip, and veto signals must, once they are on, stay on after an execution of the watchdog. New indicators can be signalled by the *watch* operation:

$$\forall s, ss: WDstate \cdot post\text{-}watch(s, ss) \; \Rightarrow \; ind(s) \subseteq ind(ss) \tag{10.1}$$

Nothing – neither the watchdog nor its environment – must change the trips or the vetoes during the execution of *watch*:

$$\forall s, ss: WDstate \cdot post\text{-}watch(s, ss) \; \Rightarrow \; tr(s) = tr(ss) \tag{10.2}$$
$$\forall s, ss: WDstate \cdot post\text{-}watch(s, ss) \; \Rightarrow \; vt(s) = vt(ss) \tag{10.3}$$

A signal must never be indicated before it has been tripped, and a signal must never be vetoed before it has been tripped:

$$\forall s, ss: WDstate \cdot post\text{-}watch(s, ss) \; \Rightarrow \; ind(ss) \subseteq tr(s) \tag{10.4}$$
$$\forall s, ss: WDstate \cdot post\text{-}watch(s, ss) \; \Rightarrow \; vt(ss) \subseteq tr(s) \tag{10.5}$$

The watchdog's mode will 'latch' in TRIP-mode:

$$\forall s, ss: WDstate \cdot$$
$$(post\text{-}watch(s, ss) \wedge md(s) = \text{TRIP}) \; \Rightarrow \; md(ss) = \text{TRIP} \tag{10.6}$$

---

[7]For example the proposition '$\frac{1}{0} = 3$' is considered undefined, and does not denote an element of the type B.

[8]Note that we use s to denote the old state, and ss to denote the new. The reason for this is, that it is easier to write in the PA, where it is not possible to write $\overleftarrow{s}$.

The watchdog will set the mode to TRIP if there is an un-vetoed trip:

$$\forall s, ss: WDstate \cdot$$
$$(post\text{-}watch(s, ss) \wedge \neg (tr(s) \subseteq vt(s))) \;\Rightarrow\; md(ss) = \text{TRIP} \tag{10.7}$$

The watchdog must always set the indicators according to the present trips:

$$\forall s, ss: WDstate \cdot post\text{-}watch(s, ss) \;\Rightarrow\; ind(ss) = tr(s) \tag{10.8}$$

One can see that the validation conditions range from simple functionality requirements (the first three) to essential safety properties of the system (the last three).

Note (again) that two validation conditions, namely the one saying that no signal
is ever indicated before it has been tripped (10.4) and the one saying that no signal is
ever vetoed before it is tripped (10.5), have been built directly into the specification –
they are part of the invariant. Whatever updates the state of the watchdog in between
the executions of *watch*, it must leave the state as a valid object in the type *WDstate*.
Thus, through the definition of a subtype, we have imposed a number of requirements
on the external world. Finally, note that without stating these properties as part of the
invariant on states, we would not have been able to assure that they were fulfilled. From
a higher level view of the system (perhaps a specification of the entire reactor system)
a variety of other safety or validation properties may be stated (such as that *watch* is
executed sufficiently often). However since we are considering the watchdog more or
less in isolation, such higher-level properties and obligations can legitimately be ignored
(and indeed are).

The validation conditions (10.2) and (10.3) could also have been build into the specification by splitting the state into four components *tr*, *vt*, *md*, and *ind* and assigning the
read only option (rd) to the components *tr* and *vt* in the watchdog specification. The reason for not doing so is that we decided to consider the state as a whole instead of splitting
it into four parts. The possibility of splitting a state into its components is often used in
[Jon90a].

Validation and consistency of first design step
By undertaking the refinement proofs (i.e. showing that *WDstate2* is an *adequate* representation of *WDstate* and showing the *domain* and *result* obligations for *watch/watch2*),
all the validation conditions are inherited from the abstract specification to the concrete
specification, since these could easily be re-proved by application of the retrieve function. All that remains is to prove the new consistency proof obligations, which arise
automatically for the concrete specification:

$$\forall s: State2 \cdot inv\text{-}WDstate2(s): \mathsf{B}$$

$$\forall l: \mathsf{B}^{*}, \; m: \mathsf{B}^{*} \cdot ptwImpliedBy(l, m): \mathsf{B}$$

$$\forall s: WDstate2 \cdot sigNotVetoed(s): \mathsf{B}$$

$$\forall s: WDstate2, \; ss: WDstate2 \cdot indsCorrect(s, ss): \mathsf{B}$$

$$\forall s: WDstate2, \; ss: WDstate2 \cdot restUnchanged(s, ss): \mathsf{B}$$

$$\forall s: WDstate2, \; ss: WDstate2 \cdot post\text{-}watch2(s, ss): \mathsf{B}$$

$$\forall s: WDstate2 \cdot \exists ss: WDstate2 \cdot post\text{-}watch2(s, ss)$$

Refinement

The refinement is proved correct in the traditional way. First a well-defined retrieve function is found, and then the *adequacy* of the concrete state to represent the abstract state is proved. The *domain* and *result* rules are proved for each operation. In this case the domain rule is trivial, since neither the abstract *watch* nor the concrete *watch2* operation carries any precondition.

$retr\text{-}WDstate : WDstate2 \rightarrow WDstate$
$retr\text{-}WDstate(mk\text{-}State2(tr, vt, md, ind)) \;\; \triangleq$
$\qquad \text{let } tr' = \{i \mid tr[i]\}$
$\qquad\qquad vt' = \{i \mid vt[i]\}$
$\qquad\qquad ind' = \{i \mid ind[i]\} \text{ in}$
$\qquad mk\text{-}State(tr', vt', md, ind')$

Definedness of retrieve function

$$\forall s\colon WDstate2 \cdot retr\text{-}WDstate(s)\colon WDstate$$

Adequacy of state

$$\forall s1\colon WDstate \cdot \exists s2\colon WDstate2 \cdot s1 = retr\text{-}WDstate(s2)$$

Result rule

$\forall s\colon WDstate2,\; ss\colon WDstate2 \cdot \; post\text{-}watch2(s, ss)$
$\qquad\qquad\qquad\qquad .\Rightarrow \; post\text{-}watch(retr\text{-}WDstate(s), retr\text{-}WDstate(ss))$

10.3.3 Representation in *mural*

Instead of using the default translation mechanism we generated the definitions by hand[9]. For types, operations, and functions introduced in the VDM specification, type symbols and constant symbols are declared in a theory in the PA. Each part of the development has its own theory. Translating composite types will result in constants for the VDM 'make' and 'selector' functions being added explicitly. In addition to a declaration (stating the expected number of arguments), each function symbol needs a definition. VDM operations are translated to a pair of Boolean-valued constants to represent the pre and postconditions. VDM functions are also translated to constants. The type information is added as definedness proof obligations, as briefly described in Section 10.2.2.

Consistency properties (traditional proof obligations: definedness, satisfiability) are generated automatically by the VST[10]. Validity properties cannot be automatically generated since in general they rely on the specifier's understanding of what the system should do and must therefore be entered by the *mural* user as unproven conjectures (yet-to-be-proven rules) in the PA.

A 'print-out' facility is included in *mural* which allows the generation of LATEX documents describing theories, rules, proofs, and so on. The following subsections contain

---

[9]As explained in the introduction of this chapter, the automatic translation mechanism was not available at the time these case studies were carried out.

[10]At least they would have been generated automatically if we had been able to use the VST's translation tool.

output generated by the PA from the theories for the abstract specification, the first design step, and the reification from the abstract specification to the first design step. The LATEX source files which are generated can easily be edited and directly included in other LATEX documents.

Representation of the abstract specification

Types

Signal $\mapsto \langle$ i : N_1 . (i $\leq$ max) $\rangle$,   State $\mapsto$ [0,0],

WDstate $\mapsto \langle$ n : State . (inv-WDstate [n]) $\rangle$,   Mode $\mapsto$ [0,0]

Signal and *WDstate* are subtypes of N_1 and *State* respectively. *Mode* and *State* are primitive types. That means that their 'meaning' will be introduced through axioms, as can be seen below.

Constants

max $\mapsto$ [0,0],	s-tr $\mapsto$ [1,0],
	s-vt $\mapsto$ [1,0],
OK $\mapsto$ [0,0],	s-md $\mapsto$ [1,0],
TRIP $\mapsto$ [0,0],	s-ind $\mapsto$ [1,0],
	mk-State $\mapsto$ [4,0],

The above constants are all primitive with arity [0,0], [1,0], or [4,0], meaning that they take 0, 1, or 4 expression arguments respectively, and that none of them take any types as argument. The *s-* symbols are selectors for the composite type, and *mk-State* is the corresponding make function. All these constants are defined by the axioms below.

inv-WDstate $\mapsto$ (((s-ind [[$e1$]]) $\subseteq$ (s-tr [[$e1$]])) $\wedge$ ((s-vt [[$e1$]]) $\subseteq$ (s-tr [[$e1$]])))

inv-WDstate is a defined constant, which takes one expression as its argument. The 'expression hole', [[$e1$]], serves as a placeholder for this argument.

post-watch $\mapsto$
   (((((s-md [[$e2$]]) = TRIP) $\Leftrightarrow$
     (($\neg$ ((s-tr [[$e1$]]) $\subseteq$ (s-vt [[$e1$]]))) $\vee$ ((s-md [[$e1$]]) = TRIP))) $\wedge$
   ((s-ind [[$e2$]]) = ((s-ind [[$e1$]]) $\cup$ (s-tr [[$e1$]])))) $\wedge$
   (((s-tr [[$e2$]]) = (s-tr [[$e1$]])) $\wedge$
   ((s-vt [[$e2$]]) = (s-vt [[$e1$]])))))

post-watch is a defined constant, which takes two expression arguments (there are *two* holes in the definition – [[$e1$]] and [[$e2$]]). For both of these defined constants a *formation rule* (to ensure well-typedness and totality) will be added as a new unproven rule.

In order to make the proofs go through more easily, an auxiliary function *watch* has been added to the theory (by hand[11]). This is a useful and fairly standard procedure when doing constructive proofs of satisfiability (and – as we shall see in Section 10.3.4 – adequacy), which generally involve proving an existential statement, and proceed using the 'exists introduction' rule (refer to Section 10.5) which requires the construction of a 'witness' element.

---

[11]Obviously, the function *watch* cannot usually be generated automatically, since it is effectively an implementation of the specification.

watch ↦
      mk-State [(s-tr [[$e1$]]),
       (s-vt [[$e1$]]),
       (if (((¬ ((s-tr [[$e1$]]) ⊆ (s-vt [[$e1$]])))) ∨ ((s-md [[$e1$]]) = TRIP))
       then TRIP
       else OK) ,
       ((s-ind [[$e1$]]) ∪ (s-tr [[$e1$]])) ,

Axioms

max is an element of N_1. Expressions OK and TRIP are distinct elements of type *Mode*. OK and TRIP are the only elements of *Mode*, and they are not equal.

max form
{ }
{ }
―
(max : N_1)

OK-formation	**TRIP-formation**
{ }	{ }
{ }	{ }
―	―
(OK : Mode)	(TRIP : Mode)

Mode closure	**Mode values unequal**
{ }	{ }
{ (g : Mode) }	{ }
―	―
((g = TRIP) ∨ (g = OK))	(¬ (TRIP = OK))

The record type *State* is defined next. By a number of axioms we give sense to the constant symbols introduced earlier. It takes 10 axioms to define the type *State*, and we show four of them below. The other six are the analogues of *s-tr-defn* and *s-tr-formation* for the other selector functions and are left as an exercise for the reader.

s-tr-defn
{ }
{ ((mk-State [e1 , e2 , e3 , e4]) : State) }
―
((s-tr [(mk-State [e1 , e2 , e3 , e4])]) = e1)

s-tr-formation
{ }
{ (t : State) }
―
((s-tr [t]) : (Signal -set))

State-formation
{ }
{ (e1 : (Signal -set)) , (e2 : (Signal -set)) , (e3 : Mode) ,
(e4 : (Signal -set)) }
―
((mk-State [e1 , e2 , e3 , e4]) : State)

State-introduction
{ }
{ (t : State) }
―
((mk-State [(s-tr [t]) , (s-vt [t]) , (s-md [t]) , (s-ind [t])]) = t)

Rules

The following three rules express the conditions that *inv-WDstate* and *post-watch* are total and correctly typed for all arguments of the correct type, and that the *watch* operation is satisfiable.

inv-WDstate form
{ }
{ (s : State) }
—————————
((inv-WDstate [s]) : B)

post-watch form
{ }
{ (s : WDstate) , (ss : WDstate) }
—————————————
((post-watch [s , ss]) : B)

watch satisfiability
{ }
{ (s : WDstate) }
—————————
$\exists$ ss : WDstate . (post-watch [s , ss])

Lemmas

As previously mentioned, the constant *watch* was introduced purely as a construction to aid the proof process, and the following two lemmas about *watch* allow the satisfiability proof to go through smoothly. The last lemma is just another one which turns out to be convenient when doing the proofs.

watch form
{ }
{ (s : WDstate) }
—————————
((watch [s]) : WDstate)

lem (s:State if s:WDstate)
{ }
{ (s : WDstate) }
—————————
(s : State)

lem watch is implementation
{ }
{ (s : WDstate) }
—————————
(post-watch [s , watch [s]])

Validation of abstract level

The validation conditions (10.1) to (10.8) are easily transformed into *mural*. They are transformed to 8 unproved theorems, of which you can see 2 below. Note – as remarked in Footnote 8 – that we do not use the usual hook notation, but let 's' denote the old state and 'ss' the new.

val 5
{ }
{ (s : WDstate) , (ss : WDstate) }
—————————————
((post-watch[s , ss]) $\Rightarrow$ ((s-vt[ss]) $\subseteq$ (s-tr[s])))

val 7
{ }
{ (s : WDstate) , (ss : WDstate) }
—————————————
(((post-watch[s , ss]) $\wedge$ ($\neg$ ((s-tr[s]) $\subseteq$ (s-vt[s])))) $\Rightarrow$ ((s-md[ss]) = TRIP))

If you carefully study 'val 5' and 'val 7' you will see why the invariant of the state cannot just require trips and vetoes to be equal.

Representation of the first design step

Here we only provide the bare translation of the specification, leaving out all the auxiliary constants and lemmas. As the representation of the first design step is very similar to that of the abstract specification no explanation should be required.

Types
Mode $\mapsto$ [0,0],
State2 $\mapsto$ [0,0],   WDstate2 $\mapsto$ $\langle$ ss:State2 . (inv-WDstate2[ss])$\rangle$

Constants
max $\mapsto$ [0,0],   s-tr2 $\mapsto$ [1,0],
                                       s-vt2 $\mapsto$ [1,0],
OK $\mapsto$ [0,0],   s-md2 $\mapsto$ [1,0],
TRIP $\mapsto$ [0,0],   s-ind2 $\mapsto$ [1,0],
                                       mk-State2 $\mapsto$ [4,0],

inv-WDstate2 $\mapsto$
    $(((($ len $[($ s-tr2 $[[\![e1]\!]]))])) = $ max$) \wedge$
    $((($ len $[($ s-vt2 $[[\![e1]\!]]))]) = $ max $) \wedge$
    $(($ len $[($ s-ind2 $[[\![e1]\!]]))]) = $ max $))) \wedge$
    $(($ ptwImpliedBy $[($ s-tr2 $[[\![e1]\!]]), ($ s-ind2 $[[\![e1]\!]]))]) \wedge$
    $($ ptwImpliedBy $[($ s-tr2 $[[\![e1]\!]]), ($ s-vt2 $[[\![e1]\!]])]))))),$

ptwImpliedBy $\mapsto$
    $\forall$ i : N_1 . $((($ i $\in$ $($ inds $[[\![e1]\!]])) \wedge ($ i $\in$ $($ inds $[[\![e2]\!]])))$
        $\Rightarrow$ $(([\![e2]\!]@$ i$) \Rightarrow ([\![e1]\!]@$ i$))),$

post-watch2 $\mapsto$
    $(((($ s-md2 $[[\![e2]\!]]) = $ TRIP $) \Leftrightarrow$
        $(($ sigNotVetoed $[[\![e1]\!]]) \vee (($ s-md2 $[[\![e1]\!]]) = $ TRIP $))) \wedge$
    $(($ indsCorrect $[[\![e1]\!], [\![e2]\!]]) \wedge$
    $($ restUnchanged $[[\![e1]\!], [\![e2]\!]]))),$

sigNotVetoed $\mapsto$
    $\exists$ i : $\langle$ ii : N_1 . $($ ii $\leq$ max $)\rangle$. $((($ s-tr2 $[[\![e1]\!]]) @$ i$) \wedge (\neg (($ s-vt2 $[[\![e1]\!]]) @$ i$))),$

indsCorrect $\mapsto$
    $\forall$ k : $\langle$ ii : N_1 . $($ ii $\leq$ max $)\rangle$.
        $((($ s-ind2 $[[\![e1]\!]]) @$ k$) = ((($ s-ind2 $[[\![e2]\!]]) @$ k$) \vee (($ s-tr2 $[[\![e2]\!]]) @$ k$)))$

restUnchanged $\mapsto$
    $((($ s-tr2 $[[\![e1]\!]]) = ($ s-tr2 $[[\![e2]\!]])) \wedge (($ s-vt2 $[[\![e1]\!]]) = ($ s-vt2 $[[\![e2]\!]])))$

Axioms
Most of these axioms are almost identical to those of the abstract specification, so we will only show four of them. Try to create the 11 axioms that are not explicitly shown.

s-tr2 defn   **s-tr2 form**
{ }   { }
{ $(($ mk-State2 $[$ e1 , e2 , e3 , e4 $])$: State2 $)$ }   { $($ t : State2 $)$ }
─────────────────────────────   ─────────────────
$(($ s-tr2 $[($ mk-State2 $[$ e1 , e2 , e3 , e4 $])]) = $ e1 $)$ $(($ s-tr2 $[$ t $]) : (\mathbf{B}*))$

mk-State2 defn
{ }
{ $($ t : State2 $)$ }
─────────────────
$(($ mk-State2 $[($ s-tr2 $[$ t $]), ($ s-vt2 $[$ t $]), ($ s-md2 $[$ t $]), ($ s-ind2 $[$ t $])]) = $ t $)$

mk-State2 form
{ }
{ (e1 : (B *)) , (e2 : (B *)) , (e3 : Mode) ,
(e4 : (B *)) }

((mk-State2 [e1 , e2 , e3 , e4]) : State2)

Rules

inv-WDstate2 form
{ }
{ (s : State2) }

((inv-WDstate2 [s]) : B)

ptwImpliedBy form
{ }
{ (l : (B *)) , (m : (B *)) }

((ptwImpliedBy [l , m]) : B)

indsCorrect form
{ }
{ (s : WDstate2) , (ss : WDstate2) }

((indsCorrect [s , ss]) : B)

watch2 sat
{ }
{ (s : WDstate2) }

∃ ss : WDstate2 . (post-watch2 [s , ss])

sigNotVetoed form
{ }
{ (s : WDstate2) }

((sigNotVetoed [s]) : B)

post-watch2 form
{ }
{ (s : WDstate2) , (ss : WDstate2) }

((post-watch2 [s , ss]) : B)

restUnchanged form
{ }
{ (s : WDstate2) , (ss : WDstate2) }

((restUnchanged [s , ss]) : B)

Refinement

Apart from giving the translation of the reification constructs, we emphasize also the constructs necessary to undertake the adequacy proof, thereby providing the (two) auxiliary constructs and lemmas. In particular we have as one auxiliary construct introduced an inject-function, which is in some sense the opposite of a retrieve-function, since such a construct – which in general may not exist – tends to make the constructive adequacy proof simpler. Like in the satisfiability proofs the problem is with the existential quantifier, so the other auxiliary construct is a 'witness'.

Constants

retr-WDstate ↦
 (mk-State [(extr-Set [(s-tr2 [[$e1$]])]) ,
  (extr-Set [(s-vt2 [[$e1$]])]) ,
  (s-md2 [[$e1$]]) ,
  (extr-Set [(s-ind2 [[$e1$]])])]) ,

inj-WDstate2 ↦
 (mk-State2 [(extr-List [(s-tr [[$e1$]]) , max]) ,
  (extr-List [(s-vt [[$e1$]]) , max]) ,
  (s-md [[$e1$]]) ,
  (extr-List [(s-ind [[$e1$]]) , max])]) ,

extr-Set $\mapsto$
 those i : N_1 . ((i ∈ (inds [[$e1$]])) ∧ ([[$e1$]]@ i)) ,
extr-List $\mapsto$
 (if ([[$e2$]]= 1)
  then ([(1 ∈[[$e1$]])])
  else ((extr-List [[[$e1$]] , (pred [[[$e2$]]])]) $^\frown$ ([[$e2$]]∈ [[$e1$]])))

Rules

retr-WDstate form
{ }
{ (s : WDstate2) }
———————
((retr-WDstate [s]) : WDstate)

Adequacy
{ }
{ (s : WDstate) }
———————
∃ s2 : WDstate2 . (s = (retr-WDstate [s2]))

Result Rule
{ }
{ (s : WDstate2) , (ss : WDstate2) }
———————
((post-watch2[s , ss]) ⇒ (post-watch[(retr-WDstate[s]) , (retr-WDstate[ss])]))

Lemmas

To give you a feel for what kind of properties you have to proof for VDM developments, we show a couple of lemmas 'at length'.

These lemmas are all related to the adequacy proof for the watchdog. One thing you will experience when using *mural* is that you have to be careful when you decide how to decompose your proofs into suitable lemmas.

inj-WDstate2 form
{ }
{ (s : WDstate) }
———————
((inj-WDstate2[s]) : WDstate2)

extr-Set form
{ }
{ (s : (B *)) }
———————
((extr-Set [s]) : (Signal -set))

lem (extr-Set[extr-List[s,max]]=s)
{ }
{ (s : (Signal -set)) }
———————
((extr-Set[(extr-List[s , max])]) = s)

extr-List form
{ }
{ (n : N_1) , (s : (Signal -set)) }
———————
((extr-List [s , n]) : (B *))

lem (length of list)
{ }
{ (s : (Signal -set)) , (n : N_1) }
———————
((len [(extr-List [s , n])]) = n)

lem (ptwImpliedBy models ⊆)
{ }
{ ((len [l]) = (len [m])) , (l : (B *)) , (m : (B *)) , (ptwImpliedBy [l , m]) }
———————
((extr-Set [l]) ⊆ (extr-Set [m]))

lem (retroinj = id-WDstate)
{ }
{ (s : WDstate) }
_____
((retr-WDstate [(inj-WDstate2 [s])]) = s)

lem (s-md2[inj-WDstate2[...]]=...)
{ }
{ (s : WDstate) }
_____
((s-md2 [(inj-WDstate2 [s])]) = (s-md [s]))

lem (s-ind2[inj-WDstate2[...]]=...)
{ }
{ (s : WDstate) }
_____
((s-ind2 [(inj-WDstate2 [s])]) = (extr-List [(s-ind [s]) , max]))

lem (s-tr2[inj-WDstate2[...]]=...
{ }
{ (s : WDstate) }
_____
((s-tr2 [(inj-WDstate2 [s])]) = (extr-List [(s-tr [s]) , max]))

lem (s-vt2[inj-WDstate2[...]]=...)
{ }
{ (s : WDstate) }
_____
((s-vt2 [(inj-WDstate2 [s])]) = (extr-List [(s-vt [s]) , max]))

lem ($\subseteq$ is impl by ptwImpliedBy)
{ }
{ (s : (Signal -set)) , (ss : (Signal -set)) , (s $\subseteq$ ss) }
_____
(ptwImpliedBy [(extr-List [ss , max]) , (extr-List [s , max])])

10.3.4   Proofs

We do not include all the proofs, since these tend to be tedious and uninteresting to read. In order to give a flavour, we show three of the more interesting examples. The first of these proofs is a derivation of the formation rule (ensuring well-typedness and totality) for the invariant (i.e. *inv-WDstate form*).

```
h1 ( s : State )
1 ( ( s-tr [ s ] ) : ( Signal -set ) )                       by s-tr-formation on [h1]; []
2 ( ( s-ind [ s ] ) : ( Signal -set ) )                      by s-ind-formation on [h1]; []
3 ( ( s-vt [ s ] ) : ( Signal -set ) )                       by s-vt-formation on [h1]; []
4 ( δ ( ( s-ind [ s ] ) ⊆ ( s-tr [ s ] ) ) )                       by δ-⊆ on [2, 1]; []
5 ( δ ( ( s-vt [ s ] ) ⊆ ( s-tr [ s ] ) ) )                        by δ-⊆ on [3, 1]; []
6 ( δ ( ( ( s-ind [ s ] ) ⊆ ( s-tr [ s ] ) ) ∧ ( ( s-vt [ s ] ) ⊆ ( s-tr [ s ] ) ) ) )
                                                            by δ∧-inherit on [4, 5]; []
7 ( δ ( inv-WDstate [ s ] ) )                                         folding from 6
c ( ( inv-WDstate [ s ] ) : B )                               by bool form on [7]; []
```

The rules to which this proof (and others in this chapter) appeals are collected in Section 10.5, so that is the place to look for rules like δ-$\subseteq$ and '$\delta\wedge$-inherit'. Note that *folding* in Lines 6-7 indicates that an instance of a right-hand-side of a definition (in this case the definition of *inv-WDstate*) has been replaced by the corresponding left-hand-side.

The second proof is of the satisfiability of *watch*. This proof goes through rather easily by an application of the lemma 'lem update is implementation' which asserts that the newly introduced constant *watch* (used as the 'witness' for an '∃-introduction') is a correct implementation.

```
h1 ( s : WDstate )
1 ( ( watch [ s ] ) : WDstate )                              by watch form on [h1]; []
2 ( post-watch [ s , ( watch [ s ] ) ]        by lem watch is implementation on [h1]; []
c ∃ ss : WDstate . ( post-watch [ s , ss ] )                  by ∃-I on [1, 2]; []
```

The more interesting proofs seem to be those establishing the correctness of the reification. Here is the proof of adequacy. In order to undertake the proof we have defined an inject function, which is part of the reification theory. The proof has been broken down into a number of lemmas. These are all part of the reification theory and were given in the previous subsection.

```
h1 ( s : WDstate )
1 ( ( inj-WDstate2 [ s ] ) : WDstate2 )                  by inj-WDstate2 form on [h1]; []
2 ( ( retr-WDstate [ ( inj-WDstate2 [ s ] ) ] ) = s )by lem (retroinj = id-WDstate) on [h1]; []
3 ( s = ( retr-WDstate [ ( inj-WDstate2 [ s ] ) ] ) )              by =-comm on [2]; []
c ∃ s2 : WDstate2 . ( s = ( retr-WDstate [ s2 ] ) )               by ∃-I on [1, 3]; []
```

Remark: When starting with the case studies, we expected to be able to concentrate on the 'interesting' proofs concerning validation and refinement, but it turned out that the consistency proof obligations required much more time than expected. The reason why we needed to spend more time on the consistency proof obligations was twofold. The first thing that one encounters is that if something is wrong in the specification that you are reasoning about, you will have to do all the proofs again, since the specification acts as a kind of assumption in your proof, and if the assumptions change the proof changes. Caused by the first reason, you start by proving that your specification is consistent, because it is tedious to do almost the same proofs over and over again. This leads directly to the second reason: even trivial proofs in *mural* take time, and since a lot of trivial proofs need to be done in order to ensure consistency, the proof of consistency takes time.

10.4   An algorithm for topological sorting

Topological sorting is the act of transforming a (finite) partial order into a linear order. This concept of topological sorting is formalized with a precise definition, which involves the definitions of a partial order and a linear order. The definition of linear orders is only needed to explain what a topological order is.

Definition 10.4.1 (Partial Order)
A partial order $(S, \preceq)$ is a set, S, and a binary relation, $\preceq$, on S which is

1. *reflexive* $\forall s \in S \cdot s \preceq s,$

2. *antisymmetric* $\forall s, t \in S \cdot s \preceq t \land t \preceq s \implies s = t, and$

3. *transitive* $\forall s, t, u \in S \cdot s \preceq t \land t \preceq u \implies s \preceq u.$

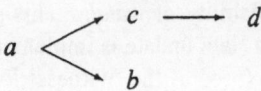

Figure 10.2: A simple Partial Order.

Definition 10.4.2 (Linear Order)
A linear order $(S, \preceq)$ *is a partial order for which any two elements of S are related by* $\preceq$:

$$\forall s, t \in S \cdot s \preceq t \lor t \preceq s.$$

Any finite linear order can be represented as a sequence, L, with indices in the set inds L.

Definition 10.4.3 (Topological order and Topological Sorting)
A topological order of a finite partial order $(S, \preceq)$ *is a sequence L of all and only all the members in S, so that no element l_i in the sequence L is preceded by an element l_j ($i > j$) for which $l_i \preceq l_j$, $i, j \in$ inds L, where inds L is the index set of L. The act of transforming a partial order into a topological order is called topological sorting.*

It is easy to see that a topological order of a partial order is always a linear order. The definition of topological sorting is best illustrated through an example.

Example 10.4.4 (Topological Sorting) *Consider the partial order* $(S, \preceq)$, *where S is equal to* $\{a, b, c, d\}$, *and* $\preceq$ *is defined by*

$$(x \preceq y) \Rightarrow ((x, y) \in \{(a, a), (b, b), (c, c), (d, d), (a, b), (a, c), (a, d), (c, d)\})$$

for all $x, y \in S$. *For the partial order* $(S, \preceq)$ *three possible topological orders exist:* $[a, b, c, d]$, $[a, c, d, b]$, *and* $[a, c, b, d]$.
In Figure 10.2 you can see a drawing of the partial order, ordered left-to-right.

10.4.1 Design guidelines

By modelling partial orders with directed acyclic graphs and linear orders with non-repeating sequences we develop an algorithm for topological sorting. In the abstract specification directed acyclic graphs are modelled as mappings from nodes to sets of immediate[12] successors and non-repeating sequences are modelled as sequences.

Example 10.4.5 (Partial Orders in Abstract Specification) *The representation as a mapping of the partial order* $(S, \preceq)$ *from Example 10.4.4 is:*

$$\{a \mapsto \{b, c\}, \; b \mapsto \{ \}, \; c \mapsto \{d\}, \; d \mapsto \{ \}\}$$

In the first design step the representation of graphs is changed to support the act of sorting. Selecting a node with no predecessors is the basis for the data structure refinement: each

---

[12]The immediate successors (predecessors) are to be opposed to all successors (predecessors) of a given node. For instance in Example 10.4.4 a has b and c as immediate successors, and b, c, and d as successors. The analogy to predecessors is straightforward.

node is represented by a triple (p, n, ns) where p denotes the number of immediate prede-cessors, n is the node name, and ns is the set of immediate successors. Directed acyclic graphs are modelled as sets of triples. The representation of non-repeating sequences is not changed. The price paid for this change in the representation of graphs is that it will become harder to update graph representations when nodes are either added or removed.

Example 10.4.6 (Partial Orders in First Design Stage) *The representation as a set of triples of the partial order* $(S, \preceq)$ *from Example 10.4.4 is:*

$$\{(0, a, \{b, c\}), \ (1, b, \{\}), \ (1, c, \{d\}), \ (1, d, \{\})\}$$

Note that for a partial order there might exist many sequences that are proper topolog-ical orders. Thus the result of applying a topological sorting algorithm to a partial order is in general non-deterministic. However, for each partial order we are only interested in computing one topological order. This is a design decision. Thus, if we again consider Example 10.4.4 the expected result of applying topological sorting to $(S, \preceq)$ could be any of the three listed topological orders.

10.4.2 Formal development

Abstract specification

Directed acyclic graphs are mappings from nodes to their set of outgoing graph edges[13].

$$G0 = Nd0 \xrightarrow{m} Nd0\text{-set}$$

$$Nd0 = TOKEN$$

where

$inv\text{-}G0 : Nd0 \xrightarrow{m} Nd0\text{-set} \rightarrow \mathbb{B}$
$inv\text{-}G0(g) \quad \triangleq \quad isClosed0(g) \land Acyclic0(g)$

The graph is closed and acyclic. These properties are the obvious criteria for a mapping modelling a directed acyclic graph since the basic data structure ensures that the graphs are inherently directed[14].

$isClosed0 : Nd0 \xrightarrow{m} Nd0\text{-set} \rightarrow \mathbb{B}$
$isClosed0(g) \quad \triangleq \quad \forall ns \in \text{rng } g \cdot ns \subset \text{dom } g$

For a graph to be closed, all outgoing edges must be nodes in the graph.

$Acyclic0 : Nd0 \xrightarrow{m} Nd0\text{-set} \rightarrow \mathbb{B}$
$Acyclic0(g) \quad \triangleq \quad \forall n \in \text{dom } g \cdot n \notin successors0(n, g)$
pre $isClosed0(g)$

For a graph to be acyclic, no node must be its own successor.

$successors0 : Nd0 \times Nd0 \xrightarrow{m} Nd0\text{-set} \rightarrow Nd0\text{-set}$
$successors0(n, g) \quad \triangleq \quad$ if $n \in \text{dom } g$
$\qquad\qquad\qquad$ then $g(n) \cup (\bigcup\{successors0(m, \{n\} \triangleleft g) \mid m \in g(n)\})$
$\qquad\qquad\qquad$ else $\{\}$

---

[13]In Example 10.4.4 the node c in the graph has $\{a\}$ as its ingoing edge(s) and $\{d\}$ as its outgoing edge(s).

[14]A way to model undirected graphs would be to choose a set of unordered pairs of nodes.

The successors of some node are all the nodes in the transitive closure of that node's immediate successors (i.e. outgoing edges).

Sequences are non-repeating sequences of node names.

$$S0 = Nd0^*$$

where

$inv\text{-}S0 : Nd0^* \to \mathbb{B}$
$inv\text{-}S0(s) \quad \triangleq \quad \forall i, j \in \mathsf{inds}\, s \cdot (i \neq j) \;\Rightarrow\; (s(i) \neq s(j))$

The sorting algorithm is specified by a relation between graphs and sequences, called an implicit definition. The partial order represented by a graph is related to the sequences that represents its topological orders. Note, as remarked in Section 10.4.1, that this relation in general will specify a non-deterministic sorting algorithm.

$TopSort0\ (g\!:\ G0)\ s\!:\ S0$
post dom $g = \mathsf{elems}\, s\, \wedge$
$\qquad \forall i, j \in \mathsf{inds}\, s \cdot i < j \;\Rightarrow\; s(i) \notin successors0(s(j), g)$

To show directly that the above relation is satisfiable, an explicit function definition is given. The function works by 'stripping off earlier nodes'. Essentially it would not have been necessary to 'strip off' nodes in the recursive calls of *TopSort0*, since we know that graphs are acyclic. But it will be difficult to prove anything about the function if you cannot use 'well-founded induction' on the actual parameters of the recursive calls[15].

$TopSort0 : G0 \to S0$
$TopSort0(g) \quad \triangleq \quad$ if $g = \{\,\}$
$\qquad\qquad\qquad\qquad$ then $[\,]$
$\qquad\qquad\qquad\qquad$ else let $n \in \{m \in \mathsf{dom}\, g \mid imPred0(m, g) = \{\,\}\}$ in
$\qquad\qquad\qquad\qquad\qquad [n] \frown TopSort0(\{n\} \triangleleft g)$

$imPred0 : Nd0 \times G0 \to Nd0\text{-set}$
$imPred0(n, g) \quad \triangleq \quad \{m \in \mathsf{dom}\, g \mid n \in g(m)\}$

The set of immediate predecessors for a node in a graph is the set of ingoing edges.

First design step

Now, directed acyclic graphs are sets of nodes represented as triples of the number of ingoing edges, their name, and the set of outgoing edges.

$G1 = Nodes1\text{-set}$

$Nodes1 \; :: \; p\!:\mathbb{N}$
$\qquad\qquad\quad nd\!:Nd1$
$\qquad\qquad\quad ns\!:Nd1\text{-set}$

$Nd1 = TOKEN$

$inv\text{-}G1 : Nodes1\text{-set} \to \mathbb{B}$
$inv\text{-}G1(g) \quad \triangleq$
$\qquad UniqueName1(g) \wedge$
$\qquad isClosed1(g) \wedge$
$\qquad Acyclic1(g) \wedge$
$\qquad ProperPred1(g)$

---

[15]This is one of the experiences gained in [Elv90], where we had to change the formulation of the explicit definition from that given in [EB89].

Nodes are distinguished on their name, and graphs can only contain one node with the same name. Still graphs must be closed and acyclic, and finally the predecessor count in each node must have the right value. These properties are expressed through the predicates and auxiliary functions listed below.

*UniqueName*1 : *Nodes*1-set → $\mathbb{B}$
*UniqueName*1(*g*) $\triangle$ ∀*t*, *s* ∈ *g* · (*nd*(*t*) = *nd*(*s*)) ⇒ (*s* = *t*)

*isClosed*1 : *Nodes*1-set → $\mathbb{B}$
*isClosed*1(*g*) $\triangle$ ∀*mk-Nodes*1(, , *ns*) ∈ *g* · *ns* ⊆ *allNodes*1(*g*)

*allNodes*1 : *Nodes*1-set → *Nd*1-set
*allNodes*1(*g*) $\triangle$ {*nd*(*t*) | *t* ∈ *g*}

*Acyclic*1 : *Nodes*1-set → $\mathbb{B}$
*Acyclic*1(*g*) $\triangle$ ∀*mk-Nodes*1(, *n*,) ∈ *g* · *n* ∉ *successors*1(*n*, *g*)

*successors*1 : *Nd*1 × *Nodes*1-set → $\mathbb{B}$
*successors*1(*n*, *g*) $\triangle$
    if (, *n*, *ns*) ∈ *g*
    then *ns* ∪ ∪{*successors*1(*m*, *g* − {*mk-Nodes*1(, *n*, *ns*)}) | *m* ∈ *ns*}
    else { }

*ProperPred*1 : *Nodes*1-set → $\mathbb{B}$
*ProperPred*1(*g*) $\triangle$
    ∀(*p*, *n*,) ∈ *g* · *p* = card {*m* | (*mk-Nodes*1(, *m*, *ms*) ∈ *g*) ∧ (*n* ∈ *ms*)}

Sequences are modelled in the same way as in the abstract specification.

*S*1 = *Nd*1*

where

*inv-S*1 : *Nd*1* → $\mathbb{B}$
*inv-S*1(*s*) $\triangle$ ∀*i*, *j* ∈ inds *s* · (*i* ≠ *j*) ⇒ (*s*(*i*) ≠ *s*(*j*))

The specification of the sorting algorithm is very similar to the abstract one. First we give an implicit definition.

*TopSort*1 (*g*: *G*1) *s*: *Nd*1*
post *allNodes*1(*g*) = elems *s* ∧
    ∀*i*, *j* ∈ inds *s* · *i* < *j* ⇒ *s*(*i*) ∉ *successors*1(*s*(*j*), *g*)

The explicit definition is still based on the principle of stripping off previous nodes.

*TopSort*1 : *G*1 → *S*1
*TopSort*1(*g*) $\triangle$
    if *g* = { }
    then [ ]
    else let *mk-Nodes*1(0, *n*, *ns*) ∈ *g* in
        [*n*] $\frown$ *TopSort*1(*upPC*1(*ns*, *g* − {*mk-Nodes*1(0, *n*, *ns*)}))

After having stripped off a node, the counters on ingoing edges are readjusted for the immediate successors to a just-removed node. This is specified through the auxiliary functions defined below (*upPC* abbreviates 'update predecessor counter').

$upPC1 : Nd1\text{-set} \times Nodes1\text{-set} \to G1$
$upPC1(ns, g)$ $\triangleq$
  $\{mk\text{-}Nodes1(decr1(q, m \in ns), m, ms) \mid mk\text{-}Nodes1(q, m, ms) \in g\}$
pre $\exists n \in Nd1 \cdot inv\text{-}G1(g \cup \{(0, n, ns)\})$

$decr1 : \mathsf{N} \times \mathsf{B} \to \mathsf{N}$
$decr1(n, b)$ $\triangleq$
  if b
  then $n\text{-}1$
  else n
pre $b \Rightarrow (n > 0)$

Proof obligations

Validation of abstract specification

To validate the abstract specification we can show that directed acyclic graphs, as represented by the specified mappings, are proper representations of partial orders, and, similarly, that non-repeating sequences are proper models of linear orders. The latter proof is trivial, since a sequence is indexed by a subset of the natural numbers, which is a linear order, and thus the sequence is also a linear order. The former proof is less trivial. To prove that any graph g: *G0* models a partial order we define a partial ordering relation on nodes of graphs in *G0*.

$$(n_1 \leq n_2 \text{ in } g) \equiv (n_2 \in \{n_1\} \cup successors0(n_1, g))$$

Based upon this order relation we can prove the properties of reflexivity, antisymmetry, and transitivity.

Note, that neither of the above 'proof obligations' can arise automatically. They arise from the informal requirements that we are specifying. They are sort of formal expressions of the customers requirements. In general such requirements are not expressible – consider for instance a requirement like 'The program must execute sufficiently fast'; there is no way in VDM to formalize such a requirement.

Consistency of abstract specification

The invariants, the implicit and explicit definition of the sorting algorithm, and the auxiliary functions must be well-defined, expressed formally by the following requirements:

$$\forall g: Nd0 \xrightarrow{m} Nd0\text{-set} \cdot inv\text{-}G0(g): \mathsf{B}$$

$$\forall g: Nd0 \xrightarrow{m} Nd0\text{-set} \cdot isClosed0(g): \mathsf{B}$$

$$\forall g: Nd0 \xrightarrow{m} Nd0\text{-set} \cdot isClosed0(g) \Rightarrow Acyclic0(g): \mathsf{B}$$

$$\forall n: Nd0,\ g: Nd0 \xrightarrow{m} Nd0\text{-set} \cdot successors0(n, g): Nd0\text{-set}$$

$$\forall s: Nd0^* \cdot inv\text{-}S0(s): \mathsf{B}$$

$$\forall g: G0,\ s: S0 \cdot post\text{-}TopSort0(g, s): \mathsf{B}$$

$$\forall g\colon g0 \cdot \mathit{TopSort0}(g)\colon S0$$

$$\forall g\colon G0,\ n\colon Nd0 \cdot \mathit{imPred0}(n.g)\colon Nd0\text{-set}$$

To aid the proofs of these properties one can develop a theory for the data types included in the specification. Such a theory would include induction rules for the data types. Such induction rules can be developed as 'generator induction' schemes, and they will extend the theory of the specification. In order for the induction schemes to be valid, one has to define a set of generators of each data type and prove that all objects in this type are finitely generated from some set of base values. One – primitive – method of doing so was described in Section 10.2.1. Finally the implicitly defined functions must be satisfiable, which is expressed as

$$\forall g\colon G0 \cdot \exists s\colon S0 \cdot \mathit{post\text{-}TopSort0}(g, s)$$

Validation of first design step
Again we need to justify that the (new) representation of graphs is also a model of partial orders, but this will be implicit from the reification proof (see below), since sets of triples are a proper implementation of the mappings from the abstract specification.

Consistency of first design step
The proof obligations that arise automatically from the first design step are very similar to those in the abstract specification. Thus we shall take the opportunity to save some space.

Reification
Both the retrieve and the inject functions are easy to define. However in the case of the inject function for the concrete graphs we need to compute some extra information, namely the number of immediate predecessors for each node in the graph. For the non-repeating sequences the inject and retrieve functions are simple identity functions.

$$\mathit{retr\text{-}G0} : G1 \to G0$$
$$\mathit{retr\text{-}G0}(g) \quad \triangleq \quad \{n \mapsto ns \mid \mathit{mk\text{-}Nodes}1(, n, ns) \in g\}$$

$$\mathit{inj\text{-}G1} : G0 \to G1$$
$$\mathit{inj\text{-}G1}(g) \quad \triangleq \quad \{\mathit{mk\text{-}Nodes}1(\mathrm{card}\,\mathit{imPred0}(n, g), n, g(n)) \mid n \in \mathrm{dom}\,g\}$$

$$\mathit{retr\text{-}S0} : S1 \to S0 \qquad\qquad \mathit{inj\text{-}S1} : S0 \to S1$$
$$\mathit{retr\text{-}S0}(s) \quad \triangleq \quad s \qquad\qquad \mathit{inj\text{-}S1}(s) \quad \triangleq \quad s$$

The inject function is not strictly part of the VDM specification model, but its presence makes the discharging of the refinement proof obligations easier; however, in general it is not possible to state the inject functions. Similarly to any other functions the inject and retrieve functions must be well-defined. The refinement proof obligations that arise from the first step of development for the topological sorting algorithm are listed below.

Adequacy Rules:

$$\forall g0\colon G0 \cdot \exists g1\colon G1 \cdot g0 = \mathit{retr\text{-}G0}(g1)$$

$$\forall s0\colon S0 \cdot \exists s1\colon S1 \cdot s0 = \mathit{retr\text{-}S0}(s1)$$

Result Rule:

$$\forall g\colon G1, s\colon S1 \cdot \ post\text{-}TopSort1(g, s)$$
$$\Rightarrow \ post\text{-}TopSort0(retr\text{-}G0(g), retr\text{-}S0(s))$$

The result rule is most elegantly expressed through the implicit definitions of the sorting algorithm, but it could as well have been expressed through the explicit definitions.

$$\forall g\colon G1, s\colon S1 \cdot \ TopSort1(g) = s$$
$$\Rightarrow \ Topsort0(retr\text{-}G0(g)) = retr\text{-}S0(s)$$

The last requirement is much more strict than the previous one, due to the non-determinancy of the implicit specification of the sorting algorithm. Thus we prefer the former to the latter.

10.4.3   Representation in *mural*

The transformation of VDM formulae into *mural* goes rather easily (even without the translation tool). This subsection explains in detail the transformation of the abstract specification for the TopSort development, together with the properties (rules and some of the lemmas) that have been necessary to prove in order to establish the validity and consistency of the algorithm. The transformation of the first design step is presented without too many comments, and to give a feel of what *mural* is able to do, the print out of the reification part is given in its raw form[16].

Representation of abstract specification

*G*0 is a domain, which can be shown to be finitely generated. Thus we can state an induction rule following the same principles as used in Example 10.2.1.

G0 ↦ ⟨ gg : (map[Nd0, (Nd0 -set)]) . (inv-G0[gg]) ⟩,

Nd0 ↦ TOKEN,

inv-G0 ↦
     ((isClosed0[[[*e*1]]]) ∧ (Acyclic0[[[*e*1]]])),

def inv-G0
{ }
{ (g: (map[Nd0, (Nd0-set)])) }
─────────────────────────────
((inv-G0[g]) : **B**)

The type information of *inv-G0* is – as explained in Section 10.2.2 – expressed in the rule 'def inv-G0', which needs to be proved. The proof of 'def inv-G0' has been included as one of the example proofs in Section 10.4.4.

isClosed0 ↦ ∀ ns : ⟨ ms : (Nd0 -set) . (ms ∈ (rng[[[*e*1]]])) ⟩ . (ns ⊆ (dom[[[*e*1]]])),

def isClosed0
{ }
{ (g : (map[Nd0, (Nd0 -set)])) }
─────────────────────────────
((isClosed0[g]) : **B**)

Acyclic0 ↦ ∀ n : ⟨ m : Nd0 . (m ∈ (dom[[[*e*1]]])) ⟩ . (¬ (n ∈ (successors0[n, [[*e*1]]]))),

─────────────────────────────
[16]Recall that *mural* is able to generate LATEX.

def Acyclic0
{ }
{ (g : (map[Nd0, (Nd0 -set)])), (isClosed0[g]) }

((Acyclic0[g]) : $\mathbb{B}$)

Note how the precondition to 'Acyclic0' is represented as an additional hypotheses in the rule 'def Acyclic0'.

successors0 $\mapsto$
$\quad$ (if ($[\![e1]\!]\in$ (dom[$[\![e2]\!]$]))
$\quad\quad$ then (($[\![e2]\!]$ at $[\![e1]\!]$) $\cup$
$\quad\quad\quad$ ($\bigcup$ those ns : (Nd0 -set) . $\exists$ m : Nd0 .
$\quad\quad\quad\quad$ ((ns = (successors0[m, ((add[$[\![e1]\!]$, {}]) $\lhd[\![e2]\!]$)]))
$\quad\quad\quad\quad$ $\wedge$ (m $\in$ ($[\![e2]\!]$ at $[\![e1]\!]$))))))
$\quad\quad$ else {}),

def successors0
{ }
{ (g : (map[Nd0, (Nd0 -set)])), (n : Nd0) }

((successors0[n, g]) : (Nd0 -set))

For the story of the proof of the rule 'def successors0', refer to Section 10.4.4.

We also want an induction rule. This can be obtained as explained in Section 10.2.1. The case is, however, a bit more complicated, so a few auxiliary constructs are applied. The generator function is called *gen-G0*, and it can only be applied to certain arguments. For this reason it has a precondition.

pre-gen-G0 $\mapsto$
$\quad$ (($\neg$ ($[\![e1]\!]\in$ (dom[$[\![e3]\!]$])))
$\quad$ $\wedge$ ($[\![e2]\!]\subseteq$ (dom[$[\![e3]\!]$]))),

def pre-gen-G0
{ }
{ (n : Nd0), (ns : (Nd0 -set)), (g : G0) }

((pre-gen-G0[n, ns, g]) : $\mathbb{B}$)

gen-G0 $\mapsto$
$\quad$ (addm[$[\![e1]\!]$, $[\![e2]\!]$, $[\![e3]\!]$]),

def gen-G0
{ }
{ (n : Nd0), (ns : (Nd0 -set)), (g : G0),
(pre-gen-G0[n, ns, g]) }

((gen-G0[n, ns, g]) : G0)

The base set of *G0* only contains the empty mapping, {}*m*. Since there is only one generator function, it can also serve as a partial ordering on *G0*. Thus we can formulate an induction rule that is a little different from the one in Example 10.2.1. The difference is caused by the precondition on *gen-G0*.

G0 ind
{ [ig, in, ins]
$\quad$ { (in : Nd0), (ins : (Nd0 -set)), (ig : G0), (pre-gen-G0[in, ins, ig]), (P[ig]) }
$\quad$ $\vdash$ (P[(gen-G0[in, ins, ig])]) },
{ (g : G0), (P[{}m]) }

(P[g])

Remark: Other induction rules can be formulated, and one should make an effort to formulate a scheme that suits one's needs best. The above induction scheme is the most primitive, and therefore the most readable, that has been formulated for *G0*.

Transformation of sequences is straightforward:
S0 $\mapsto$ ⟨ ss : (Nd0 *) . (inv-S0[ss]) ⟩ }

inv-S0 ↦
  $\forall$ i : ⟨ h : **N** . (h ∈ (inds[[$e1$]])) ⟩ . $\forall$ j : ⟨ h : **N** . (h ∈ (inds[[$e1$]])) ⟩ .
  ((¬ (i = j)) ⇒ (¬ (([[$e1$]]@ i) = ([[$e1$]]@ j)))),

def inv-S0
{ }
{ (s : (Nd0 *)) }
―――――――――――
((inv-S0[s]) : **B**)

def post-TopSort0
{ }
{ (g : G0), (s : S0) }
―――――――――――
((post-TopSort0[g, s]) : **B**)

post-TopSort0 ↦
  (((dom[[$e1$]]) = (elems[[$e2$]])) ∧
  $\forall$ i : ⟨ ii : **N** . (ii ∈ (inds[[$e2$]])) ⟩ . $\forall$ j : ⟨ jj : **N** . (jj ∈ (inds[[$e2$]])) ⟩ .
  ((i < j) ⇒ (¬ (([[$e2$]]@ i) ∈ (successors0[([[$e2$]]@ j), [[$e1$]]])))))),

TopSort0 ↦
  (if ([[$e1$]] = { }m)
   then []
   else (([ε n : Nd0 . ((n ∈ (dom[[$e1$]])) ∧ ((imPred0[n, [[$e1$]]]) = { }))]) ⌢
    (TopSort0[((add[ε n : Nd0 . ((n ∈ (dom[[$e1$]])) ∧
    ((imPred0[n, [[$e1$]]]) = { })), { }]) ◁ [[$e1$]])]))),

def TopSort0
{ }
{ (g : G0) }
―――――――――――
((TopSort0[g]) : S0)

def imPred0
{ }
{ (g : G0), (n : Nd0) }
―――――――――――
((imPred0[n, g]) : (Nd0 -set))

imPred0 ↦
  those m : Nd0 . ((m ∈ (dom[[$e2$]]))
   ∧ ((m ∈ (dom[[$e2$]])) ⇒ ([[$e1$]] ∈ ([[$e2$]]at m))))

Satisfiability of specification

sat TopSort0
{ }
{ (g : G0) }
―――――――――――
∃ s : S0 . (post-TopSort0[g, s])

lem sat TopSort0
{ }
{ (g : G0) }
―――――――――――
(post-TopSort0[g, (TopSort0[g])])

To prove the satisfiability proof obligation the lemma 'lem sat TopSort0' was stated. To undertake the proof of satisfiability tends always to demand that you construct a function and then prove that it is a correct implementation. This function acts as a 'witness' for the existential quantifier in the satisfiability proof obligation.

A few more lemmas

It is of major importance to decompose larger proofs into smaller ones. One way to do so is by stating a number of useful properties as lemmas. The above lemma is an example of such lemmas, and below you can see a few more examples. The first looks very nice

lem successors0 (def & ⊆)
{ }
{ (n : Nd0), (g : (map[Nd0, (Nd0 -set)])) }
―――――――――――
(((successors0[n, g]) : (Nd0 -set)) ∧ ((successors0[n, g]) ⊆ ($\bigcup$ (rng[g]))))

whereas

lem def TopSort0 inv-S0 (special case - ii/jj=1)
{ }
{ (¬ ((([n]) $^\curvearrowright$ TopSort0Smth) =[])),
((pred[ii]) : (6359 : $\mathbb{N}$. (6359 ∈ (inds[TopSort0Smth])))),
(jj ∈ (inds[(([n]) $^\curvearrowright$ TopSort0Smth)])), (¬ ((TopSort0Smth@(pred[ii])) = n)),
(ii ∈ (inds[(([n]) $^\curvearrowright$ TopSort0Smth)])), ((([n]) $^\curvearrowright$ TopSort0Smth) : (Nd0 *)),
((hd[(([n]) $^\curvearrowright$ TopSort0Smth)]) = n), (¬ (ii = 1)),
((tl[(([n]) $^\curvearrowright$ TopSort0Smth)]) = TopSort0Smth), (jj = 1),
(TopSort0Smth : (Nd0 *)), (n : Nd0) }

(¬ (((([n]) $^\curvearrowright$ TopSort0Smth) @ ii) = ((([n]) $^\curvearrowright$ TopSort0Smth) @ jj)))

documents that lemmas can sometimes be huge and used solely as a way of limiting the size of a proof by stating a very specialized lemma. The PA has a feature which allows you to construct such lemmas automatically from within a proof. Besides, the latter lemma makes little sense, and is meant only as an example. Also the name of the latter lemma shows that it can be difficult to come up with meaningful names for new lemmas all the time.

Validation of abstract specification
A way in which the specification can be validated is by proving that graphs as modelled by *G0* really are proper representations for partial orders. So that is what we will do.

The following constant can be defined, and proved to possess the properties of a partial order.

NLEQ ↦
     (([[e1]]=[[e2]]) ∨
     ([[e2]]∈ successors0[[[e1]] , [[e3]]]))

NLEQ refl
{ }
{ (n : Nd0), (g : G0) }

((n ≤ n in g))

NLEQ anti sym{ }
{ ((n ≤ m in g)), ((m ≤ n in g)) }

(n = m)

NLEQ trans{ }
{ ((n ≤ m in g)), ((m ≤ h in g)) }

((n ≤ h in g))

Here we have taken advantage of the possibility to define concrete syntax in *mural*. The operator 'NLEQ' is defined as ([[e1]] ≤ [[e2]] in [[e3]]).

Representation of the first design stage

The transformation of the concrete specification is very much like the abstract one. We will not discuss the formulation of induction rules for *G1*.

G1 ↦ ⟨ gg : (Nodes1 -set) . (inv-G1[gg]) ⟩

As explained previously, records cannot easily be modelled directly as defined types. To model *Nodes*1 a number of constants and axioms must be added.

Nodes1 ↦[0,0],
mk-Nodes1 ↦[3,0],
s-p ↦[1,0],
s-nd ↦[1,0],
s-ns ↦[1,0],

To give 'life' to these primitive constants, a number of axioms are added, just like for the state(s) in the reactor example. Below we only show an equality rule, leaving out eight other axioms.

mk-Nodes1 =-I
$\{\}$
$\{\,(\,\text{t1} : \text{Nodes1}\,)\,,(\,\text{t2} : \text{Nodes1}\,)$
$(\,(\,\text{s-p}[\,\text{t1}\,]\,) = (\,\text{s-p}[\,\text{t2}\,]\,)\,)\,,$
$(\,(\,\text{s-nd}[\,\text{t1}\,]\,) = (\,\text{s-nd}[\,\text{t2}\,]\,)\,)\,,(\,(\,\text{s-ns}[\,\text{t1}\,]\,) = (\,\text{s-ns}[\,\text{t2}\,]\,)\,)\,\}$

$(\,\text{t1} = \text{t2}\,)$

Nd1 $\mapsto$ TOKEN ,

inv-G1 $\mapsto$
$\qquad (\,(\,\text{UniqueName1}[[\![e1]\!]]\,) \wedge$
$\qquad (\,(\,\text{isClosed1}[[\![e1]\!]]\,) \wedge$
$\qquad (\,(\,\text{Acyclic1}[[\![e1]\!]]\,) \wedge$
$\qquad (\,\text{ProperPred1}[[\![e1]\!]]\,)\,)\,)\,)\,,$

UniqueName1 $\mapsto$
$\qquad \forall\, t : \langle\, \text{tt} : \text{Nodes1} . (\,\text{tt} \in [\![e1]\!]\,)\,) . \forall\, s : \langle\, \text{ss} : \text{Nodes1} . (\,\text{ss} \in [\![e1]\!]\,)\,) .$
$\qquad\qquad (\,(\,(\,\text{s-nd}[t]\,) = (\,\text{s-nd}[s]\,)\,) \Rightarrow (\,t = s\,)\,),$

isClosed1 $\mapsto \forall\, t : \langle\, \text{tt} : \text{Nodes1} . (\,\text{tt} \in [\![e1]\!]\,)\,) . (\,(\,\text{s-ns}[t]\,) \subseteq (\,\text{Nodes1}[[\![e1]\!]]\,)\,),$

As can be seen there is no support for pattern matching[17] in *mural*. Instead one has to rely on selector functions. This can be seen by comparing the above formulation of *isClosed*1 with the original one. In order to transform *isClosed*1 to a constant in *mural*, it had to be slightly reformulated.

Nodes1 $\mapsto$ those n : Nd1 . $\exists\, p : \mathbb{N} . \exists\, ns : (\,\text{Nd1 -set}\,) . (\,(\,\text{mk-Nodes1}[p, n, ns]\,) \in [\![e1]\!]\,),$

Acyclic1 $\mapsto \forall\, t : \langle\, \text{tt} : \text{Nodes1} . (\,\text{tt} \in [\![e1]\!]\,)\,) .$
$\qquad\qquad (\,\neg\,(\,(\,\text{s-nd}[t]\,) \in (\,\text{successors1}[(\,\text{s-nd}[t]\,), [\![e1]\!]]\,)\,)\,),$

successors1 $\mapsto$
$\qquad (\,\text{if}\, \exists\, t : \langle\, \text{tt} : \text{Nodes1} . (\,\text{tt} \in [\![e2]\!]\,)\,) . (\,(\,\text{s-nd}[t]\,) = [\![e1]\!]\,)$
$\qquad \text{then}\, (\,(\,\text{s-ns}[\varepsilon\, t : \langle\, \text{tt} : \text{Nodes1} . (\,\text{tt} \in [\![e2]\!]\,)\,) . (\,(\,\text{s-nd}[t]\,) = [\![e1]\!]\,)]\,) \cup$
$\qquad\quad (\,\bigcup\,\text{those}\, ms : (\,\text{Nd1 -set}\,) . \exists\, m : \text{Nd1} .$
$\qquad\qquad (\,(\,ms = (\,\text{successors1}[m, (\,[\![e2]\!]\text{-}(\,\text{add}[\varepsilon\, t : \langle\, \text{tt} : \text{Nodes1} . (\,\text{tt} \in [\![e2]\!]\,)\,) .$
$\qquad\qquad\qquad\qquad (\,(\,\text{s-nd}[t]\,) = [\![e1]\!]\,), \{\}\,]\,)\,)]\,)\,) \wedge$
$\qquad\qquad\qquad (\,m \in (\,\text{s-ns}[\varepsilon\, t : \langle\, \text{tt} : \text{Nodes1} . (\,\text{tt} \in [\![e2]\!]\,)\,) .$
$\qquad\qquad\qquad\qquad (\,(\,\text{s-nd}[t]\,) = [\![e1]\!]\,)]\,)\,)\,)\,)\,)\,)$
$\qquad \text{else}\, \{\}\,),$

ProperPred1 $\mapsto$
$\qquad \forall\, t : \langle\, \text{tt} : \text{Nodes1} . (\,\text{tt} \in [\![e1]\!]\,)\,) .$
$\qquad\qquad (\,(\,\text{s-p}[t]\,) = (\,\text{card}[\text{those}\, m : \text{Nd1} . \exists\, q : \mathbb{N} . \exists\, ms : (\,\text{Nd1 -set}\,) .$
$\qquad\qquad\qquad (\,(\,t = (\,\text{mk-Nodes1}[q, m, ms]\,)\,) \wedge (\,(\,\text{s-nd}[t]\,) \in ms\,)\,)]\,)\,),$

S1 $\mapsto \langle\, \text{ss} : (\,\text{Nd1} *\,) . (\,\text{inv-S1}[ss]\,)\,),$

inv-S1 $\mapsto$
$\qquad \forall\, i : \langle\, \text{ii} : \mathbb{N} . (\,\text{ii} \in (\,\text{inds}[[\![e1]\!]]\,)\,)\,) . \forall\, j : \langle\, \text{jj} : \mathbb{N} . (\,\text{jj} \in (\,\text{inds}[[\![e1]\!]]\,)\,)\,) .$
$\qquad\qquad (\,(\,\neg\,(\,i = j\,)\,) \Rightarrow (\,\neg\,(\,(\,[\![e1]\!]@i\,) = (\,[\![e1]\!]@j\,)\,)\,)\,),$

post-TopSort1 $\mapsto$
$\qquad (\,(\,(\,\text{Nodes1}[[\![e1]\!]]\,) = (\,\text{elems}[[\![e2]\!]]\,)\,) \wedge$
$\qquad \forall\, i : \langle\, \text{ii} : \mathbb{N} . (\,\text{ii} \in (\,\text{inds}[[\![e2]\!]]\,)\,)\,) . \forall\, j : \langle\, \text{jj} : \mathbb{N} . (\,\text{jj} \in (\,\text{inds}[[\![e2]\!]]\,)\,)\,) .$
$\qquad\qquad (\,(\,i < j\,) \Rightarrow (\,\neg\,(\,(\,[\![e2]\!]@i\,) \in (\,\text{successors1}[(\,[\![e2]\!]@j\,), [\![e1]\!]]\,)\,)\,)\,),$

---

[17]Please do not confuse pattern matching in the PA with pattern matching in VDM.

TopSort1 $\mapsto$
     (if ($[\![el]\!]$= {})
       then[]
       else (([(s-nd[ε t : Nodes1 . ((t $\in[\![el]\!]$) $\wedge$ ((s-p[t]) = 0))])]) $\curvearrowright$
         (TopSort1[(Remove1[(s-ns[ε t : Nodes1 . ((t $\in[\![el]\!]$) $\wedge$ ((s-p[t]) = 0))]),
         ($[\![el]\!]$- (add[ε t : Nodes1 . ((t $\in[\![el]\!]$) $\wedge$
         ((s-p[t]) = 0)), {}]))])])]))),

Remove1 $\mapsto$
     those t : Nodes1 . $\exists$ tt : Nodes1 . ((tt $\in[\![e2]\!]$) $\wedge$
       (((s-p[t]) = (decr1[(s-p[tt]), ((s-nd[tt]) $\in[\![el]\!]$)])) $\wedge$
       (((s-nd[t]) = (s-nd[tt])) $\wedge$ ((s-ns[t]) = (s-ns[tt]))))))

decr1 $\mapsto$ (if$[\![e2]\!]$then ($[\![el]\!]$- 1) else$[\![el]\!]$),

Consistency of first design step

Thirteen rules ensuring the consistency of the first design step are added in a way similar to the representation in the abstract specification. We do not show them here, but you could try to create them yourself.

Correctness of reification

The last of the theories is printed exactly in the way *mural* has done it. The reason for this is to give the reader an impression of which kind of output you can get from the *mural* system. There is also a single example of a rule and a constant printed in the original 'LaTeX source code'.

TopSort Reif 0→1
a *mural* theory

Parents

TopSort Spec 0, TopSort Spec 1, TopSort Val 0

Signature

consts{ retr-G0 $\mapsto$ m{ n : Nd0 . m} ns : (Nd0 -set) . $\exists$ p : $\mathbb{N}$.
((mk-Nodes1 [p , n , ns]) $\in[\![el]\!]$), retr-S0 $\mapsto$ $[\![el]\!]$,
inj-G1 $\mapsto$ those t : Nodes1 . (((s-nd [t]) $\in$ (dom $[\![el]\!]$)) $\wedge$ ((((
s-nd [t]) $\in$ (dom $[\![el]\!]$)) $\Rightarrow$
((s-ns [t]) = ($[\![el]\!]$at (s-nd [t])))) $\wedge$ ((s-p [t]) = (card [
those m : Nd0 . ((m $\in$ (dom $[\![el]\!]$)) $\wedge$ ((m $\in$ (dom $[\![el]\!]$)) $\Rightarrow$ (
(s-nd [t]) $\in$ ($[\![el]\!]$at m)))])))))), inj-S1 $\mapsto$ $[\![el]\!]$}

types{}

binders{}

dep types{}

Axioms

Derived Rules

adeq G1

{ }
{ (g0 : G0) }

∃ g1 : G1 . (g0 = (retr-G0 [g1]))

adeq S1

{ }
{ (s0 : S0) }

∃ s1 : S1 . (s0 = (retr-S0 [s1]))

def inj-G1

{ }
{ (g : G0) }

((inj-G1 [g]) : G1)

def inj-S1

{ }
{ (s : S0) }

((inj-S1 [s]) : S1)

def retr-G0

{ }
{ (g : G1) }

((retr-G0 [g]) : G0)

def retr-S0

{ }
{ (s : S1) }

((retr-S0 [s]) : S0)

Result Rule TopSort1

{ }
{ (g : G1) , (s : S1) }

((post-TopSort1 [g , s]) ⇒ (post-TopSort0
[(retr-G0 [g]) , (retr-S0 [s])])))

Remark: The function *retr-G0* involves an implicit map construction. To handle the implicit map construction, the primitive binders $m\{$ and $m\}$ have been defined, together with the following axiom

$$\begin{array}{c} s\text{:}\,A\text{-set;} \\ \forall x\text{:}\,A\;y,z\text{:}\,B\cdot(P[x,y]\wedge P[x,z])\;\Rightarrow\;(y=z), \\ \forall x\text{:}\,A\cdot(\exists y\text{:}\,B\cdot P[x,y]\;\Rightarrow\;x\in s) \\ \hline m\{\;x\text{:}\,A\;m\}\;y\text{:}\,B\;\cdot\;P[x,y]\text{:}\,\mathrm{map}[A,B] \end{array}$$

map comprehension form

Notice that the relation denoted by the metavariable P must be a function. This is guaranteed by the second hypotheses. The first and third hypotheses together ensure the finiteness of the constructed map.

LATEX source code

Below you can se the LATEX source code for the constant 'retr-G0' and the rule 'adeq G1'

```
retr-G0\ $\mapsto$\ m\{\ n\ :\ Nd0\ .\ m\}\ ns\ :\ (\ Nd0\ -se\t\ )\
.\ $\Exists$\ p\ :\ $\Nat$\ .\ } \\
\mbox{\ (\ (\ mk-Nodes1\ [\ p\ ,\ n\ ,\ ns\ ]\ )\
$$\in$$[\mkern-\thinmuskip[$e1$\]\mkern-\thinmuskip]$\ )\


\noindent
\mbox{\Large adeq\ G1}
\noindent
\mbox{\{\ \}} \\
\mbox{\{\ (\ g0\ :\ G0\ )\ \}} \\
\mbox{--------------------} \\
\mbox{\ $\Exists$\ g1\ :\ G1\ .\ (\ g0\ =\ (\ retr-G0\ [\ g1\ ]\ )\ )\ )\ }
```

10.4.4   A few proofs

In this subsection we give a description of some of the strategies that were applied to undertake one of the proofs, together with a skeleton of it. A few more proofs are presented – in the direct *mural*-syntax. All the rules from the VDM instantiation that have been applied in the proofs below are shown in Section 10.5.

Definedness of 'successors0'

The first proof is very simple, because we have asserted an appropriate lemma – the proof of which would have been left as an exercise for the reader in any reasonable textbook[18]. The proof is of the rule 'def successors0'.

h1 (g: (map[Nd0, (Nd0 -set)]))
h2 (n: Nd0)
1 (((successors0[n, g]): (Nd0 -set))$\wedge$ ((successors0[n, g])$\subseteq$ ($\bigcup$ (rng[g]))))
                                        by lem successors0 (def & $\subseteq$)on[h2, h1];[]
c ((successors0[n, g]): (Nd0 -set))   by $\wedge$-E-right on[1];[]

Proof of lemma 'lem successors0 (def & $\subseteq$)'

As can be seen the proof of the lemma is an induction proof. The lemma is one of the lemmas shown above. In order to finish the proof we needed a strong induction hypothesis. The reason is that the set comprehension formation axiom (refer to Section 10.5) requires that all sets are finite, i.e. that you point out a larger (finite) set. The place where this was actually used has been left out of the proof as presented here, since the whole proof takes up approximately four full pages and – partly for the same reason – is not very readable[19].

---

[18]In total the complete proof of the lemma takes up 10 to 15 tightly written A4 pages.

[19]To represent all the proofs for the TopSort development would have required more that 50 full pages. This could be formulated as a 'rule of thumb', saying that the complete proof for consistency and validity of a specification in general takes up ten times as much space as the specification itself.

h1 (n: Nd0)
h2 (g: (map[Nd0, (Nd0 -set)]))

    1[y]
    1.h1 (y: (map[Nd0, (Nd0 -set)]))
    1.c ((card[(dom[y])]): $\mathbb{N}$)   by card-form on[dom-form on [1.h1];[]];[]

2 $\forall$ ma: (map[Nd0, (Nd0 -set)]). ((card[(dom[ma])]): $\mathbb{N}$)   by $\forall$-I on[];[1]

    3[q]
    3.h1 $\forall$ p: (map[Nd0, (Nd0 -set)]). (((card[(dom[p])])< (card[(dom[q])]))) $\Rightarrow$
               $\forall$ x: Nd0 . (((successors0[x, p]): (Nd0 -set))$\wedge$
               ((successors0[x, p])$\subseteq$ ($\bigcup$ (rng[p])))))
    3.h2 (q: (map[Nd0, (Nd0 -set)]))

        3.1[nd]
        3.1.h1 (nd: Nd0)
        ┌───┐
        │ SOMETHING HAS INTENTIONALLY BEEN LEFT OUT (INCL. LINE 3.1.5) │
        └───┘
        3.1.c ((successors0[nd, q]): (Nd0 -set))   folding from 3.1.5

    3.2 $\forall$ x: Nd0 . ((successors0[x, q]): (Nd0 -set))   by $\forall$-I on[];[3.1]
    3.3 $\forall$ x: Nd0 . ((successors0[x, q])$\subseteq$ ($\bigcup$ (rng[q])))
               by lem successors0 $\subseteq$ on[3.h2, 3.h1, 3.2];[]
    3.c $\forall$ x: Nd0 . (((successors0[x, q]): (Nd0 -set))$\wedge$ ((successors0[x, q])$\subseteq$ ($\bigcup$ (rng[q]))))
               by $\forall\wedge$-dist-contract on[$\wedge$-I on[3.2, 3.3];[]];[]

4 $\forall$ x: Nd0 . (((successors0[x, g]): (Nd0 -set))$\wedge$ ((successors0[x, g])$\subseteq$ ($\bigcup$ (rng[g]))))
               by WF Induction on[h2, 2];[3]
c (((successors0[n, g]): (Nd0 -set))$\wedge$ ((successors0[n, g])$\subseteq$ ($\bigcup$ (rng[g])))) by $\forall$-E on[4, h1];[]

From the part of the proof that is presented above it can be seen that the strategy to undertake it has been by well-founded induction (Line 4). The induction step itself has been split up into two parts ending respectively in Lines 3.2 and 3.3. Line 3.3 has been proved by a lemma, the proof of which is also of size approximately four full pages. Before starting with the proofs of the TopSort example we had expected[20] such proofs to be rather simple, but they turned out to involve an incredible amount of symbol manipulations.

To motivate why we have not provided a full print-out of all the (completed) proofs, we show one of the smaller ones in its full detail. Such proofs are unreadable. Just imagine what it would be like when you have to unfold the definition of some constant with a large definition.

h1 (g : (map [Nd0 , (Nd0 -set)]))
1 (δ (isClosed0 [g])) by bool def on [def isClosed0 on [h1];
[]]; []

2 []
2.h1 (isClosed0 [g])
2.c (δ (Acyclic0 [g])) by bool def on [def Acyclic0 on [h1, 2.h1];
[]]; []

3 (((isClosed0 [g]) $\wedge$ (Acyclic0 [g])): $\mathbb{B}$)
               by bool form on [$\delta\wedge$-inherit (weak) on [1, 2]; []]; []
c ((inv-G0 [g]): $\mathbb{B}$) folding from 3

---

[20]This observation is similar to the remark on Page 281.

After all the above example is not that bad, but to give a feel for how unreadable things can be, consider the few following lines that have been extracted from the above proof. (The lines are not supposed to be readable, and the rules that have been applied in the individual proof lines are not necessarily presented in Section 10.5).

3.1.3.c
((if (nd ∈ (dom [q])) then ((q at nd) ∪ (∪
those ns : (Nd0 -set) . ∃ m : Nd0 . ((ns = (
successors0 [m , ((add [nd , {}]) ◁ q)]))
∧ (m ∈ (q at nd))))) else {}) : (Nd0 -set
)) by ITE-true-form on [3.1.3.h1, ∪-formation on [3.1.3.2,
∪-formation on [3.1.3.8]; []]; []]; []

3.1.4 []
3.1.4.h1 (¬ (nd ∈ (dom [q])))
3.1.4.c
((if (nd ∈ (dom [q])) then ((q at nd) ∪ (∪
those ns : (Nd0 -set) . ∃ m : Nd0 . ((ns = (
successors0 [m , ((add [nd , {}]) ◁ q)]))
∧ (m ∈ (q at nd))))) else {}) : (Nd0 -set
)) by ITE-false-form on [3.1.4.h1, {}-formation on []; []]; []

3.1.5 ((if (nd ∈ (dom [q])) then ((q at nd)
∪ (∪ those ns : (Nd0 -set) . ∃ m : Nd0 . ((ns
= (successors0 [m , ((add [nd , {}]) ◁ q)]))
∧ (m ∈ (q at nd))))) else {}) :
(Nd0 -set)) by ∨-E on [3.1.2]; [3.1.3, 3.1.4]

The above examples are not supposed to be a negative critique of *mural*. Rather they are justifications for the need for tools like *mural*. It would be impossible to perform proofs with such detail as described above without some tool to guard the correctness of each proof step.

10.5   Theories for VDM in *mural*

The following constant definitions and rules are brought out of their context, and they really do not give more than a feel for what the rules in the theory store are like. The reason they are here is that they have been applied in the small proofs that we presented earlier.

The symbol δ is the definedness operator from LPF [BCJ84].

$\delta \mapsto ((\llbracket e1 \rrbracket) \vee (\neg (\llbracket e1 \rrbracket)))$,

The next three rules are the well-known rules for ∧ elimination and introduction.

∧-E right	∧-E left	∧-I
{ }	{ }	{ }
{ (e1 ∧ e2) }	{ (e1 ∧ e2) }	{ e1 , e2 }
——	——	——
e1	e2	(e1 ∧ e2)

Then the rule for definedness of an expression with ⊆ as its main operator, and the rule for commutativity of equality.

δ- $\subseteq$
{ }
{ (s1 : (A -set)) , (s2 : (A -set)) }

──────────────────────

(δ (s1 $\subseteq$ s2))

=-comm
{ }
{ (s1 = s2) }

──────────────────────

(s2 = s1)

The next ten rules are all from the formalization of the predicate calculus. The rule '$\delta\wedge$ (weak)' has not been applied in any of the particular proofs in this chapter. It is however important, because it makes clear how 'conditional-and' is implicitly part of the LPF vocabulary. This question might have puzzled the reader, since it is a prerequisite for stating most of the invariants in this chapter the way we did.

bool form
{ }
{ (δ x) }

──────────────────────

(x : B)

bool def
{ }
{ (x : B) }

──────────────────────

(δ x)

$\delta\wedge$-inherit (weak)
{ [ ] { e1 } $\vdash$ (δ e2) }
{ (δ e1) }

──────────────────────

(δ (e1 $\wedge$ e2))

$\delta \Rightarrow$ -inherit (weak)
{ [ ] { e1 } $\vdash$ (δ e2) }
{ (δ e1) }

──────────────────────

(δ (e1 $\Rightarrow$ e2))

$\delta\wedge$ (weak)
{ [ ] { e1 } $\vdash$ e2 }
{ e1 }

──────────────────────

(e1 $\wedge$ e2)

$\delta\wedge$-inherit
{ }
{ (δ e1) , (δ e2) }

──────────────────────

(δ (e1 $\wedge$ e2))

$\forall$-I
{ [y] { (y : X) } $\vdash$ (P [y]) }
{ }

──────────────────────

$\forall$ x : X . (P [x])

$\forall$-E
{ }
{ $\forall$ x : X . (P [x]) , (a : X) }

──────────────────────

(P [a])

$\forall\wedge$-dist-contract
{ }
{ ($\forall$ x:X . (E1[x]) $\wedge$ $\forall$ x:X . (E2[x])) }

──────────────────────

$\forall$ x : X . ((E1 [x]) $\wedge$ (E2 [x]))

$\exists$-I
{ }
{ (a : A) , (P [a]) }

──────────────────────

$\exists$ x : A . (P [x])

The next two rules tell the conditions under which the two standard operations card and dom are well-defined.

card-form
{ }
{ (s : (A -set)) }

──────────────────────

((card [s]) : N)

dom-form
{ }
{ (m1 : (map [A , B])) }

──────────────────────

((dom [m1]) : (A -set))

This rule is the rule that was described in Section 10.2.2.

WF Induction
{ [q] { (q : PAR) , $\forall$ p : PAR .
(((ord [p]) < (ord [q])) $\Rightarrow$ (F [p])) } $\vdash$ (F [q]) }
{ (par : PAR) , $\forall$ pp : PAR . ((ord [pp]) : N) }

──────────────────────

(F [par])

Finally the rule for construction of implicitly defined sets. In order to ensure the finiteness, you must be able to point at a set that is both finite and larger than the one you are constructing. In practice this is very troublesome.

comp-formation

$$\frac{\{\,\}}{\{\,(\,s:(A\text{-set}\,)\,),\,\forall\,x:A\,.\,(\,(\,P\,[\,x\,]\,)\;\Rightarrow\;(\,x\in s\,)\,)\,\}}$$

$(\text{those } x:A\,.\,(\,P\,[\,x\,]\,):(A\text{-set}\,))$

Chapter 11

Conclusions

This chapter presents some of the reactions and reflections which resulted from experimental use of *mural*. It covers both the sort of detailed observations which have been made by the people who have used the system and indications of major developments which the designers of *mural* hope to see pursued in subsequent projects. The first section describes some of the experimental use.

The intention here is to be self-critical. This could result in a rather negative end to the book and obscure the fact that a great deal has been achieved. The project was undertaken as research and it was not intended to create an industrial product. In fact, rather more has been achieved towards industrial usability than in most research projects. Moreover, as researchers, there is greater interest in identifying the remaining research goals than in writing adverts for a commercial system

11.1 Experimental use of *mural*

Even at the stage of the 'Muffin' prototype (see [JM88]), the developers were keen to get feedback on the evolving systems by exposing them to users.[1] Because of the emphasis which was being put on achieving usability by offering a productive user interface, the reactions of users were an essential check-and-balance to our design. It was therefore natural for the group to endeavour to obtain appropriate users for *mural* as it existed in the last six months of the Alvey project (i.e. October 1989 – March 1990).

The only attempt to use *mural* by the industrial collaborators of the *IPSE 2.5* project was undertaken by Geoff Scullard of ICL. His effort was limited but the exercise was of particular interest because he had earlier run the same example through HOL. Therefore, his favourable comments on the user interface (see [Scu90]) of *mural* were particularly gratifying.

As can be seen from Chapter 10, Morten Elvang-Gøransson was one of the major users who came from outside the project. In addition to the material in this book, [Elv90, FE91] give comments on his reaction to versions of *mural*. Amongst users who were more-or-less familiar with the project were Michel Sintzoff (who had consulted for *IPSE 2.5* in general, and the work of the Manchester group in particular, most of the way through the project), Peter Lindsay (who had taken up a post in Sydney in July 1989 and flew back to review a later version of the system) and John Fitzgerald (who significantly extended

---

[1]One such user was the then Alvey Software Engineering Director.

Peter Lindsay's work on populating the *mural* theory store and wrote [Fit89a, Fit89b, Fit89c, Fit89d, Fit89e]).

Another sort of exposure of *mural* has arisen out of attempts to exploit it commercially. 'Adelard'[2] have demonstrated the system to a significant number of groups – most of whom are actively involved with safety critical systems (SCS). It was originally envisaged that revenue would be generated from use of *mural* on a consultancy basis; most excitingly, it appears that groups involved in SCS are prepared to purchase *mural* for their own use.

When reading reports of users, it is important to remember that many of the experiments were made on relatively early versions of *mural*. The system has developed and continues to do so. There has, however, been almost no use of the Symbolic Execution work (cf. Chapter 9). Because the necessary code was added at a relatively late stage, there has also been only limited use of tactics. Similarly, some early users were forced to hand generate the theories corresponding to their specifications because the VST was not available at the time of their experiments.

11.2   Detailed observations

The experiments conducted by members of the *mural* group and by outsiders gave rise to a number of detailed observations about the system. These are, in many cases, by no means trivial; but they are more specific and easier to resolve than the items discussed in the next section. This section presents items which give a flavour of users' reactions; the full lists of observations can be found in the various references (see also Section 4.11 above). Of particular importance are those items which militate against our stated objective of 'proof at the workstation'.

- Users have requested a variety of syntactic extensions. Some of these like the ability to present multiple bindings with one quantifier (i.e. $\forall i, j \in \mathbb{N} \cdot \ldots$ for $\forall i \in \mathbb{N} \cdot \forall j \in \mathbb{N} \cdot \ldots$) are relatively trivial to achieve. Some, like the ability to rename within theories (cf. Section 3.5.5), would be straightforward and non-disruptive extensions. There are, however, ideas whose implementation would require significant changes even to the specification of *mural*. One example of this is that a proper treatment of associative and commutative operators is probably best achieved on top of a model for expressions where operators take a set of arguments. Such a change could have a profound effect on the matching algorithms in *mural*.

- Structure editor input is intended to help the user with large and unfamiliar languages. It is well-known that this can become tedious, especially for the experienced user. So far, *mural* does not have a consistent policy on providing an alternative parser route whereby the user can type linear text. This is not merely an oversight: achieving the goal of parsing is far easier with simple objects – whose only structure is given by a context-free syntax – than with objects with a rich, graph-like, structure. What must, however, count as an oversight is that the well-understood ideas on natural two-dimensional presentation of large tree-like objects (cf. [KS69]) were not properly implemented.

---

[2]Adelard, Coborn House Business Centre, Coborn Road, London, E3 2DA

- It is worth reviewing a specific example where the 'proof at the workstation' objective was compromised by the lack of a specific option. Typical *mural* users frequently search for inference rules and instantiations which match particular proof situations. It must be emphasised that this is not a case of 'thrashing about': a well-populated theory base is a rich quarry and few users are likely to aspire to knowing every rule. This valuable feature can be made virtually unusable if the performance is not acceptable. There have been many technical proposals for ways to speed such searches. One which was not initially implemented was the ability to cut down the search for instantiations by allowing the user to provide a partial instantiation. Although this is now implemented, there is certainly a need for further ideas which improve the performance of searches over the theory base.

- The ability to provide different sorts of views of proofs could also be added to *mural*. Indeed, in view of the success of this idea in the prototype 'Muffin' system, its omission is to be regretted.

- There are a number of limitations to the 'logical frame' underlying *mural*. As is explained in Section 3.3.3, the intention to cover VDM's sub-typing via invariants by recognising 'inclusion polymorphism' precluded taking over the 'Edinburgh Logical Frame' of [HHP87]. But neither of these logical frames would cope with non-monotonic logics since, if the addition of new assumptions can invalidate existing deductions, a Natural Deduction proof style is inappropriate. Perhaps even more deeply, it is not easy to see how the logical frame of *mural* could cope with the sort of meta-reasoning which is used in the standard justification of the Deduction Theorem.

- The existing VST is by no means complete. But the combination of a full specification support tool and a corresponding population of a theory store would be a complete codification of a development method. Like any other effort of formalisation, it requires great insight and care. Ideally, it should be accompanied by proofs of its soundness.[3]

- The current *mural* proof assistant is very open in that most changes can be made at any time. This, in fact, was seen as an objective whose achievement has disclosed where the idea needs qualification. Users have pointed out that there are theories such as 'sets', which they would rather know can not change other than – possibly – by the addition of further derived rules. Such 'frozen' theories could also have all of the proofs removed as a way of significantly reducing the size of the Smalltalk image. The ability to freeze theories and – perhaps automatically – remove proofs could easily be added to *mural*.

- The original paper [Lin87b] about the 'Formal System for Inclusion Polymorphism' discussed the idea of *theory morphisms*. Essentially, this was intended to provide a way of placing generic results in general theories and then inheriting these general results into more specific theories. An example – prompted by the 'Larch Shared Language Handbook' – would be proving the associativity of a constructor in a theory of 'collectors' and then interpreting this variously as the associativity of

---

[3]This is not so much a pointer to a potential change to *mural* as it is a realization whose full force only became apparent after the system was in use.

sequence concatenation and set union. Although the underlying concepts are clear, many implementation problems can be identified and theory morphisms remain to be implemented in *mural*.

- Perhaps the group building *mural* concentrated on User Interface questions too exclusively. There is, of course, a wealth of algorithms related to theorem proving; in many cases, their use could contribute significantly to the objective that users should see *mural* as providing a better environment than pencil and paper. Too few of these algorithms are currently available in *mural*. It should be straightforward to code up more decision procedures, although there is an interesting issue about their correctness (see next section). A more general extension would be to add facilities for automatic use of rewrite rules. One of the authors (CBJ) experimented with the 'Larch Prover' (LP) at DEC-SRC and feels it might be possible to obtain a more controlled interface to such a tool by employing a user interface like that of *mural* to construct the outline of a proof and then drive constrained rewrites from this overall structure. So far, not even the specification of *mural* has been extended to define such features.

- (This, and the subsequent items relate solely to the implementation of *mural* and need not affect its specification.) There are several respects in which the performance of *mural* reduces its usability. The implementation strategy described in Chapter 6 has made it possible to tune *mural* based on the experience of its use. It remains true that unconstrained searches in well-populated theory stores are too slow for the user to maintain a train of thought. Ways of cutting down the search space are available to the user but a significant constant factor speed improvement could probably be sought using ideas like those in [Mor88a, Mor88b] on auxiliary representations of expressions.

- Even more worrying – because it is not possible for the user to circumvent – is the machine resource needed to run the Smalltalk implementation of *mural*. To use *mural* effectively, it must be run on a machine of at least the speed of a Sun 3/60 and with a minimum of 12MB of real store. Startup times can also be excessive unless the workstation has a local disc. The justification for listing this difficulty in the current section is the belief that it would not be too difficult to re-implement *mural*, from its formal specification, in another object-oriented language.[4] Clearly, the effort involved would depend greatly on the platform of (shallow) user-interface facilities available.

- Last, but by no means least, the current *mural* implementation is single-user because of its underlying implementation system (Smalltalk). Clearly, a system for use on large projects would have to support multi-users. At the time of writing (November 1990), Smalltalk's planned upgrade from V2.5 to the V4 presents both major worries about the cost of porting *mural* and potential gains from the fact that V4 is X-based.

---

[4]Peter Lindsay has supported a project which has re-coded the kernel of *mural* in 'Miranda'.

11.3 Further developments

The ideas listed in this section have also become clearer during the experimental use of *mural*. But, in many cases, the concern was already clear when [JLW86] was written. In most cases, the worries have been identified by the *mural* team rather than its users. In all cases, the resolution of these points requires more research and their eventual resolution will probably result in new systems being specified and built.

- The reason for wanting to show that a design or implementation satisfies a specification is to increase the confidence which can justifiably be placed in a stage of design. One aim in building *mural* has been to elevate confidence that purported proofs do indeed discharge the required proof obligations. But proof assistants like that in *mural* are themselves large pieces of software. Who is to say that the proof assistant is correct? The designers of *mural* have, as explained elsewhere in this book, worked from a VDM specification. But there is *not* a complete formal proof of the design (steps towards what was done are mentioned in Chapters 4 and 6); nor would the group recommend that such a massive proof be undertaken! There is, fortunately, a much more cost-effective way of ensuring that a flaw in *mural* could not camouflage an error in a proof: it would be straightforward to extend *mural* so that it could generate an external form of any complete proof in its store. As is pointed out in Chapter 1, it is also not difficult to write a program which checks a completely formal proof. This program could be written in perhaps ten pages of some high-level functional programming language and the proof of this could be formalised and/or widely scrutinized. The theorem proving support would then be split between, on the one hand, a large program with many modes of interaction which was carefully constructed but not formally justified and, on the other hand, a small program whose correctness is critical and treated accordingly. The former offers a user-friendly environment in which it is realistic to create proofs of significant systems; the latter requires as input excruciatingly detailed proofs which would be unlikely to see the light of day without its overweight twin.

  It would be highly desirable to create a single proof checker to cover a variety of proof assistants.[5] Unfortunately, such a plan has a pre-condition of agreement on standardized proofs which is unlikely to be easy to achieve.

  One final concern about correctness can be put into context at this point. Decision procedures offer – in special circumstances – a way of greatly reducing the burden on the user who is constructing a proof. Unfortunately, many decision procedures do not produce (even as a by-product) a proof in a formal system. The reliance on the correctness of the decision procedures would not be diminished by the construction of a slimline proof checker. Therefore, each such decision procedure should be justified.

- It could be said that the *mural* proof assistant has been built around inference rules as the fundamental unit. Steps in a proof are related by inference rules which state that, if their premises are (have been proved to be) true, their conclusion is true. There are, however, many proofs where it is useful to gather facts about other relationships. For example, chains of equalities where each new step is generated

---

[5]Chris Wadsworth attributes this idea to Malcolm Newey.

by substitution of equal subterms. Clearly, such proofs can be couched in terms of deductions, but more perspicuous presentations of proofs could be created by a system which recognised the role of equality. One reason for *not* adding such a feature as a simple extension of *mural* is that equality is clearly only one example of a large class of other relations about which one might wish to reason. Other instances which come to mind include many (irreflexive) ordering relations. There is also a deep question about capitalizing on similarities in the properties of such relationships, which is posed in [Jon90b]. It would be wise to think hard about these issues rather than make some *ad hoc* extensions to *mural*.

- It should, by now at least, be clear to the reader that specifying and constructing a proof assistant for a given family of formalisms is not a trivial task. However, in at least one crucial technical sense the task is clear-cut: it is possible to state precisely what is meant by a formal proof. In contrast, the aim to provide – in a proof assistant – support for what might be called 'rigorous proofs' is altogether more nebulous. In spite of the difficulty, this was a goal of [JLW86].

It could be claimed that some features of *mural* permit the creation of rigorous proofs. It is, for example, possible to construct a proof in which some steps are not formally proved. There is a clear distinction between steps which are (not) justified by the application of an established inference rule from identified hypotheses. As with many proof assistants, *mural* permits one proof to be completed although it relies on a number of precisely stated – but unproved – inference rules. At the other extreme, one might store a string of text as a justification. It is, alas, more difficult to pin down something useful between these extremes. The sort of thing envisaged at the beginning of the project was a facility for the user to record the claim that a certain proof could be completed 'by induction on set S' and the program to make certain minimal checks (at least that S is of type 'set'!) and to record their success or notify their failure. In a similar vein, the system should record facts like the automatic generation of a formula by unfolding a function even if this link does not constitute a full proof. In each case, the aim is to record formal links so that the potential exists for its completion if the user subsequently decides to make a rigorous proof (more) formal. During the project, it was realized that a stable version of a formal-*mural* proof assistant had to be built and appreciated before tools to assist with rigorous proofs could even be properly specified.

- The authors have reacted similarly to suggestions that AI or IKBS techniques could have been used more widely in order to lighten the burden on the *mural* user. These techniques appear to offer support in well-understood domains of knowledge. Extended use of *mural* and experience with structuring theory stores and defining tactics, could give rise to a 'knowledge base' which subsequent systems could hope to exploit.[6]

---

[6]A reluctance to promise what could not be delivered in this area led to the name '*IPSE 2.5*': the Alvey Software Engineering Strategy document [TW83] had relatively conservative objectives for second generation IPSE's whereas their third generation successors were predicated on AI techniques. To express the original commitment of the project to the support of formal methods, but to distance it from techniques which were unlikely to pay off in the timescale of the Alvey programme, *IPSE 2.5* was proposed as a working title. For better or for worse the name stuck.

- The VST (cf. Chapter 8) supports a large enough subset of BSI-VDM to permit major case studies and could be extended to support the whole of the standard. It is also believed that the same model – and even some of the code – could be used to support other formal development methods. There is however a feeling that this is not the wisest course of development. The split between the VST and the proof assistant has unfortunate consequences. It is, for example, possible to generate the proof obligations from some specifications (even to then fully formally prove them) and then to edit the specifications. The lack of warning when this is done must be contrasted with the way in which the *mural* proof assistant would flag a theorem which had been proved using a rule which is subsequently changed. The authors would like to undertake research into what might be called (in analogy to 'logical frames') 'method frames'. In fact Michel Sintzoff and his colleagues have already gone some way towards this [S$^+$89, Laf90, Web90] and the main objective might be said to be combining 'Deva' ideas with the user-interface work which has come from *mural*. There is, however, a suspicion with at least one member of the group that the frequent recurrence of problems which are expressed in terms of relations points to a more general approach.

- One last area where it is clear that an idea from the *mural* team requires more work before it comes to full fruition is the symbolic execution approach to the animation of specifications. It is clear from even limited experience with an implementation of the ideas exposed by [Kne89] that expressions are generated which become un- wieldy. Here again, it looks as though some (semi-) automatic rewrite tool is an essential component of a viable animation system. More particularly, rewriting should be aimed at eliminating state expressions since the user is likely to be in- terested in the relationship between visible (or input/output) values; the only state relationship which should be requested in most cases is equality.

11.4 Summary

This chapter presents a frank evaluation of *mural*. In case this leaves a negative feel- ing, it must be reiterated that the project produced many successful outputs. The final report [Jon90c] lists a prodigious number of papers and talks; a working system is avail- able and commercial exploitation looks viable. At the beginning of the project, a clear research direction (greater usability for a proof assistant by serious attention to its deep UI) was enunciated; a system has been specified, designed and built which must provide a benchmark for future work in this area.

The 'Kemmerer Report' [Kem86] identifies two of the key goals for 'next generation verification systems' as the use of graphics interfaces and the development of reusable theories. We believe that our project has contributed to research in these, and other, areas. Above all, the group would say 'it was fun'. Given a good group of researchers, there is probably no better measure of a successful research project.

Appendix A

Summary of VDM Notation

Logic

B	{true, false}
$\neg E$	negation (not)
$E_1 \wedge E_2$	conjunction (and)
$E_1 \vee E_2$	disjunction (or)
$E_1 \Rightarrow E_2$	implication
$E_1 \Leftrightarrow E_2$	equivalence
$\forall x \in S \cdot E$	universal quantifier [1]
$\exists x \in S \cdot E$	existential quantifier
$\exists! x \in S \cdot E$	unique existence
$\Gamma \vdash E$	sequent
$\dfrac{\Gamma}{E}$	inference rule
$\dfrac{E_1}{E_2}$	bi-directional inference rule

Numbers

N_1	$\{1, 2, \ldots\}$
N	$\{0, 1, 2, \ldots\}$
Z	$\{\ldots, -1, 0, 1, \ldots\}$
Q	rational numbers
R	real numbers

Functions

$f: D_1 \times D_2 \rightarrow R$	signature
$f(d)$	application
if ... then ... else ...	conditional
let $x = \ldots$ in ...	local definition

---

[1] With all of the quantifiers, the scope extends as far as possible to the right; no parentheses are required but they can be used for extra grouping.

Sets

T-set	all finite subsets of T
$\{t_1, t_2, \ldots, t_n\}$	set enumeration
$\{\}$	empty set
$\{x \in S \mid p(x)\}$	set comprehension
$\{i, \ldots, j\}$	subset of integers (from i to j inclusive)
$t \in S$	set membership
$t \notin S$	$\neg(t \in S)$
$S_1 \subseteq S_2$	set containment (subset of)
$S_1 \subset S_2$	strict set containment
$S_1 \cap S_2$	set intersection [2]
$S_1 \cup S_2$	set union
$S_1 - S_2$	set difference
$\bigcup SS$	distributed union
card S	cardinality (size) of a set

Maps

$D \xrightarrow{m} R$	finite maps
$D \xleftrightarrow{m} R$	one-one map
$\{d_1 \mapsto r_1, d_2 \mapsto r_2, \ldots, d_n \mapsto r_n\}$	map enumeration
$\{\}$	empty map
$\{d \mapsto f(d) \in D \times R \mid p(d)\}$	map comprehension
dom m	domain
rng m	range
$m(d)$	application
$m_1 \dagger m_2$	overwriting
$s \lhd m$	domain restriction
$s \ntriangleleft m$	domain deletion
$m \rhd t$	range restriction

Sequences

T^*	finite sequences
T^+	non-empty, finite sequences
$[t_1, t_2, \ldots, t_n]$	sequence enumeration
$[\,]$	empty sequence
len s	length
$s_1 \frown s_2$	concatenation
dconc ss	distributed concatenation
hd s	head
tl s	tail
inds s	indices
elems s	elements
$s(i, \ldots, j)$	sub-sequence

---

[2]Intersection is higher priority than union.

Composite Objects

::	compose
$mk\text{-}N(...)$	generator
nil	omitted object
$s_1(o)$	selector

Function Specification

$f\ (d\!:\!D)\ r\!:\!R$
pre $...\,d\,...$
post $...\,d\,...\,r\,...$

Operation Specification

$OP\ (d\!:\!D)\ r\!:\!R$
ext rd $e_1\ :\ T_1,$
   wr $e_2\ :\ T_2$
pre $...\,d\,...\,e_1\,...\,e_2\,...$
post $...\,d\,...\,e_1\,...\,\overleftarrow{e_2}\,...\,r\,...\,e_2\,...$

Appendix B

Glossary of terms

automatic theorem proving A style of seeking to establish theorems mechanically characterized by large systematic searches, sometimes constrained by heuristics (see below) or user advice (typically given in advance).

axiom An inference rule whose validity (in some context) is accepted without proof, either because it is considered 'self-evident' or because its justification is considered to belong to a 'lower level' (such as a more primitive logic).

Boyer-Moore theorem prover A computer system for proving theorems by induction, mainly in the style of proofs in elementary number theory. The user supplies a conjecture which the machine then tries to prove (using built-in heuristics) from axioms and already-proven results, but without direct assistance from the user. It has been used to prove many theorems, and its benchmark reaches a long way into elementary number theory. See [BM79].

CLEAR A specification language permitting modular structuring of specifications, based on Institutions (see below). See [BG81].

constructive logic A logic which accepts only direct constructions as proofs. This results, for example, in more subtle interpretations of the usual logical connectives and the rejection of the law of excluded middle. See [Bee85].

correctness An implementation is said to be *correct* with respect to a specification if it satisfies all of the properties required by the specification. Such a correctness criterion is often defined by a proof obligation; it would normally be established by a proof.

data reification A specification is likely to be written in terms of data objects which are more abstract than those available in an implementation language. Steps of design which introduce – and justify – (more) concrete representations for such abstractions are steps of *data reification*. See Section 1.2.

equational reasoning Reasoning with systematic treatment of sets of (more or less arbitrary) equations, such as term rewriting.

FOPC First order predicate calculus: the classical logic of predicates with quantification over individual elements. See Section 3.2.

formal proof A *formal* proof is one in which the validity of every step can be checked purely mechanically, without recourse to imagination or intuition. In its simplest form, a formal proof is a structure of valid applications of inference rules, in one of the following forms:

- a *sequence of lines* in which each line is either a hypothesis or follows from a number of preceding lines by an inference rule; or

- a *tree* in which each leaf is a hypothesis expression and each non-leaf node follows from its immediate subnodes by an inference rule.

For a discussion of other styles of formal proof, see Section 4.3. The *mural* proof assistant uses Natural Deduction style proofs (see below).

FRIPSE A post-Muffin (see below) prototype of *mural* supporting first order logic. See [JL88].

generic proof assistant One which can be configured for different logics.

goal-directed A *goal-directed* method of solving problems is one which proceeds by successively breaking a problem (the goal) into sub-problems (subgoals) in such a way that 'achievements of the subgoals' can be composed to form an 'achievement of the goal'. See [Mil84].

heuristics Techniques used to guide searches in automatic theorem proving. Such techniques are not usually universally applicable, but can shorten searches considerably when used on appropriate problem domains.

induction Mathematical induction is a method of proof used to establish properties of recursively defined data types by an analysis of how their elements are built up. Roughly stated, the method requires showing that an arbitrary element enjoys the property, under the assumption that all elements built up 'before' it do so. Elements without 'predecessors' give rise to *base cases*, and others to *induction steps*.

inference rules The basic building blocks of formal proofs. They generally consist of a number of *hypotheses* and a *conclusion*, the idea being that the validity of the conclusion can be inferred from the validity of all the hypotheses. In Natural Deduction proofs, however, the validity of certain hypotheses (called *sequents*) may sometimes depend on additional assumptions, which are said to be 'discharged' upon application of the rule.

Institutions Burstall and Goguen developed the notion of *Institutions* to provide an abstract model theory for program specifications; they generalize the notion of many logical systems by providing a uniform treatment of syntax and semantics, largely in the terminology of category theory – see [GB83].

lambda calculus A calculus for reasoning about and evaluating lambda expressions. See [Bar84].

lambda-expression An *untyped* lambda-expression $\lambda x \cdot E$ – where E is an expression usually involving x – denotes that function whose value (on argument x) is E. The *typed* lambda-expression $\lambda x: S \cdot E$ is defined similarly, except that x is restricted to range over S.

LCF Originally LCF stood for Logic for Computable Functions, which was a particular logic proposed by Scott. Early work on a proof checker for this logic was done by Milner and colleagues at Stanford in the early 1970s [Mil72, New75]. Experience with the Stanford system provided the basis for the development of a 'second generation' LCF at Edinburgh in the late 1970s [GMW79]. (Besides the original Edinburgh system, there are at least two other significant versions – at Cambridge [Pau85a] and at Göteborg [Pet82] – the main difference being the logics they support.) The Edinburgh work focussed on an interactive 'guided system' style for proof construction and introduced the seminal ideas of

- using a programming meta-language, **ML**, in which the user can build derived inference rules and tactics, and

- having 'theorem' as an abstract type (in ML) whose primitives are the axioms and basic inference rules of a logic.

It is these aspects which now characterize a system as being 'LCF-like' or 'descended from LCF'; notable examples are the PRL and NuPRL systems of Constable and colleagues at Cornell [PRL86], Veritas [HD86], HOL [Gor85] and Isabelle [Pau86]. (See also [Pau85b].)

logical frame A formal system in which logics can be defined. The fundamental notions it should define are 'term', 'well-formed formulae' (wffs), 'inference rule', 'proof' and 'theory'. To be suitably general, it must also define a substitution mechanism and ancillary notions, such as how capture of free variables is to be avoided. See [Lin87c].

LPF *Logic for Partial Functions* is a logic introduced in [BCJ84] to handle undefined terms in program proofs.

model-oriented A *model-oriented* specification of a system defines its operations in terms of models built up from primitive data types such as integers, sets and sequences (cf. 'property-oriented' specifications).

Muffin A prototype proof-constructor developed at Manchester University to perform experiments on user interface aspects of formal reasoning. It was not intended to have the full generic capabilities of *mural*, being restricted to propositional calculus, for example. See [JM88].

Natural Deduction A style of proof developed by Gentzen in which the set of assumptions is determined by context; this has the great advantage of allowing very succinct inference rules. The examples of proof structures in the entry for *formal proof* above must be changed to allow for assumptions to be 'discharged':

- in the linear form, 'boxes' are introduced for subcontexts;

- in the tree form, leaves can be sequents provided they are discharged further down the branch.

See [Pra65, Pra71].

NuPRL An LCF-like system for constructing proofs in a constructive theory of types similar to Martin-Löf's [Mar85, NPS90]. Besides the logical differences (such as the ability to extract 'programs' from constructive proofs), NuPRL's main non-LCF feature is its user interface, which has user-introduced abbreviations, a proof-tree manager, proof editing and a library module. See [PRL86].

operation decomposition Operation decomposition of a design entails the stepwise development of operation specifications until all of the operation steps have been refined to available primitives of the implementation language/system. Such decompositions arise because operation specifications given by pre- and post-conditions cannot be executed.

oracle A hand-coded decision procedure which checks the validity of lines in a proof.

proof obligation A logical formula whose validity must be established as part of a formal design method (such as justifying the correctness of a data reification or an operation decomposition).

proof assistant Computer Aided Proof Engineering (to coin a phrase). A software system which aids in the construction of formal proofs and checks their correctness. A *mural* credo is that the best currently achievable synergy between human and machine is to have the former guide proof creation using insight into the problem domain, and the latter performing faultless clerical steps and (constrained) searches.

property-oriented A property-oriented specification characterizes its operations implicitly via statements of their inter-relationships (rather than defining each operation over a model). Such specifications are frequently referred to as 'algebraic specifications' – see [EM85, EM90].

resolution rule A rule of inference usually of the form

$$\frac{a \vee b, c \vee \neg d}{(a \vee c)\theta}$$

where θ is the most general unifier of b and d. It is complete in the sense that a formula A of FOPC is valid iff there is a proof using only resolution rules that (the Skolemized form of) $\neg A$ leads to a contradiction.

resolution theorem provers Theorem provers adopting various search strategies to find a resolution proof – see [Lov78].

sequent A logical expression consisting of a set of *premises* and an *upshot*, usually separated by a 'turnstile' $\vdash$. A sequent holds iff its upshot follows from its premises. See Section 4.3.3.

sequent calculus A style of formal proof whereby sequents are manipulated directly: thus for example its inference rules have sequents as 'hypotheses' and 'conclusion', and the nodes of a proof tree (see the second example in the entry for *formal proof* above) are sequents. See [Smu61]. (See Section 4.3 for a discussion of different styles of formal proof.)

simplification The process of reducing an expression 'towards normal form', often by term rewriting.

Smalltalk An object-oriented programming language developed and supplied by Par-cPlace Systems, 1550 Plymouth Street, Mountain View, California 94043, USA. The implementation language of the *mural* system.

tactic The *mural* proof assistant provides a simple imperative language for expressing certain commonly-used proof strategies, called *tactics*. The *tactic language* gives the same access to basic *mural* operations as is available from the user interface, in addition to imperative constructs such as sequencing, branching and backtracking. Tactics can be parameterized, can call other tactics – including themselves – and can even poll the user for additional information at runtime. Conceptually, tactics are operations which extend the 'state' of a proof. See Chapter 5.

tactical A (possibly parameterized) operation for composing tactics, by analogy with functionals as operations for composing functions.

target logic As remarked in the early project 'concepts paper' [JLW86], *mural* was intended to be used in many different applications of formal reasoning. Perhaps the main *theoretical* problem that *mural* faced arose from the fact that these different applications call for different logics: e.g.

- extracting the computational content from proofs requires a constructive logic (cf. [PRL86])
- algebraic-style specification languages (e.g. CLEAR [San82]) call for many-sorted equational reasoning
- LARCH traits correspond to theories in FOPC (cf. [GHW85])
- VDM's proof obligations are expressed in LPF [BCJ84]
- domain theoretic reasoning is probably best done in *PPλ* (cf. [GMW79])
- Hoare logic is often used for program verification

These (and other) logics were identified as the *target logics mural* should support.

term rewriting A method for reducing expressions (with respect to a set of equations) by repeated replacement of instances of the left hand side of an equation by the corresponding instance of the right hand side.

theory 'Theory' is a heavily overloaded word. Besides its normal meaning(s) in English, there are two particular usages in the formal reasoning context. The first comes from formal logic where it is customary to refer to the set of *all* theorems provable in a logic as the (deductively closed) *theory of a logic*, or *logical theory* for short.

The second usage relates to 'theories in practice' as found in proof assistants such as *mural*. A *mural* theory consists of:

- a *signature*, indicating which symbols are available,
- a set of *inference rules*, some of which are *axioms*, some of which are *derived* from axioms using proofs, and some of which are merely *conjectures* which the user may or may not prove at some later date,
- a set of *tactics*, and
- a set of *oracles*,

with the set of *mural* theories being arranged in an inheritance hierarchy. A *logic* is just a theory of special significance: logics and theories are not distinguished in *mural*.

Further support for 'theories in practice' suggests adding a mechanism for creating yet further additional components when expedient.

UI User interface. In this book the term is used to mean not simply the visual layout of the system, but also the operations by which the user accesses and manipulates the underlying data structures.

unification A substitution θ (i.e. an instantiation of variables by terms) is said to *unify* two expressions if they become equal when θ is applied to them. The process of finding a unifying substitution (or *unifier*) is called *unification*.

VDM The *Vienna Development Method* is an (evolving) attempt to apply formal methods to the development of significant industrial computer systems. The current status can be seen in [BJ82] and [Jon90a].

verification conditions Logical formulae generated from assertions and loop invariants attached to a program which, when established, are sufficient to demonstrate that the assertions and invariants are indeed satisfied each time execution passes the points to which they are attached. Compare proof obligations.

vcg A *verification condition generator* is an automatic process for constructing verification conditions.

Veritas An LCF-like system for constructing proofs; its meta-language is Miranda – see [HD86].

VST The *mural* VDM Support Tool. See Chapter 7.

Appendix C

The Specification of the Proof Assistant

C.1 The Raw Syntax

C.1.1 Primitives

Apart from the standard VDM primitive types, the primitive types used in this spec are the following:

- Object-level 'atomic' symbols: *CESymb* (for constants and functions), *QESymb* (binders or quantifiers), *CTSymb* (types and type-constructors), *QTSymb* (dependent type constructors)

- *VSymb* (for variables), *MESymb* (expression metavariable symbols), *MTSymb* (type metavariable symbols)

- Null objects: *NullExp*, *NullType*

- Things in proofs (explained later): *Box-ref*, *Hypline-ref*, *Ordline-ref*, *Sequent-ref*

- Other names: *Rule-ref*, *Theory-ref*, *ThMorph-ref*

They are assumed to be mutually disjoint, infinite sets of structureless tokens.

Other tokens used are:

EXP, VSYMB, QEXP, OEXP, EPHOLE, NULLEXP,
TYPE, SUBTYPE, QTYPE, OTYPE, TPHOLE, NULLTYPE,
OESYMB, MESYMB, CESYMB, NULLOESYMB, QESYMB,
OTSYMB, MTSYMB, CTSYMB, NULLOTSYMB, QTSYMB,
BEXP, BTYPE, ELISTXTLIST, ELIST, TLIST

Here are some groupings which will come in useful later[1]:

NullThings = NullExp | NullType

Def = Exp | Type

NullSymbs = NullOESymb | NullOTSymb

---

[1]As an aside: all type unions (|) in this specification happen to be disjoint unions.

OTerm = OExp | OType

CSymb = CESymb | CTSymb

OSymb = OESymb | OTSymb

QSymb = QESymb | QTSymb

Atom = CSymb | QSymb

Leaf = Atom | VSymb | MESymb | MTSymb | EPHole | TPHole

ArgList = EList | TList

Construct = Exp | Type | BTerm | EListXTList | ArgList

Term = Construct | OSymb | QSymb

BTerm = BExp | BType

They are introduced mainly for simplicity and to save writing their expansion multiply. In general, they are not things that a user of the system should ever be aware of.

C.1.2 Expressions

The current preference for what an expression can be:

Exp = VSymb | QExp | OExp | EPHole | NullExp

All kinds of expression should be visible.[2]

Quantified expressions:

QExp :: SYMBOL : QESymb
*   BODY   : BExp*

See §C.1.4 for the definition of *BExp*.

Ordinary[3] expressions:

OExp :: SYMBOL : OESymb
*   ARGS   : EListXTList*

Basically, this class provides a description of constant expressions (both primitive and defined) and (parametrized) expression metavariables. The distinction between these two subclasses is made at the level of the *OESymb*:

OESymb = MESymb | CESymb | NullOESymb

---

[2]These visibility comments in bold fount relate to the export status etc. of the implementation.
[3]or *other*, or *oh, hell, I don't know what to call them!*, or ...

See §C.1.5 below for the definition of *ElistXTList* (basically pairs of *Exp* lists and *Type* lists).

Expression placeholders:

> *EPHole* :: *INDEX* : N_1

Placeholders will normally appear only in certain classes of *mural* object: viz. as instantiations of metavariable symbols, in definitions of constants, and as images of (primitive) constants under signature morphisms. Just exactly how they are used will be explained in the relevant later sections. (Basically, *mk-EPHole(n)* will be filled by the *n*th argument of a *EList*.) In practice, with a carefully chosen concrete syntax we hope to shield the user from placeholders altogether.

The *subterms* of an expression are given by:

> *subterms* : *Exp* → *Term*-set
> *subterms*(e) $\triangleq$ cases *e* of
>   *mk-QExp(qet, be)* → {*e, qet*} ∪ *subterms(be)*
>   *mk-OExp(oet, elxtl)* → {*e, oet*} ∪ *subterms(elxtl)*
>   others {*e*}
>   end

Not exported.

And its *free variables* are obtained via the following function:

> *freeVars* : *Exp* → *VSymb*-set
> *freeVars*(e) $\triangleq$ cases *e* of
>   *VSymb* → {*e*}
>   *mk-QExp(qet, be)* → *freeVars(be)*
>   *mk-OExp(oet, elxtl)* → *freeVars(elxtl)*
>   others { }
>   end

Not exported.

Similar functions (with the same names) will be defined on each of the other subclasses of *Construct* (see below).

C.1.3 Types

The various subclasses of type:

> *Type* = *SubType* | *QType* | *OType* | *TPHole* | *NullType*

All kinds of type should be visible.

A *subtype* constructor:

> *SubType* :: *BODY* : *BExp*

A *dependent type*:

QType :: SYMBOL : QTSymb
          BODY   : BType

An ordinary type is much like an ordinary expression:

OType :: SYMBOL : OTSymb
          ARGS   : EListXTList

OTSymb = MTSymb | CTSymb | NullOTSymb

Type placeholders are analogous to *EPHoles*:

TPHole :: INDEX : N_1

The subterms and free variables in a type are given respectively by:

subterms : Type → Term-set
subterms(t) △ cases t of
                    mk-SubType(be)   → {t} ∪ subterms(be)
                    mk-QType(qtt, bt) → {t, qtt} ∪ subterms(bt)
                    mk-OType(ott, elxtl) → {t, ott} ∪ subterms(elxtl)
                    others {t}
                    end

Not exported.

freeVars : Type → VSymb-set
freeVars(t) △ cases t of
                    mk-SubType(be)   → freeVars(be)
                    mk-QType(qtt, bt)   → freeVars(bt)
                    mk-OType(ott, elxtl) → freeVars(elxtl)
                    others { }
                    end

Not exported.

C.1.4 BExps and BTypes

A *BExp* is used to help define both *QExps* and *SubTypes*. It consists of a bound variable, the declared type of that variable (the *universe*), and an expression predicate (the *body*). The universe should not reference the bound variable, neither should that variable be already bound in the body. Any other variable bound in either the universe or the body should not occur in the other of these components. A *BType* is analogous, but has a type as its body instead of an expression. It is introduced only because the resulting symmetry makes some of the later stuff easier to write.

BExps **and** *BTypes* **should probably not be visible as separate objects.**

$BExp$ :: VAR : $VSymb$
          $UNIVERSE$: $Type$
          $BODY$: Exp

where

$inv\text{-}BExp(be)$ $\triangleq$ $is\text{-}OK\text{-}BTerm(be)$

$BType$ :: VAR : $VSymb$
          $UNIVERSE$: $Type$
          $BODY$: $Type$

where

$inv\text{-}BType(bt)$ $\triangleq$ $is\text{-}OK\text{-}BTerm(bt)$

$is\text{-}OK\text{-}BTerm : BTerm \rightarrow \mathbb{B}$
$is\text{-}OK\text{-}BTerm(bterm)$ $\triangleq$
    let $vt = VAR(bterm)$,
      $t = UNIVERSE(bterm)$,
      $def = BODY(bterm)$ in
   $vt \notin allVars(t) \cup boundVars(def) \wedge$
   $allVars(def) \cap boundVars(t) = \{\} \wedge boundVars(def) \cap allVars(t) = \{\}$

Not exported.

The usual functions for finding the subterms and the free variables of either a *BExp* or a *BType*:

   $subterms : BTerm \rightarrow Term\text{-set}$
   $subterms(bterm)$ $\triangleq$
      $\{VAR(bterm)\} \cup subterms(UNIVERSE(bterm)) \cup subterms(BODY(bterm))$

Not exported.

   $freeVars : BTerm \rightarrow VSymb\text{-set}$
   $freeVars(bterm)$ $\triangleq$
      $freeVars(UNIVERSE(bterm)) \cup freeVars(BODY(bterm)) - \{VAR(bterm)\}$

Not exported.

C.1.5   EListXTLists

An *EListXTList* is really just a list of expressions and a list of types. No variable bound in some expression or type in it can occur in any other of its expressions or types (part of this invariant actually appears as invariants on EList and TList, defined below).

EListXTLists **should probably be visible as a list of expressions and a list of types, with the system maintaining the invariant automatically.**

$EListXTList$ :: $ELIST$: $EList$
             $TLIST$: $TList$

where

$inv\text{-}EListXTList(mk\text{-}EListXTList(el, tl))$ $\triangleq$
  $\forall e \in rng\ el \cdot$
    $\forall t \in rng\ tl \cdot$
      $allVars(e) \cap boundVars(t) = \{\ \} \wedge boundVars(e) \cap allVars(t) = \{\ \}$

Those boring old functions *subterms* and *freeVars* again:

$subterms : EListXTList \rightarrow Term\text{-}set$
$subterms(elxtl)$ $\triangleq$ $subterms(ELIST(elxtl)) \cup subterms(TLIST(elxtl))$

Not exported.

$freeVars : EListXTList \rightarrow VSymb\text{-}set$
$freeVars(elxtl)$ $\triangleq$ $freeVars(ELIST(elxtl)) \cup freeVars(TLIST(elxtl))$

Not exported.

Plus an exciting new function for finding the *size* of an *EListXTList*. This is just a pair of integers, respectively the length of its two separate lists of arguments:

$size : EListXTList \rightarrow \mathsf{N} \times \mathsf{N}$
$size(elxtl)$ $\triangleq$ $(len\ ELIST(elxtl), len\ TLIST(elxtl))$

Not exported.

C.1.6   ELists and TLists

An EList is a sequence of expressions such that no variable bound in some element of the sequence can occur in any other element of the sequence. A EList may contain expressions which are equivalent to each other, however. A TList is analogous, but is a sequence of types rather than expressions.

ELists and TLists as such probably shouldn't appear, only their constituent parts. Their invariants should be maintained automatically.

$EList = Exp^{*}$

where

$inv\text{-}EList(el)$ $\triangleq$ $is\text{-}OK\text{-}ArgList(el)$

$TList = Type^{*}$

where

$inv\text{-}TList(tl)$ $\triangleq$ $is\text{-}OK\text{-}ArgList(tl)$

$is\text{-}OK\text{-}ArgList : ArgList \rightarrow \mathsf{B}$
$is\text{-}OK\text{-}ArgList(al)$ $\triangleq$
  $\forall m, n \in dom\ al \cdot m \neq n \Rightarrow boundVars(al(m)) \cap allVars(al(n)) = \{\ \}$

Not exported.

The *subterms* and *freeVars* functions for *ArgLists* hold no surprises:

subterms : ArgList → Term-set
subterms(al) $\triangleq$ $\bigcup\{subterms(def) \mid def \in$ rng *al*$\}$

Not exported.

freeVars : ArgList → VSymb-set
freeVars(al) $\triangleq$ $\bigcup\{freeVars(def) \mid def \in$ rng *al*$\}$

Not exported.

C.1.7   Other Accessing Functions

This section contains lots of really exciting functions for finding out what's in things. With the exception of the first, which just finds the size of the arguments of some ordinary term, they all act on constructs in general rather than on each subclass thereof individually.

argSize : OTerm → $\mathbb{N} \times \mathbb{N}$
argSize(oterm) $\triangleq$ *size(ARGS(oterm))*

Not exported.

The next function finds all variables in a construct, that is the set of subterms which are variables (*VSymbs*):

allVars : Construct → VSymb-set
allVars(c) $\triangleq$ $\{v \in VSymb \mid v \in subterms(c)\}$

Not exported.

The *bound variables* in a construct are then simply those variables which are not free!

boundVars : Construct → VSymb-set
boundVars(c) $\triangleq$ *allVars(c) − freeVars(c)*

Not exported.

In §C.1.8 below it's argued that the above agrees with the usual definition of bound variables.

The *leaves* of a construct are its symbols, variables and placeholders, and its *atoms* are its constant (i.e. not variable or metavariable) symbols[4]:

leaves : Construct → Leaf-set
leaves(c) $\triangleq$ $\{leaf \in Leaf \mid leaf \in subterms(c)\}$

---

[4]For those of you whose memory's completely shot or who just weren't paying attention earlier

Leaf = Atom | VSymb | MESymb | MTSymb | EPHole | TPHole

and

Atom = CSymb | QSymb

Not exported.

> *atoms* : *Construct* → *Atom*-set
> *atoms*(*c*) $\triangleq$ {*atom* ∈ *Atom* | *atom* ∈ *subterms*(*c*)}

Not exported.

Next, a brace of functions for finding the (expression and type) metavariable symbols in a construct:

> *meSymbs* : *Construct* → *MESymb*-set
> *meSymbs*(*c*) $\triangleq$ {*met* ∈ *MESymb* | *met* ∈ *subterms*(*c*)}

Not exported.

> *mtSymbs* : *Construct* → *MTSymb*-set
> *mtSymbs*(*c*) $\triangleq$ {*mtt* ∈ *MTSymb* | *mtt* ∈ *subterms*(*c*)}

Not exported.

The ordinary terms in some construct are found in a depressingly similar way:

> *oTerms* : *Construct* → *OTerm*-set
> *oTerms*(*c*) $\triangleq$ {*oterm* ∈ *OTerm* | *oterm* ∈ *subterms*(*c*)}

Not exported.

An object's *expression arity* is simply the largest of the set of the indices of its expression placeholders:

> *eArity* : *Construct* → N
> *eArity*(*c*) $\triangleq$
>   let *eps* = {*INDEX*(*ep*) | *ep* ∈ *subterms*(*c*) ∧ *ep* ∈ *EPHole*} in
>   if *eps* = { }
>   then 0
>   else max *eps*

Not exported.

And the *type arity* is, of course, entirely analogous:

> *tArity* : *Construct* → N
> *tArity*(*c*) $\triangleq$
>   let *tps* = {*INDEX*(*tp*) | *tp* ∈ *subterms*(*c*) ∧ *tp* ∈ *TPHole*} in
>   if *tps* = { }
>   then 0
>   else max *tps*

Not exported.

The *arity* of an object is then just the pair of its expression and type arities. This pair of integers thus says how many expression and type arguments the object expects.

> *arity* : *Construct* → N × N
> *arity*(*c*) $\triangleq$ (*eArity*(*c*), *tArity*(*c*))

Not exported.

C.1.8   Bound Variables and Free Variables

The invariants to do with nonclashing free and bound variables in the earlier sections were introduced to make it easier to specify equivalence and operations which perform substitution 'without capture'. In this section we argue that our definition of the bound variables of an expression or type agrees with the usual definition.

First, a function for extracting *BTerms* from some construct:

> $bTerms : Construct \rightarrow BTerm\text{-set}$
> $bTerms(c) \quad \triangleq \quad \{bterm \in BTerm \mid bterm \in subterms(c)\}$

Not exported.

Claim: For every $c \in Construct$, *boundVars(c)* is precisely the set

$$\{VAR(bterm) \mid bterm \in bTerms(c)\}$$

(The proof is by structural induction over *Construct*.) Hence our definition agrees with the usual one. It's also pretty clear that *VAR(bterm)* is different for each different *bterm* in *bTerms(c)*.

C.1.9   Consistency and Completeness Checks

We can now give consistency and completeness tests for syntactic objects:

A construct is *complete* if it has no null parts:

> $isComplete : Construct \rightarrow \mathbb{B}$
> $isComplete(c) \quad \triangleq \quad \forall x \in subterms(c) \cdot x \notin NullThings \mid NullSymbs$

This shouldn't be a function that the user has direct access to, though the interface should make it clear that a construct is incomplete.

A construct is *full* if it has no placeholders:

> $isFull : Construct \rightarrow \mathbb{B}$
> $isFull(c) \quad \triangleq \quad \forall x \in subterms(c) \cdot x \notin EPHole \mid TPHole$

Not exported.

C.2   Subterm Access and Editing

C.2.1   The Class of a Term

The *class* of some object is the name of the basic abstract data type to which the object belongs. Introducing an enumerated collection of tokens:

$Class$ = {VSYMB, QEXP, OEXP, EPHOLE, NULLEXP,
          SUBTYPE, QTYPE, OTYPE, TPHOLE, NULLTYPE,
          MESYMB, CESYMB, NULLOESYMB, QESYMB,
          MTSYMB, CTSYMB, NULLOTSYMB, QTSYMB,
          BEXP, BTYPE, ELISTXTLIST, ELIST, TLIST}

the *class* of a term is given by:

$classOf$: *Term* → *Class*
$classOf$(*term*) $\triangleq$ cases *term* of
                                                                                    VSymb → VSYMB
          QExp → QEXP
          OExp → OEXP
          EPHole → EPHOLE
          NullExp → NULLEXP
          SubType → SUBTYPE
          QType → QTYPE
          OType → OTYPE
          TPHole → TPHOLE
          NullType → NULLTYPE
          MESymb → MESYMB
          CESymb → CESYMB
          NullOESymb → NULLOESYMB
          QESymb → QESYMB
          MTSymb → MTSYMB
          CTSymb → CTSYMB
          NullOTSymb → NULLOTSYMB
          QTSymb → QTSYMB
          BExp → BEXP
          BType → BTYPE
          EListXTList → ELISTXTLIST
          EList → ELIST
          TList → TLIST
          end

Not exported.

The *species* of an object is the type of the most general object which can replace it (for example in structure editing). Introducing another enumerated collection of tokens:

$Species$ = {EXP, TYPE, VSYMB, OESYMB, QESYMB, OTSYMB, QTSYMB,
            BEXP, BTYPE, ELISTXTLIST, ELIST, TLIST}

$$species : Term \rightarrow Species$$

$species(term) \quad \triangleq \quad$ **cases** *term* **of**

VSymb	$\rightarrow$ EXP
QExp	$\rightarrow$ EXP
OExp	$\rightarrow$ EXP
EPHole	$\rightarrow$ EXP
NullExp	$\rightarrow$ EXP
SubType	$\rightarrow$ TYPE
QType	$\rightarrow$ TYPE
OType	$\rightarrow$ TYPE
TPHole	$\rightarrow$ TYPE
NullType	$\rightarrow$ TYPE
MESymb	$\rightarrow$ OESYMB
CESymb	$\rightarrow$ OESYMB
NullOESymb	$\rightarrow$ OESYMB
QESymb	$\rightarrow$ QESYMB
MTSymb	$\rightarrow$ OTSYMB
CTSymb	$\rightarrow$ OTSYMB
NullOTSymb	$\rightarrow$ OTSYMB
QTSymb	$\rightarrow$ QTSYMB
BExp	$\rightarrow$ BEXP
BType	$\rightarrow$ BTYPE
EListXTList	$\rightarrow$ ELISTXTLIST
EList	$\rightarrow$ ELIST
TList	$\rightarrow$ TLIST

end

Not exported.

C.2.2   Indices

In the next couple of sections we introduce some machinery which, despite looking quite formidable at first sight, is actually conceptually very easy and makes 'editing-like' operations much easier to specify by letting us 'get our hands on' the subterms of objects. An *index* will be a record of the path through the abstract syntax tree leading to the desired subterm, simply described as a list of positive integers:

$$Index = \mathsf{N}_1^*$$

Index **shouldn't be visible.**

Index is partially ordered by:

$$\prec \; : Index \times Index \rightarrow \mathsf{B}$$
$$\prec(i,j) \quad \triangleq \quad \mathsf{len}\, i < \mathsf{len}\, j \wedge \forall n \in \mathsf{dom}\, i \cdot i(n) = j(n)$$

That is, *i* is between *j* and the root.

Not exported.

An index is 'valid' if it actually refers to some subterm of the object in question (note that the subterm of some object at index the empty list is the object itself):

$isValidIndex : Exp \times Index \rightarrow \mathbf{B}$
$isValidIndex(e, i) \quad \triangleq$
    if $i = [\,]$
    then true
    else let $n = $ hd i,
          $i' = $ tl i in
      cases e of
      $mk\text{-}QExp(qet, be)$ $\rightarrow i = [1] \vee n = 2 \wedge isValidIndex(be, i')$
      $mk\text{-}OExp(oet, elxtl) \rightarrow i = [1] \vee n = 2 \wedge isValidIndex(elxtl, i')$
      others false
      end

Not exported.

$isValidIndex : Type \times Index \rightarrow \mathbf{B}$
$isValidIndex(t, i) \quad \triangleq$
    if $i = [\,]$
    then true
    else let $n = $ hd i,
          $i' = $ tl i in
      cases t of
      $mk\text{-}SubType(be)$ $\rightarrow n = 1 \wedge isValidIndex(be, i')$
      $mk\text{-}QType(qtt, bt)$ $\rightarrow i = [1] \vee n = 2 \wedge isValidIndex(bt, i')$
      $mk\text{-}OType(ott, elxtl) \rightarrow i = [1] \vee n = 2 \wedge isValidIndex(elxtl, i')$
      others false
      end

Not exported.

$isValidIndex : BTerm \times Index \rightarrow \mathbf{B}$
$isValidIndex(bterm, i) \quad \triangleq$
    $i = [\,] \vee i = [1] \vee$
    hd $i = 2 \wedge isValidIndex(UNIVERSE(bterm),$ tl $i) \vee$
    hd $i = 3 \wedge isValidIndex(BODY(bterm),$ tl $i)$

Not exported.

$isValidIndex : EListXTList \times Index \rightarrow \mathbf{B}$
$isValidIndex(elxtl, i) \quad \triangleq$
    $i = [\,] \vee$ hd $i = 1 \wedge isValidIndex(ELIST(elxtl),$ tl $i) \vee$
    hd $i = 2 \wedge isValidIndex(TLIST(elxtl),$ tl $i)$

Not exported.

$isValidIndex : ArgList \times Index \rightarrow \mathbf{B}$
$isValidIndex(al, i) \quad \triangleq \quad i = [\,] \vee$ hd $i \leq$ len $al \wedge isValidIndex(al(\text{hd } i),$ tl $i)$

Not exported.

The set of valid indices of any construct is then simply given by the following function:

indices : *Construct* → *Index*-set
indices(*c*) △ {*i* ∈ *Index* | *isValidIndex*(*c*, *i*)}

Not exported.

C.2.3   Subterm Access

The subterm situated at some (valid) index in some object is then obtained via the following functions:

termAtIndex (*e*: *Exp*, *i*: *Index*) *term*: *Term*
pre *isValidIndex*(*e*, *i*)
post *term* = if *i* = [ ]
        then *e*
        else cases *e* of
             mk-QExp(*qet*, *be*)   → if hd *i* = 1
                           then *qet*
                           else *termAtIndex*(*be*, tl *i*)
             mk-OExp(*oet*, *elxtl*)→ if hd *i* = 1
                           then *oet*
                           else *termAtIndex*(*elxtl*, tl *i*)
            end

termAtIndex (*t*: *Type*, *i*: *Index*) *term*: *Term*
pre *isValidIndex*(*t*, *i*)
post *term* = if *i* = [ ]
        then *t*
        else cases *t* of
           mk-SubType(*be*)   → *termAtIndex*(*be*, tl *i*)
           mk-QType(*qtt*, *bt*) → if hd *i* = 1
                        then *qtt*
                        else *termAtIndex*(*bt*, tl *i*)
           mk-OType(*ott*, *elxtl*)→ if hd *i* = 1
                        then *ott*
                        else *termAtIndex*(*elxtl*, tl *i*)
           end

termAtIndex (*bterm*: *BTerm*, *i*: *Index*) *term*: *Term*
pre *isValidIndex*(*bterm*, *i*)

post *term* = if *i* = [ ]
              then *bterm*
              else cases hd *i* of
                        $1 \rightarrow$ *VAR(bterm)*
                        $2 \rightarrow$ *termAtIndex(UNIVERSE(bterm)*, tl *i*)
                        $3 \rightarrow$ *termAtIndex(BODY(bterm)*, tl *i*)
                     end

termAtIndex (elxtl: EListXTList, i: Index) term: Term
pre *isValidIndex(elxtl, i)*
post *term* = if *i* = [ ]
              then *elxtl*
              else if hd *i* = 1
                     then *termAtIndex(ELIST(elxtl)*, tl *i*)
                     else *termAtIndex(TLIST(elxtl)*, tl *i*)

termAtIndex (al: ArgList, i: Index) term: Term
pre *isValidIndex(al, i)*
post *term* = if *i* = [ ]
              then *al*
              else *termAtIndex(al(hd i)*, tl *i*)

None of the above functions should be exported, though some means of accessing subterms is clearly necessary and the user interface should provide such.

The *binding points* of some construct are the indices, if any, corresponding to the *VAR* fields of the construct's *BTerms*:

bindingPoints : Construct $\rightarrow$ Index-set
bindingPoints(c) $\;\triangleq$
      $\{i \mid i \neq [\,] \wedge isValidIndex(c, i) \wedge$
                              $termAtIndex(c, truncate(i)) \in BTerm \wedge last(i) = 1\}$

Not exported.

The two functions *last* and *truncate* return respectively the last element of some index and an index consisting of all but the last element of some index:

last (i: Index) n: N_1
pre *i* $\neq$ [ ]
post *n* = *i*(len *i*)

Not exported.

truncate (i: Index) i': Index
pre *i* $\neq$ [ ]
post *i'* = $[i(n) \mid 1 \leq n \leq$ len *i* $- 1]$

Not exported.

The species at some index is given by:

speciesAtIndex (*c*: *Construct*, *i*: *Index*) *spec*: *Species*
pre *isValidIndex*(*c*, *i*)
post *spec* = if *i* ∈ *bindingPoints*(*c*)
          then VSYMB
          else *species*(*termAtIndex*(*c*, *i*))

Not exported.

C.2.4 Equivalence Testing

Constructs will be considered equivalent up to *holes* (i.e. *NullThings* and *NullSymbs*) and renaming of bound variables (α-conversion). Basically, two constructs are equivalent if they are of the same class and if their component parts are equivalent. Symbols (other than *VSymbs*) are equivalent iff they're equal. A hole is equivalent to any other hole of the same class.

isEquivalentTo : *Construct* × *Construct* → B
isEquivalentTo(*c*, *c'*) △
    let *is* = *indices*(*c*),
      is' = *indices*(*c'*) in
    is = *is'* ∧
    ∃*m* ∈ *VSymb* $\xleftarrow{m}$ *VSymb* ·
        dom *m* = *boundVars*(*c*) ∧ rng *m* = *boundVars*(*c'*) ∧
        ∀*i* ∈ *is* ·
            let *term* = *termAtIndex*(*c*, *i*),
              term' = *termAtIndex*(*c'*, *i*) in
            classOf(*term*) = *classOf*(*term'*) ∧
            (*term* ∈ *boundVars*(*c*) ⇒ *m*(*term*) = *term'*) ∧
            (*term* ∈ *leaves*(*c*) − *boundVars*(*c*) ⇒ *term* = *term'*)

Exported.

C.2.5 Building

Some renaming of bound variables may be necessary when creating new objects of those syntactic classes having invariants. For example, the invariant on *BExp* is unlikely to be satisfied by an arbitrary variable/type/expression triple. This means that you can't just create an object with an invariant out of the requisite arbitrary components. A *build-function* provides a means of doing so, however, by converting all the components to equivalent components such that the equivalent components do satisfy the invariant, then creating the desired object out of these new components. There is thus a build-function for each syntactic class which has an invariant.
All functions in this section should be used by the system whenever creating new objects of the relevant type. They don't need to be accessible to the user otherwise, though.

An *EListXTList* is therefore built out of an *EList* and a *TList* equivalent to the ones you first thought of:

build-EListXTList (*el*: *EList*, *tl*: *TList*) *elxtl*: *EListXTList*
post *isEquivalentTo*(*ELIST*(*elxtl*), *el*) ∧ *isEquivalentTo*(*TLIST*(*elxtl*), *tl*)

And similarly for an *EList* ...

> build-EList (*el*: *Exp**) *el'*: *EList*
> post len *el* = len *el'* ∧ ∀*i* ∈ dom *el* · *isEquivalentTo*(*el*(*i*), *el'*(*i*))

... and a *TList*.

> build-TList (*tl*: *Type**) *tl'*: *TList*
> post len *tl* = len *tl'* ∧ ∀*i* ∈ dom *tl* · *isEquivalentTo*(*tl*(*i*), *tl'*(*i*))

The situation for both *BExp* and *BType* is somewhat different, however, due to the presence of the extra clause in the invariant forbidding the object's bound variable from occurring free in the object's universe. The current thinking here is that the bound variable and all its occurrences in the prospective body get renamed in order to avoid this clash[5].

> build-BExp (*vt*: *VSymb*, *t*: *Type*, *e*: *Exp*) *be*: *BExp*
> post *isEquivalentTo*(*UNIVERSE*(*be*), *t*) ∧
>   *isEquivalentTo*(*renameFreeVars*(*BODY*(*be*), {*VAR*(*be*) ↦ *vt*}), *e*)

> build-BType (*vt*: *VSymb*, *t*: *Type*, *t'*: *Type*) *bt*: *BType*
> post *isEquivalentTo*(*UNIVERSE*(*bt*), *t*) ∧
>   *isEquivalentTo*(*renameFreeVars*(*BODY*(*bt*), {*VAR*(*bt*) ↦ *vt*}), *t'*)

It is perhaps worth noting at this point that, although these operations (and indeed many others appearing later) look (and are!) decidedly non-deterministic, all possible results are mutually equivalent. When it comes to implementing such operations, however, we would hope that renaming should only be carried out when it's absolutely unavoidable, and even then should be kept to the minimum necessary to ensure soundness.

C.2.6 Editing Subterms

This section contains functions for general editing of expressions, types and assertions. The basic idea is that of structure editing: any subterm of any object can be replaced by an object of the correct species; an index designates the subterm to be edited.

The first set of operations simply replaces the subterm at some given index by a given term. A subterm can be so replaced if the replacement is of the correct species, though if the subterm being replaced is actually a variable at a binding point the replacement variable should not occur free in the associated universe[6].
The structure-editing operations described by the functions in this section should be available to the user as part of the general user interface.

---

[5]Contrast this with the previous treatment in which a pre-condition on the build-functions effectively forbade creation of the object at all if the bound variable occurred free in the prospective universe

[6]This is the only case we can think of where it's not clear how to preserve the invariants by simple renaming of bound variables, courtesy of the build-functions of the previous section. Disallowing such replacements is not a problem in any of the places later in this specification where these term-replacing functions are used , however (e.g. in the treatment of unfolding definitions), though if these operations were to be thought of as simple operations for single-step structure editing it is clear that certain editing actions would have to be ruled out.

$isValidTermReplace : Construct \times Index \times Term \rightarrow \mathbf{B}$
$isValidTermReplace(c, i, term)$ $\triangle$
    let $spec = speciesAtIndex(c, i),$
       $spec' =$ if $spec = $ VSYMB
           then $classOf(term)$
           else $species(term)$
    in
    $isValidIndex(c, i) \wedge spec = spec' \wedge$
    $(i \in bindingPoints(c) \Rightarrow$
                 $term \notin freeVars(UNIVERSE(termAtIndex(c, truncate(i)))))$

Variables free in the replacement term may get captured by binders in c and variables
bound in it may need to be renamed so that they don't clash with variables bound in
c. In addition, variables bound in c but whose scope does not include the replacement
term may need to be renamed to avoid clashes with free variables being introduced in the
replacement term[7].

$replaceTermAt\ (e: Exp, i: Index, term: Term)\ e': Exp$
pre $isValidTermReplace(e, i, term)$
post $e' = $ if $i = [\ ]$
        then $term$
        else let $j = $ hd $i,$
             $i' = $ tl i in
        cases e of
        mk-$QExp(qet, be)$ $\rightarrow$ if $j = 1$
                       then mk-$QExp(term, be)$
                       else let $be' = replaceTermAt(be, i', term)$ in
                            mk-$QExp(qet, be')$
        mk-$OExp(oet, elxtl) \rightarrow$ if $j = 1$
                       then mk-$OExp(term, elxtl)$
                       else let $elxtl' = replaceTermAt(elxtl, i', term)$ in
                            mk-$OExp(oet, elxtl')$
        end

$replaceTermAt\ (t: Type, i: Index, term: Term)\ t': Type$
pre $isValidTermReplace(t, i, term)$

---

[7]These contorted conditions on what needs to be renamed are the main reason behind our return to the
rather more concrete -description of the term-replacement operations. It was felt that, although a treatment
analogous to that used in the renaming of free variables (see later in this section) would be perfectly possible,
a series of auxiliary functions would be needed to define the scope of the renaming. In the more concrete
description this is all taken care of automatically by the build-functions.

```
post t' = if i = [ ]
          then term
          else let j = hd i,
                   i' = tl i  in
               cases t  of
               mk-SubType(be)      → let be' = replaceTermAt(be, i', term)  in
                                        mk-SubType(be')
               mk-QType(qtt, bt)   → if j = 1
                                     then mk-QType(term, bt)
                                     else let bt' = replaceTermAt(bt, i', term)  in
                                              mk-QType(qtt, bt')
               mk-OType(ott, elxtl)→ if j = 1
                                     then mk-OType(term, elxtl)
                                     else let elxtl' = replaceTermAt(elxtl, i', term)  in
                                              mk-OType(ott, elxtl')
          end
```

```
replaceTermAt (be: BExp, i: Index, term: Term) be': BExp
pre isValidTermReplace(be, i, term)
post be' = if i = [ ]
           then term
           else let j = hd i,
                    i' = tl i,
                    vt = if j = 1
                         then term
                         else VAR(be),
                    t = if j = 2
                        then replaceTermAt(UNIVERSE(be), i', term)
                        else UNIVERSE(be),
                    e = if j = 3
                        then replaceTermAt(BODY(be), i', term)
                        else BODY(be)
                in
           build-BExp(vt, t, e)
```

```
replaceTermAt (bt: BType, i: Index, term: Term) bt': BType
pre isValidTermReplace(bt, i, term)
```

post *bt′* = if *i* = [ ]
      then *term*
      else let *j* = hd *i*,
             i′ = tl *i*,
             vt = if *j* = 1
                  then *term*
                  else *VAR(bt)*,
             t = if *j* = 2
                  then *replaceTermAt(UNIVERSE(bt), i′, term)*
                  else *UNIVERSE(bt)*,
             t′ = if *j* = 3
                  then *replaceTermAt(BODY(bt), i′, term)*
                  else *BODY(bt)*
          in
        build-BType(vt, t, t′)

replaceTermAt (elxtl: EListXTList, i: Index, term: Term) elxtl′: EListXTList
pre *isValidTermReplace(elxtl, i, term)*
post *elxtl′* = if *i* = [ ]
      then *term*
      else let *j* = hd *i*,
             i′ = tl *i*,
             el = if *j* = 1
                  then *replaceTermAt(ELIST(elxtl), i′, term)*
                  else *ELIST(elxtl)*,
             tl = if *j* = 2
                  then *replaceTermAt(TLIST(elxtl), i′, term)*
                  else *TLIST(elxtl)*
          in
        build-EListXTList(el, tl)

replaceTermAt (el: EList, i: Index, term: Term) el′: EList
pre *isValidTermReplace(el, i, term)*
post *el′* = if *i* = [ ]
      then *term*
      else let *j* = hd *i*,
             i′ = tl *i*,
             e = *replaceTermAt(el(j), i′, term)* in
          build-EList(el † {j ↦ e})

replaceTermAt (tl: TList, i: Index, term: Term) tl′: TList
pre *isValidTermReplace(tl, i, term)*
post *tl′* = if *i* = [ ]
      then *term*
      else let *j* = hd *i*,
             i′ = tl *i*,
             t = *replaceTermAt(tl(j), i′, term)* in
          build-TList(tl † {j ↦ t})

This next function renames metavariable symbols in some construct. Note that metavariable symbols may get 'collapsed together' in an inconsistent way as part of this process (e.g. if $m_1 \mapsto m$ and $m_2 \mapsto m$ where m_1 and m_2 expect different numbers of arguments).

$renameMSymbs$ (c: *Contruct*, *mem*: *MESymb* $\xrightarrow{m}$ *MESymb*,
$\qquad\qquad\qquad$ *mtm*: *MTSymb* $\xrightarrow{m}$ *MTSymb*) c': *Construct*
post let $is = indices(c)$ in
$\qquad indices(c') = is \wedge$
$\qquad \forall i \in is \cdot$
$\qquad\qquad$ let $term = termAtIndex(c, i),$
$\qquad\qquad\quad mm = mem \cup mtm$ in
$\qquad\qquad classOf(termAtIndex(c', i)) = classOf(term) \wedge$
$\qquad\qquad (term \in leaves(c) - \text{dom } mm \Rightarrow termAtIndex(c', i) = term) \wedge$
$\qquad\qquad (term \in \text{dom } mm \Rightarrow termAtIndex(c', i) = mm(term))$

This one's probably not very useful on its own. After all, it can be mimicked by *instantiate.*

Finally, there's a similar operation for renaming free variables (note that it is perfectly possible to rename two different free variables to the same thing with this operation. The result of renaming the free variables in some construct yields a construct which is therefore not necessarily equivalent to the original one):

$renameFreeVars$ (c: *Construct*, m: *VSymb* $\xrightarrow{m}$ *VSymb*) c': *Construct*
post let $is = indices(c)$ in
$\qquad indices(c') = is \wedge$
$\qquad \exists c'' \in Construct \cdot$
$\qquad isEquivalentTo(c, c'') \wedge$
$\qquad boundVars(c'') \cap \text{dom } m = \{\ \} \wedge boundVars(c'') \cap \text{rng } m = \{\ \} \wedge$
$\qquad \forall i \in is \cdot$
$\qquad\qquad$ let $term = termAtIndex(c'', i)$ in
$\qquad\qquad classOf(termAtIndex(c', i)) = classOf(term) \wedge$
$\qquad\qquad (term \in leaves(c'') - \text{dom } m \Rightarrow termAtIndex(c', i) = term) \wedge$
$\qquad\qquad (term \in \text{dom } m \Rightarrow termAtIndex(c', i) = m(term))$

Might be useful.

C.3   Sequents and Rules

C.3.1   Sequents

$Sequent ::\ NFV \qquad :\ VSymb\text{-set}$
$\qquad\qquad\quad PREMISES\ :\ Exp\text{-set}$
$\qquad\qquad\quad UPSHOT\quad :\ Exp$

Sequents should be visible.

The *exps* in a sequent are its *premises* plus its *upshot*:

exps : *Sequent* → *Exp*-set
exps(*s*) △   *PREMISES*(*s*) ∪ {*UPSHOT*(*s*)}

Not exported.

Its (apparent[8]) free variables are simply those of its exps:

freeVars : *Sequent* → *VSymb*-set
freeVars(*s*) △   ∪{*freeVars*(*e*) | *e* ∈ *exps*(*s*)}

Not exported.

A sequent is *proper* if its actual free variables and its apparent free variables are the same:

isProper : *Sequent* → B
isProper(*s*) △   *NFV*(*s*) = *freeVars*(*s*)

Not exported.

And a sequent can be converted into a proper sequent by making its *NFV* field the same as its apparent free variables:

properSequent : *Sequent* → *Sequent*
properSequent(*s*) △   *mk-Sequent*(*freeVars*(*s*), *PREMISES*(*s*), *UPSHOT*(*s*))

Not exported.

A sequent is *trivially true* if its upshot is amongst its premises (strictly if something equivalent to its upshot is amongst its premises):

isTriviallyTrue : *Sequent* → B
isTriviallyTrue(*s*) △   ∃*e* ∈ *PREMISES*(*s*) · *isEquivalentTo*(*e*, *UPSHOT*(*s*))

Not exported.

Renaming metavariable symbols in a sequent is achieved simply by doing the renaming on each of its component expressions:

renameMSymbs : *Sequent* × *MESymb* $\xrightarrow{m}$ *MESymb* × *MTSymb* $\xrightarrow{m}$ *MTSymb*
    → *Sequent*
renameMSymbs(*s*, *mem*, *mtm*) △
    let *mk-Sequent*(*vts*, *prems*, *up*) = *s*,
        prems' = {*renameMSymbs*(*e*, *mem*, *mtm*) | *e* ∈ *prems*} in
    mk-Sequent(*vts*, *prems'*, *renameMSymbs*(*up*, *mem*, *mtm*))

Should be possible, but covered by instantiation of sequents.

Renaming of free variables is pretty similar, but 'variable capture' (i.e. renaming some actual free variable to some variable which is apparently, but not actually, free in the sequent) is ruled out:

renameFreeVars (*s*: *Sequent*, *vm*: *VSymb* $\xrightarrow{m}$ *VSymb*) *s'*: *Sequent*
pre let *vm'* = *NFV*(*s*) ◁ *vm* in
    rng *vm'* ∩ (*freeVars*(*s*) − *NFV*(*s*)) = { }

---

[8]As distinct from *actual* i.e. the ones stated as being free in the *NFV* field

post let *mk-Sequent(vts, es, e) = s*,
  $vm' = vts \lhd vm$,
  $es' = \{renameFreeVars(\hat{e}, vm') \mid \hat{e} \in es\}$,
  $e' = renameFreeVars(e, vm')$,
  $vts' = (vts - \mathrm{dom}\ vm) \cup \mathrm{rng}\ vm'$ in
 $s' = mk\text{-}Sequent(vts', es', e')$

Exported.

Note that the precondition on the above function is trivially true for proper sequents.

A sequent can be weakened by adding hypotheses and/or collapsing free variables. A sequent *establishes* a second sequent if the second sequent is weaker than it:

establishesSequent : *Sequent* × *Sequent* → B
establishesSequent(s, s') $\triangleq$
  $\exists m \in VSymb \xrightarrow{m} VSymb \cdot$
    dom $m = NFV(s) \wedge \mathrm{rng}\ m \subseteq NFV(s')$
    $\wedge (freeVars(s) - NFV(s)) \cap NFV(s') = \{\ \}$
    $\wedge isEquivalentTo(renameFreeVars(UPSHOT(s), m), UPSHOT(s'))$
    $\wedge \forall e \in PREMISES(s) \cdot \exists e' \in PREMISES(s') \cdot$
       $isEquivalentTo(renameFreeVars(e, m), e')$

Not exported.

An expression can also establish a sequent if its free variables are disjoint from the sequent's new free variables and if it's equivalent to the sequent's upshot.

establishesSequent : *Exp* × *Sequent* → B
establishesSequent(e, s) $\triangleq$
  $NFV(s) \cap freeVars(e) = \{\ \} \wedge isEquivalentTo(e, UPSHOT(s))$

Not exported.

Claim: $\forall e \in Exp, s \in Sequent \cdot$
  establishesSequent(e, s) $\Leftrightarrow$ *establishesSequent(mk-Sequent(\{\ \}, \{\ \}, e), s)*

The following definition of equivalence of sequents is something of a cheat – it's not really a definition of equivalence of sequents at all, except in a very limited sense. As it stands, it says that sequents can only be equivalent if they're proper, which is clearly nonsense. However, this function is only used in the function *properRuleStmt* below, and its sole purpose in life is to rename the free variables in the sequent hypotheses of a rule statement in such a way that no two sequent hypotheses have (actual) free variables in common. Coupled with the fact that sequent hypotheses appearing in proper rule statements have to be proper, this means that, at least until someone comes up with a real need for a function testing for general equivalence of sequents, this one is quite adequate for all purposes for which it was designed!

isEquivalentTo (*s*: *Sequent*, *s'*: *Sequent*) *r*: B
pre *isProper(s)* $\wedge$ *isProper(s')*

post r $\Leftrightarrow$

$\exists m \in VSymb \xleftarrow{m} VSymb, m' \in Exp \xrightarrow{m} Exp \cdot$
$\quad$ dom $m = NFV(s) \wedge$ rng $m = NFV(s') \wedge$
$\quad$ dom $m' = PREMISES(s) \wedge$ rng $m' = PREMISES(s') \wedge$
$\quad$ isEquivalentTo(UPSHOT(s'), renameFreeVars(UPSHOT(s), m)) $\wedge$
$\quad \forall e \in$ dom $m' \cdot$
$\quad\quad$ isEquivalentTo(m'(e), renameFreeVars(e, m))

Not exported.

C.3.2 Rules

$Rulemap = Rule\text{-}ref \xrightarrow{m} Rule$

$Rule$ :: $STMT$ $\quad$: $RuleStmt$
$\quad\quad\quad$ $THEORY$: $Theory\text{-}ref$
$\quad\quad\quad$ $PROOF$ $\quad$: $[Proof]$

where

$inv\text{-}Rule(r)$ $\quad \triangleq$ $\quad isProper(STMT(r)) \wedge is\text{-}OK\text{-}RuleStmt(STMT(r))$

Rules should be visible.

Note that rules now have an invariant to the effect that their statement should be proper (i.e. its sequent hypotheses should be proper and shouldn't share free variables[9]) and OK (i.e. it should contain no placeholders, its ordinary hypotheses and conclusion should contain no free variables, and *OTerms* appear consistently) (see below).

Rules with a null *PROOF* field are called *axioms*; the rest are called *derived rules* – it's important not to confuse an axiom with a derived rule having an 'empty' proof. In this treatment, a rule has a single *Proof* but a *Proof* can contain multiple *proof attempts*. One of these proof attempts is designated as the actual (or currently favoured) proof by the *ROOT* field of *Proof* (see §C.8.9). Of course, different rules may have equivalent statements. This makes the circularity check on consistency of the collection of derived rules simple.

$RuleStmt$ :: $SEQHYPS$ $\quad$: $Sequent\text{-}set$
$\quad\quad\quad\quad$ $ORDHYPS$: $Exp\text{-}set$
$\quad\quad\quad\quad$ $CONCL$ $\quad\quad$: Exp

A rule statement is *proper* if its sequent hypotheses are proper and don't share free variables.

$isProper : RuleStmt \rightarrow \mathbb{B}$
$isProper(rs)$ $\quad \triangleq$
$\quad \forall s_1 \in SEQHYPS(rs) \cdot$
$\quad\quad isProper(s_1) \wedge \forall s_2 \in SEQHYPS(rs) \cdot s_1 \neq s_2 \Rightarrow NFV(s_1) \cap NFV(s_2) = \{ \}$

---

[9]This latter condition arose out of the recent UI discussions where it was decided that these free variables will be treated in much the same way as metavariable symbols, e.g. in the rule instantiator or whatever its fancy name was. Any 'instantiation' thereof by the user should be restricted to a single sequent, hence the invariant.

Not exported.

The expressions in a rule statement are naturally those in all its bits:

$exps : RuleStmt \rightarrow Exp\text{-set}$
$exps(rs) \quad \triangleq$
   let $es = \bigcup\{exps(s) \mid s \in SEQHYPS(rs)\}$ in
   $es \cup ORDHYPS(rs) \cup \{CONCL(rs)\}$

Not exported.

The oTerms in a rule statement or a sequent are naturally those in all its exps:

$oTerms : (Sequent \mid RuleStmt) \rightarrow OTerm\text{-set}$
$oTerms(sr) \quad \triangleq \quad \bigcup\{oTerms(e) \mid e \in exps(sr)\}$

Not exported.

The meSymbs in a rule statement are likewise those in all its exps:

$meSymbs : RuleStmt \rightarrow MESymb\text{-set}$
$meSymbs(rs) \quad \triangleq \quad \bigcup\{meSymbs(e) \mid e \in exps(rs)\}$

Not exported.

As are the meSymbs.

$mtSymbs : RuleStmt \rightarrow MTSymb\text{-set}$
$mtSymbs(rs) \quad \triangleq \quad \bigcup\{mtSymbs(e) \mid e \in exps(rs)\}$

Not exported.

The next function tests that the *OTerms* in a construct or a rule statement have consistent argument sizes:

$hasConsisArgSizes : (Construct \mid RuleStmt) \rightarrow \mathsf{B}$
$hasConsisArgSizes(cr) \quad \triangleq$
   let $ots = oTerms(cr)$ in
   $\forall oterm, oterm' \in ots \cdot$
    let $symb = SYMBOL(oterm)$ in
    $symb \notin NullSymbs \wedge symb = SYMBOL(oterm')$
    $\Rightarrow argSize(oterm) = argSize(oterm')$

Not exported.

A construct/sequent/rule statement (*CSR*) is consistent with some rule statement if it only contains metavariable symbols which occur in that rule statement and if they have the same argument sizes as those in the rule statement. Note that this function should probably strictly have a pre-condition to ensure that both the *CSR* and the rule statement themselves have consistent argument sizes. In the cases where this function is used, however, (see §C.8.7) this is automatically the case.

$isConsisWithRuleStmt : CSR \times RuleStmt \rightarrow B$
$isConsisWithRuleStmt(csr, rs) \quad \triangleq$
$\quad \forall oterm \in oTerms(csr) \cdot$
$\qquad SYMBOL(oterm) \in (MESymb \mid MTSymb) \Rightarrow$
$\qquad \exists oterm' \in oTerms(rs) \cdot$
$\qquad\qquad SYMBOL(oterm) = SYMBOL(oterm')$
$\qquad\qquad \wedge argSize(oterm) = argSize(oterm')$

A rule statement is OK if all its expressions are full, its ordinary hypotheses and conclusion are closed, and *OTerms* appear consistently throughout (although it might still have null parts):

$is\text{-}OK\text{-}RuleStmt : RuleStmt \rightarrow B$
$is\text{-}OK\text{-}RuleStmt(rs) \quad \triangleq$
$\quad hasConsisArgSizes(rs) \wedge freeVars(CONCL(rs)) = \{\ \} \wedge$
$\quad \forall e \in exps(rs) \cdot isFull(e) \wedge \forall e \in ORDHYPS(rs) \cdot freeVars(e) = \{\ \}$

Not exported.

A rule statement can be made proper by making its sequent hypotheses proper and renaming free variables therein so as to avoid clashes.

$properRuleStmt\ (rs: RuleStmt)\ rs': RuleStmt$
$post\ isProper(rs') \wedge CONCL(rs') = CONCL(rs) \wedge$
$\quad ORDHYPS(rs') = ORDHYPS(rs) \wedge$
$\quad let\ ss = \{properSequent(s) \mid s \in SEQHYPS(rs)\}\ in$
$\quad \exists m \in Sequent \xrightarrow{m} Sequent \cdot$
$\qquad dom\ m = ss \wedge rng\ m = SEQHYPS(rs') \wedge$
$\qquad \forall s \in ss \cdot isEquivalentTo(s, m(s))$

Not exported.

Proper rule statements are equivalent (in the sense required above) if all their components are equivalent:

$isEquivalentTo\ (rs: RuleStmt, rs': RuleStmt)\ r: B$
$pre\ isProper(rs) \wedge isProper(rs')$
$post\ let\ mk\text{-}RuleStmt(ss, es, e) = rs,$
$\qquad mk\text{-}RuleStmt(ss', es', e') = rs'\ in$
$\quad isEquivalentTo(e, e')$
$\quad \wedge \exists em \in Exp \xrightarrow{m} Exp \cdot$
$\qquad dom\ em = es \wedge rng\ em = es' \wedge \forall \hat{e} \in es \cdot isEquivalentTo(\hat{e}, em(\hat{e}))$
$\quad \wedge \exists sm \in Sequent \xrightarrow{m} Sequent \cdot$
$\qquad dom\ sm = ss \wedge rng\ sm = ss' \wedge \forall \hat{s} \in ss \cdot isEquivalentTo(\hat{s}, sm(\hat{s}))$

A rule is OK if its statement is equivalent to the rule statement of its proof (if any):

$is\text{-}OK\text{-}Rule : Rule \rightarrow B$
$is\text{-}OK\text{-}Rule(mk\text{-}Rule(rs, th, p)) \quad \triangleq$
$\quad p \neq nil \Rightarrow isEquivalentTo(rs, properRuleStmt(ruleStmt(p)))$

Background. Warning when violated.

For later convenience, we'll define a function for renaming the free variables in the sequent hypotheses of a proper rule statement according to some 1–1 map:

> *renameFreeVars (rs: RuleStmt, vm: VSymb $\xleftrightarrow{m}$ VSymb) rs': RuleStmt*
> pre *isProper(rs)*
> post let *ss = {renameFreeVars(s, vm) | s ∈ SEQHYPS(rs)}* in
>   *rs' = mk-RuleStmt(ss, ORDHYPS(rs), CONCL(rs))*

Not exported.

A rule statement can be weakened by collapsing metavariable symbols, adding hypotheses, strengthening sequent hypotheses, converting sequent hypotheses to ordinary hypotheses which establish them, or any combination thereof. A rule statement *establishes* a weaker rule statement:

> *establishesRuleStmt : RuleStmt × RuleStmt → ℬ*
> *establishesRuleStmt(rs, rs')* △
>   let *mk-RuleStmt(shs, es, e) = rs,*
>   *mk-RuleStmt(shs', es', e') = rs'* in
>   ∃*mem: MESymb $\xrightarrow{m}$ MESymb, mtm: MTSymb $\xrightarrow{m}$ MTSymb* ·
>   *isEquivalentTo(e', renameMSymbs(e, mem, mtm))*
>   ∧ ∀*h ∈ es* · ∃*h' ∈ es'* · *isEquivalentTo(h', renameMSymbs(h, mem, mtm))*
>   ∧ ∀*s ∈ shs* ·
>   ∃*s' ∈ shs'* · *establishesSequent(s', renameMSymbs(s, mem, mtm))*
>   ∨ ∃*h' ∈ es'* · *establishesSequent(h', renameMSymbs(s, mem, mtm))*
>   ∨ *isTriviallyTrue(s)*

Not exported.

Intuitively, any use of *rs'* in a proof can be replaced by a use of *rs* (with metavariable symbols renamed appropriately). A more sophisticated test might involve instantiating the metavariable symbols of *rs* instead of merely renaming them; the main point about the test given here, however, is that rules should be considered equivalent up to renaming of metavariable symbols. This function will be used to check validations of theory morphisms (cf. §C.7.5 below), so it probably doesn't matter very much if it can't be implemented very efficiently. On the other hand, if it is found to be too impractical a less sophisticated test should perhaps be substituted.

C.4 Instantiation and Pattern-matching

Instantiation consists of replacing expression metavariable symbols with expressions and type metavariable symbols with types.

> *Instantiation* :: *MEMAP : MESymb $\xrightarrow{m}$ Exp*
>   *MTMAP : MTSymb $\xrightarrow{m}$ Type*

Should be visible.

When the expressions or types introduced by the instantiation have placeholders these are filled in with the appropriate elements of the arguments of the metavariables. For this to be possible, the metavariables must have at least as many arguments as the arity of the object replacing the metavariable symbol. In order to help test that this condition is satisfied, a function testing whether an object is 'fillable' by some EListXTList (the expression arity of the object must be at most the number of elements in the ELIST of the EListXTList and the type arity at most the number of elements in its TLIST) is needed.

isFillableBy : *Construct* × *EListXTList* → B
isFillableBy(*c*, *elxtl*) ≜
  eArity(*c*) ≤ len *ELIST*(*elxtl*) ∧ *tArity*(*c*) ≤ len *TLIST*(*elxtl*)

Not exported.

isInstantiableBy : *Construct* × *Instantiation* → B
isInstantiableBy(*c*, *inst*) ≜
  let *im* = *MEMAP*(*inst*) ∪ *MTMAP*(*inst*) in
  ∀*oterm* ∈ *oTerms*(*c*) ·
    SYMBOL(*oterm*) ∈ dom *im*
    ⇒ *isFillableBy*(*im*(*SYMBOL*(*oterm*)), *ARGS*(*oterm*))

Not exported.

To avoid capture we'll need to know what free variables can be introduced by an instantiation:

freeVars : *Instantiation* → *VSymb*-set
freeVars(*inst*) ≜
  ∪{*freeVars*(*def*) | *def* ∈ rng *MEMAP*(*inst*) ∪ rng *MTMAP*(*inst*)}

Not exported.

Instantiation of objects is now straightforward. Metavariable symbols occurring in the domain of the instantiation are replaced by their image under the instantiation, and any placeholders in this image are filled in with the arguments of the metavariable so instantiated. Other metavariable symbols are left unchanged. As part of the process, some bound variables might need to be renamed in order to avoid clashes with and capture of free variables introduced by the instantiation.

There follows a suite of functions for doing simple instantiation without capture of free variables (assuming, of course, that said object is in fact instantiable!):

instantiate (*e*: *Exp*, *inst*: *Instantiation*) *e'*: *Exp*
pre *isInstantiableBy*(*e*, *inst*)

post $\exists e'' \in Exp \cdot$
       $isEquivalentTo(e, e'') \land boundVars(e'') \cap freeVars(inst) = \{ \} \land$
       $e' = $ **cases** e'' **of**
          $mk\text{-}QExp(qet, be) \quad \rightarrow mk\text{-}QExp(qet, instantiate(be, inst))$
          $mk\text{-}OExp(oet, elxtl) \rightarrow$ **let** $elxtl' = instantiate(elxtl, inst)$ **in**
                    if $oet \in$ **dom** $MEMAP(inst)$
                    then $fillPHoles(MEMAP(inst)(oet), elxtl')$
                    else $mk\text{-}OExp(oet, elxtl')$
         others e''
         end

Exported.

The *fillPHoles* operations are specified below.

$instantiate$ (t: *Type*, $inst$: *Instantiation*) t': *Type*
pre $isInstantiableBy(t, inst)$
post $\exists t'' \in Type \cdot$
    $isEquivalentTo(t, t'') \land boundVars(t'') \cap freeVars(inst) = \{ \} \land$
    $t' = $ **cases** t'' **of**
       $mk\text{-}SubType(be) \qquad \rightarrow mk\text{-}SubType(instantiate(be, inst))$
       $mk\text{-}QType(qtt, bt) \quad \rightarrow mk\text{-}QType(qtt, instantiate(bt, inst))$
       $mk\text{-}OType(ott, elxtl) \rightarrow$ **let** $elxtl' = instantiate(elxtl, inst)$ **in**
                  if $ott \in$ **dom** $MTMAP(inst)$
                  then $fillPHoles(MTMAP(inst)(ott), elxtl')$
                  else $mk\text{-}OType(ott, elxtl')$
      others t''
      end

Exported.

$instantiate$ (be: *BExp*, $inst$: *Instantiation*) be': *BExp*
pre $isInstantiableBy(be, inst)$
post $\exists be'' \in BExp \cdot$
    $isEquivalentTo(be, be'') \land VAR(be'') \notin freeVars(inst) \land$
    let $t = instantiate(UNIVERSE(be''), inst),$
       $e = instantiate(BODY(be''), inst)$ **in**
    $be' = build\text{-}BExp(VAR(be''), t, e)$

Not exported.

$instantiate$ (bt: *BType*, $inst$: *Instantiation*) bt': *BType*
pre $isInstantiableBy(bt, inst)$
post $\exists bt'' \in BType \cdot$
    $isEquivalentTo(bt, bt'') \land VAR(bt'') \notin freeVars(inst) \land$
    let $t = instantiate(UNIVERSE(bt''), inst),$
       $t' = instantiate(BODY(bt''), inst)$ **in**
    $bt' = build\text{-}BType(VAR(bt''), t, t')$

Not exported.

instantiate (elxtl: EListXTList, inst: Instantiation) elxtl': EListXTList
pre *isInstantiableBy(elxtl, inst)*
post let *el = instantiate(ELIST(elxtl), inst),*
      tl = instantiate(TLIST(elxtl), inst) in
  elxtl' = build-EListXTList(el, tl)

Not exported.

instantiate (tl: TList, inst: Instantiation) tl': TList
pre *isInstantiableBy(tl, inst)*
post *tl' = build-TList([instantiate(tl(i), inst) | i ∈ dom tl])*

Not exported.

instantiate (el: EList, inst: Instantiation) el': EList
pre *isInstantiableBy(el, inst)*
post *el' = build-EList([instantiate(el(i), inst) | i ∈ dom el])*

Not exported.

The auxiliary functions for filling placeholders follow. They sometimes need to rename
bound variables to avoid variable capture.

fillPHoles (e: Exp, elxtl: EListXTList) e': Exp
pre *isFillableBy(e, elxtl)*
post *e' =* cases *e* of
        mk-EPHole(n)   → *ELIST(elxtl)(n)*
        mk-QExp(qet, be)   → *mk-QExp(qet, fillPHoles(be, elxtl))*
        mk-OExp(oet, elxtl') → *mk-OExp(oet, fillPHoles(elxtl', elxtl))*
        others *e*
        end

Not exported.

fillPHoles (t: Type, elxtl: EListXTList) t': Type
pre *isFillableBy(t, elxtl)*
post *t' =* cases *t* of
        mk-TPHole(n)   → *TLIST(elxtl)(n)*
        mk-SubType(be)   → *mk-SubType(fillPHoles(be, elxtl))*
        mk-QType(qtt, bt)   → *mk-QType(qtt, fillPHoles(bt, elxtl))*
        mk-OType(ott, elxtl') → *mk-OType(ott, fillPHoles(elxtl', elxtl))*
        others *t*
        end

Not exported.

fillPHoles (be: BExp, elxtl: EListXTList) be': BExp
pre *isFillableBy(be, elxtl)*

    post $\exists be'' \in BExp \cdot$
        $isEquivalentTo(be, be'') \wedge VAR(be'') \notin freeVars(elxtl) \wedge$
        let $t = fillPHoles(UNIVERSE(be''), elxtl),$
          $e = fillPHoles(BODY(be''), elxtl)$ in
        $be' = build\text{-}BExp(VAR(be''), t, e)$

Not exported.

    fillPHoles $(bt: BType, elxtl: EListXTList)$ $bt': BType$
    pre $isFillableBy(bt, elxtl)$
    post $\exists bt'' \in BType \cdot$
        $isEquivalentTo(bt, bt'') \wedge VAR(bt'') \notin freeVars(elxtl) \wedge$
        let $t = fillPHoles(UNIVERSE(bt''), elxtl),$
          $e = fillPHoles(BODY(bt''), elxtl)$ in
        $bt' = build\text{-}BType(VAR(bt''), t, e)$

Not exported.

    fillPHoles $(elxtl: EListXTList, elxtl': EListXTList)$ $elxtl'': EListXTList$
    pre $isFillableBy(elxtl, elxtl')$
    post let $el = fillPHoles(ELIST(elxtl), elxtl'),$
        $tl = fillPHoles(TLIST(elxtl), elxtl')$ in
     $elxtl'' = build\text{-}EListXTList(el, tl)$

Not exported.

    fillPHoles $(tl: TList, elxtl: EListXTList)$ $tl': TList$
    pre $isFillableBy(tl, elxtl)$
    post $tl' = build\text{-}TList([fillPHoles(tl(i), elxtl) \mid i \in \text{dom } tl])$

Not exported.

    fillPHoles $(el: EList, elxtl: EListXTList)$ $el': EList$
    pre $isFillableBy(el, elxtl)$
    post $el' = build\text{-}EList([fillPHoles(el(i), elxtl) \mid i \in \text{dom } el])$

Not exported.

A sequent or a rule statement is instantiable if each of its component expressions is separately instantiable:

    isInstantiableBy : $(Sequent \mid RuleStmt) \times Instantiation \rightarrow \mathbb{B}$
    isInstantiableBy$(sr, inst)$ $\triangleq$ $\forall e \in exps(sr) \cdot isInstantiableBy(e, inst)$

Not exported.

An instance of a sequent is built by instantiating its component expressions:

    instantiate $(s: Sequent, inst: Instantiation)$ $s': Sequent$
    pre $isInstantiableBy(s, inst)$
    post let $es = \{instantiate(e, inst) \mid e \in PREMISES(s)\},$
        $e' = instantiate(UPSHOT(s), inst)$ in
     $s' = mk\text{-}Sequent(NFV(s), es, e')$

Exported.

And a rule statement is instantiated by instantiating each of its constituent parts separately:

> *instantiate (rs: RuleStmt, inst: Instantiation) rs': RuleStmt*
> pre *isInstantiableBy(rs, inst)*
> post let *ss* = {*instantiate(s, inst)* | *s* ∈ *SEQHYPS(rs)*},
>   *es* = {*instantiate(e, inst)* | *e* ∈ *ORDHYPS(rs)*},
>   *e'* = *instantiate(CONCL(rs), inst)* in
>   *rs'* = *mk-RuleStmt(ss, es, e')*

Exported.

Pattern-matching is now easy to specify:

> *matchAgainst (e: Exp, e': Exp) insts: Instantiation*-set
> pre *isFull(e)* ∧ *isFull(e')*
> post ∀*inst* ∈ *insts·isInstantiableBy(e, inst)*∧*isEquivalentTo(instantiate(e, inst), e')*

Exported.

It has been shown elsewhere (cf. 'The return of the son of FSIP' PAL021/1.2) that – given the precondition above – this operation is fully implementable, in that all possible 'relevant' instantiations can be returned. The precondition should not bother the user since, as noted earlier, placeholders only occur in a very limited class of *mural* objects, and such objects would not usually be subject to pattern matching.

C.5   Signatures

Atoms are declared or defined in a *signature*:

> *Signature* :: *CONSTS* : *CESymb* $\xrightarrow{m}$ *CEDecl*
>   *TYPES*   : *CTSymb* $\xrightarrow{m}$ *CTDecl*
>   *BINDERS* : *QESymb* $\xrightarrow{m}$ *QEDecl*
>   *DTYPES* : *QTSymb* $\xrightarrow{m}$ *QTDecl*

where

> *inv-Signature*(Σ) $\triangleq$
>   ∀*odef* ∈ *oDefs*(Σ) · *is-OK-ODef(odef)* ∧
>   ∀*qedef* ∈ *qeDefs*(Σ) · *is-OK-QEDef(qedef)*

Should be visible.

In the present treatment, the distinction between primitive and defined objects resides at the level of the signature rather than at the level of expressions and types, as it was felt that this was more natural (cf. 'Proposed Unification of Primitive and Defined Fripse Things', rm010). A symbol is thus designated as being either primitive, defined, or 'not sure which yet' according to whether its declaration is

- an *arity* (constants and types) or ZILCH (binders)

- an expression or a type

- a null declaration

CEDecl = *Exp* | N × N | *NullCEDecl*

CTDecl = *Type* | N × N | *NullCTDecl*

QEDecl = *Exp* | ZILCH | *NullQEDecl*

QTDecl = ZILCH

Decl = *CEDecl* | *CTDecl* | *QEDecl* | *QTDecl*

The declarations of all the defined constants and types in a signature is given by:

oDefs : *Signature* → *Def*-set
oDefs(Σ) $\triangleq$ {$d \in$ rng *CONSTS*(Σ) $\cup$ rng *TYPES*(Σ) | $d \in Def$}

Not exported.

And the declarations of all the defined binders are:

qeDefs : *Signature* → *Exp*-set
qeDefs(Σ) $\triangleq$ {$e \in$ rng *BINDERS*(Σ) | $e \in Exp$}

Not exported.

The declaration of a defined constant or type should contain no free variables, no metavariables and should have no missing placeholders[10].

is-OK-ODef : *Def* → B
is-OK-ODef(*odef*) $\triangleq$
    freeVars(*odef*) = { } $\wedge$ *meSymbs*(*odef*) = { } $\wedge$
    mtSymbs(*odef*) = { } $\wedge$ *hasNoMissingPHoles*(*odef*)

Not exported.

The declaration of a defined binder should contain no free variables, no placeholders, a single expression metavariable of arity $(1, 0)$, and a single type metavariable of arity $(0, 0)$.

is-OK-QEDef : *Exp* → B
is-OK-QEDef(*e*) $\triangleq$
    freeVars(*e*) = { } $\wedge$ *isFull*(*e*)
    $\wedge$ card *meSymbs*(*e*) = card *mtSymbs*(*e*) = 1
    $\wedge \forall oterm \in oTerms(e) \cdot$
        (*SYMBOL*(*oterm*) $\in$ *MESymb* $\Rightarrow$ *argSize*(*oterm*) = (1, 0))
        $\wedge$ (*SYMBOL*(*oterm*) $\in$ *MTSymb* $\Rightarrow$ *argSize*(*oterm*) = (0, 0))

---

[10]This last condition is to ensure preservation of information, i.e. that the operations of folding and unfolding definitions are mutually inverse. It might be possible to relax it, but there doesn't actually seem to be much to gain by doing so, apart from some additional potential for doing something idiotic (e.g. defining a constant to take 42 arguments, and only ever using the one at position 42).

Not exported.

The auxiliary function for checking that all placeholders are used:

$hasNoMissingPHoles : Construct \rightarrow \mathbb{B}$
$hasNoMissingPHoles(c) \;\triangleq$
$\qquad \forall m \in \mathbb{N}_1 \cdot m \leq eArity(c) \;\Rightarrow\; mk\text{-}EPHole(m) \in subterms(c)$
$\qquad \wedge\; \forall n \in \mathbb{N}_1 \cdot n \leq tArity(c) \;\Rightarrow\; mk\text{-}TPHole(n) \in subterms(c)$

Not exported.

C.5.1   Accessing Functions

A function to collect all the atoms in a signature:

$atoms : Signature \rightarrow Atom\text{-set}$
$atoms(\Sigma) \;\triangleq$
$\qquad \text{dom}\; CONSTS(\Sigma) \cup \text{dom}\; TYPES(\Sigma) \cup \text{dom}\; BINDERS(\Sigma) \cup \text{dom}\; DTYPES(\Sigma)$

Not exported.

Next, a function to collect all the primitive *CSymbs* declared in some signature (recall: these are the ones whose *CEDecl* or *CTDecl* is of type $\mathbb{N} \times \mathbb{N}$).

$primitiveCSymbs : Signature \rightarrow CSymb\text{-set}$
$primitiveCSymbs(\Sigma) \;\triangleq$
$\qquad \text{let}\; cm = CONSTS(\Sigma) \cup TYPES(\Sigma) \;\text{in}$
$\qquad \{ct \in \text{dom}\; cm \mid cm(ct) \in \mathbb{N} \times \mathbb{N}\}$

Not exported.

The defined *CSymbs* are obtained similarly, being those whose *CEDecl/CTDecl* is an *Exp/Type*:

$definedCSymbs : Signature \rightarrow CSymb\text{-set}$
$definedCSymbs(\Sigma) \;\triangleq$
$\qquad \text{let}\; cm = CONSTS(\Sigma) \cup TYPES(\Sigma) \;\text{in}$
$\qquad \{ct \in \text{dom}\; cm \mid cm(ct) \in Def\}$

Not exported.

Nothing much new in the case of the primitive *QSymbs* either; they have declaration ZILCH:

$primitiveQSymbs : Signature \rightarrow QSymb\text{-set}$
$primitiveQSymbs(\Sigma) \;\triangleq$
$\qquad \text{let}\; qm = BINDERS(\Sigma) \cup DTYPES(\Sigma) \;\text{in}$
$\qquad \{qt \in \text{dom}\; qm \mid qm(qt) = \text{ZILCH}\}$

Not exported.

Finally in this exciting mini-series of functions, the defined *QSymbs* are those with an *Exp* or a *Type* as their declaration[11].

---

[11]As yet, we've not managed to summon up sufficient strength to allow for defined dependent types (on the grounds that we can't actually think of any!) so there are only defined *QESymbs* so far. These actually

definedQSymbs : *Signature* → *QSymb*-set
definedQSymbs(Σ)   △
    let *qm* = *BINDERS*(Σ) in
    {*qt* ∈ dom *qm* | *qm*(*qt*) ∈ *Exp*}

Not exported.

The set of declared (i.e. having non-null declaration) ordinary symbols in some signature is then simply the union of the primitive and the defined *CSymbs*:

declaredCSymbs : *Signature* → *CSymb*-set
declaredCSymbs(Σ)   △   *primitiveCSymbs*(Σ) ∪ *definedCSymbs*(Σ)

Not exported.

Similarly for the declared *QSymbs*:

declaredQSymbs : *Signature* → *QSymb*-set
declaredQSymbs(Σ)   △   *primitiveQSymbs*(Σ) ∪ *definedQSymbs*(Σ)

Not exported.

The particular declaration of some symbol can be found using the following function:

declAt (Σ: *Signature*, *atom*: *Atom*) *decl*: *Decl*
pre *atom* ∈ *atoms*(Σ)
post *decl* = (*CONSTS*(Σ) ∪ *TYPES*(Σ) ∪ *BINDERS*(Σ) ∪ *DTYPES*(Σ))(*atom*)

Not exported.

C.5.2   Consistency and Completeness Checks

A construct or a rule statement is consistent with a signature if any *OTerms* in it have the correct number of arguments as far as the signature is concerned:

isConsisWithSig : (*Construct* | *RuleStmt*) × *Signature* → B
isConsisWithSig(*cr*, Σ)   △
    let *mk-Signature*(*cem*, *ctm*, *qem*, *qtm*) = Σ in
    hasConsisArgSizes(*cr*)
    ∧ ∀*oterm* ∈ *oTerms*(*cr*) ·
        SYMBOL(*oterm*) ∈ *declaredCSymbs*(Σ)
        ⇒ *size*(*ARGS*(*oterm*)) = *declaredCSymbSize*(Σ, *SYMBOL*(*oterm*))

Not exported.

The auxiliary function for finding the size of some declared *CSymb* is:

declaredCSymbSize (Σ: *Signature*, *ct*: *CSymb*) *nn*: N × N
pre *ct* ∈ *declaredCSymbs*(Σ)

---

have an *Exp* as their declaration. It's pretty clear how defined *QTSymbs* could be incorporated, though, and if we suddenly become one with the Force we might add them at some later stage.

```
post let decl = declAt(Σ, ct) in
      nn = cases decl of
              N x N → decl
              Def   → arity(decl)
           end
```

Not exported.

A signature is OK if all its declarations are consistent with it:

$is\text{-}OK\text{-}Sig : Signature \rightarrow B$
$is\text{-}OK\text{-}Sig(\Sigma) \quad \underline{\Delta} \quad \forall def \in oDefs(\Sigma) \cup qeDefs(\Sigma) \cdot isConsisWithSig(def, \Sigma)$

Not exported.

A construct is reasonable in the context of a signature if it is complete, consistent with the signature, and all its atoms are declared in the signature:

$isReasonableWRTSig : Construct \times Signature \rightarrow B$
$isReasonableWRTSig(c, \Sigma) \quad \underline{\Delta}$
$\quad isComplete(c) \wedge isConsisWithSig(c, \Sigma)$
$\quad \wedge atoms(c) \subseteq declaredCSymbs(\Sigma) \cup declaredQSymbs(\Sigma)$

Not exported.

A signature is reasonable if all its declarations are reasonable constructs with respect to itself:

$isReasonableSig : Signature \rightarrow B$
$isReasonableSig(\Sigma) \quad \underline{\Delta}$
$\quad \forall def \in oDefs(\Sigma) \cup qeDefs(\Sigma) \cdot isReasonableWRTSig(def, \Sigma)$

Not exported.

C.5.3   Equivalence Testing

Binder definitions are equivalent up to renaming of bound variables and metavariable symbols:

$areEquivalentQEDefs : Exp \times Exp \rightarrow B$
$areEquivalentQEDefs(e_1, e_2) \quad \underline{\Delta}$
$\quad is\text{-}OK\text{-}QEDef(e_1) \wedge is\text{-}OK\text{-}QEDef(e_2)$
$\quad \wedge \exists mem: MESymb \xrightarrow{m} MESymb, mtm: MTSymb \xrightarrow{m} MTSymb \cdot$
$\quad\quad isEquivalentTo(renameMSymbs(e_1, mem, mtm), e_2)$

Not exported.

The problem of collapse of metavariable symbols does not come in here because of course e_1 has only one of each kind.

So binder declarations are equivalent if they're both null, both ZILCH, or equivalent binder definitions:

$areEquivalentQEDecls : QEDecl \times QEDecl \rightarrow B$
$areEquivalentQEDecls(qed, qed') \;\; \triangleq$
    cases qed of
    Exp $\rightarrow qed' \in Exp \wedge areEquivalentQEDefs(qed, qed')$
    $NullQEDecl \rightarrow qed' \in NullQEDecl$
    ZILCH $\rightarrow qed' =$ ZILCH
    end

Not exported.

Constant and type declarations are equivalent if they're both null, equal arities, or equivalent expressions or types:

$areEquivalentCEDecls : CEDecl \times CEDecl \rightarrow B$
$areEquivalentCEDecls(ced, ced') \;\; \triangleq$
    cases ced of
    Exp $\rightarrow ced' \in Exp \wedge isEquivalentTo(ced, ced')$
    $N \times N$ $\rightarrow ced' \in N \times N \wedge ced = ced'$
    $NullCEDecl \rightarrow ced' \in NullCEDecl$
    end

Not exported.

$areEquivalentCTDecls : CTDecl \times CTDecl \rightarrow B$
$areEquivalentCTDecls(ctd, ctd') \;\; \triangleq$
    cases ctd of
    $Type$ $\rightarrow ctd' \in Type \wedge isEquivalentTo(ctd, ctd')$
    $N \times N$ $\rightarrow ctd' \in N \times N \wedge ctd = ctd'$
    $NullCTDecl \rightarrow ctd' \in NullCTDecl$
    end

Not exported.

C.5.4 New Signatures for Old

Signatures are nonclashing if common declarations are equivalent:

$areNonclashingSigs : Signature \times Signature \rightarrow B$
$areNonclashingSigs(\Sigma, \Sigma') \;\; \triangleq$
    let $mk\text{-}Signature(cem, ctm, qem, qtm) = \Sigma,$
       $mk\text{-}Signature(cem', ctm', qem', qtm') = \Sigma'$ in
    $\forall cet \in$ dom $cem \cap$ dom $cem' \cdot areEquivalentCEDecls(cem(cet), cem'(cet)) \wedge$
    $\forall ctt \in$ dom $ctm \cap$ dom $ctm' \cdot areEquivalentCTDecls(ctm(ctt), ctm'(ctt)) \wedge$
    $\forall qet \in$ dom $qem \cap$ dom $qem' \cdot areEquivalentQEDecls(qem(qet), qem'(qet))$

Not exported.

Nonclashing signatures can be merged to form a single signature[12]:

---

[12]The use of the generalised map overwrite function is valid here because the pre-condition ensures that any common declarations are equivalent. Its use does mean that this is another of those operations which

*mergeSigs (S: Signature-*set$)$ Σ: *Signature*
pre $\forall \Sigma', \Sigma'' \in S \cdot areNonclashingSigs(\Sigma', \Sigma'')$
post let $cem = \dagger\{CONSTS(\Sigma_0) \mid \Sigma_0 \in S\},$
$\qquad ctm = \dagger\{TYPES(\Sigma_0) \mid \Sigma_0 \in S\},$
$\qquad qem = \dagger\{BINDERS(\Sigma_0) \mid \Sigma_0 \in S\},$
$\qquad qtm = \dagger\{DTYPES(\Sigma_0) \mid \Sigma_0 \in S\}$ in
$\quad \Sigma = mk\text{-}Signature(cem, ctm, qem, qtm)$

Not exported.

C.5.5   Unfolding Definitions

In this section we present functions for unfolding definitions. First, a check that a term is unfoldable (the term should be an *OTerm* or a *QExp* and its symbol should be a defined symbol. If the symbol is a *CSymb* the size of the arguments expected by its declaration should be the same as the size of the term's arguments):

isUnfoldable : Term $\times$ *Signature* $\rightarrow$ B
isUnfoldable(term, Σ) $\triangle$
$\quad$ let *symb* = *SYMBOL(term)* in
$\quad$ *term* $\in$ *OTerm* $\wedge$
$\qquad$ *symb* $\in$ *definedCSymbs(Σ)* $\wedge$ *argSize(term)* = *declaredCSymbSize(Σ, symb)*
$\quad \vee$ *term* $\in$ *QExp* $\wedge$ *symb* $\in$ *definedQSymbs(Σ)*

Not exported.

The following function unfolds an occurrence of a definition *inside* a construct:

unfoldDefAt (c: Construct, Σ: *Signature, i: Index) c': Construct*
pre *isValidIndex(c, i)* $\wedge$ *isUnfoldable(termAtIndex(c, i),* Σ)
post let *term* = *termAtIndex(c, i),*
$\qquad$ *term'* = if *term* $\in$ *OTerm*
$\qquad\qquad\qquad$ then *unfoldOTerm(term,* Σ)
$\qquad\qquad\qquad$ else *unfoldQExp(term,* Σ)
$\qquad$ in
$\quad$ *c'* = *replaceTermAt(c, i, term')*

Exported.

OTerms are unfolded simply by filling the placeholders in the corresponding defienda with the relevant arguments:

unfoldOTerm (oterm: OTerm, Σ: *Signature) def: Def*
pre *isUnfoldable(oterm,* Σ)
post let *decl* = *declAt(Σ, SYMBOL(oterm))* in
$\quad$ *def* = *fillPHoles(decl, ARGS(oterm))*

Not exported.

Unfortunately the same trick can't be used for defined binders; instead we perform a few contortions with *EPHoles* and *ELists* to ensure that *EPHoles* in the expression being unfolded are preserved, then instantiate their metavariable symbols appropriately:

is in general underdetermined, of course, though again all possible results are clearly mutually equivalent.

unfoldQExp (qe: QExp, Σ: Signature) e: Exp
pre *isUnfoldable(qe, Σ)*
post let *decl = declAt(Σ, SYMBOL(qe))*,
      $\{\theta\}$ = *meSymbs(decl)*,
      $\{\phi\}$ = *mtSymbs(decl)*,
      be = BODY(qe),
      e' = bumpEPHoles((BODY(be), VAR(be)),
      decl' = growELists(decl, eArity(BODY(be))),
      inst = mk-Instantiation($\{\theta \mapsto e'\}, \{\phi \mapsto$ *UNIVERSE(be)*$\})$ in
   e = instantiate(decl', inst)

Not exported.

The auxiliary functions used in the above are:

bumpEPHoles (e: Exp, vt: VSymb) e': Exp
pre *vt* $\notin$ *boundVars(e)*
post let *is = indices(e)*,
     js = $\{i \in is \mid termAtIndex(e, i) = vt\}$,
     ks = $\{i \in is \mid termAtIndex(e, i) \in EPHole\}$,
     ls = $\{i \in is \mid termAtIndex(e, i) \in Leaf\}$,
     is' = is − js,
     ls' = ls − ks in
indices(e') = is $\wedge$
$\forall i \in js \cdot termAtIndex(e', i) = mk\text{-}EPHole(1) \wedge$
$\forall i \in is' \cdot$
    let *term = termAtIndex(e, i)* in
    classOf(termAtIndex(e', i)) = classOf(term) $\wedge$
    $(i \in ls' \Rightarrow termAtIndex(e', i) = term) \wedge$
    $(i \in ks \Rightarrow termAtIndex(e', i) = mk\text{-}EPHole(INDEX(term) + 1))$

Not exported.

growELists (e: Exp, n: ℕ) e': Exp
post let *is = indices(e)*,
     js = $\{i \in is \mid$ len $i \geq 2 \wedge termAtIndex(e, i) \in EList \wedge$
     SYMBOL(termAtIndex(e, truncate(truncate(i)))) $\in MESymb\}$,
     ks = $\{i^\frown[k] \mid i \in js \wedge$ len *termAtIndex(e, i)*+1 $\leq k \leq$ len *termAtIndex(e, i)+n*$\}$ in
indices(e') = is $\cup$ *ks* $\wedge$
$\forall i \in ks \cdot$
    *termAtIndex(e', i) = mk-EPHole(last(i)−*len *termAtIndex(e, truncate(i)))*$\wedge$
$\forall i \in is \cdot$
    let *term = termAtIndex(e, i)* in
    classOf(termAtIndex(e', i)) = classOf(term) $\wedge$
    (term $\in$ *leaves(e)* $\Rightarrow$ *termAtIndex(e', i) = term)*

Not exported.

Claim: $\forall e \in Exp \cdot growELists(e, 0) = e$

Finally, a function which tests whether a construct *c'* is equivalent to the construct obtained as a result of unfolding a definition at some given index in *c*:

$isValidUnfold : Construct \times Construct \times Signature \times Index \to B$
$isValidUnfold(c, c', \Sigma, i) \quad \triangleq$
$\quad pre\text{-}unfoldDefAt(c, \Sigma, i) \wedge isEquivalentTo(unfoldDefAt(c, \Sigma, i), c')$

Not exported.

C.6   Theories

$Theory :: PARENTS : Theory\text{-}ref\text{-set}$
$\qquad\qquad EXSIG \quad : Signature$

Visible.

$Theorymap = Theory\text{-}ref \xrightarrow{m} Theory$

where

$inv\text{-}Theorymap(m) \quad \triangleq \quad hasNoClashingAncestors(m) \wedge isNoncircular(m)$

$inheritsFromTheory : Theory\text{-}ref \times Theory\text{-}ref \times Theory\text{-}ref \xrightarrow{m} Theory \to B$
$inheritsFromTheory(th_1, th_2, m) \quad \triangleq$
$\quad$ let $ths = PARENTS(m(th_1))$ in
$\quad th_1 \in \text{dom } m \wedge (th_2 \in ths \vee \exists th \in ths \cdot inheritsFromTheory(th, th_2, m))$

Not exported.

$isNoncircular : Theory\text{-}ref \xrightarrow{m} Theory \to B$
$isNoncircular(m) \quad \triangleq \quad \forall th \in \text{dom } m \cdot \neg \ inheritsFromTheory(th, th, m)$

Not exported.

$ancestors : Theory\text{-}ref \times Theory\text{-}ref \xrightarrow{m} Theory \to Theory\text{-}ref\text{-set}$
$ancestors(th, m) \quad \triangleq \quad \{th\} \cup \{th' \in Theory\text{-}ref \mid inheritsFromTheory(th, th', m)\}$

Exported.

$definedAncestors : Theory\text{-}ref \times Theory\text{-}ref \xrightarrow{m} Theory \to Theory\text{-}ref\text{-set}$
$definedAncestors(th, m) \quad \triangleq \quad ancestors(th, m) \cap \text{dom } m$

Not exported.

$hasNoClashingAncestors : Theory\text{-}ref \xrightarrow{m} Theory \to B$
$hasNoClashingAncestors(m) \quad \triangleq$
$\quad \forall th \in \text{dom } m \cdot \forall th_1, th_2 \in definedAncestors(th, m) \cdot$
$\qquad areNonclashingSigs(EXSIG(m(th_1)), EXSIG(m(th_2)))$

Not exported.

C.6.1   Accessing functions

The *full signature* of a theory is obtained by merging the signatures of all the defined ancestors of the theory. This is well-defined because the invariant on the theorymap ensures that the ancestors are non-clashing.

> *fullSig* : *Theory-ref* × *Theorymap* → *Signature*
> *fullSig*(*th*, *thm*)   △
>   let *S* = {*EXSIG*(*thm*(*th'*)) | *th'* ∈ *definedAncestors*(*th*, *thm*)} in
>   *mergeSigs*(*S*)

Not sure.

The atoms available in a theory are those of its full signature:

> *atoms* : *Theory-ref* × *Theorymap* → *Atom*-set
> *atoms*(*th*, *thm*)   △   *atoms*(*fullSig*(*th*, *thm*))

Not exported.

The rules in a theory are all those whose *THEORY* field is that theory:

> *rules* : *Theory-ref* × *Rulemap* × *Theorymap* → *Rule-ref*-set
> *rules*(*th*, *rm*, *thm*)   △   {*r* ∈ dom *rm* | *THEORY*(*rm*(*r*)) ∈ *ancestors*(*th*, *thm*)}

Exported.

Claim: *rules*(*th*, *rm*, *thm*) ⊆ dom *rm*

And the axioms in a theory are those of its rules which have a null proof:

> *axioms* : *Theory-ref* × *Rulemap* × *Theorymap* → *Rule-ref*-set
> *axioms*(*th*, *rm*, *thm*)   △   {*r* ∈ *rules*(*th*, *rm*, *thm*) | *PROOF*(*rm*(*r*)) = nil}

Not exported.

C.6.2   Consistency and completeness checks

A rule statement is reasonable with respect to a theory if it's OK as a rule statement and all its component expressions are reasonable with respect to the theory's full signature:

> *isReasonableWRTTheory* : *RuleStmt* × *Theory-ref* × *Theorymap* → B
> *isReasonableWRTTheory*(*rs*, *th*, *thm*)   △
>   let Σ = *fullSig*(*th*, *thm*) in
>   *is-OK-RuleStmt*(*rs*) ∧ ∀*e* ∈ *exps*(*rs*) · *isReasonableWRTSig*(*e*, Σ)

Background. System should warn if violated.

A theory is reasonable if its full signature is reasonable and all its rules have reasonable statements:

> *isReasonableTheory* : *Theory-ref* × *Rulemap* × *Theorymap* → B
> *isReasonableTheory*(*th*, *rm*, *thm*)   △
>   *th* ∈ dom *thm* ∧ *isReasonableSig*(*fullSig*(*th*, *thm*)) ∧
>   ∀*r* ∈ *rules*(*th*, *rm*, *thm*) · *isReasonableWRTTheory*(*STMT*(*rm*(*r*)), *th*, *thm*)

Background. System should warn if violated.

C.7 Morphisms and Theory Morphisms

C.7.1 Morphisms

$$SigMorph :: CEMAP : CESymb \xrightarrow{m} CEMDecl$$
$$CTMAP : CTSymb \xrightarrow{m} CTMDecl$$
$$QEMAP : QESymb \xrightarrow{m} QESymb$$
$$QTMAP : QTSymb \xrightarrow{m} QTSymb$$

where

$inv\text{-}SigMorph(\sigma) \triangleq$
$\quad \forall omdef \in oMDefs(\sigma) \cdot$
$\quad\quad freeVars(omdef) = \{\,\} \wedge meSymbs(omdef) = \{\,\} \wedge mtSymbs(omdef) = \{\,\}$

Probably only need to be visible as a part of theory morphisms.

$CEMDecl = Exp \mid CESymb \mid NullCEMDecl$

$CTMDecl = Type \mid CTSymb \mid NullCTMDecl$

$MDecl = CEMDecl \mid CTMDecl$

Here, primitive constants and types will be mapped respectively to *Exps* and *Types* whilst defined ones will be mapped to defined ones. The possibility that a user hasn't yet decided which category a particular *CSymb* falls into is catered for in the usual way by the two null declarations.

The auxiliary function *oMDefs* which extracts all objects of class *Exp* or class *Type* from the ranges of the signature morphism's mappings is given by:

$oMDefs : SigMorph \rightarrow Def\text{-}set$
$oMDefs(\sigma) \triangleq$
$\quad \text{let } cm = CEMAP(\sigma) \cup CTMAP(\sigma) \text{ in}$
$\quad \{d \in \mathsf{rng}\, cm \mid d \in Def\}$

Not exported.
C.7.2 Accessing Functions

First, a function for finding the set of *CSymbs* for which morphisms are actually defined (that is the ones that don't map to null declarations).

$morphedCSymbs : SigMorph \rightarrow CSymb\text{-}set$
$morphedCSymbs(\sigma) \triangleq$
$\quad \text{let } cm = CEMAP(\sigma) \cup CTMAP(\sigma) \text{ in}$
$\quad \{ct \in \mathsf{dom}\, cm \mid cm(ct) \notin (NullCEMDecl \mid NullCTMDecl)\}$

Not exported.

Hotly pursued by one for finding the *QSymbs* for which morphisms are defined, though this one's pretty unexciting as there aren't any null declarations in this case. Thus, these are just the domains of the relevant two maps:

> $morphedQSymbs : SigMorph \rightarrow QSymb\text{-set}$
> $morphedQSymbs(\sigma) \quad \triangleq \quad \text{dom } QEMAP(\sigma) \cup \text{dom } QTMAP(\sigma)$

Not exported.

The *defined CSymbs* of a signature morphism are those which map to *CSymbs* under the mappings in its first two fields:

> $definedCSymbs : SigMorph \rightarrow CSymb\text{-set}$
> $definedCSymbs(\sigma) \quad \triangleq$
> $\qquad \text{let } cm = CEMAP(\sigma) \cup CTMAP(\sigma) \text{ in}$
> $\qquad \{ct \in \text{dom } cm \mid cm(ct) \in CSymb\}$

Not exported.

And the *primitive CSymbs* are those which are mapped to an *Exp* or a *Type*:

> $primitiveCSymbs : SigMorph \rightarrow CSymb\text{-set}$
> $primitiveCSymbs(\sigma) \quad \triangleq$
> $\qquad \text{let } cm = CEMAP(\sigma) \cup CTMAP(\sigma) \text{ in}$
> $\qquad \{ct \in \text{dom } cm \mid cm(ct) \in Def\}$

Not exported.

All atoms translated by a signature morphism are simply given by the union of the domains of all its fields:

> $translatedAtoms : SigMorph \rightarrow Atom\text{-set}$
> $translatedAtoms(\sigma) \quad \triangleq$
> $\qquad \text{dom } CEMAP(\sigma) \cup \text{dom } CTMAP(\sigma) \cup \text{dom } QEMAP(\sigma) \cup \text{dom } QTMAP(\sigma)$

Not exported.

Finally, the thing that some translated atom translates to under a signature morphism is given by its image under the relevant mapping:

> $mDeclAt \ (\sigma : SigMorph, atom : Atom) \ mdecl : MDecl$
> $\text{pre } atom \in translatedAtoms(\sigma)$
> $\text{post } mdecl = (CEMAP(\sigma) \cup CTMAP(\sigma) \cup QEMAP(\sigma) \cup QTMAP(\sigma))(atom)$

Not exported.

C.7.3   Translations

Generally speaking, an object is *translatable* across a signature morphism if the translations of all its atoms are defined, though the situation is somewhat more complicated in the case of *OTerms*, however — when its *SYMBOL* is translated to an expression or a type, that expression or type should in addition be fillable by the translated *ARGS*. Note that free variables, placeholders and metavariable symbols do not change under translation, though bound variables may change in order to avoid clashes and variable capture.

$isTranslatableOTerm : OTerm \times SigMorph \rightarrow \mathbf{B}$
$isTranslatableOTerm(oterm, \sigma) \quad \underline{\triangle}$
     let $ot = SYMBOL(oterm)$,
        $elxtl = ARGS(oterm)$ in
     $isTranslatable(elxtl, \sigma) \wedge$
     $(ot \in CSymb \Rightarrow$
     $ot \in morphedCSymbs(\sigma) \wedge$
     $(mDeclAt(\sigma, ot) \in Def$
     $\Rightarrow isFillableBy(mDeclAt(\sigma, ot), translate(elxtl, \sigma))))$

Not exported.

$isTranslatable : Exp \times SigMorph \rightarrow \mathbf{B}$
$isTranslatable(e, \sigma) \quad \underline{\triangle}$
    cases e of
    $mk\text{-}QExp(qet, be) \rightarrow qet \in \text{dom } QEMAP(\sigma) \wedge isTranslatable(be, \sigma)$
    $OExp \qquad\qquad\quad \rightarrow isTranslatableOTerm(e, \sigma)$
    others true
    end

Not exported.

$isTranslatable : Type \times SigMorph \rightarrow \mathbf{B}$
$isTranslatable(t, \sigma) \quad \underline{\triangle}$
    cases t of
    $mk\text{-}SubType(be) \rightarrow isTranslatable(be, \sigma)$
    $mk\text{-}QType(qtt, bt) \rightarrow qtt \in \text{dom } QTMAP(\sigma) \wedge isTranslatable(bt, \sigma)$
    $OType \qquad\qquad\quad \rightarrow isTranslatableOTerm(t, \sigma)$
    others true
    end

Not exported.

$isTranslatable : BTerm \times SigMorph \rightarrow \mathbf{B}$
$isTranslatable(bterm, \sigma) \quad \underline{\triangle}$
    $isTranslatable(UNIVERSE(bterm), \sigma) \wedge isTranslatable(BODY(bterm), \sigma)$

Not exported.

isTranslatable : EListXTList × SigMorph → B
isTranslatable(elxtl, σ)   △
        isTranslatable(ELIST(elxtl), σ) ∧ isTranslatable(TLIST(elxtl), σ)

Not exported.

isTranslatable : ArgList × SigMorph → B
isTranslatable(al, σ)   △   ∀*def* ∈ rng *al · isTranslatable(def, σ)*

Not exported.

Now the functions for translation. Each naturally has a precondition that the object to be translated actually be translatable.

translate (e: Exp, σ: SigMorph) e': Exp
pre *isTranslatable(e, σ)*
post *e'* = cases *e* of
        mk-QExp(qet, be)   → let *qet'* = *mDeclAt(σ, qet)*,
                                          be' = *translate(be, σ)* in
                                      mk-QExp(qet', be')
        mk-OExp(oet, elxtl)→ let *elxtl'* = *translate(elxtl, σ)* in
                                      if *oet* ∈ *CESymb*
                                      then let *md* = *mDeclAt(σ, oet)* in
                                          if *md* ∈ *Exp*
                                          then *fillPHoles(md, elxtl')*
                                          else *mk-OExp(md, elxtl')*
                                      else *mk-OExp(oet, elxtl')*

        others *e*
        end

Not exported.

translate (t: Type, σ: SigMorph) t': Type
pre *isTranslatable(t, σ)*
post *t'* = cases *t* of
        mk-SubType(be)   → *mk-Subtype(translate(be, σ))*
        mk-QType(qtt, bt)   → let *bt'* = *translate(bt, σ)*,
                                      qtt' = *mDeclAt(σ, qtt)* in
                                      mk-QType(qtt', bt')
        mk-OType(ott, elxtl)→ let *elxtl'* = *translate(elxtl, σ)* in
                                      if *ott* ∈ *CTSymb*
                                      then let *md* = *mDeclAt(σ, ott)* in
                                          if *md* ∈ *Type*
                                          then *fillPHoles(md, elxtl')*
                                          else *mk-OType(md, elxtl')*
                                      else *mk-OType(ott, elxtl')*

        others *t*
        end

Not exported.

> *translate (be*: *BExp,* σ: *SigMorph) be′*: *BExp*
> pre *isTranslatable(be,* σ)
> post let *vt* = *VAR(be),*
>   *t* = *translate(UNIVERSE(be),* σ)*,*
>   *e* = *translate(BODY(be),* σ) in
>   *be′* = *build-BExp(vt, t, e)*

Not exported.

> *translate (bt*: *BType,* σ: *SigMorph) bt′*: *BType*
> pre *isTranslatable(bt,* σ)
> post let *vt* = *VAR(bt),*
>   *t* = *translate(UNIVERSE(bt),* σ)*,*
>   *t′* = *translate(BODY(bt),* σ) in
>   *bt′* = *build-BType(vt, t, t′)*

Not exported.

> *translate (elxtl*: *EListXTList,* σ: *SigMorph) elxtl′*: *EListXTList*
> pre *isTranslatable(elxtl,* σ)
> post let *el* = *translate(ELIST(elxtl),* σ)*,*
>   *tl* = *translate(TLIST(elxtl),* σ) in
>   *elxtl′* = *build-EListXTList(el, tl)*

Not exported.

> *translate (el*: *EList,* σ: *SigMorph) el′*: *EList*
> pre *isTranslatable(el,* σ)
> post *el′* = *build-EList([translate(el(i),* σ) | *i* ∈ dom *el])*

Not exported.

> *translate (tl*: *TList,* σ: *SigMorph) tl′*: *TList*
> pre *isTranslatable(tl,* σ)
> post *tl′* = *build-TList([translate(tl(i),* σ) | *i* ∈ dom *tl])*

Not exported.

Similar functions for translating sequents and rule statements:

> *isTranslatable* : (*Sequent* | *RuleStmt*) × *SigMorph* → B
> *isTranslatable(srs,* σ)   △   ∀*e* ∈ *exps(srs)* · *isTranslatable(e,* σ)

Not exported.

> *translate (s*: *Sequent,* σ: *SigMorph) s′*: *Sequent*
> pre *isTranslatable(s,* σ)

post let *prems* = {*translate*(*e*, σ) | *e* ∈ *PREMISES*(*s*)},
     upshot = *translate*(*UPSHOT*(*s*), σ) in
  s' = *mk-Sequent*(*NFV*(*s*), *prems*, *upshot*)

Not exported.

translate (*rs*: *RuleStmt*, σ: *SigMorph*) *rs'*: *RuleStmt*
pre *isTranslatable*(*rs*, σ)
post let *shyps* = {*translate*(*s*, σ) | *s* ∈ *SEQHYPS*(*rs*)},
     ohyps = {*translate*(*e*, σ) | *e* ∈ *ORDHYPS*(*rs*)},
     con = *translate*(*CONCL*(*rs*), σ) in
  rs' = *mk-RuleStmt*(*shyps*, *ohyps*, *con*)

Not exported.

Next, we need to be able to translate a construct over a sequence of signature morphisms. In order to save writing *Construct* | *Sequent* | *RuleStmt* more than twice, we'll introduce a shorthand for it:

  CSR = *Construct* | *Sequent* | *RuleStmt*

The first function checks that it is actually possible to translate something over a sequence of signature morphisms:

isTranslatable∗ : *CRS* × *SigMorph*∗ → **B**
isTranslatable∗(*crs*, *sml*)   △
    if *sml* = [ ]
    then true
    else let σ = hd *sml*,
          sml' = tl *sml* in
       isTranslatable(*crs*, σ) ∧ *isTranslatable* ∗ (*translate*(*crs*, σ), *sml'*)

Not exported.

The next group do the translation:

translate∗ (*c*: *Construct*, *sml*: *SigMorph*∗) *c'*: *Construct*
pre *isTranslatable* ∗ (*c*, *sml*)
post *c'* = if *sml* = [ ]
       then *c*
       else let σ = hd *sml*,
            sml' = tl *sml* in
          translate ∗ (*translate*(*c*, σ), *sml'*)

Not exported.

translate∗ (*s*: *Sequent*, *sml*: *SigMorph*∗) *s'*: *Sequent*
pre *isTranslatable* ∗ (*s*, *sml*)
post let *prems* = {*translate* ∗ (*e*, *sml*) | *e* ∈ *PREMISES*(*s*)},
     upshot = *translate* ∗ (*UPSHOT*(*s*), *sml*) in
  s' = *mk-Sequent*(*NFV*(*s*), *prems*, *upshot*)

Not exported.

> *translate*∗ (*rs*: *RuleStmt*, *sml*: *SigMorph*∗) *rs'*: *RuleStmt*
> pre *isTranslatable* ∗ (*rs*, *sml*)
> post let *shyps* = {*translate* ∗ (*s*, *sml*) | *s* ∈ *SEQHYPS*(*rs*)},
>   *ohyps* = {*translate* ∗ (*e*, *sml*) | *e* ∈ *ORDHYPS*(*rs*)},
>   *con* = *translate* ∗ (*CONCL*(*rs*), *sml*) in
>   *rs'* = *mk-RuleStmt*(*shyps*, *ohyps*, *con*)

Not exported.

C.7.4 Consistency and Completeness Checks

A signature morphism is consistent with two signatures if it translates things that are consistent with the first to things that are consistent with the second:

> *isConsisWithSigs* : *SigMorph* × *Signature* × *Signature* → **B**
> *isConsisWithSigs*(σ, Σ, Σ') $\triangleq$
>   let *pcs* = *primitiveCSymbs*(Σ),
>   *dcs* = *definedCSymbs*(Σ),
>   *dqs* = *definedQSymbs*(Σ),
>   *pcm* = *primitiveCSymbs*(σ),
>   *dcm* = *definedCSymbs*(σ),
>   *qm* = *morphedQSymbs*(σ),
>   *pqs'* = *primitiveQSymbs*(Σ'),
>   *dcs'* = *definedCSymbs*(Σ'),
>   *dqs'* = *definedQSymbs*(Σ') in
>   *dcs* ∩ *pcm* = { } ∧ *pcs* ∩ *dcm* = { } ∧
>   ∀*ct* ∈ *pcs* ∩ *pcm* ·
>   *isConsisWithSig*(*mDeclAt*(σ, *ct*), Σ')
>   ∧ *declAt*(Σ, *ct*) = *arity*(*mDeclAt*(σ, *ct*))
>   ∧ ∀*ct* ∈ *dcs* ∩ *dcm* ·
>   *mDeclAt*(σ, *ct*) ∈ *dcs'* ⇒
>   *arity*(*declAt*(Σ', *mDeclAt*(σ, *ct*))) = *arity*(*declAt*(Σ, *ct*)) ∧
>   (*isTranslatable*(*declAt*(Σ, *ct*), σ)
>   ⇒ *isEquivalentTo*(*translate*(*declAt*(Σ, *ct*), σ),
>   *declAt*(Σ', *mDeclAt*(σ, *ct*))))
>   ∧ ∀*qt* ∈ *dqs* ∩ *qm* ·
>   *mDeclAt*(σ, *qt*) ∉ *pqs'* ∧
>   (*isTranslatable*(*declAt*(Σ, *qt*), σ) ∧ *mDeclAt*(σ, *qt*) ∈ *dqs'*
>   ⇒ *areEquivalentQEDefs*(*translate*(*declAt*(Σ, *qt*), σ),
>   *declAt*(Σ', *mDeclAt*(σ, *qt*))))

Not exported.

Claim:

$\forall c \in Construct \cdot$
$isConsisWithSigs(\sigma, \Sigma, \Sigma') \wedge isConsisWithSig(c, \Sigma) \wedge isTranslatable(c, \sigma)$
$\Rightarrow\ isConsisWithSig(translate(c, \sigma), \Sigma')$

A signature morphism is reasonable with respect to two signatures if it translates things which are reasonable with respect to the first signature to things which are reasonable with respect to the second, and it preserves definitions:

$isReasonableWRTSigs : SigMorph \times Signature \times Signature \rightarrow \mathbf{B}$
$isReasonableWRTSigs(\sigma, \Sigma, \Sigma')\ \triangleq$
$\quad atoms(\Sigma) \subseteq morphedCSymbs(\sigma) \cup morphedQSymbs(\sigma) \wedge$
$\quad isConsisWithSigs(\sigma, \Sigma, \Sigma') \wedge$
$\quad \forall ct \in primitiveCSymbs(\Sigma) \cdot$
$\qquad isReasonableWRTSig(mDeclAt(\sigma, ct), \Sigma')$
$\quad \wedge\ \forall ct \in definedCSymbs(\Sigma) \cdot$
$\qquad isTranslatable(declAt(\Sigma, ct), \sigma) \wedge mDeclAt(\sigma, ct) \in definedCSymbs(\Sigma')$
$\quad \wedge\ \forall qt \in primitiveQSymbs(\Sigma) \cdot$
$\qquad mDeclAt(\sigma, qt) \in definedQSymbs(\Sigma') \cup primitiveQSymbs(\Sigma')$
$\quad \wedge\ \forall qt \in definedQSymbs(\Sigma) \cdot$
$\qquad isTranslatable(declAt(\Sigma, qt), \sigma) \wedge mDeclAt(\sigma, qt) \in definedQSymbs(\Sigma')$

Not exported.

Claim:

$\forall c \in Construct \cdot$
$\quad isReasonableWRTSigs(\sigma, \Sigma, \Sigma') \wedge$
$\qquad isReasonableWRTSig(c, \Sigma) \wedge isTranslatable(c, \sigma)\ \Rightarrow$
$\qquad\qquad\qquad isReasonableWRTSig(translate(c, \sigma), \Sigma')$

C.7.5   Theory Morphisms

$ThMorph :: FROM\ :\ Theory\text{-}ref$
$\qquad\qquad\ \ TO\ \ \ \ :\ Theory\text{-}ref$
$\qquad\qquad\ \ VIA\ \ \ :\ SigMorph$
$\qquad\qquad\ \ JUSTIF :\ Rule\text{-}ref \xrightarrow{m} Rule\text{-}ref$

Should be visible.

$ThMorphmap = ThMorph\text{-}ref \xrightarrow{m} ThMorph$

Some accessing functions:

$rulesUsed : ThMorph\text{-}ref \times Rulemap \times Theorymap \times ThMorphmap \rightarrow Rule\text{-}ref\text{-}set$
$rulesUsed(\tau, rm, thm, tmm)\ \triangleq$
$\quad \mathsf{let}\ mk\text{-}ThMorph(th_1, th_2, \sigma, jm) = tmm(\tau)\ \mathsf{in}$
$\quad \mathsf{if}\ \tau \in \mathsf{dom}\ tmm$
$\quad \mathsf{then}\ \{jm(ax) \mid ax \in axioms(th_1, rm, thm) \cap \mathsf{dom}\ jm\}$
$\quad \mathsf{else}\ \{\ \}$

Not exported.

> *rulesYetToBeJustified* (τ: *ThMorph-ref*, *rm*: *Rulemap*, *thm*: *Theorymap*,
> *tmm*: *ThMorphmap*) *rs*: *Rule-ref*-set
> pre $\tau \in$ dom *tmm*
> post let *mk-ThMorph*(th_1, th_2, σ, *jm*) = *tmm*(τ) in
> $rs = axioms(th_1, rm, thm) -$ dom *jm*

Exported.

A theory morphism is consistent if its signature morphism is consistent and translates axioms from the source theory to rules in the target theory:

> *isConsisThMorph* : *ThMorph-ref* $\times$ *Rulemap* $\times$ *Theorymap* $\times$ *ThMorphmap* $\rightarrow$ B
> *isConsisThMorph*(τ, *rm*, *thm*, *tmm*) $\triangleq$
>   let *mk-ThMorph*(th_1, th_2, σ, *jm*) = *tmm*(τ) in
> $\tau \in$ dom *tmm* $\Rightarrow$
>   *isConsisWithSigs*(σ, *fullSig*(th_1, *thm*), *fullSig*(th_2, *thm*))
> $\wedge \, \forall ax \in axioms(th_1, rm, thm) \cap$ dom *jm* $\cdot$
>   *jm*(ax) $\in$ dom *rm* $\Rightarrow$
>   *jm*(ax) $\in$ *rules*(th_2, *rm*, *thm*)
> $\wedge$ (*isTranslatable*(*STMT*(*rm*(ax)), σ) $\Rightarrow$
>   *establishesRuleStmt*(*STMT*(*rm*(*jm*(ax))), *translate*(*STMT*(*rm*(ax)), σ)))

Background. Warning when violated.

A theory morphism is reasonable if its signature morphism is reasonable and translates all axioms of the source theory to defined rules in the target theory:

> *isReasonableThMorph* : *ThMorph-ref* $\times$ *Rulemap* $\times$ *Theorymap* $\times$ *ThMorphmap*
> $\rightarrow$ B
> *isReasonableThMorph*(τ, *rm*, *thm*, *tmm*) $\triangleq$
>   let *mk-ThMorph*(th_1, th_2, σ, *jm*) = *tmm*(τ) in
> $\tau \in$ dom *tmm* $\wedge$
>   *isReasonableWRTSigs*(σ, *fullSig*(th_1, *thm*), *fullSig*(th_2, *thm*))
> $\wedge \, axioms(th_1, rm, thm) \subseteq$ dom *jm*
> $\wedge \, rulesUsed(\tau, rm, thm, tmm) \subseteq$ dom *rm*
> $\wedge \, isConsisThMorph(\tau, rm, thm, tmm)$

Exported, or maybe background.

Claim:

> *isReasonableThMorph*(τ, *rm*, *thm*, *tmm*) $\wedge \tau \in$ dom *tmm*
> $\Rightarrow rulesUsed(\tau, rm, thm, tmm) \subseteq rules(TO(tmm(\tau)), rm, thm)$

Note: A reasonable theory morphism translates derived rules from the source theory into derivable rules in the target theory, provided axioms translate to *valid* rules. This is the metarule about our system which justifies the use of theory morphisms in *RuleJustif* in

§C.8.9.

A sequence of theory morphisms links up correctly if the *TO* field of an element in the sequence is in the ancestors of the *FROM* field of the next element for every element but the last:

> *linkUp* : (*ThMorph-ref**) × *Theorymap* × *ThMorphmap* → B
> *linkUp*(*tml*, *thm*, *tmm*) ≜
>   ∀*n* ∈ inds *tml* · *tml*(*n*) ∈ dom *tmm* ∧
>   ∀*n* ∈ inds *tml* · *TO*(*tmm*(*tml*(*n*))) ∈ *ancestors*(*FROM*(*tmm*(*tml*(*n* + 1))), *thm*)

Not exported.

C.7.6   More Translations

Translations over a sequence of theory morphisms:

> *isTranslatable* ∗ ∗ : *CSR* × *ThMorph-ref** × *ThMorphmap* → B
> *isTranslatable* ∗ ∗(*csr*, *tml*, *tmm*) ≜
>   rng *tml* ⊆ dom *tmm* ∧ *isTranslatable* ∗ (*csr*, [*VIA*(*tmm*(*tml*(*i*))) | *i* ∈ dom *tml*])

Not exported.

> *translate* ∗ ∗ (*csr*: *CSR*, *tml*: *ThMorph-ref**, *tmm*: *ThMorphmap*) *csr*′: *CSR*
> pre *isTranslatable* ∗ ∗(*csr*, *tml*, *tmm*)
> post let *sml* = [*VIA*(*tmm*(*tml*(*i*))) | *i* ∈ dom *tml*] in
>   *csr*′ = *translate* ∗ (*csr*, *sml*)

Exported.

C.8   Proofs

> *Proof* :: *SEQHYPS* : *Sequent-ref* $\xrightarrow{m}$ *Sequent*
>   *BOXMAP* : *Boxmap*
>   *ROOT*   : *Box-ref*
>   *NFV*   : *VSymb* $\xrightarrow{m}$ *Box-ref*

where

> *inv-Proof*(*p*) ≜
>   let *mk-Proof*(*sm*, *bm*, *b*, *vm*) = *p* in
>   *b* ∈ *roots*(*p*) ∧ *hasClosedJustifs*(*p*)
>   ∧ ∀*s* ∈ rng *sm* · *isProper*(*s*) ∧ *NFV*(*s*) ∩ dom *vm* = { }
>   ∧ ∀*b*′ ∈ *roots*(*p*) · *newFreeVarsOfBox*(*p*, *b*′) = { }

The invariant insists that the root of a proof should actually be one of the proof's roots (see below), that all sequent hypotheses should be proper, that lines, boxes and sequents used in justifications in the proof should themselves be in the same proof attempt as the line they're justifying, and that no root box should introduce new free variables.

C.8.1 Boxes

$Box :: HYPS$: $Hypline\text{-}ref \xrightarrow{m} Exp$
$\quad\quad\quad LINES$: $Ordline\text{-}ref \xrightarrow{m} Ordline$
$\quad\quad\quad BOXES$: $Box\text{-}ref\text{-set}$
$\quad\quad\quad CON$: $Ordline\text{-}ref$

where

$inv\text{-}Box(b) \quad \triangle \quad CON(b) \in \text{dom}\, LINES(b)$

The invariant on boxes forces the conclusion of a box to be one of the lines of that box.

$Ordline :: BODY$: Exp
$\quad\quad\quad\quad JUST$: $Justification$

$Boxmap = Box\text{-}ref \xrightarrow{m} Box$

where

$inv\text{-}Boxmap(m) \quad \triangle$
$\quad\quad isNoncircular(m) \land isClosed(m) \land hasNoOverlappingBoxes(m)$

The invariant says that no box should be a subbox of itself, all subboxes of any box in the boxmap are themselves in the boxmap, and no boxes are overlapping.

A box is a *subbox* of another box if it is one of its *BOXES* or is a subbox of one of its *BOXES*:

$isSubbox : Box\text{-}ref \times Box\text{-}ref \times Box\text{-}ref \xrightarrow{m} Box \to \mathsf{B}$
$isSubbox(b_1, b_2, m) \quad \triangle$
$\quad\quad b_2 \in \text{dom}\, m \land$
$\quad\quad \text{let } bs = BOXES(m(b_2)) \text{ in}$
$\quad\quad (b_1 \in bs \lor \exists b \in bs \cdot isSubbox(b_1, b, m))$

Not exported.

A boxmap is *noncircular* if no box in it is a subbox of itself:

$isNoncircular : Box\text{-}ref \xrightarrow{m} Box \to \mathsf{B}$
$isNoncircular(m) \quad \triangle \quad \forall b \in \text{dom}\, m \cdot \neg\, isSubbox(b, b, m)$

Not exported.

A boxmap is *closed* if it contains the *BOXES* of any box in it:

$isClosed : Box\text{-}ref \xrightarrow{m} Box \to \mathsf{B}$
$isClosed(m) \quad \triangle \quad \forall b \in \text{rng}\, m \cdot BOXES(b) \subseteq \text{dom}\, m$

Not exported.

A boxmap *has no overlapping boxes* if distinct boxes don't have hypotheses, lines or boxes in common:

$hasNoOverlappingBoxes : Box\text{-}ref \xrightarrow{m} Box \to \mathbb{B}$
$hasNoOverlappingBoxes(m) \quad\triangleq$
$\quad \forall b_1, b_2 \in \operatorname{dom} m \cdot$
$\qquad b_1 \neq b_2 \Rightarrow$
$\qquad \operatorname{dom} HYPS(m(b_1)) \cap \operatorname{dom} HYPS(m(b_2)) = \{\,\}$
$\qquad \wedge \operatorname{dom} LINES(m(b_1)) \cap \operatorname{dom} LINES(m(b_2)) = \{\,\}$
$\qquad \wedge BOXES(m(b_1)) \cap BOXES(m(b_2)) = \{\,\}$

Not exported.

The *Boxmap* is roughly a forest of trees representing potentially different attempts at a single proof. The *ROOT* field of the proof records the outermost proof box of that proof attempt currently of interest. Switching between proof attempts can be achieved simply by changing the proof's root. Unused trees, as well as unused lines in the relevant tree could be removed from a completed proof by means of some sort of proof 'garbage collector'.

C.8.2   Accessing Functions (Proofs and Boxes)

The *roots* of a proof are those boxes which are not subboxes of any box in the proof's boxmap, that is they are the root boxes of all the separate attempts at the proof. Note that the invariant on proof implies that the roots must have at least one member.

$roots : Proof \to Box\text{-}ref\text{-set}$
$roots(p) \quad\triangleq$
$\quad \operatorname{let} bm = BOXMAP(p) \operatorname{in}$
$\quad \operatorname{dom} bm - \bigcup \{BOXES(b) \mid b \in \operatorname{rng} bm\}$

The hypotheses of a box in some proof are precisely the hypotheses of that box!

$hypsOfBox \ (p: Proof, b: Box\text{-}ref) \ es: Exp\text{-set}$
$\operatorname{pre} b \in \operatorname{dom} BOXMAP(p)$
$\operatorname{post} \operatorname{let} bm = BOXMAP(p) \operatorname{in}$
$\quad es = \operatorname{rng} HYPS(bm(b))$

Clear from user interface.

The function to find the conclusion of a box holds equally few surprises:

$conOfBox \ (p: Proof, b: Box\text{-}ref) \ e: Exp$
$\operatorname{pre} b \in \operatorname{dom} BOXMAP(p)$
$\operatorname{post} \operatorname{let} bm = BOXMAP(p),$
$\qquad lm = LINES(bm(b)) \operatorname{in}$
$\quad e = BODY(lm(CON(bm(b))))$

Clear from user interface.

The rule statement (not necessarily proper) implicit in a proof has the proof's sequent hypotheses as its sequent hypotheses and the hypotheses and conclusion of the root box as its ordinary hypotheses and conclusion:

ruleStmt : *Proof* → *RuleStmt*
ruleStmt(p) △
    let *ss* = rng *SEQHYPS(p)*,
        es = *hypsOfBox(p, ROOT(p))*,
        e = *conOfBox(p, ROOT(p))* in
    mk-RuleStmt(ss, es, e)

Clear from user interface.

The new free variables introduced by a box are the ones which map to that box under the *NFV* field of the proof:

newFreeVarsOfBox : *Proof* × *Box-ref* → *VSymb*-set
newFreeVarsOfBox(p, b) △
    let *vm* = *NFV(p)* in
    {*v* ∈ dom *vm* | *vm(v)* = *b*}

Clear from user interface.

The subboxes of a box are the box itself plus all those which are a subbox of it:

subboxesOfBox (*p*: *Proof*, *b*: *Box-ref*) *bs*: *Box-ref*-set
pre *b* ∈ dom *BOXMAP(p)*
post *bs* = {*b'* ∈ *Box-ref* | *b'* = *b* ∨ *isSubbox(b', b, BOXMAP(p))*}

Not exported.

All the ordinary lines in a proof are given by the union of the domains of the *LINES* fields of all the proof's boxes:

ordlines : *Proof* → *Ordline-ref*-set
ordlines(p) △
    let *bm* = *BOXMAP(p)* in
    ∪{dom *LINES(bm(b))* | *b* ∈ dom *bm*}

Not exported.

For convenience, we'll call ordinary lines and (ordinary) hypothesis lines *lines*:

Line-ref = *Ordline-ref* | *Hypline-ref*

The *lines* in a box (not including its subboxes) are its hypotheses plus its ordinary lines:

lines : *Box* → *Line-ref*-set
lines(b) △ dom *HYPS(b)* ∪ dom *LINES(b)*

Not exported.

The lines in a box plus all its subboxes are precisely that:

linesOfBox (*p*: *Proof*, *b*: *Box-ref*) *ls*: *Line-ref*-set
pre *b* ∈ dom *BOXMAP(p)*
post let *bm* = *BOXMAP(p)* in
    ls = ∪{*lines(bm(b'))* | *b'* ∈ *subboxesOfBox(p, b)*}

Not exported.

Note that this is a disjoint union since boxes are non-overlapping.

The lines in a proof are simply the lines in all its boxes:

> $lines : Proof \rightarrow Line\text{-}ref\text{-}set$
> $lines(p) \quad \triangleq$
>   let $bm = BOXMAP(p)$ in
> $\bigcup\{lines(bm(b)) \mid b \in \text{dom } bm\}$

Not exported.

Claim: $ordlines(p) = lines(p) \cap Ordline\text{-}ref$

The innermost box in which a line lies is that box whose lines includes the desired line:

> $boxOfLine\ (p\text{: } Proof, l\text{: } Line\text{-}ref)\ b\text{: } Box\text{-}ref$
> pre $l \in lines(p)$
> post $b \in \text{dom } BOXMAP(p) \wedge l \in lines(BOXMAP(p)(b))$

Not exported.

Of course, for each l and p satifying the precondition, $boxOfLine(p, l)$ is uniquely determined.

Claim: $l \in linesOfBox(p, b) \Leftrightarrow boxOfLine(p, l) \in subboxesOfBox(p, b)$

The *expression labelling* of a box is a map from lines to their bodies:

> $expLabelling : Box \rightarrow Line\text{-}ref \xrightarrow{m} Exp$
> $expLabelling(b) \quad \triangleq$
> $HYPS(b) \dagger \{ol \mapsto BODY(LINES(b)(ol)) \mid ol \in \text{dom } LINES(b)\}$

Not exported.

Whilst that of a proof is just the overwrite of those of all the proof's boxes. Note that the use of the distributive map overwrite function is valid here because the invariant on *Boxmap* says that boxes do not overlap.

> $expLabelling : Proof \rightarrow Line\text{-}ref \xrightarrow{m} Exp$
> $expLabelling(p) \quad \triangleq \quad \dagger\{expLabelling(BOXMAP(p)(b)) \mid b \in \text{dom } BOXMAP(p)\}$

Not exported.

Claim: dom $expLabelling(p) = lines(p)$

The *justification labelling* of a proof is similar to its expression labelling but is instead a mapping from lines to the justifications appearing thereon. The other slight difference is that there is no contribution from any ordinary hypothesis lines as they don't have justifications.

> $justifLabelling : Proof \rightarrow Ordline\text{-}ref \xrightarrow{m} Justification$
> $justifLabelling(p) \quad \triangleq$
>   let $bm = BOXMAP(p)$ in
> $\dagger\{\{ol \mapsto JUST(LINES(bm(b))(ol)) \mid ol \in \text{dom } LINES(bm(b))\} \mid b \in \text{dom } bm\}$

Not exported.

Claim: dom *justifLabelling(p)* = *ordlines(p)*

A proof has *closed justifications* if, for each possible root of the proof, the lines, boxes and sequents (see below) of the justifications in the tree starting from that root are all in that tree:

$$hasClosedJustifs : Proof \rightarrow \mathbb{B}$$
$$hasClosedJustifs(p) \quad \underline{\triangle}$$
$$\quad \forall b \in roots(p) \cdot$$
$$\quad\quad \text{let } ls = linesOfBox(p, b),$$
$$\quad\quad\quad bs = subboxesOfBox(p, b),$$
$$\quad\quad\quad ss = \text{dom } SEQHYPS(p),$$
$$\quad\quad\quad jlab = ls \lhd justifLabelling(p)$$
$$\quad\quad \text{in}$$
$$\quad\quad \forall j \in \text{rng } jlab \cdot$$
$$\quad\quad\quad lines(j) \subseteq ls$$
$$\quad\quad\quad \land boxes(j) \subseteq bs$$
$$\quad\quad\quad \land sequents(j) \subseteq ss$$

C.8.3 Justifications

The (as yet incomplete) collection of justification kinds[13]:

Justification = RuleJustif | SeqHypJustif | UnfoldDefJustif |
$$\qquad\qquad\qquad\qquad\qquad\qquad\qquad \textit{FoldDefJustif | NullJustif | ...}$$

Each of the basic kinds of justification will be dealt with in turn below. But first, some general support functions which will be needed later.

General Support Functions for Justifications

In general, the justification of some line in a proof will consist of some particular kind of justification together with a set of *dependents*. These dependents will point off to (other) lines, boxes, or sequent hypotheses in the proof, or may themselves be justifications. In general, expression dependents can be justified by appeal to either lines in the proof or to other justifications (*ordinary dependents*), whilst sequent dependents can be justified by appeal either to lines, boxes or sequent hypotheses in the proof or to other justifications (*sequent dependents*):

OrdDependent = Line-ref | Justification

---

[13]As has become common practice, functions acting on *Justification* in general will be written as identically-named functions on each of the different kinds of justification separately in order to avoid particularly horrendous case statements (Isn't VDM wonderful?). It should be clear to those few not yet suffering from a complete mental breakdown what is meant! It is claimed that the modularity of (this version of) the specification is such that, in order to add a new kind of justification, all that is necessary is to define both it and the functions *establishesExp*, *establishesSequent*, *isReasonableAtLine*, *relevantJustif*, *justifs*, *lines*, *boxes*, *sequents*, *rules*, and *thMorphs* on it.

SeqDependent = Line-ref | Box-ref | Sequent-ref | Justification

The functions below state the conditions that an expression be established by an ordinary dependent and that a sequent be established by a sequent dependent *except* for the case *Justification*. This is dealt with below for each kind of justification in turn.

An easy one for starters – a line *l* establishes an expression at line *ol* if the expression on line *l* is equivalent to it.

$establishesExp$ (*l*: *Line-ref*, *e*: *Exp*, *ol*: *Ordline-ref*, *p*: *Proof*, *th*: *Theory-ref*,
                                    rm: *Rulemap*, *thm*: *Theorymap*, *tmm*: *ThMorphmap*) *a*: $\mathbb{B}$
pre *ol* ∈ *ordlines*(*p*)
post let *elab* = *expLabelling*(*p*) in
    a ⇔ *l* ∈ dom *elab* ∧ *isEquivalentTo*(*elab*(*l*), *e*)

Not exported.

Similarly, a line *l* establishes a sequent at line *ol* if the expression on it establishes the sequent.

$establishesSequent$ (*l*: *Line-ref*, *s*: *Sequent*, *ol*: *Ordline-ref*, *p*: *Proof*, *th*: *Theory-ref*,
                                    rm: *Rulemap*, *thm*: *Theorymap*, *tmm*: *ThMorphmap*) *a*: $\mathbb{B}$
pre *ol* ∈ *ordlines*(*p*)
post let *elab* = *expLabelling*(*p*) in
    a ⇔ *l* ∈ dom *elab* ∧ *establishesSequent*(*elab*(*l*), *s*)

Not exported.

A box *b* establishes a sequent at line *ol* if the sequent made out of the free variables, the hypotheses and the conclusion of the box establishes that sequent.

$establishesSequent$ (*b*: *Box-ref*, *s*: *Sequent*, *ol*: *Ordline-ref*, *p*: *Proof*, *th*: *Theory-ref*,
                                    rm: *Rulemap*, *thm*: *Theorymap*, *tmm*: *ThMorphmap*) *a*: $\mathbb{B}$
pre *ol* ∈ *ordlines*(*p*)
post *b* ∈ dom *BOXMAP*(*p*) ∧
    let *vsb* = *newFreeVarsOfBox*(*p*, *b*),
        con = *conOfBox*(*p*, *b*),
        hyps = *hypsOfBox*(*p*, *b*),
        s' = *mk-Sequent*(*vsb*, *hyps*, *con*) in
    a ⇔ *establishesSequent*(*s'*, *s*)

Not exported.

Lastly, a sequent hypothesis establishes a sequent at line *ol* if it does!

$establishesSequent$ (*s*: *Sequent-ref*, *s'*: *Sequent*, *ol*: *Ordline-ref*, *p*: *Proof*,
                            th: *Theory-ref*, *rm*: *Rulemap*, *thm*: *Theorymap*,
                                                    tmm: *ThMorphmap*) *a*: $\mathbb{B}$
pre *ol* ∈ *ordlines*(*p*)
post *a* ⇔ *s* ∈ dom *SEQHYPS*(*p*) ∧ *establishesSequent*(*SEQHYPS*(*p*)(*s*), *s'*)

Not exported.

Rule Justifications

$$RuleJustif :: RULE \quad : \textit{Rule-ref}$$

	VIA	: *ThMorph-ref**
	INST	: *Instantiation*
	VMAP	: $VSymb \xleftarrow{m} VSymb$
	ORDDEPS	: $Exp \xrightarrow{m} OrdDependent$
	SEQDEPS	: $Sequent \xrightarrow{m} SeqDependent$

Roughly, a *rule justification* translates the statement of a given rule across some sequence of theory morphisms and instantiates the metavariable symbols and the free variables in the sequent hypotheses of the translated rule statement according to the *INST* and *VMAP* fields respectively. The remaining fields link hypotheses of the instantiated, translated rule statement to dependents which should establish them.

A rule justification's rule statement is instantiable if it's translatable over its *VIA* field and if the result of the translation is instantiable by its *INST* field:

$hasInstantiableRule : RuleJustif \times Rulemap \times ThMorphmap \rightarrow \mathbf{B}$
$hasInstantiableRule(j, rm, tmm) \quad \underline{\triangle}$
    $RULE(j) \in \text{dom } rm$
    $\wedge$
    let $rs = STMT(rm(RULE(j)))$ in
    $isTranslatable * *(rs, VIA(j), tmm)$
    $\wedge$
    let $rs' = translate * *(rs, VIA(j), tmm)$ in
    $isInstantiableBy(rs', INST(j))$

Not exported.

A rule justification is *OK* if:

1. The rule is in the correct theory;

2. The theory morphisms link up properly;

3. It has an instantiable rule (as defined above).

$isOK : RuleJustif \times Proof \times Theory\text{-}ref \times Rulemap \times Theorymap \times ThMorphmap$
    $\rightarrow \mathbf{B}$
$isOK(j, p, th, rm, thm, tmm) \quad \underline{\triangle}$
    let $r = RULE(j),$
        $tml = VIA(j),$
        $n = \text{len } tml,$
        $th_0 = \text{if } n = 0 \text{ then } th \text{ else } FROM(tmm(tml(1)))$
        in
    $r \in rules(th_0, rm, thm)$
    $\wedge (n \neq 0 \implies TO(tmm(tml(n))) \in ancestors(th, thm))$
    $\wedge linkUp(tml, tmm, thm) \wedge hasInstantiableRule(j, rm, tmm)$

Not exported.

A rule justification *establishes an expression* at some (ordinary) line *ol* if:

1. The rule justification is OK;

2. The conclusion of the instantiated, translated rule statement is equivalent to the given expression;

3. Each ordinary hypothesis of the instantiated, translated rule statement is established by its dependent in *ORDDEPS*;

4. Each sequent hypothesis of the instantiated, translated rule statement is either trivially true or is established by its dependent in *SEQDEPS*.

establishesExp (j: RuleJustif, e: Exp, ol: Ordline-ref, p: Proof,
$\qquad$ *th: Theory-ref, rm: Rulemap, thm: Theorymap,*
$\qquad\qquad\qquad\qquad\qquad\qquad\qquad\qquad$ *tmm: ThMorphmap) a:* B

pre $ol \in ordlines(p)$
post $a \Leftrightarrow$
$\qquad$ $isOK(j, p, th, rm, thm, tmm)$
$\qquad$ $\wedge$
$\qquad$ let $rs = ruleInstance(j, rm, tmm),$
$\qquad\qquad$ $mk\text{-}RuleJustif(r, tml, inst, vm, odm, sdm) = j$ in
$\qquad$ $isEquivalentTo(e, CONCL(rs))$
$\qquad$ $\wedge\ \forall \hat{e} \in ORDHYPS(rs) \cdot$
$\qquad\qquad$ $\hat{e} \in dom\ odm \wedge establishesExp(odm(\hat{e}), \hat{e}, ol, p, th, rm, thm, tmm)$
$\qquad$ $\wedge\ \forall \hat{s} \in SEQHYPS(rs) \cdot$
$\qquad\qquad$ $isTriviallyTrue(\hat{s})$
$\qquad\qquad$ $\vee\ \hat{s} \in dom\ sdm \wedge establishesSequent(sdm(\hat{s}), \hat{s}, ol, p, th, rm, thm, tmm)$

Not exported.

A rule justification *establishes a sequent* at some (ordinary) line *ol* if:

1. The rule justification is OK;

2. Each sequent hypothesis of the instantiated, translated rule statement is either trivially true or is established by its dependent in *SEQDEPS*.

3. Each ordinary hypothesis of the instantiated, translated rule statement which has a dependent in *ORDDEPS* is established by that dependent;

4. The sequent to be established is established by the sequent whose upshot and premises are respectively the conclusion and the ordinary hypotheses with no dependent of the instantiated, translated rule statement, and whose new free variables are those which are apparently free in its premises and upshot but which are not free in either the proof at line *ol* or the established (ordinary and sequent) hypotheses.

establishesSequent (j: RuleJustif, s: Sequent, ol: Ordline-ref, p: Proof,
$\qquad$ *th: Theory-ref, rm: Rulemap, thm: Theorymap,*
$\qquad\qquad\qquad$ *tmm: ThMorphmap) a:* B

pre *ol* ∈ *ordlines(p)*
post *a* ⇔
$\quad$ *isOK(j, p, th, rm, thm, tmm)*
$\quad$ ∧
$\quad$ let *rs = ruleInstance(j, rm, tmm),*
$\qquad$ *odm = ORDDEPS(j),*
$\qquad$ *sdm = SEQDEPS(j),*
$\qquad$ *es = ORDHYPS(rs) –* dom *odm,*
$\qquad$ *es' = ORDHYPS(rs)* ∩ dom *odm* in
$\quad$ ∀ŝ ∈ *SEQHYPS(rs)* ·
$\qquad$ *isTriviallyTrue(ŝ)*
$\qquad$ ∨ ŝ ∈ dom *sdm* ∧ *establishesSequent(sdm(ŝ), ŝ, ol, p, th, rm, thm, tmm)*
$\quad$ ∧ ∀ê ∈ *es'* ·
$\qquad$ *establishesExp(odm(ê), ê, ol, p, th, rm, thm, tmm)*
$\quad$ ∧
$\quad$ let *svs =* ∪{*freeVars(s) – NFV(s) | s* ∈ *SEQHYPS(rs)*},
$\qquad$ *pvs = freeVarsAtLine(p, ol),*
$\qquad$ *evs =* ∪{*freeVars(e') | e'* ∈ *es'*},
$\qquad$ *vs =* ∪{*freeVars(e) | e* ∈ *es* ∨ *e = CONCL(rs)*} *– (svs* ∪ *pvs* ∪ *evs),*
$\qquad$ *s' = mk-Sequent(vs, es, CONCL(rs))* in
$\quad$ *establishesSequent(s', s)*

Not exported.

The auxiliary function *ruleInstance* used in both of the above returns the relevant instantiation of the *RuleJustif's* translated rule statement (assuming, of course, that such a thing actually exists!):

ruleInstance (j: RuleJustif, rm: Rulemap, tmm: ThMorphmap) rs: RuleStmt
pre *hasInstantiableRule(j, rm, tmm)*
post let *rs' = STMT(rm(RULE(j))),*
$\qquad$ *rs'' = translate* ∗ *∗(rs', VIA(j), tmm),*
$\qquad$ *rs''' = renameFreeVars(rs'', VMAP(j))* in
$\quad$ *rs = instantiate(rs''', INST(j))*

Not exported.

The *justifs* of a rule justification are those dependents which are justifications:

justifs : RuleJustif → Justification-set
justifs(j) △
$\quad$ let *dm = SEQDEPS(j)* ∪ *ORDDEPS(j)* in
$\quad$ {*j'* ∈ rng *dm | j'* ∈ *Justification*}

Not exported.

The *lines* of a rule justification are those dependents which are lines plus the lines of all of its justifs:

lines : *RuleJustif* → *Line-ref*-set
lines(*j*) △
    let *dm* = *SEQDEPS*(*j*) ∪ *ORDDEPS*(*j*) in
    ∪{*lines*(*j'*) | *j'* ∈ *justifs*(*j*)} ∪ {*l* ∈ rng *dm* | *l* ∈ *Line-ref*}

Not exported.

The *boxes* of a rule justification are those (sequent) dependents which are boxes plus the boxes of all of its justifs:

boxes : *RuleJustif* → *Box-ref*-set
boxes(*j*) △
    ∪{*boxes*(*j'*) | *j'* ∈ *justifs*(*j*)} ∪ {*b* ∈ rng *SEQDEPS*(*j*) | *b* ∈ *Box-ref*}

Not exported.

The *sequents* of a rule justification are those (sequent) dependents which are sequents plus the sequents of all of its justifs:

sequents : *RuleJustif* → *Sequent-ref*-set
sequents(*j*) △
    ∪{*sequents*(*j'*) | *j'* ∈ *justifs*(*j*)} ∪ {*s* ∈ rng *SEQDEPS*(*j*) | *s* ∈ *Sequent-ref*}

Not exported.

The *rules* of a rule justification are its *RULE* field plus the rules of each of its justifs.

rules : *RuleJustif* → *Rule-ref*-set
rules(*j*) △ ∪{*rules*(*j'*) | *j'* ∈ *justifs*(*j*)} ∪ {*RULE*(*j*)}

Not exported.

The *theory morphisms* of a rule justification are the range of its *VIA* field plus the theory morphisms of each of its justifs.

thMorphs : *RuleJustif* → *ThMorph-ref*-set
thMorphs(*j*) △ ∪{*thMorphs*(*j'*) | *j'* ∈ *justifs*(*j*)} ∪ rng *VIA*(*j*)

Not exported.

The *relevant* part of a rule justification is obtained by removing unused parts from the *INST*, *VMAP*, *ORDDEPS* and *SEQDEPS* fields (e.g. instantiations of metavariable symbols which don't appear in the translated rule, or dependents of expressions or sequents which aren't in the hypotheses of the instantiated, translated rule) and replacing all justification dependents in the resulting rule justification with their relevant part. If the justification doesn't have an instantiable rule, it's all considered to be relevant (in the absence of any evidence to the contrary!).

$relevantJustif : RuleJustif \times Proof \times Rulemap \times ThMorphmap \rightarrow RuleJustif$
$relevantJustif(j, p, rm, tmm) \quad \triangleq$
    if $hasInstantiableRule(j, rm, tmm)$
    then
        let $rs = ruleInstance(j, rm, tmm),$
           $mk\text{-}RuleJustif(r, tml, inst, vm, odm, sdm) = j,$
           $rs' = STMT(rm(r)),$
           $vm' = \bigcup\{NFV(s) \mid s \in SEQHYPS(rs')\} \lhd vm,$
           $inst' = mk\text{-}Instantiation(meSymbs(rs') \lhd MEMAP(inst),$
                                         $mtSymbs(rs') \lhd MTMAP(inst)),$
           $odm' = \{\hat{e} \mapsto relevantJustif(odm(\hat{e}), p, rm, tmm) \mid$
                                  $\hat{e} \in \text{dom}\, odm \wedge odm(\hat{e}) \in Justification\},$
           $sdm' = \{\hat{s} \mapsto relevantJustif(sdm(\hat{s}), p, rm, tmm) \mid$
                                  $\hat{s} \in \text{dom}\, sdm \wedge sdm(\hat{s}) \in Justification\},$
           $odm'' = ORDHYPS(rs) \lhd (odm \dagger odm'),$
           $sdm'' = SEQHYPS(rs) \lhd (sdm \dagger sdm')$ **in**
        $mk\text{-}RuleJustif(r, tml, inst', vm', odm'', sdm'')$
    else j

Not exported.

A rule justification is *reasonable at some ordinary line of a proof* if it's OK, if its rule instance is reasonable at that line, and if all the justifications used (see §C.8.4 below) in it are reasonable at that line:

$isReasonableAtLine\ (j: RuleJustif, ol: Ordline\text{-}ref, p: Proof, th: Theory\text{-}ref,$
                            $rm: Rulemap, thm: Theorymap, tmm: ThMorphmap)\ a: \mathbb{B}$
$\text{pre}\ ol \in ordlines(p) \wedge isConsisWithSig(ruleStmt(p), fullSig(th, thm))$
$\text{post}\ a \Leftrightarrow$
    $isOK(j, p, th, rm, thm, tmm)$
    $\wedge\ isReasonableAtLine(ruleInstance(j, rm, tmm), ol, p, th, thm)$
    $\wedge\ \forall \hat{j} \in justifsUsed(j, p, rm, tmm)\ \cdot$
        $isReasonableAtLine(\hat{j}, ol, p, th, rm, thm, tmm)$

Not exported.

Sequent Hypothesis Justifications

$SeqHypJustif\ ::\ SEQUENT\ :\ Sequent\text{-}ref$
                $VMAP\ \ \ \ \ :\ VSymb \xrightarrow{m} VSymb$
                $ORDDEPS\ :\ Exp \xrightarrow{m} OrdDependent$

Roughly, the sequent hypothesis *SEQUENT* has its free variables renamed according to *VMAP*. The remaining field links premises of the resulting sequent to dependents which should establish them.

A sequent hypothesis justification is OK if its *SEQUENT* is among the proof's sequent hypotheses.

$isOK : SeqHypJustif \times Proof \times Theory\text{-}ref \times Rulemap \times$
$$Theorymap \times ThMorphmap \to \mathsf{B}$$
$isOK(j, p, th, rm, thm, tmm) \quad \triangleq \quad SEQUENT(j) \in \text{dom } SEQHYPS(p)$

A sequent hypothesis justification establishes an expression if:
 1. The justification is OK;

 2. The upshot of the sequent obtained by renaming free variables in its *SEQUENT* field according to the (free) variable instantiation map in its *VMAP* field is equivalent to the expression;

 3. Each premise of that sequent is established by its dependent in *ORDDEPS*.

$establishesExp\ (j: SeqHypJustif, e: Exp, ol: Ordline\text{-}ref, p: Proof,$
$\qquad\qquad th: Theory\text{-}ref, rm: Rulemap, thm: Theorymap,$
$$tmm: ThMorphmap)\ a: \mathsf{B}$$
$\text{pre } ol \in ordlines(p)$
$\text{post } a \iff$
$\qquad isOK(j, p, th, rm, thm, tmm)$
$\qquad \wedge$
$\qquad \text{let } mk\text{-}SeqHypJustif(s, vm, odm) = j,$
$\qquad\quad \S = renameFreeVars(SEQHYPS(p)(s), vm) \text{ in}$
$\qquad isEquivalentTo(e, UPSHOT(\S))$
$\qquad \wedge\ \forall \hat{e} \in PREMISES(\S) \cdot$
$\qquad\qquad \hat{e} \in \text{dom } odm \wedge establishesExp(odm(\hat{e}), \hat{e}, ol, p, th, rm, thm, tmm)$

Not exported.

Claim As a proof's sequent hypotheses are proper, the precondition of *renameFreeVars* as used in the above (and, by an amazing coincidence, in the below!) is automatically satisfied.

A sequent hypothesis justification establishes a sequent if:

 1. The justification is OK;

 2. Each premise of the renamed sequent which has a dependent in *ORDDEPS* is established by that dependent;

 3. The sequent to be established is established by the sequent whose upshot and premises are respectively the upshot and the premises with no dependent of the renamed sequent, and whose new free variables are those which are apparently free in its premises and upshot but which are not free in either the proof at line *ol* or the established premises.

$establishesSequent\ (j: SeqHypJustif, s: Sequent, ol: Ordline\text{-}ref, p: Proof,$
$\qquad\qquad th: Theory\text{-}ref, rm: Rulemap, thm: Theorymap,$
$$tmm: ThMorphmap)\ a: \mathsf{B}$$
$\text{pre } ol \in ordlines(p)$

post a $\Leftrightarrow$
    $isOK(j, p, th, rm, thm, tmm)$
    $\wedge$
    let $mk\text{-}SeqHypJustif(s', vm, odm) = j,$
        $s'' = renameFreeVars(SEQHYPS(p)(s'), vm),$
        $es = PREMISES(s'') - \text{dom } odm,$
        $es' = PREMISES(s'') \cap \text{dom } odm,$
        $pvs = freeVarsAtLine(p, ol),$
        $evs = \bigcup\{freeVars(e') \mid e' \in es'\},$
        $vs = \bigcup\{freeVars(e) \mid e \in es \vee e = UPSHOT(s'')\} - (pvs \cup evs),$
        $\S = mk\text{-}Sequent(vs, es, UPSHOT(s''))$ in
    $\forall \hat{e} \in es \cdot$
        $establishesExp(odm(\hat{e}), \hat{e}, ol, p, th, rm, thm, tmm)$
    $\wedge \; establishesSequent(\S, s)$

Not exported.

The justifs in a sequent hypothesis justification are those (ordinary) dependents which are justifications:

$justifs : SeqHypJustif \rightarrow Justification\text{-set}$
$justifs(j) \quad \underline{\Delta} \quad \{j' \in \text{rng } ORDDEPS(j) \mid j' \in Justification\}$

Not exported.

The lines in a sequent hypothesis justification are the lines of all of its justifs plus those dependents which are lines:

$lines : SeqHypJustif \rightarrow Line\text{-}ref\text{-set}$
$lines(j) \quad \underline{\Delta} \quad \bigcup\{lines(j') \mid j' \in justifs(j)\} \cup \{l \in \text{rng } ORDDEPS(j) \mid l \in Line\text{-}ref\}$

Not exported.

The boxes in a sequent hypothesis justification are just those in all of its justifs:

$boxes : SeqHypJustif \rightarrow Box\text{-}ref\text{-set}$
$boxes(j) \quad \underline{\Delta} \quad \bigcup\{boxes(j') \mid j' \in justifs(j)\}$

Not exported.

The sequents in a sequent hypothesis justification are those in all its justifs plus its *SEQUENT*:

$sequents : SeqHypJustif \rightarrow Sequent\text{-}ref\text{-set}$
$sequents(j) \quad \underline{\Delta} \quad \bigcup\{sequents(j') \mid j' \in justifs(j)\} \cup \{SEQUENT(j)\}$

Not exported.

The rules in a sequent hypothesis justification are just those in all of its justifs:

$rules : SeqHypJustif \rightarrow Rule\text{-}ref\text{-set}$
$rules(j) \quad \underline{\Delta} \quad \bigcup\{rules(j') \mid j' \in justifs(j)\}$

Not exported.

The thMorphs in a sequent hypothesis justification are just those in all of its justifs:

$thMorphs : SeqHypJustif \rightarrow ThMorph\text{-}ref\text{-set}$
$thMorphs(j) \quad \triangle \quad \bigcup\{thMorphs(j') \mid j' \in justifs(j)\}$

Not exported.

The relevant part of a sequent hypothesis justification is obtained by removing unused parts from the *VMAP* and *ORDDEPS* fields and replacing all justification dependents in the resulting sequent hypothesis justification with their relevant part. If the justification's *SEQUENT* isn't amongst the proof's sequent hypotheses, it's all considered to be relevant.

$relevantJustif : SeqHypJustif \times Proof \times Rulemap \times ThMorphmap \rightarrow SeqHypJustif$
$relevantJustif(j, p, rm, tmm) \quad \triangle$
    if $SEQUENT(j) \in \text{dom } SEQHYPS(p)$
    then
        let $mk\text{-}SeqHypJustif(s, vm, odm) = j,$
            $s' = SEQHYPS(p)(s),$
            $vm' = NFV(s') \lhd vm,$
            $odm' = \{\hat{\ell} \mapsto relevantJustif(odm(\hat{\ell}), p, rm, tmm) \mid$
                                   $\hat{\ell} \in \text{dom } odm \wedge odm(\hat{\ell}) \in Justification\},$
            $odm'' = PREMISES(s') \lhd (odm \dagger odm'),$
            in
        $mk\text{-}SeqHypJustif(s, vm', odm'')$
    else j

Not exported.

A sequent hypothesis justification is reasonable at some ordinary line of a proof if it's OK and if all the justifications used in it are reasonable at that line:

$isReasonableAtLine \; (j: SeqHypJustif, ol: Ordline\text{-}ref, p: Proof, th: Theory\text{-}ref,$
                      $rm: Rulemap, thm: Theorymap, tmm: ThMorphmap) \; a: \mathbb{B}$
pre $ol \in ordlines(p) \wedge isConsisWithSig(ruleStmt(p), fullSig(th, thm))$
post $a \Leftrightarrow$
    $isOK(j, p, th, rm, thm, tmm)$
    $\wedge \; \forall \hat{j} \in justifsUsed(j, p, rm, tmm) \cdot$
        $isReasonableAtLine(\hat{j}, ol, p, th, rm, thm, tmm)$

Not exported.

Unfold Definition Justifications

$UnfoldDefJustif :: \quad TOLINE \quad : Line\text{-}ref$
                     $SUBTERM : Index$

Roughly, the subterm of the expression on line *TOLINE* designated by *INDEX* is replaced by whatever it's defined to be[14].

An unfold definition justification is OK if:

---

[14]Note that this makes no provision for unfolding definitions in sequent hypotheses. This is probably not an important omission, and, as the proof model stands, there's no easy way to accommodate such unfolding. It is therefore being ignored.

1. The *TOLINE* is one of the proof's lines;

2. The index given points to a valid subterm of the expression on that line;

3. The subterm at that index is unfoldable.

$isOK : UnfoldDefJustif \times Proof \times Theory\text{-}ref \times Rulemap \times Theorymap \times ThMorphmap$
    $\rightarrow \mathsf{B}$
$isOK(j, p, th, rm, thm, tmm)$ $\triangle$
    let $mk\text{-}UnfoldDefJustif(l, i) = j,$
      $elab = expLabelling(p),$
      $\Sigma = fullSig(th, thm)$ in
    $l \in \mathsf{dom}\ elab \wedge isValidIndex(elab(l), i) \wedge$
                          $isUnfoldable(termAtIndex(elab(l), i), \Sigma)$

Not exported.

An unfold definition justification establishes some expression if it is OK and if the result of unfolding the definition at the appropriate index in the expression on the given line yields (some expression equivalent to) that expression:

$establishesExp\ (j\colon UnfoldDefJustif, e\colon Exp, ol\colon Ordline\text{-}ref, p\colon Proof,$
               $th\colon Theory\text{-}ref, rm\colon Rulemap, thm\colon Theorymap,$
                             $tmm\colon ThMorphmap)\ a\colon \mathsf{B}$

pre $ol \in ordlines(p)$
post $a\ \Leftrightarrow$
    $isOK(j, p, th, rm, thm, tmm)$
    $\wedge$
    let $mk\text{-}UnfoldDefJustif(l, i) = j,$
      $elab = expLabelling(p),$
      $\Sigma = fullSig(th, thm)$ in
    $isEquivalentTo(unfoldDefAt(elab(l), \Sigma, i), e)$

Not exported.

An unfold definition justification establishes a sequent if it's OK and if the expression resulting from unfolding the definition at the appropriate index in the expression on the given line establishes the required sequent:

$establishesSequent\ (j\colon UnfoldDefJustif, s\colon Sequent, ol\colon Ordline\text{-}ref, p\colon Proof,$
               $th\colon Theory\text{-}ref, rm\colon Rulemap, thm\colon Theorymap,$
                             $tmm\colon ThMorphmap)\ a\colon \mathsf{B}$

pre $ol \in ordlines(p)$
post $a\ \Leftrightarrow$
    $isOK(j, p, th, rm, thm, tmm)$
    $\wedge$
    let $mk\text{-}UnfoldDefJustif(l, i) = j,$
      $elab = expLabelling(p),$
      $\Sigma = fullSig(th, thm)$ in
    $establishesSequent(unfoldDefAt(elab(l), \Sigma, i), s)$

Not exported.

An unfold definition justification has no justifs:

$justifs : UnfoldDefJustif \rightarrow Justification\text{-set}$
$justifs(j) \quad \underline{\triangle} \quad \{\}$

Not exported.

The lines (actually, there's only one!) of an unfold definition justification are simply its *TOLINE*.

$lines : UnfoldDefJustif \rightarrow Line\text{-ref-set}$
$lines(j) \quad \underline{\triangle} \quad \{TOLINE(j)\}$

Not exported.

An unfold definition justification has no boxes ...

$boxes : UnfoldDefJustif \rightarrow Box\text{-ref-set}$
$boxes(j) \quad \underline{\triangle} \quad \{\}$

Not exported.

... and no sequents ...

$sequents : UnfoldDefJustif \rightarrow Sequent\text{-ref-set}$
$sequents(j) \quad \underline{\triangle} \quad \{\}$

Not exported.

... and no rules ...

$rules : UnfoldDefJustif \rightarrow Rule\text{-ref-set}$
$rules(j) \quad \underline{\triangle} \quad \{\}$

Not exported.

... and no theory morphisms.

$thMorphs : UnfoldDefJustif \rightarrow ThMorph\text{-ref-set}$
$thMorphs(j) \quad \underline{\triangle} \quad \{\}$

Not exported.

The relevant part of an unfold definition justification is the whole thing.

$relevantJustif : UnfoldDefJustif \times Proof \times Rulemap \times ThMorphmap$
$\qquad\qquad\qquad \rightarrow UnfoldDefJustif$
$relevantJustif(j, p, rm, tmm) \quad \underline{\triangle} \quad j$

Not exported.

An unfold definition justification is reasonable at an ordinary line if it's OK:

$isReasonableAtLine \; (j: UnfoldDefJustif, ol: Ordline\text{-ref}, p: Proof, th: Theory\text{-ref},$
$\qquad\qquad\qquad rm: Rulemap, thm: Theorymap, tmm: ThMorphmap) \; a: \mathbb{B}$
$\text{pre } ol \in ordlines(p) \wedge isConsisWithSig(ruleStmt(p), fullSig(th, thm))$
$\text{post } a \;\Leftrightarrow\; isOK(j, p, th, rm, thm, tmm)$

Not exported.

Fold Definition Justifications

This is just like unfolding definitions, only backwards.

$$FoldDefJustif :: \quad TOLINE \quad : Line\text{-}ref$$
$$SUBTERM : Index$$

A fold definition justtification is OK if it's *TOLINE* is one of the lines of the proof.

$$isOK : FoldDefJustif \times Proof \times Theory\text{-}ref \times Rulemap \times Theorymap \times ThMorphmap$$
$$\rightarrow \mathsf{B}$$
$$isOK(j, p, th, rm, thm, tmm) \quad \triangleq \quad TOLINE(j) \in lines(p)$$

Not exported.

A fold definition justification establishes an expression if:

1. The justification is OK;

2. The index in its *SUBTERM* field is a valid index of that expression;

3. The subterm at that index is unfoldable;

4. The result of unfolding the definition at that subterm yields (some expression equivalent to) the expression on the justification's *TOLINE*.

$$establishesExp\ (j: FoldDefJustif,\ e: Exp,\ ol: Ordline\text{-}ref,\ p: Proof,$$
$$th: Theory\text{-}ref,\ rm: Rulemap,\ thm: Theorymap,$$
$$tmm: ThMorphmap)\ a: \mathsf{B}$$
$$\mathbf{pre}\ ol \in ordlines(p)$$
$$\mathbf{post}\ a \iff$$
$$\quad isOK(j, p, th, rm, thm, tmm)$$
$$\quad \wedge$$
$$\quad \mathbf{let}\ mk\text{-}FoldDefJustif(l, i) = j,$$
$$\quad\quad elab = expLabelling(p),$$
$$\quad\quad \Sigma = fullSig(th, thm)\ \mathbf{in}$$
$$\quad isValidIndex(e, i) \wedge isUnfoldable(termAtIndex(e, i), \Sigma)$$
$$\quad \wedge isEquivalentTo(unfoldDefAt(e, \Sigma, i), elab(l))$$

Not exported.

A fold definition justification establishes a sequent if:

1. The justification is OK;

2. The free variables in the expression on the *TOLINE* and the sequent's new free variables are disjoint;

3. The index in its *SUBTERM* field is a valid index of the upshot of the sequent;

4. The subterm at that index is unfoldable;

5. The expression resulting from unfolding the definition at that subterm is equivalent to the expression on the *TOLINE*.

establishesSequent (*j*: *FoldDefJustif, s*: *Sequent, ol*: *Ordline-ref, p*: *Proof,*
$\qquad\qquad\qquad$ *th*: *Theory-ref, rm*: *Rulemap, thm*: *Theorymap,*
$\qquad\qquad\qquad\qquad\qquad\qquad\qquad\qquad$ *tmm*: *ThMorphmap*) *a*: $\mathbb{B}$

pre *ol* $\in$ *ordlines*(*p*)
post *a* $\Leftrightarrow$
$\qquad$ *isOK*(*j, p, th, rm, thm, tmm*)
$\qquad$ $\wedge$
$\qquad$ let *mk-FoldDefJustif*(*l, i*) = *j,*
$\qquad\qquad$ *elab* = *expLabelling*(*p*),
$\qquad\qquad$ Σ = *fullSig*(*th, thm*),
$\qquad\qquad$ *e* = *UPSHOT*(*s*) in
$\qquad$ *isValidIndex*(*e, i*) $\wedge$ *isUnfoldable*(*termAtIndex*(*e, i*), Σ)
$\qquad$ $\wedge$ *NFV*(*s*) $\cap$ *freeVars*(*elab*(*l*)) = { }
$\qquad$ $\wedge$ *isEquivalentTo*(*unfoldDefAt*(*e*, Σ, *i*), *elab*(*l*))

Not exported.

A fold definition justification has no justifs:

$\qquad$ *justifs* : *FoldDefJustif* $\rightarrow$ *Justification*-set
$\qquad$ *justifs*(*j*) $\triangleq$ { }

Not exported.

The lines (again, there's only one!) of a fold definition justification are simply its *TOLINE*.

$\qquad$ *lines* : *FoldDefJustif* $\rightarrow$ *Line-ref*-set
$\qquad$ *lines*(*j*) $\triangleq$ {*TOLINE*(*j*)}

Not exported.

A fold definition justification has no boxes …

$\qquad$ *boxes* : *FoldDefJustif* $\rightarrow$ *Box-ref*-set
$\qquad$ *boxes*(*j*) $\triangleq$ { }

Not exported.

… and no sequents …

$\qquad$ *sequents* : *FoldDefJustif* $\rightarrow$ *Sequent-ref*-set
$\qquad$ *sequents*(*j*) $\triangleq$ { }

Not exported.

… and no rules …

$\qquad$ *rules* : *FoldDefJustif* $\rightarrow$ *Rule-ref*-set
$\qquad$ *rules*(*j*) $\triangleq$ { }

Not exported.

… and no theory morphisms.

$thMorphs : FoldDefJustif \rightarrow ThMorph\text{-}ref\text{-set}$
$thMorphs(j) \;\triangleq\; \{\,\}$

Not exported.

The relevant part of a fold definition justification is the whole thing.

$relevantJustif : FoldDefJustif \times Proof \times Rulemap \times ThMorphmap \rightarrow FoldDefJustif$
$relevantJustif(j, p, rm, tmm) \;\triangleq\; j$

Not exported.

A fold definition justification is reasonable at an ordinary line if it's OK:

$isReasonableAtLine\ (j\!: FoldDefJustif,\ ol\!: Ordline\text{-}ref,\ p\!: Proof,\ th\!: Theory\text{-}ref,$
$\qquad\qquad\qquad\qquad rm\!: Rulemap,\ thm\!: Theorymap,\ tmm\!: ThMorphmap)\ a\!: \mathbb{B}$
pre $ol \in ordlines(p) \wedge isConsisWithSig(ruleStmt(p), fullSig(th, thm))$
post $a \;\Leftrightarrow\; isOK(j, p, th, rm, thm, tmm)$

Not exported.

Null Justifications

These beasts cover the case when no decision has yet been made on the type of justification to be used at some given point.

A null justification doesn't establish an expression:

$establishesExp\ (j\!: NullJustif,\ e\!: Exp,\ ol\!: Ordline\text{-}ref,\ p\!: Proof,$
$\qquad\qquad\qquad\quad th\!: Theory\text{-}ref,\ rm\!: Rulemap,\ thm\!: Theorymap,$
$\qquad\qquad\qquad\qquad\qquad\qquad\qquad\qquad tmm\!: ThMorphmap)\ a\!: \mathbb{B}$
pre $ol \in ordlines(p)$
post $a \;\Leftrightarrow\;$ false

Not exported.

A null justification doesn't establishes a sequent either:

$establishesSequent\ (j\!: FoldDefJustif,\ s\!: Sequent,\ ol\!: Ordline\text{-}ref,\ p\!: Proof,$
$\qquad\qquad\qquad\qquad th\!: Theory\text{-}ref,\ rm\!: Rulemap,\ thm\!: Theorymap,$
$\qquad\qquad\qquad\qquad\qquad\qquad\qquad\qquad tmm\!: ThMorphmap)\ a\!: \mathbb{B}$
pre $ol \in ordlines(p)$
post $a \;\Leftrightarrow\;$ false

Not exported.

A null justification has no justifs ...

$justifs : NullJustif \rightarrow Justification\text{-set}$
$justifs(j) \;\triangleq\; \{\,\}$

Not exported.

... and no lines ...

> *lines* : *NullJustif* → *Line-ref*-set
> *lines(j)* ≜ { }

Not exported.

... and no boxes ...

> *boxes* : *NullJustif* → *Box-ref*-set
> *boxes(j)* ≜ { }

Not exported.

... and no sequents ...

> *sequents* : *NullJustif* → *Sequent-ref*-set
> *sequents(j)* ≜ { }

Not exported.

... and no rules ...

> *rules* : *NullJustif* → *Rule-ref*-set
> *rules(j)* ≜ { }

Not exported.

... and no theory morphisms.

> *thMorphs* : *NullJustif* → *ThMorph-ref*-set
> *thMorphs(j)* ≜ { }

Not exported.

The relevant part of a null justification is the whole thing.

> *relevantJustif* : *NullJustif* × *Proof* × *Rulemap* × *ThMorphmap* → *NullJustif*
> *relevantJustif(j, p, rm, tmm)* ≜ *j*

Not exported.

A null justification is reasonable at any ordinary line.

> *isReasonableAtLine* (*j*: *NullJustif, ol*: *Ordline-ref, p*: *Proof, th*: *Theory-ref*,
>   *rm*: *Rulemap, thm*: *Theorymap, tmm*: *ThMorphmap*) *a*: B
> pre *ol* ∈ *ordlines(p)* ∧ *isConsisWithSig(ruleStmt(p), fullSig(th, thm))*
> post *a* ⇔ true

Not exported.

C.8.4   Accessing Functions (Justifications)

The *justifications used* in some justification are the justifs of the relevant part of that justification.

> *justifsUsed* : *Justification* × *Proof* × *RuleMap* × *ThMorphmap* → *Justification*-set
> *justifsUsed(j, p, rm, tmm)* ≜ *justifs(relevantJustif(j, p, rm, tmm)*

Not exported.

The *lines used* in some justification are the lines of the relevant part of that justification.

$linesUsed : Justification \times Proof \times RuleMap \times ThMorphmap \rightarrow Line\text{-}ref\text{-}set$
$linesUsed(j, p, rm, tmm) \quad \triangleq \quad lines(relevantJustif(j, p, rm, tmm))$

Not exported.

The *boxes used* in some justification are the boxes of the relevant part of that justification.

$boxesUsed : Justification \times Proof \times RuleMap \times ThMorphmap \rightarrow Box\text{-}ref\text{-}set$
$boxesUsed(j, p, rm, tmm) \quad \triangleq \quad boxes(relevantJustif(j, p, rm, tmm))$

Not exported.

The *rules used* in some justification are the rules of the relevant part of that justification.

$rulesUsed : Justification \times Proof \times RuleMap \times ThMorphmap \rightarrow Rule\text{-}ref\text{-}set$
$rulesUsed(j, p, rm, tmm) \quad \triangleq \quad rules(relevantJustif(j, p, rm, tmm))$

Not exported.

And the *theory morphisms used* in some justification are the theory morphisms of the relevant part of that justification.

$thMorphsUsed : Justification \times Proof \times RuleMap \times ThMorphmap$
$\qquad\qquad \rightarrow ThMorph\text{-}ref\text{-}set$
$thMorphsUsed(j, p, rm, tmm) \quad \triangleq \quad thMorphs(relevantJustif(j, p, rm, tmm))$

Not exported.

C.8.5 Dependencies

A line *l* depends on some other line *l'* in a proof if *l* is an ordinary line and if *l'* is one of the lines used in justifying *l* or is the conclusion of some box used in justifying *l* or if it depends on such a line/conclusion of a box:

$dependsOnLine \ (l\text{: }Line\text{-}ref, l'\text{: }Line\text{-}ref, p\text{: }Proof,$
$\qquad\qquad\qquad\qquad\qquad\qquad\qquad rm\text{: }Rulemap, tmm\text{: }ThMorphmap) \ a\text{: B}$
pre $l, \ l' \in lines(p)$
post let $jlab = justifLabelling(p),$
$\quad bm = BOXMAP(p)$ in
$\ a \Leftrightarrow$
$\ l \in \text{dom } jlab \ \wedge$
$\ \text{let } j = jlab(l),$
$\qquad cons = \{CON(bm(b)) \mid b \in boxesUsed(j, p, rm, tmm)\},$
$\qquad ls = linesUsed(j, p, rm, tmm) \cup cons$ in
$\qquad (l' \in ls \vee \exists \hat{l} \in ls \cdot dependsOnLine(\hat{l}, l', p, rm, tmm))$

Not exported.

The lines used in a proof are those on which the proof's conclusion depends:

linesUsed : *Proof* × *Rulemap* × *ThMorphmap* → *Line-ref*-set
linesUsed(*p*, *rm*, *tmm*) △
    let *bm* = *BOXMAP*(*p*),
      ls = *linesOfBox*(*p*, *ROOT*(*p*)),
      con = *CON*(*bm*(*ROOT*(*p*))) in
    {*con*} ∪ {*l* ∈ *ls* | *dependsOnLine*(*con*, *l*, *p*, *rm*, *tmm*)}

Not exported.

This function is intended to be applied to completed proofs to determine which lines are actually needed in the proof, i.e. as part of the proof garbage collector.

The rules used in justifying some set of lines in a proof are the rules used in the justifications of those lines!

rulesUsedInLines : *Proof* × *Line-ref*-set × *Rulemap* × *ThMorphmap* → *Rule-ref*-set
rulesUsedInLines(*p*, *ls*, *rm*, *tmm*) △
    let *jlab* = *ls* ◁ *justifLabelling*(*p*) in
    ∪{*rulesUsed*(*j*, *p*, *rm*, *tmm*) | *j* ∈ rng *jlab*}

Not exported.

The rules used in a proof are those used in the justifications of the lines used therein:

rulesUsed : *Proof* × *Rulemap* × *ThMorphmap* → *Rule-ref*-set
rulesUsed(*p*, *rm*, *tmm*) △
    let *ls* = *linesUsed*(*p*, *rm*, *tmm*) in
    rulesUsedInLines(*p*, *ls*, *rm*, *tmm*)

Exported for complete proofs.

And the theory morphisms used in a proof are those used in the justifications of the lines used:

thMorphsUsed : *Proof* × *Rulemap* × *ThMorphmap* → *ThMorph-ref*-set
thMorphsUsed(*p*, *rm*, *tmm*) △
    let *ls* = *linesUsed*(*p*, *rm*, *tmm*),
      jlab = *ls* ◁ *justifLabelling*(*p*) in
    ∪{*thMorphsUsed*(*j*, *p*, *rm*, *tmm*) | *j* ∈ rng *jlab*}

Exported for complete proofs.

A proof is well-formed if it has no circular dependencies and has no dependencies which reach into boxes:

$isWfdProof : Proof \times Rulemap \times ThMorphmap \rightarrow \mathsf{B}$
$isWfdProof(p, rm, tmm) \quad \underline{\triangle}$
$\qquad \forall b \in roots(p) \cdot$
$\qquad\qquad \text{let } ls = linesOfBox(p, b),$
$\qquad\qquad\quad bs = subboxesOfBox(p, b),$
$\qquad\qquad\quad jlab = ls \lhd justifLabelling(p) \text{ in}$
$\qquad\qquad \forall l \in \text{dom } jlab \cdot$
$\qquad\qquad\qquad \neg \; dependsOnLine(l, l, p, rm, tmm)$
$\qquad\qquad\qquad \wedge boxesUsed(jlab(l), p, rm, tmm) \cap \{b' \in bs \mid l \in linesOfBox(p, b')\}$
$\qquad\qquad\qquad\qquad\qquad\qquad\qquad\qquad\qquad\qquad\qquad\qquad\qquad\qquad = \{\,\}$

$\qquad\qquad \wedge \; \forall \hat{b} \in bs \cdot$
$\qquad\qquad\qquad l \notin linesOfBox(p, \hat{b}) \; \Rightarrow$
$\qquad\qquad\qquad linesUsed(jlab(l), p, rm, tmm) \cap lines(bm(\hat{b})) = \{\,\}$
$\qquad\qquad\qquad \wedge \; boxesUsed(jlab(l), p, rm, tmm) \cap BOXES(bm(\hat{b})) = \{\,\}$

Background. Warning when violated.

Claim:

$isWfdProof(p, rm, tmm) \wedge l_1 \in lines(p) \wedge dependsOnLine(l_1, l_2, p, rm, tmm)$
$\Rightarrow \; l_2 \in lines(p) \wedge boxOfLine(p, l_1) \in subboxesOfBox(p, boxOf(l_2, p))$

Claim:

$\forall l, l' \in \textit{Line-ref}, b \in \textit{Box-ref} \cdot$
$\qquad (dependsOnLine(l, l', p, rm, tmm) \wedge$
$\qquad\qquad\qquad\qquad\qquad\qquad\qquad l \notin linesOfBox(p, b) \wedge l' \in linesOfBox(p, b))$
$\qquad \Rightarrow \; \text{let } con = CON(BOXMAP(p)(b)) \text{ in}$
$\qquad (dependsOnLine(l, con, p, rm, tmm) \wedge dependsOnLine(con, l', p, rm, tmm))$

C.8.6 When is a Proof Finished?

A function for finding the assumptions on which a line depends, by tracing back along dependencies:

$assumptionsOfLine \; (p{:} Proof, l{:} \textit{Line-ref}, rm{:} Rulemap,$
$\qquad\qquad\qquad\qquad\qquad\qquad\qquad tmm{:} ThMorphmap) \; ls{:} \textit{Line-ref}\text{-set}$
$\text{pre } isWfdProof(p, rm, tmm) \wedge l \in lines(p)$
$\text{post let } jlab = justifLabelling(p) \text{ in}$
$\qquad ls = \text{if } l \in \text{dom } jlab$
$\qquad\qquad \text{then}$
$\qquad\qquad\qquad \text{let } j = jlab(l),$
$\qquad\qquad\qquad\quad ls_1 = \bigcup\{assumptionsOfLine(p, l', rm, tmm) \mid$
$\qquad\qquad\qquad\qquad\qquad\qquad\qquad\qquad\qquad\qquad l' \in linesUsed(j, p, rm, tmm)\},$
$\qquad\qquad\qquad\quad ls_2 = \bigcup\{assumptionsOfBox(p, b, rm, tmm) \mid$
$\qquad\qquad\qquad\qquad\qquad\qquad\qquad\qquad\qquad b \in boxesUsed(j, p, rm, tmm)\} \text{ in}$
$\qquad\qquad\qquad ls_1 \cup ls_2$
$\qquad\qquad \text{else } \{l\}$

Exported.

assumptionsOfBox (*p*: *Proof*, *b*: *Box-ref*, *rm*: *Rulemap*,
$\qquad\qquad\qquad$ *tmm*: *ThMorphmap*) *ls*: *Line-ref*-set
pre *isWfdProof*(*p*, *rm*, *tmm*) ∧ *b* ∈ dom *BOXMAP*(*p*)
post let *b'* = *BOXMAP*(*p*)(*b*) in
$\qquad$ *ls* = *assumptionsOfLine*(*p*, *CON*(*b'*), *rm*, *tmm*) − dom *HYPS*(*b'*)

Not exported.

Note how hypotheses of boxes are discharged.

Claim:

isWfdProof(*p*, *rm*, *tmm*) ∧ *ol* ∈ *ordlines*(*p*) ⇒
assumptionsOfLine(*p*, *ol*, *rm*, *tmm*) ⊆
$\qquad\qquad\qquad$ {*l* ∈ *Line-ref* | *dependsOnLine*(*ol*, *l*, *p*, *rm*, *tmm*)}

A proof is finished if it is well-formed and the only assumptions on which its conclusion depends are hypotheses of its *ROOT*:

isFinished : *Proof* × *Rulemap* × *ThMorphmap* → B
isFinished(*p*, *rm*, *tmm*) △
$\qquad$ let *bm* = *BOXMAP*(*p*),
$\qquad\quad$ *root* = *bm*(*ROOT*(*p*)) in
$\qquad$ *isWfdProof*(*p*, *rm*, *tmm*)
$\qquad$ ∧ *assumptionsOfLine*(*p*, *CON*(*root*), *rm*, *tmm*) ⊆ dom *HYPS*(*root*)

Not exported.

Of course, just because a proof is finished doesn't mean that it's valid: its expression labellings must also be reasonable and complete, and its justifications must all be valid.

C.8.7   General Support Functions for Proofs

First, a function to extract the free variables available at a given line in a proof by collecting all the new free variables of boxes containing the line:

freeVarsAtLine (*p*: *Proof*, *l*: *Line-ref*) *vs*: *VSymb*-set
pre *l* ∈ *lines*(*p*)
post *vs* = ∪{*newFreeVarsOfBox*(*p*, *b*) |
$\qquad\qquad\qquad$ *l* ∈ *linesOfBox*(*p*, *b*) ∧ *b* ∈ dom *BOXMAP*(*p*)}

Not exported.

Claims:

s ∈ rng *SEQHYPS*(*p*) ⇒ *NFV*(*s*) ∩ *freeVarsAtLine*(*p*, *l*) = { }

l ∉ *linesOfBox*(*p*, *b*) ⇒ *newFreeVarsOfBox*(*p*, *b*) ∩ *freeVarsAtLine*(*p*, *l*) = { }

let *bm* = *BOXMAP*(*p*), *box* = *bm*(*b*) in
(*isWfdProof*(*p*, *rm*, *tmm*) ∧ *b* ∈ dom *bm*
∧ *dependsOnLine*(*CON*(*box*), *l*, *p*, *rm*, *tmm*) ∧ *l* ∉ *lines*(*box*))
⇒ *newFreeVarsOfBox*(*p*, *b*) ∩ *freeVarsAtLine*(*p*, *l*) = { }

It's as a result of this third property that the usual variable occurrence side-conditions will be inforced.

An expression is *reasonable at some line in a proof* if its free variables are all available at that line, if it's reasonable with respect to the relevant signature, if it contains no placeholders, and if metavariables appear consistently in the expression and the proof's rule statement:

$isReasonableAtLine$ (e: Exp, l: $Line$-ref, p: $Proof$, th: $Theory$-ref,
thm: $Theorymap$) a: B
pre $l \in lines(p) \land isConsisWithSig(ruleStmt(p), fullSig(th, thm))$
post $a \Leftrightarrow$
    $freeVars(e) \subseteq freeVarsAtLine(p, l)$
    $\land isReasonableWRTSig(e, fullSig(th, thm))$
    $\land isFull(e)$
    $\land isConsisWithRuleStmt(e, ruleStmt(p))$

Not exported.

A sequent is reasonable at some line in a proof if its apparent free variables are actually free or are available at that line, if all its exps are reasonable with respect to the relevant signature and contain no placeholders, and if metavariables appear consistently in the sequent and the proof's rule statement:

$isReasonableAtLine$ (s: $Sequent$, l: $Line$-ref, p: $Proof$, th: $Theory$-ref,
thm: $Theorymap$) a: B
pre $l \in lines(p) \land isConsisWithSig(ruleStmt(p), fullSig(th, thm))$
post $a \Leftrightarrow$
    $freeVars(s) \subseteq NFV(s) \cup freeVarsAtLine(p, l)$
    $\land \forall e \in exps(s) \cdot$
        $isReasonableWRTSig(e, fullSig(th, thm)) \land isFull(e)$
    $\land isConsisWithRuleStmt(s, ruleStmt(p))$

Not exported.

A rule statement is reasonable at some line in a proof if its conclusion, its ordinary hypotheses and its sequent hypotheses are all reasonable at that line:

$isReasonableAtLine$ (rs: $RuleStmt$, l: $Line$-ref, p: $Proof$, th: $Theory$-ref,
thm: $Theorymap$) a: B
pre $l \in lines(p) \land isConsisWithSig(ruleStmt(p), fullSig(th, thm))$
post $a \Leftrightarrow$
    $isReasonableAtLine(CONCL(rs), l, p, th, thm)$
    $\land \forall e \in ORDHYPS(rs) \cdot$
        $isReasonableAtLine(e, l, p, th, thm)$
    $\land \forall s \in SEQHYPS(rs) \cdot$
        $isReasonableAtLine(s, l, p, th, thm)$

Not exported.

C.8.8   Consistency Checks on the Expressions and Justifications in a Proof

A line has a reasonable body if the expression on it is reasonable at that line:

> $hasReasonableBody$ (l: *Line-ref, p*: *Proof, th*: *Theory-ref, thm*: *Theorymap*) a: B
> pre $l \in lines(p) \land isConsisWithSig(ruleStmt(p), fullSig(th, thm))$
> post let $e = expLabelling(p)(l)$ in
> $\qquad a \iff isReasonableAtLine(e, l, p, th, thm)$

Background. Warning when violated.

A line has a reasonable justification if it's a hypothesis line or if it's an ordinary line whose justification is reasonable at that line:

> $hasReasonableJustif$ (l: *Line-ref, p*: *Proof, th*: *Theory-ref, rm*: *Rulemap,*
> $\qquad\qquad\qquad\qquad\qquad\qquad\qquad$ *thm*: *Theorymap, tmm*: *ThMorphmap*) a: B
> pre $l \in lines(p) \land isConsisWithSig(ruleStmt(p), fullSig(th, thm))$
> post let $jlab = justifLabelling(p)$ in
> $\qquad a \iff l \in \text{dom } jlab \implies isReasonableAtLine(jlab(l), l, p, th, rm, thm, tmm)$

Background. Warning when violated.

C.8.9   Completeness Checks

A line in a proof is completely justified (with redundancies allowed) if it's a hypothesis line or if it's an ordinary line whose body is established by its justification:

> $isJustifiedLine$ (p: *Proof, l*: *Line-ref, th*: *Theory-ref,*
> $\qquad\qquad\qquad\qquad\qquad$ *rm*: *Rulemap, thm*: *Theorymap, tmm*: *ThMorphmap*) a: B
> pre $l \in lines(p)$
> post let $elab = expLabelling(p),$
> $\qquad jlab = justifLabelling(p)$ in
> $\qquad a \iff l \in \text{dom } jlab \implies establishesExp(jlab(l), elab(l), p, th, rm, thm, tmm)$

Exported.

A proof conducted in a given theory is complete if it is finished and all the lines used to establish the conclusion have complete and reasonable bodies and justifications (if appropriate):

> $isComplete$ (p: *Proof, th*: *Theory-ref, rm*: *Rulemap, thm*: *Theorymap,*
> $\qquad\qquad\qquad\qquad\qquad\qquad\qquad\qquad\qquad$ *tmm*: *ThMorphmap*) a: B
> pre $isReasonableWRTTheory(ruleStmt(p), th, thm)$
> post $a \iff$
> $\qquad isFinished(p)$
> $\qquad \land \forall l \in linesUsed(p) \cdot$
> $\qquad\qquad hasReasonableBody(l, p, th, thm)$
> $\qquad\qquad \land hasReasonableJustif(l, p, th, rm, thm, tmm)$
> $\qquad\qquad \land isJustifiedLine(p, l, th, rm, thm, tmm)$

Exported.

C.9 The Store

$$Store :: \begin{array}{ll} RULES & : Rulemap \\ THS & : Theorymap \\ THMORPHS & : ThMorphmap \end{array}$$

C.9.1 Completeness checks

The set of rules on which a proof seems to depend:

$antecedents : Proof \times Rulemap \times Theorymap \times ThMorphmap \rightarrow Rule\text{-}ref\text{-set}$
$antecedents(p, rm, thm, tmm) \quad \triangle$
$\quad\quad rulesUsed(p) \cup$
$\quad\quad\quad\quad\quad\quad \bigcup\{rulesUsed(\tau, rm, thm, tmm) \mid \tau \in thMorphsUsed(p, rm, tmm)\}$

Not exported.
(Actually, the proof also depends on any other rules which might be needed to complete the justifications of the relevant theory morphisms.)

A function to test whether a derived rule depends on another:

$dependsOnRule : Rule\text{-}ref \times Rule\text{-}ref \times Rulemap \times Theorymap \times ThMorphmap \rightarrow \mathbb{B}$
$dependsOnRule(r_1, r_2, rm, thm, tmm) \quad \triangle$
$\quad \text{let } p = PROOF(rm(r_1)),$
$\quad\quad rs = antecedents(p, rm, thm, tmm) \text{ in}$
$\quad r_1 \in \text{dom } rm \wedge p \neq nil \wedge (r_2 \in rs \vee \exists r \in rs \cdot dependsOnRule(r, r_2, rm, thm, tmm))$

Exported.

$isNoncircular : Rulemap \times Theorymap \times ThMorphmap \rightarrow \mathbb{B}$
$isNoncircular(rm, thm, tmm) \quad \triangle$
$\quad \forall r \in \text{dom } rm \cdot \neg \; dependsOnRule(r, r, rm, thm, tmm)$

Background. Warning when violated.

Although this has been relegated to the status of a consistency check, it's probably important enough that the user should be warned whenever a circularity is introduced. Similarly, when searching for rules to apply in a proof, rules which depend on the rule being proven should be rejected (remembering that there might be other rules with the same statement which need not be rejected!)

An operation to check whether a rule is established *modulo* a set of rules:

isEstablishedModRules : *Rule-ref* × *Rule-ref*-set
$\qquad\qquad$ × *Rulemap* × *Theorymap* × *ThMorphmap* → B
isEstablishedModRules(*r, rules, rm, thm, tmm*) $\quad\triangleq$
$\qquad$ *r* ∈ dom *rm* ∧ *is-OK-Rule*(*rm*(*r*)) ∧
$\qquad$ let *p* = *PROOF*(*rm*(*r*)) in
$\qquad$ (*r* ∈ *rules*
$\qquad$ ∨ *p* = nil
$\qquad$ ∨ *p* ≠ nil ∧ *isComplete*(*p*, *THEORY*(*rm*(*r*)), *rm, thm, tmm*)
$\qquad\quad$ ∧ ∀*r'* ∈ *rulesUsed*(*p, rm, tmm*) ·
$\qquad\qquad$ *isEstablishedModRules*(*r', rules, rm, thm, tmm*)
$\qquad\quad$ ∧ ∀*τ* ∈ *thMorphsUsed*(*p, rm, tmm*) ·
$\qquad\qquad$ *isEstablishedModRules*(*τ, rules, rm, thm, tmm*))

Exported.

isEstablishedModRules : *ThMorph-ref* × *Rule-ref*-set
$\qquad\qquad$ × *Rulemap* × *Theorymap* × *ThMorphmap* → B
isEstablishedModRules(*τ, rules, rm, thm, tmm*) $\quad\triangleq\quad$ *τ* ∈ dom *tmm*
$\qquad$ ∧ *isReasonableThMorph*(*τ, rm, thm, tmm*)
$\qquad$ ∧ ∀*r* ∈ *rulesUsed*(*τ, rm, thm, tmm*) ·
$\qquad\quad$ *isEstablishedModRules*(*r, rules, rm, thm, tmm*)

Exported.

A *valid* derived rule is one which is established *modulo* the empty set.

An operation which extracts a set of incompletely-proven rules on which a rule depends:

rulesYetToBeProven : *Rule-ref* × *Rulemap* × *Theorymap* × *ThMorphmap*
$\qquad\qquad$ → *Rule-ref*-set
rulesYetToBeProven(*r, rm, thm, tmm*) $\quad\triangleq\quad$ let *p* = *PROOF*(*rm*(*r*)) in
$\qquad$ if *r* ∈ dom *rm*
$\qquad$ then if *p* = nil
$\qquad\qquad$ then { }
$\qquad\qquad$ else if *isComplete*(*p*, *THEORY*(*rm*(*r*)), *rm, thm, tmm*)
$\qquad\qquad\quad$ then ∪{*rulesYetToBeProven*(*r', rm, thm, tmm*) |
$\qquad\qquad\qquad\qquad\qquad\qquad\qquad\qquad$ *r'* ∈ *rulesUsed*(*p, rm, tmm*)}
$\qquad\qquad\quad$ else {*r*}
$\qquad$ else {*r*}

Exported.
The function is called recursively, bottoming out at undefined rules and rules with incomplete proofs.

Claim: The rules returned by *rulesYetToBeProven* are necessary to establish the rule in question (at least, according to the proofs currently stored): i.e.

isEstablishedModRules(*r, rules, rm, thm, tmm*) ∧ *r* ∉ *rules*
⇒ *rulesYetToBeProven*(*r, rm, thm, tmm*) ⊆ *rules*

The set is not necessarily sufficient to establish the rule, however, since some of the theory morphisms involved may not be completely justified.

Appendix D

The specification of the animation tool

This specification makes heavy use of other work within *mural*. A simple prototype of the system SYMBEX as specified here has been built, which contains most of the functionality specified except for recursion and simplification. This implies that it is only suitable to demonstrate some of the ideas; it is not a usable system. Because of a shortage of time it was then decided to concentrate all efforts on building the proof tool, rather than continue implementing SYMBEX.

D.1 Data structure and some auxiliary functions

SEStateOp

Define

$$Index = \mathbb{N}_1^*$$

A state as used for describing the operational semantics of a language for symbolic execution is defined recursively by

$$SE\text{-}map = Name \xrightarrow{m} PredS\text{-}set$$

$$SE\text{-}elem = SE\text{-}map \mid SEStateOp$$

$$SEStateOp :: SEQ \quad : SE\text{-}elem^*$$
$$\qquad\qquad\quad INDEX : Index$$

where

$inv\text{-}SEStateOp(mk\text{-}SEStateOp(Seq, ix)) \quad \triangle$
$\quad Seq \neq [\,]$
$\quad \wedge\ \text{hd}\ Seq: SE\text{-}map$
$\quad \wedge\ \forall k \leq \text{len}\ Seq \cdot Seq[k]: SEStateOp \ \Rightarrow\ INDEX(Seq[k]) = \text{cons}(k, ix)$

This is the same definition as in the definition of the operational semantics of symbolic execution in Section 9.3.1, repeated in the theory *ThOpSem* (described in Section 9.4.1). However, it is now considered as a part of the *SYMBEXSTATE*, while before it was a type defined within the operational semantics (Section 9.3.1) or a *mural* theory (Section 9.4.1). Similarly, some of the functions defined below have been defined before in Sections 9.3 and 9.4. In the implementation of SYMBEX, a translation mechanism is needed that translates between these different versions, in particular between an *SEStateOp* in the *SYMBEXSTATE* and the equivalent one in *ThOpSem*. This is necessary so that symbolic execution on the *SEStateOp* in *SYMBEXSTATE* can be performed according to the rules of the theory *ThOpSem*.

Auxiliary functions

The function *get-element* gets a particular element of the sequence in an *SEStateOp* or one of its sub-sequences, as selected by its argument *ix*:

$get\text{-}element : SEStateOp \times Index \rightarrow SE\text{-}elem$
$get\text{-}element(S, ix) \quad \triangleq$
    if front $ix = [\,]$
    then $SEQ(S)[\text{last}\,ix]$
    else $get\text{-}element(SEQ(S)[\text{last}\,ix],$ front $ix)$
pre $ix \neq [\,]$
    $\wedge$ if front $ix \neq [\,]$
      then $SEQ(S)[\text{last}\,ix]: SEStateOp$
          $\wedge \, pre\text{-}get\text{-}element(SEQ(S)[\text{last}\,ix],$ front $ix)$
      else true

The function *current-index* finds the current or last index in an *SEStateOp*:

$current\text{-}index : SEStateOp \rightarrow Index$
$current\text{-}index(S) \quad \triangleq \quad$ if last $SEQ(S): SE\text{-}map$
               then $[\text{len}\,SEQ(S)]$
               else $current\text{-}index(\text{last}\,SEQ(S)) \oplus \text{len}\,SEQ(S)$

current-index(S) is always the index of a *SE-map*:

Lemma D.1.1

$\forall S: SEStateOp \cdot$
    $pre\text{-}get\text{-}element(S, current\text{-}index(S))$
    $\wedge \, get\text{-}element(S, current\text{-}index(S)): SE\text{-}map$

Proof By induction over len front *current-index(S)*. □

The function *previous*, given the index of an element in *SEStateOp*, finds the index of the previous element:

$previous : Index \rightarrow Index$
$previous(ix) \quad \triangleq \quad$ if hd $ix = 1$
              then tl ix
              else cons(hd $ix - 1$, tl ix)
pre $ix \neq [\,]$

We now introduce the function *collect-preds*, which collects into a set all the *PredS* in a given *SEStateOp S*, up to a certain element (given as argument *ix*) in the execution sequence of *S*. If *ix* is empty, then *all PredS* in *S* are collected:

$collect\text{-}preds : SEStateOp \times Index \to PredS\text{-set}$
$collect\text{-}preds(S, ix) \quad \triangleq$
      let $ix' = $ if $ix = [\,]$ then $[len\,SEQ(S)]$ else ix in
     $\bigcup_{i=1}^{last\,ix'} \Big($ if $SEQ(S)[i]$: *SE-map*
             then $\bigcup_{n\in dom\,SEQ(S)[i]} SEQ(S)[i](n)$
             else if $i = last\,ix'$
                  then $collect\text{-}preds(SEQ(S)[i], front\,ix')$
                  else $collect\text{-}preds(SEQ(S)[i], [\,])\Big)$
  pre if $ix \neq [\,]$
     then $last\,ix \leq len\,SEQ(S)$
        $\wedge$ if $SEQ(S)[last\,ix]$: *SEStateOp*
         then $pre\text{-}collect\text{-}preds(SEQ(S)[last\,ix], front\,ix)$
         else $front\,ix = [\,]$
     else true

Assumptions and Beliefs

$Assump ::$ *index* : *Index*
            stmt   : *PredS*

Assumptions are used for recording **assumed** predicates. They consist of an index which records *when* an assumption was made, and the assumed statement itself. The following function extracts the statements from a set of *Assump*.

$statements : Assump\text{-set} \to PredS\text{-set}$
$statements(as) \quad \triangleq \quad \{stmt(a) \mid a \in as\}$

A *Belief*, which is used to store a **believed** predicate, is similar to an *Assump*, except that it also stores the description values in the current element of the *SEStateOp*. This is necessary since a *Belief* represents a proof obligation that should later be discharged. To do so, one needs to know the hypotheses that are allowed to be used in the proof, namely all the *PredS* that are known to hold at the time when the *Belief* is stated (cf. the specifications of the operations *BELIEVE* and *DISCHARGE* in Appendix D.2).

$Belief ::$ *index*   : *Index*
         current : *PredS*-set
         stmt   : *PredS*

The function name *statements* is now overloaded to extract the statements from *Belief*s as well as *Assump*s:

$statements : Belief\text{-set} \to PredS\text{-set}$
$statements(bs) \quad \triangleq \quad \{stmt(b) \mid b \in bs\}$

Proven and provable rule statements

The following function checks whether a given *RuleStmt* is established by a given rule under a given instantiation, using various functions from the specification of *mural*:

$isProvenRuleStmt : RuleStmt \times Rule\text{-}ref \times Theory\text{-}ref \times Instantiation$
$\qquad\qquad\qquad \times Rulemap \times Theorymap \times ThMorphmap \rightarrow \mathbb{B}$
$isProvenRuleStmt(rs, rr, thr, i, rm, thm, thmm) \quad \triangle$
    let $rule = rm(rr)$ in
    let $rs' = mk\text{-}RuleStmt($
              $\{Instantiate(s, i) \mid s \in SEQHYPS(STMT(rule))\},$
              $\{Instantiate(a, i) \mid a \in ORDHYPS(STMT(rule))\},$
              $Instantiate(CONCL(STMT(rule)), i))$ in
    $Establishes(rs', rs)$
    $\wedge\ Is\text{-}Complete\text{-}Proof(PROOF(rule), thr, rm, thm, thmm)$

The operation *PROVABLE* checks whether a rule statement is provable in a theory and, if it is, adds it (including its proof) to the theory as a new rule. This operation is to be provided by *mural*.

$PROVABLE$ $(rs: RuleStmt, th: Theory\text{-}ref)$ $r: \{\text{YES}, \text{DONTKNOW}\}$
ext wr *mural* : *Store*
post $r = \text{YES} \;\Rightarrow\; rs$ is provable in *th*
                    $\wedge$ the rule with statement *rs* and a (complete) proof is
                       added to *th* in *mural*

Of course there exists a trivial implementation of *PROVABLE* that always returns the value DONTKNOW. Although this implementation would be correct with respect to the specification, obviously one would hope for something more intelligent, probably implemented by proof tactics and/or using decision procedures for decidable classes of problems. In different contexts, one should presumably use different proof tactics and decision procedures, even though they implement the same operation *PROVABLE*. An example of such a proof tactic is the algorithm *transform* given in Section 9.3.6.

The state

The state of a symbolic execution system has the following structure:

```
SYMBEXSTATE :: S        : SEStateOp
               history  : SpecName*
               assume   : Assump-set
               beliefs  : Belief-set
               module   : Theory-ref
               wmodule  : Theory-ref
               wflag    : B
               mural    : Store

where

inv-SYMBEXSTATE(mk-SYMBEXSTATE(s, h, ass, b, m, wm, wf, f))   △
    m ∈ dom THS(f)
    ∧ wm ∈ dom THS(f)
    ∧ inv-ThModule(THS(f)(m))
    ∧ inv-WThModule(THS(f)(wm))
    ∧ m ∈ PARENTS(THS(f)(wm))
    ∧ len SEQ(s) = len h + 1
    ∧ rng h ⊆ specs(m)
    ∧ h = [] ⇒ wf = false
    ∧ INDEX(s) = [ ]
```

The invariant expresses that the theories *module* and *wmodule* should be the names (in *mural*) of the theory and weak theory of the same module. The length of *SEQ(S)* should be one more than the length of the *history* to allow for the initial starting state. All the *SpecName*s in the *history* should be defined in the *module*. The *wflag* should initially be set to false to show that so far no weak symbolic execution has taken place. The *SEStateOp* should not be an element inside some other *SEStateOp*.

Copying the state

The following function copies an existing *SYMBEXSTATE*, up to a given element in the execution sequence.

$$copy\text{-}SESTATE : SYMBEXSTATE \times \mathbb{N}_1 \rightarrow SYMBEXSTATE$$
$$copy\text{-}SESTATE(mk\text{-}SYMBEXSTATE(s, h, ass, bel, m, wm, wf, f), i)\quad \triangle$$
$$\quad mk\text{-}SYMBEXSTATE($$
$$\qquad\qquad mk\text{-}SEStateOp(SEQ(s)(1, \dots, i), INDEX(s)),$$
$$\qquad\qquad h(1, \dots, i-1),$$
$$\qquad\qquad \{a: Assump \mid a \in ass \wedge \text{last index}(a) \leq i\},$$
$$\qquad\qquad \{b: Belief \mid b \in bel \wedge \text{last index}(b) \leq i\},$$
$$\qquad\qquad m,$$
$$\qquad\qquad wm,$$
$$\qquad\qquad wf,$$
$$\qquad\qquad f)$$

Initial states

A *SYMBEXSTATE* is initial, if it satisfies

$is\text{-}initial\text{-}SESTATE : SYMBEXSTATE \rightarrow \mathbf{B}$
$is\text{-}initial\text{-}SESTATE(mk\text{-}SYMBEXSTATE(s, h, ass, b, m, wm, wf, f))$ $\underline{\triangle}$
    $\mathsf{len}\, SEQ(s) = 1$
    $\wedge\, \mathsf{dom}\,\mathsf{hd}\, SEQ(s) = \{\,\}$
    $\wedge\, ass = \{\,\}$
    $\wedge\, b = \{\,\}$

The invariant on *SYMBEXSTATE* implies, for an initial *SYMBEXSTATE*, that *history* = [ ] and *wflag* = false. Different initial *SYMBEXSTATE*s at most differ in their *module*, *wmodule* and *mural*. Given any particular values for *module*, *wmodule* and *mural*, the initial *SYMBEXSTATE* will be called ARBITRARY.

D.2 Operations

All the operations specified in the following should be accessible to the user. Their user interface is discussed in [Kne89, §6.2].

Symbolic execution

Operation *SYMB_EXECUTE* symbolically executes a sequence of specifications. The pre-condition checks that there is a rule or axiom that holds in *module* and has the shape

$hyp\text{-}set \vdash \langle sn\text{-}seq, S \rangle \hookrightarrow \langle [\,], S' \rangle$

for some $hyp\text{-}set \subseteq collect\text{-}preds(S, [\,])$ and some $S' : SEStateOp$. The post-condition then applies this transition to S.

$SYMB\_EXECUTE\ (sn\text{-}seq : SpecName^*)$
ext $\mathsf{wr}\ S\ :\ SEStateOp$
    $\mathsf{wr}\ history\ :\ SpecName^*$
    $\mathsf{rd}\ module\ :\ Theory\text{-}ref$
     $\mathsf{rd}\ wflag\ :\ \mathbf{B}$
     $\mathsf{rd}\ mural\ :\ Store$
$\mathsf{pre}\ wflag = \mathsf{false}$
    $\wedge\ \mathsf{rng}\ sn\text{-}seq \subseteq specs(module)$
    $\wedge\ \exists S' : SEStateOp \cdot \exists hyp\text{-}set \subseteq collect\text{-}preds(S, [\,]) \cdot$
        $\mathsf{let}\ rs = mk\text{-}RuleStmt(\{\,\},$
                         $hyp\text{-}set,$
                         $\langle sn\text{-}seq, S \rangle \hookrightarrow \langle [\,], S' \rangle)\ \mathsf{in}$
       $PROVABLE(rs, module) = \mathrm{YES}$
       $\wedge\ \mathsf{len}\, SEQ(S') = \mathsf{len}\, SEQ(S) + \mathsf{len}\, sn\text{-}seq$

$\text{post } \exists \textit{hyp-set} \subseteq \textit{collect-preds}(S, [\,]) \cdot$

$\qquad \text{let } rs = \textit{mk-RuleStmt}(\{\,\},$

$\qquad\qquad\qquad\qquad \textit{hyp-set},$

$\qquad\qquad\qquad\qquad \langle \textit{sn-seq}, \overleftarrow{S} \rangle \hookrightarrow \langle [\,], S \rangle) \text{ in}$

$\qquad\quad \textit{PROVABLE}(rs, \textit{module}) = \text{YES}$

$\quad \wedge \textit{history} = \overleftarrow{\textit{history}} \oplus \textit{sn-seq}$

In the special case of *SYMB_EXECUTE*, one should use the "tactic" *transform* introduced in Section 9.3.6 to implement the operation *PROVABLE* and find a proof of the *RuleStmt*.

The theory of the operational semantics of a language is expected to be such that at any stage in the symbolic execution, usually (but not necessarily) only one rule will be applicable. In this case the tactic is fully automatic, no user interaction is required. Note however that this remark *only* applies to symbolic execution itself; simplification is a separate step and should certainly be user-guided. Although the operation *SYMB_EXECUTE* allows the user to symbolically execute a whole *sequence* of specifications, he will often only want to execute one at a time and then execute the next specification on the result of the previous symbolic execution.

The reason for the pre-condition *wflag* = false is that once weak symbolic execution has been used on an *SEStateOp*, any further symbolic execution can only lead to a weak result and therefore has to be dealt with using the operation *W_SYMB_EXECUTE* specified below.

Weak symbolic execution

W_SYMB_EXECUTE behaves just like *SYMB_EXECUTE*, except that it uses the 'weak' theory *wmodule* instead of *module*, and sets the *wflag* to show that the result has been derived using *weak* symbolic execution.

$\textit{W\_SYMB\_EXECUTE } (\textit{sn-seq}: \textit{SpecName}^*)$

$\text{ext} \qquad \text{wr } S \ : \ \textit{SEStateOp}$

$\qquad\quad \text{wr } \textit{history} \ : \ \textit{SpecName}^*$

$\qquad\quad \text{rd } \textit{wmodule} \ : \ \textit{Theory-ref}$

$\qquad\qquad \text{wr } \textit{wflag} \ : \ \mathsf{B}$

$\qquad\quad \text{rd } \textit{mural} \ : \ \textit{Store}$

$\text{pre rng } \textit{sn-seq} \subseteq \textit{specs}(\textit{wmodule})$

$\quad \wedge \exists S' \colon \textit{SEStateOp} \cdot \exists \textit{hyp-set} \subseteq \textit{collect-preds}(S, [\,]) \cdot$

$\qquad \text{let } rs = \textit{mk-RuleStmt}(\{\,\},$

$\qquad\qquad\qquad\qquad \textit{hyp-set},$

$\qquad\qquad\qquad\qquad \langle \textit{sn-seq}, S \rangle \hookrightarrow \langle [\,], S' \rangle) \text{ in}$

$\qquad\quad \textit{PROVABLE}(rs, \textit{wmodule}) = \text{YES}$

$\qquad\quad \wedge \text{len } \textit{SEQ}(S') = \text{len } \textit{SEQ}(S) + \text{len } \textit{sn-seq}$

$\text{post } \textit{post-SYMB\_EXECUTE}(\textit{sn-seq}, \overleftarrow{S}, \overleftarrow{\textit{history}},$

$\qquad\qquad \textit{wmodule}, \textit{mural}, \overleftarrow{\textit{wflag}}, S, \textit{history})$

$\quad \wedge \textit{wflag} = \text{true}$

Showing the results

SHOW shows the value of a program variable *name* after execution of a number of operations given by the index *ix*.

> *SHOW* (*name*: *Name*, *ix*: *Index*) *ps-set*: *PredS*-set
> ext rd *S* : *SEStateOp*
> pre *pre-get-element*(*S*, *ix*)
>   ∧ *get-element*(*S*, *ix*): *SE-map*
>   ∧ *name* ∈ dom *get-element*(*S*, *ix*)
> post *ps-set* = *get-element*(*S*, *ix*)(*name*)

To see the value of a program variable in terms of the values after *n* operations (with $n < m$), run *SHOW* and then *SIMPLIFY* the result.

Simplification

SIMPLIFY simplifies an expression by applying a rule to it (but only *returns* the result and does *not* change the state).

To specify *SIMPLIFY*, we need the auxiliary function *simp-hypotheses*. This function collects all the *PredS* in an *SEStateOp S* up to an index *ix*, except for a given *ps* which is a current description value of the given name *n*. This is exactly the set of hypotheses allowed to be used for proving a simplification of *ps*. Note that this definition does not exclude the possibility that *ps* itself is in the resulting set, since it may also be the description value of identifier *nm* ≠ *n*. In this case it is trivial to prove that *ps* ⇔ true and *ps* may be deleted from the description value of *n* since it does not affect the denotation of the *SEStateOp*.

> *simp-hypotheses* : *SEStateOp* × *PredS* × *Name* × *Index* → *PredS*-set
> *simp-hypotheses*(*S*, *ps*, *n*, *ix*)   △
>   let *nmset* = dom *get-element*(*S*, *ix*) − {*n*} in
>   *collect-preds*(*S*, *previous*(*ix*))
>   ∪ $\bigcup_{nm \in nmset}$ *get-element*(*S*, *ix*)(*nm*)
>   ∪ *get-element*(*S*, *ix*)(*n*) − {*ps*}
> pre *pre-get-element*(*S*, *ix*)
>   ∧ *get-element*(*S*, *ix*): *SE-map*
>   ∧ *n* ∈ dom *get-element*(*S*, *ix*)
>   ∧ *ps* ∈ *get-element*(*S*, *ix*)(*n*)
>   ∧ *pre-collect-preds*(*S*, *previous*(*ix*))

Now *SIMPLIFY* is defined as below. The pre-condition checks that the *SEStateOp* contains *ps* in the right place (as given by *ix*) and that *ps* can be simplified to some *ps'* by rule *rr*. The post-condition then states that this rule should be applied to *ps* to get output *ps'*.

> *SIMPLIFY* (*ps*: *PredS*, *rr*: *Rule-ref*, *inst*: *Instantiation*, *ix*: *Index*,
>   *n*: *Name*) *ps'*: *PredS*
> ext   rd *S* : *SEStateOp*
>   rd *module* : *Theory-ref*
>   rd *wflag* : **B**
>   rd *mural* : *Store*

pre *wflag* = false

$\wedge$ *pre-simp-hypotheses*(*S, ps, n, ix*)

$\wedge \exists ps''$: *PredS* $\cdot \exists hyp\text{-}set \subseteq$ *simp-hypotheses*(*S, ps, n, ix*) $\cdot$
  let *rs* = *mk-RuleStmt*({ }, *hyp-set, ps* $\Leftrightarrow$ *ps''*) in
  isProvenRuleStmt(*rs, rr, module, inst, RULES*(*mural*),
      THS(*mural*), *THMORPHS*(*mural*))

post $\exists hyp\text{-}set \subseteq$ *simp-hypotheses*($\overleftarrow{S}$, *ps, n, ix*) $\cdot$
  let *rs* = *mk-RuleStmt*({ }, *hyp-set, ps* $\Leftrightarrow$ *ps'*) in
  isProvenRuleStmt(*rs, rr, module, inst, RULES*(*mural*),
      THS(*mural*), *THMORPHS*(*mural*))

Weak simplification

The operation *W_SIMPLIFY* is specified just like *SIMPLIFY*, except that it uses the weak theory *wmodule* instead of *module*, and the conclusion of the rule is an implication rather than an equivalence. Weak simplification is not possible in the initial state when all the *PredS* that could be simplified have been introduced by *ASSUME* or *BELIEVE*.

W_SIMPLIFY (*ps*: *PredS, rr*: *Rule-ref, inst*: *Instantiation, ix*: *Index,*
      n: *Name*) *ps'*: *PredS*

ext   rd *S* : *SEStateOp*

   rd *wmodule* : *Theory-ref*

     rd *mural* : *Store*

pre len *S* $\geq$ 2

$\wedge$ *pre-simp-hypotheses*(*S, ps, n, ix*)

$\wedge \exists ps''$: *PredS* $\cdot \exists hyp\text{-}set \subseteq$ *simp-hypotheses*(*S, ps, n, ix*) $\cdot$
  let *rs* = *mk-RuleStmt*({ }, *hyp-set, ps* $\Rightarrow$ *ps''*) in
  isProvenRuleStmt(*rs, rr, wmodule, inst, RULES*(*mural*),
      THS(*mural*), *THMORPHS*(*mural*))

post $\exists hyp\text{-}set \subseteq$ *simp-hypotheses*($\overleftarrow{S}$, *ps, n, ix*) $\cdot$
  let *rs* = *mk-RuleStmt*({ }, *hyp-set, ps* $\Rightarrow$ *ps'*) in
  isProvenRuleStmt(*rs, rr, wmodule, inst, RULES*(*mural*),
      THS(*mural*), *THMORPHS*(*mural*))

Storing results of simplification

When an expression has been simplified, *REMEMBER* saves the simplified value in the state by replacing the old ps_1: *PredS* with the new ps_2: *PredS*. This is done using the auxiliary function *replace*:

replace : *PredS* × *PredS* × *SEStateOp* × *Index* × *Name* → *SEStateOp*

replace(ps_1, ps_2, S, ix, n) $\triangleq$

    mk-SEStateOp(

        $\{i \mapsto$ if $i = $ hd ix

           then if $SEQ(S)[i]$: *SE-map*

$$\text{then } \{nm \mapsto \left\{ \begin{array}{ll} SEQ(S)[i](n) - \{ps_1\} \cup \{ps_2\} & \text{if } nm = n \\ SEQ(S)[i](nm) & \text{otherwise} \end{array} \right\}$$

                  $| nm \in $ dom $SEQ(S)[i]\}$

             else *replace*($ps_1, ps_2, SEQ(S)[i]$, tl ix, n)

           else $SEQ(S)[i]$

        $| i \in \{1, \ldots, $ len $SEQ(S)\}\}$,

      INDEX(S))

pre *pre-get-element*(S, ix)

    $\wedge$ *get-element*(S, ix): *SE-map*

    $\wedge ps_1 \in$ *get-element*(S, ix)(n)

Then *REMEMBER* is specified as

    REMEMBER (ps_1, ps_2: *PredS, rr*: *Rule-ref, inst*: *Instantiation, ix*: *Index,*

                name: *Name*)

    ext   wr S : *SEStateOp*

        rd *module* : *Theory-ref*

          rd *wflag* : $\mathbb{B}$

        rd *mural* : *Store*

    pre *pre-SIMPLIFY*($ps_1, rr, inst, ix, n, S, module, wflag, mural$)

        $\wedge$ *post-SIMPLIFY*($ps_1, rr, inst, ix, n, ps_2, S, module, wflag, mural$)

    post $S = $ *replace*($ps_1, ps_2, \overleftarrow{S}, ix, n$)

Storing results of weak simplification

W_REMEMBER stores the results of *W_SIMPLIFY*. It is specified as

    W_REMEMBER (ps_1, ps_2: *PredS, rr*: *Rule-ref, inst*: *Instantiation, ix*: *Index,*

                  name: *Name*)

    ext   wr S : *SEStateOp*

        rd *module* : *Theory-ref*

         wr *wflag* : $\mathbb{B}$

        rd *mural* : *Store*

    pre *pre-W_SIMPLIFY*($ps_1, rr, inst, ix, n, S, module, mural$)

        $\wedge$ *post-W_SIMPLIFY*($ps_1, rr, inst, ix, n, ps_2, S, module, mural$)

    post $S = $ *replace*($ps_1, ps_2, \overleftarrow{S}, ix, n$)

        $\wedge$ *wflag* = true

Checking logical expressions

CHECK checks whether a given *PredS ps* is provable in the theory *module*, given all the description values in the current *SEStateOp* up to index *ix*. Of course, this will in general be undecidable, therefore *CHECK* will answer either YES, it has found a proof, or NO, it has found a proof of ¬*ps;* or DONTKNOW, it has not found a proof and therefore does not know whether the expression is provable or not.

$CHECK$ *(ps: PredS, ix: Index) r:* {YES, NO, DONTKNOW}
   ext   rd *S* : *SEStateOp*
      rd *module* : *Theory-ref*
      wr *mural* : *Store*
   post *(r* = YES ⇒ ∃*hyp-set* ⊆ *collect-preds(S, ix)* ·
                 PROVABLE(mk-RuleStmt({ }*, hyp-set, ps), module)* = YES)
         ∧ *(r* = NO ⇒ ∃*hyp-set* ⊆ *collect-preds(S, ix)* ·
                 PROVABLE(mk-RuleStmt({ }*, hyp-set, ¬ps), module)* = YES)

Assuming a logical expression

Define the auxiliary function

add-restriction : *SEStateOp* × *PredS* → *SEStateOp*
add-restriction(S, ps) △
   if last *SEQ(S): SE-map*
   then let *new* = {*n* ↦ if *n* ∈ dom last *SEQ(S)*
                     then last *SEQ(S)(n)* ∪ {*ps*}
                     else {*ps*}
               | *n* ∈ *mentions(ps)*} in
      front *SEQ(S)* ⊕ last *SEQ(S)* † *new*
   else front *SEQ(S)* ⊕ *add-restriction(*last *SEQ(S), ps)*
pre *mentions(ps)* ≠ { }

ASSUME adds a given *PredS ps* to *assume,* i.e. assumes that this expression is true. This is mainly useful for simplifying expressions, in particular conditionals. In many cases, the user will first want to make a copy of the starting state, and come back to it later to assume ¬*ps* in order to cover all cases.

The pre-condition of *ASSUME* only checks that *ps* does actually use a variable, since assuming a ground term would not make much sense.

ASSUME *(ps: PredS)*
   ext   wr *S* : *SEStateOp*
      wr *assume* : *Assump-*set
   pre *mentions(ps)* ≠ { }
   post *assume* = $\overleftarrow{assume}$ ∪ {*mk-Assump(current-index($\overleftarrow{S}$), ps)*}
      ∧ *S* = *add-restriction($\overleftarrow{S}$, ps)*

Believing a logical expression

BELIEVE also assumes that a given logical expression is true. The difference to *ASSUME* is that this leads to a proof obligation that should later be discharged — the belief has to be justified. A *Belief* thus plays the rôle of a lemma that is used before it is proven. One special case when this can be particularly useful is in symbolic execution of *incomplete* specifications, where one may use a property of some component that cannot be proven yet because the component itself has not been specified yet.

Since it does make sense to **believe** a ground term, a new auxiliary function is needed to handle this case. If *ps* is a ground term, then the user has to provide the *Name* that *ps* gets associated with, since one can no longer automatically associate *ps* with those *n*: *Name* that are mentioned in *ps*.

add-restriction-g : *SEStateOp* × *PredS* × *Name* → *SEStateOp*
add-restriction-g(*S*, *ps*, *n*) $\triangleq$
 if last *SEQ*(*S*): *SE-map*
 then let *new* = {*n* ↦ if *n* ∈ dom last *SEQ*(*S*)
         then last *SEQ*(*S*)(*n*) ∪ {*ps*}
         else {*ps*}} in
   front *SEQ*(*S*) ⊕ last *SEQ*(*S*) † *new*
 else front *SEQ*(*S*) ⊕ *add-restriction-g*(last *SEQ*(*S*), *ps*, *n*)

BELIEVE (*ps*: *PredS*, *n*: [*Name*])
ext wr *S* : *SEStateOp*
 wr *beliefs* : *Belief*-set
pre *mentions*(*ps*) = { } ⇒ *n* ≠ nil
post let *elem* = *get-element*($\overleftarrow{S}$, *current-index*($\overleftarrow{S}$)) in
 let *current* = $\bigcup_{n \in \text{dom } elem}$ *elem*(*n*) in
 beliefs = $\overleftarrow{beliefs}$ ∪ {*mk-Belief*(*current-index*($\overleftarrow{S}$), *current*, *ps*)}
 ∧ if *mentions*(*ps*) = { }
  then *S* = *add-restriction-g*($\overleftarrow{S}$, *ps*, *n*)
  else *S* = *add-restriction*($\overleftarrow{S}$, *ps*)

Discharging *BELIEVE*d proof obligations

DISCHARGE discharges a *BELIEVE*d proof obligation. The pre-condition checks that there exists a rule or axiom that holds in the theory, and whose statement expresses the assumption.

DISCHARGE (*b*: *Belief*)
ext wr *S* : *SEStateOp*
 rd *module* : *Theory-ref*
 wr *beliefs* : *Belief*-set
 rd *mural* : *Store*
pre let *hyp-set'* = *collect-preds*(*S*, *previous*(*index*(*b*))) ∪ *current*(*b*) in
 ∃*hyp-set* ⊆ *hyp-set'* ·
  let *rs* = *mk-RuleStmt*({ }, *hyp-set*, *stmt*(*b*)) in
  PROVABLE(*rs*, *module*)
post *beliefs* = $\overleftarrow{beliefs}$ − {*b*}

Appendix E

The Theorem Prover's House

The Theorem Prover's house[1] is on a high headland, above the seagulls' nests in steep cliffs above a pebbly seashore. The Theorem Prover wakes soon after the sun has appeared over the mountains behind the few miles of pasture inland, and sits up in his bed. He stares out to sea, of which he takes pleasure in observing the variations from one day to the next. To the north, only fields and mountains touch the coastline. Some distance down the coast to the south, he can see the little town where he goes, every Thursday, to pick up groceries and to spend an hour or two with the vet's wife while the vet is out on his rounds.

He descends from the transparent dome enclosing his bed, to the central space of his house. He makes a mug of tea in the peripheral alcove he calls his kitchen; thinks about shaving, but does not because it is not Monday – the vet's wife, somewhat passé, likes a three-day stubble – not Monday, he reasons (in his head), because it is Tuesday, as he determines from the calendar on the wall in his workspace under the bed.

The calendar is functional but unaesthetic, so he touches it, slides his finger down the resulting menu to the 'today's picture' slot, and stands back to admire the result. It is Turner's *The Fighting Temeraire*. He has been pleased with his subscription to this service, even if it is a shade pricey; anyway, he has few worries about money. He drags one corner with his finger, until the picture fills much of the wall; but he takes a cursory glance at the noticeboard before covering it: one or two new results advertised in the category theory section, and some ongoing political wranglings in the board of the Royal Logical Society.

He has had some ideas overnight for the problem, bits of whose proof are still littered all over the opposite wall; but before pulling it down to his desk, at which he now kneels, he will see what has arrived to be done today. Once yesterday's clutter has been moved to the wall, the desk is relatively tidy. A touch at a clear space pops up his rôle panel, and he chooses to unfurl the BUSINESS ADMIN cartouche. In it, the informal mailbox is glowing red: he presses at it and reveals a letter from his agent, who must have been up early. He listens to the message: would he review a new hyperbook? He drafts a brief acceptance, signs and despatches it, watching the route indicator show its arrival at the agent's wristerminal. The other ADMIN cartouches he ignores: they mostly give access to tax and VAT stuff, which he is content to leave to his accountant, as he is unable to comprehend such complexities. (Which was a considerable problem for himself and many others, when a date-dependent bug appeared in the accountant last April. Since then, he has changed to a formally-certified accountant; the old one was later convicted

---

[1] See also *The Verifier* by Mike Shields (Newcastle University).

of unverified behaviour, and descheduled).

Collapsing the Business Admin browser back into its cartouche, he chooses instead the Theorem Proving rôle. The summary of the Incoming Jobs Channel shows the originators, subject matter and fees of a couple of small jobs and one big one: "STL, Group Theory, 4000kW; Jones, prog transformation, 3500kW; Praxis, spec lang consistency, 32000kW". He fingers the last, getting the details showing deadline, originator's informal description, originator id and reference, agent's id and reference, expenses incurred (initialized to 0), sundry other administrative and commercial details, and of course the formal description of the problem itself. This he expands to a long scroll over the desk, then splits off some interesting bits into separate windows. He spends an hour or so just reading it, crawling over it on his hands and knees, often juxtaposing various parts, or revealing elided detail (and sometimes getting irritated when a window gets 'stuck' to his knee as he moves around).

Going back to the Theorem Proving Rôle, he opens the Resources cartouche, and within that the NCC Theorem Proving Library access, which first reveals a welcoming green and yellow logo and a money socket (female), which is flashing because it isn't connected to anything. He prods at the Praxis job's expenses cartouche, revealing the empty 'outputs' list and a picture of a stack of money plugs (male). He drags one over towards the Library's socket and as soon as they are brought together, they recognize their type-compatibility and the connection is made with a flash and a beep: the Library's socket shows the Praxis job's logo and name, and the job's expense supplies list shows the NCC library logo, together with the charges as they clock up. The NCC Library has now interrogated the TP's personal environment to find out where he likes to start navigating from, and the Library window shows this position. He navigates through, spawning off a few useful theorems and tactics in their own windows and comparing them with parts of the job's formal statement. The expenses clock up as he goes.

Finally, he sets up some short propositions to do some preliminary checks. These are very boring: he decides to set an automatic theorem prover at them while he has some tea. The Theorem Proving Library contains an Automatic TP section, to which he navigates; a number of whimsically-named ATPs are offered by various commercial concerns. They have various strengths and weaknesses, some listed in the blurb attached to each, and some which he knows from experience or reputation. He selects a couple which advertize 'no fee without termination' and applies them to his propositions, setting an audio alarm triggered by termination before making his tea and going to sit on his bed to watch the seagulls.

Variations Various reviewers have suggested alternatives to this basic scenario. Mark van Harmelen suggests a cordless keyboard is an essential accessory, hanging from a long shoulder-strap like those used by rock musicians; objects displayed on the floor are pointed to with the toes. Rather than crawling all over the theorems, Peter Lindsay would use a remote control for armchair theorem-proving, using a light-gun to zap propositions from a distance. Ursula Martin envisages the even more remote cellphone model, in which the TP works whilst jogging along the clifftops.

Bibliography

[AHM87] A. Avron, F. Honsell, and I. Mason. Using typed λ-calculus to implement formal systems on a machine. Technical Report 87-31, University of Edinburgh LFCS, 1987.

[All86] J. Allen. An investigation into the IOTA project support environment. Master's thesis, Department of Computer Science, University of Manchester, 1986.

[And88] Derek Andrews. Report from the BSI panel for the standardisation of VDM (IST/5/50). In *[BJM88]*, pages 74–78, 1988.

[B+87] F.L. Bauer et al. *The Munich Project CIP, Vol. II*, volume 292 of *Lecture Notes in Computer Science*. Springer-Verlag, 1987.

[Bar77] J. Barwise, editor. *Handbook of Mathematical Logic*. North Holland, 1977.

[Bar84] H.P. Barendregt. *The Lambda Calculus – Its Syntax and Semantics*. North Holland, second edition, 1984.

[BBH+74] H. Bekič, D. Bjørner, W. Henhapl, C.B. Jones, and P. Lucas. A formal definition of a PL/I subset. Technical Report 25.139, IBM Laboratory Vienna, December 1974.

[BCJ84] H. Barringer, J.H. Cheng, and C.B. Jones. A logic covering undefinedness in program proofs. *Acta Informatica*, 21:251–269, 1984.

[Bee85] M. J. Beeson. *Foundations of Constructive Mathematics*. Springer-Verlag, 1985.

[BF86] R. E. Bloomfield and P.K.D. Froome. The application of formal methods to the development of high integrity software. *IEEE Trans. on Software Engineering*, 12(9):988–993, 1986.

[BFM89] R. Bloomfield, P. Froome, and B. Monahan. Specbox: A toolkit for BSI-VDM. *SafetyNet*, 5:4–7, 1989.

[BG81] R. M. Burstall and J. Goguen. An informal introduction to specifications using Clear. In R.S. Boyer and J S. Moore, editors, *The Correctness Problem in Computer Science*. Academic Press, 1981.

[BG90] S. Brock and C. George. RAISE method manual. Technical Report LA-COS/CRI/DOC/3/V1, Computer Resources International, August 1990.

[BHL90] D. Bjørner, C. A. R. Hoare, and H. Langmaack, editors. *VDM '90: VDM and Z – Formal Methods in Software Development*, volume 428 of *Lecture Notes in Computer Science*. Springer-Verlag, 1990.

[BJ78] D. Bjørner and C.B. Jones, editors. *The Vienna Development Method: The Meta-Language*, volume 61 of *Lecture Notes in Computer Science*. Springer-Verlag, 1978.

[BJ82] D. Bjørner and C.B. Jones. *Formal Specification and Software Development*. Prentice Hall International, 1982.

[BJ90] M. Broy and C.B. Jones, editors. *Programming Concepts and Methods*. North-Holland, 1990.

[BJM88] R. Bloomfield, R. B. Jones, and L. S. Marshall, editors. *VDM '88: VDM – The Way Ahead*, volume 328 of *Lecture Notes in Computer Science*. Springer-Verlag, 1988.

[BJMN87] D. Bjørner, C.B. Jones, M. Mac an Airchinnigh, and E.J. Neuhold, editors. *VDM – A Formal Definition at Work*, volume 252 of *Lecture Notes in Computer Science*. Springer-Verlag, 1987.

[BM79] R.S. Boyer and J.S. Moore. *A Computational Logic*. Academic Press, 1979.

[BSI90] BSI. VDM specification language protostandard. Technical Report BSI IST/5/50, BSI, 1990.

[C+86] R.L. Constable et al. *Implementing Mathematics with the Nuprl Proof Development System*. Prentice-Hall, 1986.

[CHJ86] B. Cohen, W.T. Harwood, and M.I. Jackson, editors. *The Specification of Complex Systems*. Addison-Wesley, 1986.

[Chu40] A. Church. A formulation of the simple theory of types. *J. Symb. Logic*, 5:56–68, 1940.

[CIP85] CIP Language Group. *The Munich Project CIP—Volume I: The Wide Spectrum Language CIP-L*, volume 183 of *Lecture Notes in Computer Science*. Springer-Verlag, 1985.

[CJ91] J. H. Cheng and C.B. Jones. On the usability of logics which handle partial functions. In C. Morgan and J. Woodcock, editors, *Proceedings of the BCS-FACS Third Refinement Workshop*. Springer-Verlag, 1991.

[CJN+85] I.D. Cottam, C.B. Jones, T. Nipkow, A.C. Wills, M.I. Wolczko, and A. Yaghi. Project support environments for formal methods. In J. McDermid, editor, *Integrated Project Support Environments*, chapter 3. Peter Peregrinus Ltd., 1985.

[CJN+86] I.D. Cottam, C.B. Jones, T.N. Nipkow, A.C. Wills, M. Wolczko, and A. Yaghi. Mule – an environment for rigorous software development (final report to SERC on grant number GR/C/05762). Technical report, Department of Computer Science, University of Manchester, 1986.

[CJNW83] I.D. Cottam, C.B. Jones, T. Nipkow, and A.C. Wills. Mule: A support system for formal specification and rigorous software development. BCS-FACS/SERC Conference on Program Specification and Verification, University of York, (Proceedings not published), March 1983.

[Coh83] Donald Cohen. Symbolic execution of the GIST specification language. In *Proc. 8th Int. Joint Conference on Artificial Intelligence '83 (IJCAI-83)*, pages 17–20, 1983.

[Cra85] D. Craigen. A technical review of four verification systems: Gypsy, Affirm, FDM and Revised Special. Technical report, I.P. Sharp Associates Ltd, August 1985.

[Dah77] O-J. Dahl. Can program proving be made practical? In *EEC-Crest Course on Programming Foundations*, 1977.

[Daw88] Mark Dawson. Using the ωp generic logic environment. Technical report, Imperial College, Dept of Computer Science, September 1988.

[dB80] N.G. de Bruijn. A survey of the project Automath. In *To H.B. Curry: Essays in Combinatory Logic, Lambda Calculus, and Formalism*, pages 579–606. Academic Press, 1980.

[DDJ+85] B.T. Denvir, V.A. Downes, C.B. Jones, R.A. Snowdon, and M.K. Tordoff. IPSE 2.5 project proposal. Technical report, ICL/STC-IDEC/STL/University of Manchester, February 1985.

[Dyb82] P. Dybjer. Mathematical proofs in natural language. Technical Report 5, Programming Methodology Group, University of Göteborg, 1982.

[EB89] M. Elvang-Gøransson and D. Bjørner. TopSort: a formal software development in VDM. July, 1989.

[Elv90] M. Elvang-Gøransson. How I μral'ed TopSort. April, 1990.

[EM85] H. Ehrig and B. Mahr. *Fundamentals of Algebraic Specification 1: Equations and Initial Semantics*. EATCS Monographs on Theoretical Computer Science. Springer-Verlag, 1985.

[EM90] H. Ehrig and B. Mahr. *Fundamentals of Algebraic Specification 2: Module Specifications and Constraints*. EATCS Monographs on Theoretical Computer Science. Springer-Verlag, 1990.

[End72] H. B. Enderton. *A Mathematical Introduction to Logic*. Academic Press, 1972.

[FE91] R. Fields and M. Elvang-Gøransson. A VDM case study in μral. *IEEE Trans. on Software Engineering*, accepted for publication, 1991.

[Fit89a] J. S. Fitzgerald. mural – a preliminary wishlist. IPSE Document 060/jsf01, June 1989. University of Manchester.

[Fit89b] J. S. Fitzgerald. The mural model – preliminary evaluation. IPSE Document 060/jsf02, September 1989. University of Manchester.

[Fit89c] J. S. Fitzgerald. Some aspects of the spectool/theory store interface. IPSE Document 060/jsf04/0.1, September 1989. University of Manchester.

[Fit89d] J. S. Fitzgerald. Tactics in *mural* – an initial review. IPSE Document 060/jsf05/0.1, October 1989. University of Manchester.

[Fit89e] J. S. Fitzgerald. VDM theory store population review. IPSE Document 060/jsf03/0.1, September 1989. University of Manchester.

[Flo84] Christiane Floyd. A systematic look at prototyping. In Budde, editor, *Approaches to Prototyping*, pages 1–18. Springer-Verlag, 1984.

[GB83] J.A. Goguen and R.M. Burstall. Institutions: Abstract model theory for program specification. Unpublished Draft, January 1983.

[GB84] J.A. Goguen and R.M. Burstall. Introducing institutions. In *Lecture Notes in Computer Science, Vol. 164*, pages 221–256. Springer-Verlag, 1984.

[GG83] D. Gabbay and F. Guenthner, editors. *Handbook of Philosophical Logic Volume 1: Elements of Classical Logic*. D. Reidel Publishing Company, 1983.

[GH85] A. Geser and H. Hussmann. Rapid prototyping for algebraic specifications – examples for the use of the RAP system. Techn. Report MIP-8517, Fakultät für Mathematik und Informatik, Univ. Passau, December 1985.

[GHW85] J.V. Guttag, J.J. Horning, and J.M. Wing. Larch in five easy pieces. Technical Report 5, DEC, SRC, July 1985.

[GM82] J. Goguen and J. Meseguer. Rapid prototyping in the OBJ executable specification language. *ACM, Sigsoft*, 7(5):75–84, December 1982.

[GMW79] M. Gordon, R. Milner, and C. Wadsworth. *Edinburgh LCF*, volume 78 of *Lecture Notes in Computer Science*. Springer-Verlag, 1979.

[Gor85] M.J. Gordon. HOL: a machine oriented formulation of higher order logic. Technical Report 68, University of Cambridge Comp. Lab., 1985.

[Gri81] D. Gries. *The Science of Programming*. Springer-Verlag, 1981.

[Han83] F.K. Hanna. Overview of the Veritas project. Technical report, University of Kent, Electronics Lab, June 1983.

[Hay87] I. Hayes, editor. *Specification Case Studies*. Prentice-Hall International, 1987.

[Hay89] I. Hayes. A generalisation of bags in Z. Draft, October 1989.

[HD86] F. K. Hanna and N. Daeche. A purely functional implementation of a logic. In *8th Internat. Conf. on Automated Deduction*, 1986.

[Hen84] Peter Henderson. *me too* – a language for software specification and model building – preliminary report. Technical Report FPN-9, Dept. of Computer Science, Univ. of Stirling, December 1984. Second draft.

[HH90]   K. Havelund and A. Haxthausen. RSL reference manual. Technical Report LACOS/CRI/DOC/2/V1, Computer Resources International, August 1990.

[HHP87] R. Harper, F. Honsell, and G. Plotkin. A framework for defining logics. In *Proc. 2nd Symposium on Logic in Computer Science*, pages 194–204. Computer Society Press, 1987.

[HI88]   Sharam Hekmatpour and Darrel Ince. *Software Prototyping, Formal Methods and VDM*. Addison-Wesley, 1988.

[HJ89]   I. J. Hayes and C.B. Jones. Specifications are not (necessarily) executable. *Software Engineering Journal*, 4(6):320–338, November 1989.

[HM85]   Peter Henderson and Cydney Minkowitz. The *me too* method of software design. Technical Report FPN-10, Dept. of Computer Science, Univ. of Stirling, October 1985. Revised draft.

[Hue75] G.P. Huet. A unification algorithm for typed λ-calculus. *Theoretical Computer Science*, 1:27–57, 1975.

[Hus85] H. Hussmann. Rapid prototyping for algebraic specifications – RAP-system user's manual. Techn. Report MIP-8504, Univ. Passau, Fakultät für Mathematik und Informatik, March 1985.

[JL71]   C.B. Jones and P. Lucas. Proving correctness of implementation techniques. In E. Engeler, editor, *Lecture Notes in Mathematics, Volume 188: A Symposium on Algorithmic Languages*, pages 178–211. Springer-Verlag, 1971.

[JL88]   C.B. Jones and P.A. Lindsay. A support system for formal reasoning: Requirements and status. In R. Bloomfield, L. Marshall, and R. Jones, editors, *VDM '88: VDM – The Way Ahead*, pages 139–152. Springer-Verlag, 1988. Lecture Notes in Computer Science, Vol. 328.

[JLW86] C.B. Jones, P. Lindsay, and C. Wadsworth. IPSE 2.5 theorem proving concepts paper. Technical Report 060/00021/1.5, Manchester University and Rutherford Appleton Laboratory, June 1986.

[JM88]   C.B. Jones and R. Moore. Muffin: A user interface design experiment for a theorem proving assistant. In R. Bloomfield, L. Marshall, and R. Jones, editors, *VDM '88: VDM – The Way Ahead*, pages 337–375. Springer-Verlag, 1988. Lecture Notes in Computer Science, Vol. 328.

[Jon79a] C.B. Jones. Constructing a theory of a data structure as an aid to program development. *Acta Informatica*, 11:119–137, 1979.

[Jon79b] C.B. Jones. The Vienna Development Method: Examples of compiler development. In M. Amirchahy and D. Neel, editors, *Le Point sur la Compilation*, pages 89–114. IRIA-SEFI, 1979.

[Jon80] C.B. Jones. *Software Development: A Rigorous Approach*. Prentice Hall International, 1980.

[Jon86] C.B. Jones. *Systematic Software Development Using VDM*. Prentice Hall International, 1986.

[Jon87a] K. D. Jones. The Muffin prototype: Experiences with Smalltalk-80. IPSE Document 060/00066/1.1, August 1987. University of Manchester.

[Jon87b] K. D. Jones. The preliminary specification of FRIPSE. IPSE Document 060/00114/2.1, December 1987. University of Manchester.

[Jon87c] S. Peyton Jones. *The Implementation of Functional Programming Languages*. Prentice-Hall International, 1987.

[Jon88] H.B.M. Jonkers. An introduction to COLD-K. Technical Report METEOR/t8/PRLE/8, Philips Research Labs, Eindhoven, July 1988.

[Jon90a] C. B. Jones. *Systematic Software Development using VDM*. Prentice Hall International, second edition, 1990.

[Jon90b] C.B. Jones. Consequences. In *Beauty is Our Business*, chapter 25. Springer-Verlag, 1990.

[Jon90c] C.B. Jones. Final report on SERC Grant No. GR/D/60294: IPSE 2.5. internal communication, July 1990.

[Kem85] Richard A. Kemmerer. Testing formal specifications to detect design errors. *IEEE Transactions on Software Engineering*, SE-11(1):32–43, January 1985.

[Kem86] R. A. Kemmerer. Verification assessment study: Final report. Technical Report C3-CR01-86, Library No. S-228,204, National Computer Security Center, March 1986.

[Kin76] J.C. King. Symbolic execution and program testing. *Communications of the ACM*, 19:385–394, July 1976.

[Kle52] S. Kleene. *Introduction to Metamathematics*. North Holland, 1952.

[Kne89] Ralf Kneuper. *Symbolic Execution as a Tool for Validation of Specifications*. PhD thesis, University of Manchester, 1989.

[Kne91] R. Kneuper. Symbolic execution – a semantic approach. *Science of Computer Programming*, 1991. Accepted for publication.

[KS69]   K. Koch and F. Schwarzenberger. Introduction to formula 360. Technical Report TR 25.101, IBM Lab Vienna, 12th December 1969.

[Laf90] C. Lafontaine. Formalization of the VDM reification in the DEVA meta-calculus. In *[BJ90]*. North-Holland, 1990.

[Leh89] M.M. Lehman. Uncertainty in computer application and its control through the engineering of software. *Software Maintenance: Research and Practice*, 1:3–27, 1989.

[Lin87a] P. A. Lindsay. A formal system for interactive proofs. IPSE Document 060/pal011/2.4, August 1987. University of Manchester.

[Lin87b] P. A. Lindsay. A formal system with inclusion polymorphism. IPSE Document 060/pal014/2.3, December 1987. University of Manchester.

[Lin87c] P.A. Lindsay. Logical frames for interactive theorem proving. Technical Report UMCS 87-12-7, University of Manchester Computer Science Dept, 1987.

[Lin88] P.A. Lindsay. A survey of mechanical support for formal reasoning. *Software Engineering Journal*, 3(1), January 1988.

[LM89] P. A. Lindsay and R.C. Moore. The specification of the mural proof assistant. IPSE Document 060/00148/2.4, June 1989. University of Manchester.

[Lov78] D. W. Loveland. *Automated Theorem Proving: a Logical Basis*. North Holland, 1978.

[Mar75] P. Martin-Löf. An intuitionistic theory of types: Predicative part. In H.E. Rose and J.C. Shepherdson, editors, *Logic Colloquium '73*. North Holland, 1975.

[Mar85] P. Martin-Löf. Constructive mathematics and computer programming. In C.A.R.Hoare and J.C.Shepherdson, editors, *Mathematical Logic and Programming Languages*, pages 167–184, 1985.

[Mid90] C.A. Middelburg. *Syntax and Semantics of VVSL A Language for Structured VDM Specifications*. PhD thesis, PTT Research, Department of Applied Computer Science, September 1990.

[Mil72] R. Milner. Implementation and application of Scott's logic of continuous functions. In *Conf. on Proving Assertions About Programs*, pages 1–6. SIGPLAN Notices 7:1, 1972.

[Mil84] R. Milner. The use of machines to assist in rigorous proof. In C.A.R.Hoare and J.C.Shepherdson, editors, *Mathematical Logic and Programming Languages*, pages 77–88. Prentice-Hall, 1984.

[MN89] M.A. McMorran and J.E. Nicholls. Z user manual. Technical Report 12.274, IBM UK Laboratories, Winchester, July 1989.

[Möl90] Bernhard Möller. Formal derivation of pointer algorithms, 1990. To appear in: Informatik im Kreuzungspunkt von Numerischer Mathematik, Rechnerenwurf, Programmierung Algebra und Logic. M. Broy (Ed). Published by Springer-Verlag.

[Mon87] B.Q. Monahan. A type model for VDM. In *[BJMN87]*, pages 210–236, 1987.

[Moo88] R. C. Moore. The bumper FRIPSE spec. IPSE Document 060/00143/2.1, July 1988. University of Manchester.

[Mor88a] F. L. Morris. A data structure for representing sets of terms and some associated algorithms. IPSE Document 060/flm002, February 1988. University of Manchester.

[Mor88b] F. L. Morris. Some low-level suggestions for expression representations. IPSE Document 060/flm003, March 1988. University of Manchester.

[MP66] J. McCarthy and J. Painter. Correctness of a compiler for arithmetic expressions. Technical Report CS38, Computer Science Department, Stanford University, April 29th 1966.

[New75] M. Newey. *Formal semantics of LISP with applications to program correctness.* PhD thesis, Stanford, 1975.

[Nip86] T. Nipkow. Non-deterministic data types: Models and implementations. *Acta Informatica*, 22:629–661, 1986.

[Nip87] T. Nipkow. *Behavioural Implementation Concepts for Nondeterministic Data Types.* PhD thesis, University of Manchester, May 1987.

[Nip89] Tobias Nipkow. Equational reasoning in Isabelle. *Science of Computer Programming*, 12:123–150, 1989.

[NPS90] B. Nordstrom, K. Petersson, and J. M. Smith. *Programming in Martin-Löf's Type Theory: An Introduction.* Oxford University Press, 1990.

[Pau85a] L. C. Paulson. Interactive theorem proving with Cambridge LCF – a user's manual. Technical Report 80, University of Cambridge Comp. Lab., November 1985.

[Pau85b] L. C. Paulson. Lessons learned from LCF: a survey of natural deduction proofs. *Computer Journal*, 28(5):474–479, November 1985.

[Pau86] L. C. Paulson. Natural deduction as higher order resolution. *J. Logic Programming*, 3:237–258, 1986.

[Ped87] J.S. Pedersen. VDM in three generations of Ada formal descriptions. In *[BJMN87]*, pages 33–48, 1987.

[Pet82] K. Petersson. A programming system for type theory. Technical Report 21, Comp. Sciences Dept, Chalmers University, Göteborg, Sweden, 1982.

[Plo81] Gordon D. Plotkin. A structural approach to operational semantics. Technical Report DAIMI FN-19, Computer Science Dept., Aarhus University, September 1981.

[Pra65] D. Prawitz. *Natural Deduction.* Almqvist and Wisell, Stockholm, 1965.

[Pra71] D. Prawitz. *Natural Deduction.* Proceedings 2nd Scandinavian Logic Symposium, 1971.

[PRL86] PRL Staff. Implementing mathematics with the Nuprl proof development system. Technical report, Cornell University, 1986.

[Ram88] A. Ramsay. *Formal Methods in Artificial Intelligence.* Cambridge University Press, 1988.

[RvH89] J. Rushby and F von Henke. Formal verification of the interactive convergence clock synchronization algorithm. Technical Report SRI-CSL-89-3, SRI International, February 1989.

[S+89]   M. Sintzoff et al. Definition 1.1 of the generic development language DEVA. Technical Report RR89–35, Université Catholique de Louvain, 1989.

[San82] D.T. Sannella. *Semantics, Implementation and Pragmatics of Clear, A Program Specification Language*. PhD thesis, Department of Computer Science, University of Edinburgh, July 1982. Available as a Technical Report – no. CST-17-82.

[Sch84] P. Schroeder-Heister. A natural extension of natural deduction. *Journal of Symbolic Logic*, 49:1284–1299, 1984.

[Sch86] D.A. Schmidt. *Denotational Semantics: a Methodology for Language Development*. Allyn & Bacon, 1986.

[Scu90] G.T. Scullard. Mural evaluation, March 1990.

[Smu61] R.M. Smullyan. *Theory of Formal Systems*. Princeton University Press, 1961.

[Sno89] R. A. Snowdon. An Introduction to the IPSE 2.5 Project. *ICL Technical Journal*, 6(3), May 1989.

[Sok83] Stefan Sokołowski. A note on tactics in LCF. Internal Report CSR-140-83, University of Edinburgh, Dept of Computer Science., August 1983.

[Spi89] J.M. Spivey. *The Z Notation*. Prentice-Hall International, 1989.

[Stø90] K. Stølen. *Development of Parallel Programs on Shared Data-Structures*. PhD thesis, Manchester University, 1990.

[TW83]   D. Talbot and R.W. Witty. Alvey programme for software engineering. Published by the Alvey Directorate, November 1983.

[War90] B. Warboys. The IPSE 2.5 project: Process modelling as the basis for a support environment. In N. Madhavji, W. Schafer, and H. Weber, editors, *Proceedings of the First International Conference on System Development Environments and Factories*, pages 59–74. Pitman, 1990.

[WD88]   J. C. P. Woodcock and B. Dickinson. Using VDM with rely and guarantee-conditions: Experiences of a real project. In *[BJM88]*, pages 434–458, 1988.

[Web90] M. Weber. Formalization of the Bird-Meertens algorithmic calculus in the Deva meta-calculus. In *[BJ90]*. North-Holland, 1990.

[Wey80] R.W. Weyhrauch. Prolegomena to a theory of mechanized formal reasoning. *Artificial Intelligence*, 13:133–170, 1980.

[Wie89] Morten Wieth. Loose specification and its semantics. In *Information Processing 89*. IFIP, North-Holland, 1989.

[WL88]   J. Woodcock and M. Loomes. *Software Engineering Mathematics*. Pitman, 1988.

FORMAL ASPECTS OF COMPUTING

BCS

The International Journal of Formal Methods

Editor-in-Chief: Professor C. B. Jones; Associate Editor: Dr. D. J. Cooke

1991 Volume (3), 4 issues, £70.00 plus postage

AIMS and SCOPE

The principal aims of *Formal Aspects of Computing* are to promote the growth of computing science, to show its relationship to practice, and to help in the application of formalisms. In particular, contributions to the formal aspects of computing are to be published. The following fall within the scope of formal aspects:

- Well founded notations for system description/specifications;
- Verifiable designs;
- Proof methods;
- Theories of objects used in specifications and implementations;
- Transformational design;

- Formal approaches to requirements analysis;
- Results on algorithm and problem complexity;
- Fault-tolerant design;
- Descriptions of relevant "Project Support Environments";
- Methods of approaching development.

Applications of known formal methods as well as new results would be suitable subjects for papers. Comprehensive surveys will also be published and there is hope that some systematic coverage of major topics can be achieved over a period of years. Contributions to the teaching of formal aspects would also be welcome.

A SELECTION OF PAPERS TO APPEAR IN Volume (3) 4 issues 1991

Generator Induction in Order Sorted Algebras O. Owe and O. J. Dahl
Towards a Formal Foundation of the Specification and Description Language SDL M. Broy
A Demonstrably Correct Compiler S. Stepney et al.
The Fixed Point Theory of Unbounded Non-Determinism G. Barrett
Refinement, Conformance and Inheritance E. Cusack
Eliminating the Substitution Axiom from UNITY Logic B. A. Sanders
Real Time Process Algebra J. C. M. Baeten and J. Bergstra
Functional Specification and Proof of Correctness for Time Dependent Behaviour of Reactive Systems V. S. Alagar and G. Ramanthan
Structured Design of a Translation from LOTOS to MR W. Bouma and H. Zuidweg
A Model Checker for Linear Time Temporal Logic M. Fisher
An Evaluation of Rely and Guarantee Conditions D. Grosvenor and A. Robinson
A Proof System for Communicating Processes with Value-Passing M. Hennessy

Springer-Verlag
Berlin
Heidelberg
New York
London
Paris
Tokyo
Hong Kong
Barcelona

☐ Springer-Verlag London Ltd., Springer House, 8 Alexandra Rd., London SW19 7JZ, England
☐ Heidelberger Platz 3, W-1000 Berlin 33, F.R.Germany ☐ 175 Fifth Ave., New York, NY 10010, USA
☐ 26, rue des Carmes, F-75005 Paris ☐ 37-3, Hongo 3-chome, Bunkyo-ku, Tokyo 113, Japan
☐ Room 701, Mirror Tower, 61 Mody Road, Tsimshatsui, Kowloon, Hong Kong
☐ Avinguda Diagonal, 468-4°C, E-08006 Barcelona